UNDERSTANDING
AMERICAN GOVERNMENT
AND POLITICS

MANCHESTER
1824

Manchester University Press

UNDERSTANDINGS

Series editor **DUNCAN WATTS**

Following the review of the national curriculum for 16–19-year-olds, UK examining boards introduced new specifications, first used in 2001 and 2002. A-level courses are now divided into A/S level for the first year of sixth-form studies, and the more difficult A2 level thereafter. The **Understandings** series comprehensively covers social science syllabuses of all major examination boards, featuring dedicated A/S and A2 level textbooks. The books are written in an accessible, user-friendly and jargon-free manner and will be essential to students sitting these examinations.

Already published

Understanding criminal law
Caroline Buckley and Stephen Buckley

Understanding political ideas and movements
Kevin Harrison and Tony Boyd

Understanding British and European political issues (2nd edition)
Neil McNaughton

Understanding A/S accounting for AQA
Jeremy Renals

Understanding American government and politics (2nd edition)
Duncan Watts

Understanding US/UK government and politics (2nd edition)
Duncan Watts

Understanding A/S level government and politics
Chris Wilson

Understanding American government and politics

3rd edition

DUNCAN WATTS

Manchester University Press
Manchester and New York

distributed in the United States exclusively
by Palgrave Macmillan

Published by Manchester University Press
Oxford Road, Manchester M13 9NR, UK
and Room 400, 175 Fifth Avenue, New York, NY 10010, USA
www.manchesteruniversitypress.co.uk

Distributed in the United States exclusively by
Palgrave Macmillan, 175 Fifth Avenue, New York,
NY 10010, USA

Distributed in Canada exclusively by
UBC Press, University of British Columbia, 2029 West Mall,
Vancouver, BC, Canada V6T 1Z2

British Library Cataloguing-in-Publication Data
A catalogue record for this book is available from the British Library

Library of Congress Cataloging-in-Publication Data applied for

ISBN   978 0 7190 8683 0   paperback

First published 2012

The publisher has no responsibility for the persistence or accuracy of URLs
for any external or third-party internet websites referred to in this book,
and does not guarantee that any content on such websites is, or will remain,
accurate or appropriate.

Typeset
by Graphicraft Limited, Hong Kong
Printed in Great Britain
by Bell & Bain Ltd, Glasgow

Contents

Comparative boxes: Britain and the United States   *page* vi

The need for a third edition   vii

US presidents and their parties   ix

Map of the US: the sun belt and the frost belt   x

1 Introduction: the setting of American politics   1

2 The Constitution   27

3 Federalism in theory and practice   48

4 Presidential power   75

5 Support for the presidency   117

6 Congress   145

7 The Supreme Court   187

8 Elections and voting   218

9 Political parties   286

10 Pressure groups: the lobby at work   334

11 Civil liberties and civil rights   370

12 Conclusion: the state of American democracy   414

Index   421

Comparative boxes: Britain and the United States

Written and unwritten constitutions   *page* 42
The constitutions of Great Britain and the United States   45
Federalism and devolution   71
The president and the prime minister   110
The backgrounds of British prime ministers and US presidents   112
Cabinets   128
The bureaucracy   142
Committees in the British Parliament and the American Congress   164
Legislatures   177
Female representation in the 'top five' countries, the UK and the US   179
The social backgrounds of legislators   180
The operation of the courts   189
Judges and their role   203
The judiciaries   215
Electoral systems   227
Elections and electioneering   230
Turnout in a selection of the main democracies   235
The media and elections   249
Voting behaviour   265
Direct democracy in Britain, Europe and the US   271
The liberties and rights of people   410
Democracy   418

The need for a third edition

In the case of politics and other social science books, it is essential that they are as up to date as possible and incorporate the latest developments, thinking and research. Works such as this one need to draw upon events that have occurred subsequently to the last presidential election. The second edition was informed by the outcome of the 2004 presidential contest, being published at the beginning of 2006. Since then, we have had two sets of mid-term results, as well as the November 2008 Obama v. McCain election. This new edition allows for inclusion of the 2008 results and coverage of the 2010 congressional elections, which determined the composition of the present, 112th Congress.

Much of the original material remains relevant for this new edition. This has been retained, with any necessary updating of facts, figures and interpretations. However, the coverage of the George W. Bush era can be reflective, now that the presidency has ended, whereas previously the narrative and judgements were necessarily of an interim nature. So too, after two years of the Obama presidency, we now have some indication of its broad thrust and style and can note any relevant differences from its predecessor.

The section on the presidency has been expanded to allow for explanation and analysis of the unitary executive theory (UET), which increasingly became the theme of much writing on presidential power a few years into the Bush administration. The theory indicates how a president can exploit the latent potential inherent in the office, via a distinctive interpretation of the wording of the Constitution. Writers on the UET stress how President Bush made use of such devices as national security directives, proclamations and signing statements as a means of bypassing the more usual procedures open to a holder of the office. Coverage of this area opens up possibilities for discussion of the distinction between the power of presidents and of the presidency itself.

Also on the presidency as an institution, there was no reference in the last edition to the Wildavsky 'two presidencies' thesis, which suggests that presidents are more powerful in the conduct of foreign rather than domestic policy. This was because the Wildavsky distinction had largely gone out of fashion in the late twentieth and early twenty-first centuries. In the Bush era, it was re-assessed, and this edition includes reference to such new thinking.

Otherwise, the section on civil rights relating to the position of ethnic minorities – notably the African Americans – is now informed by Obama's swift rise to the presidency, and higher levels of black representation in Congress and the states. Coverage of other minorities, particularly the rise of the Hispanic population to positions of influence, has been expanded, an area of growing importance, as the elevation of the first Latino to the Supreme Court indicates. Relating to the latter, some recent Court rulings have been included, as well as some assessment of the changes of personnel, leanings and general tenor of the Roberts Court.

Other significant changes include: inclusion of the latest census findings; reference to the controversy over healthcare reform in the Obama administration; increased coverage of the role of the states in US federalism; mention of the declining influence of the Christian Coalition; and attention to the rise of the Tea Party movement. In addition, the comparative boxes have been set out in a way that it is hoped will make direct comparison more straightforward.

I commend this new edition to your serious consideration and trust that it will enable you, the reader, to tackle examination questions more effectively if you are a student. If you are a general reader with an interest in US politics, I hope that its comprehensive and up-to-date coverage will enhance your understanding of the subject.

Duncan Watts

Author and series editor

US presidents and their parties

President	Party	Term
1 George Washington (1732–99)	Federalist	1789–97
2 John Adams (1735–1826)	Federalist	1797–1801
3 Thomas Jefferson (1743–1826)	Democratic-Republican	1801–9
4 James Madison (1751–1836)	Democratic-Republican	1809–17
5 James Monroe (1758–1831)	Democratic-Republican	1817–25
6 John Quincy Adams (1767–1848)	Democratic-Republican	1825–29
7 Andrew Jackson (1767–1845)	Democrat	1829–37
8 Martin Van Buren (1782–1862)	Democrat	1837–41
9 William Henry Harrison (1773–1841)	Whig	1841
10 John Tyler (1790–1862)	Whig	1841–45
11 James K. Polk (1795–1849)	Democrat	1845–49
12 Zachary Taylor (1784–1850)	Whig	1849–50
13 Millard Fillmore (1800–74)	Whig	1850–53
14 Franklin Pierce (1804–69)	Democrat	1853–57
15 James Buchanan (1791–1868)	Democrat	1857–61
16 Abraham Lincoln (1809–65)	Republican	1861–65
17 Andrew Johnson (1808–75)	Union	1865–69
18 Ulysses S. Grant (1822–85)	Republican	1869–77
19 Rutherford B. Hayes (1822–93)	Republican	1877–81
20 James A. Garfield (1831–81)	Republican	1881
21 Chester A. Arthur (1830–86)	Republican	1881–85
22 Grover Cleveland (1837–08)	Democrat	1885–89
23 Benjamin Harrison (1833–1901)	Republican	1889–93
24 Grover Cleveland (1837–1908)	Democrat	1893–97
25 William McKinley (1843–1901)	Republican	1897–1901
26 Theodore Roosevelt (1858–1919)	Republican	1901–9
27 William Howard Taft (1857–1930)	Republican	1909–13
28 Woodrow Wilson (1856–1924)	Democrat	1913–21
29 Warren G. Harding (1865–1923)	Republican	1921–23
30 Calvin Coolidge (1871–1933)	Republican	1923–29
31 Herbert Hoover (1874–1964)	Republican	1929–33
32 Franklin Delano Roosevelt (1882–1945)	Democrat	1933–45
33 Harry S. Truman (1884–1972)	Democrat	1945–53
34 Dwight D. Eisenhower (1890–1969)	Republican	1953–61
35 John F. Kennedy (1917–63)	Democrat	1961–63
36 Lyndon B. Johnson (1908–73)	Democrat	1963–69
37 Richard M. Nixon (1913–94)	Republican	1969–74
38 Gerald R. Ford (b. 1913)	Republican	1974–77
39 Jimmy Carter (b. 1924)	Democrat	1977–81
40 Ronald Reagan (b. 1911)	Republican	1981–89
41 George H. W. Bush (b. 1924)	Republican	1989–93
42 William J. Clinton (b. 1946)	Democrat	1993–2001
43 George Walker Bush (b. 1946)	Republican	2001–9
44 Barack H. Obama (b. 1961)	Democrat	2009–

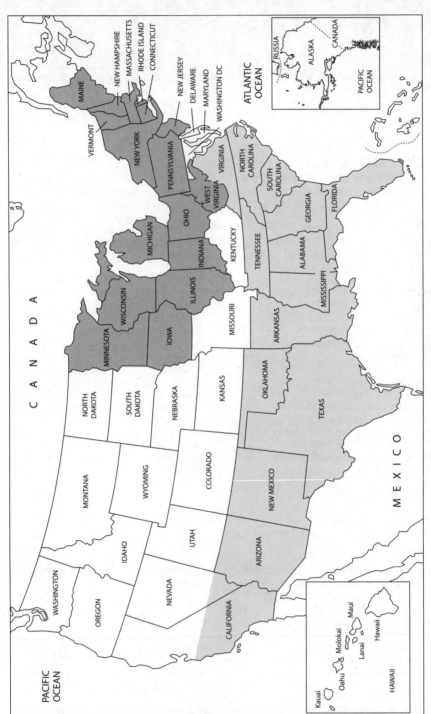

Map of the US: the sun-belt ☐ and the frost-belt ☐

Introduction: the setting of American politics

1

**A knowledge of the social and economic environment of any country is import-
ant in achieving an understanding of its government and politics. So too is an
appreciation of the ideas and values that have mattered and continue to
matter for those who inhabit that country. Many students will know little of
America's human and economic geography, or indeed of its political culture.
So here we are concerned with finding out more about the influences on American
politics, and the factors that shape attitudes and events today.**

In this section, we are concerned with examining those features of the United
States, ranging from its size and landscape to its population and religion, which
have a bearing on its political activity. Given its vast extent, it is inevitably a
country of great diversity. Differences in race, gender, religion and social class
have an impact on the way in which voters behave.

Geographically, the United States is a huge land mass, exceeding that of all
but three nations in the world: Canada, China and Russia. It borders Canada
in the North and Mexico in the South, and on its west and east coast lie two
oceans, the Pacific and the Atlantic, respectively. It is a land endowed with
considerable resources, ranging from coal to precious metals; it is also rich
in farmland. Nature has been generous and enabled America to develop as a
country remarkably self-sufficiently.

Areas have their own regional economic concerns, and political attitudes
reflect these regional differences. Some parts of the country are well suited to
ranching and agriculture, others to mining or manufacturing. For example, the
political perspectives of the automobile worker in Detroit are far removed from
those of the farmers of Kansas.

Geographical isolation

The country is not only vast, but it is also geographically rather isolated. Having
only two immediate neighbours, it faces little threat of invasion or conquest.
Moreover, as it is cut off from other continents, it has been able to keep itself
aloof from many struggles in Asia, Europe and elsewhere, unless they are conflicts
where key American interests are perceived to be involved. Between the two

world wars, the country adopted an isolationist stance, whereas after World War II it assumed a global role, including the leadership of the free, Western world. At times, as in Vietnam and more recently in Iraq, it has chosen to involve itself in conflict. In particular, during the era of the **Cold War**, its military machine was much involved in overseas struggle. In other periods, it has been more reluctant to meddle in other countries' affairs. This has enabled it to develop its own distinctive political traditions and concentrate on its own internal development.

> **Cold War**
> The period of conflict, tension and competition between the United States and the Soviet Union and their allies from the mid-1940s until the early 1990s.

Isolationist voices have always periodically been raised, particularly from politicians more remote from the European scene (such as in the Midwest). Following the experience of Vietnam, and with the Cold War over, there is again a greater wish for America to 'play in its own backyard'. Many Americans display a sense of anxiety when presidents take them into commitments, such as those in Somalia and Bosnia, from which little credit is likely to emerge. More recently, the involvement in Afghanistan and Iraq has confirmed some of their apprehensions, for it has proved longer than envisaged and difficult to bring to a close.

Sectional differences

Of all the sectional differences within the US, the most obvious is that which separates the American South from the rest of the nation. Traditionally, the South has been more rural and agricultural and the North more industrial, but the issue at the root of the distinction between them was slavery. President Lincoln and the Republicans were opposed to slavery, and it was over this issue that the eleven southern states broke away to form the Confederacy in 1860–61. Their secession led to the Civil War, fought between the forces of the Union and those of the Confederalists.

> **Civil War**
> The American Civil War (1861–65) was a civil war in which the eleven Southern slave states that formed the Confederacy (led by Jefferson Davis) fought against the United States (the Union), which was supported by all the free states and the five border slave states.

The secession made the more rural and agrarian Democrats the party of the South, because the Southern element in the Democratic Party staunchly fought to defend slavery. After the hostilities were over, the distinction of North and South remained. These differences were strengthened by the policies pursued during the era of **Reconstruction**, by differing economic interests and above all by the continuing racial problem. Today, a further difference can be ascribed to military

> **Reconstruction**
> The collective name given to federal government programmes subsequent to the Civil War, implemented in the twelve years to 1877. They established the terms on which the rebellious states would be re-integrated into the Union.

establishments, for most of the military facilities are based in the South, which tends to mean that on matters of national defence the South takes a more conservative viewpoint.

In religion, the South remains distinctive. There are strong Protestant leanings in the **Bible Belt** and religious **fundamentalism** is widespread. Above all, however, it is the treatment of the American blacks (African Americans) that has proved to be the key issue over the last century. Although black slaves were freed after the Civil War, they were for several decades still the victims of segregation, intimidation and discrimination; they were long denied basic rights, such as the franchise (right to vote). Since the 1960s, things have greatly changed. In 1960, in a southern state such as Mississippi, only one in twenty blacks were registered to vote. Today, many more blacks than whites remain unregistered, but that is true all over the country and it is not specifically a southern issue. With the advent of more civil rights and the spread of educational opportunity, the South has become less backward even if it still lags behind the rest of the nation in educational achievement and per capita income.

> **Bible Belt**
> An informal and loose term for an area broadly comprising the south-eastern quarter of the United States and stretching west into much of Texas, in which socially conservative evangelical protestantism is a dominant part of the culture, the Baptist Church flourishes and church attendance in all denominations is extremely high.
>
> **fundamentalism**
> The interpretation of every word of the Bible as being literally true.

The South has changed significantly over the last generation. It is no longer true to speak of the 'solid South', as the Democrats used to do. It is now less cohesive as a society and certainly less committed to the Democratic cause. In recent presidential elections, the Republicans have outperformed the Democrats, so that in 2004 John Kerry and in 2008 Barack Obama were able to make little headway in winning seats in the southern states, usually defined as the eleven Confederate states plus West Virginia, Kentucky and Oklahoma; in state and local elections, however, the Democrats continue to do well. White voters seem to have been disenchanted with Democratic presidential aspirants, but the voting rights won by blacks have been a re-inforcement of the Democratic position, especially at local level.

Compared to the South, no other region has such a cohesive identity, but there are nevertheless other sectional differences. The West has tended to be more isolationist (as it is further from Western Europe), as well as more committed to the alleged virtues of **rugged individualism** and less federal intervention. Such a sense of self-sufficiency made this obvious territory for Ronald Reagan in

> **rugged individualism**
> A term originally coined by Republican President Hoover to describe the widely held belief that all individuals, or nearly all individuals, can succeed on their own and that government help for people should be minimal. Personal liberty, self-reliance and free competition are Republican watchwords.

the 1980s, for he was identified with the attitudes and values of the West.

California is a state with a special importance, not least because of its 55 representatives in Congress. No candidate for the presidency has much chance of success unless he or she can win its vote in the **Electoral College** – Nixon, Reagan, Clinton and Obama, among others, all carried the state.

> **Electoral College**
> The body of 538 citizens that ultimately decides who becomes president of the United States, for presidential candidates need to win a majority of votes in the College to win the election. The College is an example of an indirect election, because the person finally chosen is not directly elected by the people.

The population and where it lives

The American population has grown by leaps and bounds. Early figures for the 2010 census show that between 2000 and 2010, it rose by 27.3 million (9.7%). In January 2011, there were almost 312 million people living in the US, making it the third-largest country by population in the world.[1]

Interim projections[2] suggest that numbers will continue to grow during the next half century, albeit at a reduced rate after 2030. By the mid-century mark, figures will approach 440 million. The country beginning to emerge will be a profoundly different America, more diverse in population. Whites, excluding Latinos, will see their influence and numbers diminish from a 70% share of the population today, to a bare majority of fractionally over 50% in 2050. The beginnings of that change are already under way. Within the next decade, minorities will account for one-third of the population, because of immigration. By 2030, there will be what William Frey,[3] demographer at the Brookings Institute in Washington, calls the 'racial generation gap' as the predominantly white generation of **baby boomers** makes way for a younger, more diverse population: 'It's the future versus the past. These old white baby boomers are being phased out and are fading away after 2030.' However, there will be plenty of company for these ageing baby-boomers as they enter their twilight years.

> **baby boomers**
> The generation born in the baby boom in the United States, between 1945 and 1955.

Not only is the population growing, it is also ageing. The median age of the population is 36.8, the highest it has ever been. The number of elderly Americans (counted as being those over 65) is now around 14% of the total. By 2050, it will be over 20%. There will also be a large population of octogenarians and the number of people aged 85 and older is expected to reach 21 million. This is politically significant for politicians, because the political outlook and concerns of this ageing population are likely to be a factor in determining election results and shaping public policy in future decades. The ageing baby boomers are going to be more concerned with security and pensions than schools or language training, which are likely to be more important to immigrants.

The growth in population

Year	Population
1900	76,212,168
1930	123,202,660
1960	179,323,175
1990	248,709,873
2000	281,421,906
2010	308,745,538

The population of every state other than Michigan grew between 2000 and 2010, but not at an even rate across the country. Of the 49 states that saw an increase, Nevada was the fastest growing (up 35.1%), Rhode Island the lowest (up 0.4%). Overall, the population of the South is increasing most rapidly (14.3%), followed by the West (13.8%), which has the two states with the highest rate of increase (Nevada and Arizona). By contrast, the Northeast and Midwest are much less rapidly increasing in size, as many inhabitants migrate to the South and West. More Americans today are seeking the warmth and other attractions of the so-called Sun Belt (the bottom 40% of the country) and deserting the Frost Belt, those states in the Northeast (see map on p. x). States such as Florida have an appeal to retired people, but also to those tempted by the job opportunities in an area of new industries and substantial economic growth.

These changes in the distribution of the population are reflected in changes to the regional pattern of congressional representation. Between 1970 and 2010, the Northeast and the Midwest were substantial losers, their representation declining from 52% to 40%. The South and West gained in the same period. They benefited from the 2010 changes. Of the beneficiaries, the South gained eight seats (Texas alone gained four), the West four. (See p. 146 for details of congressional apportionment.)

American cities, their changing size and composition (based on 2000 figures)

The 2000 census revealed that nine of the largest cities had lost inhabitants in the previous decade, a continuation of an established pattern of suburbanisation that has characterised the last few decades. For many years, America was a predominantly rural society, but in the late nineteenth and early twentieth centuries there was a movement of population from rural to urban parts as workers sought jobs in the expanding towns and cities. More recently, the trend has been away from urban centres and out to suburban areas as new housing developments have grown up and new connecting roads have been built. In Los Angeles, four times as many people live in the metropolitan outskirts as in the city itself. The overall urban population in the US is now just over 80%.

Members of the better-off white community of some city centres have been keen to move out, so that their offspring can attend all-white schools and avoid the prospect of being 'bussed' to an integrated one. The population that remains in inner cities now tends to comprise poorer whites, blacks and assorted racial minority groups. This is fertile territory for the Democratic Party. The suburbs (although they vary greatly in wealth and quality of life) tend to be places where the predominantly white people enjoy higher income levels, and vote Republican.

The top ten cities of 100,000 or more population with the largest black majorities

City	% Black majority
Gary (Indiana)	85.3
Detroit (Michigan)	82.8
Birmingham (Alabama)	74.0
Jackson (Mississippi)	71.1
New Orleans (Louisiana)	67.9
Baltimore (Maryland)	65.2
Atlanta (Georgia)	62.1
Memphis (Tennessee)	61.9
Washington DC	61.3
Richmond (Virginia)	58.1

Fourteen of the cities that have a population exceeding 100,000 now have a black majority, places ranging from Atlanta in Georgia to Detroit in Michigan, from Gary in Indiana to Washington DC. Apart from the African American population, there are many other racial minorities in this land of immigrants, ranging from Asians to Hispanics (persons of Spanish-speaking descent, who can technically be of any race) and Jews.

Racial groups

Main groups in the population of the United States (rounded to nearest million)

Year	*White	Black	Hispanic	Total
1970	178,000,000	23,000,000	n/a	201,000,000
1980	180,000,000	27,000,000	15,000,000	222,000,000
1990	187,000,000	31,000,000	22,000,000	240,000,000
2000	212,000,000	**36,000,000	35,000,000	283,000,000
2010	271,000,000	**38,000,000	50,000,000	309,000,000

* White, includes Hispanic, ** Includes black Americans of more than one racial group.

Figures for 1870–2000 are adapted from those provided by US Census Bureau; those for 2010 represent official census estimates. All have been rounded. In percentage terms, they show that some 80% are white, 13.0% are black, the rest being 'Asian', 'American Indian/African Native', 'Native Hawaiian and other Pacific Islander' and 'two or more races'. Today, more than 16.0% are Hispanics, who are seen as constituting an ethnicity rather than a race. Hispanic and Latino Americans are distributed among all the races. U.S. federal law defines Hispanic or Latino as 'those who classify themselves in one of the specific Hispanic or Latino categories listed on the Census 2000 or ACS questionnaire – Mexican, Puerto Rican or Cuban – as well as those who indicate that they are other Spanish, Hispanic, or Latino.'

Sixty-five per cent of Americans are non-Hispanic white and nearly 13% are black African American. **Black Americans** increased faster than the total population between 1990 and 2000, at a rate of nearly 16%, whereas the overall population increase was 13.2%. The black population has for much of the last one hundred years sought to improve its position in American society. Freed as a result of the Civil War, it was long denied full participation and recognition. Its struggle to advance its position and achieve civil rights has been an important feature of postwar politics. The freedom rides and sit-ins, the marches and boycotts, posed problems for white Americans, as they finally had to concede a greater measure of equal treatment than they had ever contemplated before.

Until the twentieth century, most black Americans lived in the South and 54% still do so; 19% live in the Midwest, 18% in the Northeast and 10% in the West. In the South, ten states each have a black population of over a million, and the population of four states and Washington DC is more than a quarter black. However, early in the twentieth century many left that area to seek a better lifestyle in the large cities of the West, Midwest and Northeast. Washington DC has the highest proportion of black Americans (66% of the population), but many other cities have a large black population, much of which is often to be found in poorer quarters; New York has 2.3 million and Chicago 1.1 million blacks. In places as far apart as Los Angeles and Detroit, riots have from time to time broken out in the ghettos (densely populated slum areas, inhabited by a deprived minority group) as a result of deprivation and discrimination.

Issues of racial division and race relations have bedevilled America for much of its short history. Although black Americans have achieved greater rights and political power (to the extent that a black American has even become president), the overwhelming majority tend to be worse off, with an average income substantially below that of the white population; one-third of the black population lives below the poverty line. It is a matter of political contention as to whether the black population should be helped by policies such as **affirmative action**, which provide certain groups with greater opportunities to achieve a range of positions long denied to them.

> **affirmative action**
> Policies and actions designed to compensate for the effects of past discrimination, by giving preferences to specified ethnic and gender groups.

One of the fastest-growing groups in the United States is the Hispanic population, which grew by 57.9% between 1990 and 2000. There are currently over 48 million **Hispanics** or 'Latinos' (as some Hispanics prefer to be called). For the first time they outnumbered African Americans in 2003. Indeed, as a significant minority of black Americans are also Hispanics, the historic primacy of primarily English-speaking blacks was already at an end by the turn of the century. Hispanics tend to be undercounted in surveys, a situation made more possible by the number of illegal immigrants entering the US every year. Most Hispanics have a Mexican origin, but those reporting 'other origins' are the fastest-growing group (up 96.9%).

The origin of the Hispanic population

Origin	%
Mexican	58.5
Puerto Rican	9.6
Cuban	3.5
Others, of whom largest group are Central American, South American and Dominican	28.4

Mostly better off than African Americans, half of all Hispanics live in just two states, California (11.0 million) and Texas (6.7 million). They account for 24.3% of the population in the West, the only region in which Hispanics exceeded the national level of 12.5%. Nearly two-thirds of the Cuban element live in Florida. A majority of Miami residents are Hispanic, but in cities from Dallas to Houston, Los Angeles to New York, they are also well represented.

Hispanics are expected to number 103 million by 2050 and will by then account for nearly 30% of America's population. They are a young population, their relative youthfulness being reflected in the size of the under-18 population (35.0%, against an overall figure of 25.7%) and in its median age (26, as against 36).

Hispanics hardly form a coherent group, and come from diverse places. Most of them have a Mexican origin, but there are also many Puerto Ricans, who have left their overcrowded island for the mainland with the hope of improving their position in life. Those from Cuba are a significant group. They or their parents and grandparents fled from Castro's communist revolution in 1959. They tend to be more professional and middle class, and do not share many of the social and political attitudes of the Mexican-Americans and Puerto Ricans.

Inspired by the example of black activism, Hispanics have drawn more closely together, but the diversity of their origins has prevented them from becoming a solid national grouping. Their median age is significantly younger than that of most Americans, they tend to be poorer than whites and many have not qualified as citizens. Their campaigning has been done via local groups that fight for better conditions rather than through large, nationwide associations. But they are becoming more organised and many are now acquiring citizenship. As they stand on the verge of being America's largest minority group, it is likely that issues of concern to their various sub-groups will gain greater prominence on the nation's political agenda. They may be still seriously under-represented in American institutions, but there have been recent signs of an emerging Latino-led radicalism, particularly among those who carry out many of the lowest paid and dirtiest jobs in the US. In the words of one writer:[4] 'The long history of political marginality is finally coming to an end. Latinos, all political pundits agree, are the sleeping dragon of US politics.'

The votes of Hispanics are crucial in some states, Texas, California and Florida among them. In the light of what happened in 2000 (see p. 107), Florida was a particularly interesting political battleground in the Bush years, not least because Jeb Bush, G.W. Bush's brother, was the Governor. Born in Mexico to father Jeb and his mother Columba, his articulate son George P. Bush could well prove to be the next member of the Bush dynasty to take the political stage and become a well-known figure in public life.

Of the **Asian Americans**, many originally settled in California and the Western states, having journeyed from China and Japan. More recent immigrants have come from the Philippines, South Korea and South-East Asia (especially Cambodia and Vietnam), but the area of settlement remains broadly the same: California and Hawaii, as well as the capital, Washington DC. There are more nearly 14 million Asian Americans, more than 15 million if we include those who reported Asian and at least one other race. They arrived in substantial numbers in the 1970s and 1980s, but the rate of increase has accelerated. The number of Asian alones (Asians without mixed blood) rose by nearly 50% in the decade to 2000. Today, round half of them live in the West (49%), followed by 20% in the Northeast and 19% in the Midwest. Fifty-one per cent of them live in just three states, California, New York and Hawaii.

In the past, the Chinese and, especially, the Japanese were the victims of regular discrimination; in 1942 many of the latter were interned in camps because of their 'doubtful' allegiance. Since then, much of the anti-Asian prejudice has disappeared. Most Asian groups have advanced in American society, though there are occasional outbreaks of hostile feeling.

America's Asian and Hispanic population is set to triple over the next fifty years. Waves of immigration from Asia and Central America are likely to keep the country young and vital.

The **Native American population** was originally called 'Indian' by the explorers and colonists who found it. By prior usage, the land belonged to the Native Americans, but these tribal peoples were gradually displaced as the settlers move westwards and the buffalo herds on which they depended were wiped out. They were eventually granted certain reserved areas, and many of the present Native Americans still live in or near these reservations, in Arizona, New Mexico and Utah. In a sense, it is wrong to group these Native Americans together, for they include representatives of many tribes whose cultures and lifestyles were once very different. Only about 3.1 million Native Indians and Alaskan Natives remain, the two groups generally being categorised as American Indian for census purposes. Forty-three per cent live in the West, the next largest group living in the South (31%). Only about one-third of Native Americans still live on reservations.

Generally they experience inferior standards of living, the reservations being enclaves of social disadvantage. Native Americans are much more likely to live in poverty; they also earn less and achieve less via the educational system. Some left their reservations because of the low quality of life there, and inhabit towns and cities such as Chicago and Los Angeles. However, those who have left have in many cases yet to become integrated into American society, and lack the occupational skills and cultural background to sustain themselves. They are prone to a variety of social problems, ranging from alcoholism and family disintegration to, at worst, suicide. Only recently have activist Native Americans begun to organise and press for changes in their quality of life.

Other than the Native Americans, all Americans are immigrants. The poor and oppressed from different parts of the world gathered in the country, so that it has developed as a land of diversity. In theory, all of those who entered the United States could benefit from the **American Dream**, by which every enterprising person could improve his or her position in a land of opportunity.

Not all groups have benefited equally from this possible social mobility, but individuals of any race and background have been able to change their lifestyle and prospects, and via education, occupation and intermarriage have altered their status. America is often seen as a '**melting-pot**', and groups from different backgrounds and of differing cultures have been able to mix with members of other groups, and have become assimilated into the American way of life.

American Dream

The widespread belief that by hard work and individual enterprise even the most poor and lowly Americans can achieve economic success, a better way of life and enhanced social status, in a land of immense opportunity. According to the Dream, there are no insurmountable barriers that prevent Americans from fulfilling their potential, even if many individuals and groups do not do so.

melting pot

The process by which people of diverse lands, cultures, languages and religions are blended or assimilated into American society.

The religious mix

Given the diversity of races represented in the United States, it is inevitable that many varieties of religious belief are to be found. There is no national or 'established' church for the whole country, though there were until the 1830s established state churches. Religious allegiances are active at all levels of society and religious beliefs, language, symbols and values are important to

Americans. They impact upon politics, as faith groups seek to organise voters, and play an active part in the selection of candidates and the appointment of judges.

Religious beliefs feature strongly in policy debate. Candidates for office routinely acknowledge the Almighty in their speeches and discuss issues in moralistic terms. In the 2000 election, both George W. Bush and his Democrat opponent, Al Gore, frequently referred to their status as **'born again' Christians**. In 2004, like the president, John Kerry was willing to parade details of his personal faith. In 2008, Barack Obama seemed to be the most comfortable presidential aspirant when talking about issues of belief. (The title of his political testament, *The Audacity of Hope*, was taken from a sermon by the pastor of his church.) He was keen to win the backing of a group known as progressive evangelicals, or Red Letter Christians, who are theologically conservative but strikingly radical on poverty, the environment and Iraq. Every White House incumbent from Jimmy Carter onwards has claimed to be 'born again'.

> **'born again' Christians**
> Christians who claim that their religious life has been dramatically altered by a conversion experience that has made them see issues very differently.

Unlike many countries, the United States does not include a question about religion in its census, so that information concerning religious allegiance has to be taken from survey and organisational findings. These indicate that the US has a greater number of religious groups than any other country in the world (well over 1,200). According to the CIA *World Factbook* (2010), the top organised religions are Christianity (78.5% of all Americans, by far the largest), Judaism (1.7%), Islam (0.6%), other and unspecified (2.8%), unaffiliated (12.3%) and none (4.1%).

Today, there are many more faiths than ever before, part of a remarkable upsurge in religious feeling. Religious toleration is a long-standing tradition, extending to groups with all manner of idiosyncrasies and eccentricities. It applies to the growing number of Islamic supporters, some of whom have been associated with more radical black political attitudes. Adherence to the Muslim faith poses a challenge to some traditional attitudes and values, the more so since the attack on the Twin Towers (see p. 17), which placed many American Muslims in an uncomfortable and unenviable position. But as yet America has been spared the kind of religious tension that has bedevilled many other parts of the globe.

Within the Christian church, there are many different denominations. Fifty-one per cent of all adult Americans classify themselves as Protestants, 25% as Catholic, 1.4% as Mormon (Latter Day Saints). Most Protestant denominations have European roots. Among adherents, the largest group belong to the Baptist church, which itself has many splinter offshoots; the Methodists, Lutherans, Presbyterians and Episcopalians are also well represented.

Comprising approximately a quarter of the population, Roman Catholics out-number any single Protestant group, as the table below indicates.

Religious affiliations in the United States

Religion	Number	%
Christian denominations	173,402,000	76.0
Roman Catholic	57,199,000	25.1
Baptist	36,148,000	15.8
Methodist/Wesleyan	11,366,000	5.0
Lutheran	8,674,000	3.8
Presbyterian	4,723,000	2.1
Other religions	8,796,000	3.9
Jews	2,680,000	1.2
Muslims	1,349,000	.6
Buddhists	1,189,000	.5

Adapted from figures provided in the American Religious Identification Survey (ARIS), 2008. Their estimates based on polling evidence vary slightly from those given in the CIA *World Factbook*.

This is the national picture, but the number of members of each particular sect varies widely from state to state. Baptists are very strong in Alabama, Georgia and Mississippi, and comprise more than half of the population in those states. The South has a strong Protestant majority. There are clusters of very firm allegiance in other areas, so that whereas Catholics are well represented in Connecticut, Massachusetts and Rhode Island, the Mormons (numerically small in the country as a whole) dominate the religious life of Utah, with 70% membership. In New York State, as one would expect, there are members of any sect and none; in New York City, 14% of the population is Jewish.

The importance of religion in American life

Religious groups operate at all levels of the political system, seeking to ensure that those who would attain political power share their beliefs. Religion has shaped and informed the character of political movements. It can be a powerful cata-lyst of social change. In the Civil Rights Movement of the 1950s and 1960s there were many promi-nent church ministers, notably Martin Luther King (see p. 379). The black church played an influen-tial role in communicating ideas and information. Jesse Jackson was a younger member of the crusade for social justice and equal rights, and remains influential in the Democratic Party.

The **Religious Right** (many of whose members are part of the Christian Coalition – see p. 318–319)

Religious Right

A broad movement of conservatives who advance moral and social values. It first attracted attention as the Moral Majority, but later became known as the Christian Coalition. Highly active in the Republican Party, it seeks to take America back to its true heritage and to restore the godly principles that made the nation great. Most of its members emphasise that they have been 'born again'. They tend to be fundamentalist and are unquestioning in accepting Christian doctrines.

is an increasingly significant force in the Republican Party. On issues such as abortion and school prayer its contribution to discussion and action has had a considerable effect on politicians and voters. In 2004, its members played a significant role in the victory of George W. Bush. They were less enthusiastic about the candidature of John McCain four years later.

A candidate's religion can be a factor in determining his prospects, though the choice of Senator John F. Kennedy showed that a Catholic could be chosen, despite some initial reservations. In 2004, the Democrats again nominated a Catholic, John Kerry. Whereas in 1960, some 80% of them voted for Kennedy, today they are less likely to vote as a bloc. But on an issue such as abortion or stem cell research, church leaders listen to the words of any candidate with much interest. The stand adopted may influence the prospects of election in certain states.

Broadly speaking, Jews (although they tend to be prosperous and better educated than members of other minority groups) are more likely to be Democrats than Republicans, as are Catholics and members of minority denominations. The fact that the Democrats were willing to choose Catholics in 1928 and 1960 as presidential candidates meant that many of that religious leaning were well disposed towards the party. It is perceived as being more accessible to them; they are welcome to join. Protestants, especially outside the South, incline strongly towards the Republicans, which is seen as the natural home for White Anglo Saxon Protestants – often referred to as WASPS.

Religious belief and practice are important in American family life and in the political process. God is alluded to in many public speeches, and religion is taken seriously. Americans are more likely to believe in God, pray, attend a place of worship. More than two-thirds of all Americans belong to a church or synagogue, more than half say religion is 'very important' in their lives and more than 40% go to a religious service at least every week. This amounts to a remarkable level of religiosity, suggesting that America has resisted some of the secularising influences familiar in European nations. In Europe, only citizens of the Irish Republic exhibit a similar degree of religiosity to the Americans. The scale and intensity of belief is such that it influences the discussion of many issues from abortion to gay rights, from pornography to school prayer. It can also influence the conduct of foreign policy.

Education, class, inequality and occupation

America is much less preoccupied with social class than is Western Europe, and the Marxian division of bourgeoisie and proletariat has never been much applied to American society. Sociologists often talk of socio-economic status (SES) as a convenient tool by which to analyse the population, and this SES measurement is decided on the basis of education, income and occupation. The usual difficulty about any such categorisation applies, namely that people whose income places them in one stratum have a higher status than some who earn more than they do.

Whereas 'subjective social class' refers to the position in society in which a person places himself or herself, 'objective social class' depends on the position assigned by a social scientist. Many people assume that they are middle class, as befits a land in which people believe that they can achieve whatever they want if they seize their opportunities. In fact there are many people whose occupation and income place them lower down the social scale. Such persons may also wish to distance themselves from organised labour in the trade union movement, which has an unfavourable connotation for many Americans. Overall, the emphasis on class-based analysis fits the American experience less comfortably than in other countries, for the ethos of individualism and enterprise does not sit easily alongside any notion of class solidarity.

About one-third of Americans have stayed on and attended some kind of college, and education is valued in the United States as both a desirable thing in itself and a necessary precondition for a successful economy in which skills and training assume ever-greater importance. However, the learning experience is not evenly shared, for among blacks and Hispanics there has traditionally been a much greater likelihood that they will not complete their high-school course. Most younger blacks do finish their high-school education, but relatively few go on to college; Hispanics are less likely to stay with their courses than blacks, and their drop-out rate is high even in the early years. Such differences in achievement have an impact on job prospects and earnings levels, and on the likelihood of political participation in adulthood.

In the early years of the Republic, agriculture was by far the most common occupation, but in the twentieth century America became the leading industrial country in the world. The invention of new machines and of techniques of mass production along with the super-abundance of natural resources paved the way for economic success as an industrial nation. Today, commentators often describe the country as being in a post-industrial phase, in which success and rewards depend more on skill and training than on the old industrial structure in which labour and management were often in conflict. The numbers now employed in manufacturing have diminished and those in farming have reduced dramatically. In 1800, 83% of the labour force was employed in agriculture; today the figure is below 1%.

In total, 91% of Americans are employed by the private sector. Small businesses are the largest employer in the country, representing 53% of US workers. Large businesses employ another 38%; amongst them, Walmart, the largest company and the largest private sector employer in the world, employs 1.4 million. White-collar work has grown rapidly as more and more people enter the professions and management of some kind. Many people work in government (8%), education and defence.

Relatively few African Americans are employed in supervisory or higher positions. Blacks are more often engaged in the service industries or, if more educated, in clerical work; in 2009, there were about 4.5 million (30%) working in education and health services. Hispanics often work as labourers, operators and on the farms.

Employment of the labour force (153.9 million), by sector: 2009

Sector	% of population
Farming, forestry and fishing	0.7
Managerial, professional and technical	37.2
Manufacturing, extraction, transportation and crafts	20.3
Sales and office	24.0
Other services	17.7

Source: 2010 Census.

Income levels vary enormously, as one would expect in a land in which enterprise and initiative are encouraged. According to the Census Bureau, in the year 2008:
- 8% of US households had incomes of $15,000 and under
- 14% had incomes between $15,001 and $30,000
- 14% had incomes between $30,001 and $45,000
- 12% had incomes between $45,001 and $60,000
- 26% had incomes between $60,001 and $100,000
- 21% had incomes between $100,001 and $200,000
- 5% had incomes over $200,000 (44% of whom had incomes of $250,000 or more.)

Income distribution in the United States has remained relatively constant since World War II, but by the 1990s the wealthiest groups had gained a larger share of the nation's wealth. In 1950, the richest 20% of Americans controlled 42.8% of wealth, the middle 20% controlled 17.4%, and the poorest controlled just 4.5%. By 1980, the figures were 41.6%, 17.5% and 5.1%, respectively. However, by 2010 the poor and middle groups had lost some ground to the wealthy, the figures being 58%, 13% and 4%. The trend toward the greater concentration of wealth by the rich accelerated throughout the 1990s.

The wealth gap has obviously been widening between white households and Hispanic and African American families.[5] According to census figures (2010), the median net worth of white households was $113,822, nearly ten times greater than Hispanic families ($13,375) and more than thirteen times greater than African American ones ($8,650). Hispanic and black Americans are much less likely to participate in politics, although they are the people who most depend on government help via federal and state welfare programmes.

Poverty in the US in the early twentieth century

Poverty is usually defined as the lack of those goods and services that most members of society take for granted. The usual measure employed by the federal government, annually adjusted for inflation, is the 'poverty threshold'. The amount set is tied to a relative level, based on total income received. For instance, for 2011 the level was set at $22,350 for a family of four. The Census Bureau uses the same approach to estimate the number of people in poverty throughout the United States each year and classifies them by type of residence, race and other social, economic and demographic characteristics.

Official Census Bureau figures for 2010 show that 46.2 million (15.1%) are living in poverty. This represents the third consecutive annual increase in the proverty rate and is the largest figure recorded in the 52 years for which records are available. In part, the increases of recent years reflect the rapid increase in the US population.

The 2009 poverty rate increased for non-Hispanic whites from 8.6% to 9.4%, for Hispanics from 23.2% to 25.3% and for blacks from 24.7% to 25.8%. For Asians, the 2009 poverty rate (12.5%) was not statistically different from a year earlier.

Source: Census Bureau.

A sense of unity, despite diversity

America is a multi-lingual, multi-racial society of great social diversity. Yet many of the immigrants and their descendants have taken on board many traditional American values, such as a commitment to liberty and equality. There are forces that bring Americans together and give them a sense of common identity.

Part of this sense of national unity can be explained by the pursuit of the American Dream by which, in a land of opportunity, all may prosper – if they are sufficiently enterprising. The Dream is often referred to in American literature and has been a theme of many a Hollywood film. Former President Clinton spoke of it as the 'dream that we were all raised on'. It was one based on a simple and powerful idea: that 'if you work hard and play by the rules you should be given a chance to go as far as your God-given ability will take you'. Americans are valued as individuals, according to what they make of their chances in life.

Adversity has also helped to bring them together. War and the threat of war often serve to bind a nation; in World War II, Americans of all types could recognise the service and patriotism of others from a different background. So too in September 2001 and thereafter, the terrorist attacks on the World Trade Center, which destroyed the well-known image of the Twin Towers on the New York skyline and killed nearly 4,000 people of diverse backgrounds, also had the effect of uniting New Yorkers and their fellow Americans. They were determined both to hunt down those who perpetrated the outrage and to show the world that the spirit of the city could not be crushed.

Finally, shared values, a common culture, the prevalence of the mass media and intermarriage serve to blur the differences between different groups, for we have seen that in the melting-pot of modern America all national groups are to some extent assimilated into the mainstream of American life. They come to accept and embrace American values, and to share a common attachment for democratic ideals and processes.

Common values: the political culture of the United States

The term 'culture' refers to the way of life of a people, the sum of their inherited and cherished ideas, knowledge and values, which together constitute the shared bases of social action. **Political culture** is culture in its political aspect. It emphasises those patterns of thought and behaviour associated with politics in different societies, ones that are widely shared and define the relationship of citizens to their government and to each other in matters affecting politics and public affairs. Citizens of any country or major ethnic or religious community tend to have a common or core political culture, a set of long-term ideas and traditions that are passed on from one generation to the next. As Heywood[6] explains, 'political culture differs from public opinion in that it is fashioned out of long-term values rather than simply people's reactions to specific policies and problems'.

Political culture in the United States derives from some of the ideas that inspired the pioneers, who made the country, and the **Founding Fathers**, who wrote its constitution. It includes faith in democracy and representative government, the ideas of popular sovereignty, limited government, the rule of law, equality, liberty, opportunity, support for the free market system, freedom of speech and individual rights. But of course at different stages in history, the existing political culture serves some individuals and groups better than others. Until the 1960s, the prevailing political culture suggested that women and ethnic minorities were

political culture
The widely shared underlying political beliefs and values which most citizens of a country share about the conduct of government, the relationship of citizens to those who rule over them and to one another.

Founding Fathers
The men who attended the Philadelphia Convention in May 1787 and devised the American Constitution.

not full members of the political community. Not surprisingly, these two groups sought to change the political culture. They wanted to see ideas of equality and opportunity applied to them as much as to other groups. Since then, there has been a 'rights culture', as activists have sought to demand the rights they regard as their due.

Political culture is not an unchanging landscape, a fixed background against which the political process operates. Attitudes evolve and change over time, for there are in society often a number of forces at work which serve to modify popular attitudes, among them migration and the emergence in a number of liberal democracies of a substantial underclass. Both can be a cause of greater diversity in popular attitudes, for immigrants and those alienated from majority lifestyles may have a looser attachment to prevailing cultural norms. In the words of one author,[7] 'culture moves'.

American political culture is tied up with **American exceptionalism**, the view that American society and culture are exceptional in comparison with other advanced industrial countries. In a sense this is true of all societies and cultures, and one might equally point out that there are several things that they have in common with each other. But supporters of this 'exceptionalist' viewpoint suggest that there are several features peculiar to US politics and society that distinguish the country from other western democracies. A number of American politicians and writers have reinforced this idea that theirs is a 'chosen people' that has made

> **American exceptionalism**
> The idea that the United States is different from all other nations, distinctive in its political development and – according to some advocates – unique in its contribution to mankind. Most Americans consider their country to be a unique bastion of freedom and some suggest that the values of this exceptionalism (individualism, liberty and populism) could beneficially be exported elsewhere.

a special contribution to mankind and whose actions have been guided by a 'special providence'.[8] In his second inaugural speech in January 1997, Bill Clinton echoed such thinking, in his listing of his country's many achievements:

> What a century it has been. America became the world's mightiest industrial power, saved the world from tyranny in two world wars and a long cold war, and time and time again reached across the globe to millions who longed for the blessings of liberty. Along the way, Americans produced the great middle class and security in old age; built unrivaled centers of learning and opened public schools to all; split the atom and explored the heavens; invented the computer and the microchip; made a revolution in civil rights for minorities; and extended the circle of citizenship, opportunity and dignity to women.

It was the Frenchman **Alexis de Tocqueville**[9] who first wrote of American exceptionalism, back in 1835. He saw the United States as 'a society uniquely different from the more traditional societies

> **Alexis de Tocqueville (1805–59)**
> A liberal French aristocrat, writer and politician who visited the United States as a young man, was impressed and wrote his *Democracy in America*.

and status-bound nations of the Old World'. It was 'qualitatively different in its organising principles and political and religious institutions from . . . other western societies', some of its distinguishing features being a relatively high level of social egalitarianism and social mobility, enthusiasm for religion, love of country, and ethnic and racial diversity.

One of its characteristics is a strong belief in **liberal individualism**, dating back to the ideas of the English political philosopher John Locke (1632–1704), who wrote of people's inalienable natural rights. By contrast, the culture of the Old World has emphasised ideas of hierarchy and nationality. What Hames and Rae[10] refer to as **messianism** is another characteristic. Americans tend to see themselves as the 'Last, Best, Hope of Mankind', a theme apparent in foreign policy, where some are isolationists who reject the rest of the world as beyond redemption, while others are idealists who want to save the world and make it better (i.e., adopt American values and goals).

> **messianism**
> A sense of mission, the idea that some people are the exceptional and long-awaited liberators of a country or people.

Sometimes, the different values identified conflict with each other. If liberal individualism is one element of the American outlook, stressing as it does freedom from overbearing governmental interference, the republican strand is another. As we see below, it is associated with the idea of political involvement by a concerned and interested citizenry, what Welch[11] describes as 'a marked tilt towards participation'. At times, the dislike of central government and fear of 'governmental encroachment' is more influential than the commitment to the ideal and practice of participation.

What are the key elements of American political culture?

Analyses of political culture are inevitably replete with generalisations that must be regarded with a degree of scepticism. There is and can be no definitive listing of shared political values and the ones suggested in any contribution often tend to overlap with each other. At times, they have been ignored or at least denied in regard to certain social groups. But none the less, we can point to a number of shared American interests and concerns. Among these are:

1 **Liberalism** – a recognition of the dignity and worth of the individual and a tendency to view politics in individualistic terms. Classical liberals believed in government by consent, limited government, the protection of private property and opportunity. They also stressed the importance of individual rights, some of which were regarded as 'inalienable'. Americans have great faith in the common sense of the average citizen and believe that all individuals have rights as well as responsibilities. All should have the chance

to fulfil their destiny, and no individual or group should be denied recognition of their worth or dignity. Individual liberties must be respected and opportunities for economic advance unimpeded. By contrast, collectivist policies and solutions (those based around the idea of the state – on behalf of its citizens – acknowledging society's collective responsibility to care about those in need) have never been embraced (see the section on socialism below and on p. 300–303).

The word 'liberal' derives from the Latin *liber*, meaning 'free' or 'generous', from which we can detect an attachment to qualities such as liberty and tolerance. The Americans have a strong attachment to liberty, as symbolised by the statue erected in its name. The War of Independence was fought in its name, and the Constitution, like the American Revolution, proclaims this commitment. The late Clinton Rossiter,[12] a renowned American political scientist, saw liberty as the pre-eminent value in American political culture: 'We have always been a nation obsessed with liberty. Liberty over authority, freedom over responsibility, rights over duties – these are our historic preferences.'

2 **Equality** – the words in the Declaration of Independence are clear enough: 'We hold these truths to be self-evident, that all men are created equal.' As a relatively young nation, America lacks the feudal past that was a feature of many European countries. There has always been a strong belief in social equality, and although there are sharp inequalities of income and wealth, the divisions are not associated with a class system as they have been in Britain. The equality Americans favour is not equality of outcome, but rather of worth. They do not want a society in which all are reduced to the same level, for this would conflict with their belief in the opportunities they value in the American Dream. They do believe that every American is entitled to equal consideration, equal protection under the law and equal rights, even if at times there has been considerable reluctance to acknowledge that this applies to African Americans as well as to whites.

Equality is more about prospects of advancement than about result. No one should be limited by his or her social background, ethnicity, gender or religion. All should have the chance to climb the ladder of success and share in the American Dream, in a land of opportunity. Even those of humble origins can still rise to greatness, so that Bill Clinton, the lad from Hope (Arkansas) could reach the White House.

3 **Democracy** – a belief in government by the people, according to majority will. Today, this might be seen as similar to liberalism, with its emphasis on personal freedom and rights, but at the time of the writing of the American Constitution in 1787 there was far more support for liberalism (as set out in the writings of John Locke) than for democracy, seen as rule by majorities and mobs.

Liberalism and democracy have roots in an older classical republican tradition. This dates back to the days of ancient Rome and in particular to the writings of the Roman consul and writer Cicero. The speeches and writings of the Founding Fathers often employed republican imagery and symbols, and statues of George Washington have often shown him wearing Roman costume. The ancient Romans believed in the idea of self-governing republic ultimately ruled by a knowledgeable and involved citizenry. In this sense, the term 'republic' refers to a form of government that derives its powers directly or indirectly from the people. In a representative democracy, Americans could select representatives to govern and lay down the rules by which society operates. For the Founding Fathers, republic seemed preferable to democracy, with its overtones of demagogy and mass rule.

Such fears have long disappeared and there has, throughout much American history, been a strong consensus in support of democracy and the values that underpin it, including:
- **a deep interest in the exercise of power**, who has it, how it was acquired and how those who exercise it can be removed;
- **a general acceptance of majority rule**, but also respect for minority rights so that minorities can have the opportunity to become tomorrow's majority. Pluralism in society, involving the existence and acceptance of distinctive groups and political toleration, has been important as the country has become more ethnically and religiously diverse and people have adopted new lifestyle arrangements;
- **a firm commitment to popular sovereignty**, the idea that ultimate power resides in the people themselves;
- **strong support for the rule of law**, with government being based upon a body of law applied equally and with just procedures. The principle of fairness applies, with all individuals entitled to the same rights and level of protection and expected to abide by the same codes of behaviour. No one is above the law, for in the words of Chief Justice Marshall,[13] 'the government of the United States has been emphatically termed a government of laws, not of men';
- **a dislike and distrust of government and a fear of the tyrannical rule and exercise of excessive authority that can accompany it**, not surprising in a land whose pioneers tamed the wilderness, created new frontiers and tried to build themselves a better future. Americans have always been wary of those who exercise power over them – a distrust which has roots in Lockean liberalism, but was primarily based upon the experiences of the colonists in their dealings with King George III. This suspicion of government and things associated with it may be a factor in the low turnouts in many elections. At the approach of the new millennium, the number of

Americans who expressed 'confidence in Washington to do what is right' is markedly lower than a few decades ago. The loss of faith has affected the Obama administration, just as at times it affected its predecessor (see box below). Many Americans are indifferent to what goes on in Washington. It seems remote from their experience and – for some of them – the policies that emerge from the capital seem often wasteful, ineffective and ill judged. Such anti-government feeling is widely held, even its intensity varies considerably. At the one end of the spectrum are moderates who are wary of overbearing Washingtonian attitudes and too much interference. At the other, there are strong devotees of states' rights who much resent the intrusion of central government and who wish to see far more decision making conducted at state or local level.

- **a liking for politicians who seem to articulate the thoughts and feelings of the common man**. Populists who have railed against the special interests, the East Coast establishment or communists have often found a ready response. Anti-politicians à la **Ross Perot** and those who blend religion and politics in the fashion of Jesse Jackson have at times found themselves backed by a surge of popular enthusiasm.

Other features could be mentioned, such as love of God and of their country, eternal optimism and idealism. As we have seen, religion (see pp. 10–13) matters in American life in a way that it does not in most of Europe. The Declaration of Independence affirms that all men are 'endowed by their Creator' with certain rights, and ends with a recognition of the 'firm reliance on the protection of divine Providence' necessary to make the Declaration a success. Religious faith – the Christian faith – has been and remains all important.

Intense admiration for and love of country is another American quality. Americans also tend to be very patriotic and to support emblems that help them to identify with their country. They acknowledge their Constitution, their anthem, their flag and other symbols of their nationhood. Morning in many schools begins with young Americans facing the flag and renewing their **Pledge of Allegiance**.

Ross Perot

A billionaire Texan businessmen who had created and managed a highly successful computer firm and who in 1992 made known his interest in running for the presidency. In the November election he did very well, attracting some 19% of the popular vote – although he failed to win in any single state. He stood again in 1996, as the candidate for the newly created Reform Party. This time, he made little impact.

Pledge of Allegiance

I pledge allegiance to the flag of the United States and to the Republic for which it stands, one nation, under God indivisible, with liberty and justice for all.

Pew research findings on trust in government, 1958–2010

Public trust in the federal government in Washington is at one of its lowest levels in half a century. Just 22% of Americans say they trust the government to do what is right 'just about always' (3%) or 'most of the time' (19%). The current level of scepticism was matched previously only in the periods from 1992 to 1995 (reaching as low as 17% in the summer of 1994), and 1978 to 1980 (bottoming out at 25% in 1980). When the National Election Study first asked this question in 1958, 73% of Americans trusted the government to do what is right just about always or most of the time.

The Pew research paper diagnosed prevailing feelings in this way: 'The forces contributing to the current wave of public distrust include an uncertain economic environment, overwhelming discontent with Congress and elected officials, and a more partisan environment. The bitter and drawn-out healthcare debate exacerbated negative feelings about government – particularly Congress. During the final House debate over healthcare reform, public perceptions of Congress reached an all-time low. And the public's impressions of elected officials as corrupt, wasteful, self-centered, unwilling to compromise, and indifferent to the concerns of regular Americans are widespread.'

Pew Research Center findings, 18 April 2010, 'Distrust, Discontent, Anger and Partisan Rancor'.

In particular, Americans respect the office of president, if not the behaviour of individual presidents. The figure in the White House operates as a focal point of their national loyalty and, especially in times of crisis, he speaks up for the interests of all Americans. He and they possess the same vision. They want to build a better world for themselves and their families. They want a share in the American Dream. That Dream encompasses many of the values listed above – individualism, limited government, liberty and equal opportunities among them. It is in essence the belief that the United States is a land of opportunity for those prepared to work hard, get ahead and make a fortune. Americans are valued as individuals according to what they make of their chances in life.

Given the commitment to the American Dream and the ideas that underpin it, it is no surprise that **socialism** has never taken root in the United States. Indeed, for Seymour Lipset and Gary Marks,[14] its absence is a cornerstone of American exceptionalism. They point out that opinion polls in America continue to reveal a people whose atti-

socialism
Socialists share in common a belief that unrestrained capitalism is responsible for a variety of social evils, including the exploitation of working people, the widespread existence of poverty and unemployment, gross inequality of wealth and the pursuit of greed and selfishness. Socialists would prefer to see a social system based on cooperative values and emphasise the values of community rather than of individualism. They also believe strongly in the need for a more equal and just society, based on brotherhood and a sense of social solidarity. Marxian socialism is a variety of socialist thinking associated with the ideas of the left-wing German thinker, Karl Marx. It has a strong economic, as well as an ethical, dimension.

tudes are different to those of people in Europe and Canada. Americans do not favour an active role for government in the economy or a desire for large welfare programmes. They favour private efforts in business and welfare and rely more on philanthropic giving. The two writers point to the absence of those conditions that the left has always seen as a prerequisite for the development of any 'mass allegiance' to socialism, but draw attention to the diversity of explanations given for the failure of American socialism (see also pp. 300–303 for a more detailed analysis): 'Explanations for [socialism]'s weakness are as numerous as socialists were few. Some . . . attribute the weakness of socialism to the failures of socialist organisations and leaders. Another school ascribes socialism's bankruptcy to its incompatibility with America's core values, while still others cite the American Constitution as the decisive factor.'

In their analyses of the development of socialism, Karl Marx and Friedrich Engels contributed a Marxist perspective to the debate on the failure of American socialism. Marx had assumed that the working class was destined to organise revolutionary socialist parties in every capitalist society. He and Engels noted, however, the respects in which the United States differed from other European societies. Above all, it was a new nation and society, a democratic country lacking many of the institutions and traditions of previously feudal societies. It had a 'modern and purely bourgeois culture'. After Marx's death in 1883, Engels[15] gave more thought to the non-emergence of socialist movements on a mass scale. He attributed the 'backwardness' of the American workers to the absence of a feudal past. In his view, 'Americans [were] born conservatives – just because America is so purely bourgeois, so entirely without a feudal past and proud of its purely bourgeois organisation'.

CONCLUSION

The United States is a land of great diversity, even if there are factors that bind the nation together. Jews, Irishmen, Poles and many others have been part of successive waves of past immigration, leaving America as what Robert Singh[16] calls 'a kaleidoscopic mosaic of racial, ethnic, religious, regional and linguistic differences'. Some enthuse over the positive benefits of multiculturalism and multiethnicity, seeing it as an indication of vigour and energy. But diversity also creates special problems in a democracy, for it is associated with wide differences of opinion that can make it difficult to reach agreed solutions to political problems. Administering America presents a strong challenge to the governing institutions and those who run them. As de Tocqueville[17] observed more than 150 years ago: 'A confused clamour is heard on every side and a thousand simultaneous voices demand the immediate satisfaction of their social wants.'

De Tocqueville's words carry considerably more weight today. The distinguished historian and one-time adviser to President Kennedy, Arthur Schlesinger,[18] wrote of 'the fragmentation of the national community into a quarrelsome spatter of enclaves, ghettos, tribes'. Others too fear fragmentation, the possibility of what alarmists refer to as a Balkanisation of the United States that could ultimately undermine the forces that pull it together.

REFERENCES

1 *The World Factbook*, CIA, 2010
2 US Census Bureau, 2010 projection. Other figures in this section, apart from those relating to cities, are adapted from the official figures produced for the 2010 Census, unless otherwise stated in the text. Those relating to city sizes and composition relate to the 2000 Census (the 2010 material was unavailable at the time of going to print)
3 W. Frey, Brookings Institute, as quoted in *The Guardian*, 19 March 2004
4 M. Davis, *Magical Urbanism: Latinos Reinvent the US City*, Verso, 2001
5 Pew Hispanic Centre, analysis of US census data, as quoted in *The Guardian*, 27 August 2000
6 A. Heywood, *Politics*, Macmillan, 1997
7 T. Rochon, *Culture Moves: Ideas, Activism and Changing Values*, Princeton University Press, 1998
8 W. Mead, *Special Providence: American Foreign Policy and How It Changed the World*, Knopf, 2001
9 A. de Tocqueville, *Democracy in America*, vol 2, reissued by Vintage, 1954
10 T. Hames and N. Rae, *Governing America*, Manchester University Press, 1996
11 S. Welch, 'Pressure Groups, Social Movements and Participation', in G. Peele, C. Bailey, B. Cain and B. Peters (eds), *Developments in American Politics* 4, Palgrave, 2002
12 C. Rossiter, *Conservatism in America*, Vintage, 1962
13 J. Marshall, judgment in Marbury v. Madison, 1803
14 S. Lipset and G. Marks, *Why Socialism Failed in the United States: It Didn't Happen Here*, W.W. Norton, 2000
15 F. Engels, letter quoted in 14 above
16 R. Singh, *American Government and Politics: A Concise Introduction*, Sage, 2003
17 A. de Tocqueville, as in 10 above
18 A. Schlesinger Jr, *The Disuniting of America: Reflections on a Multicultural Society*, W.W. Norton, 1992

USEFUL WEB SITES

www.americansc.org.uk The American Studies Resources Centre. A useful starting point for the discussion of all aspects of American government and politics, with links to many other sites.

www.census.gov Bureau of the Census. Statistics on the US and its citizens.

www.norc.org/GSS+Website/ General Social Survey. Mass of polling evidence.

www.electionstudies.org/ National Election Studies. More evidence from the polls.

The Constitution

2

Constitutions are important in all countries, for they set out the principles, rules and conventions according to which people should be governed. They normally outline the powers of the various parts of the governing body and the relationship that exists between them. Almost always, as in the case of the United States, they are written documents. Usually, they contain a declaration of rights, providing for civil and political liberties. However, the mere existence of a constitution and some written statement of freedoms is no guarantee that these will be respected.

In this chapter, we examine the drafting of the Constitution; its nature and contents; and the process by which it can be amended. We can then attempt some assessment.

POINTS TO CONSIDER

- How did the Articles of Confederation and the 1787 Constitution differ from each other?
- What are the main characteristics of the American Constitution?
- What is meant by the theory of a separation of powers and the notion of checks and balances?
- What role did the idea of a Bill of Rights play in discussions on the new Constitution?
- How easy is it to amend the American Constitution?
- How effectively has the US Constitution adapted to changing circumstances?
- Why do Americans attach such importance to their Constitution?
- What issues of constitutional reform have been debated in recent years and why has the cause of constitutional reform not aroused greater enthusiasm?
- What are the similarities and differences in the constitutions of Britain and the United States?

THE CONSTITUTION IN THEORY

In the Declaration of Independence (1776) drafted by Thomas Jefferson, he produced a classic justification for breaking the British connection. To Jefferson and those around him, the only legitimate basis for government was the consent of the governed, a revolutionary sentiment at the time and an ingredient missing from the relationship between Britain and the colonists:

> We hold these truths to be self-evident, that all men are created equal, that they are endowed by their Creator with certain inalienable Rights, that among these are Life, Liberty and the Pursuit of Happiness. – That to secure these Rights, Governments are instituted among Men, deriving their just Powers from the Consent of the Governed, – That whenever any Form of Government becomes destructive of these Ends, it is the Right of the People to alter or to abolish it, and to constitute new Government . . .

The colonies – or the United States as they later called themselves – drafted a compact that bound them together as a nation whilst hostilities were still raging. This agreement was known as the Articles of **Confederation** and Perpetual Union. It was adopted by a Congress of the States in 1777, and signed in July 1778. Not until March 1781 did these Articles become binding, when Maryland finally ratified them.

The Articles provided for a loose association, establishing a central government that had only modest powers. On many key issues – including defence, finance and trade – it was at the mercy of decisions made by the state legislatures. George Washington recognised the weakness of the union that hung by only 'a rope of sand'. The new nation was near to chaos, for it lacked political and economic strength. The Confederation was inadequate for the task of governing such a diverse area and there was no stability in the arrangements that had been agreed.

In particular, Congress, the main institution in the Confederation, had insufficient power to fulfil its duty, 'the management of the general interest of the United States', for it was too beholden to the thirteen colonies and lacked any means of enforcing its views. It was especially difficult for Congress to gain acceptance for a common foreign policy, for any agreements made might not be enforced by other colonies. Disillusion with the existing governing arrangements was rife. This was the background to the drawing up of the American **Constitution**.

confederation

A political system in which there is a loose alliance of self-governing states, with a weak central government to bind them together.

constitution

A constitution sets out the formal structure of the state. It specifies the institutions and powers of central government and its relationship with other levels; articulates the relationships between the central institutions, the pathways of power and the procedures for law making; and usually includes a declaration of rights of the citizen and – by so doing – thereby establishes the limits on governmental power. It embodies the fundamental principles by which a country is governed.

The Philadelphia Convention, 1787

In 1787, the legislative body of the Republic, the Continental Congress, put out a call to all the states inviting them to send delegates to Philadelphia on 25 May 1787. The meeting was to be held in Independence Hall, where the Declaration of Independence had been adopted eleven years earlier. The delegates (better known as the Founding Fathers) met to consider 'the situation of the United States, to devise such further Provisions as shall appear to them necessary to render the Constitution of the federal Government adequate to the emergency of the Union'. They were authorised to amend the Articles, but in the event they cast them aside and proceeded to draw up a charter for a more centralised form of government. It was this Constitution that was completed on 17 September 1787 and formally adopted on 4 March 1789.

Inevitably, there were disappointments with the outcome of the deliberations, causing some delegates to depart before the signing ceremony (of the 39 who did sign, few were completely satisfied with what had been accomplished). The settlement had to be a compromise, given the obvious differences between large and small states, and between those who wanted and those who baulked at an extension of federal power. Benjamin Franklin articulated the viewpoint of those who had doubts but still gave their acquiescence: 'There are several parts of this Constitution which I do not at present approve, but I am not sure I shall never approve them.' Acceptance was justified because 'I expect no better and because I am not sure that it is not the best.'

It was in theory desirable for every state to ratify (give formal approval to) the new document, but the convention delegates realised that this would be difficult to achieve quickly. They boldly declared that the proposed Constitution should become effective when nine had given their approval. Delaware was the first to sign, followed by Pennsylvania and New Jersey, and then by Georgia and Connecticut, where comfortable majorities were achieved. There was a fiercely contested struggle in Massachusetts over the absence of any Bill of Rights, but in early 1788 it too narrowly endorsed the document. In June 1788, the ratification by Maryland, New Hampshire and South Carolina meant that nine states had given their support, enough to see the document accepted.

The nature of the Constitution

The US Constitution is explicit and straightforward, its original, unamended contents comprising 4,543 words expressed in seven long articles and printed on four pages of parchment; it is the shortest and oldest written constitution still in use by any nation in the world today. It sets out the basic structure and

A note on the Founding Fathers

The Founding Fathers of the United States (also known as the Framers) were the political leaders who met at Philadelphia between May and September 1787 and agreed the Constitution. Chaired by the widely respected George Washington, the delegates benefited from the political brilliance and insight of Alexander Hamilton and James Madison, whilst the 81-year-old Benjamin Franklin added the moderation of age to the proceedings. Overall, the delegates possessed a blend of experience and learning, forty-two out of fifty-five having served in the Continental Congress and more than half having received a college education and studied the classics of political thought. Their average age was only 40 and, having politically matured during the revolutionary period, they were less tied to state loyalties than were older men whose outlook was formed before the war. Only six had signed the Declaration of Independence. Those who assembled were nationalists building a nation, not merely defending the interests of their states.

Socially, the Framers were not a representative sample of the population. Among them were several wealthy bankers, land speculators, lawyers, merchants and planters, fifteen being slaveholders. They constituted a conservative, propertied group in which small farmers and workers were unrepresented. There were divisions among them during the writing and ratification process, in part reflecting whether the representatives came from large or small states. Those from large states tended to favour a strong national government that they hoped to dominate, whereas those from the smaller states were fearful of a strong centre. The division is often expressed in the distinction between the Federalists and the Anti-Federalists. All delegates supported a republican form of government and all were constitutionalists who opposed arbitrary, unrestrained rule.

On 27 September 1787, the Founding Fathers assembled for the ceremony of signing the document that they were commending to the nation. All but three of those present signed. By then, those who had doubts about the general tenor of the proposals being made had already departed.

functions of the various branches of government – executive, legislative and judicial – and the relationship between them.

The Constitution is designated as the 'supreme law of the land', and this was taken to mean that in any conflict with state constitutions or state laws, the federal Constitution and federal laws take precedence. Over the succeeding two centuries, decisions by the Supreme Court have confirmed and reinforced this idea of constitutional supremacy.

The Constitution is the framework against which all political activity occurs, and laid down within it are the answers to key questions of governmental organisation. It explains the method of election for the federal executive and legislature, and the system of appointment to federal offices (including the Supreme Court). It itemises the powers of the central government, and denies certain powers to the states while giving them others. It provides certain civil, legal and political rights for the citizens that may not be taken away. It sets out the procedure for its own amendment.

The Constitution sets out general political ideas, but its first three articles describe the three branches of the national government: legislative, executive and judicial, each with its own duties and responsibilities. The powers of the president are outlined, as are the topics on which the legislative branch can make laws, and as is the structure of the federal courts. Since its introduction, the Constitution has changed in a number of respects, but its underlying principles remain unaltered. These are:

- The three branches of government are separate and distinct, and the powers given to each of them are carefully balanced by the powers granted to the other two. Each branch therefore acts as a check upon the potential excesses of the other (see the box on checks and balances, and the separation of powers, below). It is therefore a **presidential system**, in which the executive is separately elected and is, in theory, equal to the legislature, as opposed to a parliamentary system (such as that of the UK), in which the government governs in and through parliament, thereby fusing the two branches.

- A belief that government should be restricted to doing only that which is strictly necessary, in order that the rights and freedoms of the individual citizen are recognised and respected. Such **limited government** had been advocated by James Madison in the **Federalist Papers**, which put it this way: 'If men were angels, no government would be necessary . . . In framing a government which is to be administered by men over men, the great difficulty lies in this; you must first enable the government to control the governed; and in the next place oblige it to control itself.'

- The Constitution, and the laws passed under its provisions, and any treaties entered into by the president which have the approval of the Senate, take precedence over all other laws, executive acts and regulations.

limited government
A situation in which the role of government is constrained by a higher authority, usually a constitution, thus ensuring that there is no more than minimal governmental intrusion into personal liberties and the running of the economy. All US governments – federal and state – are limited in that none of them can exceed the powers designated to them by the US Constitution. The Bill of Rights is the clearest statement of the limits of the government's powers.

Federalist Papers
A series of 85 articles published in *The Federalist* newspaper (1787–1788), written by Hamilton, Jay and Madison (under the name of Publius) with the purpose of persuading individual states to ratify the newly negotiated constitution. They are widely regarded as an invaluable statement of the values that the document embraces.

- A commitment to **democracy** (see Chapter 11) and the **rule of law**. The view of the American philosopher John Dewey[1] was that a democratic system was superior in form and purpose to other systems, for it embodied the idea that each individual possesses intrinsic worth and dignity. As for the rule of law, the principle is not specifically mentioned in the Constitution, yet it is one of the most important legacies of the Founding Fathers. It is implicit in a number of constitutional provisions, such as Article IV ('The Citizens of each State shall be entitled to the Privileges and Immunities of Citizens in the several States') and the Fifth Amendment, which requires 'due process of law' and 'just compensation', whenever government initiates adverse actions against a citizen.
- All free men are equal before the law and are equally entitled to its protection (but not slaves and women, until the passage of the Fourteenth Amendment). Similarly, all states are equal, none being entitled to special treatment from the federal government.
- Each state must acknowledge the laws passed by other states.
- State government must be republican in form, with final authority resting in the hands of the people. The opening words of the document proclaim: 'We the People of the United States . . . do ordain and establish this Constitution.' This commitment to the **sovereignty of the people** echoes the ideas of the French writer and philosopher Jean Jacques Rousseau,[2] who argued that the best form of government was one that reflected the general will of the people, which was the sum total of those interests that all citizens had in common. It finds expression in the use of methods of **direct democracy** (see p. 266–274).
- The people must have the right to change their form of government by legal means defined in the Constitution itself.

democracy
Rule by the people ('people power'), as in Abraham Lincoln's phrase, 'government of the people, by the people and for the people'. Democracy involves control of the government by the governed, in free and regular elections. It implies both popular participation and government in the public interest.

rule of law
Government based on the idea of the supremacy of the law, which must be applied equally and through just procedures. The law governs the actions of individual citizens towards one another and also controls the conduct of the state towards them. No one is above the law, regardless of their status or position.

sovereignty of the people (popular sovereignty)
The belief that the legitimacy of the state is created by the will or consent of its people, who are the source of all political power.

direct democracy
Government in which citizens come together in one place to make laws and select rulers. The term often nowadays refers to populist measures such as the initiative and referendum, or procedures such as the New England Town Meeting.

The Founding Fathers, who devised the Constitution, had several clear-cut objectives in mind, and these were set down in the fifty-two-word preamble to the principal document. They may be summarised as:
- 'to form a more perfect Union'
- 'to establish justice'
- 'to insure domestic tranquillity'
- 'to provide for the common defense'
- 'to promote the general welfare'
- 'to secure the blessings of liberty to ourselves and our posterity'.

CHECKING POWER: CHECKS AND BALANCES IN THE AMERICAN SYSTEM

The idea of **checks and balances** is one of the key principles underpinning the US system of government. It is designed to prevent tyranny, by avoiding an undue concentration of power in any one individual or agency. It requires different parts of the government to work together in a constructive fashion, thereby encouraging a spirit of bipartisanship and compromise – particularly in the relationship between the president and Congress. However, when the executive and legislature are under the control of different parties, such 'divided government' can result in gridlock, a kind of political traffic jam in which it is difficult for a president to fulfil the programme on which he fought the previous presidential election.

> **checks and balances**
> The principle of government under which its separate branches are empowered to prevent actions by other branches and are encouraged to share power. Checks and balances are applied primarily in constitutional governments. In the US, checks and balances are exercised by each of the three branches of the central government in Washington upon the other two branches.

The federal system

The framers of the Constitution wanted a stronger and more effective national government than they had experienced previously. But they were aware of the dangers of excessive central control. They needed to balance the efficiency and good order that might come from central control against the liberties of the subject, which might be threatened by an all-powerful administration in Washington DC. The answer was to establish a federal system, in which certain powers would be allotted to the national government and others reserved for the individual states. (See Chapter 3 for a full discussion of federalism in theory and practice.)

The separation of powers

All political systems need to have three arms of government, each performing one of three basic tasks – the executive, to make decisions and put laws into effect; the legislature, to create and pass laws; and the judiciary, to adjudicate in cases of dispute or to determine whether the law has been broken.

> **separation of powers**
> The principle that executive, legislative and judicial power should be separated through the creation of three independent branches of government, ensuring that power is fragmented and that the different divisions of government cooperate.

Montesquieu (1689–1755), the French philosopher who wrote *De l'Esprit des Lois*, argued that each arm needs to be separate, so that no one person can take control of all three functions of government. His influence is to be found in the work of the Founding Fathers, who drew up the US Constitution, for they instituted a number of checks and balances to prevent any danger of a powerful individual or group from dominating the whole structure by concentrating power in too few hands. In the 47th *Federalist Paper*, Madison quotes

presidential system
A system of government in which the executive branch exists and *presides* (hence the term) separately from the legislature, to which it is not accountable and which cannot in normal circumstances dismiss it.

Montesquieu to that effect: 'There can be no liberty where the legislative and executive powers are united in the same person or body of magistrates, or if the power of judging be not separated from the legislative and executive powers.'

Some writers have questioned the appropriateness of the term 'separation of powers' in the case of the American Constitution. Richard Neustadt[3] pointed out that in the US it is the institutions that are separate, rather than the powers. In his view, rather than having created a government of 'separated powers', the Founding Fathers created a system of 'separated institutions sharing powers'. The distinction is a valid one, for what they did was to devise a system in which each of the three branches of government can act as a brake on and balance to the others. In the case of the president and the two houses of Congress, a further check is introduced by virtue of the fact that they each serve for different terms of office and are elected by different constituencies. In the words of Alan Grant:[4] 'Negativity is the chief characteristic of the separation of powers doctrine, as it is concerned with producing limitations and constraints on government rather than looking at the positive use to be made of such authority.'

Having separated the three branches of government, the delegates of the Philadelphia Convention allowed a certain amount of participation in, and checking of, the activities of one branch by the others. Thus, key presidential appointments have to be confirmed

Amending the Constitution

The framers of the Constitution recognised the need to make provision for amendment of the document, should this become necessary. As the nation developed and circumstances altered, change would become necessary, but it must not be so easy that it opened up the possibility of ill-conceived changes, nor so unduly difficult that any proposal could be blocked by a minority of the nation. The answer was a dual process. Congress was given the right to initiate an amendment, by a two-thirds majority vote in each chamber. Or the legislatures of two-thirds of the states could request Congress to summon a national convention to discuss and draft amendments, a method never yet employed. Whichever procedure was adopted, there must be approval from three-quarters of the states before any amendment entered into force.

by a majority of the Senate; all legislation the president wishes to see enacted has to pass through Congress; and the Supreme Court can declare the president's actions and policies (and those of Congress) to be 'unconstitutional' (though this latter idea was not made explicit in the Constitution). The president has the opportunity to reshape the Supreme Court by making nominations in the event of vacancies, and can veto bills passed by Congress that are considered to be unnecessary or undesirable.

Other checks and balances

As we have seen, many checks and balances are written into the Constitution – although some have developed subsequently. Two examples of more recent checks are:

1 Political parties

The president and members of Congress belong to political parties, and therefore there are bonds between those who share the same affiliation. This may help the president pass his or her legislative programme through Congress, for if Congress has a majority of members who share the president's political allegiance then there are likely to be common legislative goals.

2 Congressional committees

Although neither the president nor the cabinet secretaries may belong to Congress, executive branch officers may be questioned in committee about their work and responsibilities. Like parties, committees do not feature in the American Constitution.

Over the years, the system of checks and balances can be seen to have been effective in several ways: presidents have vetoed more than 2,500 acts of Congress; Congress has overridden more than 100 of these; the Supreme Court has ruled more than forty federal laws 'unconstitutional'; the House has impeached several federal officials; and the Senate has refused to confirm several nominations.

This was the direct procedure for amending the constitution. It can also be changed by judicial interpretation, for in the landmark *Marbury* v. *Madison* ruling (1803), the Supreme Court established the doctrine of judicial review, the power of the Court to interpret acts of Congress and decide on their constitutionality or otherwise. This doctrine enables the Court to offer its verdict on the meaning of various sections of the Constitution as they apply in changing economic, social and political circumstances, over a period of time. In other words, without any substantive changes in the Constitution itself, the thrust of constitutional law can be changed.

In the same way, congressional legislation can also broaden and change the scope of the Constitution, as also can rules and regulations of the various agencies of the federal government. Everything depends upon whether such legislation and rules conform to the intentions of those who devised the Constitution.

The machinery for formal amendment of the Constitution, in action

More than 5,000 constitutional amendments have been suggested, but only thirty-three have been submitted to the states. Twenty-seven alterations to the Constitution have been made, although it is likely that there will be further revisions in the future. Most of these changes were made in the very early period after it was adopted; the first ten were made in the first two years.

Subsequent amendments have covered a wider range of topics, among them the method of electing the president, the outlawing of slavery, the right of Congress to levy income tax and the direct election of US senators. Most recently:

- **The Twenty-Fifth Amendment (1967)** provided for filling the office of vice-president when it becomes vacant in mid-term. The president must make a nomination which then requires majority approval in both chambers. (The procedure was used shortly afterwards, in 1973, when President Nixon required a new vice-president on the resignation of Spiro T. Agnew, and again the following year, when, on the elevation of that vice-president – Ford – to the presidency, a new second-in-command was needed.)
- **The Twenty-Sixth Amendment (1971)** lowered the voting age to 18.
- **The Twenty-Seventh Amendment (1992)** concerned congressional salaries; no pay rise under consideration can come about until an election has intervened.

  This emerged in an unusual manner. A student at Texas University was working on a paper dealing with the proposed Equal Rights Amendment. He came across an amendment which was suggested as part of the original Bill of Rights. Six of the original thirteen states had ratified it, and later on another three had done so. The student launched a ratification movement, and found six more states that were willing to do so. As anti-Congress sentiment increased in the late 1980s and early 1990s, the movement for ratification gained ground. Finally, in May 1992, Michigan became the thirty-eighth state to give its approval. This showed that even when 200 years had elapsed it was still possible for a proposed amendment to be put into effect. In recent years, however, Congress has included a deadline for ratification within the text of a proposed amendment, seven years being the usual time frame imposed. Within that period, if thirty-eight states do not ratify the amendment, it fails. In the case of the failed Equal Rights Amendment (see p. 394), its original deadline was extended from 1979 to 1982, but even with the unusual extension, a sufficient number of states failed to ratify the amendment.

Overall, amendment of the Constitution has been rare. Relatively few amendments have been introduced and ratified. The thirteen proposals initiated in the House during the first six years of Republican control of Congress from January 1995 all failed to achieve the necessary majorities in the Senate, only two (flag desecration and the balanced budget) having passed the lower chamber with the necessary majority. Even these issues tended to be ones of broader national policy, albeit with constitutional implications, rather than straightforward issues directly affecting some aspect of institutional arrangements. Term limits do fall into this category (see pp. 181–182), but despite being a high-profile part of the Republican 'Contract for America' programme in the November 1994 election, they have failed to materialise.

Issues covered in the first ten amendments proposed during the 111th Congress (2009–11)

- A balanced budget for the United States government and greater accountability in the enactment of tax legislation.

- Abolition of the Electoral College and provision for the direct popular election of the president and vice-president of the United States.

- Authorisation for the Congress and the states to prohibit the act of desecration of the flag of the United States and to set criminal penalties for that act.

- Healthcare reform.

- Limits on the amounts of contributions and expenditures that may be made in connection with campaigns for election to public office.

- Limits on the number of consecutive terms that a member of Congress may serve.

- Presidential election voting rights for residents of all US territories and commonwealths.

- Provision that Representatives shall be apportioned among the several states according to their respective numbers, counting the number of persons in each state who are citizens of the United States.

- Removal of the limitation on the number of terms an individual may serve as president.

- Voluntary school prayer.

Several suggestions for amendments have been proposed over and over again, in different sessions of Congress. Some are proposed every year. Up to 200 amendments are typically proposed in each term of Congress. According to a study by C-Span (www.c-span.org/questions/weekly54.asp) in 2000, the number of amendments proposed in each of the sessions of Congress in the 1990s was as follows:

101st (1989–90)	214
102nd (1991–92)	165
103rd (1993–94)	156
104th (1995–96)	158
105th (1997–98)	103
106th (1999 only)	60

Amendments may be proposed outside of government by experts on the Constitution, but most are proposed by a member or members of the legislature. Most never emerge from Congressional committees, failing to overcome even the first constitutional hurdle, approval by two-thirds majorities in both chambers.

Why has so little constitutional change come about?

One answer is that, in comparison with peoples of other nations, Americans have been broadly contented with that which the Founding Fathers devised. Many regard their constitution with considerable awe and reverence, their deference emerging in poll findings and other expressions of popular opinion. These indicate that Americans are both familiar and content with their constitutional arrangements. Indeed, according to US historian Theodore White,[5] the nation is more united by its commonly accepted ideas about government (as embodied in the Constitution) than it is by geography.

On becoming president in 1974, Gerald Ford observed that 'our constitution works'. He was speaking in the aftermath of the **Watergate Crisis**, which led to the downfall and ultimate resignation of President Nixon. Nixon was judged to have been involved with a cover-up and various illegal operations, and thereby to have abused his position. As the Americans firmly believe in the idea that 'we have a government of laws, not of men', Ford and many other Americans saw his removal as a vindication of their constitution. It had served to protect freedom, restrain the behaviour of those in high office and define the limits of executive power.

Watergate crisis
The collective name for a series of abuses that began with a break-in at the Democratic national headquarters in the Watergate building, Washington DC, but later involved revelations of many other acts of wrong-doing, ranging from wire-tapping to 'misleading testimony'. As the episode unfolded, it became evident that President Nixon was personally involved. This led to his becoming the first and only president to resign in disgrace.

Given such widespread approval of the form of government, it is not surprising that America has not shown the same interest in constitutional reform that has characterised other nations. Very few people publicly advocate radical changes in the structure of government established in 1787. Those who would tamper with it have to make a strong case for change and tend to talk in terms of restoring it to its original glory rather than making fundamental alternations.

In addition to a broad measure of popular satisfaction with the Constitution, there are other factors that help to explain the fact that the original document has survived more or less intact:

- The most obvious is the relative difficulty of achieving change. The fate of the Equal Rights Amendment shows that the hurdles created more than two hundred years ago are difficult to surmount. In the two attempts to outlaw flag desecration in the Senate, it was possible to muster sixty-two and sixty-three votes in favour, in 1995 and 2000 respectively. This was an impressive figure, but still five and four votes short of what was needed. Even if the Senate had passed the measure, then the hurdle of getting thirty-eight states to ratify the change would have been a hard one to achieve.
- The very lack of clarity in the wording of the Constitution means that the vague phrases can be interpreted over time in accordance with the needs of the day. The language is retained, but the values mean different things in different eras. Congress is allowed to 'provide for the common defense and general welfare of the United States', a broad remit that enables the document to adapt to changing circumstances without formal amendment to its language.
- In particular, the ability of the Supreme Court to make 'interpretative amendments' means that the Constitution is kept up to date. When the Bill of Rights (the first ten amendments to the Constitution) was introduced, it applied only to the national government. But over time, its provisions were extended by Court judgments to the states. Phrases such as 'due process' and the 'equal protection of the law' have been instrumental in allowing this adaptation to changing circumstances.

Assessment of the Constitution

Without flexibility of the type we have seen, it is unlikely that the arrangements made more than 200 years ago would have survived in a country that has changed dramatically. The diversity of the nation has increased: the country has spread westward across the entire continent; a stream of migrants have been absorbed; the population has soared; new resources have been exploited; and all sorts of differing interests have developed, be they those of the east-coast ship owners who favoured free trade, the mid-west manufacturers who wanted protection for their goods from foreign competition, farmers who wanted low freight charges or railroad operators who wanted high ones. Like all these groups, Texas ranchers and Oregon lumbermen have their own priorities and concerns. Yet all these interests have been taken on board and the essential unity of the nation has grown stronger. That this has happened is in no small part because of the success of the working arrangements drawn up in 1787, which had enough built-in flexibility to cater for changing circumstances.

Americans pride themselves on having the world's oldest written constitution, and many still marvel at the wisdom of the Founding Fathers in devising a document that has stood the test of time and been capable of adaptation to changing conditions and circumstances. An American writer[6] has captured some of the appeal that it has for many Americans:

> Along with the flag, the Constitution stands alone as a symbol of national unity. America has no royal family, no heritage of timeless and integrative state institutions or symbols, no national church. Add to that America's history of being peopled by diverse religious, national and racial stocks, many of whom came long after the founding, and one can see how the Constitution could become such a focus of national identity and loyalty. There is precious little else to compete with it as an integrative symbol and evocation of America . . . Unlike the flag . . . which has changed dramatically over the years, with the constantly expanding number of states, the Constitution has endured virtually unchanged . . . This is, surely, another important source of its status as the focus of American identity, its stability and unchanging quality.

Disadvantages and advantages of the Constitution

Not all writers have supported the various provisions of the Constitution. It has been found deficient by some critics, who have been exasperated with the diffusion of power that was basic to its operation. The young Woodrow Wilson,[7] then a professor of government but a future president, wrote his analysis, *Congressional Government* in 1890, before the extension of federal and presidential power occurred in the 1930s. He argued that the American arrangements made it difficult to achieve coherence in policy making or responsible government. In his view, there were too many people involved in the evolution of policy and there was too little likelihood of progress being achieved.

Wilson lamented the absence of strong parties. He particularly disliked the low quality of Congressional debate that – largely because of party discipline – in his view lacked coherence. Too much discussion took place in obscure committees headed by entrenched and autocratic senior members, a point not effectively addressed until the 1970s. He much preferred the British system of government, with its clear allocation of power and responsibility.

A common point of criticism is the failure of the Constitution to permit quick and decisive action, except in times of crisis. One can understand why an American president might envy a British prime minister, whose ability to achieve his programme within a parliamentary session is so much greater. But this was how the Founding Fathers wanted it. They were not looking for speedy action. They preferred to create machinery that would function at a slower pace, once all interests had had a chance to expound their viewpoints and to influence the outcome of the debate on any issue. This is what characterises the American approach, the fact that particular groups can frustrate the pace of advance where they think that change would damage their interests.

A contemporary of Wilson's, the British Liberal statesman William Gladstone,[8] saw things differently to the future president. He described the American Constitution in this way: 'As the British Constitution is the most subtle organism which has proceeded from the womb and long gestation of progressive history, so the American Constitution is, so far as I can see, the most wonderful work ever struck off at a given time by the brain and purpose of man.' For all of its alleged defects, many writers and commentators might still agree with him over a century later. The Constitution has now survived for over 200 years and proved its durability over years of extensive and often rapid economic and social change. It may have been amended twenty-seven times but, after all, ten of these modifications were made at the beginning of its existence, and in any case the amendments and their subject matter suggest that there has been no fundamental alteration in its character.

In other words, the Constitution remains much as it was originally written. The whole **New Deal** was carried through without amendment of the Constitution. Leaders – such as Franklin Roosevelt – who wish to innovate tend to use the wording of the Constitution, rather than seek to get it changed. Political fashion and practices have made the system viable in the twenty-first century. Presidents now rely on the Supreme Court to interpret their actions favourably.

> **New Deal**
> The programme introduced by President Roosevelt in the 1930s to combat the depressed condition of the US. Several 'alphabet laws' (named after their initials) were passed to achieve the '3Rs' of relief, recovery and reform. The package greatly extended the role and authority of the federal government.

It may well be that if the framers of the Constitution were alive today, they would be surprised at the way in which its practical operation has evolved, for it has provided the political framework for a society immeasurably different from the one they knew. For instance:

- The Founding Fathers had fears about democracy. They felt that the principle needed to be controlled, but subsequently the American system has become markedly more democratic. Politicians quickly saw merit in accepting the guidance of the electorate, and the importance of the popular will has become much greater than was ever intended.
- The balance of power has tipped in favour of the federal government at the expense of the states, most evidently since 1933, when President Roosevelt began his New Deal programme to lift the country out of serious economic depression.
- The presidency has become more powerful. Although it was envisaged as being remote and above the political fray, it has in fact become the most identifiable institution and an essential part of the political battleground. However rigid a written constitution may appear to be, in the American case it is as flexible as most citizens wish it to be.

What has remained, as the Fathers envisaged, is the built-in conflict between the various institutions. They wanted no part of the machinery to acquire excessive power at the expense of the others. Accordingly, they created a system in which it was difficult to get all parts moving in the same direction and at the same speed. They were happy at the prospect of disputation between the federal government and the states, and between the institutions of the federal government. In this, their wishes have remained intact.

Written and unwritten constitutions: a comparison

Advantages of a written constitution:

- They provide a clear statement of the position as to what is and what is not constitutional.

- They have an educational value, helping to curb the behaviour of those in government office.

- It is easier for the courts to interpret what is constitutional behaviour when a document lays down clear limitations on institutions and individuals.

- They are difficult to amend or tamper with, because the procedure for so doing is normally difficult.

Disadvantages of a written, codified constitution:

- Constitutions do not necessarily provide a clear protection for people's rights. American experience proves this, for the original document recognised slavery and the Fifteenth Amendment, passed in 1870, provides that 'The right of citizens to vote shall not be denied or abridged by the US or by any states on account of race, color or previous condition of servitude . . . Congress shall have the power to enforce this by appropriate legislation; yet in many states blacks were excluded on grounds of illiteracy from exercising their democratic right to vote until the 1960s.

- Constitutions can be inflexible and rigid, incapable of being easily adapted to the needs of the day. Whereas the British constitution is adaptable and has evolved according to circumstances, a formal document can be difficult to amend, and therefore may act as a barrier to much-needed social change. Several US presidents have been attracted to the idea of gun control as a means of combating crime, but they have run into fierce opposition from the National Rifle Association (see p. 340), which reminds people about the statement in Article 2 of the Bill of Rights concerning 'the right to bear arms'. The Supreme Court was similarly able to restrict some of the New Deal on the grounds that it was a breach of the Constitution, restricting states' rights and giving too much power to the president.

- Constitutions can be hard to change. In America, the fate of the Equal Rights Amendment (see p. 394) illustrates the difficulty of gaining adequate support.

THE CONSTITUTION IN ACTION: THE PROTECTION OFFERED BY THE BILL OF RIGHTS

Much of the early opposition to the Constitution itself was not centred on resistance to increased federal power at the expense of the states, but more on anxiety that the rights of individuals were insufficiently protected. There was widespread agreement that a set of constitutional amendments must be drafted to provide specific guarantees of individual rights, although this would not happen until after a government under the new Constitution had been established.

THE BILL OF RIGHTS

The first ten amendments to the Constitution were added as a block by the Congress in September 1789, and ratified by eleven states by the end of 1791.

The first ten amendments to the Constitution and their purpose

Protections afforded fundamental rights and freedoms
- Amendment 1: Freedom of religion, speech, press and assembly; the right to petition the government.

Protections against arbitrary military action
- Amendment 2: The right to bear arms and maintain state militias (National Guard).
- Amendment 3: Troops may not be quartered in homes in peacetime.

Protection against arbitrary police and court action
- Amendment 4: There can be no unreasonable searches or seizures.
- Amendment 5: Grand jury indictment is required to prosecute a person for a serious crime. No 'double jeopardy' – a person cannot be tried twice for the same offence. It is prohibited to force a person to testify against himself or herself. There can be no loss of life, liberty or property without due process.
- Amendment 6: The right to speedy, public, impartial trial with defence counsel, and the right to cross-examine witnesses.
- Amendment 7: Jury trials in civil suits where the value exceeds 20 dollars.
- Amendment 8: No excessive bail or fines; no cruel and unusual punishments.

Protections of states' rights and unnamed rights of the people
- Amendment 9: Unlisted rights are not necessarily denied.
- Amendment 10: Powers not delegated to the United States or denied to states are reserved for the states or for the people.

The Bill of Rights was ratified in 1791, but its application was broadened significantly by the Fourteenth Amendment to the Constitution, which was ratified in 1868. A key phrase in the Fourteenth Amendment – 'nor shall any state deprive any person of life, liberty, or property, without due process of law' – has been interpreted by the Supreme Court as forbidding the states from violating most of the rights and freedoms protected by the Bill of Rights.

The contents of the Bill of Rights

James Madison did much of the drafting of the ten amendments. He was unconvinced about the adequacy of the existing protection and wanted to see clear constitutional guarantees of the liberties of the people. Those that he laid down in 1791 included a list of civil, religious and legal rights that remain intact today, in the same form in which they were originally set out. The first four set out individual rights, the next four deal with the system of justice, and the last two are broader statements of constitutional intention.

The new document applied to the federal government only, for many Americans were unworried about possible tyranny in their own states. It was the central government of which they were suspicious, although this fear has proved largely unfounded and many infringements of liberty have occurred at state and local level.

The Fourteenth Amendment, adopted in 1868, includes a 'due process' clause, and this does apply to the states. It lays down that no person can be deprived of life, liberty and property without the due process of law, and this was seen as meaning that states were bound by the Bill of Rights in the same way that the national government was. For many years, the Supreme Court did not so rule, but in 1925, in a landmark judgment in *Gitlow* v. *New York*, it was decided that:

> For present purposes, we may and do assume that freedom of speech and of the press – which are protected by the First Amendment from abridgement by Congress – are among the fundamental personal rights and liberties protected by the due process clause of the Fourteenth Amendment from impairment by the States.

The ruling was of profound importance, and once it had been accepted that freedom of speech and of the press were protected at state and local level by the First Amendment, so it was inevitable that other provisions of that same amendment would be enforceable in the same way. Those rights laid down in 1791 – including rights of religion, assembly and petition – are now applicable to all levels of government.

Although the First Amendment has been accepted as binding, this is not true of all of the other nine. A minority on the Supreme Court wished to proceed from the 1925 decision to make all freedoms protected by the Bill of Rights binding on the states. In other words, this would mean that the Bill of Rights would be incorporated fully into the Fourteenth Amendment.

This has not been the predominant opinion. The majority has taken the view that some provisions of the Bill of Rights should be included, in other words, selective incorporation. Gradually the number of those original amendments that have come within the scope of the Fourteenth Amendment has been extended. Today, only the second, third, seventh and tenth do not apply at state and local level – along with the Grand Jury requirements of the fifth. Other liberties not in the Bill of Rights also receive protection today – among these are the right of association, the right of privacy, the right to be presumed innocent and the right to travel freely.

Once much of the Bill of Rights was interpreted as being applicable at all levels, judges in state courts began to place more emphasis upon its provisions than upon those set out in state constitutions. More recently, however, there has been a more conservative leaning among the Supreme Court justices, and this has led to a greater interest in the protection offered by state guarantees. Justice Brennan became concerned about the way in which the Court was narrowly interpreting the scope of the Bill of Rights. Back in 1977 he urged judges in state supreme courts to take up the challenge, noting that: 'State con-stitutions . . . are a font of individual liberties, their protection often extending beyond those required by the Supreme Court's interpretation of federal law.'[9]

The constitutions of Great Britain and the United States: a comparison

A summary of the differing characteristics of the two constitutions

The British Constitution	The US Constitution
Unwritten (not codified in a single text)	Written/codified
Oldest constitution in world	Oldest written constitution in world
Flexible/easy to amend	More rigid/less easy to amend
No entrenchment of basic rights	Rights are entrenched
Unitary rather than federal system	Federal
Fusion of powers	Separation of powers
Parliamentary system	Presidential system
Parliamentary sovereignty	Popular sovereignty/more direct democracy
Monarchy	

NB See also the box **Written and unwritten constitutions: a comparison** on p. 42 for a further comparison of the workings of the two constitutions.

CONCLUSION

The American Constitution is based upon key, underlying principles, notably:
- democracy and the values that underpin it, such as consensus, compromise, consent, discussion, tolerance and the rule of law;
- popular sovereignty, with an emphasis on direct democracy;
- limited government, by which the scale and scope of the federal govern-ment in Washington is restricted to what is necessary for the common good;
- a federal division of power (of which more in the next chapter);

- separation of powers (often more accurately described as 'separate institutions sharing power', for it is the institutions that are separate, the powers being shared via the checks and balances introduced by the Founding Fathers);
- judicial review – the power of the courts to declare presidential actions or congressional legislation as unconstitutional.

These principles are enduring and remain intact, but as a result of formal amendments, judicial interpretation and legislation the Constitution itself has been much modified. The changes made have enabled it to survive and retain acceptance in a country whose circumstances differ substantially from those of the late eighteenth century.

Documents depend upon their implementation and interpretation. At different times, the US Constitution has been differently applied. Sometimes its provisions have been ignored, much to the detriment of minority groups, for whom the Bill of Rights has proved to be an inadequate form of protection.

NB For fuller information on the protection offered in the area of civil liberties and rights, see Chapter 11.

REFERENCES

1 J. Dewey, 'On Democracy', *School and Society* 45, 1937
2 J. Rousseau, *The Social Contract: or Principles of Political Right*, 1762, reprinted as a Cosimo Classic, 2008
3 R. Neustadt, *Presidential Power: The Politics of Leadership*, Wiley & Sons, 1960
4 A. Grant, *The American Political Process*, Dartmouth, 1994
5 T. White, 'The American Idea', *New York Times Magazine*, June 1986
6 I. Kramnick, 'Editor's Introduction' to J. Madison, A. Hamilton and J. Jay, *The Federalist Papers*, Penguin, 1987
7 W. Wilson, *Congressional Government*, revised edition, Meridian Books, 1956
8 W. Gladstone, 'Kin Beyond the Sea', *The North American Review*, September 1878
9 W. Brennan, 'Constitutional Adjudication and the Death Penalty', *Harvard Law Review* 100: 2, 1977

USEFUL WEB SITES

www.nationalarchives.gov.uk/education/ National Archives Classroom web site. Many key historical documents on American government can be found here, notably the Declaration of Independence, the Constitution, etc.

www.gpoaccess.gov/constitution/browse.html Congressional Research Service, Library of Congress. Online copy of the Constitution, annotated with commentary and relevant Supreme Court cases, etc.

www.constitutioncenter.org/ National Constitution Center. A useful starting point for study of the Constitution.

www.americanstrategy.org/foundations.html An introduction to American constitutional history.

www.foundingfathers.info The Federalist Papers

SAMPLE QUESTIONS

1 Has the American Constitution been an aid or an obstacle to good government?
2 Do the checks and balances written into the American Constitution still work today?
3 How difficult is it to amend the American Constitution?
4 Should the American Constitution be rewritten?
5 Discuss the view that the main difference between the US and UK constitution is that one is flexible and the other is not.
6 Does the written constitution of the United States make the country harder to govern than the United Kingdom?
7 Examine the difficulties faced in effecting constitutional change in the United States compared to the United Kingdom.

Federalism in theory and practice

3

Even the most authoritarian government would find it difficult to take all decisions at the centre. It would be impractical for any set of ministers to understand the needs of every area and to involve themselves in the minutiae of its public administration. Hence the need to allow some scope for regional or local initiative.

The Founding Fathers well understood that the structure and character of the governmental system that they were creating for the United States would shape the path of the country's development. It was important for them to strike the right balance between nationalism and states' rights. Since the Philadelphia Convention, that balance has changed and developed, and the emphasis on Washington DC has markedly increased. Yet in recent decades, there has been a movement to return power to the states, a tendency broadly encouraged by presidents from Reagan to Clinton.

POINTS TO CONSIDER

- Why did the US move away from its original system of 'dual federalism'?
- To what extent has there been a conservative backlash against the growing power of Washington in public affairs since the 1970s?
- What was the impact of George W. Bush on federalism?
- Why has there been a resurgence of the states since the early 1980s?
- By what label would you characterise American federalism today?
- What are the benefits of American federalism?
- Have the dangers and complexities of the modern world made it inevitable that national rather than regional or local government is the main focus of power in any political system?
- Is local/state government better than national government because it is closer to the people?
- What are the differences between federalism and devolution?

In addition to the national government in Washington DC and the fifty state governments, there are in the United States more than 87,500 units of local government. How to balance the relationship between these elements has been at the heart of discussion about federalism ever since the passage of the Constitution. There have been several descriptions of that relationship, which has fluctuated in different periods of American history.

The system of government devised by the Founding Fathers at the Philadelphia Convention (1787) resulted from the compromises necessary to reconcile conflicting political and economic interests. Federalism was seen as a 'halfway house' between the concept of a centralised unitary state, which was unacceptable to thirteen states jealous of their independence, and the idea of a confederation, which would have been a weak association of autonomous states. As Alan Grant has written:[1] 'It arose out of a desire to bolster national unity whilst . . . accommodating regional diversity'.

The Constitution does not mention the words 'federalism' or 'federation', but the United States has always been recognised as a major example of this compromise form of unity. Other nations later adopted the federal principle, which Zimmerman[2] describes as 'a government system in which constitutional authority is divided between a central and state or provincial governments'. Wheare[3] wrote more elaborately of federalism as 'the method of dividing powers so that the general and regional governments are each, within a sphere, coordinate and independent'.

The federal principle as originally envisaged was a system of **dual federalism**. In other words, powers are divided between a general (that is, a national or federal) government, which in certain matters is independent of the governments of the associated states, and state governments, which are in certain matters independent of the general government. To illustrate its workings, Bryce[4] offered the image of two sets of machinery, both of which worked well because they generally avoided contact with each other. In the eighteenth century, the distinction between the autonomous spheres of national and state government could be maintained, for extensive cooperation between them was neither necessary nor, at the time, practical.

dual federalism

A variety of federalism in which the national and state governments retain separate spheres of action, each level independently performing the functions allocated to it in the Constitution. No one government within the system should encroach upon the sovereignty of the others.

Every American citizen is therefore subject to two governments that act directly upon the people; the system was not designed as a pyramid structure with the federal government at the apex, the states below it and then local government at the bottom. The Constitution lays down the binding division of power. In constitutional terms, the federal and state governments are seen as being of equal status within their own distinctive realms of authority. The Supreme

---

The division of power in American federalism: some examples

Delegated powers (powers delegated to federal government)

- Declare war

- Make treaties

- Coin money

- Regulate interstate and foreign commerce

Concurrent powers (powers shared by the federal and state governments)

- Levy taxes

- Shape public health

Types of governmental systems: getting the terms right

In **unitary states**, legal power flows from one source, for instance the queen-in-Parliament in the United Kingdom and the Knesset in Israel; most European governments are of the unitary type. Power is concentrated in national government, and the operation of lower tiers of government derives not from a written constitution but from the centre. In Britain, local authorities exist but they do so at the behest of Westminster, and they are entirely subordinate to it. Some devolution of power is possible (as in the case of Northern Ireland, Scotland and Wales), but this does nothing to breach the idea that control derives from Parliament; local and devolved power can be revoked.

Devolution involves the idea that there should be some redistribution of power away from the centre to subordinate assemblies that can, if necessary, still be overridden by the parent authority. It usually springs from dissatisfaction with centralised government when ministers appear to be unwilling to recognise local needs.

In **confederacies**, the regional authorities exercise much of the power, and central control is relatively weak. Historically, the best example of a confederacy was probably that

---

Court settles any disputes about the division of powers between them. Its judgments are accepted as binding on the federal and state governments.

The relationship outlined at Philadelphia entails that no state may unilaterally secede from the Union; neither can a state be expelled against its will. The interests of smaller states are protected in most federations by equal representation, or by additional members to those warranted by the size of their population. An important part of the Philadelphia compromise was to secure the support of the less populous states by giving them equal representation in the Senate – two seats per state.

- Regulate auto safety

- Control drugs

Reserved powers (powers reserved for state governments)

- Draw electoral districts

- Regulate intra-state commerce

- Create local units

- Determine police powers

found in the United States under the Articles of Confederation, but many years later the eleven Southern states seceded from the Union in the American Civil War and they too declared themselves to be a Confederacy. Switzerland today is often described as having confederal administration, its twenty-six cantons exercising much of the power in the country.

In **federal states**, power is shared between different tiers of government, a federal (central) government and regional governments – known as states in the US and Länder in Germany. Under federalism, the states have guaranteed spheres of responsibility, and the central government conducts those functions of major importance that require policy to be made for the whole country. Both tiers may act directly on the people, and each has some exclusive powers. Federalism thus diffuses political authority to prevent any undue concentration at one point. Under federalism, it is still likely that there will also be a system of local government, although it can vary significantly in form. In the US, the federal government has little role in regulating the functioning of this tier, which falls under the direction of the states.

The growth in central power from 1787 to the late 1960s

Under dual federalism, the central government in Washington was expected to limit its activities to the tasks explicitly allotted to it in 1787. The idea represents the federal spirit as originally conceived and it retains significance in American culture. In practice it was never likely to survive for very long in its original form, but it remains the benchmark against which modern developments in the workings of federalism in the United States today are assessed.

As it evolved in the nineteenth century, dual federalism was often undermined by the developments listed below. In the twentieth century, the influence of the federal government was much strengthened as the country became a world power. This led to huge increases in the budget and a massive expansion of personnel, both civilian and military. The decisions of the federal government, as a major contractor and provider of jobs, vitally affected the well-being of the states and of the people.

The Great Depression of the 1930s greatly increased the expectation that the federal government would intervene to deal with the major social and economic ills of the country. Washington's attempts to ease these problems by direct works programmes and various schemes of assistance for businessmen, farmers and whole areas in dire need filled a vacuum. Given the scale of the task confronting the country, the states were unable to act themselves, as a result of the strain on their finances as well as out of an ideological unwillingness in some cases to do so.

Some rurally dominated state legislatures neglected the urgent difficulties afflicting the nation's urban areas, and not surprisingly the city administrations turned to the federal government for a lead. The lack of a positive response by many state governments to the crisis of the cities only served to increase the tendency towards centralisation. Since 1939, the very nature of problems faced in a highly complex industrialised society has provided a challenge to the federal system. The federal government has also often stepped in to coordinate governmental programmes when problems have cut across state boundaries. The demands of an integrated economy, world war and – much later – international terrorism have combined to overwhelm dual federalism.

Such a combination of economic and social factors led to pressure, over a century and a half, for a change in the political and constitutional relationships within the federal system. In the nineteenth and twentieth centuries, three specific developments served to increase the influence of Washington over the states and transform the relationship between them:

1 **Constitutional amendments.** Some amendments since 1787 affected the federal system – for example, the Fourteenth Amendment provided 'equal protection' of the law to all citizens and the Sixteenth gave the federal government the right to raise graduated income tax.
2 **Decisions of the Supreme Court.** At times, Court decisions have allowed a considerable expansion of national intervention by emphasising the broad and permissive character of some clauses in the Constitution – for example, the congressional power to 'tax for the common defense and general welfare of the United States'.
3 **The financial relationship.** After the passage of the Sixteenth Amendment, on income tax, the financial base of the federal government was expanded. This led to a considerable increase in the size of its budget. (Americans now

pay the majority of their taxation to Washington, a smaller amount to the states and slightly less again to their local governments.)

With the growing demands on hard-pressed local and state governments for education, health and welfare, police protection and environmental services, the federal government increasingly stepped in with more financial aid. This growing dependence of the states on federal financial resources to support their services inevitably coloured the relationship. Since the Great Depression, the main financial assistance has been in the form of **grants-in-aid**. Some existed before 1900, but most have developed since the 1930s, and this has led to federal supervision in areas not normally in Washington's power. In other words, this financial assistance is money 'with strings attached'. The federal government began to lay down minimum

> **grants-in-aid**
> Transfers of money from federal government to states and localities in order to finance their policies and programmes.

standards and to inspect the results of its funding, and matching funds had to be provided by the states to qualify for federal aid. The more a state was prepared to develop programmes, the more it was likely to receive national funds or contracts.

The move towards centralisation until the late 1960s: differing conceptions of federalism

Before the New Deal, America had a system of dual federalism, in which the two levels of government were supposed to be independent, each with its own clearly defined sphere of influence and responsibility. The concept was interpreted in different ways, between those on the one hand who wanted a more nation-centred form of federalism and those who wanted a more state-based form. The version that emerged triumphant was the nation-centred one, the issue being finally resolved on the battlefields of the Civil War in the 1860s, in which the Lincoln approach of keeping the country united was vindicated.

The model of dual federalism was a conservative one. Those who have supported it (right through to the present day) would prefer to see a strictly limited role for Washington. They stress the importance of the idea of 'states' rights', with its emphasis on a large and secure place for the states within the federal system. As we have seen, it is doubtful if such a situation ever really existed in anything like its pure form. From as early as the nineteenth century, the federal government was 'stepping in' to provide grants for improvements on expensive and necessary items such as road building.

Roosevelt's energetic response to the deteriorating economic situation in the Great Depression involved deploying the resources of central government in a series of interventionist measures known as the New Deal, 'an extraordinary assumption of federal authority over the nation's economy and a major expansion of its commerce and taxing powers'.[5] More and more decision making moved to Washington, with numerous grant-in-aid programmes bringing federal, state and local tiers into close, if not always harmonious, cooperation.

The New Deal programme inaugurated the era of **co-operative federalism**. This emphasised the partnership of different levels of government in providing effective public services for the nation. As Cummings and Wise[6] put it: the two levels were 'related parts of a single government system, characterised more by cooperation and shared functions than by conflict and competition'. Writing in 1966, Grodzins[7] did not view the American system as a 'layer cake' of three (national, state and local) distinct and separate planes, but rather as a 'marble cake', an inseparable mixture of differently coloured ingredients. In the nature of the relationship, the federal government supplements, stimulates and assists states, rather than pre-empting them. The distinguishing features of co-operative federalism were, then, a sharing of responsibilities over many governmental functions and the recognition that all the players were partners rather than adversaries.

The 1960s witnessed a marked expansion of the role of the federal government in initiating programmes and gaining state/local compliance. President Kennedy had promised to 'get the country moving again' with the use of federal money. The policy was vigorously taken up by his successor. In his Great Society programme (including such initiatives as the War on Poverty scheme), President Lyndon Johnson spoke of **creative federalism**, a more active form of co-operative federalism. This involved a massive expansion of federal aid, with grants to state governments increasing from nearly $7.5 billion in 1960 to $32 billion in 1978. Much of the

co-operative federalism
The system of federalism that evolved in the Great Depression and afterwards, that involved growing collaboration between national and state institutions, which were increasingly expected to govern as partners, in the interests of the whole community. A variant often described as 'marble-cake federalism'.

creative federalism
A 1960s form of federalism in which the central government increasingly intervened directly in political jurisdictions traditionally associated with the states and sought to persuade them to abide by federal guidelines. Washington was interpreting the Constitution 'creatively', in order to establish national standards. States were viewed as less important, the less influential partner in the central–state relationship.

The trend towards decentralisation of power since the 1970s

By the late 1960s, states and localities had become ever more dependent on federal funding, and the conditions attached to the aid had become stringent. At the same time, the deteriorating state of the American economy led many people to believe that the country could not afford such vast and expensive social programmes. To President Johnson's political opponents, the proliferation of policies and grants had brought about confusion and an excess of bureaucracy.

Conservatives never liked high-spending federal programmes. In their view, they involved an unnecessary amount of regulation and encouraged the states to initiate schemes that they did not want or need – simply to obtain the available federal funds. They claimed that problems were better tackled locally by

funding came in the form of **categorical grants**, money being offered with the proviso that the recipient organisation carried out a specific task in such a way as to comply with detailed federal requirements. Such grants grew in number. There were only five in 1900. By 1960, there were 132; eleven years later there were 530.

Creative federalism was not supposed to be a means of imposing programmes from the centre, although it did involve a great expansion in the role of the federal layer. The idea was that Washington, the top tier, would seek out and respond to local ideas and demands, and be able therefore to provide the type of service and the money which was wanted by those who lived in each locality. The role of state governments and legislatures was less important, and a wide-ranging series of civil rights and other measures imposed a greater degree of regulation upon state capitals. Johnson was able to work with an overwhelmingly Democratic Congress to carry out his programme. In the process, he was helped by a series of decisions taken by the federal judiciary, which was in a mood to end racial discrimination and segregation, protect civil liberties, reform criminal justice procedures and grant new rights to both the accused and the convicted.

categorical grants
Grants made from the central government to states and localities for specific, often narrow, purposes and to be used in specified ways; they are based upon a clear procedure for applying, implementing, and reporting back on the use of, the money.

coercive federalism
The name applied by many critics to the way in which creative federalism had developed by the end of the 1960s. They disliked the way in which central government was demanding that states perform certain tasks and adopting strong regulatory powers to ensure that they complied. If the functions were not carried out appropriately, states were liable to lose funding.

Some writers, particularly those opposed to the Great Society vision, wondered whether what had happened by the end of that decade was that creative federalism had become **coercive federalism**, a situation in which there was, in Kincaid's[8] words, 'unprecedented federal reliance on conditions of aid, pre-emptions of state and local authority, mandates, court orders, and other devices intended to ensure state and local compliance with federal policies'.

people who understood the needs of the area, rather than by wasteful and inefficient national programmes. They disliked the idea of federal interference in the affairs of states and local authorities, and argued the case for a preservation of 'states' rights'.

The New Federalism of the 1970s and 1980s

As a conservative President, Richard Nixon had the opportunity both to preach and to practise his ideas of a **new federalism**. To him, the relationship between all tiers of government was in need of redefinition. Yet his approach was not essentially about curtailing the amount of money that reached the localities, but more about how it got

new federalism
An approach to federalism that aimed to return certain powers and responsibilities from Washington to state governments. New Federalists felt that the balance in the federal–state relationship had been tilted too heavily in favour of central government.

there. Money was provided by a **block grant**; the need was identified locally and the money was then spent.

block grant
A discretionary grant handed over by the federal government to states or communities; recipients can choose how the money is spent within the broad area covered by the transfer.

Despite the efforts of President Nixon to stem the flow of power from the states to Washington, it was still commonplace until 1980 for academics and commentators to speak of the erosion of states' rights. The growth of grants-in-aid, the expansion of federal regulations, and the decisions of the Supreme Court (especially on desegregation), had all signalled a decline of the states as a significant force. In the words of one exam question of the 1970s: 'States' rights' are no more than an empty slogan for those who do not like the government in Washington.'

In January 1981, in his inaugural speech, Ronald Reagan observed that: 'Our government has no special power except that granted it by the people . . . All of us need to be reminded that the federal government did not create the states; the states created the federal government.' He cast himself firmly in the dualist mode, emphasising his determination to 'demand recognition of the distinction between the powers granted to the federal government and those reserved to the states or to the people'. For him, it was not enough merely to adjust the delivery systems. He wanted to tackle the basic problem, namely that government was trying to do too much. ← more libertarian approach

The Reagan version of 'new federalism' was more radical in its intention and in its impact. His intention was to bring about a restructuring of the federal system. In his vision of the future, the federal government would withdraw from several areas, the states would gain the right to take more initiatives and operate more programmes (if they so wished) and city governments would lose much of the power they had accumulated. He had little sympathy for 1960s schemes designed to help the cities. Of the War on Poverty, he observed: 'I guess you could say poverty won the war.' For him, this all added up to a 'new federalism', which would reverse a situation in which 'our citizens feel they have lost control of even the most basic decisions made about the essential services of government . . . A maze of interlocking jurisdictions and levels of government confronts average citizens in trying to solve even the simplest of problems.'[9]

The changes on which he embarked included:
- a reduction of grants-in-aid;
- a merging of those grants directed to specific purposes into block grants, which allowed for far more state discretion;
- a removal of many federal regulations;
- an emphasis on urban and other problems being solved by a concentration on

    (a) achieving an increase in the overall prosperity and wealth of the country and

    (b) encouraging local private/public initiatives;

- a recasting of welfare arrangements, by which the federal government would take care of Medicaid health funding, whilst the states would look after the AFDC (Aid to Families with Dependent Children) and food stamp programmes.

What had been created by the end of the 1980s was not a replica of the pattern that existed before the days of Franklin Roosevelt and the New Deal. Federal funding may have been reduced, but the Supreme Court decisions that had done so much to change the nature of American federalism survived intact. National standards were also largely preserved. The number of regulations was reduced and they were imposed with less zeal than was once the case.

By the end of the 1980s, in areas such as environmental regulation there remained a strong federal role. Americans were now used to turning to their president in Washington for a response to pressing national problems, and whether they were worried by rising crime, the system of welfare or any other aspect of policy, they expected a lead from the White House (and Congress) – even if they did not always like the policy that emerged. The outcome therefore was a situation that, in Kincaid's[10] words, was something of a paradox, combining 'federal dominance and state resurgence . . . If the states are so resurgent, why is the federal government [still] so dominant? The main reason is that the federal government has established a significant regulatory role in most domestic policy fields.'

The Bush to Obama years, 1989 to 2010

Reagan's successors had markedly less impact on the balance of the federal–state relationship. George H. Bush did not share his view of the appropriate role for government in the nation's life, so that, if anything, there was a modest swing back to emphasising the role of Washington. But the scale of the budget deficit meant that there was unlikely to be a return to the heyday of co-operative federalism. In any case, in the words of David McKay,[11] 'Lower level governments had been taught to be more self-reliant and to cut spending and services rather than increase taxes or plead for aid from the federal government.'

When Bill Clinton entered the White House, many commentators initially viewed him as a centraliser in intergovernmental relations, someone who believed in more active national leadership than did Bush or Reagan. But as he was a southerner, some hoped that the former Governor of Arkansas would be likely to be a defender of states' rights. After all, he came from an area where

SOUTHERN STANDARDS

there was a history of resistance to federal demands and had a reputation as an innovator who understood and appreciated the role of the states in the federal system. Moreover, he was not a traditional high-spending Democrat of the Kennedy–Johnson variety. Indeed, in his State of the Union message in 1996, he was forthright about the change of circumstances, declaring that the 'age of big government is over'.

Once he was elected, one of Clinton's primary concerns was to cut the budget deficit, which had grown dramatically in the 1960s and 1970s. By the time Nixon left office, more than a quarter of all spending at state and local level was provided from Washington. Jimmy Carter had begun to trim the amount of national support but, as we have seen, it was Reagan who set about slashing it. Clinton continued in this vein, redirecting financial resources and responsibility for programmes back to the states, a process intensified after the Republican congressional successes of November 1994. He was more generous with federal money than Reagan had been, and more than his Republican opponents desired, but the increased funding was modest by the standards of his party predecessors.

Two examples that illustrated the willingness of Bill Clinton to devolve power to the states concerned welfare policy and **unfunded mandates**. The welfare reform proposals introduced in 1996 ended the federal commitment to providing assistance to low-income mothers and to children brought up by them, thereby shifting the burden of welfare entitlement from Washington to the states. Many Democrats had doubts about the cessation of a policy that had survived since the days of the New Deal, but whatever his personal reservations, the president signed the measure. He recognised the prevailing mood, as registered in the 1994 mid-term elections, and with a presidential campaign ahead he had no intention of obstructing welfare reform. A less significant but none the less useful symbolic change was to make it more difficult for Congress to impose new unfunded mandates, those orders imposed by the federal government on state governments that required them to implement certain programmes without providing the means for them to do so. Other measures involving the relaxation of central control included the repeal of national speed limits and allowing states and local authorities more freedom to decide how they wished to apply the terms of the Safe Drinking Act. Taken together, the measures indicate a federal retreat from social programmes on which uniformity was previously seen as desirable.

unfunded mandates
Orders imposed by the federal government on state and local governments requiring them to carry out certain tasks, for which there has been no reimbursement of the costs involved. The high cost of such mandates became a cause of tension between the federal and state governments because the latter found them excessively burdensome.

Francis[12] labelled the policy of transferring programmes once under federal direction to the
states as '**devolutionary federalism**'. The concept of
devolution is in some ways a dubious one to apply
to the United States, for it is traditionally associated with the idea of a transfer of specific powers
to a subordinate tier of government, under a unitary system. But inasmuch as the term pointed to
a rebalancing of the federal system in such a way

> **devolutionary federalism**
> A variant of new federalism,
> the emphasis being on
> devolving responsibility for
> once federally run programmes
> to the states which – being
> closer to the people – are
> thought to be better placed
> to respond to local needs.

as to boost the power of the states, its use has subsequently been accepted by
several writers.   *seems He Held up on his Promise*

Clinton stressed the importance of improved cooperation between the federal
and state/local governments, and spoke of increased opportunities for local experimentation. Within two weeks of assuming office, he had invited the nation's
state governors to meet him so that he could listen to their complaints and ideas.
Over the following years, he established a framework in which federal
officials were able to loosen programme requirements to allow states and localities greater flexibility.

The impact of George W. Bush on federalism

When George W. Bush assumed the presidency, he labelled himself a 'faithful
friend of federalism', as might be expected from a Republican ex-governor. He
drew on his experience in Texas to show what might be achieved at state level.
He showed his leanings towards local initiative in his early days, by seeking
out the advice and services of leading state officials. He quickly established a
study group to see how the role of states might be advanced. His early implementation of the campaign promises he had made on tax cutting was justified
on several grounds, but one of them was that if the central government had a
reduced role and spent less on national programmes, then money could be left
in the pockets of individual Americans.

Yet other factors conspired to distance the president from such a pro-devolution
policy: the business community was sometimes unenthusiastic about regulatory state laws that were often pro-consumer or pro-environment, and urged
congressional intervention to pre-empt state legislation; the Religious Right
disliked some features of state autonomy (not least Oregon's suicide law and
Massachusetts' contentious policy on same-sex marriages) and would have
preferred to see a stricter moral code, more uniform in its application – Bush
himself argued for a constitutional amendment to outlaw gay marriages. And
the president's strong backing for improved standards in education implied
stricter central controls, to an extent that worried some sympathetic state
governors who were fearful of the possible adverse electoral consequences of
an increased federal role.

Two more serious issues emerged, both of which required vigorous federal leadership. Firstly, national security: the September 11 attacks on the Twin Towers and their aftermath shifted the focus of attention away from the states and more to Washington, where policy makers were engaged in measures to safeguard the interests of all Americans. Secondly, after the 'good years', in which the economy had been performing well, recession made it more difficult for states to fund programmes for which they had in recent years assumed responsibility. In July 2008, Congress sought to respond to the sub-prime mortgage crisis and increasing number of mortgage foreclosures by passing the Housing and Economic Recovery Act; the Treasury Department was given authority to bail out **Fannie Mae and Freddie Mac**; and local governments were given $4 billion in grants for use in purchasing and then rehabilitating foreclosed houses.

> **Fannie Mae and Freddie Mac**
>
> Two US mortgage giants, the Federal Home Mortgage Corporation (nicknamed Freddie Mac) and the Federal National Mortgage Association (nicknamed Fannie Mae), at the heart of the US housing market.

Overall, Bush was 'notably inattentive to federalism considerations in office – supporting expansion of federal authority even on issues where Republicans had traditionally deferred to state authority, such as education, prescription drug coverage, driver's licenses and welfare policy, and rarely perceiving any tension between his policy priorities and state prerogatives or concerns'.[13]

The early impact of Barack Obama on federalism

In the early days of the Obama presidency,[14] the most significant developments for federal–state relations were the presidential election and economic recession. In the 2008 election campaign, there was no indication that Barack Obama had a guiding approach to the issue, so that after his election he had no clear mandate to implement any changes in the distribution of federal and state power. None the less, his election and the accompanying Democratic gains in Congress had some implications for federalism. Firstly, federal power was used to promote different policy priorities, for instance the use of federal regulation in areas such as regulation of greenhouse gas emissions. Secondly, state experimentation was encouraged on a different range of issues than had been apparent during the Bush administration, particularly by permitting state auto-emission standards that exceeded federal requirements, as well as state expansion of coverage by the Children's Health Insurance Program (CHIP). Thirdly, there was greater willingness on the part of the White House and Capitol Hill to respond to state pleas for additional funding, whether for particular programmes such as Medicaid or for general emergency stabilisation assistance.

Above all, the election of Barack Obama returned the issue of health reform to the national agenda. He made comprehensive reform a high priority,

↖ Still apparent today!.

emphasising the need to get reform enacted during his first year in office. The goals included providing coverage to the uninsured, financing that coverage with some combination of new tax revenues and effective cost containment measures, and more generally slowing the rising cost of the nation's health-care bill. A reform package to implement Obama's proposals finally reached the statute book in May 2010. It is as yet premature to assess the impact of the health reforms on the relationship of the central government and the states. Their critics fear that 'Obamacare' will have far-reaching effects on traditional state roles and authority – as well as on the freedoms of American citizens.

Federal-stategovernment relations reviewed: yesterday, today and tomorrow

Relations between the states and the centre are at the very heart of federalism, for federalism seems to provide for an in-built tension between the two levels of government. Hague and Harrop[15] point out that in the United States

> the original principle was that the national and state governments would operate independently, each tier acting autonomously in its own constitutional sphere. In particular, the federal government was required to confine its activities to functions explicitly allocated to it, such as the power 'to lay and collect taxes, to pay the debts and provide for the common defense and welfare of the United States'. In the circumstances of eighteenth century America, extensive coordination between federal and state administration was considered neither necessary nor feasible. This model of separated governments . . . has long since disappeared, overwhelmed by the demands of an integrated economy and society.

The experience of American history reveals that the nature of federalism has changed over time. There was a broad tendency towards central control from the early days of the Republic, and it accelerated with the greater state intervention and regulation following the establishment of the New Deal. The trend reached its peak in the 1960s. Sometimes, this greater central power came about as a result of constitutional amendment; more often it was a response to prevailing economic and social conditions. Sometimes, too, the tendency towards central control was given a push by judicial decisions, so that clauses in the Constitution were interpreted widely to provide the federal government with a broad scope for legislation. The result was that in America the centre gained power at the expense of the fifty states, especially in the area of major economic policy. However, the centralising tendency was arrested in the closing decades of the twentieth century.

At the end of the first decade of the twenty-first century, states are more active than they were thirty years ago. They have enjoyed a resurgence and renewal that came about in part as the result of a backlash against the activist government of the Great Society years. The Johnson presidency had some important achievements to its credit, not least for the poor and ethnic minorities who were the main beneficiaries. These achievements came at a time when state and local governments often seemed inert and inefficient. But his changes generated opposition, and political opinion turned against them. Americans have always been lukewarm about 'big government', and opponents found increasing evidence that too many programmes had been badly run, were wasteful and undermined individual and local initiative.

Agreed!

There were several other reasons for the state resurgence that began in the late twentieth century, among them:

- the strong performance of the Republicans in congressional and gubernatorial elections, encouraging the adoption of policies based on less federal intervention and more respect for states' rights;
- increased wariness of congressional politicians on Capitol Hill, who had responsibility for introducing and passing federal laws. (The choice of ex-governors rather than congressmen as presidential candidates over the last generation was an indication of a growing distrust of Washington politicians.) These former Governors – Carter, but especially Reagan and Clinton – were well versed in state perspectives on the appropriate national–state relationship;
- a feeling that the federal government had failed to respond to assorted economic and social problems, so that the states had to act on their own; the cutting of many grants-in-aids further enhanced the tendency towards state self-reliance, spurring state politicians to reform;
- the handing over to the states of decision-making powers on important subjects such as welfare, especially via the 1996 Welfare Reform Act. From then onwards, although there was a national framework, it was increasingly left to the states to decide whether to hand over money to individual claimants, and the level at which help should be given;
- rulings of the Supreme Court, a number of which supported the states in their attempts to make important inroads on topics such as the availability of abortion;
- the increased willingness – indeed enthusiasm – of some states to experiment with new policies; state administrations became notably more vigorous and creative than they were in the heyday of 'big government'.

Broadly, the degree of national government interventionism has tended to vary according to economic and political necessities and the tide of popular opinion. As the economy became national, there was an increasing need for national leadership to sort out problems such as urban decline, worker protection and the regulation of large corporations; state activity seemed inadequate to meet the challenge. When government became too big, then many voters came to see the federal government as part of the problem, rather than as part of the solution.

The late twentieth-century Supreme Court and the federal–state balance

In the last decade of the twentieth century, the Rehnquist Court was instrumental in helping to shape the character of American intergovernmental relations. It leaned towards a more state-centred approach.

- In 1992, in *New York* v. *United States*, the justices took the view that the national government could not 'simply compel' a state to take particular policy actions.

- In 1999, the justices decided that Maine was not subject to Federal Labor Standards legislation.

- In 2000, in *Kimel* v. *Florida Board of Regents*, they went significantly further in exempting states from the requirements of federal laws designed to prevent age discrimination.

Sometimes people have had confusing aspirations, wanting smaller but decisive national leadership. Even those who deride big government and Washington 'meddling' sometimes find themselves calling for leadership on key issues. Robert Dole, a presidential contender in 1996, illustrated the ambiguity in a remark on law and order. He upheld states' rights by saying that: 'Republicans . . . believe that our country's increasingly desperate fight against crime is an area where more freedom is needed at the state level.'[16] He went on to promise that the proposed 'crime bill [would] impose mandatory minimum sentences on those who use guns in the commission of a crime, and make sure the jails are there to lock them up!'

The complexity of the relationship today

In practice, American federalism has experienced growing interdependence. There is a developing trend to improve relations between federal, state and local governments and find common ground between them. In several areas of policy, such as education and transport, policies are made, funded and applied at all tiers. States have regained much of their lost autonomy and are very important in their own right, but on occasion the national government steps in. When California experienced a serious electrical power shortage in 2000, Washington became unavoidably involved as the state began to make demands on the supplies of surrounding states.

In the last few years, there have been numerous examples of states acting in an imaginative and more assertive fashion. They have advanced their own interests by effective lobbying in the national capital; have tried out different forms of revenue raising and cost cutting; and developed alternative policy approaches. A spirit of innovation and vitality has spread through several state capitals, in many cases supported by both liberals and conservatives. As federal, state and local administrations vie with each other to provide the public services that the voters demand, the atmosphere is one of what Thomas

Dye[17] called '**competitive federalism**'. Washington is no longer seen as 'knowing best' and there has been greater recognition of the role and importance of the states in producing effective government.

> **competitive federalism**
> Competition is a mix of cooperation and conflict. Competitive federalism stresses the conflict between the national government and the states, and between the states themselves; for example regional or local governments compete with other regional or local governments.

The relationship between states and the centre is not static. America has, as Gillian Peele[18] points out, 'a vibrant but complex system which displays enormous variety and contradiction . . . Bush may expect, or indeed, want to continue the rebuilding of a genuine partnership with the states. The evolution of the American system has, however, produced a complex labyrinth of relationships that are less than easily navigated. It is thus likely that although the American federal and intergovernmental system will continue to tilt away from Washington, change will be relatively slow and incremental.'

In the George W. Bush era, there was indeed ambivalence with regard to federal–state developments. Several factors combined to push the 'faithful friend of federalism' into taking strong central action. Yet, in the last two years of the Bush era, states were more successful in securing relief from some unpopular federal directives regarding the National Guard, homeland security, education and welfare than in the previous six years. They also continued to be the primary innovators in areas such as immigration, environmental protection and healthcare, although they encountered new constraints in the form of federal court challenges and agency rulings.

The debate about the appropriate level of federal intervention is unresolved, for the relationship cannot be fixed for all time. As Woodrow Wilson[19] wrote, back in the early twentieth century, the matter is not for 'one generation, because it is a question of growth, and every new successive stage of our political and economic development, gives it a new aspect, makes it a new question'. Federalism has proved to be a flexible system, suitable for the administration of a large and diverse country, and capable of adaptation to changing needs and interests as the situation requires.

State and local government in operation

In the past, textbook writers have concentrated on the national scene at the expense of what happens in the states and localities. Examiners still tend to see American politics in this way. Yet not to be aware of the revival in sub-national politics would be to underestimate seriously the importance of the trends of recent years and also to misinterpret the essence of American federalism. In the words of Hames and Rae,[20] 'states are the basic building-blocks of American life, and they remain highly individual and distinctive'.

The fifty states vary enormously, all of them having distinctive histories, constitutions, governmental institutions and policies. As we have seen, they have a substantial degree of autonomy, so that the quality of public service provision, the level of taxation and the degree of tolerance extended on matters sexual and social are very different in liberal Massachusetts than in conservative Kansas. Singh[21] points out that on sexual matters the variation is marked, there being laws theoretically forbidding adultery in twenty-four states, fornication in seventeen, oral sex fifteen and the sale (but not use) of marital aids in eight:

> the state of Alabama allows sex with donkeys and corpses, but punishes oral sex between husbands and wives . . . Most of these laws are unenforced . . . and unenforceable. Nevertheless, the differences illustrate how domestic regulations can differ sharply even on the most intimate and private of matters, according to the particular state's moral traditions and political culture.

In general, matters that lie entirely within the borders of the fifty states are their exclusive concern. These include such things as:

- regulations relating to business, industry, property and utilities;
- the state criminal code;
- working conditions within the state.

All of the states are bicameral (two legislative chambers), except for Nebraska, which is unicameral. As with the federal government, the lower house is normally the larger of the two, and generally senators or members of the upper house serve for four years, as against two for members of the lower chamber. Many of the states impose **term limits** on their legislators (see also p. 181–182), largely because of the movement in recent decades towards greater professionalism in legislatures and the resulting development of **career politicians**. Until the 1960s, many state legislatures had met only in alternate years, and even then had short sessions. Today, their operation varies across America. Some states, such as California, are highly professionalised and have regular sessions and paid, full-time members. On the other hand, Kansas, Montana and seven other legislatures do not have annually paid members, but make payments for each day when the chambers are in session. They meet much less regularly.

Each state has an elected governor, but again the substance of the position varies considerably. All but two of the governors serve for four years. In New Hampshire and Vermont they have only a

term limits
Restrictions on the number of terms for which a member of an executive position (for example governor) or an elected state representative may serve. In 1995, the Supreme Court prevented states from introducing limits on the length of time their federal legislators can serve, but within the state legislatures there are no federal requirements. Thirty-nine states have a limit on governorships, eighteen on legislators.

career politicians
People committed to politics, which they regard as their vocation. They know little else beyond the worlds of politics, policy making and elections.

two-year term, but no limit on the maximum number of consecutive terms for which they can hold their position. There has been a trend towards greater gubernatorial power in recent years. In forty states, the governor has full responsibility for proposing the budget and, to the envy of most recent presidents, forty-one of the fifty also have some version of the **line-item veto**.

The fact that four of the last five presidents were at one time governors suggests the degree of respect that the office now carries. In most states, there has been greater recognition in recent years of the need to modernise gubernatorial authority, the more so as the states are now assuming some responsibilities that were once the prerogative of the federal government. This changed atmosphere has given governors a greater opportunity to make their mark, by introducing or urging the use of state initiatives in economic, environmental and social policy.

> **line-item veto**
> The authority of the president (or state governor) to delete part of a bill passed by the legislature and referring to matters of spending and/or taxation, thereby preventing those provisions from becoming law. The need for a presidential line-item veto was urged by presidents Nixon, Ford, Reagan, Bush senior and Clinton. It became law in 1996 and was overturned in the Supreme Court two years later.

Innovation across American states

Several states have been active in Washington DC in recent years, lobbying on their own behalf and employing professional lobbying companies to help them in their bid for federal help. However, they have also recognised the need to become more self-reliant. This has led to more creative thinking and some states have been fertile in devising initiatives.

- Alabama state insurance plans have imposed a monthly surcharge on smokers who refuse to quit.
- California has been restrictive on the rights of entry of illegal immigrants and the use of affirmative action programmes. These and many more policies have resulted from the widespread use of direct legislation, as described on pp. 226–227.
- Hawaii has introduced a British-style scheme of healthcare, and Oregon too has promoted a new system for the delivery of health provision.
- Wisconsin has experimented with parental choice and a voucher system in state education.
- Several states have tried out different approaches to issues of law and order, the main common factor between them being that policies have generally veered towards 'toughness'. Texas is noted for its frequent use of the death penalty and its 'boot camps' for young offenders; other states have employed policies ranging from 'zero tolerance' to registration of sex offenders.

THE GOVERNMENT OF MASSACHUSETTS: A CASE STUDY

Massachusetts is the most populous state in New England. Most of its population of 6.6 million lives in Boston and its surroundings. The eastern half of the state comprises urban, suburban and rural areas, while the west is mostly rural.

Massachusetts has been significant throughout American history, Plymouth being the second permanent place of English settlement; indeed, it was colonists from England who created many of the other towns in the state in the 1620s and 1630s. In the eighteenth century, it was the place where revolt against the Mother Country began. Boston became known as the 'Cradle of Liberty' because of the agitation that led to the American Revolution and the independence of the United States from Great Britain. In addition:

- the state has contributed many prominent politicians to national service, most notably the Adams and Kennedy families;

- it has always been the capital of higher education in the United States. Besides Harvard and the Massachusetts Institute of Technology, other noted institutions include Amherst College, Boston College, Simmons College and Brandeis University;

- it was also a centre of the temperance movement and abolitionist activity before the Civil War. In 2004, it became the first state to legally recognise same-sex marriage.

Government and politics in Massachusetts

The Massachusetts Constitution was ratified in 1780 while the War of Independence was still in progress, nine years before the US Constitution was adopted. It is the oldest written Constitution now in use in the world. It specifies the three traditional branches of government, an executive, a legislature and a judiciary.

The Governor of Massachusetts heads the executive branch. Elected for a four-year term, the incumbent has a range of duties including: signing or vetoing legislation; filling judicial and agency appointments; granting pardons; preparing an annual budget; and commanding the Massachusetts National Guard. Unusually, governors are addressed as His/Her Excellency. The executive branch also includes the Executive Council, which consists of eight elected councillors and the Lieutenant Governor. It confirms gubernatorial appointments and certifies election results.

The Massachusetts legislature, known as the General Court, has a House of Representatives with 160 members and a Senate of 40 members; all members serve two-year terms. The state sends ten Representatives and two Senators to the US Congress and has twelve votes in the Electoral College, which are granted on the usual American winner-takes-all system.

The judicial branch is headed by the Supreme Judicial Court, which serves over a number of lower courts. The Supreme Judicial Court is made up of a Chief Justice and six associate justices.

In 1913, the legislature approved a bill establishing a procedure for advisory initiatives to be placed on the ballot by voters across the state. The proposal must not be, either affirmatively or negatively, substantially the same as any other measure which has qualified for submission or been submitted to the people at either of the two preceding biennial state elections. Also, it must contain only subjects not excluded from the popular initiative. The state constitution excludes subjects that relate to religion, judges, the courts, particular localities, specific appropriations and certain provisions of the state Declaration of Rights from the initiative.

Massachusetts also has provision for popular referendum, an example being Question 4 on the 1998 state-wide ballot. In 1997, the Massachusetts General Court passed a law deregulating the state's electricity utility industry. Citizens who opposed this new law gathered enough signatures to have the law placed on the ballot. Sixty-five per cent of the voters in Massachusetts voted to retain the law. If they had voted 'no', the law would have been repealed.

Massachusetts is not one of the eighteen states that permit recall elections to remove state officials, but they are used in some local jurisdictions. It does make use of town meetings (see p. 242). In operation for over 300 years, they have proved to be a valuable means for many residents to voice their opinions and directly effect change in their communities.

A liberal state

In the mid-twentieth century, Massachusetts gradually moved from being Republican-leaning to being largely dominated by the Democrats; the 1952 victory of John F. Kennedy over the incumbent Republican senator is seen as a watershed moment in this transformation. The state has subsequently gained a reputation as being politically liberal and is often used as an archetype of modern liberalism, hence the term 'Massachusetts liberal' to describe Democrats of generally progressive leanings.

States do not get much more Democratic than Massachusetts. For several decades, it has routinely voted for the Democrats in federal elections, although it does not always live up to its national stereotype as a bastion of liberalism:

- it twice voted for Ronald Reagan in presidential elections;
- in the most recent state-wide contest (a special election in 2010 for the US Senate, following the death of Senator Edward Kennedy), Republican Scott Brown was victorious, causing a major political upset.

In state elections, Democrats hold every state-wide office and control both houses of the legislature with lopsided majorities. Surprisingly, from 1991 to 2007 Massachusetts had only Republican governors, albeit ones on the party's more progressive wing. In November 2006, Democrat Deval Patrick became the first African American to be elected as the state's governor.

A number of contemporary national political issues have been influenced by events in Massachusetts, such as the 2003 state Supreme Court decision that declared the prohibition of gay marriage to be a violation of the state's constitution. As a result, gay couples gained an unprecedented opportunity to marry in Massachusetts and receive all of the legal rights, protections and benefits associated with marriage (see also pp. 406–407). In another liberal vote, the outcome of a 2008 initiative decriminalised possession of small amounts of marijuana.

Local government

In addition to its fifty state governments, America has a vast and complex maze of local government units. Generalisation is difficult, because they range from the extremes of small, rural, sparsely populated townships to huge, densely populated metropolitan areas, with cities, towns, counties and districts in between. Every American lives within the jurisdiction of the national government, a state government and perhaps ten to twenty local bodies. For instance, the six-county Chicago-Illinois metropolitan area has more than 1,200 different governments, some serving the people in broad ways, others providing more specialised services. *Wow!*

Governments in the USA in 2010: a summary

Type	Number
Federal	1
State	50
County	3,034
Municipal (city, town, village etc.)	19,429
Township (in some states called town)	16,504
School district	13,506
Special purpose (for example fire, police, library, etc.)	35,052
Total	87,576

Since the Reagan era, states have been willing to decentralise their governing arrangements to the local level ('second order devolution') and the smaller units encourage individual participation and promote the value of individualism. There is a strong tradition of grassroots democracy in America that fits in well with the widely shared belief that government should be kept as close to the people as possible. The very existence of so many governments to deal with so many different and necessary services seems to indicate that democracy flourishes in the localities, a situation far removed from British experience.

Yet the health of local democracy in America can be overstated. As in Britain, local politics is often poorly covered by the media and consequently the public often remains ill-informed about what goes on. This in turn makes it difficult for people to hold those who represent them accountable. Moreover, levels of turnout in some elections are often very low. Some cities, such as Birmingham (Alabama), have done much to encourage neighbourhood democracy by creating neighbourhood boards that have meaningful control over important policy decisions. In this way, voters can see that participation is worthwhile and they feel that it is worth the effort to take their involvement beyond voting alone.

Writing of Britain and the United States, McNaughton[22] gets the balance about right:

In the USA, if anything, citizens are more interested in the politics of their state and their community than in the goings-on in Washington. Their daily lives are clearly affected more by the nature and performance of local government than those of British citizens. American local democracy is, therefore, more lively, more meaningful and more cherished than it is in the UK.

Debatable

The benefits of federalism today

With the growth of the federal government since the New Deal, it might have been expected that the states would become mere appendages of Washington. Yet, despite the development of 'co-operative federalism' (see p. 54) and the fact that states were no longer 'coordinate and independent' as Wheare envisaged, in practice many writers could see them as a still important, indeed vital, part of the system. To Daniel Elazar,[23] writing in 1987, the states 'remain viable because they exist as civil societies with political systems of their own'.

Each state has its own distinctive history and traditions, and Americans identify with their state as well as with the nation as a whole; they are broadly popular as a form of government. In recent years, most of them have improved the quality of their services and the personnel who deliver them. Political institutions have been reformed and more efficient management of programmes has been introduced. They have, particularly in some cases, acted in an innovatory manner, and have been a testing-ground for experiments that others can follow.

They also provide to many citizens an opportunity for involvement in the political process, and have been a training ground for national leadership. It is through securing election in a particular state that national politicians build up their reputation, either by serving in the legislature, by becoming governor of the state or by representing the state in Congress.

The fifty states are important in their own right, and they are preferable to a more centralised system that would be unsuitable for a country of the size and regional diversity of the United States. Although there are ways in which the federal government can directly intervene to force the states to adopt certain programmes and policies – as happened over the ending of racial segregation – nevertheless the central powers are limited. The relationship between Washington and the states is more one of negotiation and compromise, rather than one of coercion.

Americans think of their states as being important. Until well into the nineteenth century, they identified first with, for example, Virginia and second with the United States. The motto of Illinois reflects the ambiguity of loyalty even today: 'State Sovereignty, National Union'. States are still a powerful reference point in their culture, and it is state laws that citizens encounter more frequently than any enactments of the federal government. Many federal laws are actually implemented through the states, which modify them to suit their circumstances.

Federalism today has particular appeal to the many Americans who have become increasingly sceptical about the desirability of federal intervention. They show greater distrust of politicians who work in federal government than was the case forty years ago. They often feel that Washington is too remote from their experience. They have more confidence in their state governments, for the politicians who run them are more in touch with the people. Several opinion polls have pointed to this preference for state over national government and to the widespread belief that state administrations are better able to handle responsibility over several areas of policy. In answer to the question of which government they trusted to perform certain tasks, most Americans

Federalism and devolution in Britain and the United States: a comparison

	Britain	The United States
Unitary or federal?	Unitary.	Federal.
Degree of centralisation	Traditionally centralised, but now a 'developing unitary' system.	Decentralised, but as a broad trend, more power at the centre now than 200 years ago. Move from 'dual federalism' to other forms such as 'creative federalism'.
Developments in devolution and federalism	Devolution introduced in Scotland, Wales and Northern Ireland, in differing degrees; a kind of 'creeping federalism'. Scotland in particular developing distinctive policies.	Despite broad trend above, more initiative at state level since the 1980s – new emphasis on partnership and local experimentation since days of 'new federalism'.
Quangos	Development of quango state: quangos replaced many traditional local government functions. Attract much criticism; Coalition government committed to axing 192 and reviewing others.	Term originated in US politics, where there was concern about the growth of independent regulatory agencies which emerged at the end of the nineteenth century as essential instruments to discipline of free enterprise; widely disliked in a country noted for commitment to the elective principle.
Local government	Flourished after World War II, but increased central control, especially after 1979, and attempts to rationalise structure and reduce number of authorities. Much talk of death of local democracy – low election turnouts. Labour attempted to re-invigorate council activity, by introduction of elected mayors.	Responsibility of each individual state. Vast range of local units. Great theoretical interest in public participation, but local democracy not as flourishing as some would like. As in Britain, suffers from low level of media coverage and interest.

told interviewers from the *Washington Post*[24] that they felt that the state was preferable to the federal administration in:

- running things (70%–27%);
- establishing rules on welfare entitlement (70%–25%);
- setting rules for workplace safety (55%–42%);
- setting Medicaid and Medicare regulations (52%–43%);
- and setting environmental rules for clean air and water (51%–47%).

Only on issues such as conducting foreign policy, protecting national security and safeguarding civil rights did the federal tier come off best.

CONCLUSION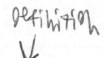

Federalism is a form of government that divides political responsibility. Its underlying ideas are that:

- too much political power is dangerous and it is therefore desirable that there should be diverse levels of government to prevent undue concentration;
- particular powers are best assigned to particular tiers best suited to exercising them.

An understanding of federalism is crucial to unlocking the secrets of the American political system. It decentralises American politics, helps to decide which president is elected, enhances judicial power and decentralises policies as well. In the distant past, the debates were about whether the national government should regulate the railroads or adopt minimum wage legislation. Today, they are about whether it should regulate abortion, determine speed limits on highways or lay down that 18-year-olds cannot legally drink alcohol. Policies relating to the economy, the environment and many other issues are subject to the centralising force of the national government and the dispersing force of the fifty states. Because of the overlapping powers of the two tiers of government, most discussion of policy is also a discussion about federalism.

The neat arrangements devised at Philadelphia have been adapted to changing circumstances at different periods in American history because special situations have required a new approach. The broad drift has been towards a centralisation of power since the early days of dual federalism. But in recent years there has been a significant reversal, and today it is meaningful to talk of states' revival and renewal.

State and local government are and always have been important parts of the American system. The Constitution would not have been ratified had it not recognised the rights of the states. Today, much of American government still operates at the sub-national level and state and local identity remains strong.

REFERENCES

1 A. Grant, *The American Political Process*, Dartmouth, 1994
2 J. Zimmerman, *Contemporary American Federalism: The Growth of National Power*, Praeger, 1992
3 K. Wheare, *Federalism*, Oxford University Press, 1946 (reissued 1963)
4 J. Bryce, *The American Commonwealth*, Macmillan, 1907
5 J. Burns, J. Peltason, T. Cronin and D. Magleby, *Government by the People*, Prentice Hall, 1994
6 M. Cummings and D. Wise, *Democracy under Pressure*, Harcourt College Publishers, 2000
7 M. Grodzins, *The American System*, Rand McNally, 1966
8 J. Kincaid, 'American Federalism: The Third Century', in *Annals of the American Academy of Political and Social Science*, May 1990
9 R. Reagan, as quoted in G. Wasserman, *The Basics of American Politics*, Longman, 1997
10 J. Kincaid, as in 8 above
11 D. McKay, *American Politics and Society*, Blackwell, 2001
12 J. Francis, 'Federalism', in R. Singh (ed.), *Governing America: The Politics of a Divided Democracy*, Oxford University Press, 2003
13 J. Dinan and A. Conlan, 'Federalism, the Bush Administration and the Transformation of American Conservatism', paper presented to the American Political Science Association, Chicago, 2007
14 J. Dinan and S. Gamkhar, 'The State of American Federalism, 2008–9: The Presidential Election, the Economic Downturn, and the Consequences Federalism' *The Journal of Federalism*, Publius/Oxford University Press, 2009
15 R. Hague and M. Harrop, *Comparative Government and Politics*, Palgrave, 2004
16 R. Dole, as quoted in G. Wasserman, as in 9 above
17 T. Dye, *American Federalism: Competition among Governments*, Lexington Books, 1990
18 G. Peele, 'Introduction: The United States in the Twenty-first Century', in G. Peele, C. Bailey, B. Cain and B. Peters (eds), *Developments in American Politics* 4, Palgrave, 2002
19 W. Wilson, *Constitutional Government in the United States*, Columbia University Press, 1908
20 T. Hames and N. Rae, *Governing America*, Manchester University Press, 1996
21 R. Singh, *American Government and Politics: A Concise Introduction*, Sage, 2003
22 N. McNaughton, *Success in Politics*, John Murray, 2001
23 D. Elazar, *Exploring Federalism*, University of Alabama Press, 1987
24 *Washington Post* – ABC poll, fieldwork conducted in March 1995

USEFUL WEB SITES

www.governing.com *Governing* magazine (published by Congressional Quarterly); useful information and links on issues relating to the states and local government.

www.usmayors.org US Conference of Mayors; the official non-partisan organisation of cities with populations of 30,000 or more.

www.ncsl.org National Conference of State Legislatures; information about the policy and effectiveness of state legislatures and state innovation.

www.nga.org National Governors' Association; contains analysis of issues affecting the states and information on current policy initiatives.

www.csg.org Council of State Governments; information about and links to the states and the way their systems of government are organised.

www.urban.org The Urban Institute (a Washington think tank); monitors changes in federal social policies that affect the states and local governments.

In addition, the web sites of particular state and local governments can be consulted.

SAMPLE QUESTIONS

1 To what extent has there been a change in the relationship between the federal and state governments, and why has any change come about?
2 'The devolution of power from Washington since the 1980s is the most significant change in the balance of the national–state relationship since the time of the New Deal.' Discuss.
3 'American federalism works well because although the constitutional structure has been largely unchanged, in practice the system operates with flexibility and in a spirit of partnership.' Discuss.
4 What is the role of the states in the American federal system?
5 Does the cry of 'states' rights' have any meaning in the present-day US?
6 To what extent would the Founding Fathers recognise the concept of federalism as it is practised today?
7 What are the advantages and disadvantages of American federalism as it operates in the twenty-first century?
8 Outline the major consequences of American federalism.
9 'America has a federal and Britain a unitary form of government, but in reality the influence of the national government over the states and local and devolved authorities respectively is broadly similar.' Discuss.
10 Discuss the similarities and differences of American federalism and British devolution.

Presidential power

4

The president is the head of but one of the three branches of government, but he is – in the words of one writer[1] – the 'superstar of the American political game'. As the only nationally elected official, other than the vice-president, he is the symbol of both the federal government and the nation. Much is expected of American presidents, but in reality there are limitations to the power that any modern president can wield. He is an 'emperor with few clothes'.[2] Power is his for a fixed term only and is held on trust from the people who elect him. It is checked by the restraints of a separate legislature and an independent judiciary.

In this chapter, we will examine: the roles presidents perform; the development of presidential power in the era of the modern presidency; the expectations of modern presidents and their ability to fulfil them; and the academic debate surrounding the power of presidents and the presidency.

POINTS TO CONSIDER

- How wide-ranging are the powers of the president, as outlined in the Constitution?
- What is the role of the US president?
- Who controls the conduct of US foreign policy: president or Congress?
- What do we mean by 'presidential power' and why has this power tended to increase over the last 100 years?
- What factors determine the success or failure of presidents in their dealings with Congress?
- What is the current balance of power in the relationship between the president and Congress?
- What are the limits of presidential power?
- In what ways did Neustadt and Schlesinger disagree about the nature of presidential power?
- What is meant by unitary executive theory?

- What makes a good president?
- How can we measure presidential success?
- Was George W. Bush (a) a strong president and (b) an effective president?
- Is the prime minister stronger within the British system of government than the US president within the American system?

The role of the president as outlined in the Constitution

The American Constitution has relatively little to say about what the American president can and should do. Key terms such as 'the executive' are not clearly defined. Furthermore, the functions set out are subject to restraints.

The actual powers outlined in the document are set out mainly in Article II:
- Article I.7: to veto congressional legislation;
- Article II:2 to act as commander-in-chief of the US armed forces;
- Article II.2: to grant pardons;
- Article II.2: to make treaties;
- Article II.2: to appoint ambassadors;
- Article II.2: to appoint judges;
- Article II.2: to appoint members of the executive;
- Article II.3: to comment on the State of the Union;
- Article II.3: to recommend legislation to Congress;
- Article II.3: to summon special sessions of Congress.

The Founding Fathers had in mind a presidency the holder of which would stand above the political process and act as a symbol of national unity. He would not depend directly on the people or any political party for his support. This would enable him to act as a kind of gentleman-aristocrat, remote from the political arena. Congress was supreme, as far as the actual government of the country was concerned. In the words of Maidment and McGrew,[3] the presidency would be 'the brake, the restraining hand of the federal government; it would provide the balance for the congress, and the House of Representatives in particular'.

It has not worked out in this way, for from an early stage presidents have stepped in to resolve national problems. In the twentieth century, wars and domestic crises provided the opportunity for assertive leadership from the man in the White House, so that there was a broad, underlying trend towards greater presidential power. But as we shall see, the combination of weak presidents and variations in the national mood has meant that at different times the presidency has been either a power-house or a motionless engine. There has been no continuous accumulation of power, more a waxing and waning of the degree of leadership and control.

The roles of the president in practice

Head of state

The president is the symbolic head of state and, as such, a focal point of loyalty. He has ceremonial functions, ranging from visiting foreign countries to attending important national occasions. At one time, he throws the first baseball of the season, at another he reviews parades. These opportunities for favourable media coverage give him an advantage over his opponents, for he can be seen to speak and act in a 'presidential' manner.

George Washington was acutely aware of the value of such ceremonial occasions in enhancing his prestige, leading John Adams[4] to observe that 'if he was not the great President, he was the best actor that we ever had'.

Chief executive

The ability of the president to carry out or execute laws is laid down in Article II of the Constitution – 'The executive power shall be vested in a President of the United States'. He has overall responsibility for ensuring that a network of fifteen executive departments and a range of diverse agencies and bureaux work effectively. He heads a vast federal bureaucracy, employing nearly three million civilians in the executive branch. He appoints to some 2,000 posts and can hire and fire the heads of executive agencies.

Other than embracing the appointment of key members of the bureaucracy, the presidential power of appointment extends widely to include a number of key offices. In Article II.2, the Founding Fathers divided the power of appointment as follows:

> **Advice and Consent**
> The power granted in the Constitution to the Senate to advise the president, ratify treaties he makes with foreign nations and give consent to presidential appointments. On occasion, it is denied or delayed for political reasons.

He shall nominate, and by and with the **Advice and Consent** of the senate, shall appoint Ambassadors, other public Ministers and Consults, Judges of the Supreme Court, and all other Officers of the United States, whose Appointments are not herein otherwise provided for, and which shall be established by Laws.

These nominations require approval by a simple majority of the Senate. Often, this is a routine process, although on occasion approval has been denied or there has been a prolonged delay before it has been granted. Some of President Clinton's appointees to the Supreme Court came under close scrutiny, as they were deemed to be too liberal.

Presidents can also grant pardons, perhaps the most famous being that granted by President Ford to Richard Nixon, in a bid to consign the long nightmare of Watergate (see p. 85) to history. In this capacity, they have also asserted the right of **executive privilege**, although, following the cases of *United States* v. *Nixon* (1974) and *Clinton* v. *Jones* (1997), the courts have applied strict limitations to the exercise of that claim.

> **executive privilege**
> The right, asserted by presidents since Washington, to refuse to appear before, and to withhold information from, the legislature or a court. Its existence was recognised in the case of *United States* v. *Nixon*, although the ruling imposed strict limits on the circumstances when it might be exercised.

Chief legislator

Although the president is not part of the legislative branch of government, he has the constitutional right to recommend measures to Congress. In the twentieth century, presidents increasingly found themselves in the position of producing their own proposals to encourage the legislature. They have used the State of the Union address every January to present their annual programme, and today most measures passed by Congress have their origins in the executive branch. Much depends on the political situation. A president without a congressional majority – such as Bill Clinton in his last six years – is in the position of responding to and attempting to modify measures, rather than initiating them. In general, presidents are more successful in securing their legislation in the earlier than in the latter years of their term. The first two years of the Obama presidency saw the passage of contentious legislation, but after the mid-term results it was to be expected that he too would have to seek bipartisan cooperation if he was to obtain congressional approval for his proposals (see p. 92–94 for the fate of his early legislative initiatives).

In this role, presidents make extensive use of arm-twisting techniques to impose their will or fend off policies that they dislike. This may involve invitations for senators and representatives to attend the White House or a round of golf ('killing opposition by kindness'), or threats to obstruct public works projects in a congressman's district. Senator Byrd[5] of West Virginia gave an indication of the sort of meeting that might occur:

> [President] 'I respect you for your opposition to that funding [for the Contras in central America], but I wish you would see your way to vote with us next time on that. Can you do it?'

> 'Well, I will certainly be glad to think about it, Mr. President . . . '

> 'Well, Bob, I hope you will. And by the way, that money for the heart research center in Morgantown that you have worked for, I will bet your people love you for that . . . I have given a lot of thought to that. Be sure and take another look at that item we have, funds for the Contras.'

In addition to subtle and more blatant arm-twisting, presidents can also use the presidential veto (see p. 158), as a means of blocking unwanted policies.

Head of party

The president is the leader of his party, a role that itself involves several duties. The president:
- tries to fulfil its programme, the platform on which he was elected;
- is its chief fund raiser and campaigner;
- appoints its national chairperson;
- distributes offices and favours to the party faithful.

As party leader, the president's control is limited, the more so given the decentralised nature of American political parties. He can use party identification to gain support in Congress, if his party has a majority. Yet in the case of Bill Clinton this did not guarantee support even in the first two years, when he had a congressional majority. If members of either chamber oppose the president, there is little he can do about it, other than appeal directly to the people over their heads. The president has no formal disciplinary sanctions.

Presidents vary in their attempts to keep the party within their control. President Carter placed little emphasis on this party responsibility, which did little to ease his relations with Congress. At first, Clinton was more aware of party feelings and the need to 'manage' his legislative colleagues, but his policies came unstuck. By the time he was seeking re-election in 1996, there was an air of detachment between the presidential and congressional wings of the party.

Chief diplomat

The president has the power to develop relations with representatives of foreign powers, appoint ambassadors to those countries and sign treaties that become effective once the Senate has consented by a two-thirds majority. As we have seen, in the postwar years, presidents have become the initiators and executors of foreign policy. Although Congress officially declares war, there is presidential primacy in this area and this has provided incumbents with a formidable source of influence and power, doing much to enhance or diminish their political stature at home.

On occasions, the president may personally participate in summit conferences, where heads of state meet for direct consultation. President Woodrow Wilson headed the American delegation to the Paris Peace Conference at the end of World War I. Every president from Franklin Roosevelt onwards has met world statesmen to discuss economic and political issues and pursue bilateral and multilateral agreements.

Commander-in-chief of the armed forces

Closely related to the role of chief diplomat is the position of commander-in-chief, for it is the ability to use the might of the armed forces that makes a president's foreign policy credible. Presidents have very extensive powers in wartime, deciding when to intervene abroad. They have embarked on intervention in episodes ranging from wars in Korea to Vietnam, from Afghanistan to Iraq, deploying troops as necessary. In practice, much of the authority is delegated to the secretary of state for defense, who in turn normally delegates his command to leading figures in the military establishment.

In reaction to presidential war making in Vietnam, Congress passed the **War Powers Act** in 1973 to curb presidential freedom. However, as with some other legislation that appears to restrict executive actions, its meaning is open to interpretation and its effectiveness is questionable. Presidents from Reagan to Clinton have basically ignored the limitations it was designed to impose upon them. It is often mentioned at times when troops are deployed, but in 1991 during the war with Iraq President George H. Bush described it as being 'unconstitutional', and three years later, in

> **War Powers Act**
> An Act that imposes a 60-day limit on the time for which a president can keep American troops abroad without congressional approval. Without such authorisation, the troops have to be withdrawn; overall, 90 days can be allowed, to enable the withdrawal to be carried out successfully.

sending troops to Haiti, his successor also did not seek congressional approval for his intervention. Neither was there much congressional oversight of the war initiated by President George W. Bush in Afghanistan.

Originally the Act was passed over President Nixon's veto. Ever since, Congress and a succession of presidents have failed to reach agreement over its status and relevance. In recent years, some congressmen have recognised that the attempt to control presidents in this way was ineffective and perhaps not even prudent. Whilst some would like to strengthen the Act to give it more teeth and others would wish see it made more workable, there are many who would prefer to scrap it altogether. Members of the latter group accept that in an age of fast-moving crises on the international scene, it is unwise to undermine the president as he performs his role on America's behalf.

Others

The late Clinton Rossiter,[6] an American political scientist, listed other presidential roles – 'Voice of the People' in American affairs, 'Protector of Peace' (intervening in race riots etc.), 'Manager of Prosperity' and 'Leader of the Western World'.

PRESIDENTS AND THE MAKING AND HANDLING OF FOREIGN POLICY

Crisis management

The president's roles as chief diplomat and commander-in-chief are related to another presidential responsibility: crisis management. A crisis is a sudden, unpredictable and potentially dangerous event. Most occur in the realm of foreign policy. Crises often involve hot tempers and high risks. Quick judgements are needed, despite the availability of only sketchy information. Whether it was the discovery of Soviet missiles in Cuba (1962), American hostages held in Iran (1979) or the events associated with 9/11, crises have challenged the president's ability to make difficult decisions. In origin, crises are rarely the president's doing, but handled incorrectly they can be his undoing.

With modern communications, the president can instantly monitor events almost anywhere. Moreover, because situations develop more rapidly today, there is a premium on rapid action, secrecy, constant management, consistent judgement and expert advice. Congress usually moves slowly (one might say deliberatively), is large (making it difficult to keep secrets) and composed of generalists. As a result, the president – who can come to quick and consistent decisions, confine information to a small group, carefully oversee developments and call upon experts in the executive branch – has become more prominent in the handling of crises.

Throughout the century, crises have allowed presidents to become more powerful, and crisis management is a natural role for most who assume the presidential position. Most have been only too willing to step into the vacuum and seize their chance to lead, whether it be Kennedy over the Cuban missiles, Bush senior over the Iraqi invasion of Kuwait, Clinton over Bosnia or George W. Bush over the terrorist attacks on Washington and New York in September 2001.

The machinery of foreign policy

Presidents have their own style of management, and their own priorities. Some wish to be more involved with the detail of foreign policy than others, and wish to centralise decision making on all aspects of foreign and national security matters into their own hands. The foreign policy-making machine in the United States is a vast one, with the president at the apex of the structure. He or she appoints key personnel such as the secretary of state and the secretary of state for defense, and the heads of important agencies such as the Central Intelligence Agency (CIA).

In its original form, the Department of State was not concerned with overseas policy alone, but over the years most of its domestic workload was gradually transferred elsewhere. The department retains the Great Seal of the United States, and if the president or vice-president resigns it is to the secretary of state that the resignation is officially submitted. The main work of the department is concerned with:

- promoting of the security interests of the US and its allies;

- protecting foreign trade and commerce;

- helping negotiate and enforce treaties and other agreements with foreign countries;

- administering the Agency for International Development, the Peace Corps and most non-military aid to foreign nations;

- maintaining friendly contacts between the US and other countries, including such things as arranging the reception of new foreign ambassadors by the president and advising on the recognition of new foreign countries and governments;

- informing the American public about developments in the field of foreign policy, by publishing appropriate documents, official papers and other publications;

- protecting American citizens, their welfare and property abroad. This last function involves the supervision of the Foreign Service of the United States, including the ambassadors and administrative, consular, economic and political officers who manage the country's foreign relations. It is also concerned with the treatment of any Americans abroad, and it issues passports for their visits and processes visa applications for those entering America.

In the Executive Office, see pp. 128–134, the president has his own advisers, and the special assistant for national security affairs (SA) has a highly significant position in the presidential team. Presidents like the advice and support of the SA, for not only is he conveniently located (in the White House) but he also owes prime loyalty to the person who chose him for the position. By contrast, the secretary of state – once appointed – has a department to represent, the views of which can shape his or her own in a way which the president may not like.

The National Security Council (NSC), created by the National Security Act of 1947, meets irregularly to advise the president on foreign and defence policy. By the terms of the statute, it comprises the president, vice-president and secretaries of state and defense, along with advisers such as the heads of the CIA and the joint chiefs of staff. Originally, the position of SA was little more than that of a secretary to the NSC, but it has grown vastly in scope. Today, some presidents prefer to rely on an informal group of advisers and the SA, rather than the statutory body.

Despite intentions to the contrary, Ronald Reagan allowed his SA unprecedented freedom of manoeuvre, and in the Iran–Contra affair his office operated what was in effect an independent foreign policy. The State Department and Congress were in the dark about the way in which the SA and some members of the NSC were engaged in trading arms with Iran in return for the release of American hostages, just as they were about the use of the proceeds of arms sales to supply the Contra guerillas in Nicaragua with weaponry – and thus evade a congressional ban on such a distribution of military supplies. 'Irangate' (see p. 85), as it became known, illustrated the difficulties of establishing democratic control of the SA and his office. It also showed how powerful that office is, for the SA has special access to the president. Whatever they may say before assuming office, presidents like this source of extra and independent advice, for it frees them from the bureaucratic preoccupations of any department or agency.

The growth of presidential power

Presidential power is judged according to the ability of a president to achieve the identifiable goals he has set himself. Those presidents who set themselves clear priorities and manage to accomplish them are widely viewed as successful. Some do not set themselves clear objectives, or if they do so have difficulty in fulfilling them. Presidential power has increased since the days of the Founding Fathers, as people turned to the presidency for initiatives to get things done. Presidents stepped in to fill the vacuum left by the inertia or inaction of Congress, the states or private enterprise.

1933 to the 1970s: the imperial presidency

The **modern presidency** really began in 1933, for the Great Depression, created (or, at least, certainly accelerated) a fundamental change in political behaviour in the United States. The sheer scale of economic dislocation and hardship overwhelmed the states, and their inadequacy was revealed. The public and the special interests turned to the federal government to promote measures of recovery. The administration of Franklin D. Roosevelt was not reluctant to respond.

modern presidency
Usually dated from March 1933, the term refers to the fundamental change that followed FDR's entry into the White House. Four key developments were that the president: acquired a regular role in the legislative process; made increased use of unilateral powers such as executive orders (see p. 88); had a significantly larger staff to support him; and became more visible to the public and a symbol of government.

Since then, the American political system has become a very presidential one and the political process now requires a continued sequence of presidential initiatives in foreign policy and in the domestic arena to function satisfactorily. Modern presidents impose themselves with far greater effect on the political environment than did their counterparts of the nineteenth century.

The early 1960s saw the peak of enthusiasm for presidential power. A broad spectrum of commentators welcomed its expansion, for post-1945 there was a consensus about domestic and foreign policy which encouraged a delegation of power to the president. There was a greater degree of agreement about the fundamentals of policy making, and the level and extent of debate over public policy was less intense and robust than at other times.

Of course, there was dispute and division, but many things were agreed. The legacy of the New Deal, the great postwar economic expansion, the growing confidence over the management of the economy, the belief in the solubility of problems and the increasing claims on the federal government combined to create a feeling of well-being. It was felt to be prudent to allow the president a relatively free hand to lead his country. There was broad agreement that the federal government should have a significant role in the nation's economy and in creating and maintaining a welfare system.

The Johnson era (1963–69) was the high point of the postwar domestic consensus that was about to crumble. Till then, there was a belief that social ailments were amenable to the application of money, and this confidence in the power of economic growth and social engineering enormously enhanced the presidency. It seemed to be the only institution that could solve problems. It had the expertise to devise new policies; Congress did not, and looked to the president for a lead.

In foreign policy, the postwar consensus aroused even less dissent than its domestic counterpart. Few raised a voice against the direction of American policy after Truman had laid down the 'Truman Doctrine', which outlined America's place in the world and was to become the foundation of foreign policy to the late 1960s. America was the world's policeman and had abandoned its prewar isolationism, stationed troops abroad and played an increasingly interventionist role.

Congress had willingly accepted presidential leadership, and gave Truman and his successors more or less carte blanche in matters of national security. The nation was united, and congressmen had no desire to create an impression of disunity. A bipartisan coalition acquiesced in most presidential initiatives. Foreign policy was the president's policy, and received the almost automatic ratification of Congress. It was an unsatisfactory position, which opened up the possibility of the abuse of power.

Such abuses of presidential power did occur – the **Vietnam War** and Watergate were but the most significant. In 1974, many Americans became aware for the first time of the tremendous accumulation of power in the hands of the president. The 'separation of powers' principle had been incorporated into the Constitution to prevent a concentration of power in one part of the government. Watergate and the revelations of the misuse of power by the executive branch by several past presidents reminded people of the message spelt out by the Founding Fathers – a system that placed too much responsibility in the hands of one man must offer temptations for wrong-doing.

This growth of executive power did not happen suddenly under President Nixon. Arthur Schlesinger[7] argued that the concept of the constitutional

Vietnam War

The war begun under Kennedy and escalated under Johnson to prevent communist North Vietnam from taking over South Vietnam and to contain the spread of communism in Southeast Asia. It ended with an American withdrawal in 1973, America's first defeat in war. In 1975, Vietnam was united under communist rule.

> **Watergate**
>
> Watergate is the collective label for a series of abuses of power that began with a break-in at the national headquarters of the Democratic Party in the Watergate Building, Washington DC, in June 1972, as part of an attempt to find out the Democrats' election plans and thereby assist the chances of a Republican victory.
>
> As the story unfolded, many malpractices were uncovered. Several members of the Nixon administration were indicted and convicted on charges ranging from burglary and wire-tapping to 'misleading testimony' and 'political espionage'. It became apparent that Nixon had been taping conversations in the Oval Office and that he had been tapping the phones of his political enemies. When parts of the tapes were released, many began to become more than ever suspicious that the president had himself been involved. With talk of his being impeached, he resigned in August 1974, the first president to do so. He left the White House in disgrace.

presidency had given way by the 1970s to an **imperial presidency**, a revolutionary use of power very different from what had originally been intended. The presidency no longer seemed to be controllable via the constitutional checks and balances.

The 1970s to the present day

In the aftermath of these concerns, power passed to two presidents, Ford and Carter, who were widely perceived as anything but 'imperial'. Neither projected the image of an assertive leader and both were rejected by the voters after one period in office. Observers began to refer to the limitations of the presidency rather than to the strength of the office, with Franck[8] writing of the 'tethered presidency', one too constrained to be effective in providing the leadership America required.

Ronald Reagan was the first postwar president since Eisenhower to complete two terms in office. Despite the lapses that occurred (in particular, **Irangate**), he is widely perceived as having achieved much of what he wished to accomplish. After the setbacks of the 1970s, there was talk of a 'restored presidency'. Many Americans seemed to warm to the Reaganite style, which is why he has

imperial presidency

A label for the increased authority and decreased accountability of the presidency, at its peak in the late 1960s/early 1970s. It signified an era in which there was a high-handed and often secretive handling of foreign policy issues and in which, in domestic policy too, presidents were able to evade the usual system of checks and balances.

Irangate (the Iran–Contra affair)

'Irangate', the major crisis of the Reagan presidency, concerned the sale of arms by the US to Iran in return for the release of American hostages detained in the Middle East. The proceeds of the arms sales were channelled to the Contras, rebel forces that were seeking to overthrow the left-wing Sandinista government of Nicaragua, which the US administration wished to destabilise. Altogether, at least four main laws were breached, and the sale of weapons to states sponsoring terrorism was something that the president himself had publicly denounced.

President Carter's difficulties with Congress

In domestic policy, the president was little versed in the methods of Washington politics and failed to understand the rudimentary facts about the policy-making process. He found Congress unresponsive to his requests.

A congressman[9] produced his impression of the exchanges between the president and Speaker Tip O'Neill, which went as follows:

> **O'Neill:** A fine speech, Mr President. Now here's a list of members you should call, you know, to keep the pressure on. We need their votes.
>
> **Carter:** Tip, I outlined the problem to the people of the United States of America. It was rational, and my presentation was also rational. Now the American people are the most intelligent people in the world, Tip, and I am sure that when they see their Representatives think my program over, they will see that I was right.
>
> **O'Neill:** Lookit, Mr President. We need you to push this bill through. This is politics we are talking here, not physics.
>
> **Carter:** It is not politics, Tip, not to me. It's what is right and rational and necessary and practical and urgent that we do . . . Say, do you like my sweater?
>
> **O'Neill:** [later to a congressional colleague] That guy is hopeless. It's gonna be a long winter.

been immortalised in numerous ways, with an airport, an aircraft carrier and highways being named in his honour. He was able to make many Americans feel good about themselves and their country. After years in which its reputation had taken a severe blow over episodes such as the Vietnam War and Watergate, he was able to restore morale and there was a resurgence of patriotic feeling and confidence about the future.

Unlike his predecessor, G.H. Bush, **Bill Clinton** was not initially faced by a Congress dominated by his political opponents, but the advantage was more apparent than real and his initiatives were rebuffed on several occasions. After the November 1994 elections, he was confronted by two Republican-dominated chambers, a situation which lasted throughout the rest of his presidency. Relations with Congress were often strained, the more so as the president became more deeply immersed in the problems which led to his impeachment (see p. 94–96).

Not only was Clinton constrained by the power of the legislature. More than any other recent president since F.D. Roosevelt, he had to deal with an angry and deeply conservative opposition, mainly of southern Republicans. It was not so much his policies as his origins that alienated them. Their sense of propriety was offended by his background ('white trash'), his affinity for black Americans, his career-minded and intelligent wife and the scandels of his presidency.

The presidency of **George W. Bush** moved into a higher gear following the events of 9/11, the president becoming more focused and purposeful than in his early months in office. Washington reorganised itself around the executive branch and Bush reorganised his administration around the struggle against terrorism. Almost at once, he persuaded Congress to approve a substantial recovery package that also made additional provision for strengthening of the intelligence and security services. Congress also quickly passed an anti-terrorism bill that greatly increased the potential of executive power.

Although having long been suspicious of the power exercised by 'big government' in Washington, many Americans now rallied behind President Bush. They were in a mood to accept more assertive presidential leadership. They were unsure of what was happening to them and yearned for a sense of direction. This gave the president a chance to take a firmer grip upon events. He began to shape the political agenda, and his early actions were accepted with little dissent. Some commentators began to use phrases such as 'the revived presidency' or 'the re-imperialised presidency'. War – in this case on terrorism – was the catalyst for change. It demanded personalised control from the man who symbolised the unity of the country.

For further information on the performance and declining appeal of the Bush administration, see pp. 107–108. For information on George W. Bush's approach to power, see pp. 88–89.

The limits of presidential power

Several presidents from Franklin Roosevelt to Bill Clinton have at times spoken of the constraints under which they operated whilst in the White House. They have complained about the difficulties they experienced in carrying out policy, particularly on the domestic front. Clinton's failure to restructure healthcare was an obvious example, but so too did George W. Bush find it hard to achieve reform of the tax system in his first administration. Sometimes, this was because of their personal deficiencies as leaders. On leaving office, Lyndon Johnson[10] – who was far more adept at manipulating the levers of power than was Carter – pointed out to his successor, Richard Nixon, some of the realities of political power. He observed: 'Before you get to the presidency, you think you can do anything. You think you're the most powerful leader since God. But when you get in that tall chair, as you're gonna find out, Mr President, you can't count on people. You'll find your hands tied and people cussin' you.'

In *Presidential Power*, first published in 1960, Richard Neustadt[11] pointed to the limitations on the power of the president, as well as to the strength of his position. He was writing before the days of the 'imperial presidency', but even

The George W. Bush presidency and the approach to presidential power

Some members of the Bush administration – including the president himself – regularly advanced the **unitary executive theory**, which addresses aspects of the separation of powers. It argues for strict limits on the power of Congress to deprive the president of control of the executive branch. It relies heavily on the clause of Article II which states: 'The executive Power shall be vested in a President of the United States of America'.

Proponents of the unitary executive use this language, along with the **take-care clause**, to argue that the Constitution creates a hierarchical, unified executive department under the direct control of the president. The ways in which Bush used this broad remit shed an interesting light on the debate on presidential power.

As part of his determination to use the powers of the presidency to their fullest extent, Bush:

* used his tightly knit team of close advisers to focus carefully on what he wanted to achieve;

* was keen to assert executive privilege over information;

* made effective use of **executive orders**;

unitary executive theory

A theory of US constitutional law that asserts presidential control over the entire executive branch of government. Relying on the second article of the Constitution (Sections 1 and 3), its supporters claim that executive authority is solely concentrated in presidential hands. The theory was widely quoted by President George W. Bush, when issuing his signing statements (see p. 89).

take-care clause

Article II, Section 3 of the Constitution requires that the president 'take Care that the laws be faithfully executed'. Presidents from Lincoln onwards have interpreted this seemingly innocuous and straightforward requirement as a demand that they both efficiently administer US laws and also ensure that they are 'faithfully executed' by the government and respected by the citizenry. In extraordinary circumstances – for example involving the defence of the nation – the clause may be seen as allowing the administration to take extraordinary actions, even if they are beyond the law and Constitution.

executive orders

Regulations or rules issued by the president that have the effect of law. Such orders must either be derived from the president's constitutional powers or based on laws passed by Congress. Many have far-reaching importance – for example Kennedy's instruction in 1963 prohibiting racial discrimination in housing subsidised by the federal government.

- regularly used **national security directives, proclamations** and **signing statements**;

- made appointments in the recess to avoid the need for Senate confirmation;

- made extensive use of the opportunity to appoint ideologically sympathetic conservatives to the federal judiciary.

Bush benefited from having Republicans in control on Capitol Hill for six of his eight years in office. Although control of the Senate was lost in the 107th Congress following the defection of Senator Jeffords from the Republican Party, it was restored by the 108th and 109th Congresses, so that his position was well established until the setbacks in November 2006, which resulted in Democratic control of both chambers. He did not antagonise congressmen by frequent use of the presidential veto, in part because his party's domination for six years left the administration with a block of solid supporters. Where necessary, he often proved willing to make compromises with Congress, whilst being careful always to take the credit for any legislative successes.

national security directives

A form of executive order issued by the president and having the effect and force of law. All recent presidents have used them, though under different names. For Kennedy and Johnson, they were National Security Action Memorandums; for Clinton, Presidential Decision (or Review) Directives; and for George W. Bush, National Security Directives, so named because they are issued with the advice and consent of the National Security Council. Bush also issued Homeland Security Directives, with the approval of the Homeland Security Council, which he initially created, one such directive being to change immigration policy in the light of the perceived terrorist threat.

proclamations

During the Civil War, President Abraham Lincoln issued two proclamations that freed slaves from states in secession. In January 2008, George Bush issued Proclamation 8217, regarding the National Sanctity of Human Life Day.

signing statements

Written observations made by a president at the time of signing legislation, sometimes merely comments on a bill's value in fulfilling some pressing need, but in more controversial cases involving claims by presidents that they believe some part of the legislation is unconstitutional and therefore they intend to ignore it or implement it only in ways they believe is constitutional. Bill Clinton issued more such statements than his successor, but the G.W. Bush variety seemed geared towards undermining legislative intent. He routinely asserted he would not act contrary to the constitutional provisions that direct the president to supervise the unitary executive branch, a formulation originally made in the first signing statement of Ronald Reagan. Basically, it asserts that Congress cannot pass a law that undercuts the constitutionally granted authorities of the president, a key theme of the unitary executive theory (see p. 88).

at that time took the view that the presidency was actually rather weak in US government, being unable to effect significant change without the approval of Congress.

Neustadt soon found himself in demand by the president-elect, John F. Kennedy and, began his advisory role with a memo suggesting how the new president might approach his term in office. As a liberal who believed in an activist presidency such as that of FDR, he urged Kennedy to get off to a good start, creating 'a first impression of energy, direction, action and accomplishment'. But it is his diagnosis of how a president might overcome the limitations of his role that has been much quoted. He concluded that 'the power of the presidency is the **power to persuade**, its professional reputation and its public prestige'. In a system in which there is shared power, the president must do his best to bargain with rival power centres to get what he believes to be needed.

> **power to persuade**
> The 'power' identified by R. Neustadt (see p. 87) as the means by which the president could achieve his goals. Because the machinery of US government is vastly dispersed, the president cannot simply command and receive. Rather, he must bargain, and persuade others that what he wants is in their best interest.

In a revised edition of *Presidential Power* (1990), Neustadt confirmed his original findings. Indeed, he detected a further blow to presidential power. The Cold War had contributed to the increase in post-1945 presidential power. With its disappearance, the role of commander-in-chief might be more fraught with problems than it was when he had first written: 'Presidents will less and less have reason to seek solace in foreign relations from the piled-up frustrations of home affairs. Their foreign frustration will be piled high too.'[12] In the later work, he reiterated his emphasis upon the importance of the personal qualities of the incumbent. It takes, in Neustadt's view, a person of extraordinary temperament to make a really significant impact and achieve all the goals he sets for himself.

Among the specific factors which Neustadt's work highlighted are:

1 **Congress**

The Constitution places a joint responsibility on the president and Congress to govern the nation. Real leadership can only be brought about when both bodies (and sometimes the Supreme Court as well) are facing in the same direction. At times, as we have seen, Congress has the upper hand, but in the last sixty years of the twentieth century presidents were usually in control, despite attempts by federal legislators to lay down specific restraints. In 1995 Stephen Weissman[13] went so far as to refer to the 'culture of deference' within Congress, suggesting that there was 'a distinct set of norms, beliefs, customs and institutions, that confine[d] it to the margins of power'. He claimed that Congress had regularly bowed to presidential leadership, particularly in matters of foreign policy.

Yet despite this broad tendency, the politics of shared power have at times been stormy. Conflict can easily arise, whether over Watergate, the Iran–Contra affair, Supreme Court confirmations or Clinton's/Obama's healthcare proposals. Indeed, in recent decades one major area of contention has been over the conduct of foreign policy, the area identified by Weissman as the one in which presidents have often assumed the upper hand. Initiatives are usually launched by the president, but Congress still has an overseeing role. It has imposed statutory limits on presidential action, such as the **Case v. Zablocki Act (1972)**, and the War Powers Act of 1973 (see p. 80). It has the power to raise taxes to fund a conflict, to create and maintain armed forces, to regulate arms sales and for the signing of treaties. It has the power also to make war. Johnson never formally declared war against North Vietnam, but the hostilities there led to Congress re-assessing its position. In the Nixon presidency, there was a

> **Case v. Zablocki Act (1972)**
>
> An Act requiring the president to inform Congress of every foreign policy agreement that he makes, thus ending the practice of presidents concluding executive agreements in secrecy.

continuing struggle between the White House and Capitol Hill over the control of foreign policy. So too George W. Bush increasingly faced opposition and obstruction from Congressional Democrats over policy towards Iraq.

A hostile Congress can make life difficult for any president, by refusing his nominations, failing to fund his programmes and refusing approval for treaties he has carefully negotiated. If the president has public support, he is much less likely to meet this degree of obstruction; he can take to the media to rally public support on his side. Congressmen will watch the popular reaction with interest. Theodore Roosevelt was an exponent of the 'bully pulpit' approach, for he saw the opportunities for inspirational leadership if he could get his message across to the nation at large – as though it was a religious congregation. Wilson, Kennedy, Franklin Roosevelt and Reagan all knew how to 'preach' to the nation and strengthen their position by winning acquiescence and support.

The president needs congressional support, but in the more assertive mood of Congress in recent years incumbents have found this difficult to achieve, even with their own party in control. Faced by a hostile Congress, G.H. Bush and Clinton (in his last six years) had difficulties in carrying out aspects of their programme, resulting in 'gridlock', a situation in which the two branches of government were locked in conflict. So too George W. Bush experienced a range of problems with Congress as his power and influence waned in his second term, particularly after the November 2006 mid-term elections (see p. 108).

EARLY LEGISLATION OF THE OBAMA PRESIDENCY: PRESIDENTIAL DIFFICULTIES WITH CONGRESS

President Obama used his decisive majority in both houses of the 111th Congress to push through a range of legislative changes in the face of obstructive Republican opposition. Notable measures included:

The American Recovery and Reinvestment Act (February 2009), which was a direct response to the economic crisis. The intention was to create new jobs and save existing ones; to spur economic activity and invest in long-term growth; and to foster unprecedented levels of accountability and transparency in government spending. To achieve those goals there were to be tax cuts and benefits for millions of working families and businesses, worth $288 billion; increased federal funding for education and healthcare as well as entitlement programmes (such as extending unemployment benefits), to the value of $224 billion; and $275 billion available for federal contracts, grants and loans. Congressional voting was largely along party lines. The Senate passed the bill, 60 to 38, with all Democrats and Independents voting for the bill, along with three Republicans. In the House of Representatives, seven Democrats opposed it, as did all Republicans.

The Patient Protection and Affordable Care Act (March 2010), passed after a year-long legislative roller, fulfilled a key campaign promise and a priority legislative aspiration of Obama's. In the original 1,017-page plan for overhauling the health system, the wide-ranging scheme included provision to spend $900 billion over ten years on improved health provision. It include a government insurance plan, also known as 'the public option', to compete with the corporate insurance sector as a chief component of lowering costs and improving the quality of healthcare. The proposal would also make it illegal for insurers to drop sick people or deny them coverage for pre-existing conditions. The bill in its final form extended coverage to 32 million more Americans, imposed new taxes on the wealthy and outlawed restrictive insurance practices, such as that concerning pre-existing medical conditions. It marked the biggest change to the US healthcare system in decades. But it included no public option clause, because this was sacrificed by the administration in order get the bill through a reluctant House of Representatives. Republicans were unanimous in opposing the legislation.

Obama was tough and tenacious – some might say stubborn – in sticking with this legislation after so much opposition and so many setbacks. Although Democrats pushed the measure through the House with three votes to spare, thirty-four members joined the Republicans in voting against it, worried about paying a political price in the coming November elections. In a last-minute move designed to win the support of a block of anti-abortion law makers, the president announced plans to issue an executive order assuring that healthcare reform would not change the restrictions barring federal money for abortion.

Healthcare reform became a rallying point for Republicans, who were convinced that the American people did not want the changes and that it would be a vote winner for them in the November 2010 mid-term elections. They claimed that the measures were unaffordable and represented a government takeover of the health industry. No Republicans voted in favour of the bill. Once it was signed into law, they and other opponents of healthcare reform shifted from parliamentary and procedural opposition to challenging the constitutionality of the legislation in the courts.

In contrast to the fate of the healthcare reform bill, climate-change legislation in the form of the **Comprehensive Energy Reform Act (CERA)** stalled in Congress in 2010 amidst partisan bickering. The 'postponement' of climate and energy legislation reflected the heavy pounding taken by the administration over Obama's plans for healthcare reform. The administration took a decision to deprioritise the energy bill and focus instead on trying to get an immigration reform bill passed. Some critics said that this was a nakedly political attempt to mobilise the Hispanic vote prior to the mid-term elections.

The lame-duck period of the 111th Congress

After the congressional elections (2010), which Obama labelled a 'shellacking' for himself and the Democrats, Congress passed a series of bills on major issues that had appeared to be mired in legislative stalemate. The president and legislators stayed in Washington five days longer than planned to wrap up work on several major issues in the lame-duck session of the 111th Congress. Among the significant accomplishments:

- A compromise was reached between Obama and Senate Republican leaders that resulted in the extension of the Bush-era tax cuts to everyone for two more years, while also extending unemployment benefits for 13 months and reducing the payroll tax by 2 percentage points for a year – measures intended to bolster the slow recovery from economic recession.

- The President signed the repeal of the 'don't ask, don't tell' (DADT) policy, which banned gays from serving openly in the military. Its implementation was delayed for sixty days, to give the president, the secretary of defense and the chairman of the joint chiefs of staff the time to certify in writing that they had reviewed a Pentagon report on the effects of DADT repeal and ensured that repeal regulations were 'consistent with the standards of military readiness, military effectiveness, unit cohesion, and recruiting and retention of the Armed Forces'. As of June 2011, certification has not occurred, and it is still the policy of all branches of the US military to discharge individuals under the provisions of DADT.

- The Senate ratified a long-sought arms reduction treaty with Russia, a document that required the support of two-thirds of the chamber and which could not be changed without both nations returning to the negotiating table.

- The Senate also passed a bill to provide health benefits and compensation for 9/11 first responders and victims.

Obama called the lame-duck session 'a season of progress for the American people' that reflected the message voters had sent in November for Democrats and Republicans to work together. At the same time, he recognised that deep ideological differences existed between his party and its opponents. He anticipated a 'robust debate' on government spending and deficit reduction when the 112th Congress began its work, given that Republicans were in control of the House and held a stronger minority position in the Senate. Obama also cited issues left unresolved, mentioning the failure of Congress to pass an immigration bill that would create a path to citizenship for illegal immigrants who had come to the country as children as 'maybe [his] biggest disappointment'. This was the Development, Relief and Education for Alien Minors Act (the so-called Dream Act) that would have given hundreds of thousands of young, undocumented immigrants a conditional path to legal residency. It ran into serious Republican opposition in the aftermath of the elections.

The tendency of Congress to appoint special prosecutors to probe every aspect of a President's affairs, and the relentless media interest which this creates, has a paralysing impact on presidential policy. Investigations drag on, seemingly for partisan reasons, and – as Clinton found to his cost (see pp. 96–97) – there is always the ultimate horror of the threat of **impeachment** at the end of the road.

2 The Supreme Court

In many cases, especially those involving situations of national emergency or in a state of war, the Supreme Court will be supportive of the president. Indeed, on matters of foreign policy, the judiciary has played a significant part in establishing executive primacy, as in the case of **United States v. Curtiss-Wright Export Corporation** (1936). More generally, Clinton Rossiter[14] wrote of how 'for practical purpose, the president may act as if the Supreme Court did not exist. The fact is that the Court has done more over the years to expand than contract the authority of the presidency.'

> **impeachment**
> The process by which Congress can remove officers of the national government, including the president. The House votes on a charge or series of charges and a trial on the charges is then conducted in the Senate.
>
> **United States v. Curtiss-Wright Export Corporation**
> A ruling in which the Supreme Court upheld a 1934 Act allowing the president to embargo arms ships to foreign combatants in a South American war. In the words of one Justice on the Bench, the president is 'the sole organ of the federal government in . . . international relations'.

However, on rare occasions, the Court can damage a president and negate a particular activity, as it did to FDR over his 'Court-packing' scheme (see pp. 201–202) and to President Nixon over the Watergate tapes. During the Clinton presidency too, it became clear that proceedings could be brought against an incumbent, with the president and his closest staff being compelled to give evidence under oath.

3 The Constitution and constitutional amendments

The Founding Fathers had in mind a more limited view of executive power than that which prevails today. They were nervous about allowing the president a general prerogative, granting only the power to pardon without significant strings attached. Most of the other executive powers, whether they concern legislative and administrative matters, or foreign policy and military affairs, were hedged in by restrictions – for this was a system of divided government.

In developing his New Deal programme, President Roosevelt found that the Constitution could be used as a barrier to social progress. More recently, any president seeking to bring about a measure of gun control faces the difficulty that the right to bear arms is written into the document. Again, some amendments to the Constitution of the last few decades of the twentieth century weakened the presidency. The Twenty-Second Amendment limited the incumbent to two terms of office and the Twenty-Fifth provided for the removal of a person physically or mentally unfit.

4 The federal system

Whereas points (1) and (2) above are limitations which derive from the operation of the 'separation of powers' principle, so too are there hurdles for any president which reflect the operation of the idea of federalism. The fifty states have a large degree of fiscal and legislative autonomy, which acts as a check on the role of the federal government and therefore of the president, who has to negotiate with state representatives in several areas of decision making.

5 The mass media

Television can be a source of power to a telegenic president, but it can also act as a 'double-edged sword'. It can damage his reputation, for a poor performance or gaffe (for example the Ford blunder in the presidential debates of 1976 – see p. 246) is seen by so many viewers that credibility is undermined. Moreover, press journalists can be vigilant in exposing presidential wrong-doings, as over Vietnam, Watergate, Irangate and Whitewatergate/ Monicagate. The press was generally indulgent towards President Kennedy's personal indiscretions, but in the post-Watergate atmosphere it has been more disposed 'to seek out the dirt' in the private lives of politicians.

6 Pressure groups

Individual groups achieve prominence at particular times. Today, a Republican president has to contend with the Christian fundamentalists of the Religious Right, pro-lifers and big corporations. A Democrat has to deal with the labour unions and environmentalists. In Bill Clinton's first few months in office, the clashes between groups concerned over 'gays in the military' inflicted serious damage to his reputation. So too over healthcare legislation, he faced organised opposition from the American Medical Association (AMA), a group that had opposed attempts to reform health provision in the preceding forty years, ever since the creation of Medicare. President Obama was aware of the damage that the AMA could inflict on his own proposals in that area, but found elements within the organisation less hostile to change than did Clinton. He was able to work with them to achieve a reform that was acceptable to both the group and the White House.

IMPEACHMENT: THE CLINTON EXPERIENCE

Article II:4 of the American Constitution states that: 'The President, Vice President and all civil officers of the united States, shall be removed from Office on Impeachment for, and Conviction of, Treason, Bribery or other high Crimes and Misdemeanours.' Impeachment, then, involves a charge of misconduct against an officer of the national government being laid. In the case of the president, he is then committed for trial and, if convicted, removed from office.

In the process of impeachment, the House acts as the prosecutor and the Senate as judge and jury. Any member of the House may initiate impeachment proceedings by introducing a resolution to that effect. The House Judiciary Committee conducts proceedings in the lower chamber and then decides in favour of or against impeachment. It delivers a verdict to the whole House, which requires a 50% vote to impeach. If the process goes ahead, the case is then tried in the Senate, the Chief Justice presiding on this occasion. A two-thirds vote of those present is needed to secure a conviction and subsequent removal.

Impeachment is one of the most potent checks upon the abuse of power. It can also be a means of undermining a president's authority. But – being a rather partisan, cumbersome and time-consuming means of ensuring accountability – it has only sparingly been used. Charges have been considered by the House against more than sixty officials, including nine presidents. But in only seventeen of these cases has the issue resulted in a Senate trial. Only two of the nine cases involving a president have got that far, those of Andrew Johnson in 1868 and Bill Clinton in 1999. The Senate failed to convict Johnson by just one vote, whereas in the Clinton case the Senate was at least twelve votes short of the necessary number. The case of Richard Nixon's obstruction of justice in the Watergate inquiry never reached the Senate, for he resigned as president in August 1974. Had he not done so, he might well have been the first incumbent of the White House to be impeached successfully.

The impeachment of Bill Clinton

Clinton was not impeached for sexual misconduct, although the case against him originated in a case of sexual harassment concerning Paula Jones. As part of the Clinton deposition (testimony), he was asked about his relationship with Monica Lewinsky, a former White House intern. Clinton's answers were untruthful and the perjury involved enabled the (Republican) prosecutor, Kenneth Starr, to recommend that the president be impeached. (The Jones case was eventually settled out of court. If this had happened earlier in the proceedings, impeachment might have been avoided.)

Four articles of impeachment were laid before the House Judiciary Committee, which in December 1998 voted to approve further action on all of them, namely:

7 Public opinion

Levels of popular support can fluctuate, as they did for George Bush senior (high at the time of Gulf War, then down as the state of the domestic economy failed to impress Americans). Clinton was able to retain a high degree

- **article 1**, charging perjury before Ken Starr's Federal grand jury;

- **article 2**, charging perjury in the Paula Jones deposition;

- **article 3**, charging obstruction of justice in the Paula Jones case;

- **article 4**, charging failure to respond to the eight-one questions posed by the House Judiciary Committee during the impeachment inquiry.

The whole House decided to go ahead on two counts, articles 1 and 3. House Representatives handling the prosecution in the Senate emphasised how the obstruction of justice involved in the third article involved a threat to the rule of law that the president had sworn to uphold. They professed concern that if he was allowed to escape punishment, this set a bad precedent. It would permit one system of justice for the powerful, another for other people. Some Democrats might have agreed with the view that Clinton had behaved badly and violated his oath, but the majority of them – and a few Republican moderates – were unconvinced that this amounted to 'high crimes and misdemeanours'. As Senator Jeffords put it: 'I am gravely concerned that a vote to convict the president on these articles may establish a low threshold that would make every president subject to removal for the slightest indiscretion, or that a vote to convict may impale every president who faces a Congress controlled by the opposing party. In other words, this would be a potentially devastating precedent'.

The Senate agreed and voted to reject both articles, with ten Republicans defecting on the perjury count and five on article 3.

Why did the impeachment proceedings fail?

As we have seen, some Republicans could not accept that the gravity of the offences merited such a drastic punishment as was being proposed. They realised too that the way in which the charges were brought by a near-obsessed special prosecutor and passed by a Republican-dominated House smacked of undue partisanship. It seemed like a Republican witch-hunt against Clinton. If this was the public perception, then their party might suffer for its behaviour at the polls. Beyond this, senators were only too aware of the public mood. The president's personal popularity was increasing, at the very time impeachment proceedings were being debated. To impeach him would have been particularly risky for the Republicans, bearing in mind that many Americans did not seem sufficiently troubled to want to be rid of him. They were able to distinguish between the flawed man (whose failings were well known to them at the time of his re-election in 1996) and the successful president who was presiding over a seemingly strong economy.

of public approval, in spite of his personal misdemeanours. He was able to bounce back after the disastrous 1994 elections and to win re-election. Many have been less fortunate, and this can be damaging not only because of the need to win re-election. A president who is losing popular backing, or at least acquiescence, may find that opposition in Congress, the media and the bureaucracy will increase, so that other checking mechanisms come into play.

8 Bureaucracy

The president has plenty of constitutional authority, but the problem is sometimes how to get the bureaucracy to work for him. He needs to be able to persuade as well as to direct, but even then he can find that his will is frustrated by bureaucrats who tend to see the world through a lens which is focused largely on their own departments. No modern president seems to have been able to stop the growth of bureaucracy, so that the majority of the agencies created since the 1930s have survived intact into the twenty-first century.

There are other factors, ranging from the power of the Federal Reserve to determine interest rates to prevailing attitudes to presidential power, that may limit a president's freedom of manoeuvre. The American writers Burns et al.[15] make a series of fair observations when they write of

> one of the persisting paradoxes of the American presidency . . . on the one hand, the institution is too powerful, and on the other, it is always too weak. It is too strong because in many ways it is contrary to our ideals of government by the people and decentralization of power. It is too weak because presidents seldom are able to keep the promises they make. Of course, the presidency is always too strong when we dislike the incumbent. And the president is always too constrained when we believe a President is striving to serve the public interest – as we define it.

Neustadt, as quoted above, makes the point that the power of the president always did depend upon personal leadership rather more than the formal position: 'powers are no guarantee of power'. This was true in the days of the imperial presidency. Indeed, it is easy to overstress the power of presidents before Watergate and to overemphasise the decline or difficulties of the presidency from the 1970s onwards. John Hart[16] reminds us that FDR, the first of the so-called modern presidents, was untypical in the power that he exercised:

> None of his successors faced anything like the enormity of the Depression of the early 1930s, and none took over the White House during a national emergency so clearly and unambiguously defined. Neither has any post-FDR president had such a comparable level of public support for presidential initiative and leadership. As the beneficiary of a landslide election victory in a realigning election (one in which the voters opted for a complete change of direction and which resulted in a permanent shift in popular support), a strong coat-tails effect in the congressional races, and as head of a political party that behaved as a 'cohesive office-seeking team', FDR enjoyed a political environment that none of his successors have shared, and most could only fantasise about.

In other words, the Roosevelt presidency was the exception rather than the rule. Personality, ability and circumstance all play their part in determining presidential power, but whoever is in the White House operates in a system which specifically denies too much power to the executive.

THE ACADEMIC DEBATE ON PRESIDENTIAL POWER, AS IT STANDS TODAY

Perceptions of the power of individual presidents and 'presidential power' have varied significantly. Some of the contributions have tended to emphasise the approach to the office adopted by incumbents, and also to equate their strengths and successes with the powers of the presidency as an institution. The use of labels such as the 'tethered', 'restored' or 're-imperialised' has been dependent on the performance of an individual president in office. However, there is a distinction to be made between the way in which individuals approach the presidency and the amount of power inherent in the office, although the two aspects are clearly related.

In *The Imperial Presidency*, Schlesinger[17] argued that by the end of the 1960s/early 1970s, the presidency had become excessively powerful, with presidents being able to commit America to disastrous policies without the true facts of situations ever becoming known. For a long while, the debate on presidential power centred on whether there ever was such an imperial presidency. Those who questioned its existence suggested that in reality the idea was an exaggerated response to the circumstances of the time. In particular, it referred to a period in which there was a high-handed and often secretive handling of foreign policy and in which, in domestic policy, presidents were able to evade the usual system of checks and balances.

If 'the imperial presidency' was a description for the excesses of the Johnson and Nixon administrations, Schlesinger later applied it with even greater urgency to the presidency of George W. Bush. He saw his fears realised in ways that even he had not dared to imagine. John Nichols[18] quotes the story of how, when John Dean (a Nixon aide jailed as a result of the Watergate scandal) suggested to Schlesinger that the misdeeds of Bush and Vice-President Dick Cheney were 'worse than Watergate' and asked whether the Bush presidency met the classic definition of executive excess, the by-then elderly historian replied: 'I'd certainly say this is an imperial presidency.'

Neustadt and the limitations of presidential power

Since Schlesinger first wrote of an over-mighty, all-powerful presidency, the weakness or strength of the office has been much debated, with two broad views emerging: those represented by Richard Neustadt and by William Howell. In *Presidential Power* (1960), written before Schlesinger first expounded his thesis, Neustadt[19] introduced his major theme, that far from being all-powerful, presidents find that their wishes do not automatically become policy. Unable to depend upon the support of anyone, not even their own appointees, they must rely upon persuasion. Hence, the relevance of considerations such as: the president's prestige and his ability to lead public opinion; his temperament, style and bargaining skill; his relations with Congress, and in particular the ability to strike deals with congressional leaders; his ability to communicate, involving managing press relations and being impressive and convincing on television; and his ability to mobilise constituencies and conserve political capital. In the system of shared powers, the president must convince others that what he wants is in their interests as well.

For two or three decades, the Neustadtian approach came to dominate study of the presidency. His final edition of *Presidential Power*,[20] published in 1990, again stressed the weakness of the president's formal powers and the difficulty of acting unilaterally to achieve his desired aims, in a situation where he was in competition with other actors with their own independent sources of power. The decline in US international hegemony after the ending of the Cold War, the growing assertiveness of Congress, the confrontational and often hostile style of media coverage, the proliferation of interest groups and the difficulties in managing a vast bureaucracy all served to make it more difficult for a president to act decisively and effectively, except under the most extraordinary circumstances. Presidents found it increasingly difficult to meet public expectations. This weakness was aggravated by the gulf between what the public expects of the presidency and what occupants can deliver.

In the late twentieth century, many political scientists were much influenced by Neustadt's preoccupation with political leadership and strategy, rather than with the constitutional origins of presidential legal authority. With few exceptions, scholars of the presidency continued to view the institution in personal rather than in legal terms. Study of the formal powers of the presidency or questions of constitutional interpretation seemed to be less interesting than the drama of the political dimension to presidential activity.

Howell and others and the reassertion of presidential authority

In the post-Nixon years, presidents have been conscious of the difficult time they have had in relying upon the traditional powers of bargaining and persuading, of which Neustadt had written. In the words of Gillian Peele,[21] 'they have attempted to squeeze every ounce of advantage from their position to overcome the constraints of the constitutional order'. As a means of circumventing the restrictions that have limited their effectiveness, recent incumbents, from Reagan to George W. Bush, have taken unilateral actions. They have tried to control the executive branch, claiming in the process to be protectors of the prerogative of the office, whilst at the same time being able to advance their policy agenda.

Much of the recent writing on the presidency has been heavily influenced by the experience of the Bush administration and its employment of direct power, as part of the whole controversial theory of presidential discretion that uses as its cover the label 'unitary executive theory' (see pp. 88–89), a theory that some commentators regard as 'imperial'. In his study *Power without Persuasion* (2003), William Howell[22] has produced the most theoretically substantial and far-reaching re-evaluation of presidential power written for many years. He takes an entirely different view to that expressed by Neustadt. He denies that presidential power is limited to the 'power to persuade', the power of bargaining and convincing other political actors to do things the president cannot accomplish alone.

Howell notes the striking ways in which President Bush used presidential powers following the attack on the Twin Towers, often in the absence of congressional legislation. Although the circumstances of late 2001 were extraordinary, Howell argues that Bush's actions are otherwise typical: in his view, presidents often exercise power without persuasion.

He argues that there is a long history of strong presidents acting unilaterally, taking initiatives and pursuing and implementing the policies in which they believe. As he puts it:

> Going back to the Louisiana Purchase and the Emancipation Proclamation, presidents have set landmark policies on their own. More recently, Roosevelt interned Japanese Americans during World War II, Kennedy established the Peace Corps, Johnson got affirmative action under way, Reagan greatly expanded the president's powers of regulatory review, and Clinton extended protections to millions of acres of public lands. Since September 11, Bush has created a new cabinet post and constructed a parallel judicial system to try suspected terrorists.

Howell's emphasis is on the dramatic initiatives a president can take with relative freedom from Congress and customary deference on the part of the courts. He shows that presidents often determine public policies, whatever the objections on Capitol Hill or from interest groups and the bureaucracy. In particular, he stresses the importance of executive orders (see p. 88) as a means of bypassing the constraints that Congress, interest groups and the bureaucracy can impose.

When Howell was writing *Power without Persuasion*, the impression of the Bush presidency was very different to what it had become by 2007. The constitutional means by which George W. Bush sought to circumvent Congress still existed and continued to be used. However, following his re-election in 2004 – and in particular after the 2006 mid-term elections – political circumstances had become markedly less favourable to a display of presidential leadership – an illustration of the importance of the distinction between the fluctuating power of individual presidents and 'presidential power'.

Wildavsky and revival of the 'two presidencies' thesis

One further theory merits consideration. In 1966, Aaron Wildavsky[23] first advanced the idea that there are really 'two presidencies'. Wildavsky argued that presidents have a much easier time exercising power in foreign policy than on domestic questions. As evidence, he drew on quantitative research showing that between 1948 and 1964 Congress enacted 65% of presidential foreign policy initiatives and only 40% of domestic ones. He further noted that there had 'not been a single major issue on which presidents, when they were serious and determined, have failed'. He went so far as to claim that for the president 'foreign policy concerns tend to drive out domestic policy'. For some years the theory was restated on several occasions, by Wildavsky and by other writers. However, by the 1980s it had become discredited and Wildavsky himself concluded that it had lost its relevance, largely because of changes on the international scene, notably the ending of the Cold War. The distinction between the foreign policy president and the domestic one had lost its validity, the 'two presidencies' having become one.

Recent re-evaluation of Wildavsky's thinking by Brandice Canes-Wrone[24] and others (including Howell) has given broad endorsement to the original thesis. They note how, in recent presidencies incumbents have turned to unilateral action to bypass congressional control and gain influence over policy making, concluding that the effects of such action 'are especially noteworthy in the area of foreign policy'. Their research indicates that in the enactment of budget appropriations and inagency creation, 'the results suggest that presidents exercise significantly greater influence over foreign than domestic policy'.

Presidential leadership and power today

As the size and influence of the United States in the world has developed, so has the machinery of government, and with it, the informal power and influence of the president. He is a national leader and by many is seen also as the leader of the Western world, the person who will represent the country on the global stage.

Factors in the broad growth of presidential power and influence: a summary

1 **The growth of 'big government' in the years after 1933**, as Roosevelt became identified with increased federal intervention in the Depression.

2 **The importance of foreign policy.** With the development of an American world role after World War II, the country became the leader of the free West and the world's policeman. The constitutional role of commander-in-chief enabled the president to send American troops around the world, even though Congress has only formally declared war on five occasions. Successive presidents have made **executive agreements** with foreign governments that have enabled them to circumvent the need for Senate ratification.

> **executive agreements**
> Agreements negotiated between the executive branch of the US government and a foreign government that do not require confirmation by the Senate. They have the same legal force as treaties.

3 **The personality of the incumbent and the conception of the office held by him.** Individual presidents have by their performance enlarged the scope of the office and changed expectations of what it can achieve. Sometimes, a passive president has seemed appropriate for the time, as in the 1920s, whilst at other times an active presidency has been required.

4 **The inertia of Congress and erosion of balance.** At times, Congress surrendered much influence and allowed strong 'liberal' presidents to pursue and achieve reform, as part of what Stephen Weissman[25] has called 'a culture of deference'.

5 **Supreme Court judgments**, which on occasion have enlarged the scope of the presidential office – for example the *United States* v. *Curtiss-Wright Export Corporation* (1936).

6 **The development of an administrative apparatus to serve the president.** For details of the Executive Office of the President and the White House Office, see pp. 128–134.

7 **The mass media.** The media can easily focus on one national office and on the person of the president, for he is news. Telegenic leaders have used the medium of television to their advantage, notably Kennedy, Reagan, Clinton and Obama.

In discussing past presidents, commentators often refer to 'presidential leadership' and 'presidential power'. Sometimes the two terms are used interchangeably. Yet there is a difference between them. Political leadership implies the capacity to chart the course of events, set out goals and persuade and inspire others to follow. It suggests influence. Power is the ability to achieve goals. This implies command over the personalities, institutions and events involved. All presidents have a substantial degree of power, deriving from the office they hold, but there are serious limitations in its exercise. When presidents leave office, they lose power. Those who have exercised leadership and sought to reshape the political landscape in pursuit of what they see as the public good are the ones most often remembered.

Americans recall FDR, JFK and Ronald Reagan long after they have left office. In recent decades, they have generally expected leadership, wanting to be assured that presidential candidates have a clear vision of where and how they are going to lead the country, if elected. On the other hand, a reaction can set in when presidential initiatives founder or the approach of the incumbent seems overbearing.

Presidential powers are set out in the Constitution, but they are also influenced by political and personal considerations. They may be limited by circumstances. To exercise a high degree of power requires careful utilisation of the available resources. If the president has qualities of leadership, then his chances of 'changing the constellation of political forces about him in a direction closer to his own conception of the political good'[26] are much increased. A display of presidential leadership can focus attention on what needs to be done and help the White House to overcome any inertia and obstruction in the political system.

The nature of the presidency at a particular moment depends considerably upon the incumbent. Great men make great presidents. Personality is important to the style and impact of the presidency, but the active presidential leadership of the 1960s and the habit of congressional compliance are out of fashion.

Popular expectations of presidents

Many Americans want more from their president than somebody who is merely efficient while in office. They also want someone who looks 'presidential' and who embodies the American creed and reflects the 'spirit of the people'. Like the flag and the Constitution, presidents are a symbol of national identity. Some have been successful in capturing the public's imagination and winning popular support, as Kennedy and Reagan were able to do. If they can do this, then their influence and informal power will increase as well.

In the age of television, the personality and style of leadership of anyone who would be president have become all-important. The need to perform well is crucial, and Reagan, for all of his seeming lack of familiarity with some key issues and his occasional verbal stumbles, was a man who embodied the

American Dream. His resolute optimism, his old-fashioned values and his promise to help America 'stand tall' after the malaise of the 1970s were very popular. His background as a film and TV actor enabled him to communicate well (his supporters called him 'the Great Communicator'), so that he represented a merger between the worlds of entertainment and politics.

How Americans evaluate their presidents varies over time. In part, it depends on who has recently been president and who is the present incumbent. In different eras, Americans have a different idea of what their president should be like. At times, they demand vigorous leadership, but they may then become troubled by the consequences of that assertiveness and yearn for a less active presidency. After a while, such inactivity can be portrayed as weakness and ineffectiveness. In Wasserman's[27] words: 'Americans have swung back and forth in how powerful they want their presidents . . . [they] have walked a thin line between too much and too little power.' He illustrates this by pointing to the worries felt by many citizens about the abuse of power by Nixon, and the perception only a few years later that Jimmy Carter was too weak to solve the nation's difficulties. In actual fact, it was the reaction against Vietnam and Watergate (as well as changes in the organisation of Congress) that made it difficult for Carter to stamp his authority on the legislature.

Qualities often admired in presidents are honesty, decision-making ability, good judgement, intelligence and toughness. Yet although the average voter seems to value credibility and truthfulness as admirable qualities for anyone in the White House, the example of Bill Clinton shows that even if they distrusted him when it came to truth telling, many of voters none the less admired him for other reasons. They recognised that he was a creative, resourceful and smart politician, a man with fine rhetorical skills who excelled on the public platform. Ironically, some of his best approval ratings came at the very time when the Lewinsky scandal (see p. 94) was exposing aspects of his more irresponsible behaviour.

The differing approaches to the office adopted by past presidents

The presidency is what its holder makes of it, being as large and important, or as weak and as insignificant, as the holder of the office. Academics have tended to divide past presidents into 'active' leaders of the nation or 'constitutional or passive' ones. The two views of presidential power can be seen by contrasting the approaches of past incumbents, and reactions to them.

Theodore Roosevelt[28] remarked in his *Autobiography* that he 'declined to adopt the view that what was imperatively necessary for the nation could not be done by the president unless he could find some specific authorisation to do it. My belief was that it was not only his right, but his duty to do anything that the needs of the nation demanded, unless such action was forbidden by the Constitution or by the laws . . . I did not usurp power but . . . did greatly broaden the use of executive power.' He was of the Lincoln school, and like him, a Republican. He favoured a policy of active leadership, setting out national goals. Others of this type have wanted to make a mark on the national scene, not being content with mere stewardship of the presidency. Roosevelt, Truman, Kennedy and Johnson were of this type, as was Bill Clinton.

By contrast, under President Lincoln, the leaders of his party in the two chambers of Congress gave a warning in what has become known as the Wade–Davis manifesto:[29] 'the authority of Congress is paramount . . . if [the president] wishes our support he must confine himself to his executive duties – to obey, and to execute, not to make laws'. Those who take this view have a custodial view of the presidency, by which the incumbent confines himself to carrying out those powers expressly mentioned in the Constitution and leaves Congress to take the lead in deciding what is to be done. Examples included Harding and Coolidge in the 1920s – significantly, they were both Republicans, many of whom tend to have a more sceptical view of the role of government.

Some writers[30] have detected a third genre, referred to as the 'Eisenhower type'. Exponents of this style combine elements of the two views described above. They tend to delegate responsibility (and thus shield themselves from blame when things go wrong), using the rhetoric of being 'above the political battle' to conceal a more active engagement with the political process. It is sometimes called the 'hidden-hand' approach, and its adherents have sometimes been willing to take a decisive stand and wield a surprising degree of power. Nixon tried to convey the impression of being a national figure and statesman beyond the heat of battle, whilst at the same time using the White House as a centre for powerful and partisan leadership.

Most modern presidents have by inclination been more activists than stewards. Bill Clinton began his period in office by taking several initiatives, helped as he was by his majority in both chambers of Congress. But his intentions were stalled in November 1994 and the political agenda was increasingly set on Capitol Hill rather than in the White House, with Clinton reacting to policies rather than shaping them. Some of his later 'triumphs' were more in the way of fending off the impact of congressional inroads into social programmes than as a result of his preferred lines of action. Not surprisingly, some commentators wrote of the 'constrained presidency'. Yet in Clinton's case his qualities as an effective campaigner, with a knack for appealing over the heads of congressmen to the nation at large, often enabled him to stage a comeback. He was able to use the presidential office as a pulpit from which to preach his values on issues that mattered to him, such as the family, race and even religion.

Presidential success?

It is unclear what constitutes presidential success. The views of academics (see pp. 109–112) and the voters do not necessarily coincide, the two groups not sharing the same priorities. Success depends on what the president is supposed to do. If the criterion is dynamism and/or creativity, then Eisenhower was not a success. But in other respects, given his more limited conception as a steward of national affairs, he was arguably successful, being a popular national leader who was suitable for the mood of the times.

Qualities admired by Americans (%)		Top 10 popular rankings of post-1945 presidents (11 possibilities)
When Americans were asked by interviewers to rate the importance of ten characteristics that might be found in any president, the findings were:		Reagan Clinton Kennedy
Sound judgement in a crisis	78	Truman
High ethical standards	63	Eisenhower
Compassion for the average citizen	63	Carter
Saying what one believes, even if it is unpopular	57	Bush, G.W. Bush, G.H.
Having consistent positions on issues	50	Johnson, L.
Forcefulness and decisiveness	46	Nixon
Experience in public office	38	
Loyalty to one's party	33	Quinnipiac University poll, May 2006:
Willingness to compromise	33	'Best president since 1945': Ford
Experience in Washington	27	came bottom of the list.

Adapted from a survey conducted for the Pew Research Center, July–September 1999, entitled 'Essential Qualities Americans Want in a President'.

Certain eras require more vigorous leadership and legislative action than others. By the criterion of the proportion of his legislative programme achieved, President Johnson was an undoubted success. But he presided over a country that was becoming increasingly troubled and divided, and his memory has been tarnished by the events in Vietnam. Bill Clinton was able to speak to the hearts of many Americans at times of crisis and presided over eight years of economic success. Yet he stained the presidency by his personal conduct and harmed his party's prospects in the 2000 election.

Some presidents operate in a situation in which there is an opportunity to show real leadership. But of recent presidents, those from Ford to Clinton found it more difficult to make an impact on the political system The Bush presidency was an example of power sometimes exercised without persuasion. It operated in exceptional circumstances. President Obama is not functioning against the same situation that faced George W. Bush. Given Bush's damaged reputation in the latter years of his presidency and growing unease about his use of presidential power, it has been important for his successor to deploy the power of persuasion with some dexterity.

Fred Greenstein[31] has singled out six characteristics that might be used in assessing the effectiveness of presidential leadership:
- **effectiveness as a public communicator**, the ability to convey ideas to party, public and the international community;
- **organisational capacity**, effectiveness in planning and executing policies – in other words, the skills exhibited as manager of the executive branch;
- **political skill**, the ability to persuade Congress, mobilise support and campaign effectively;
- **political vision**, the ability to articulate clear goals;
- **cognitive skills**, the ability to understand a range of key issues;
- **emotional intelligence**, the character and temperament to work under pressure.

The list in not exhaustive and some of the criteria might be questioned, much depending on the qualities sought after in a political leader. Others that might be added, in the light of earlier comments, are the ability to achieve legislative goals, to maintain steady judgement in an international crisis and to preside over a strong economy. Some might add the ability to maintain popularity and to get re-elected.

Academic rankings of presidents

American academics, particularly historians and students of government, have often been invited to compile lists of presidents whom they admire or consider great. Greatness is difficult to define. For some, it conjures up an impression of idealism in thought or action. Others think of the accomplishment of heroic deeds. Judgement, integrity, talent, vigour of mind and vision are other qualities that might be identified as important criteria. Experts tend to place more faith in intellectual capacity, experience and ability to impart a sense of direction than do members of the public, who, as we have seen, regard honesty as especially important. Landy and Milkis[32] make the point that: 'The great presidents were great because they not only brought about change, but also left a legacy – principles, institutional arrangements and policies that defined an era . . . When decisive action was required, they took it . . . the need to execute requires presidents to be willing to flout the popular will.'

In early 2000, the findings of a survey of fifty-eight American history professors were published for the public affairs TV channel C-Span. Ten qualities were tested, ranging from crisis leadership to moral authority, from vision to

THE PERFORMANCE AND DECLINING APPEAL OF PRESIDENT GEORGE W. BUSH: A 'SUCCESSFUL' PRESIDENT?

George Walker Bush was the 43rd president of the United States. He was sworn into office on 20 January 2001, re-elected on 2 November 2004 and sworn in for a second term on 20 January 2005. He won the presidency in 2000 as the Republican candidate in a close and controversial contest in which he lost the nationwide popular vote but won by 271–266 votes in the Electoral College.

First term, 2001–5

After such a narrow and contentious victory, many Americans indeed hoped that Bush would recognise his limited mandate and seek to govern from the centre, as a man of the consensus. This did not prove to be the case, for he and his supporters were serious in their intent to mark a distinct break from the Clinton years. Although he tended to use the rhetoric of bipartisanship, humility and healing, this was a cover for the pursuit of a radically conservative agenda.

Following the terrorist attacks of 9/11, many Americans rallied behind President Bush. They were in a mood to accept more assertive presidential leadership, for the times seemed to require more personalised control. Bush became an international statesman on the world scene and a popular leader at home. His Pew approval ratings soared from 61% in July 2001 to over 90% in mid-September 2001.

The short and initially successful war against the Taliban proved to be the first stage of a wider '**war on terror**'. Vice-President Cheney and others in the White House became obsessed with the link between international terrorism and the existence of weapons of mass destruction (WMD). He became the administration's most aggressive voice in favour of confronting Iraq, hyping the nuclear threat from Saddam Hussein. Saddam had long been a thorn in America's side and Cheney and other hawks were keen to see America launch a pre-emptive strike against one of American's enemies. A 'coalition of the willing' was assembled to fight in Iraq, consisting primarily of American and British forces. On this occasion, world opinion was much less united behind the president, and at home the war soon generated opposition.

War on Terror

A term employed by Bush in 2001 to describe the military campaign led by the US, UK and other countries against al-Qaeda in Afghanistan. Its use was broadened to cover action against states such as Iraq that were seen as sponsoring or allowing the operation of terrorist cells of extreme militants whose actions were seen as endangering the security of the Western world. As it is now widely recognised there is no single, unified, transnational enemy, the term is less commonly used. President Obama talks instead of the Overseas Contingency Operation.

Many early supporters of military action against Iraq later became alarmed at the seeming lack of a plan for peace keeping after the cessation of hostilities. The failure to find WMD, the excesses of some American troops and the continuation of insurgency against the occupation of Iraq caused continuing disquiet. Bush nevertheless continued to assert that the war had been worthwhile and confirmed that he would have made the same decision if he had known more.

Running as a self-styled 'war president' in November 2004, George Bush was a strong performer on the campaign trail. If his style did not travel well across the Atlantic, it went down well in parts of the United States. He was re-elected, in the process winning more votes than any presidential candidate had ever done before. His victory was decisive, not just in the battle for the White House but also in the congressional elections, in which Republicans tightened their grip, adding seats in both the House and the Senate.

The second term, 2005–9

Iraqi elections and a referendum to approve a constitution were held in January and December 2005, respectively. From 2004 through 2007, however, the situation in Iraq deteriorated further, with some observers arguing that the country was heading towards a full-scale civil war. Bush's policies regarding the war in Iraq met increasing criticism, and demands within the United States to set a timetable to withdraw troops from Iraq. The 2006 report of the bipartisan Iraq Study Group led by James Baker concluded that the situation in Iraq was 'grave and deteriorating'. While Bush admitted that strategic mistakes had been made in regard to the stability of Iraq, he maintained that he would not change his overall strategy. In a speech in January 2007, he addressed the nation on Iraq and announced a surge (see p. 278) of 21,500 more troops for Iraq, as well as a job programme for Iraqis, more reconstruction proposals and $1.2 billion for these programmes. On 1 May 2007, Bush used his veto to reject a congressional bill setting a deadline for the withdrawal of US troops from Iraq.

Bush was also criticised for what was widely seen as the slow and inadequate response to the devastation caused by Hurricane Katrina in Louisiana, Mississippi and Alabama in late August 2005. On 13 September, in a vague answer to his critics, Bush admitted responsibility to the extent that the federal government had failed to perform its job properly.

Prior to the mid-term elections (2006), Bush went on the campaign trail, stressing that the Republicans were strong on national security and would keep taxes low, unlike the Democrats. This time, his party suffered a serious rebuff, losing the majority of state governorships and control of both houses of the bicameral legislature to the Democrats. Thereafter, he never again exercised the same power, and his administration became engulfed in growing problems as the recession deepened and his personal reputation declined. Of course, the constitutional means by which he had sought to circumvent Congress (see pp. 88–89) still existed and continued to be used, but the political circumstances had become markedly less favourable to a display of presidential leadership.

As a lame duck president in his final years in office, George Bush saw his popular reputation descend to its lowest ebb. His Pew approval ratings of 36% in November 2005, 41% in November 2006 and 30% in November 2007, had dropped by November 2008 to 24%. (A CBS poll placed his approval rating at 20%, the lowest figure since polling began in the 1930s.) According to a poll taken in early 2009, a majority of Americans thought he would be remembered as a below-average or poor president. A mere 17% believed he would go down in history as outstanding or above-average, a figure at variance with Bush's own confidence that his presidency would be appreciated over a longer period of time. Another 23% predicted that he would be remembered as 'average', whilst 59% labelled the likely verdict as being 'below average' or 'poor'.

The president and the prime minister: a comparison

Issue	Prime minister	President
A parliamentary versus a presidential system of government	Prime minister (PM) chosen by his party as leader and becomes PM by virtue of being the head of the majority party in the House of Commons. Is therefore part of legislature and answerable to it. Must defend himself in Commons – for example Prime Minister's Questions.	President elected by the people in a national election. Detached from legislature and not required to justify his performance before Congress – unless impeached. Delivers State of the Union speech there.
Chief of the executive branch or head of state?	Chief of the executive only – smaller ceremonial role.	Chief of the executive and head of state – dual role makes job more burdensome, but also enables him to appear as embodiment of the people.
A single executive: position of the Cabinet	PM has to work with the Cabinet, which meets regularly, and share collective responsibility with it, even if he or she may on occasion choose to side-line it when key decisions are made.	President has a Cabinet, but it has considerably less status in American politics than in the UK. He may not consult it when making key decisions. It does not include several powerful politicians, personalities in their own right.
Security of tenure – length of time that can be served in office	May serve for as long as the public and party want him/her, but in practice this is rarely more than for 7–8 years; service may not be continuous. Determines the date of the next election.	Limited by Constitution to two whole terms, though may also finish out the existing presidential term if vice-president. Has no power to determine the date of the next election.
Party leadership	Strong party leader: can count on support of back-benchers in the Commons in most circumstances. Also, powerful party machine behind him, to rally party beyond Westminster.	Cannot count on party loyalty or support – for example in voting lobbies of Congress. National party leadership much weaker. Impact of federalism/ separation of powers.
Ability to achieve desired policies and implement programme	High success rate for governmental policies, in terms of amount of programme implemented. Even controversial programmes usually pass into law, although in Tony Blair's third term difficulties were experienced with Labour backbenchers.	Presidential policies may not be carried out: several presidents have had difficulty with Congress (for example Clinton and healthcare reform).
Role in foreign policy and management of crises: national strength	Several PMs have been very powerful in times of war: opportunity for strong leadership. But Britain's global influence has declined postwar; lack of former industrial or military might.	Presidents tend to thrive on crisis management – for example Kennedy and Cuba, 1962, George W. Bush and crusade against terrorism post 9/11. Country most powerful in world. USA leader of free world and able to act strongly to try to enforce its world-view.

The top and bottom five presidents in a series of scholarly rankings

Survey	Schlesinger senior 1948[33]	Schlesinger senior 1962[34]	Murray-Blessing 1982[35]	Schlesinger junior 1996[36]	Ridings-McIver 1996[37]	C-Span 2000[38]	Wall Street Journal/Federalist Society 2005[39]
Number of presidents surveyed	29	31	36	39	41	41	40
Top 5	Lincoln	Lincoln	Lincoln	Lincoln	Lincoln	Lincoln	Washington
	Washington	Washington	Roosevelt, F.D.	Washington	Roosevelt, F.D.	Roosevelt, F.D.	Lincoln
	Roosevelt, F.D.	Roosevelt, F.D.	Washington	Roosevelt, F.D.	Washington	Washington	Roosevelt, F.D.
	Wilson	Wilson	Jefferson	Jefferson	Jefferson	Roosevelt, T.	Jefferson
	Jefferson	Jefferson	Roosevelt, T.	Jackson	Roosevelt, T.	Truman, H.	Roosevelt, T.
Bottom 5	Taylor	Coolidge	Johnson A.	Hoover	Pierce	Harrison	Fillmore
	Buchanan	Pierce	Buchanan	Nixon	Grant	Harding	Johnson
	Pierce	Buchanan	Nixon	Johnson, A.	Johnson, A.	Pierce	Pierce
	Grant	Grant	Grant	Buchanan	Buchanan	Johnson A.	Harding
	Harding	Harding	Harding	Harding	Harding	Buchanan	Buchanan

Note: 1 The number of presidents surveyed here varies, for the obvious reason that the earlier studies could not include the more recent presidents. The 2005 ranking is based on only forty presidents because it was considered that the durations of the William Harrison and James Garfield presidencies were too brief for an adequate analysis.

2 A 2006 Siena College poll of professors in 2002, taken shortly after 9/11, ranked President G.W. Bush 23rd of forty-two presidents. Five years into his presidency, the assessments were: great, 2%; near great, 5%; average, 11%; below average, 24%; failure, 58%. The latest Siena survey (2010) ranked Bush thirty-ninth out of forty-three, with poor ratings in handling of the economy, communication, ability to compromise, foreign policy accomplishments and intelligence. The early judgement on Barack Obama placed him fifteenth, with high ratings for imagination, communication ability and intelligence and a low rating for background (family, education and experience).

THE BACKGROUNDS OF BRITISH PRIME MINISTERS AND US PRESIDENTS: A COMPARISON

Prime ministers

The road to the premiership in Britain is usually a long one, a prime minister normally having experienced a good innings as a backbencher and then served in a variety of ministerial posts. They become leader of the nation by first becoming the choice of their party. In the two main British parties, the leader is now chosen by a combination of MPs and party members (the trade unions also, in the case of the Labour Party), so that many thousands of people are involved (see below) – or have the opportunity to become involved – in the decision. Once the party leader has been chosen, everything depends upon the outcome of the general election. The leader of the largest party becomes prime minister and forms his or her administration. Only when one party fails to win a majority – as in 2010 – might a coalition of two or more parties be formed.

Of recent premiers, most have had some experience of ministerial office before they reach 10 Downing Street. James Callaghan was elected as an MP in 1945 and served for thirty-one years before he became prime minister. Unusually, he had served in all three great offices of state (chancellor of the Exchequer, home secretary and foreign secretary). By contrast, Tony Blair lacked ministerial experience when he assumed the premiership. He entered the House of Commons in 1983, became the leader of the Labour Party eleven years later, and within another three years became prime minister, following a landslide election victory. David Cameron similarly lacked ministerial experience, having served as an MP only since 2001 and as party leader since 2005, prior to becoming prime minister in 2010.

Presidents

American presidents gain their position by one of two basic routes. They either take the normal route to the White House, running for the presidency via the electoral process previously described, or else they are elevated to the presidency from the vice-presidency. About one in five presidents have reached the Oval Office not by the normal road of elections, but because they were the number two when the incumbent died of natural causes, was assassinated or was discredited.

Candidates for the White House have tended to come from the Senate or a state governorship rather than the House of Representatives, where the period of two years in office gives them little time to make their mark. Gerald Ford was the last member of the House of Representatives to become president, although in his case he was vice-president immediately prior to his elevation.

administrative skills, and from the pursuit of equal justice to performance in the context of the times. The top ten in the rankings were (in order) Lincoln, Franklin Roosevelt, Washington, Teddy Roosevelt, Truman, Wilson, Jefferson, Kennedy, Eisenhower and Lyndon Johnson, whose reputation has risen

Until the Obama victory in 2008, John F. Kennedy was the last person to rise from the Senate to the presidency, although since the 1960s several senators have attempted to gain their party's candidacy. The main route of successful candidates has been the vice-presidency or a governorship. Johnson, Ford and Bush senior were each vice-president immediately prior to becoming president, and Nixon had served in that office for eight years before having a further eight years in the political wilderness. Carter, Reagan, Clinton and George W. Bush were all previously state governors. Reagan was well known to Americans, his face being familiar on cinema and television screens as a movie actor, whereas Carter (the peanut farmer from Georgia) and Clinton (the governor of Arkansas) were little known outside their states. George W. Bush served as governor of Texas for six years, prior to becoming president.

What qualities are needed to be a successful leader in Britain, the United States and elsewhere?

Politicians come in all shapes and sizes, although the demands of the media today make it less likely that anyone who becomes their party's nominee for the highest office will be fat, ugly, or unconvincing on television. The tendency in any modern democracy is to choose leaders who are thought to be likely to be 'good on television'. Those who are not 'naturals' for the medium, or at least effective in handling it, such as Michael Foot and Iain Duncan Smith, have often failed to be elected. In Ronald Reagan, Americans found the perfect blend of the worlds of television and politics. Ideally, leaders need to have wide popular appeal.

The qualities needed to obtain the leadership and stay there are varied. What is evident from a study of recent prime ministers and presidents is that politicians of very different personalities can occupy high office and achieve success. Important qualities might include, among other things, affability, ability (not necessarily the highest academic distinction, but rather, nimbleness and vigour of mind, and a certain astuteness), industriousness (not necessarily a massive command of detail), an ability to delegate and to concentrate on essentials, a capacity for decision making, high ideals, vision, judgement, good timing, courage and the willingness to tackle difficult events and, where necessary, to give a clear steer to events. Determination and perhaps ruthlessness also feature in the mental equipment of most successful politicians.

steadily in recent years. Almost without exception the presidents considered 'great' by academic commentators have been 'leaders'. Most of the more passive ones have been long forgotten or remembered only because of the futility or scandals of their administrations.

CONCLUSION

Many Americans have an ambivalent attitude towards the presidency. Like the framers of the Constitution, they both fear and admire leadership. At times, they seem to expect their president to rise above the party battle and represent the broad consensus of the nation at large. At others, they expect to see him provide a lead, both to Congress and to the people.

The presidency has been described by Malcolm Walles[40] as 'the focal point of the United States system of government'. The Constitution may have shared power between the executive and the legislature, but it is the president who symbolises the nation. When people think of the achievements or failures of any particular epoch, they see these in terms of presidential rather than congressional eras. The curtailment of the imperial presidency accelerated during the 1990s. It is a trend that is widening the gulf between the electorate's expectations and a president's capacity to deliver. Presidential aspirants scatter promises on the campaign trail, but find them increasingly hard to fulfil.

REFERENCES

1 G. Wasserman, *The Basics of American Politics*, Longman, 1996
2 T. Hames and N. Rae, *Governing America*, Manchester University Press, 1996
3 R. Maidment and D. McGrew, *The American Political Process*, Sage/Open University, 1992
4 J. Adams, as quoted in B. Schwarz, *George Washington: The Making of an American Symbol*, Cornell University Press, 1990
5 R. Byrd, *New York Times*, 27 July 1985
6 C. Rossiter, *The American Presidency*, Harcourt Brace, 1960
7 A. Schlesinger Jnr, *The Imperial Presidency*, Houghton Mifflin, 1973
8 T. Franck, *The Tethered Presidency*, New York University Press, 1981
9 J. Beatty, as quoted in D. Mervin, *The President of the United States*, Harvester Wheatsheaf, 1993
10 L. Johnson, as quoted in B. Baker and L. Nixon, *Wheeling and Dealing*, W.W. Norton, 1978
11 R. Neustadt, *Presidential Power: The Politics of Leadership*, Wiley & Sons, 1960
12 R. Neustadt, *Presidential Power and the Modern President*, Free Press, 1990
13 S. Weissman, *A Culture of Deference: Congress's Failure of Leadership in Foreign Policy*, Basic Books, 1995
14 C. Rossiter, as quoted in 6 above
15 J. Burns, J. Peltason, T. Cronin and D. Magleby, *Government by the People*, Prentice-Hall, 1994
16 J. Hart, *The Presidential Branch: Executive Office of the President from Washington to Clinton*, Chatham House, 1995
17 A. Schlesinger Jnr, as quoted in 7 above

18 J. Nichols, 'Arthur Schlesinger *v.* The Imperial President', in *The Nation*, 2 March 2007

19 R. Neustadt, as quoted in 11 above

20 R. Neustadt, as quoted in 12 above

21 G. Peele, 'The Presidency', in G. Peele, C. Bailey, B. Cain and B. Peters (eds), *Developments in American Politics* 5, Palgrave, 2006

22 W. Howell, *Power without Persuasion: The Politics of Direct Presidential Action*, Princeton University Press, 2003

23 A. Wildavsky, 'The Two Presidencies', in *Trans-Action* 4 (December 1996), reproduced in *Perspectives on the Presidency*, Little Brown, 1975

24 B. Canes-Wrone, W. Howell and D. Lewis, 'Towards a Broader Understanding of Presidential Power: A Re-evaluation of the Two Presidencies Thesis', in *Journal of Politics*, 70.1, 2008

25 S. Weissman, *A Culture of Deference: Congress's Failure of Leadership in Foreign Policy*, Basic Books, 1996

26 T. Cronin and M. Genovese, *The Paradoxes of the American Presidency*, Oxford University Press, 2004

27 G. Wasserman, as quoted in 1 above

28 T. Roosevelt, *An Autobiography*, Scribner, 1913

29 As printed and explained by G. Welling and G. Wiersema, *From Revolution to Reconstruction: And What Happened After*, University of Groningen Press, 2001

30 G. Wasserman, as in 1 above

31 F. Greenstein, *The Presidential Difference: Leadership Styles from FDR to Clinton*, Martin Kessler Books (The Free Press), 2000

32 M. Landy and S. Milkis, *Presidential Greatness*, University Press of Kansas, 2000

33 A. Schlesinger Snr, *Life Magazine*, 1 November 1948 (the results of this and the 1962 survey are given in full in W. Degregorio, *The Complete Book of U.S. Presidents*, Barricade Books, 2009)

34 A. Schlesinger Snr, *New York Times Magazine*, 1962

35 R. Murray and T. Blessing, 'The Presidential performance Study: A Progress Report', in *Journal of American History*, 70, December 1983

36 A. Schlesinger Jnr, 'Rating the Presidents: Washington to Clinton', in *Political Science Quarterly*, 179, 1997

37 W. Ridings Jnr and S. McIver, *Rating the Presidents: From the Great and Honorable to the Dishonest and Incompetent*, Carol Publishing, 1997

38 C-Span, *Survey of Presidential Leadership*, 2000

39 J. Lindgren, *Presidential Leadership*, Wall Street Journal/Federalist Society, 2005

40 M. Walles, *British and American Systems of Government*, P. Allan, 1988

USEFUL WEB SITES

www.whitehouse.gov/ Official presidential site for the White House. Useful for following the day-to-day activities of the president, including daily briefings and press releases.

www.whitehousehistory.org White House Historical Association. General overview of the presidency and the White House; offers a virtual tour of the White House, showing its objets d'art.

www.presidency.ucsb.edu The American Presidency Project, an archive of more than 85,000 documents relating to the study of the presidency.

www.millercenter.org/ The Miller Center for Public Affairs, on the role and history of the presidency, University of Virginia.

In addition, the various presidential libraries offer additional insights, for example **www.jfklibrary.org/**, the John F. Kennedy Presidential Library and Museum.

SAMPLE QUESTIONS

1 What factors determine the ability of a president to exercise control over Congress?
2 Assess the effectiveness of presidential power in relation to either (a) domestic or (b) foreign policy.
3 What factors determine the power of the president? In what ways are his powers limited?
4 Distinguish between the 'power' (personal influence) and 'powers' (as in the Constitution, laws and customs of the United States) of the US President.
5 In what ways might the presidency of G.W. Bush be regarded as 'imperial'?
6 'The fundamental and irreducible core of presidential power rests not on influence, persuasion, public opinion, elections or party, but rather on the successful assertion of constitutional authority to resolve crises and significant domestic issues' (Richard Pious, 1996). Do you agree?
7 What was the impact of George W. Bush on the presidency? How would you assess his performance in office?
8 The presidency was described as 'imperial' in the 1960s, 'tethered' in the 1970s, 'restored' in the 1980s, 'constrained' in the 1990s and 're-imperialised' early in the new millennium. How might we categorise presidential power today?
9 'The power to persuade.' Is this a valid description of presidential power today?

Support for the presidency

5

The presidency is an institution based on a set of powers, procedures and expectations that are to be found in the Constitution, laws, precedent and custom. It is also an institution in the sense that it contains a group of people – such as the White House staff and those working in the Executive Office of the President – who directly serve the president and are there to support him in fulfilling his roles. Indeed, although the White House is the presidential home, it is also an office building where the president and a part of the presidency work; most of its rooms are taken up by the hundreds of staffers who work there.

The president is, in effect, the chief bureaucrat, the person who administers the executive branch, including the departments of state and unaffiliated agencies. So numerous, diverse and sprawling are the institutions of the federal bureaucracy that such a task would be impossible, as no single person could personally supervise a vast range of organisations, employing millions of personnel and spending billions of dollars.

In this chapter, we are concerned with the help available to the president, from: his deputy, the vice-president; the Cabinet, and in particular the departmental heads within it; and those who are employed in the Executive Office. We also examine the constituent parts of the federal bureaucracy and the difficulties the president experiences in controlling it.

POINTS TO CONSIDER

- What considerations influence a president as he chooses his vice-presidential running-mate?
- Has the position of vice-president grown in political significance in recent years, and if so, why?
- How important is the Cabinet today?
- In what respects are the British and American Cabinets (a) similar and (b) dissimilar?
- What is meant by 'the bureaucracy'?
- What are the key problems relating to the size and scale of the federal bureaucracy?
- How has the federal bureaucracy changed over recent decades?

The vice-presidency

For many years the office of vice-president ('Veep') was viewed as little more than a joke. Its first incumbent, John Adams, spoke of it derisively: 'My country has in its wisdom contrived for me the most insignificant office that ever the invention of man contrived or his imagination conceived.' The majority of his successors would probably have shared his view, and a disillusioned John Nance Garner, Franklin Roosevelt's deputy, suggested that the office was 'not worth a pitcher of warm spit'. Even Walter Mondale,[1] Carter's mostly successful vice-president, referred to the job as 'handmade for ridicule and for dismissal. In the nature of it, you always look like a supplicant, a beggar, a person on a string'.

The office was created only as an afterthought by who devised the Constitution. The document simply says that he will be chosen by an Electoral College, outlines the circumstances when he or she will be acting president and lays down that he or she will preside over the Senate. Given that there are so few formal responsibilities, some vice-presidents make little of it. One such occupant was Charles Dawes, who served under President Coolidge. Dawes declared that his position was 'the easiest job in the world'.

Choice of the vice-president

Presidential candidates want a running-mate who will be an asset to the ticket and boost their electoral prospects. Ideally the person chosen will balance their own background and characteristics, so that geographical, demographic and ideological factors come into play. It may be that the choice will be pleasing to an area, to a group of voters or to some faction within the party. Kennedy, a northern liberal and a Catholic, chose Johnson, a Texan Protestant likely to appeal to southern conservatives. Nixon chose Spiro Agnew (a Maryland governor) to please the same group. Clinton chose Al Gore, for although he came from a similar geographical background and shared many similar beliefs, he offered definite advantages that might extend the appeal of the ticket. In particular, he was seen as a 'Mr Clean', reassuring on the topic of 'family values', a subject on which Bill Clinton was thought to be vulnerable. George W. Bush opted for Dick Cheney, who had served as defense secretary in his father's Cabinet and was expected to provide some experience and weight to the presidential challenge in 2000. He had the experience of handling foreign affairs and national security issues that the presidential candidate so obviously lacked.

Barack Obama appointed Joe Biden, who became the first Roman Catholic to assume the office and also the first Delawarean. Biden did not represent a swing state or one with a significant a vote in the Electoral College. Neither did his selection sit naturally with the Obama message of change. Yet he brought important strengths to the Democratic ticket, most obviously gravitas, deep foreign policy and national security expertise, a willingness and ability aggressively to attack John McCain (in a way that did not come easily to Obama) and an easy connection with middle-class and blue-collar Americans.

Responsibilities and role

The vice-president assumes some of the ceremonial tasks of the president, and represents him on formal occasions, whether it is the funeral of a foreign leader or the commemoration of some past event. The vice-president is formally the presiding officer of the Senate, refereeing its proceedings and interpreting the rules. In this capacity, vice-presidents usually put in few appearances, for there is little kudos to be won and little chance to exert political influence – given that he or she is not a member of the chamber. In the event of a closely divided chamber, he has a casting vote, although such tie-breaking votes are very rare, as the figures indicate. Otherwise, vice-presidents take on ad hoc assignments, their number and character depending on the use that the president wishes to make of them. Joe Biden was named as the head of a new White House Task Force on Working Families, an initiative aimed at improving the economic position of the middle classes.

Tie-breaking votes by vice-presidents

Mondale	1
Bush, G.H.	7
Quayle	0
Gore	4
Cheney	8

Since 1789, 244 tie-breaking votes have been cast by thirty-five of the vice-presidents. John Adams holds the record, at twenty-nine votes, followed closely by John Calhoun with twenty-eight. Since the 1870s, however, no vice-president has cast as many as ten tie-breaking votes. Twenty were cast by the five incumbents prior to Biden, who has yet to do so.

A frustrating role

For those with presidential ambitions, the post takes them that much nearer the White House. There is always the chance that their services might be needed should a death or assassination occur, or that electors will choose them as the next president. About one-third of vice-presidents eventually become president: five have done so since World War II: Truman, Johnson, Nixon, Ford and Bush senior.

Yet it is still difficult for vice-presidents to carve out a useful and distinctive role. The job is a frustrating one, particularly when the administration is nearing its end – even more so if it is unpopular. On the one hand, the 'Veep' is expected to remain loyal and act as a mouthpiece of the presidential team. On the other, he may wish to carve out a distinct persona and, if things are going badly for the president, to show a degree of detachment. Hubert Humphrey was in such a dilemma over Vietnam, in the latter days of the Johnson presidency. Whatever his personal reservations, he was unable to oppose official policy whilst he remained a member of the White House team. Al Gore faced a similar problem. In his case, there was no dispute over political direction, but he was embarrassed by the scandals which so damaged the Clinton reputation. Especially in the latter days, he kept himself as detached as possible when it was apparent that the administration was in political difficulty.

The office provides the incumbent with an opportunity to see the workings of government at the highest level, and gain a useful insight into the problems that arise and the way in which they are handled. But it is easy for the occupant to seem faceless and lacking independence of outlook. Few presidents would appreciate an outspoken understudy, or one who diverted too much attention from them. Many have preferred to keep their number two in the dark on key issues. Roosevelt took this isolation of his vice-president so far that he did not even tell his 'Veep' that America was developing the atomic bomb.

Nixon did not find work under Eisenhower fulfilling, and neither did Johnson under Kennedy. In both cases, the relationship was a poor one before they were ever chosen as running-mates. Nixon's own vice-president, the much-despised Spiro T. Agnew,[2] found it a 'peculiar situation to be in, to have . . . a title and responsibility with no real power to do anything'. Indeed, Nixon barely knew Agnew at the time he chose him as his running-mate. Having felt humiliated in the vice-presidential job himself, he inflicted even greater humiliation on Agnew. By most accounts, Agnew was scorned by the White House staff and given little of importance to do. Johnson too was snubbed by White House staffers, who reputedly mocked him behind his back as 'Uncle Cornpone'.

Presidents rarely feel that they can totally trust the person they have chosen to run with, for such associates have their own ambitions. It is usually a 'marriage of convenience' on the part of the president, rather than an expression of deep regard for the person selected. Political rather than personal considerations dictate the original choice.

The growing significance of the position

Until well into the twentieth century, the vice-presidential role was to act as what Cronin and Genovese[3] describe as 'ceremonial ribbon-cutters'. It was generally regarded as a 'semi-retirement job for party stalwarts, acting as a resting place for mediocrities' or as a 'runner-up'. Two constitutional amendments helped to raise the status of the office. The Twenty-Second limited the president to two full terms in office, and thereby increased the chances of the vice-president taking over. The Twenty-Fifth, in 1967, confirmed the previous practice of making the vice-president not an acting one but the real thing, in the event of a national emergency such as the incapacity of the president to fulfil his tasks. A procedure is laid down to determine if and when the deputy should take over, and for how long and under what conditions he or she should exercise presidential duties. (In 1985, George Bush senior was the first vice-president to assume such responsibilities, when President Reagan had an operation for skin cancer.)

Although these amendments boosted the importance of the role, its influence still varies, according to who is in the White House. For some presidents, their deputies can be useful in an advisory capacity on matters of politics and policy. Jimmy Carter made more use of his vice-president, Walter Mondale, than had been usual in the past, because he needed the support of a Washington 'insider' who could give good advice based upon his knowledge and experience. Reagan allowed Bush senior to attend many meetings and to represent him in many engagements. However, activity and influence are very different, and whereas Mondale was allowed more say in the decision-making process, this was much less true of his successor.

During the Clinton administrations, it became fashionable for writers to describe Al Gore as 'probably the most influential vice-president in American history'. Not only did he preside over important projects such as the 'Reinventing Government' initiative, he also took an active interest in issues ranging from the environment to science and technology. On foreign affairs, he was deeply involved in discussions such as policy towards the Middle East, Russia and South Africa, as well as in issues of nuclear non-proliferation. On these and other matters, Bill Clinton valued his advice. Often, he would remain in the Oval Office when all other advisers had departed, so that his voice was the last the president heard. He was credited with wielding considerable influence over the composition of the revamped Cabinet at the beginning of the second term, the idea being that this would give him influential supporters in key positions to help him prepare his bid for the November 2000 contest. Clinton seemed to feel less threatened by his vice-president than had some of his predecessors.

In several ways, the two men complemented each other, a point spotted by the labor secretary, Robert Reich,[4] who noted that: 'Al [Gore] is . . . methodical where B is haphazard, linear where B is creative, cautious where B is impetuous, ponderous where B is playful, private where B shares his feelings with everyone. The two men need one another, and sense it. Above all, Gore is patient, where B wants it all now.' For Gore, the position was a good training ground for the job he badly wanted. He used it as an opportunity to prepare himself for the presidency, carefully studying the operation of power at the highest level.

Joe Biden has been heavily involved in aspects of Obama's decision-making process, holding an oversight role on the issue of infrastructure spending within the economic stimulus package targeted at counteracting recession. However, commentators have generally regarded him as being less influential than his predecessor, Dick Cheney (see p. 122). On occasion, they have noted his capacity for making embarrassing verbal gaffes.

Dick Cheney as vice-president

In the events leading up to war in Iraq, the 'most influential vice-president' label was applied to Dick Cheney, who was often described as 'the power behind the throne'. His was an unusual case, for if he qualified as the most-powerful ever vice-president, he was also among the least visible. As a running-mate, he was a surprise choice.

Cheney had several apparent disadvantages as vice-president. He was an uninspiring and rare public speaker, a mediocre election campaigner, lacking an obviously warm and appealing personality to charm the electorate. He brought little to the presidential ticket, coming from a small, conservative state that almost any Republican presidential candidate would expect to win. Moreover, ever since he was selected as vice-presidential running-mate by George W. Bush, there were serious doubts about his health. After all, he has had four heart attacks and uses a 'pace-maker plus' to give his heart an electric shock, should it lose its normal rhythm. A further potential source of weakness might be the fact that, according to polls, he was not trusted by a significant element among those interviewed. His recent past as chief executive at Halliburton oil services company, at a time when it dabbled in questionable accounting, made him appear as the embodiment of America's corporate ills.

There has been discussion in recent years of 'a new vice-presidency'. Yet in spite of the developing trend towards providing vice-presidents with a more worthwhile role, for much of the time they are effectively 'waiting in the wings' in case their services are called upon to assume the burden of the presidency. They stand in readiness to assume command, in the event of death (either through natural causes or assassination), of resignation or of removal from office. Nine presidents have failed to complete their allotted terms, eight through death, and one (Nixon) because of his forced resignation. The possibility of assassination is a real one: four presidents have been killed, two in the twentieth century (McKinley and Kennedy), and several others have been the victims of life-threatening attacks. Because of this, Vice-President Adams was right in his summary of the strengths and weaknesses of his position: 'I am vice-president of the United States. In this, I am nothing, but I may be everything.'

Unsurprisingly, because he is a heartbeat away from the supreme office, there is often a tension between the vice-president and the president he serves. Henry Kissinger,[5] an eminent figure in the Nixon administrations, noted that the relationship between the occupants of the two posts was never easy: 'it is, after all, disconcerting to have at one's side a man whose life's ambitions will be achieved by one's death'. Lyndon Johnson[6] was clearly aware of this unusual aspect of his office, on one occasion admitting that whenever he was in the

However, as vice-president, from a Bush point of view, Cheney had several assets. He was uncommonly and fiercely loyal to his boss, and the president trusted him with absolute confidence. Particularly after 9/11, Bush leaned on him for advice, seeing him as a heavyweight with gravitas who could deal with day-to-day issues effectively. Although he was taciturn and rarely showed his cards in meetings, Cheney used private opportunities to speak his mind. His judgement and views commanded respect. His importance in the Bush administrations was recognised by admirers and critics alike. He was useful to the president in several ways, able to say things that the president might feel but dare not publicly say. Whereas George Bush often spoke in terms of 'compassionate conservatism', see p. 316, his vice-president had licence to betray the innermost thinking of some Republicans around the White House. He famously derided environmentalism as a 'personal virtue' and broke the 'no gloating' rule after the fall of Baghdad. Above all, Cheney had one quality that endeared him to the president. He did not covet his office. He did not need to be seen often in public, for he was not seeking to build a popular reputation as part of a build-up to some presidential bid. He had no political ambitions.

presence of JFK, he felt 'like a goddam raven hovering over his shoulder'. In his case, a tragic death forced him to make the transition from acting as a standby to assuming the awesome responsibilities of the presidency.

The Cabinet

The Constitution allows the president to invite the opinions of the main officers of the executive departments of government, but there is no mention of summoning them together as a Cabinet. Yet this has always happened, from George Washington onwards. The influence of the **Cabinet** has varied according to the tastes and inclinations of the president. As a broad generalisation, it was a more powerful body before the 1930s than it has been subsequently. Yet the 'decline' has not been a continuous one, and from time to time individual presidents have promised to use such gatherings more. A very few have fulfilled their initial promise.

> **Cabinet**
> Cabinet meetings comprise the president, vice-president, the officers who head the fifteen departments, plus a few other officials whom the president considers to be of appropriate rank.

Abraham Lincoln is usually credited with the comment 'seven noes, one aye – the ayes have it', following a cabinet discussion in which his proposal was unanimously rejected by those around the table. True or otherwise, the remark indicates the view that most presidents have of the people they appoint to serve under them. Presidents tend to view them as spokespersons for their departments who have nothing to contribute on other matters.

This means that presidents lack the political support that the British Cabinet gives to the prime minister. The American Cabinet does not contain party notables, high-ranking members with a power-base and standing in their own right. Neither do cabinet members have a place in the legislature, and so they are of little assistance to the president in pushing his programme through Congress. An American cabinet bears little relation to one operating in a parliamentary system. It does not work as a team, as the British one does, and American and British cabinets have little in common other than the name.

Some presidents have begun their presidency with the intention of using the Cabinet more. They have spoken of its value and how they intended to utilise the talents of those appointed to it. Truman[7] spoke of 'a body whose combined judgement the president uses to develop fundamental policies of the administration'. Reagan flattered his new appointees, saying that they were to be used rather like a board of directors in a corporation. He would discuss issues frankly with them and take on board their input when making decisions. In 1969, Richard Nixon saw the cabinet members as having an important role in policy making. But whatever the initial promises, the relationship between president and cabinet officers tends to deteriorate within a year or so. Any honeymoon romanticism about the office begins to wear off and the more trusted White House staff come to outstrip the Cabinet in power and influence. In Truman's administration, 'important decisions were made by ad hoc groups consisting of cabinet officers and others. He did not wish to . . . formalise the meetings.'[8]

The number of meetings tends to decline as the years go by. By 1972, Nixon was down to eleven meetings in the course of the year. As Watergate enveloped his administration, he came to regard the Cabinet with intense suspicion and conceived a strong dislike for its individual members, whom he had originally appointed and praised as people capable of providing an 'extra dimension . . . superior and even great leadership'. He got rid of more of them than most of his ever predecessors had. Those who retained their positions found the meetings boring and rather 'bland': 'Nothing of substance was discussed. There was no disagreement because there was nothing to disagree about. Things over which we might have disagreed were not discussed.'[9] Similarly, Jimmy Carter's good intentions were never fulfilled. The number of his Cabinet meetings declined significantly and members felt that they lacked any proper agenda or coherent theme.

Especially in the early years of his administration, Reagan was keen on the idea of Cabinet government, and at meetings was likely to go round the table and invite individual views. He also made use of cabinet councils of five or six cabinet members on topics such as economic affairs and human resources, and these worked with White House staff to provide a source of new ideas for the president – a system which was analogous to the British system of cabinet committees. Bill Clinton formed committees of cabinet and sub-cabinet members, as in the case of the National Economic Council. Again, the purpose was to better integrate departmental heads and White House officials around particular policy areas. The original precedent for such committees was the National Security Council, formed shortly after World War II with the intention of providing the president with quality advice on matters concerning the security of the nation against external threat.

Every Cabinet has its key players who matter more as individuals than as members of a collective team. John Foster Dulles was a key figure in the Eisenhower administration; Warren Christopher and Madeleine Albright had the same status under Bill Clinton. Along with Dick Cheney, Donald Rumsfeld and Condoleeza Rice were important personnel for much of the George W. Bush presidency. Every Cabinet has its dominating personalities; sometimes their influence varies according to personalities involved and the department they represent. Their influence depends more on their individual worth to the president, rather than on their role as part of team. Presidents lack the time and often the inclination to deal with individual cabinet officers. Only those whose views are valued and who handle matters of national security and foreign policy are likely to gain regular access to the White House.

Choosing the Cabinet

One of the first tasks of a new president before the inauguration is the choice of the Cabinet, and the selection is watched by commentators eager to get an indication of the likely tone and style of the administration. The president can choose whom he wishes, although it is wise to nominate people who are likely to be acceptable to the Senate. The Cabinet is the president's personal creation, and he will seek out people felt to be useful, and effective within their departments. Few people can assume that they will be included, for it does not follow that prominent people in the presidential election campaign will be rewarded with a position in the Cabinet; other rewards may be awarded and preferred.

The president will want to include people who are loyal to him and to presidential programmes. Other considerations include the need to reward prominent politicians who helped the campaign nationally and within the president's state. There are often political debts to repay. Kennedy, as a northern liberal, was even prepared to include a southern segregationist within the cabinet – though this seemed to be in direct contradiction of his expressed support for civil rights. The choice did enable him to achieve a geographical balance, with representation of regions different from his own. A broad social balance is desirable, and recent presidents have been aware of the desirability of acknowledging the existence within the US of women and of different racial groups, such as the black and Jewish communities.

The president will also want people of administrative competence who may bring expertise and specialist knowledge to their work. It does not matter if they have not previously served in a government position, and many have no political background. There will sometimes be an attempt to persuade congressmen from either house to serve the administration, but in most cases figures who have won re-election are unlikely to be interested in forsaking the legislature for administrative responsibilities that are lacking in influence over the overall direction of policy. Moreover, from their own experience they will know what it is like to grill members of the administration, and may be unwilling to submit themselves to the procedure. Republican Cabinet appointees often come from a business background. Eisenhower, Nixon, Bush senior and Reagan all plucked people from the worlds of commerce and manufacturing. Those chosen may be elevated from obscurity, and when the administration comes to an end they often return to such a status – having made little impact on the public mind.

The twenty-two members of the Obama Cabinet (October 2011)

Office	Holder
Secretary of State	Hillary Clinton
Secretary of the Treasury	Timothy Geithner
Secretary of Defense	Leon Panetta
Attorney General	Eric Holder
Secretary of the Interior	Ken Salazar
Secretary of Agriculture	Tom Vilsack
Secretary of Commerce*	Rebecca Blank (acting)
Secretary of Labor	Hilda Solis
Secretary of Health and Human Services	Kathleen Sebelius
Secretary of Housing and Urban Development	Shaun Donovan
Secretary of Transportation	Ray LaHood
Secretary of Energy	Steven Chu
Secretary of Education	Arne Duncan
Secretary of Veterans Affairs	Eric Shinseki
Secretary of Homeland Security	Janet Napolitano
Vice-president of the United States	Joe Biden
White House Chief of Staff	William Daley
Administrator of the Environmental Protection Agency	Lisa Jackson
Director of the Office of Management and Budget	Jacob Lew
United States Trade Representative	Ronald Kirk
United States Ambassador to the United Nations	Susan Rice
Chair, Council of Economic Advisers	Christina Romer

*Acting Secretary

The role and practice of American cabinets

As we have seen, the Cabinet is not even mentioned in the Constitution, although the Twenty-Fifth Amendment lays down a procedure to be followed in the case of the president's incapacity. Congress determines the lines of succession after the vice-president, and beyond the speaker and Senate president *pro tempore*, the Cabinet personnel are listed in order of status, starting with the secretary of state.

The Cabinet is an advisory body only, and in the final analysis the president consults whom he or she wishes and may choose to ignore what the cabinet members say – assuming they are consulted in the first place. As the president does not have to refer to the Cabinet in times of crisis, the sole responsibility for decision making rests with him. The role can be a lonely one. The president may choose to seek out the advice of individuals whose counsel is trusted, but for many members there is little incentive to offer backing and support. There is no question of the president seeking and feeling the need to act upon the advice of all of the cabinet members. He or she may prefer to seek the advice of the White House Office and the Office of Management and Budget when advice is needed.

Presidents use the Cabinet as they feel appropriate or necessary. They may choose to hold meetings regularly, as Eisenhower did, or perhaps allow the Cabinet to meet only irregularly, and consult individuals where they are likely to be in a position to contribute usefully. Kennedy regarded the Cabinet as an anachronism as a consultative body and felt that full meetings were usually unproductive. He posed the question that sums up the way in which many presidents regard Cabinet discussion: 'Why should the postmaster sit there and listen to a discussion of the problems of Laos?' In other words, members can more usefully employ their time on the work of their own departments rather than engage in general discussions.

Cabinet unanimity does not exist in the sense to which the British are accustomed. It may be desirable where it can be achieved, but it is not a constitutional principle such as 'collective responsibility' is in Britain. Members do differ in their views, and may do so publicly, as happened at the time of the Vietnam War and at the time of the Argentinean dispute with Britain in the early 1980s. In both cases, spokespersons gave different responses when questioned about the policy decisions taken by the administration in which they served.

No cabinet member feels that he or she has to rush to defend a colleague (or president) under attack, and when there are disagreements no one feels obliged to resign – though members may choose to do so if they are at odds with the president. Disagreement is not in itself an automatic reason for resigning, and Congress would not call for resignation because cabinet members are not responsible to the legislature, only to the president.

Cabinets in Britain and the United States: a comparison

- In both countries, cabinet membership is usually just over twenty, the British model being the larger of the two. In 2010, in addition to the president and vice-president, there are in the Obama Cabinet the heads of the fifteen departments and six other persons of Cabinet rank. David Cameron has a Cabinet of twenty-three, although five (sometimes six) others attend Cabinet meetings.

- In Britain, meetings are held regularly (every Thursday). American cabinets meet irregularly, much depending on who is president and whether it is early or late in the lifetime of the administration.

- In Britain, other than a few peers in the House of Lords, most members are elected politicians, drawn from the House of Commons and answerable to it. Some are powerful figures in their own right, with a political standing in the party and country. They may even be potential rivals to the prime minister. US cabinet appointees have not been elected, are not figures of prominence within the party (occasionally, one or two may be members of the other main party), are not members of Congress and are not viewed as potential rivals to the president.

- In Britain, the Cabinet is the main decision-making body. It takes decisions, coordinates policy and acts as a court of appeal when agreement cannot be reached in the

The Executive Office of the President

As presidential responsibilities widened in the years following the Great Depression, it became increasingly difficult for the president to cope with the demands of the job. He lacked the necessary support, a point noted by the president's Committee on Administrative Management in 1937: 'The president needs help', it proclaimed.

A Commission on the Organisation of the Executive Branch of the Government, set up by President Truman and headed by Herbert Hoover, reported twelve years later. It was troubled by the lack of clear lines of authority from the president down to the civil service, and felt the modern president faced an impossible task unless there was an extensive regrouping of executive departments and agencies into a number of smaller, non-overlapping units, and an increased use of the Cabinet. These changes would give the president the chance to achieve an effective supervision of the governmental activities for which he was constitutionally responsible.

Both analyses drew attention to the burdens of the presidency, and argued the case that because executive power was centred on one person he needed help from better support services rather than from other people. The Cabinet might have seemed a possible choice to relieve the burden. But as the officers who serve in it are unelected and therefore lack political or moral authority – and

Cabinet Committee. Even if the prime minister is very powerful, the role of the Cabinet is still a major one, although commentators debate the balance of power between the premier and his or her colleagues. Major issues come before the Cabinet and ultimately, prime ministers need cabinet backing. The president looks elsewhere for policy advice, coordination and support. He may choose to consult the Cabinet, but does not feel bound to do so. Discussions are frequently regarded as pointless or boring, often not dealing with the matters that might cause controversy.

- In Britain, the doctrine of 'collective responsibility' applies to cabinet members. In the US, there is no such doctrine and disagreement in public is more apparent. For instance, in the George W. Bush administration, the secretary of state and the defense secretary took a different line on European Union defence policy.

- In both countries, the tendency in recent years has been for the Cabinet meeting to be bypassed. In Britain, those who allege that we have prime ministerial government often point to the increased use of a Kitchen Cabinet of key advisers and to the tendency of strong prime ministers to consult with Cabinet members on a bilateral basis. In the US also, matters tend to be resolved in small, informal groupings or between the president and the appropriate departmental secretary.

in any case, are not usually front-rank politicians – they have little incentive to relieve the president of any duties. In particular, they have little experience of managing relations with Congress. In other words, even if the president wished to make greater use of the Cabinet, several of its members have little interest in offering the necessary backing, for their reputation does not depend on the president's political success. Each secretary looks after his or her patch; however, the president looks after his own duties, but also has to answer for any secretary's shortcomings.

The president is in a solitary position, with overall responsibility for the activities of an enormous governmental machine that he or she must direct and coordinate. To do this, the president requires information about operations, assessments of policy needs and means of ensuring that his or her decisions and those of Congress are efficiently carried out, in the ways and spirit in which they are intended.

The establishment and operation of the Executive Office

As a result of the recommendations of the 1937 Committee, Roosevelt agreed that new machinery should be established. Two years after it reported, an enlarged presidential office was created, far larger in scale than had existed previously. Instead of a few clerks and secretaries, there was to be a new Executive Office of the President. In the words of Clinton Rossiter,[10] the

ELEMENTS OF THE EXECUTIVE OFFICE

Presidents vary in the way in which they allocate roles to particular entities within the Executive Office. Depending on the priority they attach to particular problems, they may abolish one body or transfer its brief to another. For instance, the functions of the National Economic Council and the Office of Policy Development have now been incorporated into the Office of White House Policy, housed in the White House Office.

The White House Office

The president's closest aides, his personal staff, work in the White House Office, the nerve centre of the Executive Office. Of those located in the White House, only a few dozen of the most senior advisers will see the president regularly. There are special assistants to advise on foreign and domestic affairs, speech writers, liaison officers who maintain contact with Congress, and, of course, the press secretary. There is nowadays a special counsellor to the president, and also many whose services are more concerned with basic personal needs, such as a personal secretary, a social secretary and a physician.

The office ensures that urgent priority issues reach the president's desk quickly, and members seek to ensure compliance by the departments with presidential policies, and so obtain for the president control over the federal administration. These assistants obtain their real authority from their closeness to the president, and the trust that he places in them. By deciding who should see the president and the issues to prioritise, they have much discretionary power. The danger is that the office can so 'protect' the president that he becomes remote from the political world. He becomes surrounded with 'yes-men' who say what they think the president wants to hear, and thus prevent him from making a balanced assessment.

Under Kennedy, several members were used more to help the president carry out the tasks he set himself, rather than to act as key advisers. In contrast, other presidents have given this inner circle enormous influence, so that some administrations are remembered in terms of the president himself and the immediate associates with whom he surrounded himself – Nixon had Haldeman and Ehrlichman, Carter had Jordan and Powell, and Reagan had Baker (later his secretary of state), Deaver and Meese. During the Nixon presidency the size of the White House Office grew substantially, with well over 500 personnel. Nixon downgraded his Cabinet, and so, to get the coordination of policy which he required he established the post of counsellor to the president. The appointee was given the prime responsibility for coordinating the handling of home and overseas affairs, and was included within the Cabinet – a status denied to previous White House aides.

presidency was converted 'into an instrument of twentieth century government . . . it gives the incumbent a sporting chance to stand the strain and fulfil the constitutional mandate as a one-man branch of our three-part government'. In his view, the innovation saved the presidency from paralysis, and the Constitution from radical amendment.

The Office of Management and Budget

Nixon reconstituted the Bureau of the Budget into the Office of Management and Budget (OMB) in 1970, as a major managerial instrument for the president. Its main task is to prepare a federal budget to submit to Congress, and all appropriations requests from the departments come through the office for approval. The departments use their influence to retain maximum financial autonomy, and the president needs support if he is to keep overall control of their plans. The office can be a powerful instrument, for it also provides a mechanism by which the president can coordinate governmental activities and ensure, in his role as manager of the executive branch, that programmes are carried out as efficiently as possible.

The National Security Council

Established in 1947, the National Security Council (NSC) was given the role of advising the president on domestic, foreign and military matters relating to national security. Its duty was to consider 'policies on matters of common interest to the departments and agencies of the government concerned with national security, and to make recommendations'. As with the Cabinet, the NSC does not make decisions for the president, but it provides evidence and advice from which the president can come to his own conclusions. At times of crisis, the Council does not usually seem to be the place where key assessments are made.

In the Obama Administration, the NSC has become part of a wider entity that also incorporates the Homeland Security Council (HSC). The HSC and NSC exist by statute as independent but closely coordinated councils of leadership advising the president.

The Council of Economic Advisers

Economic policy is increasingly important to the performance and reputation of any administration, and for presidents, few of whom are economic experts, assistance is needed. Since 1946, a three-person panel of professional economists has been appointed with the consent of the Senate to advise on key issues. Often they are university academics, but new presidents select people of their own persuasion and outlook. The Council of Economic Advisers is a purely advisory body, but it is an important counter to the Treasury and the OMB, which have a narrower and more immediate focus. Such advice helps presidents to bear in mind longer-term considerations in their economic thinking. One specific responsibility is to assist in the preparation of an annual economic report to be given by the president to Congress; this outlines the administration's view of economic trends.

From the earliest days, it was obvious that the new office would be highly significant, but even so the extent of its eventual impact on American government could not have been judged. At the time, it comprised barely 1,000 staff, whereas at the beginning of the twenty-first century the total exceeds 5,000. But the extent of its operations and of its importance is not to be judged by numbers alone, but more by the centrality of its position in the workings of the executive branch. It has become what Maidment and McGrew[11] call 'the principal instrument of presidential government'.

The modern president relies on the Executive Office to come up with the background information, detailed analysis and informed policy recommendations that are needed to enable him or her to master the complexities of a task. It has taken its place at the heart of the administration, giving the president the advice he depends upon, conducting many dealings with Congress, and helping to publicise and supervise the implementation of presidential decisions. The president is freed to deal with top-level matters of the moment and to engage in future planning.

The component parts of the Executive Office change from president to president, for it is the president's personal bureaucracy. Individuals have varied in the use made of it and amended its internal organisation to reflect their own priorities, interests and needs. New parts of the office have been established, some have been developed or transformed from their original character, and others have become redundant.

The Executive Office is an umbrella under which exist a number of key agencies which cover the whole range of policy areas and which serve the president directly. The Office of Management and the Budget already existed in 1939, but otherwise only the White House Office has been there since the original machinery was set up. Elements have changed in different administrations, but central to the work of the office are the White House staff, personal appointees who are likely to be the closest advisers for general and particular policies (see p. 130).

Assessment of the Executive Office

It was because of the growing demands on the president that some help was necessary if he was to be adequately equipped for the necessary tasks. As the president's responsibilities grew, so did his need for expert assistance. At the time of the creation of the Executive Office few commentators realised just how important it would become. It is now far larger than in the year after its establishment, and its influence has grown even more dramatically than its number of personnel. What makes it so important for the president is that it is beholden only to him. Its members are appointed by the president, and they know that they owe their position to him and therefore seek to serve him loyally.

The Executive Office is the main instrument of presidential government, and all modern presidents rely upon it to a greater or lesser degree, for information, analysis and policy recommendations. In some cases, their dependence is greater than others, and certain key aides emerge as the linchpin of the administration. For them, their focus of attention is inevitably the presidency, as it must be. It is easy for them to become so obsessed with the protection of the president that they ignore the limitations of the office designed by the framers of the Constitution. In other words, the Executive Office – and especially those assistants who serve in the White House Office – can become out of touch with the viewpoints and requirements of those who inhabit other areas of the system of government.

The danger can be that, having appointed an advisory team of people who share his personal and political preferences, the president receives advice only from those who share the same outlook. Other people in different branches of the

---

THE EXECUTIVE OFFICE OF THE PRESIDENT AND WHITE HOUSE OFFICE UNDER BARACK OBAMA

The Executive Office of the President
Council of Economic Advisers
Council on Environmental Quality
National Security Staff
Office of Administration
Office of Management and Budget
Office of National Drug Control Policy
Office of Science and Technology Policy
Office of the United States Trade Representative
Office of the Vice President
Executive Residence

The White House Office
Domestic Policy Council
National Security Advisor
National Economic Council
Office of Cabinet Affairs
Office of Chief of Staff
Office of Communications
Office of First Lady
Office of Legislative Affairs
Office of Management and Administration
Oval Office Operations
Office of Presidential Personnel
Office of Public Engagement and Intergovernmental Affairs
Office of Scheduling and Advance
Office of the Staff Secretary
Office of the White House Counsel

Details as provided on www.whitehouse.gov/administration/eop/ (October 2011).

governmental process also have insights worthy of an audience, and some congressmen and bureaucrats may find that their route to the president is barred. Presidents can come to rely too much on those around them, and in that way allow themselves to become out of touch with the views of a wider section of the American public.

The federal bureaucracy

Bureaucracy refers to what Burns et al.[12] describe as a 'professional corps of officials organised in a pyramidal structure, and functioning under impersonal, uniform rules and procedures'. By the term 'bureaucrats', we refer to people who operate in the executive branch, whose career is based in government service and normally work there as a result of appointment rather than election; they work for presidents and their political appointees. They serve in government departments, and in the more than fifty independent agencies embracing some 2,000 bureaus, which are sub-units of the agencies.

This **federal bureaucracy** grew from 1,000 employees in 1790 to more than 2,800,000 in 1979. It began to decline after the end of the Cold War and now comprises about 2,600,000 officials. Federal bureaucrats serve in a wide variety of positions and geographic locations both in the United States and around the world.

> **federal bureaucracy**
> The official executive; the unelected administrative system of the national government, comprising executive departments, government agencies, government corporations and independent regulatory commissions that carry out policy on a day-to-day basis.

Who is part of the federal bureaucracy?

- Some five million people work in the executive branch.

- Of these, 60% are civilians; the rest are military personnel.

- About 12% of them operate in Washington.

- The rest are based around the country.

- In California, there are more than a quarter of a million federal employees.

- Of the three million civilians, about one million work in the area of national security – for the air force, army, navy and various defence organisations – and nearly half a million work for the welfare agencies.

- There are some 15,000 different categories of federal employee. The majority are white-collar workers, ranging from inspectors and engineers to secretaries and clerks.

It is sometimes assumed that the administration is primarily concerned with putting into effect decisions taken elsewhere, so that politics and administration are separate compartments. According to this view, bureaucrats are the neutral instrument of elected politicians and their concern is only to pursue their tasks with the utmost efficiency, free from considerations of personal gain or political advantage. Such a view is naive, and the executive branch is deeply involved in politics at many levels.

Much of the legislation that goes before Congress begins its life in the departments and many agencies of government, and pressure group activists and congressmen realise this and may seek to influence proposals from the administration at an early stage. Equally, much discretion is granted to those who implement the law when enacted, and they seek to influence congressmen on matters such as appropriations. In the same way, they seek to influence other agencies and departments whose interests conflict with their own, and so administration and politics cannot be isolated from each other.

Key positions in the American bureaucracy are held by persons appointed by the president (see p. 136). Because these are normally people who share the president's outlook, this might be expected to result in presidential control of the bureaucratic process. Yet this often does not happen, for once in position, those appointed may 'go native' and become part of the administrative machine – rather than agents of the president's will. As with relations with Congress, presidents soon find out that it is important to persuade, for they lack the power to command. In the frustrated words of President Truman: 'I thought I was the President, but when it comes to these bureaucracies I can't make 'em do a damn thing.'

The importance of political appointments can be exaggerated. They may seem to provide the president with an opportunity to change the direction and character of government policy, but in reality the number of appointments that he can make amounts to only a small percentage of those who work for the federal bureaucracy. For his first administration, President Clinton was able to nominate 222 personnel in the Department of Commerce, less than 1% of those working in the department; overall, he chose less than 0.2% of the total civilian, non-postal federal workforce. Moreover, the appointments have to be made in the brief period between the day of the presidential election and Inauguration Day. Inevitably, the presidents must concentrate their attention on appointments at cabinet level and leave many of the rest to other members of their team.

The American bureaucracy has a large degree of autonomy, each agency having its own clientele, power base and authority. Much of that authority derives from Congress, which creates or destroys agencies, authorises and approves reorganisation plans, defines powers and appropriates agency funds. Yet even Congress is unable to control the operation of bodies once they are established, and many of them have a life of their own. Walles[13] sees the bureaucracy as 'an active and largely independent participant in the political process, negotiating and bargaining with Congress, groups and the presidency alike'.

The presidential power of appointment

At one time, political appointees made up the vast majority of the federal bureaucracy. Appointments were made on the basis of patronage, 'who you knew, rather than what you knew', and membership of the successful party was important in gaining government jobs. Andrew Jackson (1829–37) developed the patronage system to its maximum extent, for he believed that 'to the victor go the spoils'. By the 'spoils system', employment was given to members of the party that won political office, not just as a reward for political support but also as a way of ensuring that many offices were opened up to ordinary citizens.

The Jacksonian approach survived for several decades and it helped to make the federal bureaucracy responsive to the needs of the White House. However, it later came to be associated with corruption. Congress tackled this problem by passing the Pendleton Act (1883), which limited the number of political appointments that a president could make and established a merit system for about 10% of federal jobs. This stressed ability, education and job performance as the key criteria for appointment, rather than political background. The merit system now applies to some 95% of federal civilian jobs.

Today, the president has an opportunity to influence the nature of the bureaucracy via his power of appointment over the most strategically important positions in government. He can nominate more than 3,000 senior civil servants to serve in the administration, and these include the heads of the fourteen major departments (the secretaries), as well as assistant and deputy departmental secretaries, deputy assistant secretaries and a variety of other appointive positions. Nearly 700 of the top presidential appointments have to be confirmed by the Senate. Once in office, their tenure depends on how the White House judges their performance.

The president is likely to choose personnel whom he regards as loyal and competent, and who share his political outlook. Abernach[14] notes that whereas in the past many appointees had been people who had established good connections with interest groups or congressional committees, in the Reagan era 'ideology was the key'. Before coming to office, he established an appointment system that ensured that appointees would be faithful to him and pursue his objectives of reduced governmental activity.

There are some 2,000 federal agencies, which are not directly amenable to presidential command or congressional directive! There is no collectivity of purpose, and the decisions and actions of one body may easily conflict with those of another. The Federal Reserve Board, which supervises the private banking system of the US and regulates the volume of credit and money in circulation, may pursue policies that are at variance with those of the administration, just as the secretary of the Treasury may publicly cross swords with the director of the OMB.

The types of organisation involved

The federal administration is organised around most of the same vital functions that exist in any other national bureaucracy. The administrative apparatus responsible for fulfilling them is divided into three broad categories:

1 *Government or executive departments*

The heads of departments (or ministries) are picked by the president and hold office at his pleasure. As we have seen, they constitute the American Cabinet, although they do not share collective responsibility for government policy as they do in Britain. There are fifteen cabinet-level departments, which vary greatly in size. They are subdivided into bureaux and smaller units, often on the basis of function. Within the Commerce Department, there is the Bureau of the Census, and others such as the Patent and Trademark Office.

By far the most important department is the State Department (see pp. 81–82 and 139), but others include the Treasury, the Defense Department, and the Justice and Interior departments. Others include Agriculture, Commerce, Labor, Health and Human Services, Education, Housing and Urban Development, Transportation and Energy.

2 *The independent agencies*

In addition to the executive departments, which are the major operating units of the federal government, there are many other agencies that help to keep the government and economy functioning smoothly. As they are not part of the executive departments they are often known as 'independent agencies'. They are powerful and important bodies in the executive branch: *in* it but not *of* it. They include several types of organisation, and have differing degrees of independence. They carry out functions laid down in statute, but have a complex set of formal and informal relationships with president and Congress, unlike those of a normal executive department.

These agencies vary considerably in character and purpose. Some provide special services either to the government or to the people (the forty or so **executive agencies**, such as the Veterans' Administration), whilst others are supervisory, monitoring sections of the economy (**regulatory commissions**, such as the Federal Reserve Board and the Environmental Protection Agency). Some have substantial independence, others rather less so. In many cases, the agencies have been created by Congress to tackle areas or issues that are too complex to come within the scope of ordinary legislation.

The independence of regulatory commissions is considerably greater than that of the executive agencies, this substantial autonomy having been

executive agencies

Executive agencies – such as the Agency for Toxic Substances and Disease Registry (ATSDR) – exist outside of the federal executive departments, but nonetheless carry out functions of the executive branch of government. While constitutionally part of the executive, they are independent of presidential control, usually because the president's power to dismiss agency personnel is limited.

regulatory commissions

Regulatory commissions have the federal government's authority to oversee and regulate by law a specified area of government activity. For example, the Nuclear Regulatory Commission is an independent federal agency which licenses and regulates nuclear power plants.

deliberately arranged by Congress. Regulatory commissions have a different function: they remove supervision of particular areas from presidential hands, and are run by independent boards of commissioners. Often there are only five to seven commissioners, who serve for a fixed term of anything varying from three to fourteen years.

Such commissions are part of the executive branch, but they are not under direct presidential control. When vacancies arise, the president appoints appropriate personnel. However, once their appointment has been confirmed by the Senate, incumbents have security of tenure, and remain in office until their term has expired. Commissioners are not responsible to the president for the work of the commission, and because of their autonomy they can pose considerable problems for any president. Such commissions are sometimes described as the 'headless fourth branch of government'.

Commissions have quasi-judicial and quasi-legislative functions, as well as executive ones. Their number grew considerably during the twentieth century, for as new problems arose so new machinery was needed to watch over developments and resolve situations. Congress established these commissions in a way designed to keep them free of White House influence. It has given them much power, but their relationship to the president is unclear. Any president will be concerned with their activities because of the way in which they regulate economic activity, but presidential power over them is limited, given their conditions of appointment.

A new president will be confronted with a complex number of commissions whose leading figures have been selected by a predecessor, and it may be two or three years before he or she can tip the balance of agency thinking by making new appointments on the retirement of existing officials. President Kennedy felt particularly limited by the fact that eight years of Republican patronage under Eisenhower meant that he was unable to get his own people into important offices, and direct policy along the lines he favoured. Crucially, the president lacks the power of dismissal over such appointees. Moreover, the legislation regulating the commissions requires that members should be drawn from both political parties, a further limitation on presidential control of their operations.

3 *Government corporations*

The United States avoided nationalisation of the type that was introduced in Britain by the postwar Labour government. However, the federal government has become involved in conducting numerous activities that are commercial or industrial in nature. For this purpose, the corporation has been seen as the most appropriate form to enable activities to be carried out according to commercial or industrial needs. The intention was to give those directing such corporations the same sort of freedom to take decisions as that enjoyed by a director of any private enterprise organisation. As such, they are a cross between business corporations and regular governmental agencies. Examples of corporations include the Panama Canal Company, the St Lawrence Seaway Development Corporation and the Tennessee Valley Authority (TVA).

These and other bodies have a huge annual turnover and are responsible for projects of massive importance. The attempt to allow them freedom of manoeuvre has not always worked, for as with British nationalised industries there is a temptation for the administration and Congress to seek to exert control over the decisions taken. The 1945 Government Corporation Control Act was passed to integrate them more closely into the normal machinery of the executive branch.

Making the bureaucracy function better; presidents and their bid for reform

The president is the chief executive. It is his responsibility to ensure that 'laws are faithfully executed'. Yet in spite of his formal authorities and titles that place him at the top of the bureaucracy, it is not easy for him to exercise control; bureaucrats seem to manage not to be controlled by presidents. Once they are secure in office, they learn how to avoid or neutralise the power emanating from the White House. Thus, when a president tries to change a bureau's policy, cut its budget or reorganise its structure, the chief and his or her congressional allies in Congress, in the press, in other agencies, in organised interest groups and among the public at large, will fight a rearguard action and extol the virtues of the agency's programme and its staff. The bureaucracy has also often successfully resisted reform. Most recently, the FBI, CIA and the US Immigration Service proved highly resistant to the reform efforts of the Bush administration in the wake of the 9/11 attacks.

In particular, presidents have often viewed the State Department as a slow-moving barrier to innovation, an inhibition to getting things done and a body that crushes new ideas and new thinking in favour of traditional ways of looking at the world. John F. Kennedy, for instance, felt that the State Department often got in his way. When offered advice by a colleague, Kennedy famously quipped: 'I agree with you, but I don't think the government will.'

Presidents understand the difficulties of their situation vis-à-vis the bureaucracy and are wary of confrontations with powerful individuals or groups of bureaucrats. They know the tactics that might be deployed against them. For this reason, reform of the bureaucracy is difficult to achieve. As soon as a proposal is made specific, its implications for particular groups are understood and they may then lobby against change.

Efforts to make the bureaucracy more efficient and more responsive are none the less regularly mentioned at election time, but they continue to run into difficulties. Ronald Reagan was deeply sceptical of bureaucrats and their work, and he committed to a series of changes. These included privatisation of some operations, contracting out, and handing over federal programmes to the states as part of the New Federalism project. The outcome was less dramatic than he had anticipated, but there were some successes, such as bringing in private-sector enterprise to root out inefficiency and waste. Inasmuch as cuts in personnel were made in areas such as welfare, they tended to be balanced by increases in staffing in the Justice, Defense and State departments.

The *Reinventing Government Report*, September 1993

In 1993, President Clinton gave Al Gore the task of reviewing the bureaucracy and making recommendations for promoting efficiency and flexibility, and improving morale. His National Performance Review (NPR) made several criticisms of the federal bureaucracy, including:
* the wastefulness of many governmental organisations;
* their traditional preoccupation with familiar working practices;
* the lack of incentive for them to experiment and innovate;
* the relative absence of penalties for inadequate performance.

The Gore Report (known as the *Reinventing Government Report*) made wide-ranging recommendations which among other things stressed the need to cut red tape, place more emphasis on customer service, give more authority to those operating at lower levels of employment and prune unnecessary expenditure. The broad thrust of the review was accepted, but it was less easy to command agreement when individual measures were to be implemented. Critics made the point that many changes were impossible to achieve, for it was not in the interest of Congress or the White House to insist on measures which were upsetting to groups of voters across the country.

The NPR has had some modest successes, not least in pruning the number of federal employees by more than 300,000, transforming the Federal Emergency Management Agency into a highly efficient disaster-relief unit and removing thousands of pages of governmental rules and regulations written in largely incomprehensible language. Progress was made and meaningful reform of the bureaucracy has occurred in recent years. But other factors have been at work besides the Gore review, notably:
* the ending of the Cold War. The reduction in personnel was at least in part related to the defence cuts which followed from the thaw in international relations;
* the fact that both parties supported the Government Performance and Results Act of 1993, which required every government agency to publicise its performance criteria, to enable Americans to have a more effective assessment of how well public bodies were performing;
* the political climate created by Republican stress on 'smaller government' following the 1994 mid-term elections. Promises were made to axe

departments such as Housing and Urban Development and Energy, but they were not abolished. More modest ambitions were to lessen the impact of the Food and Drug Administration and to privatise some NASA programmes; these were fulfilled. Overall, however, the changes made in the 1990s were fewer than many Republicans had wanted to see.

The term 'bureaucracy' conjures up an image of 'red tape' and inefficiency, and in the 1990s it was fashionable for many Americans to deride 'faceless bureaucrats' whose actions were wide -ranging and difficult to control. Anti-government politicians (many of whom were to be found in the Republican Party) were able to capitalise on this mood and urge the need for smaller government. There are problems in large and complex bureaucracies, for those working in them tend to acquire expertise in their own area and in the immediate problems confronting them, and also to extend their sphere of activity. Presidents have always found difficulty in ensuring that federal employees at all levels relate their expertise to the wider public interest. In the twentieth century, they initiated eleven reviews to try to make bureaucracy more responsive and efficient, and less costly and intrusive.

George W. Bush's Management Agenda

In 2001, President Bush created the President's Management Agenda (PMA), a bold plan to improve the management and performance of the federal government. In the PMA, the president focused on initiatives where reform was most needed, where there was the greatest opportunity for improvement and where practical solutions could be readily implemented. After the PMA programme was rolled out, the federal government concentrated on becoming more citizen centred and results oriented, more efficient and more effective, in an effort to ensure that the American people received the first-class programmes and services they deserved.

In order to increase the likelihood that the PMA initiatives would succeed, President Bush developed the President's Management Council. The council comprised executives from various federal agencies who convened monthly to discuss new issues, opportunities and best practices regarding the PMA. Its brief was to fulfil the Bush maxim: 'What matters in the end is completion. Performance. Results. Not just making promises, but making good on promises.'

The agenda emphasised regular performance reviews for departments, increased managerial flexibility and greater accountability for employees, in all cases drawing on techniques and models popular in the private sector. Reviews were established to examine five areas: human capital; financial accountability; competitive sourcing; e-government; and budget and performance integration.

An early assessment of President Obama's management agenda – written by a team of analysts, including industry and former government executives –

The bureaucracy in Britain and the United States: a comparison:

	Britain	United States
Key personnel	Permanent secretary and higher civil servants who serve for several years and acquire wealth of knowledge and expertise, derived from functioning under different party administrations.	No comparable job to permanent secretary; senior figures are political appointments of incoming administration.
Use of outside personal advisers	Less used in past, though recent governments have employed more in a bid to ensure that the political will of ministers is reinforced as they seek to impose a sense of direction on their departments. Act as minister's eyes and ears.	Secretaries of various departments surrounded by a coterie of appointees, political figures who help departmental heads to impose their will on the career civil servants below them. System most evident in Executive Office, especially White House Office, where advisers act as a counter-bureaucracy.
Traditional principles	British civil service noted for its permanence, neutrality and anonymity. Now less neutral and anonymous, with increasing comment about a 'politicisation' of service under Thatcher and Blair administrations. Senior civil servants now liable for interrogation by parliamentary select committees, making them more accountable.	Ninety-five percent permanent civil service, politically neutral, though appointments made by president undermine the idea. Political appointees not anonymous or neutral, but discussions between departmental heads and their advisers are kept secret to allow officials to 'think the unthinkable'. Never same reluctance to allow officials to appear before congressional committees.
Power and influence of bureaucracy	Increasing comment in recent years about influence of civil service over policy making. Suggestion that they wield real political power and dominate their political masters. But theory remains that civil servants advise and ministers decide. Minister takes praise or blame for conduct of department and its officials, answering in Parliament for what is done.	Bureaucracy not a single, monolithic institution, and various elements of bureaucracy differ in the degree of independence they exercise – for example bureaux in departments have great autonomy. Bureaucracy a powerful institution, large and complex, often seen as burdensome by American public. All senior members are appointed by the president, who can remove them, but once in office they often act independently.
Recent characteristics	Increased politicisation. Use of political appointees. Use of agencies and other unelected bodies. Appointment of chief executives in agencies in gift of government of the day	Characteristics of modern British bureaucracy long familiar in United States – for example politicisation/political advisers.

appeared in the Winter 2010 issue of the *Public Manager*, the journal of a not-for-profit and non-partisan organisation devoted to furthering knowledge and best practice at all levels of government. One article examines the Office of Personnel Management's (OPM) performance under Obama and OPM Director John Berry. It gave the administration no grade lower than B-minus for performance and resource management and an A-plus for leadership.

CONCLUSION

The president needs and gets support from a multitude of advisers – the vice-president, the Cabinet and the Executive Office of the President, which includes the smaller White House Office. The policies deriving from the decision makers in the executive branch are implemented by the federal bureaucracy, which has grown in size as its responsibilities have expanded. All who work in the area of making and carrying out governmental policy spend their time trying to match the expectations of a demanding electorate.

Presidents have regularly complained about the power of the permanent bureaucracy, and there are often tensions between the White House and the departments and agencies which are responsible for implementing presidential directives.

For the president, it can be a daunting task to impose his will. The power of the bureaucracy is informal, based on experience, expertise, information and group support. The sheer size of the bureaucracy is an obstacle. Although the president can appoint some of the personnel at its head, these are vastly outnumbered by the millions beyond presidential control. Hence the story told concerning the FDR presidency, of how Roosevelt awoke one morning, read a newspaper and then called in one of his aides, to whom he said:

> When I woke up this morning, the first thing I saw was a headline in the *New York Times*, to the effect that our navy was going to spend two billion dollars on a shipbuilding program. Here I am, the commander in chief of the navy having to read that for the first time in the press. Do you know what I said to that? I said 'Jesus Chr-rist.'

REFERENCES

1 As quoted in D. Broder and B. Woodward, *The Washington Post National Weekly Edition*, 2 February 1992
2 As quoted in T. Cronin and M. Genovese, *The Paradoxes of the American Presidency*, Oxford University Press, 2004
3 As quoted in T. Cronin and M. Genovese, as in 2 above

4 R. Reich, *Locked in the Cabinet*, Knopf, 1997
5 H. Kissinger, *White House Years*, Little Brown, 1979
6 D. Kearns, *Lyndon Johnson and the American Dream*, Harper & Row, 1976
7 H. Truman, Message to Congress, 19 December 1945
8 H. Gosnell, *Harry S. Truman*, Greenwood Press, 1980
9 As quoted in T. Cronin and M. Genovese, 2 above
10 C. Rossiter, *The American Presidency*, Harcourt Brace, 1960
11 R. Maidment and D. McGrew, *The American Political Process*, Sage/Open University, 1992
12 J. Burns, J. Peltason, T. Cronin and D. Magleby, *Government by the People*, Prentice Hall, 1994
13 M. Walles, *British and American Systems of Government*, P. Allan, 1988
14 J. Abernach, 'The President and the Executive Branch', in C. Campbell and B. Rockman (eds), *The Bush Presidency: First Appraisals*, Chatham House, 1991

USEFUL WEB SITES

www.whitehouse.gov/ Official presidential site for the White House. Useful for following the day-to-day activities of the president, including daily briefings and press releases. Also useful on the tasks assigned to the vice-president and for a listing of EOP entities.

www.usgovinfo.about.com/ Browse the section on the president and Cabinet; listing of departments and secretaries of the Cabinet.

See also individual departments, such as the Department of State at **www.state.gov/**.

SAMPLE QUESTIONS

1 'In this, I am nothing, but I may be everything' (John Adams). Evaluate the role and importance of the vice-presidency, in the light of this remark.
2 How successfully do presidents direct and coordinate the work of their administrations?
3 Examine the evolution and present importance of the Executive Office of the President.
4 How important has the Cabinet been in the era of modern American government?
5 Should we be concerned that White House staffers have displaced members of the Cabinet as the president's closest advisers?
6 Which is the more useful to the president, the Cabinet or the Executive Office?
7 Examine the part played by the federal bureaucracy in government and policy making in the United States.
8 Assess the attempts made by the Clinton and George W. Bush administrations to modernise and streamline the workings of the federal bureaucracy.

Congress

6

Congress is a bicameral legislature, comprising two bodies, the Senate and the House of Representatives. They are both directly elected law-making chambers. They have broadly equal powers, the Senate being the most powerful upper house in the world. Although representation and law-making are its primary roles, Congress also has other duties. For example, the Senate approves or rejects the US President's choices for the heads of government departments, Supreme Court justices and certain other high-ranking jobs. The Senate also approves or rejects treaties that the president makes.

In this chapter, we investigate the role and status of Congress and its members in the American system of government, the way it is organised, the attempts at reform in the past and proposals for further reform in the future.

POINTS TO CONSIDER

- How is Congress constituted?
- Why might an ambitious American politician prefer to serve in the Senate rather than the House of Representatives?
- What are the major stages through which legislative proposals must pass before they become law?
- What factors influence members of Congress as they make legislative decisions?
- How important is the role of congressional committees?
- How might Congress be usefully reformed?
- What are the social characteristics of members of Congress? In what respects have they undergone change in recent years?
- In what ways do the duties and responsibilities of US congressmen coincide and conflict with those of Members of Parliament?
- How do the memberships of Congress and Parliament compare in terms of age, gender, race and social background?

How Congress is organised

Congress is bicameral. In other words, it has two chambers:
- **The Senate** consists of two senators from each of the fifty states.
- **The House of Representatives** has 435 members. Members of the House of Representatives are elected from congressional districts of about equal

---

APPORTIONMENT OF MEMBERSHIP IN THE HOUSE OF REPRESENTATIVES

Apportionment is the process of dividing the 435 seats in the House of Representatives across the country. A reapportionment has been made on the basis of each decennial census from 1790 to 2000 (except following the 1920 census), in line with the growth or decline of population in each of the fifty states.

The average size of a **congressional district** based on the 2010 census is 710,767, more than triple the average district size of 193,167 based on the census taken in 1900. Of the seven states with one seat, Montana is the largest, having a population of 994,416.

> **Congressional district**
> An area established by law for the election of a representative to the House of Representatives.

Wyoming, which also has one seat, is the smallest congressional district, having a population of only 568,300. Overall, eighteen states were affected by change. Eight states were granted additional representation and ten lost out in the process of reallocation. The changes become effective in time for the 2012 presidential election, provided that there are no significant legal challenges to them.

After the number of seats assigned to each state is determined (apportionment), the task of drawing House districts (redistricting) is up to the state governors and legislatures, who have often used these powers to advantage their own party and penalise their opponents. In the past, malapportionment (large differences in the populations of congressional districts) was common in many areas of the country. Districts could be devised in such a way that minority party districts included more votes than majority party districts, so that each minority party voter would count for less. For instance, in Michigan (1960) the sixteenth district had 802,999 inhabitants whereas the twelfth had only 177,431.

The two main malpractices are packing (drawing up a district so that it has a large majority of supporters, to make it safe) and cracking (splitting up an opponents' supporters into minorities in a number of districts, in order to lessen their impact). Such practices are often referred to as gerrymandering, a technique named after Governor Elbridge Gerry of Massachusetts. It is said that one of the constituencies he created had the shape of a lizard. 'Why, this district looks like a salamander!' remarked an observer. 'Say rather a Gerrymander', replied an opposition 'wit'.

Malapportionment has long been criticised by reformers, who were supported in their efforts by a Supreme Court judgment in 1964. In the case of *Reynold* v. *Sims*, the nine justices held that legislative districts at both the state and national levels should be as close to equal in population as possible, so that each individual was weighted equally in legislative apportionment and the principle of 'one person, one vote' was maintained. Yet controversy continues, being notably a feature of the post-1990 census. North Carolina's legislators created a twelfth district that snaked across thirteen counties in half the state,

population into which the states are divided (see the box on apportionment). Every state must have at least one House seat. For example, Alabama has two senators and seven House seats, Delaware two senators and one House seat, and New York State two senators and twenty-nine House seats. Representatives are often called congressmen or congresswomen, though technically the term applies to senators as well.

---

in a bid to include as many black voters as possible. This ploy, by the controlling Republicans, helped to lessen support in surrounding districts for the Democrats, because they contained fewer Democrat-voting minorities.

Figures on apportionment adapted from those provided by the Bureau of the Census.

The representation of Washington DC

One area of the United States mainland – Washington DC, the federal capital – has no governor, state legislature or voting representation in Congress. It has one non-voting delegate in the House and has three votes in the Electoral College.

Washington is run like a state, but has only a mayor and city council (a largely power-less body). Its budget and social policies are determined by the federal government, as is true of territories such as Guam, Puerto Rico and the Virgin Islands. But although the capital looks and acts like a state, many of its residents believe that as US citizens they are being denied their constitutional rights.

A constitutional amendment proposed in 1978 was designed to give it voting represen-tation, but it was not ratified by a sufficient number of states and therefore 'died' in 1985. A petition requesting admission to the Union as the fifty-first state was filed in Congress in 1983 and new statehood bills were introduced ten years later. The campaign for full voting rights and statehood continues.

Arguments over representation

Opponents of District of Columbia (DC) voting rights argue that the Founding Fathers never intended that District residents should have votes in Congress, because the Constitution makes it clear that representation must come from the states. Those opposed to making DC a state claim that such a move would destroy the notion of a separate national capital and that statehood would unfairly grant Senate representation to a single city.

DC residents seek statehood because it is the most appropriate mechanism to grant US citizens who reside there the full rights and privileges of American citizenship. These rights would include not only full voting rights in the House of Representatives and the Senate, but also full control over local affairs.

The United States is the only nation in the world with a representative democratic con-stitution that denies voting representation in the national legislature to the citizens of the capital.

The Democrats and the Republicans have long been the only major parties in Congress. In each chamber, the party with more members is the **majority** party, the other the **minority** one. Before each new session of Congress, Republicans and Democrats in each house meet in what is called a caucus or conference to choose party leaders and to consider legislative issues and plans.

The role of speaker in the House of Representatives

Members of the majority party in the House choose the speaker in a party caucus (gathering of party members) at the beginning of each two-year session of Congress. The person chosen is not necessarily the oldest or longest serving, but is usually someone who commands respect and has served a lengthy apprenticeship in other party offices in the House.

The speaker's is the only House role mentioned – although not described – in the Constitution. As presiding officer of the lower chamber, he or she fulfils several functions including opening each session, ruling on procedural matters, deciding who shall speak and referring bills to committees. Beyond this, he or she has several powers of appointment, including membership of the Rules Committee and of ad hoc committees that may be created. The speaker is third in line to the presidency, should the president and vice-president resign, be impeached or killed. Because of this, he or she is expected to inform the White House of his or her whereabouts at all times. He or she also represents the House on ceremonial occasions.

The two most recent Republican incumbents were Newt Gingrich and Dennis Hastert. Taking over in January 1995 after the Republican success in the mid-term elections of the previous November, Newt Gingrich became the first Republican speaker for forty years. His period of office was highly influential. He was concerned not only to make the lower chamber operate more efficiently, but also to introduce a system of party government within the chamber. Accordingly, he:

- ushered in several rule changes;

- tightened the coordination of activities among House leaders;

- limited the number of subcommittees within each committee and reorganised several committee jurisdictions;

- introduced greater cohesion among the Republicans, so that in the first hundred days of his speakership the 'Contract for America' programme was pushed through the House with an average of only five dissenting voices on thirty-three roll-call votes;

- handpicked committee and subcommittee chairs, often ignoring the claims of seniority; chairs were to be limited to six years' service in future, in order to prevent their becoming too powerful and independent;

- created taskforces of carefully chosen colleagues to consider issues and make proposals, and thereby bypass the characteristic blockages often found within the committee system;

Committees form an important feature of each chamber's organisation. They prepare the bills to be voted on. The committee system divides the work of processing legislation and enables members to specialise in particular types of issues. The majority party in each chamber elects the head of each committee and holds a majority of the seats on most committees.

- freed himself from the day-to-day business of running the House by handing over such tasks to the House Majority Leader, so that he was able to concentrate on determining the party agenda;
- used frequent media appearances to turn his office into a powerful role from which he could advance an alternative and more conservative programme than that of the president.

By virtue of his forceful personality and the backing he received from several freshmen Republicans, Gingrich became the most powerful speaker of modern times. But his tenure did not last long and he did not achieve all that he hoped. Aspects of the 'Contract for America' programme stalled because of opposition in the Senate. Moreover, his personal brand of leadership created enemies who disliked the concentration of power in his hands. This led to his downfall shortly after disappointing mid-term elections in 1998. After four years, the mantle of leadership was taken up by Dennis Hastert, a legislator with no national profile at the time.

The Hastert approach to the speakership was traditional in its mode of operation. More of a conciliator, he sought a consensus. By spending more time in the chamber and involving himself in legislative details and procedures, he opted for a 'return to regular order'.[1] Although, at the time, his appointment was expected to be a short-lived affair, he none the less outlasted his more high-profile predecessor.

The speaker from 2007 to 2011 was the Democrat Nancy Pelosi the first woman, the first Californian and the first Italian American to hold the speakership. She was also a self-confessed liberal. Republicans and their allies in the media criticised her political positions and voting record and sought to portray her as the embodiment of everything they disliked about their opponents. They disapproved of her alleged willingness to raise taxes and her 'soft line' on help for illegal immigrants and backing for same-sex marriage. In the early days of the 111th Congress, she worked with President Obama to pass the American Recovery and Reinvestment Act, designed to provide relief for American families and to create or save 3.5 million jobs.

The speaker in the 112th Congress is John Boehner, a Republican from Ohio. He is the sixty-first occupant of the speakership.

As we have seen, the speaker is a highly influential figure, possessing considerable power via his or her control over the majority party and influence over how the committee system operates. This is why more powerful holders of the office, such as Gingrich, have sometimes been referred to as the equivalent of prime ministers.

The vice-president serves as head of the Senate and presides over its proceedings. In fact, he or she usually only appears on special occasions or to break a tie, and for everyday work the Senate elects a president pro tempore to serve in the vice-president's absence. The speaker of the House serves as presiding officer and party leader. He or she is chosen by the majority party, the choice then being ratified by the whole chamber. The speaker is the most important member of Congress, because of the broad powers the post provides within the assembly (see box on pp. 148–149).

A new Congress is organised every two years. Voters elect all the Representatives at that time, and a third of the Senators come up for election every two years. The Senate is therefore a continuing, stable body because its membership is never completely new. The two chambers elected in November 2010 form the 112th Congress.

The 112th Congress: party representation in January 2011

	Democrats	Republicans	Independents
House	193	242	0
Senate	51	47	2*

* Both caucusing with the Democrats.

Each house of Congress has the power to introduce legislation on any subject, except revenue bills, which must originate in the House of Representatives. The large states may thus appear to have more influence over the public purse than the small states. In practice, however, each chamber can vote against legislation passed by the other house. The Senate may disapprove a House revenue bill – or any bill, for that matter – or add amendments that change its nature. In that event, a conference committee made up of members from both houses must work out a compromise acceptable to both sides before the bill becomes law.

The concurrent and exclusive powers of the two chambers

Type of powers	House	Senate
Concurrent (both chambers involved)	Pass legislation Override presidential veto Begin process of amending constitution Declaration of war Confirm choice of newly appointed vice-president	
Exclusive	Introduction of money bills Initiation of impeachment procedure Election of president, should there be deadlock in Electoral College	Confirmation of appointments and ratification of treaties (known as the 'Advice and Consent' role) Staging of impeachment trials Election of vice-president, should there be deadlock in Electoral College

The Senate also has certain powers especially reserved to that body, including the authority to confirm presidential appointments of high officials of the federal government, as well as to ratify all treaties by a two-thirds vote. Unfavourable action in either instance nullifies the wishes of the executive.

In the case of impeachment of federal officials, the House has the sole right to bring charges of misconduct that can lead to an impeachment trial. The Senate has the sole power to try impeachment cases, and to find officials guilty or not guilty. A finding of guilt results in the removal of the federal official from public office.

The eighteen broad powers of the whole Congress are spelled out in the eighth section of the first article of the Constitution. The first seventeen are specific duties, but the eighteenth sets out the task of making 'all Laws which shall be necessary and proper for carrying into execution the foregoing Powers, and all other Powers vested by this Constitution in the Government of the United states, or in any Department or Officer thereof'.

THE POWERS OF THE HOUSE AND OF THE SENATE

The two primary functions of Congress are to represent the will of the people and to make laws for the country. The two tasks overlap, for if the laws do not represent the people's wishes then the law makers may suffer defeat at the next election.

Which chamber has the higher status?

Whereas, in Britain, one chamber is dominant, this is not so in the United States. In powers, they are virtually co-equal, having some concurrent powers (as in the passing of legislation or in overriding a presidential veto) and some exclusive ones. Many commentators would argue that the Senate's responsibilities with regard to treaties and ratification of appointments give it a greater degree of authority. Even the restriction that all bills on revenue raising must originate in the House is hardly a limitation, as the Senate has the same full power of amendment as it has with other types of bill.

Indicative perhaps of the Senate's higher status is the fact that candidates for the presidency and vice-presidency tend to come from the upper house (or after serving a period in office as a state governor). Few come from the House of Representatives. Senators tend to get higher levels of media coverage and so find it easier to build personal reputations. More of them are known nationwide, the names of Elizabeth Dole, Edward Kennedy, John Kerry and John McCain all being recognisable well beyond the confines of their states. Richard Pear[2] has elaborated in this way:

> Great senators have made the Senate great, and have influenced the course of American history in ways which can be recorded in the history books . . . [Some] sitting for safe seats have spent their lives in the Senate, becoming the embodiment of national or regional thinking on certain topics. Great senators are competitors for the limelight with presidents. They know their power and can use it for long-term objectives.

An important difference is the length of service of a senator and a representative. Senators have the opportunity to acquire a working knowledge of their subjects of concern, without the problem of constantly having to campaign for their return to Washington. They can take part in a genuine debate rather than speaking and listening with the likely reactions of the voters in mind. Also, they have been elected by the whole state rather than a district within it. For instance, senators Scott Brown (R) and John Kerry (D) represent the entire state of Massachusetts, whereas Ed Markey is the Democrat House representative for the Seventh District.

By comparison, members of the House are at a disadvantage. Maidment and McGrew[3] quote the example of one newly elected representative, who described his four years in the House in this way: 'The first two years, I spent all of my time getting re-elected.' Two years is perhaps too short a time in which to achieve anything substantial. For this reason, membership of the lower chamber is not a particularly satisfying form of activity, nor a particularly honoured position. Every two years, there are some representatives who do not seek re-election, but return from whence they came. Some are put off by the nature of their work, which they may find unrewarding. Little can be achieved by a 'freshman' unless the committee on which he or she serves suddenly bursts into prominence because of a sensational investigation or contentious bill. For many of them, the job leads no further. If they wish to advance their careers, they may well seek a seat in the Senate. Senators, by contrast, do not look for an opportunity to enter the House.

Americans are healthily sceptical about all those who represent them in Washington, and all politicians are held in low esteem. They tend to have a higher regard for those who have improved themselves by their own industry and perseverance in the fields of business, law and the other professions, rather than for those who operate in government.

The functions of Congress

The overall role of Congress is extensive. As with any other Western democracy, it performs a key representative task. People choose representatives to make decisions for them, and if they do not like the decisions made they can reject those previously chosen at the next election. In this way, a link between the people and the national government is formed, and the consent of the governed is achieved. **Representation** is a difficult concept, and is open to a number of interpretations, but it involves the basic idea that legislators are responsive to those who put them in their position (see box).

representation

The term has several meanings in political science. Usually, it means the authority to act on behalf of another, as gained through the process of election; in this sense, the representative acts to safeguard and promote the interests of the area represented. It can also mean the extent to which a representative mirrors or is typical of the characteristics of the person he or she formally represents – for example is the House representative: does it have an appropriate balance of women and ethnic minority members? (see pp. 178–180).

The role of representation

The House of Representatives was originally viewed by the framers of the Constitution as the chamber that would represent the wishes of the mass of the people. The Senate, not directly elected, was seen as a more detached, dispassionate body that could operate as a check upon the House, which was liable to be influenced by considerations of short-term popularity. When direct election of the Senate was introduced, the House lost its unique position as the body reflecting the mood of the mass electorate. Since 1913, both chambers can claim to be representative of the people.

The importance attached to this function of representation is one of the distinguishing features of Congress, compared with other legislatures. The Senate and the House have always attached the highest priority to the attitudes and concerns of those who elected them; considerations such as party figure much less in their thinking.

Much of the work of Congress takes place within committees, rather than on the 'floor' of the House or Senate. Its day-to-day tasks can be conveniently classified according to three main headings: legislation, investigation and finance. The legislative role is the prime function, for it affects the lives of the American people most directly. An efficient and responsive legislature has the power to further national goals at home and abroad, by the way in which it handles its law-making task.

Legislative work

Bills are introduced by a variety of methods. Some are drawn up in standing committees, some by special committees created to examine specific legislative issues, and some may be urged by the president or other executive officers. Individuals and outside organisations may suggest legislation to congressmen, and individual members may themselves have ideas they wish to see pass into law.

Such is the volume of legislation proposed by senators and representatives that much of it has no chance of getting any further. It is introduced in the first place more as a way of securing the goodwill of lobbyists or constituents than with any expectation of further progress. After the initial introduction, the leadership sends bills to designated committees, where many of them die. Ninety per cent of those before a subcommittee get no further, for lack of time or lack of support. This is the justification for the existence of committees. They act as a screening mechanism for the flood of measures presented, and thereby prevent the Senate and House being overwhelmed.

For those bills with significant backing, the committee schedules a series of public hearings that may last for weeks or months and that allow for outside input

COMMITTEES IN CONGRESS: MAIN TYPES

Writing in *Congressional Government*, Woodrow Wilson[4] (later to become a Democrat president) argued that 'Congress in session is Congress on public exhibition, whilst Congress in its committee rooms is Congress at work.' Committees are indeed the principal means via which the House and Senate carry out their legislative duties. In the 112th Congress, there are 20 permanent committees in the Senate and 21 in the House, with 74 and 105 subcommittees respectively. The smallest committee in the Senate is the Ethics Committee (6 members) and in the House the Administration Committee (9). The largest committee in the Senate is the Appropriations Committee (30) and in the House the Transportation and Infrastructure Committee (62).

There are several types of committee, notably:

1 Standing committees

Standing committees are by far the most important committees of both chambers, the focus of much of the work performed by the legislature. They are permanent, having fixed jurisdictions that operate from one session of Congress to another. In the House, the Rules Committee (see p. 156) has a crucial role, with the power to delay or even stop legislation. The Ways and Means Committee raises money; the Appropriations Committee deals with how government spends that money. Many members of the House Budget Committee are drawn from these two bodies, with one member from each of the other standing committees. In the Senate, the Appropriations, Budget, Finance and Foreign Affairs committees are prestigious. Membership of the committees mentioned is highly prized and congressmen and senators may have to wait years to get assigned to them. Usually, congressmen serve on one or two standing committees only, whereas in the smaller Senate members are expected to serve on three or four.

Most standing committees spawn subcommittees. The House and Senate Appropriations committees each have twelve. The standing committees carry out the committee stage of the legislative process, holding hearings and taking evidence from witnesses who might be representatives of the administration, pressure groups or even ordinary members of the public. They also conduct investigations within their broad policy area, ascertaining – among other things – why problems occurred, whether legislation is working and what

from interested bodies. The subcommittee then discusses and amends the bill, and – assuming there is a vote in its favour – the bill is sent ('reported') to the full chamber, where it is debated and again a vote occurs. (In the House, the bill will first go to the Rules Committee (see p. 156), which determines the time limits to be allowed and decides whether or not amendments from the floor will be permitted.)

Usually, both chambers consider their own bills, at approximately the same time. To succeed, the approval of both the Senate and the House is necessary. If there

action might be taken. In the Senate, they additionally carry out the role of 'advice and consent' (see p. 150).

2 Select and special committees

There is no substantive difference between select and special committees. They may be asked to study or report on a particular topic, but they do not receive or report bills. Their investigations are often time consuming and detailed, and tend to cover areas that would not be catered for in the investigative capacity of standing committees. They are temporary bodies that cease to exist once their final reports have been submitted, unless specifically renewed at the beginning of each new Congress.

An example taken from the Clinton years is the Senate Committee on Whitewater, established in the 104th Congress. It was given the task of uncovering any illegal activity in the president's involvement in a failed Arkansas real estate project back in the 1980s. Today, there are a Special Committee on Aging and a Select Committee on Intelligence.

3 Joint committees

Permanent bodies, these include members drawn from both houses and have continuing oversight of a particular area of policy (for example taxation) or housekeeping matter (for example printing). The Joint Economic Committee has the important tasks of studying and reporting on the president's annual economic report. Joint committees may also initiate legislation.

4 Conference committees

Again drawn from both houses, these are temporary committees charged with resolving the differences between legislative proposals dealing with the same topic. These differences come about because of amendments attached to the bill by one chamber but not the other, or because the two houses have passed different bills relating to the same subject. Before a bill goes to the president, both chambers must pass it in identical language.

are differences in the versions passed, then a conference committee will seek a compromise.

The bill must have successfully endured the procedure of both houses, and have been approved in identical form, for it to become law. If this does not happen in the lifetime of one Congress, the attempt has failed: the whole process needs to be started again.

At this point, the bill goes to the White House for the approval of the president. He may sign it, veto it or do nothing. If Congress is sitting and he does

The House Rules Committee

The House Rules Committee of only thirteen members is the most influential committee in the lower chamber. Comprising some of the most senior members of the House and having a 2:1 membership in favour of the majority party, it organises the timetable of the House and thereby effectively determines the fate of proposed legislation. The dominance of the majority party reflects the Committee's status in recent decades as an arm of the leadership and as legislative gatekeeper.

The committee decides on a rule, which sets the time limit for debate and states whether amendments can be allowed on the floor of the House. It may decide that there can be debate and amendments subject to the overall time available ('open rule') or it may limit debate and insist that only members of the reporting committee may offer amendments ('closed rule', usually used only for tax and spending bills). Normally, without such a rule, the bill will not reach the floor.

Before Congress was reformed in the 1970s, the committee was even more powerful than is the modern one. The 'old guard' (a coalition of southern Democrats and Republicans) used their influence to block proceedings. The committee was then much disliked by liberals and those who wanted to see reform; they saw it as dictatorial and unrepresentative.

Today, the committee is less controversial and more representative of the membership of the majority party. If it wants a bill to be passed, the committee can expedite its passage by sending it quickly to the floor of the House for immediate debate.

NB The Senate Committee on Rules and Administration is less powerful than its counterpart in the House, having a more administrative role. There are no official time limits for debate and the legislative procedure is usually determined on a more consensual basis between the majority and minority party leaders.

nothing, then after ten working days the bill becomes law without his signature. If the Congress has adjourned and the president waits ten days before signing, then this is a pocket veto. Other than in this case, a vetoed bill is returned to the Congress, with the reasons for rejection. The presidential veto can be overturned, if both chambers can muster a two-thirds majority against it.

Figures produced some years ago by Professor Davidson[5] showed that on average only about 3% of bills received by the president were vetoed and only about 4% of all presidential vetoes up to and including George Bush senior were overridden by Congress. (The experiences of presidents Nixon, Ford, Reagan and George W. Bush highlight the difficulties of some post-1945 Republican presidents – particularly when faced with Democrat predominance in Congress.) Presidents have chosen to veto a particular bill for several reasons – perhaps because it differs from their own legislative preferences, or because they feel it is unconstitutional, costs too much, or is hard to enforce.

The legislative procedure of Congress has often been described as an 'obstacle course', for bills have to get past the appropriate standing committee, be given time by the Rules Committee and then survive the debate on the floor of the House or Senate. To have got this far, there must have been a substantial degree of support, but in the Senate this is no mere formality and the bill can always be subject to a **filibuster**, by which senators hold the floor of the chamber, speak at length and seek to delay proceedings to avoid a vote being taken. The aged Strom Thurmond holds the record: in seeking to delay the 1957 Civil Rights Act, he spoke for 24 hours 18 minutes!

> **filibuster**
> A device that enables a senator or group of senators to kill a bill by the use of delaying tactics. As there is unlimited debate in the Senate, they can carry on talking for as long as they wish. Only a cloture vote of 60% can end a filibuster and there has not been a successful one for more than twenty-five years. The word filibuster derives from the Spanish word meaning 'pirate', one who plunders freely. Filibusters are part of the normal political process, a means by which a legislative minority can prevent a vote.

It is not surprising that few bills successfully navigate the procedure. In the 106th Congress (1999–2001), just over 5% of those introduced went on to become law. For the two years of the 110th Congress (2007–9), the overall success rate dropped to under 4% (1.5% and 5.8%, in 2007 and 2008, respectively). It dropped again in the 111th Congress, to an average for the two years of 2.5%.

Percentage of bills/resolutions introduced and enacted into law:
selected years 1996–2010

	Introduced	Passed
1996	2,759	8.9
2000	4,247	9.7
2004	3,656	8.2
2008	4,815	5.8
2009	9,071	1.4
2001 (as of 30 November 2010)	4,358	3.7

Based on figures provided in the *Resume of Congressional Activity*, 2 January 2010 and for 2010 provided on TheCapitolNet at www.thecapitol.net.

The legislative procedure is not without advantages. The separation of powers is there to stop the domination of one section of the governmental machinery by another, and the law-making process reflects this aim of preventing tyranny. It is impossible for the whips to force through changes at the wish of the executive branch, and there is no elective dictatorship of the type often said to exist in Britain. Instead, those who seek to get a bill passed onto the statute book need to build a consensus in its support, and if it does pass it is likely to have substantial backing. The system offers a built-in advantage to those who would thwart legislation, which is why Denenberg[6] describes Congress as 'a bastion of negation'. The legislative procedure enables a dissenting minority

The presidential veto

After passing through both houses of Congress, bills are sent to the White House for the president to sign. If the president fails to act within ten days (excepting Sundays), a bill automatically becomes law. But in the last ten days of a session, a failure to act amounts to a pocket veto; in other words, as Congress is not sitting and cannot fight back, the bill is effectively killed.

When a president vetoes a bill within the allotted time, Congress can override the decision, as long as two-thirds of those present in each chamber support the initiative. Presidents

Number of vetoes and overrides for presidents 1933–2011

President	Number of bills vetoed	Number and percentage of vetoes overridden
F. Roosevelt (1933–45)	635	9 (1.4%)
H. Truman	250	12 (4.8%)
D. Eisenhower (1953–61)	181	2 (1.1%)
J. Kennedy	21	0 (0%)
L. Johnson (1963–69)	30	0 (0%)
R. Nixon (1969–74)	43	7 (16.3%)
G. Ford	66	12 (18.2%)
J. Carter	31	2 (6.5)
R. Reagan (1981–89)	78	9 (11.5%)
G.H. Bush	44	1 (2.3)
B. Clinton (1993–2001)	37	2 (5.4%)
G.W. Bush	12	4 (33.0%)
B. Obama*	2	0 (0%)
Total for all presidents	2,564	110 (4.3%)

Source: Figures adapted from those available from the Research Division, Congressional Quarterly, Washington, DC.
* As of 31 May 2011.

to prevent the passage of bills by obstructing them at several access points – and thereby kill the proposal off.

The legislative process is lengthy and complex, there being so many obstacles that a bill may fail to overcome. It is not surprising that so few bills survive this 'legislative labyrinth' and become law, for the odds are stacked heavily against success. Because of the number of bills introduced, the standing committees – to whom so much power is given – are overwhelmed. Much depends on the drive and forcefulness of the committee chairpersons. It also helps if the two chambers are under the control of the same party, as in the era of Republic predominance since November 1994. But even when the majority has been more cohesive, as in recent years, there is no certainty that members will vote with their parties in support of the legislative programme.

know that Congress only very rarely successfully overrides their vetoes, so the mere threat of using the veto is often enough to enable them to extract concessions from the legislature. As long as the power is sometimes used, the threat is a credible one. Presidents vary in their use of the veto, some using it extensively, as the figures suggest.

For many years, critics of the procedure argued that the presidential veto was a blunt weapon, for the president either had to sign or reject an entire bill. Knowing this, congressmen sometimes attached extra (and unpalatable) provisions (riders) to a bill that they knew the president really wanted. By so doing, they were trapping him, for he either had to sign the whole bill with the unwanted features, or lose it altogether. After much discussion, Congress finally passed a line-item veto in 1996, giving the president the power to veto 'objectionable' parts of an appropriations (expenditure) bill whilst agreeing to the rest of it. This innovation was soon tested in the Supreme Court. In *Clinton* v. *New York* (June 1998), the judges were asked to decide whether Bill Clinton's rejection of some aspects of a tax bill was legitimate. They concluded that the line-item veto was unconstitutional, in that it violated the requirement that any bill must pass both houses and be signed by the president in the same form. If the president was allowed to strike out particular features, then in effect a new bill was being created.

The loss of the line-item veto means that presidents are left with one weaker power which they can employ if they are unhappy with a piece of legislation. Having signed the bill, they can withhold the funds (impoundment) appropriated by Congress for its implementation. Generally, impoundment has been used sparingly, but President Nixon used it regularly against a Democrat-dominated Congress, both as a means of controlling spending and as a means of controlling its behaviour. Congress responded by passing the Budget and Impoundment Control Act in 1974 (see pp. 170–171). This laid down restrictions on the presidential use of impoundment. What remains is a much weakened alternative to the defunct line-item veto.

If in a crisis the machinery is often less responsive than the situation demands, there are none the less exceptions. Franklin Roosevelt and Lyndon Johnson, each aided by a Congress controlled by his own party, were able to introduce a package of measures speedily. So too was President Obama able to work with Speaker Pelosi to smooth the passage of the stimulus package contained in the American Recovery and Reinvestment Act in 2009. Introduced on 26 January, it passed through the House two days later. Although 206 amendments were scheduled for floor votes, they were combined into only eleven, which enabled quicker processing of the bill. No Republicans in the House and only three Republican senators voted for the bill, but it was signed into law on 17 February.

THE ROLE OF THE ADMINISTRATION IN LEGISLATION

The amount and character of legislation has changed significantly over the years. In the 1960s and 1970s, there was a burst of legislative action, but in the following decade the pace of change – especially on substantive issues – slowed down.

Federal governments cannot in theory make laws, and their proposals have no priority in congressional procedure. Presidents can propose legislation, but if congressional leaders prefer their own, then the White House has no means of redress. Departments, in consultation with committee chairpersons and party leaders, draw up the measures seen as desirable. They are then introduced by sympathetic members.

Although most successful legislation now originates in the executive branch, the administration cannot be sure of its passage in the form that it favours. Whereas in Britain the system of party discipline ensures that a government with a parliamentary majority may get its way, this is not the case in the US. Presidents cannot depend on congressional support, and Congress remains a major force in determining the shape and timing of legislation.

The president and Congress: cooperation in the legislative arena

The separation of powers and the divided government that it involves present an obstacle to policy making. They set the scene for a continuous struggle, although the Constitution requires the two branches to work together. The administration and Congress can legislate when the president and congressional leaders bargain and compromise. President Johnson was skilled in this process, for as an ex-Senate majority leader he understood the need for the White House to build bridges with his former colleagues. He urged his aides and cabinet members to get to know more about the key figures on Capitol Hill and what mattered to them. What was sometimes known as the 'Johnson treatment' 'ran the gamut of human emotions', from accusation and cajolery to tears and threats. Writing of the relationship with congressmen, two journalists, Evans and Novak[7], noted the technique:

> Johnson anticipated them before [interjections] could be spoken. He moved in close, his face a scant millimeter from his target, his eyes widening and narrowing, his eyebrows rising and falling. From his pockets poured slips, memos, statistics. Mimicry, humor and the genius of analogy made The Treatment an almost hypnotic experience and rendered the target stunned and helpless.

But Johnson had more than personal skills working to his advantage. He was president at a time of strong Democrat majorities in both chambers. Some of his more recent successors would have been delighted to receive such party backing. Moreover, his opponents were less ideologically driven and cohesive than has been the case over the last decade or so. In today's circumstances, a president needs to be in regular consultation with his opponents, as well as his supporters. The Clinton experience, following the Republican victory in the mid-term elections of November 1994, showed that to rescue his legislative proposals, he needed cooperation and agreement. When he obtained this, his success record improved (other than in the year of impeachment proceedings), as the figures indicate:

Year	%
1993	86.4
1994	86.4
1995	36.2
1996	55.1
1997	56.6
1998	51.0
1999	37.8
2000	55.0

The legislative success of presidents Bush and Obama

In his first year, George W. Bush achieved a success rate of 87%, almost identical to that achieved by Clinton in the equivalent period. He did even better the following year, scoring 88%. He had a thin legislative agenda that he pursued with modest vigour, whereas his predecessor had a more difficult ride, not least because he had a busy programme on which he was seeking to drive a reluctant Congress to take action. Moreover, Bush took fewer public policy positions, often taking a stand only when the intentions of Congress had already become clear. He could then support a bill drafted in a form that he knew was likely to pass. By the end of his administration, following the setbacks in the November 2006 mid-term elections, his success rate fell to approximately the same figure as that achieved by Clinton in his seventh year.

In 2009, President Obama racked up the highest presidential support score in Congress since *Congressional Quarterly* inaugurated its study in 1953. In the Senate, legislators agreed with the president on 96.7% of the occasions when he took a position; in the House, 94.4% of the time.

Given the persistent media coverage of numerous hard-fought legislative battles in the two chambers and his declining levels of public approval, Obama's figures may seem surprising. The answer is that Obama and his team picked their battles carefully, the president taking a public position on only 79 of 397 Senate roll-call votes and losing on only one of them. In the House, he won on sixty-eight out of seventy-two battles on which he took a position.

In his first two years, Obama clearly benefited from large Democratic majorities in both chambers and a historically high level of party unity within the party – even the wayward Senator Joseph Lieberman voted with him over 90% of the time. Also, as we have seen, he was careful in his choice of issues on which to take a public position. Like several recent presidents, he has avoided declaring his viewpoint on several matters, his advisers adopting the strategy of allowing him to do so only when there was a strong chance of success. A final ingredient of his success was that in the Senate thirty-two of the seventy-eight victories took place on confirmation votes, ranging from the well-known Hillary Clinton as secretary of state to the re-nomination of the relatively unknown Andre Davis as a judge on the US Court of Appeals on the Fourth Circuit. It was unlikely that Democrats would desert Obama on such appointments.

Investigation

One of the most important non-legislative functions of Congress is the power to investigate. This power is usually delegated to committees, either the standing committees, select (special) committees set up for the specific purpose or joint committees composed of members of the two houses. As the legislative initiative in Congress has diminished in recent years, so the investigatory role has assumed a greater importance.

It is in the scrutiny of the executive that the extent of congressional power becomes most apparent. Two factors give Congress greater power than the British Parliament. The first is the separation of powers, which was designed to prevent undue concentration of power in one location and which denies the executive the chance to sit in Congress. Secondly, the absence of strong party discipline means that congressmen can act as free agents, and act and vote as they please; they do not feel beholden to their party leaders for their advancement.

Investigations may be conducted to gather information on the need for future legislative action, to test the efficacy of laws already enacted, to inquire into the qualifications and performance of members and officials of the other branches of government, and to lay the groundwork for impeachment proceedings. Often, these hearings will involve the use of outside experts to assist in conducting the investigation and to enable a detailed study of the issues involved.

Most of these hearings are open to the public, and they are widely reported in the media. Witnesses can be compelled to testify, and those who refuse may be cited for contempt; those who give false testimony can be charged with perjury. Investigations of a special type (such as that by the 1987 Joint Committee on the Iran–Contra affair) attract much publicity and through their findings can provoke much public and political controversy. Congress can examine anything it considers appropriate within the legislative sphere, and added to the overseeing aspect of investigation (i.e. acting as a watchdog on the executive), this indicates the power of the two houses in the political process. Investigations over the years have covered topics such as drug addiction, the Ku Klux Klan, foreign aid programmes, the American role in NATO, foreign commitments in China and Vietnam, and the possible abuses of power involved in the Watergate/Irangate operations. Whitewatergate (and allied/ other scandals) was the subject of investigation during the Clinton years.

Finance

The presidential budget proposals may begin their existence in the White House, but they have to survive the detailed scrutiny of Congress. Most policies cost money, and thus require congressional authority to raise and spend it. Once the president and Congress are agreed upon a programme (authorisation), it is Congress that has to appropriate the funds to pay for its implementation. Such appropriations are processed by a committee in either house, and until the president signs the annual appropriations bill the original authorisation of expenditure amounts to nothing.

In recent years, the federal budget has been a continuing source of controversy between the president and Congress. The conflict originally dates back to the growth in the costs of federal programmes in the Great Society programmes of the 1960s, and in the years since then there has been an insufficient amount of revenue to match the expenditure. This has resulted in budget deficits, which by the 1990s were increasingly viewed with much alarm by many commentators and politicians.

Congress could accept the increase in military spending in the Reagan years, for it shared the goal of keeping America strong. It also liked the idea of low taxation. But the growing deficit could only be tackled by reduced spending in other areas, and this posed political difficulties for congressmen. A large part of the expenditure could not be cut without tackling the controversial social security and medical programmes, which used up so much federal money but were popular with recipients. These programmes and other entitlements such as pensions (adjusted for annual cost-of-living increases) were difficult to control.

Without cuts in defence spending, welfare and other areas, there was little scope for tax cuts unless the deficit was allowed to increase – which is what happened. The reason, as given by President Reagan's Director of the Office of Management and the Budget,[8] was that: 'Deficits create many winners and few losers . . . Every legislator is in a position to confer benefits on his or her favourite constituencies, and the incentive for any individual legislator to refrain from such behaviour is virtually non-existent.'

The work and responsibilities of members of Congress

Since 1789, more than 12,000 individuals have had the distinction of serving in the House of Representatives or Senate. None of them had a written job description to guide his or her work. Article I of the Constitution sets out the composition and powers of the Congress and the qualifications necessary for election. However, it does not outline the specific duties of the individual members. Accordingly, each member of Congress defines his or her own duties and sets his or her own priorities.

Congressmen have to be decision makers. Members are faced with hundreds of decisions in both recorded and unrecorded votes on matters major and minor.

COMMITTEES IN THE BRITISH PARLIAMENT AND THE AMERICAN CONGRESS: A COMPARISON

- Modern assemblies require a comprehensive array of committees to assist them in their work. Such is the volume and complexity of business, that they are indispensable.

- Committees are used in the areas of examination of bills and of financial proposals, acting as a check upon government administration and investigating issues of current importance and concern.

- Effective committees tend to have a membership of fifteen to thirty, with a core of long-serving members who have the opportunity to acquire specialised knowledge and expertise. Given sufficient numbers, they can cover the whole range of government business and provide detailed scrutiny of legislation, spending and the controversies surrounding key issues.

- To be truly effective, they need the power to summon witnesses and interrogate them intensively; their own staff and expert advisers; the ability to ensure that their reports are accorded good media coverage; and the power to require government action.

- In America, much of the main work of Congress is done in the committee rooms, which is why Congress can be described as a working assembly. In Britain, it is on the floor of the House of Commons that reputations are made, key issues discussed and government held to account. The British system is floor-oriented rather than committee-oriented which is why Hague and Harrop[9] describe the House of Commons as a talking rather than a working assembly.

Legislative committees

- Congress developed a comprehensive network of highly specialised standing committees well in advance of the House of Commons; it also has far more subcommittees. For example, the House Agriculture Committee has six subcommittees. Whereas standing committees have legislative jurisdiction, subcommittees generally handle specific areas of any committee's work.

- Legislative committees in Britain are non-specialist, as is apparent from their labels, Standing Committees A–H. Bills are assigned to them at random. Fewer members participate in the committee system of the House of Commons than in that of Congress, where every Senator serves on two committees, every Representative on at least one. Because they may serve for several years on the same committee, they develop spe-

Many decisions must be made quickly. Each decision, whether spontaneous or studied, balances the conflicting perspectives received from private citizens, public officials and party leaders.

Any senator or representative is concerned with five broad spheres of responsibility: the national interest, the constituency interest, the party interest, the

cialist knowledge of the issues involved in their subject area and, given their more important role in the legislature, it means that members on committees exercise real influence and power.

- Chairmen of congressional committees have often served for some years; chairs of committees and subcommittees always belong to the majority party. At Westminster, standing committee chairmen have no comparable specialist knowledge, powers or status.

- Scrutiny of legislation in American standing committees is much more meticulous because it is carried out by specialists. The party allegiance and degree of party cohesion of congressmen matters less than it does in Britain. In their consideration of bills, they are willing to think beyond the convenience of those who lead the party.

Committees of scrutiny

- US select or special committees are established in either chamber for a limited time period to perform a particular study or investigation. Special investigating committees, such as the 1973 Senate Select Committee to Investigate Presidential Campaign Activities (the Watergate Committee), expire after they submit their final report to the Senate. One high-profile committee of recent years was the one that inquired into the events of 9/11.

- The task of Westminster committees is to examine 'the expenditure, administration and policy' of the department whose activities they monitor. Via their investigations, members acquire detailed information about the work and problems of departments, which is essential if they are to engage in intelligent debate. As a result, those in the executive are called to account for their policies and administration by effective watch-dogs, who throw the spotlight of publicity on their actions.

- British committees cannot match their American counterparts in terms of personnel, nor are their reports always taken as seriously. Often, there is a lack of time for debates on their reports and findings. Governments have been reluctant to countenance any strengthening of their resources and powers, being wary of their influence.

- American select (or special) committees are appointed to perform a special function that is beyond the authority or capacity of a standing committee. They are often invest-igative in nature, rather than legislative. Their work generally expires on completion of their assigned duties, though they can be renewed.

lobbyists and the Political Action Committees who supported his campaign, and his/her own personal convictions. Any member of Congress must seek to balance the importance of these spheres to him or herself.

Several congressmen represent areas where their re-election is likely. They know that party discipline is much looser than in Britain, and the party label counts for less. Some of them may not feel particularly beholden to special interests. In other words, they can make up their own minds on issues, in the light of what they think is best for the country, best for their constituency and most in accordance with their own wishes. Independence of judgement in the light of their own conscience and beliefs is still a determinant of their vote.

Congressmen and party voting

Members of either chamber are required to vote on many occasions every year, more so in the House than in the Senate. In 2003, there were 675 House votes and 459 Senate ones. Among other things, the votes may cover bills in their various readings, amendments to them, budgetary details and (in the Senate) treaties or appointments made by the president.

In recent years, there has been an increase in party loyalty, against the background of a more intense ideological struggle. The attempt to drive through the Republican 'Contract for America' programme (see p. 314) inspired greater loyalty among party members than had usually previously been the case. So too it provoked greater unanimity among the Democrat minority. Contentious issues ranging from abortion to taxation and from gun control to school prayer have often been the cause of increased partisanship, as also was the failed attempt to impeach President Clinton. For all these reasons, there was a marked polarization in party attitudes, and intra-party rancour and invective became more common.

Apart from the Republican takeover in November 1994, other factors too have contributed to greater party unity, among them:

* the break-up of the so-called Solid South (see pp. 2–3) a few decades ago, meaning that the Democrats in Congress are altogether more homogeneous, being notably more urban based and liberal;
* the declining influence of the liberal element within the Republican party, in an age when the Religious Right has been in the ascendancy. As party support has been increasingly concentrated on the South and West, so too has the conservative element been strengthened;
* the influence of ideologically based pressure groups, including think-tanks (see p. 362), which have tended to push parties in a more partisan direction. As they often provide funding for election campaigns, their influence is important. As a price for their backing, they expect some adherence to their preferences. Such a pressure discourages party negotiators in Congress from the politics of bargaining and compromise.

For the reasons given, party voting (a situation in which the bulk of the members of one party vote with each other and against the opposition) has become markedly more common than it was a few decades ago, but it is by no means the norm, as the figures given below indicate:

Party voting in Congress 1958–2008

	House (%)	Senate (%)
1958	40	44
1968	35	32
1998	56	56
2003	52	67
2008	53	52

NB The year of the greatest intensity of party voting was 1995, when on 73% of the possible occasions a party vote was recorded in the House, and on 69% in the Senate. In the last years of the Clinton presidency, in spite of the impact of impeachment proceedings in 1999, partisanship was actually at the lowest level recorded since the late 1980s, with only 43% of the House votes and 49% of those in the Senate being party votes. By then, Republican leaders lacked a clear majority in both chambers to push through their agenda, although there were still some highly partisan confrontations.

The more partisan atmosphere of recent years has not just been a feature of votes on the floor of the chambers. It also influences members' conduct in committees and in relationships with the White House.

Party has never claimed the allegiance of congressmen as it does that of Members of Parliament (MPs) in Britain. Except on rare occasions, MPs see support for the party as a primary obligation. In the United States, the situation is different. As Walles[10] puts it: 'While party membership provides a natural starting point for action, ultimately it may well take second place to activity related to committee and constituency pressures.'

Parties are of course the routes via which the senators or representatives reach Congress, but as Mayhew[11] argues, once the journey is successfully accomplished 'it is the pressure for re-election which colors congressional activity'. He distinguishes three forms of likely activity that to a greater or lesser degree might influence a congress member's behaviour in pursuing this goal:

1 Self-promotion, via postal communication and diligent attention to social and other occasions in the constituency. Engagements include conducting surgeries with constituents, making tours around local factories, hospitals and schools, appearing on local radio stations, addressing lunches and giving interviews to local journalists.
2 Credit claiming, as members point to what they have done for their district (jobs, contracts, support for local industry, etc.) and for individuals. This is especially relevant to the representatives, facing as they do the prospect of a re-election battle within two years, although no senator wants to antagonise important interests within the state.
3 Position taking, undertaken to help promote a favourable image of what the representative really believes in – what Mayhew calls 'the public enunciation of a judgmental statement on anything likely to be of interest'.

The constituency 'welfare' role

Since the early 1980s constituency responsibilities that consume much of the time of the legislators. They hire more staff to work in their state and local offices, make more trips to the constituency, receive and send more mail to voters and generally treat such work as a priority demand upon their time. For many of them, it has come to be a more important responsibility than drafting legislation.

In American government, there has always been talk of **'pork-barrel' politics**, by which congressmen are judged according to the success with which 'they bring home the bacon'. It used to mean 'delivering the goods' in terms of bringing rewards to the constituency. Today, constituency service has a wider connotation than merely gaining 'pork' or advantages. It is also about assuming the role of welfare worker or ombudsman, as citizens feel that they need assistance in their dealings with those who work in government offices and who are part of what is seen as an unresponsive bureaucracy.

pork-barrel politics
Pork-barrel politics are all about congressmen being able to secure advantages for their constituents, because bills are pieces of legislation designed to produce visible (usually economic) benefits – for example defence contracts, local highways and post offices. By the passage of legislation covering local projects, congressmen hope that they will find political favour in their states. If they can serve on committees such as that dealing with transportation and infrastructure, there are ample opportunities for practising pork-barrel politics.

Helping constituents in difficulty is more likely to ease the path to re-election than speaking and voting on controversial issues. Christopher Bailey[12] has highlighted this change of emphasis, and quotes the example of a Democratic senator from Alabama who observed:

> Many freshmen view their role differently than 25 years ago, when a Senator was only a legislator. Now a Senator is also a grantsman, an ombudsman, and a caseworker, and cannot ignore [these activities] . . . When we are asked by our constituents to help, we can't say we don't have time because we are focusing on national and international issues.

Bailey concludes that 'the increased emphasis on constituency service has transformed members from national legislators to narrowly focused ombudsmen'. He shows how many of them see themselves as lobbyists furthering the interests of their constituents in dealings with federal bureaucrats, by interceding on their behalf.

The danger of such an approach, in which Congress members see themselves as acting as advocates for the people, is that they may be tempted to act more forcefully on behalf of those who are the most influential persons in the community, particularly those who have contributed to campaign funds. The Ethics Committee of the House advises that the member must treat all constituents equally, 'irrespective or political or other considerations', and warns against favouritism or arm-twisting tactics. This has become the more important in recent years, given the number of cases involving questions of ethics.

Bailey also makes the point that, in spending more time on matters of welfare and other matters of constituency service, Congress members may boost their reputations, but do so at the expense of their effectiveness:

> By ensuring that grandma gets her social security cheque, the member may enhance his chances of gaining re-election, but the consequences are profound. Mismanagement and corruption within the federal agencies go unnoticed, and federal benefits are distributed on the basis of political clout rather than need. The cost to the taxpayer of the expanded notion of constituency service runs into billions of dollars, and the cost to the American people is a Congress filled with ombudsmen rather than legislators.

Congressmen are acutely aware of their prospects for political survival. They know that these depend to a large extent on their ability and effort, and accordingly they spend a large part of their time in discovering, assessing and acting upon the wishes of those who sent them to Washington. Maidment and McGrew[13] quote a Republican who described his task in the House as 'taking care of home problems, case work, not necessarily having anything to do with legislation at all. Taking care of constituents'. The member continues: 'if Senators and Representatives are to be believed, they are constantly looking over their shoulders for guidance. Few, if any, are willing to ignore the interests of their constituents. In that sense, the Congress is an extraordinarily representative legislative body. It is sensitive to the slightest shift in electoral opinion.'

The roles of congressmen: conflicts involved

There is no easy answer to the question of which is the most important responsibility of congressmen. Many voters expect that they will represent the wishes of the people of the district, for that is why they are sent to Washington in the first place. They are there to voice feelings 'back home', and not to take an independent line based on some perception of the national interest or personal feelings. If the needs of the US as a whole happen to be in line with those of the folks 'back home', so much the better, but if they are not, then constituents will draw this to the attention of their elected representative.

In the eyes of the voters, this is not just a matter of constitutional theory, but one of tangible benefits that the congressman can and should be able to win. The title 'representative' is therefore not lacking in significance – they do or should represent the people of their district.

Congressmen inevitably perceive their roles differently. This was highlighted by the findings of the final report of The Commission on Administrative

Review (in the House, 1977), which analysed the responses of 140 representatives about what they saw as their most important responsibility. The
priorities were:

- 45% the nation only;
- 28% the nation and district;
- 24% the district only;
- 3% unsure.

When a conflict arose between these differing pressures upon them,

- 65% professed to following the dictates of conscience;
- 25% thought it depended on the issue;
- 5% wished to follow the wishes of the district;
- 3% were uncertain.

In practice, any congressman, senior or junior, must react according to the pressures of the moment. It is unrealistic to expect that he or she will ignore the
chances of re-election in making a decision, and for that reason he or she is
likely to pay heed to the prevailing mood of fellow citizens – especially those
in his or her locality. Yet on many issues where there is no clearly expressed
constituency view or obvious local involvement, the congress member can argue
a more exalted case as a trustee of the national interest.

Congressional reform: the 1970s onwards

Congress can be, and often is, very parochial, run as it is by senators and
representatives who have their own individual ambitions and constituency
problems to preoccupy them. Because of this, it can seem as though it is more
concerned with safeguarding its own interests and those of the members'
localities, than of acting for the general good. Several presidents have criticised
the preoccupation with immediate local pressures that has prevented congressmen from seeing what needs to be done over the longer term. Since the
1970s, Congress has become much more assertive, but some writers (and some
presidents) wonder if it has become any more constructive.

Legislative curbs

The struggle in the Nixon years over the bombing of Cambodia made
Congress act. It overrode the president's veto and passed the 1973 **War
Powers Act** (see p. 80), which reasserted congressional oversight of foreign
policy by curbing the scope for the commander-in-chief to wage war abroad.
Another limitation that Congress imposed was the **Budget and Impoundment
Control Act**, which was an attempt made in 1974 to allow a more effective
check on the president's budgetary and economic planning. Congressmen
objected to the way in which the president impounded (refused to spend)

huge sums of money set aside for social programmes. Both chambers set up their own budget committees, and a Congressional Budget Office, with its own specialist staff, was created, to boost their expertise and enable them to seek out and acquire the sort of information that presidents tended to deny them.

The internal workings of Congress

Apart from the legislative control over the presidency, the other changes made were more to do with the internal organisation of Congress itself. The time was appropriate for an expansion of internal democracy.

Problems with the committee structure

Many younger congressmen felt that the workings of their chambers were beyond their control. Power lay with the committee chairpersons (see p. 172), and in the hierarchical structure new entrants saw little chance of being able to play a significant part and wield real influence for many years. Yet they were elected to look after the position of their constituents, and could not do so as effectively as they wished if they did not have the backing of powerful committee chairpersons.

Congressional committees are very important, and the House in particular has always devolved much power to them. Even though there is more debate on the floor of the Senate, its committees are also what one writer[14] has called 'the nerve centre of its legislative process'. To serve on one of the more prestigious committees is an ambition of many congressmen, and the position of chair is regarded as especially influential.

Until the 1970s, Congress operated via a **seniority rule**, so that length of service was the main determinant of committee allocation. It favoured the congressmen who came from areas where their party always won, so that they would gain the opportunity for years of unbroken membership (as long as they could survive their party's primary election). For the Democrats, it paid to represent the South or the northern cities, for the Republicans advancement came for those who hailed from the agricultural Midwest. Representatives and senators who were elected for these areas were accordingly overrepresented on committees.

The seniority rule applied especially to advancement within the committees, and those who became chairpersons were those who were the most

seniority rule
The rule stating the chair of a congressional standing committee will be the person of the majority party with the lengthiest unbroken period of continuous service on that committee. Reforms in the 1970s undermined the principle, as the Democrats in the House moved to elect their chairperson each session. But it remains the case that the more senior and experienced a person is, then the greater the likelihood that he or she will become the chair. However, there are exceptions and these make the change significant and worthwhile.

Committee chairpersons

Chairpersons of committees occupy an important position in American government. They are key figures in the work of Congress, whether it is in investigation and scrutiny, in examination of scandals and complex and/or controversial issues or in the passing of legislation. After the majority party leaders, chairs are the most influential members. There is one-party domination of chairmanships. In both houses, all are currently in Republican hands.

As we have seen, the House Rules Committee, the Senate Foreign Relations Committee and several others are prestigious, and membership is highly prized, the chairmanship much sought after. In the days of the seniority rule, the position had great security of tenure because the incumbent was usually experienced and respected and often served for several years. Today, that situation has changed and there are some able, younger persons of more diverse backgrounds who achieve the chairmanship. It can no longer be assumed that the chair will be reappointed from session to session, survival depending in part on the ability to command support within the ruling circles of the party. There is also today media coverage of committee hearings and media scrutiny of what goes on in committee, particularly in cases where there is a high-profile investigation under way. Power has also been diluted by the greater number of subcommittee chairmanships, a rival source of influence.

None the less, chairpersons are key figures in the legislative process:

• They tend to be active and effective legislators, often experienced in making the system work.

• They appoint members to subcommittees.

• They have a major influence over the legislative agenda, determining the bills that will be considered and the priority attached to them.

• They also have influence over the amendments called and the order in which they are discussed.

• They direct financial resources.

• In the days of the iron triangles of the past (see p. 348), the significance of the role was even greater, for between them the relevant departmental secretary, interest group representative and long-serving committee chair could largely shape policy in areas such as agriculture, tobacco and nuclear power. President Johnson was adept at gaining the support of the 'inner circle' of senior members of Congress, when pushing his Great Society programme through the legislature.

senior members of their party on the committee. This provided enormous influence, for it was the chairperson who determined the agenda for discussion and the number and composition of subcommittees. The Democrats were the victorious party in almost all of the congressional elections from 1930 to 1970, so that many chairpersons were unrepresentative, and often conservative, southern Democrats. This had a significant bearing on legislation, for too much influence lay in the hands of those who represented rural – and white – America.

The old system had few defenders, but it had one main advantage. The existence of an 'inner club' of senior members whose attitudes and behaviour could be predicted meant that presidents knew who to do business with. These people counted, for they had so much influence over congressional proceedings. If their approval was sought and won, then Congress could be managed. When reform finally came, this was not the case – as President Carter found to his cost. No longer were the reactions of Congress as coherent as they once were. Anything could happen, without the strong will of senior chairmen to steer legislation and impose control.

Reform of the structure

In 1973 the Democrats in the House decided, at a caucus meeting, to abandon the automatic use of the seniority system. In future, chairpersons would be nominated by the steering and policy committee of the party, and the nominees would then be subject to an election by secret ballot of all Democrats in the chamber. Most of the senior members were actually elected in the first elections, but there was now an opportunity for change. Two years later, with an influx of younger and more liberal representatives, three elderly chairmen were removed.

Another change prevented chairpersons of key committees from serving as the chair of other significant ones. They also lost some of their control over the subcommittees, which became less beholden to the parent body. The Republicans saw the need to exhibit a similar 'democratic' interest, and implemented similar changes within their party.

Nowadays, less-senior members of Congress have more authority, subcommittee chairs are more independent and, especially in the Senate, subcommittee chairs may be offered to congressmen who have served for only one or two terms. Often, chairpersons are still chosen on the basis of seniority, with the longest-serving majority-party member on the committee being selected.

Since the 1980s, Democrats from the South have lost their disproportionate strength, and those from safe northern industrial areas have frequently been chosen. Whereas once the system discriminated against organised labour, civil rights and urban-based interests, that is no longer the case. Over time, women and members of racial minorities should benefit from the seniority rule as it now operates, whereas if there were a free choice without recognition for long service they might get selected only rarely.

Power in Congress has become more dispersed than ever before, and the seniority rule for choosing chairpersons is much less of a bone of contention than it used to be. In the Senate, most members who belong to the majority party chair a subcommittee, several a full committee. In the House, many Republican representatives now have such a responsibility.

Improved staffing

The formation of the Congressional Budget Office (via the Budget and Impoundment Control Act, see p. 170–171) was an indication of the wish of many congressmen to improve their professionalism and acquire a new expertise. An Office of Technology Assessment had already been formed two years earlier, and the General Accounting Office and other research services were reformed to allow for the use of more analysts and experts.

In addition, the number of aides to congressmen of both houses has been increased, as has the staffing of committees. According to C-Span (www.C-Span.org), some 24,000 congressional staff currently support the work of Congress and its members. They work in several categories, all of which have different roles, job descriptions and salaries. Their numbers include:
- **11,692 personal staff**, working for individual members of Congress. (A House member employs an average of 14 staff; the Senate average is 34. House members may not exceed 18 full-time and 4 part-time staff. Senators have no limit on the number of staff they can hire.)
- **2,492 committee staff**, working for either the majority or minority on congressional committees
- **274 leadership staff**, working for the speaker, majority leader, minority leader, majority whip or minority whip
- **5034 institutional staff**, majority or minority party floor staff, and non-partisan staff: police, legislative clerks, building, janitorial workers, etc.
- **4479 support agency non-partisan staff**, of whom 747 work in the Congressional Research Service, 232 in the Congressional Budget Office and 3,500 in the General Accounting Office.

Congress ought to be able to perform its task with greater efficiency, having equipped itself with an increased capacity to handle and investigate presidential initiatives.

Letting the cameras in

Reforms of the legislative procedure in 1970 allowed each house to decide whether to televise its proceedings. A new generation of legislators was more comfortable than its predecessors with television, and eager for coverage of floor debate. Members quickly agreed to experiment with a closed-circuit debate. The House first opened its chamber to television in 1979; the Senate held out for a further seven years. But long before there were broadcasts of floor debate, television had been allowed to record more impressive and/or dramatic events on Capitol Hill, among them the State of the Union messages and Senate committee hearings such as those concerned with the possible impeachment of Richard Nixon.

Representatives and senators have learnt to exploit television by consenting to interviews, appearing on news programmes and crafting photo opportunities with constituents. Some of them now devise a video version of their press releases, so that they can be sent – or beamed via satellite – back to local stations.

What more can and should be done?

By the turn of the twenty-first century, the balance of power had significantly altered from the situation a generation earlier. Congress became assertive, and the change in overall party control in both houses (from Democrat to Republican) meant that there was a much greater willingness – indeed enthusiasm – to challenge presidential policy. As the continuing saga of Whitewatergate and alleged sexual lapses unfolded, great damage was done to Bill Clinton's authority, but also – some would say – to the presidency itself.

Congress now has the expertise and will that it had lacked for many years, and if it wishes to challenge the president it has the capacity to do so. Yet the reforms carried out, especially the weakening of the importance of seniority, have actually made it less easy to organise congressmen to act in concert and produce a united response. If anything, they are even freer to concentrate on acting in a way pleasing to their constituents, and are an easy prey for the special-interest groups who lobby for their support.

Much of what is done is designed to enhance the chances of re-election, and this does not make for effective long-term thinking. It does, however, ensure that congressmen think about the wishes and needs of those who elected them, and this helps to ensure that there is continuous accountability.

Criticism still surfaces from time to time of a 'do-nothing' or 'obstructive' Congress, which is portrayed as timid, obsessed with internal bickering, narrow-minded and self-interested. Those who seek further congressional reform ask:

1 **Is Congress efficient?** Congress has to deal with a vast number of complex bills, and criticism often relates to the pace of legislation. David Brinkley, the TV anchorman, expressed public frustration[15] when he said that 'it is widely believed in Washington that it would take Congress thirty days to make instant coffee work'. There is much talk of a 'paralysis in Congress', brought about by the number of subcommittees and their overlapping juris-diction. Again, with more independently minded members less committed to the party line, it is more difficult for leaders to create coalitions to get business conducted and the agenda kept on time. For instance, much-needed reforms on healthcare have been particularly difficult to achieve.

2 **Does Congress defend the national interest?** Are legislators so anxious to ensure their re-election that they neglect to think of the national interest? Are they willing to tackle controversial issues which may be unpopular with their constituents? One House Republican leader[16] suggested that congressional behaviour was too concerned with 'perpetuating the longevity and comfort of the men who run it'. Are those representatives too concerned with the views of special interests? Think of the way in which expensive congressional elections are financed. Are congressmen beholden?

3 **Is Congress representative?** In both parties, there is a notable overrepresentation of middle/upper-middle-income groups. Women and racial minorities remain seriously underrepresented.

Such questions are often asked and the responses are invariably critical. If it is true that Congress does not often perform its legislative and investigative tasks as effectively as it should, this perhaps reflects the fact that it is, in Walles's[17] words, 'better organised for obstruction than for promotion'. The overlapping jurisdictions between committees and subcommittees provide opportunities for affected interests to delay or halt action. Walles suggests that the machinery seems 'ill-equipped to establish priorities which can be readily translated into action'.

Dominated by 535 sets of individual considerations, Congress can be an ineffective body, unable to devise policy initiatives coherently and pass them into

---

Public perceptions of Congress

Public opinion poll ratings asking people if they approve of the job Congress is doing have, in the last few decades, generally indicated low levels of popular support. Approval ratings over the last 25 years have varied within a range from 20% to 50%, the only 'high' being the 84% registered in October 2001 after the 9/11 attacks. From 2006 to 2011, ratings have usually hovered in the 20–30% range, with the occasional high (37% in early 2007) and an all-time low of 14% in late 2008 (*USA Today*/Gallup).

In a recent poll for *USA Today* (23 June 2010), Gallup found that many Americans wanted most members of Congress ousted, seeing the body in which they served as 'ineffective, self-serving and entrenched'. They claimed that most members of Congress did not deserve to be re-elected, many of them supporting their position with observations along the lines that representatives were doing a bad job, had been in office too long, were not making decisions based on what was best for the country and were too focused on self-interest, special interests and partisanship. Relatively few cited Congress's performance on specific issues (although a minority referred to topics including debt, financial bailouts, the economy as a whole, healthcare legislation, wars and immigration issues) and many were less harsh on their own representatives than on the performance of the 435 representatives as a collective body.

law. It can sometimes seem that those 535 interests take precedence over the overall needs of the nation, and this is why major national problems – from tax reform to energy policy, from welfare to gun control – have been so difficult to resolve.

Congress is not rated highly in popular esteem (see p. 176). The public seems to admire its local representatives more than it approves of the legislature as a whole. In surveys, interviewees tend to advance similar criticisms to the ones considered above, notably that Congress is cumbersome, negative, slow to respond and too often beset by gridlock. This is certainly true of its legislative work, in comparison with many other legislatures around the world. But in other respects, members of legislatures in Europe might well envy the facilities, independence and influence of their American counterparts, who are less beholden to their party and able to exert important powers of oversight.

Legislatures in Britain and the US: a comparison

	Britain	United States
Unicameral or bicameral	Bicameral	Bicameral
Size	House of Commons 646	Representatives 435
	House of Lords 753	Senate 100
Method of selection	Commons: direct election	Representatives and
	Lords: mainly appointment	Senate: direct election
Nature of membership	Both unrepresentative: too few women and minorities	Both unrepresentative: too few women and minorities. Congress in particular fails to reflect the full diversity of the US
Status of chambers	Commons: significant	Theoretically equal, but
	Lords: secondary role	Senate has higher prestige
Type and role of committees	Standing (non-specialist) for legislation; select for scrutiny	Standing (specialist) for legislation and scrutiny; select for special inquiries
Law making	Commons has main role, Lords does work of revision; most bills pass and impact of revision process limited	Key legislative role for both houses, though relatively few bills pass into law; lack of party support
Watchdog role, investigation	Questions, official Opposition and select committees	Powerful investigatory committees; no question time or official opposition
Relative power	Loss of power: talk of 'Parliament in decline' and need for reform	Most powerful legislature in world, though often talk of 'congressional paralysis'
Pay and facilities	Pay low by European standards; conditions poor	Generous pay and excellent facilities, especially staff support

Issues for consideration

Is Congress socially representative of the nation?

By this use of 'representative', we mean 'typical of a class'. Sociologists use the term this way when they speak about a 'representative sample' of the people. In the case of America, the suggestion is that congressmen should possess characteristics that are broadly similar to those possessed by the people as a whole. If this is the case, then Congress as a whole will be a microcosm or mirror image of the nation.

Congress is not such a microcosm, for congressmen – judged by attributes such as socio-economic status, education, race, gender and age – are not representative of Americans as a whole. Like the House of Commons, Congress is overwhelmingly white, male, middle class and middle aged.

Most senators and representatives are professionals: lawyers, business people, accountants, journalists, doctors, teachers, university professors or farmers. Lawyers have traditionally been the most sizeable contingent: their numbers are lower now than in the 1970s, but they remain the largest group in the Senate and still constitute just over 37% of the 112th Congress. Today, 209 out of 535 members have worked in business and/or banking, 208 in public service/ politics and 200 in the legal profession. There are few blue-collar workers (16), and in the usage of the term, the poor, the underclass of the big cities and others near the bottom of the social pile are unrepresented, although of course this does not mean that present congressmen are incapable of representing their interests. Some rich senators are active in seeking to protect the underprivileged and can be vociferous advocates of their cause.

Black Americans (44 members) and Hispanics (25) are present in smaller numbers than is justified by their presence in the community. They and other ethnic minorities as a whole still have a long way to go to achieve anything like equality, as do women. There are fewer women (88) in the 112th Congress than in its predecessor. Groups such as Jews (38) and Catholics (148) are now represented in greater numbers than in the past, Jews being significantly overrepresented.

The profile of congressional membership in recent years

	107th Congress		109th Congress		112th Congress	
	House	Senate	House	Senate	House	Senate
Women	59	13	65	14	73	15
African American	36	0	42	1	44	0
Hispanic	19	0	26	2	23	2

NB To aid comparison, the figures for some twenty-five years ago (the 99th Congress, 1985–86) were 22/2 women, 19/0 African American and 11/0 Hispanic.

Representatives and senators in particular are older than the average of all Americans. Senators are usually older, on average, than representatives (62, as against 56, in the 112th Congress), partly perhaps because of the minimum entrance qualification (30, as opposed to 25), but also because many senators build up a reputation over six years and then, as incumbents, are difficult for opponents to remove. They may survive for many years, as the example of Strom Thurmond illustrates. Originally elected in 1954, he remained a senator until the end of the 107th Congress, the month in which he celebrated his 100th birthday (December 2002).

It is very doubtful whether any freely chosen assembly ever could constitute a cross-section of the electorate, for the choice is largely at the mercy of the voters. But this having been said, the discrepancies between different groups and categories and their representation in Congress is clearly a considerable one.

This underrepresentation obviously matters to the groups who feel largely unrecognised. If they are not well represented among the membership, it is all the more important that there should be members who in their approach can show empathy with those less fortunate than themselves. In the nineteenth, twentieth and twenty-first centuries there have always been legislators who – whilst socially untypical of and unlike those whom they seek to serve – can nevertheless imagine what it is like to be disadvantaged and are prepared to articulate their concerns for such people.

For the practice of their profession, congressmen need the education and skills normally associated with middle-class professionals. In a system reliant upon volunteers to come forward, it is unlikely that the least-educated, those from the poorest backgrounds and the majority of people who do manual work

---

Female representation in the 'top five' countries, the UK and the US: a comparison

Country	Year of last election	% of women MPs	Electoral system
Rwanda	2008	56.3	List PR
Sweden	2010	45.0	List PR
South Africa	2009	44.5	List PR
Cuba	2008	43.2	Double ballot
Iceland	2009	42.9	List PR
UK = 51st	2010	20.1	FPTP
USA = 70th	2008	15.3	FPTP

Table and figures in the text are adapted from information provided by the Inter-Parliamentary Union (www.ipu.org), as calculated at 31 January 2011, and are based on lower houses in two-chamber legislatures. The world average, calculated from the countries for which data was available, was 19.2%; the European average was 21.4%; and the average for the Americas (inflated by those for Latin America) was 23.1%. In the European Parliament elected in 2009, 257 out of 736 MEPs (34.9%) were women, the figure for the UK being 23/72 (31.9%).

The social backgrounds of legislators in Britain and the US in 2010: a comparison

A comparison based on the outcomes of the US congressional elections and the UK general election

- In general, legislatures in European democracies and the United States tend to be male, middle aged, middle class and white.

- The number of women has increased in most assemblies, although the situation is patchy. It is poor in the US and in some European countries such as France, Greece, Ireland and Italy. In Britain, the representation of women moved forward in 1992 and significantly so in 1997 (120/635). It fell back slightly in 2001, to 118. It increased to 128 in 2005 and again to 143 (22%) in 2010, helped by a significant increase in the number of female Conservatives elected.

- Most representatives attain their position only after doing some other job and making a mark in their chosen careers. This may give them experience of life, but it also means that the voice of the young is largely excluded. In 2010, the average age of Conservative members upon election to the House of Commons was 47, of Labour members 52. The number of under-40s was 129 (19.8%), Labour having ten members who were under 30. In the US, the average age is usually a few years higher, the number of under-40s being only twenty-nine (5.4%).

- The middle-class nature of elected representatives is more marked now than it used to be in Britain. Labour evolved as a party to represent the working classes in Parliament. In 1918, the Parliamentary Labour Party (PLP) had 87% working-class membership. Since the 1960s, the parliamentary party has been dominated by members with a university education and middle-class professions, many of them in higher education. Following the 2001 election, the manual-worker element diminished to 12%, the lowest ever; in 2010, it diminished further, to only 9%. The Conservatives have always found it difficult to get working-class candidates to stand, and if this happens it is usually in unwinnable constituencies. Business people (24%) and professionals (33.5%), especially lawyers (13.2%) and those in the communicating professions (8.3%) are well represented in Britain. So too are business (39.1%), the law (37.4%) and academia (15.1) strongly represented in the US, where the blue-collar contingent accounts for just 3%.

- Twelve British MPs elected in 2001 belonged to ethnic minorities; in 2005, the number rose to fifteen, in 2010, to twenty-seven (4.2%), of whom sixteen were Labour (including the first female Muslims, three) and eleven Conservative. Hispanic and black Americans have generally fared badly in Congress, but among religious groups Jews are well represented.

- Of course, both countries use the 'first past the post' electoral system. This does not encourage the representation of minority groups, for everything is staked on one candidate in a single-member constituency. Parties encourage the choice of candidates who are likely winners. They have traditionally been reluctant to adopt candidates who might cost them votes.

NB For further information on the backgrounds of senators and congressmen, see p. 178–179.

are likely to put their names forward. Few would wish to forsake their existing lifestyle and live the life of a congressman, who spends much of the time in Washington, away from the family. That being the case, it is desirable that those who emerge as candidates and win election should understand the conditions and outlook of people drawn from all 'walks of life'.

Should there be term limits for congressmen?

In the 1990s, there was renewed interest in 'term limits', although the debate on how long any incumbent should serve has a much longer history. The Founding Fathers considered limiting the period for which any member of the executive or legislature should sit, but decided to avoid setting a limit on the number of terms anyone could serve.

In the nineteenth century, however, it was customary for elected politicians to limit themselves. It was only in the twentieth century that congressmen began to exceed two terms in the House and one in the Senate. The development of the seniority rule for committee chairmanships inspired representatives to seek a longer term. The introduction of direct election for senators in 1912 encouraged them to seek an extra six years.

Recent developments

Term limits were approved in the 1990 elections in Colorado, and thereafter in several – mainly western – states. In the 1994 elections, the tenth item in the Contract with America (see p. 314), the Citizen Legislature Act, dealt with the issue. It urged the need for a first-ever congressional vote to place limits on career politicians and replace them with citizen legislators.

In 1995, the Supreme Court ruled in the case of US Term Limits, Inc. v. Thornton that states could not impose term limits on their congressional delegations, but the ruling did not apply to state legislators. Fifteen states now have limits on legislative service, but there is little uniformity in their application (in 2002, the Idaho legislature became the first to repeal its own term limits). Thirty-six have limits on the period of gubernatorial service.

Why the interest today?

Several factors inspired the desire to curb career politicians from staying in power on Capitol Hill:
1 All politicians – and congressmen foremost amongst them – are increasingly viewed with disdain by many voters, who have a deep scepticism about the motives of those who serve them. They wish to 'throw the rascals out', and believe that they can 'clean up' a sleazy Congress by ensuring that fresh faces appear to replace older, seasoned Washington politicians who can 'play

the system'. Yet despite this distaste for Congress and many congressmen, voters seem more than happy to re-elect their own representatives in either chamber, a point that leads to the second explanation.

2 In recent years, incumbents have been re-elected with great regularity. In 1994, no Republican incumbent was defeated in any gubernatorial, Senate or House race, and even the Democrats lost only two incumbent scalps in the Senate – though they lost thirty-four in the lower house. For a variety of reasons, incumbency presents an advantage over opponents, so that once elected some congressmen have stayed on Capitol Hill for a long (too long?) time.

3 Allied to the point about long-time career politicians is the feeling that there are too many incentives for congressmen to stay 'on the Hill'. Perquisites and salaries are generous: too lavish for the many Americans who have a much less comfortable life.

A beneficial change?

Against:

1 Term limits are unnecessary in that the American system provides a check on those in power through regular (in the case of the House, frequent) elections. The incumbent can be challenged from within his/her party in a primary election, and by the voters as a whole in the general election.

2 It seems undemocratic to impose limits on the electorate's right of choice, for limits on congressmen are actually limits on voters. They cannot reward able men and women who have given good service.

3 If there are problems of low ethical standards and scandalous or self-interested behaviour, the answer is to legislate against the evil or to vote against the offending congressman.

For:

1 Term limits would weaken the stranglehold of long-servers in Congress, people who command excessive influence by virtue of their seniority. Fresh faces may be talented, as well as less 'corrupted' by long service in the system.

2 A 'citizen legislature' would replace a chamber of career politicians. Congressmen would be more in touch with those who elect them, and Congress would contain 'ordinary people'.

3 Applying term limits to congressmen is a logical extension of the curbs on presidential service. In thirty-six states, governors also have a limited period of office.

Are congressmen paid enough and do they have good facilities?

Members of both houses of Congress are paid $174,000 per year, as of October 2010. The figure is high by most American standards, although well below that

THE MAIN PERQUISITES OF CONGRESSMEN AND SENATORS

Retirement benefits

A member becomes eligible for benefits upon retirement from Congress if he or she is 62 years old with five years of congressional service; 50 years old with twenty years of service; or any age with twenty-five years of congressional service.

Personal staff allowances

These enable members to hire aides for clerical, administrative, legislative and media support. Representatives' staff allowances can be used to hire up to eighteen permanent and four non-permanent aides divided between the member's Washington and district offices. Up to $75,000 of a representative's staff funds can be transferred to his or her official expense account for use in other categories, such as computer and related services.

Senators' personal staff allowances vary with the size of the member's state. Senators may hire as many aides as they wish within their allowance. Typically this ranges between twenty-six and sixty, depending on the size of the state and the salary levels offered to the staffers. (In addition to their personal staffs, senators and representatives are assisted on legislative matters by the staffs of the committees and subcommittees on which they serve.)

Expense allowances

These cover domestic travel, stationery, newsletters, overseas postage, telephone and telegraph service, and other expenses in Washington and in the members' state or congressional districts. Foreign travel by members for the conduct of government business is financed through special allowances. For instance:

1. Money is appropriated by Congress through the Mutual Security Act to pay travel and other expenses of congressional committees for routine and special investigations.

2. Members may use the funds of various government agencies when they speak on foreign policy issues at overseas posts.

3. Members may travel on military aircraft, including cargo planes, at no charge.

Outside employment income

Income from non-congressional sources is generally limited to 15% of members' pay. There are, however, certain prohibited categories. Members may not receive compensation for employment in real estate, insurance sales, the practice of law, the practice of medicine or service as an officer or board member of a company.

In addition, members have awarded themselves a variety of expense allowances, which are generally considered a necessary accessory to members' regular salaries. They range from generous staff assistance and accommodation to free use of video-recording facilities and sophisticated computer services. Congressional leaders receive additional remuneration. Once they leave office, they receive handsome retirement benefits.

of several corporate presidents, who earn several times as much. For many members of the public, the amount seems excessive and whenever there is an increase there are expressions of popular disquiet. In fact, the most recent amendment to the Constitution, the Twenty-Seventh, concerned this very issue. As law makers debate and set their own levels of pay, there is a feeling that any such change should not take effect until an election has intervened, thereby allowing the public the opportunity to vote out those who have enhanced their own salary levels!

Pay and facilities of elected representatives in Britain and the US: a comparison

- In terms of accommodation, equipment, staffing, library assistance and other amenities, congressmen are notably better placed than their British counterparts.

- Each senator or representative has a suite of offices in a building connected to Capitol Hill by an underground railway, and the member has access to office equipment, gymnasia and many other facilities, as well as generous expense allowances.

- For many years, it was customary for MPs to lament their inadequate facilities, the vast size and splendour of the Palace of Westminster being little consolation for the conditions in which they had to operate. Today (October 2011) an MP has a salary of £65,738, as well as a range of allowances for office help and accommodation. Some members still voice criticism of the lack of constituency help they receive, whilst others feel that they could do with more research assistance at Westminster. The lack of office equipment, and in particular of information technology services, are frequently condemned, for the House of Commons makes no central provision for such facilities.

CONCLUSION

The effectiveness of Congress and the need for congressional reform have been periodically analysed in recent decades. The changes of the 1970s went some way towards enhancing Congress's powers and made it more assertive in relation to the presidency. Yet doubts about the performance of Congress and its members remain, as the preoccupation in the 1990s with 'term limits' indicates.

The public expects that Congress will be both responsive to popular needs and efficient. Many Americans lack confidence in the performance of those who represent them and feel that congressmen are too swayed by lobbyists and party leaders and insufficiently committed to serving their interests. They also decry a 'do-nothing' Congress, complaining that it is often slow to identify, define and effectively tackle the problems facing the nation. But if Congress is sometimes slow to act, this may be because the American people themselves do not agree on what the problems are and how they should be resolved.

REFERENCES

1 A. Grant and E. Ashbee, *American Government*, Manchester University Press, 2002
2 R. Pear, *American Government*, MacGibbon & Kee, 1963
3 D. Maidment and D. McGrew, *The American Political Process*, Sage/Open University, 1992
4 W. Wilson, *Congressional Government*, rev. edn, Meridian Books, 1956
5 R. Davidson and W. Oleszek, *Congress and its Members*, Congressional Quarterly Press, 1998
6 R. Denenberg, *Understanding American Politics*, Fontana, 1976
7 R. Evans and B. Novak, *Lyndon B. Johnson: The Exercise of Power*, New American Library, 1966
8 As quoted in C. Jillson, *American Government*, Harcourt Brace, 2007
9 R. Hague and M. Harrop, Comparative Government and Politics: An Introduction, Palgrave, 2007
10 M. Walles, *British and American Systems of Government*, P. Allan, 1988
11 D. Mayhew, *Congress: The Electoral Connection*, Yale University Press, 1974
12 C. Bailey, 'Ethics as Politics: Congress in the 1990s', in P. Davies and F. Waldstein (eds), *Political Issues in America*, Manchester University Press, 1991
13 D. Maidment and D. McGrew, as in 3 above
14 G. Wasserman, *The Basics of American Politics*, Longman, 1997.
15 D. Brinkley (TV anchorman), as quoted in T. Conlan, M. Wrightson and D. Beam, *Taxing Choices: The Politics of Tax Reform*, Congressional Quarterly Press, 1990
16 J. Rhodes (one-time House Republican leader), *The Futile System*, EPM Publications, 1976
17 M. Walles, as in 10 above

USEFUL WEB SITES

www.thomas.gov/ Named after Thomas Jefferson, the Library of Congress site that offers a comprehensive look at Congress in the past and today; useful information about current activities.

www.cq.com *Congressional Quarterly*. The authoritative site of the weekly magazine covering congressional activities, committees etc.

www.house.gov/ (House of Representatives) and **www.senate.gov/** (Senate). Both give valuable details about the work of the two chambers, reports about current legislation, the activities of congressmen, their conditions etc.

www.vote-smart.org/ Vote Smart. An easy-to-understand guide to current legislation going through either chamber.

SAMPLE QUESTIONS

1 Why is the US Senate more powerful and prestigious than the House of Representatives?
2 Examine the role of Congress in making the law. Is Congress an efficient law-making body?
3 Discuss the view that the real work of Congress is done in its committee rooms.
4 What is the most important responsibility of congressmen?
5 What factors affect the way in which members of Congress vote?
6 Discuss the view that Congress is more effective at representation than it is at law making.
7 Does Congress exercise effective scrutiny over the executive branch of government?
8 What reforms might lead to an improvement in the public perception of Congress?
9 Should Congress be more socially representative of the nation?
10 Why is Congress a more powerful legislature than the British Parliament?
11 Compare the background and roles of MPs and congressmen. What might an MP like and dislike about the American legislature?

7

The Supreme Court

The judiciary wields considerable political power in the US and for this reason must be considered in any discussion of the political process. Its members may not act overtly in the manner of a politician seeking election or re-election, but in a more passive way their influence is highly significant. They do not take the initiative, but rather wait for cases to be brought before them. At that stage, in the light of the facts presented, they can make judgments that may have important political implications.

In particular, the Supreme Court has a key role in making the Constitution relevant to modern needs and circumstances. It is not bound by past precedent and can specifically or implicitly overrule, ignore or modify rulings given in previous cases. Its decisions have important political significance. In this chapter, we examine the judiciary in general, but our attention will be particularly directed to the Supreme Court, its history, judgments and personnel.

POINTS TO CONSIDER

- What are the differences in role and method of appointment between the state and federal court systems in the USA?
- What are the qualifications for membership of the Supreme Court? Are the personalities and opinions of judges relevant?
- Why is the presidential choice of justices considered so important?
- What principles should guide judges as they interpret the American Constitution?
- Has judicial activism gone out of fashion?
- To what extent can the political role of an unelected judiciary be defended?
- Is the Supreme Court still a strong defender of the rights of the individual?
- Does the social background of leading judges matter?
- To what extent is the judiciary a powerful political factor in politics on either side of the Atlantic?

The judiciary is the branch of government that determines the outcome of legal disputes. It is responsible for the authoritative interpretation of law and the application of it to particular cases. Accordingly, judiciaries resolve disputes between individuals, adjudicating in controversies within the limits of the law; interpret the law, determining what it means and how it applies in particular situations, thereby assessing the guilt or innocence of those on trial; and act as guardians of the law, taking responsibility for applying its rules without fear or favour, as well as securing the liberties of the person and ensuring that governments and people comply with the 'spirit' of the constitution.

In democratic countries, it is expected that the judicial system will be enabled to function freely, without any interference from those who exercise political power. **Judicial independence** implies that there should be a strict separation between the judiciary and other branches of government.

> **judicial independence**
> The constitutional principle that there should be a strict separation of powers, in which there is a clear distinction between the judiciary and other branches of government.

The range of state and federal courts

There are today two parallel systems of courts in the United States that between them cover the range of **civil and criminal** cases. There are the state court systems established under the individual state constitutions: these decide actions and settle disputes concerning state laws. There is also the federal judicial system, which has become relatively more important as the country has expanded and the amount of legislation passed by Congress has increased. In effect, there are therefore fifty-one different judicial structures.

> **civil and criminal law**
> Civil law relates to private and civilian laws, and deals with relationships affecting individuals and organisations (for example family or property matters).
> Criminal law relates to crimes against the state. It is concerned with such things as theft, violence and murder.

The practice of state courts may vary significantly, for it is the essence of federalism that the states may run their own affairs in the way best suited to their own wishes and requirements. Differences of operation and terminology are inevitable, and this makes general comment on their structure more difficult. For instance, judges are elected in approximately three-quarters of the states, whilst in others they are appointed.

States are responsible for passing and enforcing most of the civil and criminal law of the United States. For every person in a federal prison, there are at least eight times more in a state one. The vast majority of cases are resolved in state municipal or justice courts in town and cities, with a right of appeal to the state appeals courts or, in a small minority of cases involving the interpretation of the state constitution or basic constitutional rights, to the state supreme court.

Federal courts enforce federal law and state courts enforce state law, but the relationship between the two systems is more complex than this. The federal

Constitution is the supreme law of the land, and if state law conflicts with it or with federal laws made under that Constitution, then state law gives way. This is made clear in the 'supremacy clause' of the Constitution (Article VI). Because of it, decisions made in the federal courts can have a broad impact on those made in the state courts.

We are primarily concerned with the federal judicial system, the structure of which is relatively simple. There are three layers of courts. At the bottom of the pyramid are the district courts, above them are the circuit courts of appeal and at the apex of the system is the Supreme Court, the highest court in the land.

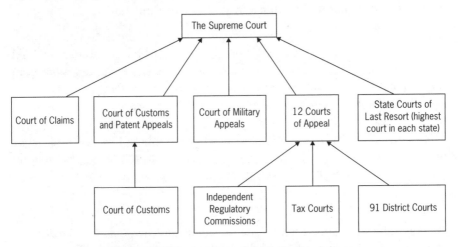

Figure 2 The structure of the federal judiciary

The operation of the courts in Britain and the United States: a comparison

- In both countries there is an elaborate network of courts that have responsibility for upholding the law. The guilt or innocence of those involved in criminal offences is determined after defendants have been given the opportunity to defend themselves. Those involved in civil disputes can get them resolved.

- In Britain, there is one basic judicial system for criminal law and a second that handles civil law. The United States has a more complex judicial structure. As a federal country, it has two court systems, a series of federal courts and a series of state/local ones. It is the state system which is used in the overwhelming majority of cases.

- In Britain and America, courts operate along adversarial lines, with the prosecution and defence each seeking to discredit the arguments advanced by the other side and to persuade the judge and/or jury of the merits of their case.

- Whereas in America those who handle cases are all attorneys, in Britain there is a distinction between barristers, who in most cases put forward the arguments before judge and jury, and solicitors, who are the initial point of contact for those in need of legal assistance. Solicitors do much of the preliminary, out-of-court work.

Judges in federal courts

In the United States, the term 'federal judge' usually refers to a judge who is nominated by the president and confirmed by the United States Senate, as laid down in Article III of the Constitution. The Senate Judiciary Committee typically conducts confirmation hearings for each nominee. Article III states that these judicial officers are appointed for a life term. Other judges serving in the federal courts, including magistrates and bankruptcy judges, are also sometimes referred to as 'federal judges'. However, they are not appointed in accordance with the procedures outlined in Article III. They are not 'Article III judges' because their power does not derive from Article III of the Constitution.

Although the number of Supreme Court justices has remained the same for well over a century, the number of court of appeals judges has more than doubled since 1950 and the number of district court judges has increased more than three times in that period. The number of federal judges at any particular time is liable to fluctuate, partly because there are always vacancies needing to be filled because of retirement or death. In addition, from time to time Congress will increase (or, less frequently, decrease) the number of federal judgeships in a particular judicial district, usually in response to shifting population numbers or a changing workload in that district.

The appointment of federal judges

Federal judges are appointed by the president, on the advice of the Department of Justice and the office of the deputy attorney-general. The names of potential nominees are often recommended by senators, or sometimes by members of the House who are of the president's political party. This power of appointment is highly significant. As Vile[1] puts it: 'No president can afford to ignore either the partisan advantages of such appointments or the fact that the men he appoints will be able, to say the least, to give a particular emphasis to the way in which policy is carried out.'

The power of appointment gives the president the opportunity to influence the balance of opinion in the courts. By 1940, Roosevelt had achieved a Democratic majority among federal judges, but the high point was reached during the presidency of Johnson, when more than 70% were of his party. In his 1980 election campaign, Reagan undertook to choose conservative judges who would abandon the social activism of many earlier appointees. His overt concern with the ideological stance of judges was in line with the Nixon approach, but a departure from the usual practice whereby party label was a more important consideration. For Reagan, Republican leanings alone were not a sufficient guarantee of suitability. He had the opportunity to appoint more lower-court judges than any of his predecessors since Franklin Roosevelt, filling about half of all the judgeships at that level.

Reagan's appointees were singularly conservative by nature, much more so than most previous Republican nominations. George H. Bush followed a similar approach in his selection of another 185 judges. The combined effect of the appointments made between 1981 and 1993 was to transform the type of personnel who sat in judgment on legal issues. Overwhelmingly, the nominees were young, white males who were deeply conservative. Few women, African Americans or members of other minority groups were selected, but in one respect the choices were unusual for Republican administrations. More Roman Catholics were chosen than usual, perhaps because the Justice Department was in sympathy with the Catholic stance on the controversial matter of abortion, and saw a chance to win some popularity with the Christian Right on the topic.

Appointments made in the Clinton era were quite distinctive. As a result of a rush of retirements, Clinton was able to nominate almost a quarter of all federal judges, and he used the opportunity to diversify the composition of the judiciary. Almost all of his nominees were Democrats, but many of them were more moderate and less ideological than some party members would have liked. George W. Bush also demonstrated an interest in a diversified bench, continuing the pattern established by his recent predecessors.

The tables below illustrate the different approaches of some past presidents, in particular those since 1981. They give an early indication of the background of judges appointed by Barack Obama:

Presidential appointments to the federal judiciary

1. Party affiliation of appointees under selected presidents		
President	Party	Party appointees (%)
Roosevelt	Democrat	97
Kennedy	Democrat	92
Nixon	Republican	93
Reagan	Republican	94
Bush snr	Republican	89
Clinton	Democrat	88
Bush jnr	Republican	92
Obama	Democrat	80

2. Profile of appointees under selected presidents				
Characteristic	Reagan	Bush senior	Clinton	George W. Bush	Obama
Female	28	36	110	69	25
Black	7	12	62	24	14
Hispanic	15	8	24	29	5
Asian	2	0	5	4	6
Total	368	185	376	325	55

Figures adapted from those provided by T. Cronin and M. Genovese, *The Paradoxes of the American Presidency*, Oxford University Press, 2004.

NB Figures for the G.W. Bush and Obama (to 4 November 2010) presidencies have been kindly provided by Sheldon Goldman, Professor of Political Science, University of Massachusetts at Amherst.

A determined Republican campaign in the Senate has side-tracked so many of the men and women nominated for judgeships by President Obama that he has put fewer people on the bench than any president since Richard Nixon at a similar point in his first term forty years ago. At the time of writing, fewer than half of his nominees have been confirmed. As of October 2010, most federal courts still had a majority of Republican appointees, reflecting Republican dominance of the White House in recent times. However, the party allegiance of the president who appointed a judge is not always a good indicator of that judge's judicial philosophy and place on the political spectrum.

The Supreme Court

Courts tend to have a reputation for conservatism. Often, they resist the tide of innovative enthusiasm, interpreting the law as it is, guarding precedents and securing rights that have been traditionally recognised. The American Supreme Court has at times acted in a remarkably radical way, and rather than reacting to the wishes of politicians it has sometimes forced them to deal with great issues of the day. In particular, it was the Court that was instrumental in the drive to establish the rights of American blacks on a firmer footing in the postwar era. By so doing, it was effecting a major change – one resisted by a large section of the population.

The Court has not regarded the American Constitution as fixed and unalterable, but rather as an evolving body of ideals. It has preserved the fundamental principles which underpin the whole political system and create its basic character, but it has sought to reformulate them at various times in a way which makes them relevant to the problems of the day. It was not expected to exhibit such extraordinary influence when the Constitution was devised.

The Constitution said little about the judiciary, and the status of the Court is only briefly sketched. Judicial power was vested in one Supreme Court 'and in such inferior courts as the Congress may from time to time ordain and establish', but it was unclear as to how important the main Court was to be. Few specific powers were set out, the document did not seek to limit its role. The expectation in the very early days of the Republic was that it would play a lesser role in the newly established governing arrangements than the other two branches of government.

Much of the Court's present-day influence stems from a series of remarkably vigorous interpretations of the law and Constitution by the fourth Chief Justice, John Marshall, who was the leading figure on the bench from 1801 until his death in 1835. He established the Court's pre-eminence in judicial matters, and helped to make it a major influence in American politics. His contribution was threefold. He:

- helped to establish the independence of the judiciary from other branches of government;
- developed the role of judicial review (see pp. 197–200);
- ensured that the Court's decisions were supreme over all courts in the land. He firmly believed in the importance of upholding national power over that of the states, and from this it followed that it was the duty of the Court to see that states did not infringe on the sovereignty of the federal government.

Size and composition

The Constitution is silent on the qualifications of judges. There is no requirement that judges be lawyers, although, in fact, all federal judges and Supreme Court justices have been members of the bar. Since the creation of the Court more than two hundred years ago, 120 justices have been appointed. The original Court comprised a Chief Justice and five associates. Thereafter, the number varied until, in 1869, the total was fixed at one Chief Justice and eight associates, and nine has been the figure ever since. Each justice has one vote, and rulings do not have to be decided unanimously. The Chief Justice is *primus inter pares* (first among equals), in relation to his colleagues.

Prior judicial service is not essential for service on the Court, and some 40% of all appointees since 1789 have had no kind of previous judicial experience in federal or state courts. Some leading figures on the bench have had a mainly political background. Earl Warren was a Californian politician, state attorney-general and governor before his elevation, and several others have been actively (some controversially) involved in political struggles before they gained recognition. It can be argued that such a background is more of an asset than a liability, for many of the decisions taken by justices are essentially political ones.

In making appointments to the Court, it follows that presidents have not been primarily concerned with the judicial expertise of their nominees. They want to choose people who share a broadly similar political outlook and judicial philosophy to their own, so that the passage of contentious legislation has an easier ride both now and in the future. John Adams did not appoint John Marshall solely because of the brilliance of Marshall's mind, but because they shared a number of beliefs. Ever since then, presidents have been interested in finding people who broadly share their own opinions.

Appointments are an opportunity to change the direction of the Court's approach, and thereby to influence the evolution of public policy. For any president, therefore, the primary concern is to find someone who represents his or her own thinking (almost certainly someone of the same party) and who will be acceptable to the congressmen who have to confirm the appointment.

Beyond these considerations, other factors may come into play, all of which have the merit of maximising the president's political advantage. Presidents may wish:

1 to make a gesture of recognition to some disadvantaged group, by appointing someone who is a member of, or sympathetic to, that community. In the distant past, it was sometimes considered prudent to ensure that there was a Catholic or Jew on the Court. In 1967, Lyndon Johnson saw the advantage of appointing a black justice (Thurgood Marshall); in 1981, President Reagan appointed the first woman, Sandra Day O'Connor; and in 2009 President Obama appointed the first Hispanic (Sonia Sotomayor). In such a way, the president may hope to boost his or her standing with the under-represented group;

2 directly to influence the Court's direction, as did Roosevelt with his Court-packing scheme, and Reagan with his attempt to curtail **judicial activism**;

3 to give favours in recognition of some past service. Warren backed Eisenhower at the 1952 Republican Convention, and in return was given a seat on the bench.

Richard Nixon consciously set out to change the balance of the Court, for like many conservatives he had become increasingly irritated by the persistent judicial activism of many who sat on the bench. He wanted to tip the balance by appointing people who would exercise **judicial restraint**: whose interest was in interpreting the Constitution and the law, rather than in breaking new ground via their adventurous decisions. 'Strict constructionists' were his preferred type of judges: in his words, those who would be 'caretakers of the Constitution . . . not super-legislators'. He was fortunate in having the opportunity to nominate four out of the nine justices on the Court at the time of his departure, and indeed if he had continued his presidency in the normal manner he would have been able to make another choice, and thereby gain a theoretical majority in his favour.

> **judicial activism**
> The view that the courts should be active partners in shaping government policy – especially in sensitive cases, such as those dealing with abortion and desegregation. Supporters are more interested in justice, 'doing the right thing', than in the exact letter of the text. They see the courts as having a role in looking after groups with little political influence, such as the poor and minorities.
>
> **judicial restraint**
> The idea that the courts should not seek to impose their views on other branches of government, except in extreme cases. Supporters of this view are constructionists: those who want the courts to limit themselves to implementing legislative and executive intentions. They want a passive role for the courts.

The plans of presidents do not always work out in the ways intended. In the Nixon years, two of his nominees – Harold Carswell and Clement Haynsworth – fell foul of Senate approval, the first time this had happened since the 1920s. Carswell had been involved in a conflict of interest, and Haynsworth was seen as a mediocre figure with a marked tendency towards racial bias. In 1987, Robert Bork, a distinguished former professor of law and later a well-known judge of conservative persuasion, was rejected following heated battles over his confirmation. The Senate Judiciary Committee questioned him for five days before it came to its verdict. The choice proved to be too controversial, for he had been associated with the dismissal of the special prosecutor during the Watergate scandal, and was seen as having contentious views and too partisan a past. Bork aroused deep suspicion among American liberals, who pledged millions of dollars in an attempt to fight the nomination; conservatives were willing to spend freely to defend his cause.

Other Republican nominees also had difficulties. The preferred replacement for Bork, Douglas Ginsberg, was rejected. President Reagan withdrew him when it became apparent that many senators were worried about his earlier use of marijuana. Clarence Thomas – accused by Anita Hill, a professor of law at Oklahoma Law School, of sexual harassment – was only confirmed after twelve days of embarrassing revelations at the Senate hearings in 1991, as graphic descriptions of his sexual habits were laid before the national television audience.

Altogether, 151 people have been nominated to the Supreme Court. The Senate has rejected twelve, taken no action on five and postponed votes on three; seven have declined the offer. On eight occasions, the president has withdrawn his nominee, most recently in the case of Harriet Miers (2005). Her nomination by G.W. Bush immediately ran into criticism from politicians and commentators across the political spectrum. She was widely perceived as unqualified for the position, and in recognition of the problems she was causing the president she asked him to withdraw her name.

In putting names forward, timing is often a consideration, for whereas most nominations in the first three years of a presidency are confirmed, the chances are less favourable in the fourth year. The broad general trend is for hearings to be longer than was once the case, so that in the more intensive scrutiny which now takes place a candidate needs to have a very clean record to get an easy passage. Controversial nominations inevitably are more likely to fail.

President Clinton was aware of the importance of his decision when his first opportunity arose to make an appointment. The existing Court had been chosen entirely by Republican presidents, and he faced a body that had become markedly conservative in character. He wanted to arrest the rightward drift of the Court's membership and find someone who would take a pro-choice line on abortion, as he had pledged to do in his campaign. Yet he was aware that an overtly liberal person could easily be 'Borked' by conservative opponents in either party.

When Byron White retired in 1993, this was the first opportunity for a Democrat to make an appointment for twenty-six years, and Clinton set out to find 'a person that has a fine mind, good judgement, wide experience of the law, and in the problems of real people, and someone with a big heart'. His selection of Ruth Bader Ginsburg was readily confirmed by the Senate, for she had a reputation for fairness and moderation, was obviously well qualified and was seen as someone who would interpret the law rather than become an advocate of special causes. Clinton's second nominee, Stephen Breyer, similarly survived the hearings without damage to his reputation or credibility.

The number of Supreme Court appointments made by recent Presidents

President	Period in office	Number of nominations	Number of appointments
Kennedy	Under 3 years	2	2
Johnson	Over 5 years	3	2
Nixon	Over 5 years	6	4
Ford	Over 2 years	1	1
Carter	4 years	0	0
Reagan	8 years	6	4
Bush senior	4 years	2	2
Clinton	8 years	2	2
George W. Bush	8 years	2	2
Obama	2 years (to January 2011)	2	2

Sometimes presidents find that the choice they have made turns out to be a wrong one from their own point of view. Harry Truman claimed that his biggest mistake was putting 'that damn fool from Texas' (Tom Clark) on the bench. Earl Warren proved to be a talented and innovative Chief Justice, but Eisenhower had not selected him as such, and never imagined that the Court would move in such a liberal direction under his leadership when he appointed him. 'Ike' was equally disenchanted with another of his appointments, Justice Brennan. Nixon was similarly disappointed with the performance of his appointees Blackmun and Powell. Appointed primarily for short-term political reasons, justices have a habit of becoming more independent and sometimes more creative when they are safely installed in office.

Procedure

The Court term begins in early October and runs through until June or July, depending on the workload. Throughout the term, it alternates between two weeks of open court, known as sessions, and two weeks of recess, during which the justices read petitions and write opinions. In the period when the Court is in session, the justices attend from Monday to Wednesday to hear oral arguments presented by the attorneys, whose presentations are strictly time-limited. **Briefs** (written documents) will have been presented before the hearing, so that in the oral sessions attorneys are supposed to discuss the case rather than read from a prepared text.

The more crucial stage is the **conference work**, during which the justices meet on two occasions a week to discuss and decide cases. The Chief Justice will initiate the discussion of each case, by outlining and commenting on the main issues as he or she sees them. Then, in order of seniority, the other eight members of the court are invited to comment. If the position of some justices is not clear at this stage, a formal but still preliminary vote will be taken. After the vote, the Chief Justice assigns the writing of the opinion to one of his or her colleagues. Others may decide to write **concurring opinions** (in agreement with the conclusion but not the reasoning of the majority) or **dissenting opinions** (that disagree with the majority conclusion). As the drafts are completed, the others comment upon them and may suggest changes in wording and reasoning. Sometimes this is a time-consuming procedure, for opinions may sharply diverge. The opinion-writing stage is only completed when all the justices have decided which opinion they support. When this has happened, the Court judgment is announced.

Role

The Supreme Court stands at the apex of the federal court system and is the only court specifically created by the Constitution. A decision of the Supreme Court cannot be appealed to any other court. Congress has the power to fix the number of judges sitting on the Court and, within limits, decide what kind of cases it may hear – but it cannot change the powers given to the Supreme Court by the Constitution itself.

The Supreme Court has original jurisdiction in only two kinds of cases – those involving foreign dignitaries, and those in which a state is a party. In all other cases, the Court is involved on appeal from lower courts or from the supreme courts of the fifty states. It decides on no more than 160–170 cases a year, although thousands are filed annually. Most are concerned with the interpretation of a particular law or the intentions of Congress in passing it.

An important part of the work of the Supreme Court involves the determination of whether executive acts or legislation conform to the Constitution. This is the power of **judicial review**,

> **judicial review**
> The power of any federal court to refuse to enforce a law or official act based on law because, in the view of the judges, it conflicts with the Constitution.

which is not specifically referred to in the original document. However, it is a doctrine inferred by the Court from its reading of the Constitution, and it was propounded very clearly in the *Marbury* v. *Madison* case (1803):

> A legislative act contrary to the Constitution is not law . . . it is emphatically the province and duty of the judicial department to say what the law is.

Judicial review is necessary because the Constitution provides only broad and rather vague principles for the organisation and operation of government. It

GEORGE W. BUSH AND BARACK OBAMA: THE IMPACT OF THEIR APPOINTMENTS

G.W. Bush

Much media interest centres on the nominations for judicial office made by modern presidents. In the 2000 election campaign, commentators speculated on the differing approaches to nomination that George W. Bush and Al Gore might adopt. It was realised that the impact of a Bush or Gore presidency on abortion rights and other controversial issues could be considerable, if a vacancy arose on the Supreme Court.

As president, G.W. Bush quickly indicated that he was seeking to adjust the composition of the judiciary in a more conservative direction. In so doing, he took advice from the **Federalist Society for Law and Public Policy**. Federalists were keen to steer the judiciary away from the liberalism of the past, and as a means of fulfilling this agenda they sought out ideologically acceptable candidates who might become suitable judges. Most members of George W. Bush's vetting panel for nominees belonged to the organisation.

> **Federalist Society for Law and Public Policy**
>
> Formed in the early 1980s to challenge the perceived liberal orthodoxy in most law schools, the Federalist Society serves as a haven for conservatives and libertarians who wish to ensure that the judiciary says what the law is and not what it should be. Members played an influential role in the impeachment proceedings against President Clinton and in the Florida legal offensive that brought G.W. Bush to power in 2001.

The president did not have an opportunity to make any nominations to the Supreme Court in his first administration. However, following his victory in 2004 he was able to make two appointments: John Roberts (initially nominated as an associate justice to replace Sandra Day O'Connor, but then – on Rehnquist's death – as Chief Justice) and Samuel Alito, a Roman Catholic of Italian descent whose nomination proved highly controversial, on account of his alleged record of restricting freedoms (in the eyes of the American Civil Liberties Union) and his anti-abortionist stance (in the eyes of pro-life activists). Alito was eventually confirmed by a narrow vote of 58–42.

Barack Obama

President Obama has made two successful nominations to the Supreme Court: that of an Appeals Court judge, Sonia Sotomayor, a Hispanic, to fill the vacancy created by the retirement of Associate Justice Souter; and that of former Solicitor General Elena Kagan to fill the vacancy created by Associate Justice Stevens, who announced his intention to retire at the end of the court's term in June 2010. Speculation has also focused on the potential retirement of Justice Ruth Ginsburg for health reasons.

Obama's views on judicial appointments had been made clear in his observations on the Bush nominations of Roberts and Alito, respectively.

> *On Roberts:* The problem I face . . . is that while adherence to legal precedent and rules of statutory or constitutional construction will dispose of 95% of the cases

that come before a court so that both a Scalia and a Ginsburg will arrive at the same place most of the time on those 95% of the cases – what matters on the Supreme Court is those 5% of cases that are truly difficult. In those . . . the constitutional text will not be directly on point . . . In those difficult cases, the critical ingredient is supplied by what is in the judge's heart . . . The problem I had is that when I examined Judge Roberts' record and history of public service, it is my personal estimation that he has far more often used his formidable skills on behalf of the strong in opposition to the weak.

On Alito: I have no doubt that Judge Alito has the training and qualifications necessary to serve. He's an intelligent man and an accomplished jurist. And there's no indication he's not a man of great character. But when you look at his record – when it comes to his understanding of the Constitution, I have found that in almost every case, he consistently sides on behalf of the powerful against the powerless; on behalf of a strong government or corporation against upholding Americans' individual rights.

Obama's views were reiterated in the 2008 election campaign. In a speech to the Planned Parenthood Fund (17 July 2007) he elaborated on his thinking:

I think the Constitution can be interpreted in so many ways. And one way is a cramped and narrow way in which the Constitution and the courts essentially become the rubber stamps of the powerful in society. And then there's another vision of the court that says that the courts are the refuge of the powerless. Because oftentimes they can lose in the democratic back and forth. They may be locked out and prevented from fully participating in the democratic process. . . . And we need somebody who's got the heart – the empathy – to recognize what it's like to be a young teenage mom. The empathy to understand what it's like to be poor or African American or gay or disabled or old – and that's the criteria by which I'll be selecting my judges.

Such observations give a clear indication of the kind of justice Obama favours and of the direction in which he would like to see the Court move. He has frequently spoken of the need to appoint people who are vulnerable in the political process, the outsiders, the members of minority groups, those who are voiceless or lack clout and any others for whom the system does not work. Whilst dissociating himself from some aspects of the judicial philosophy that pervaded the Warren Court, he praised the Chief Justice's empathy and feelings for ordinary people. In particular, he upheld David Souter (a G.H. Bush nominee of pragmatically liberal inclinations, who sat as an associate justice from 1990 to 2009) and Stephen Breyer – people of common sense rather than strict ideological commitment – as the sort of justice he would like to see on the Bench:

They take a look at the facts and they try to figure out: How does the Constitution apply to these facts? They believe in fidelity to the text of the Constitution, but they also think you have to look at what is going on around you and not just ignore real life. (Article in *The Detroit Free Press*, 3 October 2008)

establishes three branches based on the principle of the separation of powers, and it sets out a federal structure and guarantees certain individual rights. These rules have remained largely unaltered, but they require elaboration and interpretation. Somebody has to decide what the Constitution actually means, and then interpret its relevance to specific cases. The Supreme Court acts as the arbiter of the constitutionality of the acts of the legislature and the executive. In the words of Alexander Hamilton in the *Federalist Papers* (no. 78) the duty of the Court 'must be to declare all acts contrary to the manifest tenor of the Constitution void'.

After the 1803 case, the authority of the courts to act as the final arbiter on constitutional matters was confirmed in other cases in 1810 and 1821, and it has been accepted ever since. Maidment and McGrew[2] have calculated that some eighty federal statutes and more than 700 pieces of state legislation have been struck down in the subsequent period as 'unconstitutional'. The frequency of such rulings may be an indication that the federal and state governments have too often acted without due recognition of the constitutional proprieties involved, or of the assertive stance taken by Supreme Court justices. But two other possible explanations are:

1 that the Constitution has not proved to be a straightforward document to interpret. Maidment and McGrew ask whether the First Amendment ('Congress shall make no law . . . abridging the freedom of speech, or of the press') literally means that Congress cannot legislate on matters such as libel or pornography. Was the intention of those who devised the Constitution really to prevent Congress from passing any legislation at all in such areas, or was it really meant to be a safeguard of political liberty, to prevent undue exercise of governmental power which might curb beliefs and the expression of ideas on matters political, social and economic?

2 that the courts have had to deal with a changing country. Even if the intention of the framers of the Constitution was to create a system that would last indefinitely, a society in rapid development clearly needs some machinery to accommodate the pace of change. The Court has had to be faithful to the original document, yet seek to interpret its provisions in a way relevant to the times. The increased role of government in the social and economic lives of the people has posed a clear challenge to those on the bench. From after the Civil War through to the Great Depression of the early 1930s, the regulation of economic activity by the government became a key issue. From the presidency of Franklin D. Roosevelt, the scale of federal intervention has grown dramatically, and the Supreme Court found much of the New Deal legislation unacceptable in its original form.

Case load

Ten thousand cases are tried annually by the American courts, 2% of them by federal ones. Of these, around seven or eight thousand reach the Supreme Court.

In an average year, around ninety are the subject of oral argument, and seventy or eighty are decided by a signed, written opinion. The broad trend of recent decades has been for the justices to hear fewer cases than their predecessors did. In William Rehnquist's first term the Court disposed of 175; in the equivalent period for John Roberts, it dealt with only 82. Only a handful of the judgments delivered have such an impact that they define the Supreme Court in the eyes of the American public.

The Supreme Court has made decisions affecting every aspect of American life, decisions which have shaped the course of development in every sphere of governmental activity. The earliest ones were often concerned with the division of responsibility between the federal and state governments at a time when the nation was rapidly expanding in size. The question of slavery was relevant to that discussion. Thereafter, the degree of economic regulation by the government was a controversial subject, as was later the massive expansion of federal activity in the New Deal in the 1930s. Since World War II, the issues tackled by the Court have often been of a different type, for by then the debates over the degree of economic regulation and intervention had been resolved. The issues of the postwar era have been ones of civil liberties and rights.

The Court and political controversy

The Supreme Court is a complex body, for it is neither a completely judicial nor a completely political/policy-making body. As Grant[3] observes: 'Politics play a crucial role in the appointment, working and decision-making of the . . . Court, and many of its judgements have broad policy implications.' Yet if its work and personnel are involved in political controversy at various times, it is also supposed to interpret the Constitution, a function that places it above the everyday political fray.

The Court has constantly been involved in political matters, even though in theory it has generally stayed clear of questions of direct political controversy. Its rulings can and often have had political implications, so that when, in *Dred Scott* v. *Sandford* (1857), the Court declared that a slave was a property and had no rights, this was a serious blow to those campaigning for an end to slavery. In other words, a judicial judgment had impacted on the political process.

In the 1930s, a Court reflecting the conservatism of the 1920s overturned eight statutes aimed at fighting the economic devastation of the Great Depression. Roosevelt was dissatisfied with the Court's performance, for its members posed a threat to the New Deal by their willingness to strike down key measures as 'unconstitutional'. The broad objection raised was that the federal government was exceeding its authority, and that the president and his advisers were too willing to downplay constitutional considerations. Since then, there has been much debate about the rights and wrongs of the issue, some writers believing that legislation should have been more carefully drafted, others taking the view that political malice was involved. Four of the nine justices were hostile to the New Deal, seeing it as a threat to property rights and the powers of the states. Several of them were elderly and conservative.

As a result, FDR came up with a Court-packing scheme, which would have enlarged its size and curtailed the power of older members. The plan ran into opposition, for it seemed to some Americans to be a bending of the rules. However, in the end Roosevelt got his way, for after 1937 the president had no further problems with the Court, as its members – reinforced by new appointments – began to allow legislation to pass onto the statute book ('a switch in time, saved nine').

In the 1950s and 1960s, the judgments of the Warren Court (see pp. 204–206) ushered in one of the most liberal periods in the history of the Supreme Court. Some of its decisions aroused intense controversy, as indicated by the abortive movement at one time during his stewardship to replace the existing Court with a new Constitutional Court of fifty members.

The decisions of the Court are not mere exercises in constitutional exegesis (interpretation). They are related to the great questions of the day, and the verdicts delivered impinge upon the nation's economic, political and social life. Can a tax be levied? Can an abortion be performed? If so, under what conditions? Can pornography be banned? Can races be segregated? These are all issues of primary concern to many Americans, and decisions broadly seen as liberal or conservative can greatly affect the tone of political debate. On some controversial questions, such as church–state relations, affirmative action programmes and abortion, the Court was evenly balanced, often voting 5–4 one way or the other, until the early 1980s. The choice of justices was therefore a highly significant one. It had political, as much as judicial, implications.

The political role of the Court is well established, and the justices play an important part in the political process. They are appointed for political reasons, and after their appointment they inhabit an intensely political atmosphere. It may seem strange to many people that matters affecting the fate of society are ultimately decided by nine unelected justices who, once on the bench, have no direct contact with public opinion. But as has often been pointed out, 'they read the election returns, too'. In other words, they understand prevailing pressures, and react to changing moods among the population, as in their decisions on affirmative action in recent years.

At various times, the Court runs into difficulties with the left and the right, for both liberals and conservatives sometimes find its decisions controversial and unacceptable. This is because it is charged with handling issues that are of vital importance to democracy and society at large. Yet justices use their powers sparingly, for they realise that if they allow themselves to become out of step with popular opinion for too long, then the reputation of the Court will be damaged. They also wish to avoid open confrontation with the other branches of government. They understand the need to interpret the Constitution in the light of the requirements of today's industrialised society, and thus ensure that it remains a living document which continues to command general assent. The Court has performed its role rather well, and Professor Archibald Cox,[4] the Watergate special prosecutor, has explained the reasons for this success:

> The Court must know us better than we know ourselves . . . the roots of its decisions must already be in the nation. The aspirations voiced by the Court must be those the community is willing not only to avow but in the end to live by, for the power of the constitutional decisions rests upon the accuracy of the Court's perceptions of this kind of common will and upon the Court's ability, by expressing its perception, ultimately to command a consensus.

Judges and their role in Britain and the United States: a comparison

One of the most significant political developments in Britain in recent decades has been the growing importance of judges and the courts. Previously, the role of the courts in British politics had been restricted and sporadic, whereas it is now often said to be central and constant. Today, the power of judges to review the legality of governmental action has become an important stage in the public policy process. Its increased relevance was apparent when in 1987 government lawyers produced a document for civil servants, entitled *The Judge over your Shoulder*. It showed them how to avoid the pitfalls into which they might tumble.

Between 1981 and 1996, the number of applications for judicial review rose from just over 500 to nearly 4,000; in the latter year alone, there were 1,748 immigration applications and 340 concerning homelessness. The increasing resort to review and the decisions which judges reached in several cases, ranging from criminal injuries to deportation, caused resentment under the Major government. Tension became acute, for ministers were overtly critical of judges and complained about judicial activism, whilst some judges felt there was a campaign to discredit them. The tabloid press joined in the 'judge-bashing', complaining of the 'galloping arrogance' of the judiciary.

Opponents of a British Bill of Rights – many of whom are Conservatives – often claim that it would remove power from the hands of elected MPs and give it to the judges. Similar fears about the transfer of power to the judiciary are at the heart of much anxiety about the 1998 Human Rights Act, which incorporated the European Convention on Human Rights into British law. If today that suspicion is often voiced on the political right, in the past it was the labour movement that felt uneasy about judicial power. Its suspicion was not based solely on a number of well-documented and unfavourable verdicts. It had much to do with a feeling that these judgments derived from problems about the selection, backgrounds and attitudes of those 'on the bench'.

Many British judges have formerly practised at the bar, membership of which has long been thought to be elitist and unrepresentative. Members tend to have professional, middle-class backgrounds, and have often been educated at public school before attending Oxbridge. In other words, they are said to be conservative, wealthy and out of touch. A privileged lifestyle might not by itself render judges unsuitable to exercise greater political influence. But – it is alleged – the nature of their training, and the character of the job they do, tends to give them a preference for traditional standards of behaviour and make them particularly impressed by traditional values in matters of behaviour, family life and respect for the law. They are unlikely to be overly sympathetic to demonstrators, minority activists and those who are strident in seeking justice for their cause.

Courts of law are part of the political process in most democratic countries, for governmental decisions and acts passed by the legislature may require judicial decisions to be implemented. Courts need to be independent to be respected, but in practice this is difficult to achieve. There is rarely full independence as far as appointment is concerned, though in America the process is more overtly political.

As a broad trend, the role of judges in the political system has increased in liberal democracies. Some fear that this political involvement has gone too far, and that there are dangers for the standing of judges if this is unchecked. Others worry less about the damage which may be done to their reputation, but instead place their emphasis upon fear of judicial power. In both countries, alarm is sometimes raised about the politicisation of the judiciary, and interest centres on the character and leanings of those who are appointed judges.

Nowadays, to see the judiciary purely as being preoccupied with the legal system would be to ignore its key political role. As Chief Justice Holmes once put it: 'We are under the Constitution, but the Constitution is what the judges say it is.' In Britain too, judges are now much more willing to step into the political arena, an area long inhabited by justices of the Supreme Court. The same fear about their activities is voiced in both countries: those on the bench are unelected, unaccountable and invariably rather elderly.

Four Chief Justices and their courts

Earl Warren, 1953–69

At the time of his appointment, Warren was not thought of as being progressive. He was widely expected to be a consolidator, so Eisenhower could feel comfortable with his choice. Yet the Warren Court was to be noted for its judicial activism. Decisions taken in that era were of fundamental importance, and concerned such things as the rights of individuals, especially minorities, equal representation and equality before the law. This was an innovative Court, one of the most liberal in its history. It made a huge impact on many aspects of American life, so that the years 1953–69 witnessed what has widely been seen as a constitutional revolution.

Some of the reasons for this 'judicialisation' of politics have been listed by Richard Hodder-Williams:[11]

1. 'the failure of the political process to meet the aspirations of those who are governed under it';

2. 'the rise of the administrative state and a bevy of bureaucracies the decisions of which affect so much of so many people's lives';

3. the rise of 'a more educated, more challenging electorate that is less deferential to government in all its forms and is more aware of deficiencies through a lively, and often vulgar, press';

4. the development of 'an ideological shift throughout Europe and America, which has enhanced the status of rights-based demands and has redefined a substantial part of what politics is about, away from struggles between classes and religious groups towards conflict between the coercive powers of the state and the individual';

5. the influence of particular and influential individuals 'like Lord Denning in Britain and Earl Warren in the United States, who had the strength of character and self-belief to challenge the old orthodoxies and help usher in new values and expectations';

6. the increased use of international conventions in the modern world and the proliferation of international or transnational courts to enforce them, ranging from the European Court of Human Rights to the European Court of Justice, from the World Trade Organisation panels to the North American Free Trade Agreement panels. They test national law against some other body of law, usually treated as being superior. In some cases, these agreements or conventions have involved members of the Bench in any member country ruling against the decisions of the party in power.

It was in the field of civil rights that Warren made his greatest impact. Segregation had developed in the United States under the constitutional doctrine laid down in *Plessey* v. *Ferguson* (1896), when it was decided that it was constitutional to segregate people according to colour on the railways, as long as the separate facilities were equal in quality. In the landmark judgment in *Brown* v. *Board of Education in Topeka, Kansas* (1954), it was declared that segregation in schools was unconstitutional, for separate facilities were seen as inherently unequal, and thus a breach of the Fourteenth Amendment, which declared that no state could 'deny to any person within its jurisdiction the equal protection of the laws'. The verdict applied only to segregation in schools, but it soon became apparent in other judgments that no service offered by the state could be provided on a segregated basis. The Court later ruled that it was constitutional to bus children across school district lines to achieve racial equality, a decision which upset many northerners, just as the 1954 ruling was greeted with dismay in the South.

The Warren Court exhibited a new spirit of tolerance on other issues of civil liberty, but it was the liberal approach it adopted on the treatment of criminals that aroused fury on the political right. Justices took the view that it was necessary to impose new guidelines on the police because the balance of opinion had swung too much in the direction of the prosecution rather than those on trial. Those opposed to this change of direction were often moved to outrage, as indicated by the posters that appeared – 'Impeach Earl Warren'. Some used 'hang' instead of 'impeach'!

THE WARREN COURT AT WORK: TWO RULINGS THAT ILLUSTRATE ITS LIBERAL TONE

Gideon v. Wainwright (1963)

Under the Sixth Amendment, the accused has a right to representation by a lawyer. But states were not required to provide attorneys to poor defendants until 1932, when this right was established for capital offences. In 1963, the Court ruled that states would have to pay to ensure legal representation for everyone on a low income who was a defendant in a case of serious crime.

Griswold v. Connecticut (1965)

The Court struck down a Connecticut state law banning the use of contraception even by married couples, basing the judgment on a 'right to privacy' that Justice Douglas decided could be inferred in the Bill of Rights. This was **'loose constructionism'** in practice and the new right so established was to be quoted more controversially a few years later in Roe v. Wade (1973).

loose constructionism
A doctrine that allows the Constitution to be interpreted more loosely or liberally than would be suggested by a strict reading of the document. Loose constructionists do not feel bound by the exact meaning of particular words or phrases and tend to be sympathetic to notions of judicial activism. They are broadly willing to extend the scope of federal governmental power.

Such judgments aroused dismay and opposition. Critics felt that via the new liberal line, the Court was becoming too immersed in political controversy. In the 1968 election, the performance of the Warren Court came under much scrutiny. Richard Nixon promised to appoint **'strict constructionists'** to the Supreme Court: those who would confine themselves to the task of interpretation, rather than engage in 'political meddling'. When Warren resigned shortly afterwards, Nixon (as president) had his opportunity. He nominated Warren Burger as his successor.

strict constructionists
Supporters of the view that judges must examine the exact wording of the Constitution and identify its plain, literal meaning. Generally conservative, they are supporters of judicial restraint and tend to be strongly in favour of the rights of individual states.

The Burger Court 1969–86

The Burger Court was again intended to be a consolidating one, but the counter-revolution that Nixon favoured never really took place. Although the new nominees appointed in this period were generally conservative, they did not seek to undo the work of Earl Warren and his colleagues. The Court may not have been as innovative as its predecessor, but it produced some surprisingly bold judgments – especially on racial matters, abortion and Watergate.

The Court decided that affirmative action could be constitutional (see the Baake case of 1978, p. 402); made a landmark judgment on abortion (in *Roe* v. *Wade*, 1973, it struck down state anti-abortion laws and ruled in favour of the right of women to control what happened to their own bodies); and although in matters of criminal justice it was sympathetic towards police powers, there was no attempt to return to the pre-Warren era.

THE BURGER COURT AT WORK: TWO RULINGS THAT ILLUSTRATE ITS BALANCED TONE

Swann v. *Mecklenberg Board of Education* (1971)

De jure (legal) segregation had been outlawed in 1954, but de facto segregation was still in place; if blacks lived in one part of the town, then the local school would be overwhelmingly black, and vice versa. The Court permitted the bussing of black and white students across cities, in order to ensure a racial balance in schools.

Miller v. *California* (1973)

Having been made more conservative in composition by the four Nixon appointees, the Court moved to limit the spread of sexually explicit materials. It decided that prosecutors no longer needed to be able to demonstrate that a work was 'utterly without redeeming social value'. They only had to show that it did not possess 'serious literary, artistic, political or scientific value', for it to lose its protection as speech under the First Amendment.

It was the Burger Court that ruled against President Nixon in the matter of the Watergate tapes, recordings made by those around the president to provide him with a clear record of conversations that had taken place in the Oval Office. As the scandal unfolded, with its allegations of a massive cover-up and obstruction of justice following the break-in at the Watergate building, a federal district court judge issued a subpoena, ordering the president to release sixty-four tapes. The president claimed executive privilege, and refused to release them to the special prosecutor. The Supreme Court insisted unanimously that the tapes must be handed over, and Nixon complied with the decision – an illustration of the status of the Supreme Court. The executive and legislative branches of government abide by its decisions, even though it lacks any direct means of enforcement. The impact of the 'tapes issue' was enormous, and within a fortnight Nixon had resigned. The action of the Court had again been of momentous consequence.

The Rehnquist Court 1986–2005

Given the disappointment felt by many conservatives over the performance of the Burger Court, President Reagan was determined to appoint justices of conservative persuasion. He opted for William Rehnquist as Chief Justice on Burger's retirement. The Rehnquist Court lasted until 2005.

Commentators of more liberal leanings were wary of Rehnquist's elevation. At the time of his appointment, they saw him as the most conservative member of the existing nine justices. However, even many of those who were uneasy about the direction in which he might lead the Court could recognise his intellect and diplomatic skill. Observers from the left and the right noted his early efforts to improve the Court's efficiency and his effectiveness in dealing with colleagues.

THE REHNQUIST COURT AT WORK: SIX RULINGS THAT ILLUSTRATE ITS CAUTIOUSLY CONSERVATIVE TONE

Bowers v. Hardwick (1986)

By then rather more conservative in tone, the Court decided by 5–4 in 1986 that the 'right to privacy' did not extend to consensual gay sex. States were permitted to pass their own laws on matters relating to single-sex relationships.

Texas v. Johnson (1989) and US v. Eichman (1990)

In this early 5–4 ruling, the Court decided that the burning of the 'Stars and Stripes' represented a form of protected free expression under the First Amendment. Two conservatives, Kennedy and Scalia, found the action deplorable, but given the wording of the Constitution, they felt they had little choice but to permit it. When Congress passed a law outlawing desecration of the national flag, the Court stepped in with another judgment. In 1990, it found the congressional statute unconstitutional, in that violated the guarantee of free speech as set out in the Bill of Rights.

Reno v. American Civil Liberties Union (1997)

The Court unanimously struck down the Communications Decency Act (1996) that had prohibited 'indecent' and 'patently offensive' material on the Internet or in e-mails. It adjudged that the statute lacked precision and undermined the protection offered under the First Amendment.

With the benefit of hindsight, it is now easier to review the performance of the Rehnquist Court. Overall, it handled proportionately fewer cases than previous courts and struck down fewer federal and state laws. Its judgments were generally cautious and less spectacular than some given by its predecessors.

The Court took a notably less progressive line than its two predecessors. The majority of justices did not see it as their task to act as the guardian of individual liberties and civil rights for minority groups. Yet their broad approach was to nibble away at the edges of contentious issues, rather than make a direct challenge to the whole direction of past policy in areas such as abortion and affirmative action. As Biskupic[5] and some other commentators noted: 'Gone is the self-consciously loud voice the Court once spoke with, boldly stating its position and calling upon the people and other institutions of government to follow.'

The failure to reverse many liberal judgments of an earlier era disappointed many conservatives, but none the less Schwartz[6] detected in the Rehnquist Court a series of cumulative decisions 'limiting the use of habeas corpus by prisoners, broadening the power of the police to search automobiles, applying the harmless

Washington v. Glucksberg (1997)

The justices found that euthanasia, 'mercy-killing' or 'assisted suicide', was not a constitutional right and was therefore a matter for state decision.

Boy Scouts of America v. Dale (2000)

By 5–4, the Court decided that the requirement that the Boy Scouts admit homosexuals as scout leaders was a violation of the rights of scouting groups to free association.

Virginia v. Black (2003)

By 6–3, the justices declared that the ritual burning of a cross (as done by the Ku Klux Klan) can be banned by states if the purpose of the event is to intimidate or terrorise. The act of burning can be interpreted as threatening and therefore cannot be regarded as protected expression.

NB Several of the judgments of the Rehnquist Court were decided on the basis of narrow majority verdicts, often by 5–4 (for example twenty-one out of seventy-four in 1999–2000). Many commentators detected a lack of consistency in them, some extending rights under the First Amendment, others curbing them.

The Supreme Court and the 2000 presidential election

The final decision of the Court in the *George W. Bush* v. *Albert Gore Jnr* case was among the most momentous of its history. In addition to deciding this particular presidency, it could have the effect in future of pushing the nation's highest court into more election battles – an area it has traditionally avoided.

The Court was dealing with an appeal by George Bush Jnr against a ruling in the Florida Supreme Court to order a manual recount in the state. The Court basically had three options:

1. It could have found for Bush on the grounds that the only votes usually counted in Florida are those clearly marked, so that the state's Supreme Court decision to allow other votes to be included was a departure from normal practice. Justices Rehnquist, Scalia and Thomas were supporters of this viewpoint, which, if handed down, would have been final and stopped all recounts without qualification.

2. It could have ruled clearly for Gore, deferring – as federal courts normally would do – to state courts on matters of state law. This might have involved issuing guidance to the Florida Supreme Court on how the recount should proceed. Justices Breyer and Ginsburg wanted to do this. To do so would have made the process lengthier, but would have meant that ultimately the choice lay with the voters.

3. The third option, which it actually took, was to seem to do the second, whilst actually doing something akin to the first. By 7–2, it sent the case back to the Florida Supreme Court (FSC) 'for further proceedings not inconsistent with this opinion'. In practice, as the various dissenting opinions made clear, this meant that by 5–4 the FSC had to have the votes counted, allow sufficient time for judicial review of these proceedings and do it all by midnight, 12 December, two hours after the Supreme Court issued its ruling (the date by when the Electoral College votes were supposed to be over).

---

error doctrine to a constitutional error committed at the trial, and upholding regulations prohibiting abortion counselling, referrals or advocacy by federally funded clinics'.

This widely held view of the Rehnquist Court and its alleged judicial restraint has been questioned. Its greater ideological conservatism is generally accepted, although its record on civil liberties was more mixed than the term might imply. Some commentators have suggested that it was highly activist in its willingness to challenge the elected branches of government. Comparing the Warren and Rehnquist eras, Rosen[7] argues that both courts were committed to an increase in judicial power: 'Both combine haughty declarations of judicial supremacy with contempt for the competing views of the political branches.' Others too[8] have observed that for all of the lip-service paid to judicial self-restraint, 'most of the current justices appear entirely comfortable intervening in all manner of issues, challenging state as well as national power, and underscoring the Court's role as final arbiter of constitutional issues'.

By opting for the impossible, this meant that the Court effectively handed victory to Bush.

In the Court's defence, seven justices had found serious constitutional violations in the way that the manual recounts had been conducted. Even Associate Justice Ginsburg, a Democrat appointment, called the process 'flawed'. They were uneasy about the way in which decisions on vote counting were being taken away from the officials whom the legislature had appointed for the task of managing the election, and handing them over to the judiciary. Neither was the recount to include 'all ballots', a requirement of state law. All in all, the Court had brought finality to a messy business and produced a result.

To Gore sympathisers, any outcome of the Court's deliberations would have been questionable, but the final decision seemed to be intellectually less than rigorous. Doubts were expressed about the reasoning and remedy that led to the verdict. The verdict expressed implied that the Supreme Court knew better than the Florida Supreme Court what was meant by Florida state law, a strange judgment from a generally constructionist court which has generally been very sympathetic to states' rights. As Justice Breyer pointed out, the Florida Supreme Court would have preferred a recount finished on 18 December (when Electoral College votes were due to be certified), for it had stressed 'the will of the voters' and its willingness to recount ballots in its decision.

By rejecting some ballots, as it effectively did, and acting in a way that seemed to reflect its Republican majority, the Supreme Court involved itself in controversy. The case created intense excitement and partisan feeling, and Americans and observers worldwide were waiting to see how the verdict would go. By its judgment, it has risked eroding public confidence in its collective wisdom and fairness, what Justice Breyer called 'a public treasure that has been built up over many years'.

The Roberts Court 2005–

John Roberts is the seventeenth and current Chief Justice of the Supreme Court. George W. Bush appointed him as an associate justice in mid-2005, but on the death of Rehnquist the president nominated him as his successor, thereby making him the youngest person to be appointed as Chief Justice since John Marshall took the bench in 1801. He is a Catholic, with generally conservative social and political views.

In his earlier career, Roberts spent fourteen years in private law practice and held positions in Republican administrations in the Department of Justice and Office of the White House Counsel. Immediately prior to joining the Court, he served as a judge on the Court of Appeals for the District of Columbia Circuit for two years.

In the Senate Judiciary Committee hearings, Roberts spoke of his wish to see the Supreme Court issue more unanimous opinions, something difficult to achieve because the Court sometimes seems as divided as the nation over abortion and other contentious social issues. He indicated his support for some abortion restrictions, but did not commit himself to overturning *Roe* v. *Wade*. His nomination was approved by a vote of seventy-eight to twenty-two. He received support from many Democrats as well as Senate Republicans.

The Roberts Court at work

Early on in his period as Chief Justice, the associate justice Antonin Scalia remarked that Roberts 'pretty much run[s] the show the same way' as did his predecessor, albeit 'let[ting] people go on a little longer at conference . . . but [he'll] get over that.' In line with his previously expressed preference, Roberts

---

THE ROBERTS COURT AND ITS WORK: SIX RULINGS THAT ILLUSTRATE ITS TONE

Gonzales v. *Oregon* (2006)

The judgment in a case concerning physician-assisted suicide does not allow the Attorney-General to prevent physicians from prescribing drugs for the assisted suicide of the terminally ill. In Oregon, euthanasia had been legalised in 1994 and the case before the Court represented the final stage of a challenge by the first Attorney-General of the George W. Bush administration to this state decision. He argued that the use of drugs to end lives was not a legitimate medical purpose and therefore was not legal under the Controlled Substances Act. The decision went against the Attorney-General and made clear that it was not possible for the federal law officer to declare illegal a medical practice authorised under state law. Along with justices Scalia and Thomas, Roberts dissented from the ruling.

Georgia v. *Randolph* (2006)

The majority decision prohibited police from searching a home if, as in this case, both occupants are present but one occupant objects while another consents. Roberts wrote his first dissent in this case, expressing the fear that the Court's ruling would limit the ability of police to combat domestic violence. He also noted that although the purpose of the Fourth Amendment was to protect individual privacy, any person who shares a dwelling (or, as Roberts points out, a locker or a hard drive) with another person, may anticipate that the other person sharing access to their belongings might turn them over to authorities. In short, to share a home with someone is to surrender privacy to that person, who might consent to an invasion of it. Roberts also asserted that the majority opinion was arbitrary, being inconsistent with prior case law.

Jones v. *Flowers* (2006)

In a case involving the due process requirement that a state should give notice to an owner before selling his or her property because of unpaid taxes, the Court ruled that

achieved unanimity in over 49% of the cases in his first year and has been similarly on track ever since. There has been the same search for agreement, but there are limits to the power of any Chief Justice to obtain consensus. However, to a greater degree than his predecessors, he urges that avoidable disagreements be resolved in the Court's internal conference, rather than being aired in unnecessarily provocative passages or footnotes in an opinion.

From the beginning, the Roberts Court has been portrayed as a consistent advocate of conservative principles by legal analysts such as Jeffrey Toobin,[9] an American lawyer and legal analyst for CNN and *The New Yorker*. Others have noted his commitment to judicial restraint. In reviewing Roberts's first term on the court, Seventh Circuit Judge Diane Sykes[10] concluded that:

---

due diligence must be demonstrated and proper notification be sent to the owners prior to any sale. Roberts sided with the liberal majority on this issue.

Gonzales v. Carhart (2007)

In a majority ruling, the Court upheld the constitutionality of the Partial-Birth Abortion Ban Act. Whereas Justice Thomas urged in his concurring opinion that the 1973 Court judgment on *Roe* v. *Wade* should be reversed, Roberts did not join him. He supports some restrictions on abortion.

Morse v. Frederick (2007)

The Court ruled that a student in a public school-sponsored activity does not have the right to advocate drug use, for the right to free speech does not prevent the exercise of school discipline. Roberts authored the judgment.

Presley v. Georgia (2010)

The Court ruled that the right to a public trial under the Sixth Amendment extends to the jury-selection phase of the trial. The Court noted an existing precedent establishing a right of the press under the First Amendment to access to the jury-selection phase of a trial. The Court extended this right to the criminal defendant, holding that the Sixth Amendment gives criminal defendants a personal right to have the jury-selection phase of their trial open to the public. The Court said that while the right is not absolute, trial courts are obligated to take every reasonable measure to accommodate a request for public attendance at a criminal trial. Because the trial court in this case did not consider any reasonable alternatives to closing the courtroom during jury selection, the Court reversed the judgment (by 7–2, with only Scalia and Thomas dissenting) of the Georgia Supreme Court and remanded the case for further proceedings.

his jurisprudence 'appears to be strongly rooted in the discipline of traditional legal method, evincing a fidelity to text, structure, history, and the constitutional hierarchy. He exhibits the restraint that flows from the careful application of established decisional rules and the practice of reasoning from the case law. He appears to place great stock in the process-oriented tools and doctrinal rules that guard against the aggregation of judicial power and keep judicial discretion in check: jurisdictional limits, structural federalism, textualism, and the procedural rules that govern the scope of judicial review.

The Roberts Court in 2011

The Court currently consists of six males and three females; one African American and eight Caucasians (one of whom is Latino); six Roman Catholics, three Jews and therefore, unusually, no Protestants. As of October 2010, the average age of the justices was 64 years 9 months, and their average length of service was 12 years 2 months.

The Court currently comprises five justices appointed by Republican presidents and four appointed by Democratic presidents. In journalistic, legal and political circles, justices Roberts, Scalia, Thomas and Alito are usually categorised as being conservatives, Ginsbsurg, Breyer and Sotomayor as liberals and Kennedy as a conservative who is liable to vote with the liberals – especially on matters of civil liberties – and is therefore potentially a 'swing vote'. Recent appointee Elena Kagan had at the time of writing not yet cast a vote.

The current Supreme Court justices

	Year of birth	Year of appointment	President who made appointment
Chief Justice			
John Roberts	1955	2005	George W. Bush
Associate justices			
Antonin Scalia	1936	1986	Reagan
Anthony Kennedy	1936	1988	Reagan
Clarence Thomas	1948	1991	Bush
Ruth Ginsburg	1933	1993	Clinton
Stephen Breyer	1938	1994	Clinton
Samuel Alito	1950	2006	George W. Bush
Sonia Sotomayo	1954	2009	Obama
Elena Kagan	1960	2010	Obama

The judiciaries of Britain and the United States: a comparison		
	Britain	*The United States*
Liberal democracy	Liberal democracy, based on rule of law	Liberal democracy, based on rule of law
Approach to judicial review	Modest form of judicial review of executive actions	Strong version of judicial review, courts able to strike down laws or other official acts as 'unconstitutional'
Selection of judges	Judicial appointments made by new Judicial Appointments Commission	President appoints Supreme Court justices and federal judges (election of judges in state judicial systems)
Security of judges	Judges very hard to remove	Appointments normally made for life, though impeachment possible in theory
Background of judges	Chosen from narrow social base, often seen as white, male and middle class, and deeply conservative. Few women and ethnic minority members on bench.	Presidential appointees vary, Democrat presidents traditionally more likely to appoint women and members of ethnic minorities – for example Clinton's willingness to diversify composition
Judicial activism v. judicial restraint	Judges traditionally confined themselves to interpretation of law, shunning political involvement or controversy. The courts are now more willing to take a more active role in government. Influenced by European experience, many are now more willing to take on ministers, and criticise their policies and review their actions.	Republican presidents tend to prefer judges who adopt a more passive approach to their role and seek only to interpret the Constitution. Many Democrats favour judges who take a more activist approach and who see courts as having a key role in shaping policy. Such activism was evident in the 1950s, over the promotion of racial integration.

CONCLUSION

Much interest centres on the composition of the Court at any time, with the past records of the nine coming under much scrutiny. It is common to portray justices as conservatives, liberals or moderates. Yet the reality is that such categorisations are simplistic, perhaps seeming to imply more division than actually exists. Tom Goldstein,[12] a lecturer, attorney and regular blogger on the Supreme Court who specialises in analysing and summarising its decisions, argues that the popular view of the Court as sharply divided along ideological lines, with each side pushing an agenda at every turn, is 'in significant part a caricature designed to fit certain preconceptions'. His research indicates that in the

2009 term almost half the cases were decided unanimously and only about one-fifth by a close 5–4 vote; barely one in ten cases involved the straightforward liberal/conservative divide.

Those who serve on the Supreme Court invariably survive those who put them there. This means that there is a thread of judicial continuity from one presidential administration to another and that the Court can act as a powerful counter to the other two branches of government. As a result of its rulings over the last fifty years, it has taken a central role in the political process. An early twentieth-century president, William Taft, summed up the situation. He observed that: 'Presidents come and go, but the Supreme Court goes on forever.'[13] True enough, but the fact that the nine justices and those who serve as judges across the country are political appointments does help to shape the development of public policy. On occasion, as in the 2000 election, it may be thought to play too large a role when the justices reach their verdicts.

Because the courts have so much power, the role they play in addressing important social issues is much discussed. Dispute centres on whether judges should confine themselves to interpreting the Constitution, implementing the letter of the existing law, or whether they should actively seek to broaden the nature of justice by identifying and redressing grievances. On occasion, as with the Warren Court, judicial activism is triumphant. Usually, and certainly more recently, judicial restraint is the norm.

REFERENCES

1 M. Vile, *Politics in the USA*, Hutchinson, 1978
2 R. Maidment and D. McGrew, *The American Political Process*, Sage/Open University, 1992
3 A. Grant, *The American Political Process*, Dartmouth, 1994
4 A. Cox, *The Court and the Constitution*, Houghton Mifflin, 1987
5 J Biskupic, 'The Rehnquist Court: Justices Want to Be Known as Jurists, not Activists', *Washington Post*, 9 January 2000
6 B. Schwartz, *A History of the Supreme Court*, Oxford University Press, 1993
7 J Rosen, 'Pride and Prejudice', *New Republic*, 10/17 July 2000
8 For instance: T. Yarborough, 'The Supreme Court and the Constitution', in G. Peele, C. Bailey, B. Cain and B. Peters (eds), *Developments in Modern Politics* 4, Palgrave, 2002
9 J. Toobin, 'No more Mr. Nice Guy', *The New Yorker*, 25 May 2009
10 D. Sykes, 'Of a Judiciary Nature: Observations on Chief Justice Roberts's First Opinions', *Pepperdine Law Review* 1027, 2007
11 R. Hodder-Williams, *Judges and Politics in the Contemporary Age*, Bowedean, 1996.
12 T. Goldstein, SCOTUSblog
13 Quoted in H. Pringle, *The Life and Times of William Howard Taft*, Farrar, 1939

USEFUL WEB SITES

www.uscourts.gov Federal Judiciary Home Page. Comprehensive guide to federal court system, with court statistics, answers to frequently asked questions etc.

www.supremecourtus.gov The official site of the Supreme Court, providing information relating to its background, history and procedures.

www.Oyez.org/ The Oyez Project hosted by Northwestern University, a site that offers information about the justices, answers frequently asked questions and provides a virtual tour of the Court buildings.

www.law.cornell.edu/supct/ Cornell Law School. Provides a diverse array of legal sources and full text of Supreme Court judgments.

www.findlaw.com Comprehensive guide to the US Constitution and legal system, as well as coverage of all rulings since 1893.

SAMPLE QUESTIONS

1 How 'supreme' is the Supreme Court within the American political system? Would the Founding Fathers be troubled by the way in which its role has evolved?
2 'A judicial body certainly, but its decisions often have a major impact on the political scene.' Discuss this verdict on the Supreme Court.
3 Do Supreme Court judgments follow popular opinion? Should they?
4 Is it true that the judgments of the Supreme Court have a greater impact on American society than the actions of the president or Congress?
5 To what extent can presidents mould and influence the Supreme Court?
6 To what extent are the decisions of the Supreme Court influenced by its changing membership?
7 'In view of the political influence it exercises, it is unacceptable that the Supreme Court is an unelected body.' Discuss.
8 'Legislatures may make laws by passing statutes, but judges have to apply them in particular situations.' To what extent do judges in Britain and the United States make the law?
9 Does the Supreme Court exercise too much influence in American government and society?
10 Discuss the view that the Founding Fathers would be uneasy about the powers exercised by the Supreme Court today.

Elections and voting

8

Elections, campaigns and voting are central features of democratic life. America has more elections than other democracies and voters are faced with alternative visions, programmes and personalities at all levels of administration. Many of them decline the opportunity to make up their minds about their preferred choice, even in the four-yearly presidential contests.

In this chapter we are concerned to find out why elections are so basic to thinking about democracy in the United States and to see how the various types of election are conducted, particularly that for the presidency. We ask why so many Americans do not turn out to vote and what influences those who do. We also consider the growth in popularity of initiatives and referendums in recent years. Finally, as a case study, we look at the 2008 presidential election.

POINTS TO CONSIDER

- Why are there so many elections in US politics? Why are they so important?
- In what ways has television changed the nature of election campaigns?
- How is the president elected? Could the system be improved? Does it need to be improved?
- Which is more important in the choice of President: money, personality or any other consideration?
- Why do so many Americans not vote in important elections such as those for president, Congress or governors?
- What changes have occurred in voting behaviour since the 1980s?
- Why might Americans 'split the ticket' when they vote?
- Is direct legislation a good thing?
- What similarities and differences are there between elections, electioneering and voting behaviour in Britain and the United States?
- Why was Barack Obama successful in the 2008 presidential contest?

GENERAL FEATURES OF ELECTIONS AND ELECTIONEERING

The importance of elections to American democracy

Elections are basic to the American democratic process. At every tier of political life, the incumbent (occupant) is selected by election. In some states, even such offices as the municipal judge and the registrar of wills are contested. Americans who turn out to vote have the chance to choose the president (via the electoral college), a representative, a senator, state legislators, a governor, state administrative officials, local councillors, local administrative officials, mayors and county officials. They might also help to choose judges and party officials, and take part in referendums (votes on single issues). There are in excess of a million elected offices, though because many of these are local they fail to make headline news. When allowance is made for the primary elections that are held to determine who will represent the parties in the main contests, it is obvious that elections in America occur with considerable frequency.

The vast number of elections is a reflection of the general growth of the democratic principle since the eighteenth century. Americans have long believed that the greater the direct involvement of the citizen, the better the likely outcome in terms of the quality of output. More participation is thought to lead to superior government. But it has another explanation: the belief in limited government. From the days of the Founding Fathers, Americans have always had a fear of too much power residing in one pair of hands. Elected officers should not be trusted too much or for too long. It is desirable for citizens to retain as much power as possible under their own control.

How people get elected

The selection of elected representatives is done via a two-part process, comprising the nomination stage, which is carried out by the party, and the final stage (polling day), in which all the voters in a particular town or state can express their allegiances.

The method of selecting candidates has evolved over the 200-year history of the United States. In colonial times, the method adopted was the **caucus** (literally, 'a meeting of wire-pullers'), an informal meeting of party leaders at which

caucus
A meeting of members of a political party, in this case a reference to the caucuses arranged by state parties as an alternative to the presidential primaries (see below). Local activists meet precinct by precinct within the state (some 1,800 in Iowa) to choose delegates from amongst themselves to attend the national party conventions (see pp. 253 and 325). Those who turn out to attend caucuses tend to be support more ideological candidates who adhere to fundamental party principles.

agreement was reached on the individuals who merited support. As the country evolved, different forms of political organisation developed, and the various local caucuses began to delegate representatives to meet with representatives from other local caucuses to form county and then state

> **primary elections**
> Preliminary elections held within a party to choose the candidate for that party in the general election.

groups, which finally selected candidates. These enlarged bodies were known as conventions, the early prototypes of the presidential nominating conventions used today (see pp. 253–254). The third development was the use of **primary elections**. Primaries are state-wide intra-party elections. Their basic purpose is to give voters the opportunity to select directly their party's candidates for various offices.

THE USE OF PRIMARY ELECTIONS

At the beginning of the twentieth century, many 'progressives' were concerned at the power exercised by party bosses and their political organisations. They wanted to curb the corruption felt to be endemic in public life, and pressed for reforms to break the control of the party machines and the 'bosses' who ran them. In this spirit, they urged the use of primary elections that would transfer power away from the party regulars meeting in smoke-filled rooms to the interested ordinary voter. This was seen as a significant step towards greater democracy.

The use of primaries gradually spread, although for many years the system was still not widely used for choosing presidential candidates. By the 1970s they had become nation-wide for almost all forms of election: local, state and federal. It was not only the large city machines that lost power with the advent of primaries – party organisations every-where lost their hold. Even where there was no suspicion of doubtful propriety, they lost the key function of nomination – for any candidate could stand for election, whether or not he or she had rendered some service in the local party.

Types of primary

Practice varies from the restrictive to the generous. In some states everyone can vote, whereas in others only those who are registered as members of the party have the right. Where only registered members can vote, this is a **closed primary**. Where anyone, regardless of party affiliation, can vote, this is an **open primary**. In Connecticut and Delaware in the Northeast, only party members are eligible. In the same region, Vermont holds open primaries. So does Rhode Island, which none the less requires a voter to state his or her affiliation. By contrast, Alaska in the Northwest uses open primaries, allowing voters to vote in both parties, should they wish to so do.

Open and closed primaries: the procedures

As we can see, the exact procedure for use in primary contests varies between different states, each of which makes its own regulations for the conduct of the election. Broadly, the position is as follows:

In general elections, the candidates of the political parties are pitted against each other. Usually, the party candidates for all offices – federal, state and local – run as a block or 'slate'. In addition each party draws up a statement of its position on various issues, called a **platform**. Voters thus make their

> **platform**
> A statement of party aims and policies that the candidate will officially support but by which he/she does not feel bound.

decisions not only for or against persons who run for office, but also on the political, economic and social philosophies of the parties they represent.

Candidates may run for office without the support of a political party, as independents. To do so, they must present a petition, signed by a specified number of voters (varying from state to state) who support the candidacy.

1 In **open primaries**, the elector is given two ballots, one for each party. He or she fills in one to go in the ballot box, and the unused one is discarded in a sealed container. He or she cannot use both, and there is no way of knowing which one has been filled in. Some object to this process on the grounds that it is possible for the voter to use their vote not to distinguish between the candidates in his or her favoured party, but rather to seek to 'wreck' the chances of the other party by voting for its least impressive candidate. If that weak person were to be chosen, this might increase the chances of the voter's preferred party.

2 In **closed primaries**, this 'wrecking' cannot occur, but neither is the process so secret for, on entering the polling station, the voter must express his or her affiliation. The appropriate ballot paper is then handed over, and if the party officers of one side question the allegiance it can be challenged.

The merits and disadvantages of primaries

There are obvious benefits in the use of primaries: they are more democratic than the system they replaced, they emphasise the personal qualities of the candidates rather than their party label, and they sometimes produce good candidates who would otherwise not have been chosen. They can provide a chance for the different wings of the parties to air their points of view, and so indicate where the preferences of members really lie. They have drawbacks, in that they are an additional expense – often the party machine still fights hard to ensure victory for its favoured candidate – and they demand that the voter turns out for yet another election: the frequency of elections is one reason sometimes given for low turnouts, for many ordinary voters lack the stamina or interest.

Another device is the **write-in vote**: a candidate's name does not appear on the ballot, but is 'written in' by voters in a space left blank for this purpose.

> **write-in vote**
> The process operated in some US states that allows voters to cast a vote for a candidate whose name does not appear on the ballot. Having one's name printed on the ballot confers an enormous advantage over candidates who are not named; it is extremely rare for write-in candidates to get elected. (In some cases, write-in votes are simply not counted.)

The timing of elections

Most issues relating to elections are decided within the states, although the Constitution lays down the general requirements on how often they are to take place for each institution.

American elections are used to choose representatives for a fixed term of office, so the date of future elections is known in advance. They are scheduled in such a way that every fourth year (2000, 2004, 2008 and 2012) there is a presidential election. They are always held on the Tuesday after the first Monday in November, in an even year. This contrasts with the situation in countries such as Britain and Canada, where an election can be called at any time as long as there is at least one every five years.

According to the Constitution, two years is the fixed period served by a member of the House of Representatives. The election occurs on the day of the presidential election and two years later (for example November 2008 and November 2010, 2012 and 2014). For the Senate, the period is considerably longer – six years – and the election again occurs in November. Whereas members of the House are all elected together, this is not so with the Senate: senators are elected on a staggered basis, one third at a time. There are, then, congressional contests every two years, those in the non-presidential election years being known as mid-term elections (see pp. 224–225).

The electoral system

For almost all elections, the method employed is the one used in Britain and Canada, the 'first past the post' (FPTP) or simple majority system. In other words, the candidate with the most votes in the single-member constituency is elected; the 'winner takes all'. It is a straightforward and familiar means of deciding the outcome, but one that is becoming increasingly rare around the world. In several countries, **plurality systems** are out of favour, the preference being for systems in which candidates and parties are to some degree rewarded in proportion to the share of the vote they obtain.

> **plurality systems**
> Those electoral systems in which the winning candidate is the one who obtains more votes than any rival candidate. In the most straightforward form, the simple majority system, there is no requirement that the winner gain an overall majority of the votes cast.

FPTP is widely seen as making it more likely that a two-party system will result, for third parties are discouraged; they may win many votes in an area, but unless they can win an individual contest they get no tangible reward. By comparison, proportional methods of voting, such as those used in most of continental Europe, are said to encourage the formation and development of small parties. They have a chance of gaining representation in the legislature, even on the basis of relatively small support.

In elections to Congress, there is an overwhelming preponderance of two main parties that totally dominate the legislature. The same applies in state legislatures as well. The use of 'winner-takes-all' has worked against the development of minor parties, which usually obtain scant reward for their efforts. Plurality systems convert seats into votes in a way that damages the interests of small parties, particularly if their limited support is spread across many constituencies. The effects of the system are evident in the fortunes of the American Socialist Party (see p. 302). Even during its peak years of electoral support (1912–20), when it won 3–6% of the national vote in presidential elections, it was barely represented in Congress. At its high point of 1912 (6%), it failed to elect a single representative to Congress. The evidence suggests that it makes more sense for an existing or would-be third party to form an alliance with a major one than to struggle on its own with little hope.

The American situation is different in one important respect from that of Britain, because, under its presidential system, no government is formed on the basis of a party majority in either chamber in Congress. In elections for presidents (and governors and mayors), there is only one prize. The presidency cannot be shared; there can be no coalition. In presidential elections the party with a plurality in a state receives all the electoral votes of that state, other than in Maine and Nebraska, which divide their votes in the Electoral College on the basis of the number of votes cast. In 2000, there was much disquiet about the outcome of the presidential election in America, in which George W. Bush defeated Al Gore. For the fourth time in American history, more people voted against the eventual winner than for him – a situation that can arise in any country where a plurality system is used.

In single-member constituencies there can be a close relationship between the elected representative and his/her constituency. One member alone has responsibility for an area that he/she can get to know well. He or she represents all who live in it, not just those who voted for one particular party; all citizens know whom to approach if they have a problem or grievance needing resolution. This is very different from what happens under some proportional systems, in which several elected members represent a broad geographical area. The relationship between individual legislators and their constituencies is highly valued by many commentators in Britain and America, where these local

MID-TERM ELECTIONS AND THEIR SIGNIFICANCE

Mid-term elections take place every two years, between presidential elections (for example 2002, 2006, 2010 etc.). All members of the House of Representatives are due for re-election, as are a third of the members of the Senate. There are gubernatorial contests and initiative/referendum votes taking place at the same time.

In mid-term elections, existing members usually get re-elected should they decide to stand, because of the incumbency factor. For instance, in 1998, 98.5% of House members and 90% of senators won re-election. Even in a year when there is an anti-incumbency mood (1992, 1994), many more members leave office due to retirement than to defeat at the polls.

Mid-term elections are a chance to assess the mood of the country and the president's chance of re-election. They can inspire or demoralise the person in the White House and his would-be challengers. They can be particularly significant during some presidencies. In November 1994, the Republicans scored a convincing victory, capturing both chambers of Congress for the first time for many years and thereby dealing a blow to the future legislative and other prospects of the Clinton presidency. The Republican resurgence proved costly for the president over the following years, for a partisan House was able to pursue him vigorously over the Lewinsky and other scandals. The party's revival significantly reshaped the political agenda, moving it sharply to the right.

In mid-term elections, some candidates benefit from a coat-tails effect. When there is a popular president, it can help their cause for they are able to associate themselves with his glories. This has not often happened in recent years, but in 2002 many Republicans were delighted to have George W. Bush lend support to their campaign and to bask in his popularity. On that occasion, the party consciously tried to 'nationalise' the campaign, so that candidates could be associated with his success in Afghanistan and the early stages of the war on terrorism. By contrast, in 1994, Democrats were keen to dissociate themselves from President Clinton, for his political stock was low at the time, after the failure of his health reform project. The president's party often suffers losses in mid-term, as the voters express disappointment or disapproval of what has been done over the previous two years.

More usually, local rather than national factors are relevant to voting in mid-term elections. Voters assess the performance of the incumbent in 'bringing home the bacon'. Their wants and needs will differ from state to state. For instance, logging is a key issue in Oregon and cross-border immigration in Texas. In all cases, they will want to see ample evidence that their elected representative has pursued every opportunity to achieve economic advantages for the district, perhaps by gaining some defence contracts or public works projects for the area. Mid-term elections determine the fate of members of the lower chamber, for their tenure expires with them. Because of the brief period in which they can make a difference, pork-barrel politics assume great importance to them.

The 2010 mid-term elections

President Obama and the Democratic Party received a drubbing in the mid-term elections. Resurgent Republicans gained sixty-three seats in the House to win their largest majority there since the 1940s. They won six Senate seats (among them Obama's old seat in Illinois). This was not enough to achieve a majority in the upper house, but enough to make it more difficult for Democrats to overcome a Republican filibuster. In addition, although they lost five governorships to the Democrats, they took eleven from them. They control the governorship in twenty-nine out of fifty states, giving them a majority at gubernatorial level for the first time since before the 2006 contests.

In his first post-election message from the White House, President Obama claimed that voters were feeling frustrated with the pace of economic recovery. He ruefully noted that 'some election nights are better than others', and referred to his 'shellacking' at the hands of the voters. For many commentators, it seemed like a rout. Yet the picture was not quite as bad as may have immediately appeared, because:

1 Heavy mid-term defeats are not uncommon, for the elections act as a kind of safety valve in which Americans let off steam when the voters are in a discontented mood. Presidents Roosevelt, Reagan and Clinton, among others, all took a hammering and went on to win control of the White House for a further term. They were galvanised into action, whereas the victors mistook a protest vote against the incumbent president for enthusiasm for themselves. In this case, Republican promises to undo Obama's financial and health measures could be seen as a misinterpretation of the popular mood, for in both cases, if large numbers opposed the changes, so too in similar numbers did many Americans accept them or even want to see them go further.

2 Although President Obama would inevitably find it harder to introduce new legislation, so too the Republicans – not popular themselves – would have to show themselves to be cooperative rather than obstructive, if they were not to antagonise the voters. The president immediately offered to work with his political opponents; if that offer were to be rebuffed, moderate voters might not relish a confrontational stance. Moreover, the Republican Party has clear divisions between mainstream, traditional Republicans and – further to the right – the Tea Partyists. The latter may have energised the conservative cause in the elections, by firing up the enthusiasm of many activists. Yet arguably, the party would have performed better in some seats if it had chosen more mainstream, centrist candidates, rather than persons identified with fringe viewpoints.

3 The Democrats retained control of the Senate, which had seemed unlikely a couple of months earlier.

For the outcome of the elections to the 112th Congress, see p. 150

relationships are highly significant. In the US, elected representatives are judged according to their ability to 'bring home the pork'.

There is little pressure for reform in America. **Proportional representation** (PR) could be used only in limited circumstances. As we have seen, there are difficulties in using it in presidential elections, although each state could at least follow the Maine/Nebraska example of dividing its vote

> **proportional representation**
> The collective name for the variety of electoral systems under which a party wins seats in the legislature in proportion to the number of votes it receives on polling day. Elections take place in multi-member constituencies.

in the Electoral College on the basis of the votes cast. Because PR works in multi-member constituencies, it would not work for elections to the Senate, because individual states elect only one senator at a time. In the case of elections to the House, there are again problems. Six states return only one representative and would therefore be unable to employ multi-seat constituencies. PR could be used for congressional districts in larger states, but their average size is already around 600,000, so a multi-member constituency of five representatives would have a population of of 3 million. Moreover, except in small states, the geographical areas which the successful candidates would have to represent would be very large, destroying much hope of keeping the sense of connection with a district, and making electioneering particularly exhausting and expensive.

Experimentation with proportional representation in America

During the early century two dozen American cities for a time employed the single transferable vote (STV). Its use was urged by the Progressive Movement, which sought to clean up government in the major cities and blunt the power of the party bosses. Progressives argued that winner-take-all, single-member district elections served to reinforce the power of – often Democratic – urban political machines, sometimes enabling them to win almost all the seats on city councils, on the basis of only 50%–60% of the popular vote. PR was seen was a way to break these one-party monopolies and to allow for the fair representation of a variety of political parties.

The Proportional Representation League – founded in 1893 – was also instrumental in promoting the use of PR. As an attainable goal, it urged the adoption of PR at city level, for cities could easily introduce PR elections by a change of charter following a referendum, without the need to persuade government officials of the case for reform. In 1936, voters in New York City approved the adoption of PR elections by a large margin, a development that inspired several other cities to take up the cause.

Why was the flirtation with PR abandoned?

In several cities, the system came under attack from those politicians and parties who lost power and privileges. Legal challenges were mounted in Michigan and California, the courts ruling that PR violated their constitutions. More usually, change was brought about by popular referendum. Just as their use had made it easy to get PR adopted, so too they were a tool deployed by well-financed opponents who eventually succeeded in ending the use of PR in some cities. In New York City, a 'red scare' campaign was mounted by the Democrats, who attempted to link PR with Soviet communism. A handful of Communists had served on the STV-elected city council since 1941, but it was the onset of the Cold War that enabled party leaders to exploit this issue and portray the method as essentially an un-American practice. The voters opted by a solid margin to end the use of PR, their example soon being followed in the 1950s in other cities.

By 1962, only Cambridge, Massachusetts retained this system. It is still used in elections to its nine-member city council and six-member school committee. Representatives are elected every two years by STV. Once a laborious process that took several days to complete by hand, vote counting is now done by computer.

Electoral systems in Britain and the United States: a comparison

Britain

General and local elections:	FPTP
European elections:	Closed list PR
Scottish Parliament and Welsh Assembly elections:	Additional Member System (AMS) mixed
London: Mayoralty	Supplementary vote (a cross between the French double ballot and the alternative vote)
London: Assembly	AMS

NB Northern Ireland uses FPTP for Westminster elections, but STV for local, Assembly and European elections.

United States

Most settings, including national, state and most local elections, use the single-member, FPTP system. In some states, a candidate in a given election must win a majority of the votes cast: Georgia requires a run-off in the election of senators, as do both it and Arizona for the election of governors.

NB Scotland uses the proportional voting system, STV, in local elections.

Election campaigns

In past generations, candidates have needed to be effective 'on the stump', addressing a gathering in the local marketplace or school hall. Sometimes those running for office addressed electors from a platform at the back of a train, most famously Harry Truman, whose 'whistle-stop' tours involved the train pulling up at every local station. He was the last campaigner to deploy this method of electioneering on such a scale, though others subsequently (for example John F. Kennedy) conducted very active speech-making tours and sometimes spoke from the rear of a railway carriage.

Election campaigns have never been the same since the televising of politics began in the 1950s. New styles of campaigning have developed, so that in recent years there have been innovative polling techniques, the wider use of **focus groups**, the introduction of **political consultants** and an emphasis on the training of candidates. This greater professionalism of campaigns has been fairly general in all political systems, as has put increasing emphasis on the qualities of the candidate rather than the party. In this world of more **candidate-centred campaigning**, professional political consultants have acquired a new importance. For years, both candidates and their parties have brought in outside agencies to advise them. Now, they maintain a core of image and marketing specialists, who are either employed permanently at headquarters or are readily available.

Today, the demands of television – and the need for candidates to ensure the best possible coverage – have taken over campaigning, but the purpose remains the same: to encourage the electorate to support the personality and policy platform on polling day. Reaching the maximum number of the electorate has always been a priority, but whereas at one time an audience could be counted in tens or hundreds, now it can be counted in millions for a single programme. The

focus groups

Focus groups are a form of qualitative research in which a group of perhaps ten or fifteen carefully selected individuals are asked about their attitudes towards a product or service. The participants are led through an in-depth discussion of their thoughts on and reactions to particular policy issues, candidates or campaign themes and arguments.

political consultants

'Political consultants' is the label applied to the group of people that advise and assist those engaged in political campaigns. Most specialise in some aspect of campaigning, such as fund raising, polling, speech writing or voice projection. Others help to manage the news, spin stories or develop policy positions. All are in the business of 'selling' politicians.

candidate-centred electioneering

A campaign in which the emphasis is on the role and activity of the individual candidate, rather than on the party he or she represents. Consultants (see above) and volunteers coordinate campaign activities, develop strategies and raise funds, although parties still are likely to be involved to some degree.

whistle-stop tour could last weeks and the candidate might see a hundred thousand altogether.

Candidate-centred campaigning

The process of electioneering has always demanded certain qualities from the person chosen – a pleasing voice, a gift for public speaking, the ability to sell one's personality and to persuade people of the merits of a particular case. However, over recent decades, deficiencies in any of these aspects have become a serious liability exposed before the whole nation, whereas previously many voters did not know about them. Other personal failings are also highlighted in the blaze of publicity surrounding a modern election campaign.

Elections are nowadays far more focused on the candidate and his or her positive qualities and/or failings than on party labels. What candidates must do is put together a winning coalition of support. They do this by making sure that there are sufficient funds to allow them to get the message across as widely as possible, so that everyone knows who they are and what they stand for. Those who run their campaigns are skilled in the latest campaign technology. They use the direct mail-shot – targeted to individual voters – to arouse interest and obtain funding. They use computers to analyse the voters of a particular precinct. They employ professional opinion pollsters and media gurus – specialists who are able to advise on the best means of exploiting the potential of the candidate and downplaying or destroying the qualities and reputation of an opponent.

Once candidates are chosen, parties are obviously concerned to help them to sell themselves and their message. They send out their voluntary workers to canvass on the doorstep, they use the phone to call possible voters, they arrange lifts for those who otherwise might not make it to the polling booth, as well as involving themselves in fund raising, commissioning and studying opinion polls and advertising. However, the role of parties in electioneering has been downgraded, for increasingly – with the breakdown of the party machines, after the reform of the arrangements for financial contributions in the early 1970s – it is the individual candidate and the team of supporters he or she puts together which has become important. With the backing of Political Action Committees (PACS, see p. 352–353) – whose primary function is to help finance election contests – candidates now tend to run their own campaigning.

The purpose of the campaign is not only to reach as many people as possible, but to ensure that those who are sympathetically disposed actually turn out to vote. Given the relatively low turnouts in the United States, it is important for the parties and PACs to do anything they can to assist in the process of voter registration and to encourage those who are registered to go to the polls.

Elections and electioneering in Britain and the United States: a comparison

British election campaigns are much shorter than American ones. Even though there is much speculation and a pre-election atmosphere in the third or fourth year of the lifetime of a Parliament, the campaign proper lasts only three to four weeks. Campaigns for all elective offices in America are longer, but this is especially true of presidential ones.

Despite the increasing personalisation of British politics – for example the emphasis on the gladiatorial aspect of the Cameron versus Miliband contest – it remains the case that the voter is still voting for a party rather than just one person: other key figures in the Cabinet or Shadow Cabinet play a significant role in the campaign, as do the local and national party organisations. By contrast, the American experience is more candidate centred. More stress is placed upon the personal qualities of the candidates than on their party allegiance. 'Personal qualities' can include many things, from the superficial, such as looks and friendliness, to others including character, temperament and outlook. As the person, once elected, will make up his or her own mind on political issues, personality and views can be very significant.

In the USA, the organisations that provide the contestants with support (parties and PACs) have more of a personal than a party loyalty. They are concerned especially with the funding of the campaign and political advertising, aspects which are still more developed on the other side of the Atlantic – though Britain is moving in the American direction, with increased use of public relations advisers and negative advertising on posters, and via the style of some party election broadcasts.

Britain does not allow unlimited access by the parties to television time, which is strictly regulated. America does not have the British-style election broadcast, but candidate-centred structures make extensive use of the media, to which their access is limited only by the funds they have available.

The role of money in American elections

The role of money in American elections has long been controversial, as have been the sources of funding. Several sources exist. Money can come from the individual candidate, interested individuals, interest groups operating through PACs and political parties. There are also several purposes for which the money is made available. It may derive from the generosity of a benefactor, it may be given out of idealistic support for a particular individual, idea or set of principles, or it may be offered in the hope of securing some goal of personal or group benefit.

Whatever the motive of the donor, what is important is that the representative – once elected to public office – does not feel unduly beholden to those who have financed the campaign, at the expense of the general public whom they are there to represent. The fear is that money given is 'interested money', in that those who donate it are looking for favours from the persons they back.

Given the new technology and methods of electioneering, national elections have become very costly, whether for Congress or for the presidency. An individual is – in most cases – unlikely to be able to meet those costs on his or her own. The difficulty is all the greater if the candidate is not an incumbent congressman, for incumbents find it easier to raise money from affluent individuals and from PACs, which prefer to contribute to sitting tenants than to challengers.

Spending in the 2008 presidential election

The costs of presidential elections have risen dramatically in recent years. In 2008, spending was significantly higher than ever before.

Figures from the Federal Election Commission indicate that in the 2008 contest:

- Barack Obama raised $745 million and spent $730 million on his primary and general election campaigns;

- John McCain raised $368 million and spent $333 million.

Legislation on campaign finance

There are, then, problems surrounding the sources of money and the unequal distribution of the money available. Attempts have been made to regulate political money, for by the 1960s many commentators were concerned at the escalating costs of election campaigns, the incidence of very rich candidates who could easily outspend their rivals and the possibility of undue influence being exercised by those who handed over money.

The first significant piece of legislation was the **Federal Election Campaign Act (FECA) of 1971**, which replaced all earlier laws on the subject. All candidates for political office, as well as the individuals, campaign committees, parties and PACs that backed them, were made to declare their contributions. As a result of evidence heard in the Watergate hearings, it was felt necessary to tighten up on violations of the 1971 measure – hence the 1974 Act, which was designed to reduce further the impact of money on the democratic process.

Two main themes were tackled in the second measure: the importance of tough limits on contributions and the need for public funding of election campaigning (see p. 233). The new legislation tightened up the rules on disclosure of campaign income, and restricted the influence of wealthy individuals. Strict limits were imposed. Donations of more than $100 had to be disclosed. Individuals could pay up to $1,000 towards a single campaign, with primaries and general elections being counted as separate entities; a maximum expenditure of $25,000 per year was permitted. There was no overall limit on the amount that PACs could provide in a single year, but they were restricted to

$5,000 per campaign. PACs were thus placed at an advantage over other donors, so that, as Grant[1] has pointed out, 'the law effectively increased candidates' reliance on them'.

A further amendment to FECA was made in 1979. It allowed parties to raise and spend money to be used on party-building and get-out-the-vote activities ('**soft money**'). These were purposes not easily distinguishable from supporting party candidates. As the amount of spending on these activities significantly increased over the following years, there was growing suspicion about the ways in which money was used. Parties were using soft money to complement their publicly financed presidential campaigns, in effect bypassing the official 1974 limits. There was therefore a considerable gulf between legislative intention and prevailing practice.

In 2002, the McCain-Feingold Campaign Finance Reform Act was passed, against the preferences of President Bush, who, however, did not use his veto against it. This bipartisan measure addressed the role of soft money in campaign financing and the proliferation of issue ads. Among other things, the Act:

- banned the national party committees from raising or spending soft money;
- prevented business and labour unions from directly funding **issue advertisements**;
- prohibited the use of business and labour money to broadcast advertisements that named a federal candidate in the thirty days prior to a primary election and the sixty days prior to a general election;
- outlawed any fund-raising activities on public property.

soft money

Money contributed in ways and for purposes (such as registration and mass-mailing) that do not infringe the law, as opposed to 'hard money' contributions, which are strictly regulated. Soft money is collected at state and local level, but is often used for national purposes.

issue advertisements

Ads that are similar to the usual political advertisements on behalf of a candidate (see pp. 248–249), but do not use words such as 'support' or 'vote'. Moreover, whilst candidate ads are sponsored by a candidate or his/her organisation, issue ads are sponsored by individuals not running for office, corporations, unions or other organisations. Some advocate or oppose the election of a candidate in an implied way (sham issue ads), whereas others seek to mobilise constituents, policy makers or regulators in support of or opposition to legislation (pure issue ads). By purporting to be about issues, sham or candidate-centred issue ads evade restrictions that would otherwise apply.

The Federal Election Commission, which oversees FECA legislation, is often portrayed as ineffectual and lacking 'teeth'. But as a result of the passage of the above package of restrictions, we now have a clearer idea of where politicians get their money from and how they use it. Voters and interested commentators can check the disclosures made, and see the resources available to candidates, who have to declare their personal wealth, their property and their debts. This means that there is greater transparency, and people can assess the impact of any financial considerations that may influence the policy pursued by those who rule.

State funding for candidates

A scheme of public financing for presidential candidates was introduced in 1971, and subsequently substantially amended in 1974, 1976 and 1979. It provided, inter alia, for funding of the primary contests and for the main election. For every candidate who could raise $5,000 across twenty states from small individual contributions (under $250), there was to be a matching sum available from the federal government. State aid was not, then, unconditional, but triggered by the decisions of private individuals.

Funds are provided for candidates by means of a tax check-off box on the declaration of income from individual income tax returns. The money collected is then distributed to those candidates who have chosen to opt for public funding. They must accept stringent restrictions upon the raising or spending of corporate money. Most have willingly accepted the offer of financial assistance, even wealthy candidates such as Ronald Reagan and the two George Bushes.

On 19 June 2008, Barack Obama became the first major-party presidential candidate to turn down public financing for a general election campaign since the system was created. He was expected to raise $265 million between the time of the announcement and election day. By rejecting the funds in favour of private donations, the campaign was in a position to outspend John McCain prior to the election. Had he signed on to the plan, the campaign would have been able to spend only $84.1 million between the party convention in August and the general election in November. John McCain, who was the first candidate in the contest to accept public financing, was highly critical of Obama for refusing it. He claimed that it illustrated his undue reliance on wealthy private donors.

Could more be done?

McCain-Feingold's two major pillars – the ban on soft money and regulation of issue ads – have been generally successful in achieving their purposes. However, the legislation imposed no new restrictions on large individual donors beyond the existing limit of $5,000 for individual contributions to non-party political committees. Indeed, it was agnostic about the total amount of money raised and spent in federal elections, even though some of the bill's supporters in Congress and outside reformers made clear that they favoured further controls.

Proposed reforms have been opposed by those who see election spending as proportionate with the costs of goods and services in today's economy. In this regard, election spending is seen as the price a democracy pays for electoral competition, with large contributions and expenditures by interest groups as the contemporary expression of America's long-standing pluralism. It is hard to prove any specific connection between interest-group donations and government policy. Courts have also questioned whether further restrictions on campaign giving and spending might unduly limit donors' constitutionally protected right to free speech in the political arena. Given the immense expense of modern campaigning, certain extremely wealthy individuals simply fund their own campaigns for public office – there is no rule against it. Sometimes they win, sometimes they don't.

Other things could be done to control the influence of wealth in American politics. For instance, airtime could be made available freely to each party for a fixed period, so that no longer would being poor or modestly well off be a disadvantage. This might have the effect of encouraging more blacks and other minority candidates to come forward, as well as introducing an element of greater fairness. Candidates could still be expected to pay for the making of their own advertisements, but this is not the problem. It is the frequency with which advertisements are repeated that makes election campaigns so expensive, for what happens is that at present one candidate with greater means available can outgun his or her opponent simply by reiterating the message over and over again.

Participation in American politics

Democracy implies participation, by which we mean that people should be able to take part in the formulation, passage or implementation of policies. Democratic standards are more likely to prevail where people are well informed and willing to get involved. In the *polis*, the city state of ancient Greece, it was considered natural that people would take part in politics; then, to be able to do so was the privilege of a few.

The United States has always attached great importance to the ideas and values of democracy. Although the founders of the American Republic were wary of majority rule, they none the less believed that most people would be able to take part in the electoral process and thus be able to play a key role in determining the direction which government policy should take. Yet at a time when the electorate is more informed about politics than ever before in its history, we find that turnout in elections is lower than it has been for many years and involvement in party activity is on a downward slide.

Turnout in presidential and congressional elections

In much of the twentieth century, the successful presidential candidate has won an election in which less than half of the eligible electorate turned out to vote, so that the decisions about who should govern the country and the direction in which it should be led are in the hands of a minority of the population. The 1960 presidential contest had a better turnout than usual, but since then the percentage voting has declined more or less continuously, as the figures below indicate. However, in 2004 the interest of the voters was more engaged by the Bush versus Kerry contest, when there seemed to be the prospect of a close race between candidates who were dissimilar in much of their political thinking. Again, in 2008, there was expectation of a higher than usual turnout. The final figure released by the Federal Election Commission was 61.7%, the highest in four decades.

Turnout in presidential elections since 1960

Year	Turnout of voting-age population (%)
1960	63.1
1964	61.9
1968	60.8
1972	55.2
1976	53.6
1980	52.6
1984	53.1
1988	50.1
1992	55.1
1996	49.1
2000	51.3
2004	55.3
2008	56.9

Source: Federal Election Commission.

NB Voting-age population (VAP) includes all persons over the age of 18. It therefore includes a significant number of persons who are ineligible to vote in federal elections, including legal and illegal aliens, persons under sentence of a felony conviction and those individuals who have been declared non-compos mentis by a court of law. The VAP is therefore considerably larger than the pool of potential voters.

The figures are unimpressive by European standards, and the table below suggests that the US lags well behind Britain, which itself has a smaller turnout than most other countries. Whereas Britain has usually achieved a turnout of almost 75% in general elections (a figure that dropped decisively in 2001, however), 55% is good by American standards. The comparison is not, however, an entirely appropriate one, for British figures relate to the number registered who vote, whereas American figures are based upon the number of Americans over the minimum voting age who actually do so. According to V.O. Key,[2] the difference may be worth as many as six or seven percentage points.

Turnout in a selection of the main democracies: a comparison

	Turnout %	Compulsion?
Australia	93.8	Yes
Austria	75.6	No
Denmark	86.6	No
Finland	65.0	No
Ireland	67.0	No
Malta*	93.3	No
New Zealand	79.5	No
South Africa	77.3	No
Sweden	82.0	No
United Kingdom	65.1	No

* Malta invariably has the highest turnout of any country not using compulsory voting.
NB Figures based on the general election most recent to November 2010.

The US presidential campaign certainly gets massive television exposure, for it dominates the media from the time of the first primaries through to November. This might be expected to generate interest and excitement, but yet in the media age we are faced by decline. The drop in turnout rates is the more notable if we bear in mind the increase in the size of the potential electorate since the 1970s. The passage of the 1965 Voting Rights Act added many black voters to the list of those eligible to vote. Moreover, women have become more politically involved in that period, and their turnout levels have risen to such an extent that more women turned out than men in the 1996 and 2000 elections. Finally, given the overall increase in education and living standards, one expect that more would be inspired to vote, the more so as it is traditionally the least well-off who are the category the most reluctant to vote.

Yet some half the registered electorate does not turn out even in presidential contests, and for other elections the number is considerably greater still. In an off year (when there is no presidential contest), the figure for turnout is usually between 35–40% in congressional elections (in 2002, it was 37.0%, in 2006, 37.1% and in 2010, 37.8%). In primaries, the figure is generally considerably lower, although it was at historically high levels in the 2008 primaries and caucuses. Voter turnout on **Super Tuesday** was 27% of eligible citizens, breaking the previous record of 25.9% set in 1972.

> **Super Tuesday**
> Super Tuesday is the Tuesday in February or March of a presidential election year when the greatest number of states hold primary elections. In 2008, twenty-four states held primaries or caucuses on this day. Because choices are being made in a large range of states representing geographically and socially diverse regions, Super Tuesday typically represents a presidential candidate's first test of national electability.

Why are turnouts so low?

Several reasons for low turnouts have been given, but among them **registration** emerges as a key issue. In most states it is up to individuals to register themselves as qualified voters before election day. Failure to do so disqualifies anyone from using their right, even if in other respects they are eligible to do so. Registration involves either meeting a registrar or filling out a form at the country courthouse. When allowance is made for this responsibility and for age and residential qualifications, it is evident that there is built-in discouragement to vote.

A change was introduced in 1993 when President Clinton signed the so-called **motor voter** bill, designed to ease the process of registration. Citizens are now able to register when they apply for a driving licence (hence the name) or some other form of public document. Furthermore, states must designate a public office concerned with providing help to the public as a place where assistance is also available with voter registration – such as a state welfare agency. The effects should have been to enable and encourage more people to turn out on election day, for it has long been the case that in those states with same-day or no registration turnout is considerably above the national average.

The new legislation operated from 1995, and within eight months some 5,000,000 new voters registered. Some commentators predicted that if this momentum were maintained, almost four out of every five voters would be registered by the end of the century. It was not, and today some 66% of Americans are registered to vote, a few percentage points up on the situation before 'motor voting' was introduced. Yet in 1996 and 2000, the turnout figures were disappointingly low. As president, George H. Bush had vetoed such a measure, perhaps in the belief that the Democrats would benefit more from a higher turnout. His fears seem to have been largely unjustified.

Alternative explanations include the following.

1 **Apathy**: some have used apathy as an explanation, but surveys of political interest suggest that if anything Americans are rather more politically interested than people in many other democracies. Voting does, however, require more personal effort than elsewhere for the reasons we have given, and the frequency of elections could result in voter fatigue and a loss of interest.

2 **Lack of a meaningful choice between the parties**: some commentators would suggest that voters who are registered fail to detect any real difference between the parties, and that the electors feel that a choice between Tweedledum and Tweedledee is not one worth attempting to make. They say 'a plague on both your houses', and see parties as increasingly irrelevant to their lives. No party really addresses their concerns.

3 **The lack of an inspiring choice of candidates**: others say that the quality of political leaders fails to inspire, and there are too many unattractive personalities who become candidates. Discontent with the available choice was a much-discussed feature of the Bush versus Dukakis contest, the 'Wimp' v. 'the Shrimp', (1988), the Clinton versus Dole contest in 1996 and the Bush versus Gore contest in 2000.

4 **The composition of the electorate**: broadly speaking, middle-class people, those with a professional education and with a college education, are more likely to turn out than unskilled working people or those whose qualifications are only a high-school diploma or less. Again, family influence may be significant. In those homes where there is a tradition of participation, it is more likely that future generations will turn out to vote and become more generally involved in political life.

Certain groups have persistently been more reluctant to vote. Non-voting is greater in the South and in rural areas, among the young, the less-educated and among the minorities such as the black population and Hispanics. Young people (under 24) have regularly been less disposed to involve themselves in the electoral process, although those who claim a clear allegiance towards one of the main parties are markedly more willing to vote than those who are apathetic about politics and current affairs. Whites are more likely to vote than blacks, blacks than Hispanics. An important consideration is that the groups that shun the democratic process are ones that make up an increasing proportion of the electorate.

5 **The nature of electioneering**: it may be that negative advertising produces disillusion with the Washington politicians and the political system in general, and that this contributes to the falling turnouts of the last generation. In the 1994 elections, it was suggested that one of the most toxic campaigns in living memory had left many people turned off politicians. American voters have become more disengaged from political strategy, as the style of advertising increasingly antagonises them. Overall, they are seen, in Hames's words, as 'over-long, over-slick and dominated by the mass media with a premium on character attacks on political opponents'.[3]

6 **Other factors**: the theory has been advanced[4] that America is now in a post-electoral era. More and more voters see parties and elections as no longer very significant. Now, major decisions are made by investigating committees and the courts, and through media revelations. The traditional processes have had their day.

Another idea is that non-voting is broadly a sign of contentment with the political system. If Americans felt worried, because their country was in crisis, they might feel inclined to turn out to avert a national catastrophe. But in times of peace and prosperity, most Americans are happy to leave the politicians to get on with their task; there is less need to vote.

Alternative forms of participation

Political issues are not the be-all and end-all of most people's lives, and – like most people – Americans are concerned with bread-and-butter matters such as making a living, improving their family position and enjoying their leisure. The level of interest varies sharply between different groups of the community, but the findings of the 2008 American National Election Study, conducted jointly by the University of Michigan and Stanford University, show that only 26% were interested for 'most of the time', 37% for 'some of the time' and 25% 'only now and then'; 12% were 'hardly at all' committed. As one blogger explains: 'Many Americans follow politics like they follow Major League baseball; they are interested only in the World Series' (www.huffingtonpost.com/). So too, Americans assume greater interest when there is an election or when a great issue such as health reform regularly hits the headlines.

Moreover, an increasing number of Americans 'have lost confidence in the three institutions of federal government – the Congress, the president, the Supreme Court – over the past 30 years'.[5] Whereas in 1964, 76% of the people trusted

Turnout in the United States: a cautionary word

Turnout figures in the United States are much disputed, the outcome depending on the basis of calculation employed. We have already noted that the calculation usually used is based upon the percentage of the voting-age population (VAP) which votes, as opposed to limiting calculations to those who are registered to so do. A further area of contention concerns the basis on which the VAP is calculated. Many academics tend to talk in terms of the decline in turnout, but research by the United States Election Project (USEP) (www.electionstudies.org) suggests that the 'much-lamented decline in voter participation in presidential, congressional and state elections is an artifact of poor measurement'.

The VAP includes many persons ineligible to vote, mainly non-citizens and ineligible felons, and excludes overseas eligible voters. USEP figures, as calculated by Dr Michael McDonald, calculate the voting-eligible population (VEP), those eligible to vote for the highest office once the non-eligible have been excluded. This provides a new picture of turnout, for the 'non-eligibles' constitute a significant number, as the 2010 figures at the bottom of the box indicate. Using VEP figures, there has been no decline in the turnout for presidential elections since 1972 and in the last two elections a return to the very high levels of the 1960s. On average, the difference between VAP and VEP figures appears to be around 3–4%.

McDonald's figures for turnout in presidential elections since 1980, are given below, with the official figures provided by the FEC in brackets:

1980	54.2 (52.6)
1984	55.2 (53.30)
1998	52.8 (50.3)
1992	58.1 (54.7)
1996	51.7 (48.1)
2000	54.2 (50.0)
2004	60.1 (55.4)
2008	61.6 (56.9)

In response to the calculations used in the US Elections Project, the Census Bureau and the Center for the Study of the American Electorate now report citizen VAP turnout rates which take into account the largest ineligible group, non-citizens. The figure given for the 2010 mid-term elections was 40.3%, as opposed to the provisional VAP figure of 37.3% (10 November 2010).

VAP	Total ineligible felons (incl. prisons, those on probation and those on parole)	Overseas eligible voters	VEP
235,809,266	3,148,613	4,972,217	218,054,301

Source: United States Election Project.

NB This turnout rate estimate is almost certain to rise because the number of votes reported to date did not include all absentee and provisional ballots in many states; neither did it include candidates whose name were written-in. In a mid-term election, the 'vote for highest office' is the vote tally for gubernatorial and congressional elections.

and had confidence in 'the government in Washington to do what was right', as the millennium approached the figure was down to 29%. A series of events, from the war in Vietnam to the Watergate scandal, from the Iran-Contra affair to the impeachment trial of President Clinton had combined to fuel a high level of public cynicism concerning government and politics.

Many people may find politics a complicated – as well as a dirty – process. Surveys of political knowledge and understanding reveal widespread public ignorance. According to a survey by the *American Political Science Review* (September 1980), 40% of those interviewed could not name one of their state's senators. Ignorance covers personalities and policies. Given such a lack of interest and information, participation in the political process is inevitably unlikely to be very high.

Levels of knowledge about politics

On average, today's citizens are about as able to name their leaders and as aware of major news events as was the case some twenty years ago. In 2007, somewhat fewer were able to name their governor and the vice-president, but more respondents than in the earlier era gave correct answers to other questions relating to national politics. For instance, in 1989, 74% could name Dan Quayle as vice-president, whereas in 2007 only 69% could name Dick Cheney. However, more Americans in 2007 knew that the Chief Justice was generally considered to be a conservative and that Democrats controlled Congress, than knew these things in 1989. Some of the largest knowledge differences between the two time periods may reflect differences in the amount of press coverage of a particular issue or public figure at the time the surveys were taken. But taken as a whole, the findings suggest little change in overall levels of public knowledge.

Source: Pew Research Center, *Public Knowledge of Current Affairs Little Changed by News and Information Revolutions: What Americans Know: 1989–2007*, 15 April 2007.

Those who possess interest, knowledge and understanding tend to participate more. They are often the better-educated people who read a newspaper, watch current affairs programmes and engage in political discourse with their relatives and friends. At the other end of the scale, are those who participate very little, the least-educated, who may feel isolated from the political world, which they may see as having let them down. Many of those who are some-where in between, having a sporadic interest in politics, will join in from time to time. They will vote in certain elections that seem relevant or interesting to them – as we have seen, more often in presidential ones than the rest. They will occasionally discuss political issues at times of peak media attention, but for much of the time choose not to read about or view what is going on.

The issue of political participation has been one of lively debate. Back in 1835, the liberal French aristocrat Alexis de Tocqueville[6] visited America and was much impressed by what he saw of the way it was governed and of how society functioned. He observed that 'Americans of all ages, all stations in life, and all types of disposition are forever forming associations'. He portrayed them as belonging to 'the most democratic country in the world', extolling their involvement in groups which helped them pursue 'the objects of common desires'.

In a controversial study, Robert Putnam[7] suggests that the willingness of Americans to engage in political life has diminished in recent decades. He argues that there is now a 'degree of social disengagement and civic connectedness' that has damaging consequences for political life. He believes that social participation is declining in the USA, observing that today more people spend time watching *Friends* than making them! More seriously, he points to static levels of political knowledge in spite of the development of university education: in addition, fewer people engage in volunteer work (there may be more pressure groups but average membership is only 10% of its 1962 level and members tend to take a less active role), belong to trade unions, attend church or public meetings, and vote in elections or trust government.

Of course, there are more opportunities for participation than voting alone. Americans can involve themselves in election campaigns, join political parties and pressure groups, and take part in protest marches and forms of direct action (see p. 351). The American system also offers the citizens of some states an opportunity for direct participation in decision making that is generally denied to the British electorate except on rare constitutional issues. This is done via the **town meeting** (see pp. 242–243) in New England, and via the initiative and **referendum** (see p. 266) in many areas of the country.

Participation in various forms of electoral activity (% of total US population)

Type of activity	% of total US population
Discuss politics from time to time	81
Try to persuade others	35
Wear button, sport sticker or sign	10
Attend meetings, rallies	6
Do other campaign work	3
Contribute to candidate	7
Contribute to political party	6

Adapted from figures produced in the 2000 National Election Study, University of Michigan.

Town meetings in New England: direct democracy in action

The purest form of direct democracy was to be found in ancient Greece. All qualified citizens were allowed to participate in the government of their city-state. They were encouraged/expected to play a positive role in controlling their own life, rather than leaving it to others to act on their behalf. Such direct democracy is no longer seen as possible in large, modern industrial societies and the nearest approximation in most countries is the use of the referendum and/or initiative. However, in New England, town meetings have operated ever since the first British settlements.

The experience of meetings in the six states of that region has been variously described as 'the Secret Flame of democracy'[8] and 'a bedrock form of democratic expression'[9] Of Maine's 493 incorporated municipalities, 440 have a town-meeting form of government, in which residents attend for a morning or a day to chart their communal course. Topics debated range widely, from property taxes to budgets for administration, from same-sex marriages to nuts-and-bolts issues concerning local facilities.

Town meetings are not without their critics and there are problems with the way they function today. In particular:

• Often meetings are not well attended. Rarely do more than 10% of registered voters turn out to participate, and the trend has been consistently downwards in recent years. In a recent study, Joseph Zimmerman[10] has examined figures collected for the last three decades and finds the trend is common to all six states. He sees declining attendance as a parallel to the downward trend in voter turnout in state and national elections and as correlating with towns' increasing difficulties in finding candidates to run for local office and volunteers to run fire departments.

• Those who can attend are often self-employed, retired or otherwise not working in regular daytime jobs and therefore cannot accurately reflect the opinions of local citizens. An article in a local newspaper in Maine[11] carried a report that in Kingfield '65 people are calling the shots for the entire town', and that reports from officials in Eustis and Strong also reported low, unrepresentative turnouts: 'in Farmington, a town of 7,600, only 80 people attended the annual meeting'.

THE MASS MEDIA AND ELECTIONS

Democracy requires the free flow of ideas, information and comment, and the role of the **mass media** is central in influencing public opinion; they both reflect it and help to mould it. For many people, it is through the media that they become acquainted with what is happening in the world and form their own viewpoint on issues. There is

mass media
Those means of communication such as newspapers, radio and television that permit messages to reach the mass public. Today, they operate in an arena of intense competition, with 24/7 cable TV networks, talk radio, Internet sites, blogs and ever-proliferating new media like Facebook, MySpace, and YouTube, all playing a significant role.

Several reasons have been advanced for declining turnout. For instance, it is sometimes claimed that:

- Even at the level of a small New England town, society is now too large and complex for direct democracy to be a complete success. Towns used to be smaller, with more of a sense of community. Urbanisation has affected even New England, and people are now too busy, often travelling some distance to work. Meetings take too long for those with little time available. They can spend their spare time on various forms of entertainment.

- Voters are frustrated and disenchanted with government at all levels.

- Many people are better off than ever before and therefore feel that it is not a matter of serious personal self-interest whether they attend.

- There are no burning issues in municipal government.

Town meetings have been described[12] as 'alive, but troubled'. In some towns they have actually ceased to exist, ten out of the thirty-one towns in Rhode Island having abandoned them; turnout in the remaining towns in that state is often exceptionally low, at 4–5%. Voters are experimenting with alternatives to the traditional open town meeting, some opting for meetings where the time is spent in directly voting on a series of referendum questions, others preferring either representative town meetings for which residents elect representatives to vote on their behalf (anyone can stand and speak, but only the representatives can vote), straightforward town councils or citizen-initiated referendums. It is in the smaller towns and more rural areas of northern New England that town meetings continue to function best.

Supporters of town meetings portray them as providing a useful opportunity for community involvement in decision making. In addition, Town Meeting Day serves a social purpose: it brings people together who might not otherwise know each other. This can strengthen social ties within a town and help people to work together to tackle community problems.

much academic debate as to whether television, in particular, actually creates opinions or reinforces them.

By the media, we mean the various forms of communication available. By the mass media, we mean those that in the modern day are available on a large scale. All are concerned with the dissemination of ideas in the form of information, entertainment and persuasion. However, if the term is all embracing, in popular usage it is applied particularly to broadcasting and the press.

The media are sometimes described as 'the fourth branch of government', rivalling the three main official branches in their political influence and power. Here we are concerned to examine the ways in which they influence modern electioneering.

Television has now become the most important of the ways via which the candidates seek to gain popular approval and support. Although party managers may still be interviewed and seek to use the medium to promote the party cause, it is the candidates who are the focus of media attention. They and their team of consultants are constantly on the look-out for opportunities to ensure that they gain favourable coverage, and are vigilant in watching out for any signs of bias against them. They attempt to 'manage the news'.

Managing the media involves ensuring that journalists get the right stories (information slanted to the candidate's particular viewpoint) backed up with good pictures. It can range from crude political arm twisting to more subtle means. Advisers dream up sound-bites and photo-opportunities, and use their spin-doctors to put across an appropriate line (see p. 245).

> **news management**
> The techniques used by politicians and their advisers to control the information given to the media.

POLITICAL MEDIA MANAGEMENT

Photo-opportunities

Carefully stage-managed episodes in which the leading figure is set against a particular background – perhaps to demonstrate concern for the area or its industry. For example, Ronald Reagan favoured the image of the all-American cowboy, riding on horseback into the sunset, thereby conjuring in the mind of the electors an image of the great outdoors as part of the wholesome American dream.

In 2008, Sarah Palin was noted for her ability to seize photo-ops. On one occasion, she was photographed with Henry Kissinger. Seated on blue couches, they were separated by an end table with photographs of two former Republican presidents, Nixon and Reagan, on it. The McCain–Palin campaign aroused some criticism from media figures who disliked the decision to limit coverage to brief photo-ops for a still photographer and a television camera, with no producer present to provide editorial guidance.

Sound-bites

Short sayings, full of concentrated meaning, which consist of a few easily remembered words and yet convey a particular message. Examples are Reagan's 'You ain't seen nothin' yet' and George H. Bush's 'Read my lips. No new taxes', a slogan that backfired when, as president, he found himself supporting higher taxation. Sound-bites are often phrases lifted from larger speeches and used to summarise the speech's overall message; they developed largely out of necessity, as broadcasters typically lack the time to run entire statements.

In 2008, Obama's 'Yes we can' was a successful sound-bite, positive in tone. It perfectly reflected the campaign of a liberal presidential candidate. If just as void of content as any other election phrase, it none the less managed to convey openness to change and

They try to book interviews with 'softer' interviewers, rather than undergo a potentially damaging interrogation. They seek to control the agenda, sticking to themes on which they are strong and avoiding (or downplaying) embarrassing issues.

Presidential debates

Presidential debates are held late in the election cycle, a few weeks after the nominating conventions and a few weeks before polling day. There are normally three debates between the candidates for the presidency and one between the challengers for the vice-presidency. The gatherings are staged in a large public place, such as a university hall. The formats of the debates have varied from election to election, the details in each case being governed by a memorandum of understanding between the two major candidates, under the

a sense of optimism. Moreover, it was not merely a message sent downwards from a politician through the media to the electorate; rather, it had the power to engage the public. Beginning with the candidate's concession speech in the New Hampshire primary (after Hillary Clinton had won only a narrow victory over him), crowds began to chant it at all of Obama's appearances. The slogan became really popular at the grassroots level of campaigning.

Spin

The label applied to a heavily biased portrayal in one's own favour of an event or situation. The intention is to bring about the most positive result possible. It has become an accepted feature of campaigns in the US. The term derives from the spin given to a ball in various sports, originally baseball, to make it go in a direction that confuses the opponent.

Spin-doctors

Part of the media team, their task being to change the way the public perceive some happening, or to alter their expectations of what might occur. They try to forestall potentially negative publicity by putting a favourable gloss on information and events. In 2008, as soon as each presidential debate was over, commentators and spin-doctors began declaring victory for one candidate or the other. At the end of the second one, the Republican party chairman, Mike Duncan, tried to sway early reactions by claiming victory for McCain, praising his 'commitment and decisiveness', noting that while Barack Obama postured for political expediency and contradicted his record, John McCain showed true leadership and clarity on the issues. In spite of this, most early polls crowned Barack Obama the victor.

auspices of the Commission on Election Debates. Sometimes questions have been posed by one or more journalist moderators, in other cases by members of the audience.

The presidential and vice-presidential debates have been of varying quality, and the rules of engagement have differed from election to election. The one that has been endlessly quoted is that held in 1960 between Kennedy and Nixon. Kennedy looked handsome, impressive and youthful, whereas his opponent looked unshaven and untrustworthy. The debate was broadcast on radio and television, and significantly, whereas polling showed that a majority of listeners thought that Nixon had emerged on top, a majority of viewers were in no doubt that Kennedy had won. When he did win, it was by the narrowest of margins, by 0.5% of the popular vote. It may well be that television swung the outcome.

Thereafter, debates did not take place for several years. They were resumed in 1976, since when they have been a regular feature of the presidential campaign. In part depending on the format adopted, they have been useful in clarifying the policies of those participating. They make it easier for the audience and the viewers to come to a verdict on the merits of the rival candidates, enabling them to judge their sincerity and to see how they react under pressure.

The debates have almost certainly made a difference to the outcome of some elections, on occasion a decisive one. In a close-run contest the importance of appearing steady and in control is supreme. If you cannot win, it is crucial to avoid mistakes. Errors have been made, and some have been costly. Apart from the Nixon performance in 1960, the other famous or infamous gaffe was the moment in 1976 when Jimmy Carter benefited from a fatal howler committed by his opponent, Gerald Ford, the Republican president. At a time when the Cold War was still a determining factor in international diplomacy, Ford said that Poland was not then under Eastern European domination! On other occasions, comments made by one candidate have opened up an opportunity for the other to hit back and score effectively. When George Bush senior attacked Governor Clinton for protesting against the Vietnam War, the challenger was smart in his response:

> When [Senator] Joe McCarthy went around this country attacking people's patriotism, he was wrong. And a Senator from Connecticut stood up to him named Prescott Bush. Your father was right to stand up to Joe McCarthy; you were wrong to attack my patriotism. I was opposed to the war, but I love my country.

Presidential debates have become the pre-eminent media event of the campaign. They attract a vast, if – until 2004 – generally declining, audience. The first of the three debates in 1960 attracted 66 million out of 179 million viewers; in 2000, 46 million out of 280 million watched the first debate, with 10 million fewer watching the subsequent debates that year; and in 2004, 62.5 million out of 292 million people watched the first debate.

At their best, they are a useful means of providing each candidate with an opportunity to reach a mass audience. Their impact is unlikely to change the allegiances of the committed voters. More often, it will confirm them in their predisposition. However, on the increasing number of non-aligned voters, a strong or weak performance have an all-important. Debates help viewers to assess character and ability, and may also increase their knowledge and understanding of politics. This is why media advisers are so concerned to get the details right.

The debates in 2008

The three ninety-minute presidential debates took place in late September to early October at various locations around the country, in Mississippi, Tennessee and New York. The vice-presidential one was held in Missouri.

In the debates, McCain repeatedly referred to his experience, drawing on stories from his background and achievements and contrasting his past involvement with the relative inexperience of his rival. Obama tried to pin down McCain on what he characterised as mistakes made by the Bush administration and elaborated on aspects of his own pro-gramme in some detail. He stressed the issues that seemed to be of major concern to the voters, seeming to be more in touch with their feelings.

The first debate (watched by more than 52 million viewers) was meant to be about for-eign and national security policy, although given the financial situation, inevitably much of the time was spent on finance and the broader economy. The second ranged widely, questions coming from the audience and via Internet contact. The third concentrated primarily on domestic policy. In particular, Joe Wurzelbacher of Ohio, who became known in the debate and thereafter in the campaign as Joe the Plumber, made his first appear-ance. The plumber had met Obama on the campaign trail and was worried that if he went ahead with plans to buy the business in which he then worked, his chances of grow-ing the business and taking on new employees would be damaged by the candidate's tax plans.

Obama was widely judged to have won the first and second debates comfortably. In the third, simply by avoiding any gaffe, he did enough to emerge with his reputation firmly intact, even if his superiority was less evident. Throughout, he was seen by many impartial commentators as strong on domestic issues, in particular the economy, with McCain having a lead on the security of the nation. McCain inspired some criticism – particularly among women and undecided voters – for his seeming disrespect for Obama, as instanced by his habit of wandering aimlessly around the stage whilst his opponent was speaking, not looking at or addressing him directly, and on occasion refer-ring to him as 'that one'.

Political advertising

The quality of individuals and the image they present is also important in political advertising. Here, the emphasis is often less upon the assets of the candidate, more upon the deficiencies of the opponent. Advertising can be blatantly unfair.

Political advertising began in 1952, with Eisenhower's 30-minute biographical portrait as 'the man from Abilene'. Its scale has significantly increased in recent years, and the advertisements have become much shorter. Advertisers know that the public can take in only so much information at any one time. During the vice-presidential race of that same year, Richard Nixon took thirty minutes of paid television time to answer charges of corruption in front of 58 million viewers. Nowadays, advertisers specialise in the 60-second or (more often) the 30-second or even 15-second commercial that makes a point briefly, yet dramatically.

Americans have often used advertisements that are autobiographical in style. Television is good at handling personalities and stories, and some of the most effective advertisements judiciously combine the two elements. Not all advertisements are of this style. Advertising is overwhelmingly negative, and goes for the jugular. Often, it pinpoints alleged deficiencies in the moral character of an opponent, as with the candidate in Tennessee who was congratulated by his opponents for 'kicking [his] chemical dependency'. Sometimes, it highlights inconsistency, as when the Bush senior campaign team in 1992 showed two politicians expressing directly opposite views on issues ranging from the first Gulf War to drug use. As the faces became clear, a voice-over observed that: 'One of these politicians is Bill Clinton. Unfortunately, so is the other!'

In 2008, the McCain team initially claimed that it would not be making personal attacks of Barack Obama of the type that he himself had suffered at the hands of George W. Bush in the Republican primaries, 2000. But as the polls looked increasingly discouraging in the later stages of the campaign, it set out to destroy the credibility of the Democratic candidate by making reference to alleged past associations with terrorists.

According to *The Wall Street Journal*[13] 'almost all of McCain's ads and one-third of the Obama ads were negative'. In defiance of conventional thinking that negative campaigning must be about an issue already worrying voters, both candidates brought up past associations of their rival. Obama used McCain's involvement in a 1980s savings-and-loan scandal. McCain widened his attacks, for instance (in response to Barack Obama's perceived rise in popularity following his July 2008 trip abroad) by releasing the 'Celeb' ad, in which he compared Obama to Paris Hilton and Britney Spears. Members of his team also drew attention to Obama's racial background, often not in an overt way. Attack ads showed Obama playing basketball, an overwhelmingly black sport in the USA. Republican vice-presidential nominee Sarah Palin emphasised the importance of electing someone committed to defending true American and Christian values, the implication being that Obama could not be relied upon to so do. This was in line with the advice apparently given to Hillary Clinton during the primary season that she needed to portray Obama as someone whose roots to basic American culture and values were at least limited.

Bill Schneider, an American political scientist, sees[14] negative advertising as a very efficient tool: 'For one thing, it's easier in 30 seconds to turn people off your opponent than to build a positive case for yourself – especially since television is a medium particularly suited for carrying negative, warning-style messages . . . you get more bang for the buck by running negative ads.'

THE MEDIA AND ELECTIONS IN BRITAIN AND THE UNITED STATES: A COMPARISON

In both countries, the media fulfil similar functions of entertaining and informing the public. Both have a privately owned press that is often accused of political bias, and there are similar worries about concentration of ownership in too few hands and a consequent lack of diversity of opinion. In Britain, there is a much more vigorous national press, whereas in the USA many people read a more local paper; in both countries, newspaper readership is in decline.

Television has come to dominate political coverage, especially at election time. It has tended to personalise politics, so that there is now more emphasis on the qualities of those who lead and less on serious discussion of issues. American campaigns are more candidate centred (see p. 228), but in recent years commentators have frequently portrayed British party conflict in terms of the Blair–Major, or Cameron–Miliband clash. Similar allegations of trivialisation are made on both sides of the Atlantic, a recognition of the fact that television is primarily a means of entertainment.

What the British have learned from US experience

- Britain has in many ways learnt from the American experience. Campaigners have visited the United States and sometimes participated in elections there. Inevitably, their findings have been relayed to their colleagues back home. In addition, people in Britain see pictures of presidential electioneering, and there has often been discussion in the media of the techniques employed. As a result, America has been a source of innovation in British campaign techniques.

- In recent years, there has been an increasing British obsession with walkabouts, photo opportunities and other **pseudo-events** created for the media. In the late 1980s and 1990s, there were several examples

pseudo-events

Events that have been staged in order to attract media publicity and, as a consequence, public interest – for example, many photo-opportunities. Other than the journalistic coverage, little of significance actually happens.

of the Americanisation of politics at work, not least in the style of some party broad-casts (*Kinnock – the Movie*, 1987), and in the Sheffield Rally of 1992, a triumphalist occasion very reminiscent of the American convention.

Differences between US and UK media coverage

There are differences between media coverage on either side of the Atlantic and – from the British point of view – some safeguards:

- In Britain, we elect a party rather than just one person, and politics is not about personality alone.

- The in-depth interview provides a kind of antidote to the dangers of shallow but media-friendly leaders being chosen, for their personal qualities come under heavy scrutiny and in the in-depth, Sunday-lunchtime type of programme policy deficiencies can be much exposed. We also can now see our representatives in action in the House of Commons, and Prime Minister's Questions at least is an occasion that shows those in power being forced to defend their position, even if it does little to inform people of the issues. The interviews conducted during the election in a range of television programmes are a reminder of how leading figures can be put on the spot by skilful members of the public who can unsettle their composure.

But most people do not watch such encounters, and the likelihood is that those people who use television the most to obtain their information may be the very people who are least the discerning and able to come to a reasonable conclusion based on knowledge. They probably don't read other sources, and therefore what they see and hear has a potent effect on the least-sophisticated electors.

Is there a danger of the Americanisation of British politics?

A number of observers see dangers in the way in which American techniques of elec-tioneering have impacted on electioneering in Britain and other countries. Martin

ELECTING THE PRESIDENT: A CHOICE BY ELECTORAL COLLEGE

Running for the presidency involves three stages:
- winning the support of delegates to the party convention;
- winning the approval of the convention itself;
- winning in the presidential race following the autumn campaign (the general election).

Winning delegates to the convention

The first stage in the process of choosing a new president is for the parties to choose their nominee, and this consumes several months of the election year.

Rosenbaum,[15] who has written widely on postwar British campaigning, comments that of late 'An Americanization [of British politics] is clearly occurring'. Some would call it 'trivialization, with politicians speaking in shorter and shorter sound bites'. Even before this trend accelerated in the mid-1990s, Kavanagh found that elections already had become 'more leader-centred, increasingly stage-managed for the media, particularly television, and a greater role is played by public relations advisors, advertisers, and opinion pollsters'.[16]

To illustrate the point symbolically, the Labour Party's 100th anniversary celebration, attended by then prime minister, Tony Blair, was sponsored by the American fast-food chain McDonalds, giving rise to its naming by one pundit[17] as 'the McLabour conference'. He commented rather sardonically that, like the food chain, 'Labour's packaging is rather more wholesome than the contents'.

Party broadcasts rather than political advertisements, free airtime, vigilant journalists, in-depth political interviews and politicians more prepared to answer questions about their proposals, help to differentiate the British from the US experience in certain respects and are some kind of protection against the adoption in Britain of the more questionable aspects of American electioneering methods. Yet as we have seen, the party broadcasts themselves have to some degree 'gone American' in style and form.

Some would argue that on this side of the Atlantic we are less susceptible to the excesses of emotionalism and negative campaigning that beset American politics. However, the advent of television, opinion polls and campaign consultants – among various other features – has transformed British elections in a way that makes them more akin to the US experience. The form of 'Americanisation' has been different in different countries, in line with national traditions and practices.

Any person who hopes to become a presidential candidate has to decide when to launch his or her bid for the White House. Some make a decision to stand soon after the last election is over, but any announcement of the intention is not usually made until the year before the election at the earliest, even if campaign planning is already actively under way. Candidates and those who manage their campaigns know the importance of lining up support and raising funds before their declaration.

Candidates have to decide how to navigate the primaries and caucuses that take place in the early months of the presidential year, and this decision involves a number of considerations. Until the 1970s, it was not common for candidates to take the primary route, but this has become the accepted procedure for any 'hopeful' to adopt. A decision not to stand entails the risk of losing momentum whilst others secure the support of party delegations.

The arrangements vary in detail from state to state, and in some cases the parties in a particular state employ different approaches. But today the use of primaries is the accepted method used by both parties in most states. Eight states use a caucus and/or convention system, the details of which are laid down by its legislature. In those using caucuses, the party organisation is still important, whereas in those using conventions the choice of national delegates is made by people who are themselves delegates from local meetings.

The primary route

More than 80% of the delegates in 1992 were chosen as a result of primary contests, and most candidates now take the primary route. They need to decide which primaries to enter, but whereas it was once common for a candidate to miss some of the early ones, this is now seen as a high-risk strategy. Jimmy Carter decided to seek the Democratic nomination by staging a nationwide primary campaign and involved himself in the early contests and as many as he could thereafter. This is now the usual policy, and most commentators believe that it is wise to enter as many as possible. Candidates tend to choose contests where they are likely to make a good showing. The number of rivals, their personal standing in the opinion polls, local interests, the timing of the contest and their level of financial backing all play a part in the decisions made.

The first primary takes place in New Hampshire, and a strong performance in the early contests can lend a useful momentum to the campaign and help to demoralise rivals who do less well. Many states have now brought their primaries forward, hoping that this will give their voters a greater influence on the final choice of candidates. As a result of this 'front-loading', some 70% of the delegates to the convention have been selected by the end of March.

To do well in the primaries, candidates need to manoeuvre with some skill. The opposition in each primary will vary, and tactics used to defeat a strong rival in one state may not work in another. Media coverage, as well as financial and human resources, is also relevant to the outcome, and candidates looking for good coverage will spend heavily on the early contests in their bid to gain popular momentum. It is important for the candidates and those who support them to use the media wisely and to downplay the expectations of what they might achieve. If they then do well, this gives their campaign a boost. If it is widely expected that they will perform well as the front runner, then a disappointing outcome (even though it is a technical victory) can cost valuable momentum.

The presidential primaries are the arena in which lively personal battles are fought, and they are conducted under intense public scrutiny by the media and commentators. Sometimes, the battles have been so savage at this stage that great damage is done to party unity.

Winning support at the convention

The national nominating conventions are held over a four-day period in July and August. By then, the outcome is usually a foregone conclusion, and normally the successful candidate is chosen on the first ballot. Delegates are now forced to pledge themselves to a definite candidate for at least the first two ballots, although in the past this was not the case and delegates arrived with varying degrees of commitment.

Once the candidate has been chosen, the nominee makes an acceptance speech and receives homage as the party's standard-bearer for the forthcoming struggle. At this point, the intra-party battle that has dominated the political scene for so many months becomes unimportant, and the concentration of those present has to be on the contest with the other party. As Malcolm Vile[18] has observed: 'This switch from the bitterness of internal conflict to the competition between parties is one of the perennial wonders of the American political scene.'

The convention comprises those delegates elected in primaries, caucuses or state conventions. Their task is to choose the presidential candidate (in effect, already done) and the vice-presidential nominee – a choice actually made by the presidential candidate and invariably ratified by those assembled. Delegates also help to write the party platform, and at this stage there is often a tussle between different factions, which seek to move the party in their direction. The policy statement is not binding on the two people chosen to run for the White House, but as it indicates prevalent feeling in the party, candidates do not usually ignore such an expression of the mood of the faithful.

The conclusion of the national convention season brings to an end a long-drawn-out process for which the candidates have been planning and working for many months – if not years. As a result, the two main presidential candidates have been chosen and are ready for the main battle ahead. But there is an alternative way by which presidential candidates can be placed on the ballot for the November election, one that shuns the primary/convention route. This involves a would-be challenger complying with the petition requirements in each individual state (difficult in Maryland, where 3% – approximately 60,000 signatures – are required, simple in Louisiana, where payment of a filing fee of $500 is sufficient).

Ross Perot fulfilled these requirements in each individual state in 1992, for his funding and voluntary support enabled his cause to be well represented across the nation. Once on the ballot paper, it is these days much more possible to achieve national prominence without the backing of a political party, as the candidacy of Perot showed. Television can provide ample exposure, via chat-show and other appearances. It was a matter of some pride to Perot that he was able to run an efficient and effective campaign without dipping too heavily into his own substantial private fortune. Without any established party organisation, he was able to launch a highly successful bid in 1992 and eventually win 19% of the popular vote in November.

Winning the presidential race

There is only a short pause between the end of the party conventions and the beginning of the campaign, and in this time each party is concerned to pull together again after what can be a wounding primary process. They also devise their strategies for the final stage – the bid for the White House.

The campaign, and in particular the ever-growing importance of television, are discussed on pp. 228–230 and 242–250. Some of the important features include:

- the growing use of market research;
- the use of professional consultants and assorted media gurus;
- the increasing attention to the importance of photo-opportunities, to provide the media with pictures as well as words;
- a concentration on themes which appear appropriate for the national mood;
- the use of television opportunities, ranging from chat shows to interviews and, of course, the presidential debates.

Much depends on creating the right image for the candidate, who at this stage needs to adopt a stance that can appeal to many Americans of all social groups, well beyond the confines of traditional party support. The candidate needs to be attuned to the mood of the hour. Franklin Roosevelt caught the popular imagination in 1932 with his promise of dynamic action; John F. Kennedy seemed to embody the hopes of those who wanted to see America move forward to the challenge of New Frontiers, in 1960; Bill Clinton was presented as a man who might get America moving again in 1992, after a period in which domestic policy had been neglected.

Of course, doubts about a candidate's personal standards of behaviour can throw the strategy off course. But in Clinton's case in 1992, he was able to keep the economy in the forefront despite the attempt of the Bush team to portray him in a negative way – just as it had successfully painted a picture of the Democratic presidential nominee Dukakis in 1988 as 'soft' on issues of public concern, such as crime. In 1992, it was perhaps easier for the Democrat to stick to his emphasis on the pivotal role of the economy, for Ross Perot was also making this the central element in his campaign.

The election takes place on the first Tuesday after the first Monday in November.

The Electoral College and how it works

The method of becoming president in the United States is in many ways a clumsy and protracted process. A candidate needs to acquire 270 votes in the Electoral College, out of the 538 available. Each state is apportioned a number of votes according to the number of seats it possesses in Congress: two for the Senate and a variable number for the House of Representatives. Thus, in 2008, California had 55, Texas 34, New York State 31, Florida 27, Illinois and Pennsylvania 21 each, and Hawaii 4.

Because of the equal representation of each state in the Senate, the smaller states are over-represented in the Electoral College, so that Delaware and Vermont, with well under a million people each, still have three votes. The electors in the college formally make the choice of the person to become president, just as they separately decide on the vice-presidency also. The choice is not made by the ordinary voter, who when he or she went to the polling station actually voted for electors who were pledged to Obama/Biden or McCain/Palin. In each state, the candidate who received the largest popular vote won the entire electoral vote, though Maine and Nebraska have a slightly different procedure.

If, when the electors in the college are making their choice, no candidate gains a majority, then the choice is thrown open to the House of Representatives, which chooses from among the top three candidates. If there is no majority for the position of vice-president, then the choice goes to the Senate, which chooses between the first two candidates. If it became necessary to use this process, then it is the new Congress just elected (for example November 2000) rather than the old one that makes the choice. Theoretically, it would be possible for the two houses to choose candidates from different parties, so that in 2000 the House could have opted for Gore, the Senate for Cheney.

From this short account, it becomes apparent that it is essential for any presidential candidate to win in the Electoral College. To achieve this, he or she needs to perform strongly in the large urban and suburban states that have so much influence. Indeed, it has often been said that to become president it is necessary to win in California; its fifty-five votes are a greater number than those of the twelve least-populated states and the District of Columbia all combined. As we have seen, states such as Texas, New York, Illinois and Pennsylvania have a significant number of votes and – as the 2000 result indicated – so does Florida. The candidate is likely to focus attention particularly on such large states and on those where he or she can expect to fare well.

The importance of certain individual states dictates the strategy of any would-be contender. A candidate who can win in California or New York is more important than one who can do fairly well in every state, for most candidates do not aim to win across the nation and often fight less than enthusiastically in some hostile territory. For this reason, it is important for the main parties to have a candidate of wide appeal in the states that are liable to go one way or the other. To choose a candidate from a safe state wastes the possible bonus of choosing a local person in a state or region in which there is a chance of success. For the Democrats in 1992, the choice of Clinton was a useful way of trying to restore the party's fortunes in a region where its support had been eroded over the Reagan years.

Such considerations are in the mind of the parties and commentators as they ponder the campaign scene in a presidential year. But the other factor of great significance is television, the impact of which is enormous. It has made the country one vast constituency, and concentrated attention on the personal appeal and overall abilities of the candidate. Because of this, the campaign is increasingly in the hands of the advisers and gurus, who collectively enjoy the label of 'political consultants'.

Yet as we have seen, this is not the end of the process. The result of the contest may be known within a few hours of the close of polling, but it is another

---

What qualities make a good presidential candidate?

Ideally, the person should represent a large, pivotal state which they will have a chance of winning. They should have broad appeal, having the ability to carry some, preferably most, key states, which means being well received in California, on the east coast and in the South. They also need the flexibility to cope with the demands of the primary struggle – requiring an ability to enthuse the party faithful – and then, having won the nomination, to seem a less partisan figure who can their his area of potential support by reaching out to many non-committed Americans.

Candidates normally have a record of public service, sometimes as senators, but recently more likely as state governors. Preferably, they will not be identified too strongly with particular views, for it is likely that on contentious issues this will create many opponents. Broad intelligence and a certain vagueness on policy is a useful recipe. It is desirable, if not strictly necessary, to show an appropriate interest in and knowledge of significant topics, and by the tone of one's observations to seem to be in touch with public concern. Neither Ronald Reagan or George W. Bush proved to be intellectually high powered, but the former, and the latter for four or five years, managed to create the impression that their hopes and fears resonated with those of the average American.

Occasionally, a candidate comes along who is a national hero, and has not stood in the usual offices prior to candidacy. Eisenhower was a good choice for the Republicans in 1952, though retired generals do not always make strong candidates. They were more common a century ago, although from time to time the name of such a man still emerges. Colin Powell, having achieved honour and distinction in the Gulf War, has the sort of reputation that could override considerations such as lack of political experience. This is why many moderate Republicans would have liked to see his candidature in 1996.

month before the actual election of the president takes place – when the members of the Electoral College cast their votes. The event is largely unnoticed in the outside world, yet it is of profound importance even if the actual outcome is a formality in almost every case.

Because the smaller states are proportionally over-represented in the college, it is possible for a candidate to win the largest share of the popular vote in the country but not the majority of the votes in the Electoral College. This has happened in the past – in 1824, in 1876 and in 1888 – and it happened again in 2000. It nearly happened in 1960 and 1976, elections that were closely contested. Neither of the men elected in those years, Kennedy or Carter, received a popular majority of the votes cast, and neither did Bill Clinton in either of his two victories.

The method of choosing the president assessed

The process of choosing an American president is long, complex and expensive in the eyes of many outside observers. It certainly tests the mettle of any

Other considerations include the desirability of being a Protestant in religion, although the choice of Kennedy in 1960 showed that a Roman Catholic could make it to the White House; the nomination of John Kerry showed that this factor has now become less important. JFK was an untypical candidate for, apart from his religion, he was spectacularly wealthy which could have been off-putting and made him appear out of touch with ordinary Americans. He also showed no great interest in agriculture, which at the time was unusual, given the political importance of the farm vote. Yet he had one obvious virtue: he was a glamorous candidate and one of the first to see the potential of television as a means of selling his personality. Today, being personable and of good appearance is especially important. Television is not generally regarded as a medium in which bald, fat or ugly figures fare well. The ability to speak fluently and with seeming sincerity is another asset.

Presidential elections today have become major media events and the successful candidate will be subjected to the glare of the cameras and the gaze of an interested public over many months. They need to avoid negative coverage, for there are many who have fallen because of media scrutiny of some impropriety in their private life, be it sexual or financial. Bill Clinton obtained the nomination in spite of damaging allegations about his private life in 1991–92, helped by his and his supportive wife's appearance together on television frankly admitting to their marital difficulties and their determination to overcome them. Being married is an asset. No bachelor was elected president in the twentieth century.

It requires a special stamina to endure the run for president and to withstand the pressures imposed by such endless attention. It is a long and arduous struggle, enough to tax the energies and finance of even the most dedicated and ambitious politician.

candidate for the highest office, and, particularly in an age of television, any contender who can emerge relatively unscathed after such a prolonged procedure must have considerable powers of endurance and stamina. Hence Vile's[19] reference to 'almost lethal' demands.

The system enables the person chosen to become established as a national figure. In the case of someone such as General Eisenhower, his reputation was already well known. This is not the case with many of the persons who seek to win the presidency via the primary route. Jimmy Carter was an 'outsider' from Georgia, unknown to the Washington elite in 1975, a year before he was elected to the White House. Others may be more familiar, but the way in which a presidential candidates emerge does ensure that they become national figures by the time they come to take office. Either by travel in the past or, especially, via television today, they have been exposed to the critical gaze of millions of American voters, have been forced to sell their personality, to demonstrate an understanding of the needs and wishes of the voters, and to show that they are worthy of the voters' respect, trust and support as the country's leader.

Yet there are many criticisms that can be made of the way in which the US chooses its national leader. Some concern the primaries, some the Electoral College and others the system of election and the nature of the campaign. There is a heavy reliance on the media, increasing professionalism and expense, yet the result is low turnouts and mounting public cynicism.

The primary system is often criticised because of the number and timing of the various contests, a situation which forces candidates to navigate the primary season with some dexterity. They need to stand in as many contests as possible, although this can be very costly and involves putting their names down in several states which ballot on the same day; for instance, several primaries in the South are held on Super Tuesday, in early March. This makes a campaign difficult to organise and conduct.

A possible improvement would be to hold a national presidential primary, an election on a single day across the whole country, in the late spring or autumn. As an alternative, the separate state primaries could all be held on the same day. Such a one-off election would reduce the demands on the candidates, attract much media publicity (and therefore a higher turnout?) and produce a fair and representative verdict. But would it increase the role of television and emphasise the professionalism of the modern campaign, with all of its advisers, consultants and preoccupation with image building? Would it not favour the wealthy or well-resourced candidate who could afford to advertise his cause in every state?

It would, of course, be possible to revert to the older system, and rely more on caucuses to make the choice. We have examined the reasons for the

greater use of primaries (see pp. 220–221). It is unlikely that there would
be any strong support for scrapping their use today, although for those who
wish to strengthen the role of political parties in the American system of
government there could be a benefit in so doing.

Most of the anxiety about the American system relates to the use of the
Electoral College, for it is from the use of this approach that several potential
problems derive. Criticism centres on several aspects, notably:

- the over-representation of very small states and the excessive concentration on those which have many college votes;
- the use of the simple plurality method of voting;
- the possibility that members of the college may vote for a person other than
  the one to whom they were pledged;
- the fact that it is possible to win the popular vote and yet lose the election;
- the fact that there may be no clear victor in the college, if no one emerges
  with a majority. This could have happened in 1992, if Ross Perot had actually managed to carry some states. It was the strategy of George Wallace
  in 1968 to aim for deadlock, and thereby throw the decision into the
  House. A choice made in Congress could be contrary to the people's will
  as expressed in the ballot box in November.

Why have an Electoral College? Does the system work well?

The Founding Fathers wanted a method of choosing their president that
would shun 'mob politics'. Democracy was then not yet in fashion, and as they
were creating an elected office they wanted to ensure that they were not handing power to demagogues who could manipulate popular opinion. They were
suspicious of the mass of the people. Choice by college, after the voters had
expressed their feelings, could be conducted in a more leisurely and rational
manner. As Hamilton put it in the *Federalist Papers*:[20] 'The immediate election
[of the president] should be made by men most capable of analysing the qualities needed for the office.' In this spirit, the Founding Fathers set up a system
in which the electorate actually chooses between two competing lists or
'slates' of Electoral College candidates, although on the ballot papers it is the
names of the candidates for the presidential office which are actually given.

There was never any serious likelihood that members of the Electoral College
meeting in December would ignore the expression of public feeling in early
November, and candidates for the college soon became pledged to cast their
vote for one of the presidential challengers. In other words, they do not use
their individual discretion, but reflect the feelings of voters in their state. In
fact, the college does not even meet as one deliberating body. Members meet

in their state capitals, and their choices are conveyed to Washington. Very rarely, an elector in the Electoral College has changed his or her mind and not voted for the person to whom he or she was pledged. In 1948 a Tennessee elector did not vote for Truman, who had carried the state, but opted instead for the states' rights candidate. Twenty years later, an elector in North Carolina switched from Richard Nixon to the third party candidate George Wallace. In 1988, a Democrat voted for Lloyd Bentsen, the vice-presidential nominee, rather than Michael Dukakis, the candidate for the presidency.

Some writers have also drawn attention to the way in which balloting takes place. Instead of there being a proportional split in the Electoral College vote of a particular state, to reflect the division of the popular vote, the candidate who gets the most votes carries the whole state allocation. This simple plurality or 'winner takes all' method may seem unfair, especially when the result is very close. In 1960, Kennedy obtained all of New York's 45 college votes, despite the fact that he only obtained 52.5% support; a proportional split would have given him 24 votes, to 21 for his opponent. This method makes the impact of geography on the outcome very important, for as we have seen, a candidate who can carry California and other populous states has an enormous advantage. This would not be the case if the college vote were divided. The importance of urban states with dense populations is unduly emphasised under this process.

For all of its disadvantages, the system has so far worked tolerably well. When there is a close popular vote, as in 1960, the outcome in the college makes the result clear cut. Until 2000, the same has been true in other contests where the gap between the main candidates is a narrow one.

Is there a better alternative to the Electoral College?

There have been many suggestions for the use of an amended college system, and others for its total abolition. Modifications could take the form of using an electoral system other than 'winner takes all'. A proportional division of the college votes is an alternative to the simple plurality.

The most obvious change would be to jettison the Electoral College and opt for a straight popular election of the president by the voters, instead of using the present indirect process of election. If it proved to be the case that no candidate could overcome a 40% hurdle on the first round of voting, then there could be a replay, a run-off between the two candidates who had scored most successfully. The person elected could then claim to have wide national backing, and not be unduly beholden to the voters in especially populous states. No longer is there the same apprehension about democracy as prevailed when the Founding Fathers made their choice.

It is true that such a method could further enhance the power of television, for few candidates could ever get across the nation to tour every state to encourage popular support. Yet effectively this is what happens now; the campaign is already organised for its television impact. More seriously for some critics of reform along these lines, it might weaken further the two main parties and encourage the candidature of third-party nominees.

For defenders of states' rights, such a proposal might seem to be a threat to the federal system, for it undermines the importance of each state and region in the contest. In particular, the smaller states might feel uneasy, for their current influence in deciding the outcome would be diminished.

Is change likely?

It is far more likely that the present system will continue indefinitely, for although there is periodic unease about the Electoral College, this mainly coincides with the prospect of an indecisive outcome in the next presidential election. When a clear winner emerges, as eventually happened in 1992, much of the earlier talk of change vanishes.

There is no agreement on any alternative. Direct election was supported by Jimmy Carter early in the life of his presidency, when he described the existing arrangements as 'archaic'. Many analysts might concur with such a view, but there are strong forces ranged against it. The federal system was designed to protect the influence of the states, especially small ones, and they would not readily vote for a change, either via their congressmen or in their state legislatures. For the Dakotas or Vermont, the Electoral College gives them an influence beyond their size, and why should they wish to surrender it?

HOW AMERICANS VOTE AND WHY THEY VOTE AS THEY DO

Ever since the time of the New Deal, there has been a marked trend for urban workers with low incomes, who generally live in the poorest districts and have a lower level of formal educational qualification, to vote Democrat. In contrast, well-to-do voters, often with a higher level of educational attainment and living in suburban areas, have usually inclined to the Republican side.

The Democrats have had the support of minority groups such as blacks, who suffered in the Great Depression and regarded the party as the one that conferred benefits and was more likely to be interested in advancing their economic interests. The majority of Catholics, mainly of Irish immigrant stock, have inclined to the same party, and so have groups such as the Jews and other minorities. However, just as white southern Democrats were often noted for their deeply ingrained Protestant fundamentalism, so Republicans always had some voters who were poor whites, Catholics, Jewish or black. There was never a complete racial, religious or socio-economic divide.

A changed picture in recent years

The pattern of voting behaviour in Britain and America has changed over the last generation and some of the broad generalisations previously made by political scientists and strategists were found to be inadequate by the 1980s and 1990s. The changing class structure, with fewer people working in manufacturing industry, greater prosperity for most classes in the population and more upward social mobility, challenged some previous assumptions about the way Americans vote. Voting behaviour has become more volatile, and as Stephen Wayne[21] has written:

> While class, religion and geography are still related to party identification and voting behaviour, they are not as strongly related as they were in the past. Voters are less influenced by group cues. They exercise a more independent judgement on election day, a judgement that is less predictable and more subject to be influenced by the campaign itself.

Political scientists today talk more about partisan identification, the appeal of the candidate and issues, than they did in the past. There is, of course, no clear-cut division between them, for the party one associates oneself with will often help to determine what one thinks about the candidate and the topic under discussion. By partisan identification, we mean the long-standing identification that a person has with a particular party, a preference that often will have been formed over many years. It will have been influenced by family background, education and the influence of peers in the early years, and this sense of attachment stays with people for much of their lives, modified by life experience, especially economic considerations and the impressions formed of the effectiveness of particular administrations in delivering the goods and making people feel content. The underlying assumption in studies of 'partisan identification' is that most Americans will stick by their normal party affiliation unless there are seemingly good reasons for not doing so.

However, partisan identification is a less powerful tie than it was in the past. In the shorter term, there are other determinants of voting behaviour, less stable factors that fluctuate from election to election. They include the attractiveness of the individual candidate and the issues that are in the forefront of people's minds. Martin Wattenberg[22] has argued that there has been a change of focus in recent years from party allegiance to concentration on the merits of the nominee: 'The change . . . is an important historical trend, which has been gradually taking place over the last several decades.' Voters now seem to be more interested in the qualities the candidate possesses – not surprisingly, as these are now featured in the media more than ever before. Via television, voters can assess candidates' leadership ability and charisma, their honesty and experience, their knowledge or their ignorance. 'Strength' and 'leadership' are much-admired qualities, as is what George Bush senior called 'the vision thing'; many people like to be led by a person who knows where he or she wishes to lead them.

THE TREND TO SPLIT-TICKET VOTING

By **split-ticket voting**, we mean the practice of casting ballots for the candidates of at least two different political parties when multiple offices are being decided in the same elections. This is in contrast to straight-ticket voting, in which a voter chooses candidates from the same political party for every office on the ballot paper.

Since the days of Democratic ascendancy, which ended in 1968, there has been a clear reduction in voter loyalty. Voters are more willing to vote differently between elections and within them – by split-ticket voting. The trend to split-ticket voting actually has a longer history, going back to 1952, but it has intensified in recent years. Whereas in 1952, 12% voted differently in their choice of party for the president and their member of the House of Representatives, by 1968, 26% did so, and in 1980 the figure was 34%. Voters were enthusiastic about electing Ronald Reagan, but less willing to vote for his party in the congressional elections.

In 2008, the state of Montana illustrated the willingness of voters to split their vote. For the Presidency/Vice-presidency, they opted for Republicans McCain/Palin, just as for the House they chose Republican Denny Rehberg. Yet for all other posts, ranging from the Senate vacancy and the governorship/lieutenant governorship to the secretary of state and superintendent of public instruction, they elected Democrats.

The trend is notable at all levels, with more voters behaving differently in choosing a candidate for the White House and candidates for Capitol Hill, more voting one way for the Senate and a different way for the House, and – particularly marked – a larger number voting differently in their choice of state and of local representatives.

Why is split-ticket voting common?

1 The desire of many Americans to divide power in order to prevent an undue concentration in the hands of one person or party – for example they may have preferred Clinton to Dole as their president in 1996, but chose to balance this choice by electing a Republican-dominated Congress.

2 Voter attachment to one party has declined, there being less strong partisan identification and more voter volatility. There are more votes 'up for grabs' and voters make a judgement on the qualities and policy positions of the candidates, both of which matter more in a media age of candidate-centred electioneering.

3 Some voters may feel that the candidate of one party is better at providing leadership in the White House, whereas in Congress they prefer to see the other party predominate. They may feel safer with a Republican president who might be expected to be tough on America's enemies, but prefer a more progressive Democrat agenda on domestic policy.

Restrictions on split-ticket voting

A few states refuse to accept split tickets for primary elections and force voters to select all candidates from one of the main parties. For instance, on the Michigan general election ballot paper in November, voters can vote a straight party ticket by indicating their wish to do so at the top of each political party's column, but are able to vote for candidates of different parties for the various offices by marking accordingly in the appropriate place. For the August primary, they must confine their votes to a single party column. In the 2010 South Carolinian primary, the prohibition was extended in the case of the Democratic Party ballot paper to include resolutions as well as candidates and offices. In the case of the Republicans, voters had the option of approving or disapproving resolutions to pass legislation.

Issues are also important, but rather less so than party identification and candidate appeal. Voters are often uncertain about where a contender stands on a particular issue, for politicians realise that clarity can sometimes antagonise people and groups whom the candidate hopes to attract. If they have taken the trouble to find out rival policy positions and understand them clearly, then it may be that they incline to one side on one issue, the other on a different one.

More broadly, voters think in terms of what the last administration has done for them (**retrospective** issue voting) and what the candidates are offering for the next four years (**prospective** issue voting). In 1992, many were unimpressed by the domestic performance of the Bush presidency, particularly Bush's handling of the economy. They felt that Bill Clinton offered a better future – reform of healthcare, and a new emphasis on recovering from the recession and creating jobs ('It's the economy, stupid!'). However much Bush might try to stress the 'character issue', by suggesting that his opponent was untruthful, evasive and not to be trusted, this appeared to matter less on this occasion than the promise of movement on the domestic front.

These shorter-term considerations have become more significant over several decades. Otherwise, the Democrats would always be more successful than their opponents, for American National Election Study researchers have consistently found that considerably more Americans describe themselves as 'strong', 'weak' or 'independent-leaning' Democrats than as Republicans, as the table below shows.

Party identification (percentages), 1958–2008

Leaning identified	1958	1968	1978	1988	1998	2008
Strong Democrat	28	20	15	18	19	19
Weak Democrat	23	26	24	18	18	15
Independent Democrat	7	10	14	12	14	17
Independent	8	11	16	12	12	11
Independent Republican	5	9	10	13	11	12
Weak Republican	17	15	13	14	16	13
Strong Republican	12	10	8	14	10	13

Source: American National Election Studies.

NB Note that the table indicates two trends, towards a broad reduction in strong/weak Democratic Party identification and towards more independently minded thinking in both parties. (see also 290)

NB For further information on voting behaviour see the information on African American and female voting on pp. 384–385 and 398–400, respectively. For data relating to voting behaviour in the 2008 presidential election, see p. 281.

Voting behaviour in Britain and the United States: a comparison

The academic study of voting behaviour became popular in the 1960s on either side of the Atlantic. Early studies such as *The American Voter* and *Political Change in Britain*[23] showed how voting was influenced by long- and short-term influences. Since those early days, theories of voting behaviour have undergone substantial modification. Social changes have occurred in all developed countries, and as a result the old certainties have vanished. Voting is now less predictable than in the past. In an age of greater volatility, short-term influences are likely to be more significant, and parties cannot count on traditional loyalties to provide them with mass support.

Short-term influences relate to a particular election, and include:

- the state of the economy;

- the personality and performance of political leaders;

- the nature of the campaign;

- the mass media;

- events leading up to the election.

Long-term influences include:

- party loyalty;

- social class;

- factors relating to the social structure such as age, gender, occupation, race and religion.

In Britain, the features most noted in the postwar years up to 1970 were:

- the stability of voting patterns, as people stayed loyal to the party they had always supported;

- the relevance of social class (Pulzer[24] could once memorably write that: 'Class is the basis of British politics; all else is embellishment and detail');

- the recognition that elections were determined by a body of floating voters in key marginal constituencies;

- the uniform nature of the swing across the United Kingdom;

- the domination of the two main parties, which between them could count on the support of the majority of the electorate.

Since the 1970s many of these assumptions have lost their validity. The main parties can no longer anticipate the degree of support they once enjoyed, and the rise of third parties has made inroads into the share of the vote the two parties can command. In 1994, Madgwick concluded[25] that: 'Voting is still related to social class, but the relationship is complex, and there is less confidence about the significance of the term.' His conclusion was heavily influenced by Ivor Crewe,[26] whose researches showed that not only was class identification weakening, but so was party identification generally.

The publication of *Decade of De-alignment* was a psephological milestone. Bo Sarlvik and Crewe showed the extent to which the two parties had steadily lost their once-reliable supporters. They found that the bulk of the electorate was now liable to switch votes, and become actual or potential floating voters. In particular, they discovered that demographic changes were taking their toll of Labour, for the old working-class communities were being destroyed by redevelopment schemes and the inner cities were emptying. Labour's

referendum

A vote on a single issue in which all registered electors are eligible to take part. Instead of being asked to give a verdict on the administration as a whole – as in a general election – they are asked their opinion on one measure or act presented to them by the legislature.

initiative

A device by which an individual citizen (or group of citizens) can – if they collect a given number of signatures on a petition – have a proposal placed directly on the ballot in a state-wide election. As such, the initiative is particularly useful in cases where law makers refuse to enact or even consider a law that the people want.

DIRECT LEGISLATION: THE REFERENDUM, INITIATIVE AND RECALL

The United States is one of only five democracies that have never held a nationwide **referendum**. However, in forty-six states and many cities there is provision for at least one of the three forms of direct legislation, the **initiative**, recall (see box on p. 268) and referendum. The facility has been more widely used in several of them in the last generation.

traditional electoral base was being eroded, a point which led Peter Kellner[27] to write that the 'sense of class solidarity which propelled Labour to power in 1945 has all but evaporated'. Tony Blair's New Labour party recognised that Labour needed to extend its appeal, particularly in Middle England. Particularly in 1997 and 2001, Labour gained broad support from across the ages, sexes and social classes. By 2005, the last election Blair fought, Labour's appeal was waning among all groups. Five years later, New Labour only received just over 8.6 million votes, its appeal to all groups having significantly narrowed.

In the US, broad trends in voting behaviour in recent years are that:

- party identification means less today than was once the case;

- voting has become more candidate-centred. In a television age, voters know much more about the candidates, and considerations of perceived competence, integrity and visual appeal matter more than ever before. In presidential debates, the electorate can easily assess these qualities;

- policy issues may play a greater role than in the past. Today, those who stand for office are regularly grilled about how they respond to particular issues and events.

In both countries, voters are now less committed to their long-term allegiances. Partisan de-alignment has occurred, and this means that there has been a weakening of the old loyalties, and a new volatility among the electorate. Other key points of comparison are that:

- social class, once a key determinant of voting, especially in Britain, has lost much of its impact;

- the personality of the candidate has assumed greater importance in a media age, particularly in America, where the party label anyway counts for less;

- issues and the election campaign become more significant, as there are today more votes 'up for grabs'.

Early twentieth-century progressives supported the use of direct democracy and many states where it is now employed adopted it around that time, originally South Dakota in 1898 and Oregon in 1902. Most of the 'early' ones opted for the initiative and referendum, but as David Magleby[28] points out, the states that have incorporated direct legislation since World War I have decided in several cases not to go for the whole package:

> In short, in the early going, states were much more likely to embrace all aspects of direct legislation, and provide the most direct forms of the process . . . While many states permit both the initiative and the popular referendum, it is the initiative that is much more frequently used. Since 1980, there have been roughly five initiatives for every popular referendum.

The recall

The recall is a device that allows the voters to petition for a vote on whether an elected official should be 'recalled' or removed from office. Employed in the days of Athenian democracy, its use is uncommon today. In the United States, recall elections do not take place at the federal level. The majority of states allow them in local jurisdictions, but only eighteen states have provision for them to remove state officials.

In states such as Alaska, Georgia and Montana, specific grounds are required for a recall, such as some form of misconduct while in office. Via a November 2010 referendum, Illinois voters opted to amend their state constitution to allow a recall, in the light of an alleged corruption scandal involving ex-Governor Blagojevich. In these and some other states, the official may choose to dispute the validity of the grounds in court, where judges decide whether the allegations merit a recall. In eleven other states that permit state-wide recall, no grounds are required and recall petitions may be circulated for any reason. However, the target of a recall is permitted to submit responses to the stated reasons for recall.

Successful cases of recall are rare, the most famous being that in California (2003), where Democrat Governor Gray Davis was recalled because of controversy over the state budget. In California, a recall triggers a simultaneous special election, where the vote on the recall, as well as the vote on the replacement should the recall succeed, are on the same ballot. There had been previous attempts to recall governors of the state (one

Direct democracy is most commonly used in the western states. Their political systems were still relatively undeveloped at the turn of the twentieth century, so that they were much more open to the arguments of the progressive movement. Progressivism was firmly entrenched in the region, supporters urging anti-institutional reforms that allowed for popular involvement. It never took root in the same way in the older South and Northeast, which provide less opportunity for this form of direct democracy. (NB Some towns in New England have a different form of direct democracy, the town meeting – see p. 242).

Issues and frequency

Initiatives have in recent years offered Americans tough choices on a wide array of subjects, from animal welfare to gay rights, from abortion to firearms purchases. Initiatives were used in several western states in the 1990s, among other things to test how many terms a person could serve in a state legislature or on Capitol Hill, to restrict (or enhance) personal liberty and to prohibit the trapping of black bears out of season.

The state most frequently associated with the use of initiatives and referendums is California. There can be as many as thirty propositions on the

targeted Ronald Reagan), but the Davis case was the first in which opponents gathered the necessary signatures to qualify for a special election. Davis himself had faced an unsuccessful recall petition in 1999, but that effort failed to gain enough signatures to qualify for the ballot.

An unsuccessful attempt at recall was adjudicated in November 2010 in the New Jersey Supreme Court. The effort of a Tea Party group (Sussex County Tea Party Patriots) to recall Senator Robert Menendez was thwarted when the court ruled that a recall is not allowed by the US Constitution. In a 4–2 verdict, the New Jersey judgment argued that the federal Constitution has precedence over the state one. The former does not allow for recall of senators, even though the state constitution does. The majority ruling, written by Chief Justice Stuart Rabner,[29] noted that: 'The historical record leads to but one conclusion: the Framers rejected a recall provision and denied the states the power to recall U.S. Senators.' The case is likely to be appealed to the Supreme Court in Washington.

The group seeking to recall Menendez did not claim that he had been embroiled in any particular scandal or that he had voted in the Senate differently than he said he would when he was elected in 2006. Their problem was simply that they disagreed with his liberal views, including his support for the reform of healthcare provision passed by Congress in March 2010.

biennial November ballot paper, where they are placed alongside the contests for federal and state offices. The protagonists on either side are allowed to draw up statements of the pro and anti cases; these are freely distributed to the voters, in weighty booklets. In 1998, topics ranged from tribal gaming to an animal-trap ban, from air quality to the sale of horsemeat. In 2000, they covered the treatment of non-violent drug offenders, the use of school vouchers and the issuing of bonds as a means of raising money for schools. The nine votes in 2010 and their outcome were:

	Issue
Yes votes	Redistricting the congressional districts
	Prohibiting the state from taking some local funds
	Requiring only a simple majority vote to pass a budget
	Requiring a two-thirds vote for changes to some state/local fees
No votes	Legalising the purchase of small quantities of marijuana for personal use
	Imposing a vehicle license surcharge
	Suspending the air pollution control legislation
	Repealing the allowance of lower business tax liability
	Eliminating the State Redistricting Commission

Ballot proposals and their fate in November 2010

At the time of the November 2010 mid-term elections, 160 measures in thirty-seven states qualified for the November ballot, another 24 measures having appeared on primary and special election ballots. Twenty-four states allowed voters to petition to place measures on the ballot. Three proposals that did not get placed on the ballot paper, were:

- allowing slot machines in Ohio;

- banning drift nets that hurt endangered whales and sea turtles in Massachusetts;

- banning drilling in the Great Lakes, in Michigan.

In various state ballots, as a result of some of the votes:

- legalising marijuana was rejected in Arizona, California, Oregon and South Dakota;

- measures to block federal healthcare reforms were approved in Arizona and Oklahoma, but rejected in Colorado;

- making English the official language and prohibiting courts from using Sharia law and international law in making decisions was approved in Oklahoma;

- allowing 17-year-olds to vote in primaries if they will have turned 18 by the general election was approved in Vermont;

- banning felons from some public offices was approved in Michigan and North Carolina;

- changing the official state name of Rhode Island from its real name (the 'State of Rhode Island and Providence Plantations') to the most commonly used form was rejected.

As a general trend, the outcome of the ballots meant that balancing the budget was made more difficult in several statehouses across the country. Voters made it more difficult for legislatures to pass tax increases, yet gave consent to programmes with high price tags and no revenue stream; for instance, in Oregon they approved a new mandatory minimum sentencing law that will cost $1.4 million in the first year and grow to an estimated $29.1 million in the fourth year, without making any provision for funding the policy.

Why has direct democracy become more popular?

There are several explanations for the upsurge in the popularity of initiatives and referendums in the last two decades. Key factors include:

1 Activists have discovered their value as a means of advancing particular interests – for liberals, this might be an issue such as environmental protection and for conservatives tax-cutting or curbing abortion.

2 Some politicians have been keen to associate themselves with initiative proposals as a useful means of raising public awareness of particular subjects and their own profile. This can win them the backing – and finance – of issue activists.

3 An industry has developed to professionalise the use of initiatives and popular referendums. Pollsters, media consultants, petition circulators and others have brought their expertise to the field and thereby made it easier to get an issue 'off the ground'. The 'initiative industry' operates not just in getting measures onto the ballot, but in challenging or defending in the courts measures that have already been approved by voters.

4 The news media particularly thrive on initiatives, because the attempts to raise or block contentious issues provide good stories, often with a strong human interest and great headline potential.

Participation and turnout

Citizens are involved in direct democracy via a number of activities. For the more active, this may involve organising and circulating petitions, campaigning to maximise support or running a fund-raising lunch. For most people, the limit of their involvement is voting.

Sometimes a contentious issue may provoke an enthusiastic response, but usually turnout is high only if the initiative is being held at the same time as a general election. Magleby quotes[30] the example of Maine, which stages initiatives in general election years and in the odd-numbered years in between, when there is no other vote. Far more people take part in the years when offices are being contested than when there is just an issue or issues up for election. Also, in general election years, he detects a mean drop-off of 15% in the number who cast a vote on the propositions, compared with the number who cast a vote for the candidates.

DIRECT DEMOCRACY IN BRITAIN, EUROPE AND THE US: A COMPARISON

Referendums are a means of giving the electorate a chance to have a direct influence over the decision makers on specific policies. In recent years they have been much more widely used in many parts of the world. As we have seen, a growing number of American states have used them to decide on contentious moral, social and constitutional issues. Some member states of the European Union have used them to confirm their membership of the EU or to ratify important constitutional developments. The new democracies of Central and Eastern Europe, particularly the fifteen republics of the former USSR, have used them to decide a range of issues relating to the form of their new governments.

In the past, referendums were often associated with dictatorial systems such as that of Nazi Germany, or with democratic ones with authoritarian overtones such as the French Fifth Republic of Charles de Gaulle. Often they were then known as plebiscites. It is the memory of such past experience that troubles some democrats who fear the purpose and management of such means of consultation with the public. Hence the attitude of British Prime Minister Clement Attlee after World War II. Worried about the countries that had practised 'direct democracy', he described referendums as 'devices alien to our traditions' and saw them as instruments of 'demagogues and dictators'. He pointed to their often suspiciously high turnouts. Such overtones have largely disappeared, and initiatives and referendums are now used with increasing regularity in countries and states that have impeccable democratic credentials.

Britain and the US

Americans have been more enthusiastic than the British about direct legislation. They do not employ it at the national level, for the Constitution does not provide for referendums and/or initiatives at the federal level; a constitutional amendment would be required to allow them. In a country in which the proper role of government is much discussed, issues of public spending and taxation, matters of public morality and governmental or political reform have all been seen as suitable subjects for popular consultation. By comparison, the British have been wary of resolving controversial matters such as drug use or abortion in this way. They have embraced the referendum only slowly and with some reluctance.

In the US, the status of initiatives and referenda varies from state to state. Advisory referenda are rarely used. In this form of the process, the legislature, and in some states the governor, may place a question on the ballot to gauge voter opinion. The results of the election on this question are not binding. An example of an advisory referendum is Question 5, which appeared on the Rhode Island ballot in 2002. Placed on the ballot by the governor, it asked voters if they favoured changing the state constitution to make the three branches of government co-equal. Although voters overwhelmingly voted yes, the question was non-binding and the governor and legislature were not obligated to act upon the measure.

In Illinois, but not in every state, state-wide initiatives are advisory only, except for those amending the constitution; there is no process for creating statutes via initiatives. Historically, advisory initiatives have been ignored by the legislature and therefore have become less common over time. There are no state-wide referendums in Illinois. Both binding and advisory referendums and initiatives are used by local governments.

Britain has until recently had very little experience of voting on a single issue, even though the case has often been canvassed in the twentieth century. A Conservative leader and

When there is a general election, the task for the voter can be lengthy. In November 2010, the *Complete Voter Information Guide* ran to 127 pages. A long ballot paper is sometimes needed, as when in 1988 the voters of San Francisco were asked to decide on fifty-two separate questions. Voter weariness means that even some of the more enthusiastic citizens do not answer every question, although the fewer the questions, the better the response.

Are initiatives and referendums a good thing?

There has been some discussion of the idea of initiatives for the federal government, but as yet no national vote has taken place. Many who exercise power are reluctant to opt for more direct democracy and argue that whilst it may

former prime minister, Arthur Balfour, told the House of Commons back in 1911 that 'so far from corrupting the sources of democratic life [they] would only be a great education for political people'. The Conservatives held a referendum on the border issue in Northern Ireland in 1973, and the Scottish and Welsh electorates were allowed to vote on whether they wanted devolution in 1979. Yet the only occasion when all of the voters have been allowed to vote on a key national issue was four years earlier, when they were asked whether or not they wished the country to remain in the European Economic Community. There have been local votes on the future status of schools and the ownership of council estates, and in Wales the issue of 'local option' on the Sunday opening of pubs has been decided in this way. Some councils are now consulting their electorates as to whether they should preserve public services by raising the level of council tax.

During the Labour administrations of Tony Blair (1997–2007), referendums were used to resolve the issue of devolution, and the future shape of London's government. Also, in concurrent votes, popular approval of the Good Friday Agreement was supported by electors on both sides of the border in Ireland. More recently, Coalition ministers gave the voters a chance to vote in May 2011 on whether to replace FPTP with the alternative vote electoral system, an opportunity that they overwhelmingly declined. Should there at any time be any change affecting the constitutional relationship between Britain and Europe, then this too is likely to be submitted to the people for popular backing.

Unlike the situation in some other countries, in Britain the outcome of such referendums is only advisory. Given its commitment to the idea of parliamentary sovereignty, only Parliament can cast a decisive vote on any issue. Yet it is unlikely that a majority of legislators would make a habit of casting their parliamentary votes in defiance of the popular will as expressed in a popular vote. Ministers have accepted that to consult and then to ignore the verdict is worse than never to have sought an opinion. In 1975, Prime Minister Wilson accepted that a majority of even a single vote in favour of so doing would be enough to take Britain out of the European Community. In other words, both governments and MPs accept that they should treat the popular verdict as mandatory, in the sense that it is morally and politically binding.

be appropriate for deciding local and state issues, it has disadvantages in national politics. Conservatives tend to fear its use on key questions of defence and foreign affairs. Liberals worry about the repercussions for minority groups. Many members of both categories feel safer with traditional methods of representative democracy.

In favour of votes on single issues, it may be said that:

1 They give people a chance to take decisions that affect their lives, whereas in a general election they can only offer a general verdict.
2 They stimulate interest and involvement in public policy.
3 They may exert pressure on the legislature to act responsibly and in the public interest.

4 They help to counter the special interests to which legislators can be beholden.

5 They help to overcome the obstructionism of out-of-touch legislators and therefore make reform more likely.

Against:

1 Proposals can be ill thought out and badly drafted.

2 Campaigns can be expensive and therefore to the advantage of well-funded groups. Money is too dominant in the process. Business interests have far more scope to influence the outcome.

3 There are too many issues for voters to handle – they elect representatives to decide. This is what representative democracy is all about. If the voter dislikes the decisions made, he or she can vote against the controlling party in the next election.

4 Initiatives and allied devices undermine political parties and therefore weaken the democratic process.

5 They encourage single-issue politics, rather than debate based on a conflict of broad principles.

6 They can work to the disadvantage of minorities, who can be persecuted by the majority – for example blacks and gays.

Despite all of the reasons that may be used to oppose direct democracy, no state that possesses the provision for initiatives and/or referendums has ever repealed it. The process is likely to continue to be a major factor in the political life of many states.

THE PRESIDENTIAL ELECTION, NOVEMBER 2008: A CASE STUDY

The fifty-sixth presidential election was held on 4 November 2008. Six candidates stood in a sufficient number of states to allow them a theoretical chance of winning enough votes in the Electoral College to be elected. In the event, only two candidates were successful in capturing any college votes. Barack Obama won the general election, and became the 44th President of the United States on 20 January 2009.

The two main candidates

Barack Obama (Democrat)

In January 2007, Senator Obama of Illinois officially formed an exploratory committee to investigate the possibility of standing as the Democratic Party's nominee for the presidency. Less than a month later, he formally declared his candidacy, on 10 February 2007, at Springfield, Illinois. He did so in a symbolic setting outside the old state Capitol, from where Lincoln had famously issued his denunciation of slavery. From the beginning of his campaign, Obama urged the need for change in Washington. He claimed that a leader who represented a new generation that wanted to see a better tomorrow could best bring this about. Like Martin Luther King and John F. Kennedy before him, he spoke with the uplifting rhetoric of hope, recognising that a hopeful message would embolden his supporters. As he said to his supporters on the evening of his defeat in the New Hampshire primary:

> We know the battle ahead will be long. But always remember, no matter what obstacles stand in our way, nothing can stand in the way of the power of millions of voices calling for change.

The Democrats' candidate was selected via a series of primary elections and caucuses that culminated in the party convention held in Denver, Colorado, from 25 to 28 August 2008. To secure nomination, a candidate needed to receive at least 2,117 votes from delegates, a simple majority of the 4,233 delegate votes – a total that included votes from superdelegates (party leaders and elected officials). The contest between Senators Obama and Hillary Rodham Clinton remained hotly competitive for longer than expected, neither candidate receiving enough delegates from the primary races and caucuses to achieve a majority without the support of superdelegate votes. Obama received enough superdelegate endorsements on 3 June to claim victory, having secured approximately 54% of the available total; Clinton conceded the nomination four days later.

John McCain (Republican)

Senator McCain had made a challenge for the Republican Party presidential nomination in 2000, but lost a heated contest against George W. Bush. He announced that he would form an exploratory committee for a second run at the presidency on 15 November 2006. In late February 2007, he announced that he would seek the Republican presidential nomination, and on 25 April he made a formal announcement of his decision to stand. Having overcome early setbacks, McCain became the presumptive presidential nominee on 4 March 2008 by obtaining the 1,191 delegates necessary to receive the party's nomination. He was officially nominated at the Republican Party National Convention, held in Saint Paul, Minnesota from 1 to 4 September. He won the nomination almost unanimously, having secured 2,343 of the available 2,380 delegate votes (98.4%).

The campaign

The general election campaign centred on two key themes, firstly the policies and performance of the outgoing Bush administration, and secondly the issue

OBAMA VERSUS CLINTON: THE PRIMARIES AND CAUCUSES

In 2008, Hillary Clinton was expected to win the Democratic nomination and become the first female presidential candidate of either main party. Her career had been moving in this direction from the time that she became the first American First Lady to run for public office. Elected as the first female senator for New York State in November 2000, she was a high-profile figure within the Democratic Party and over the next few years acquired much experience along her political journey. Her victory in 2008 seemed assured, yet in June 2008 she found herself conceding defeat to someone who, at the time of his election as the junior senator for Illinois (2004), was little known beyond his state.

How did this major political upset come about?

In some respects, Clinton's background and reputation told against her as the campaign got under way. Few doubted her ability, experience or understanding of political issues. But her qualities reflected the fact that she had been prominent in Democratic circles ever since her husband had been elected to the presidency in 1992. In 2008 there was a widespread desire for change. Many Americans wanted something new, a fresh face, fresh thinking and a move away from the Clinton–Bush era. Obama benefited from being less well known and being better able to offer an inspiring vision for the future. By contrast, Hillary Clinton seemed a figure of the past, someone who had initially supported the Bush policy on key foreign policy issues (she had voted for the Iraq War resolution). Though she subsequently opposed the president's handling of events concerning the war, as well as sharply criticising his record on most domestic issues, she seemed ill placed to embrace the politics of hope, which were so well represented by her rival.

of change and the public appetite for it. Much of the discussion was on two elements that were basic to both themes: domestic policy and the state of the economy as the 2008 financial crisis unfolded.

Opinion polls indicated a growing dissatisfaction with the performance of George W. Bush during his second spell in office, events such as Hurricane Katrina and the continuing wars in Afghanistan and Iraq taking their toll. By 2008, his approval ratings were fluctuating in the area of 20%–30%. In the light of such levels of unpopularity, he did not make a single appearance for McCain during the campaign proper, although he had earlier endorsed his nomination. McCain supported policy on Iraq, but in other respects attempted to distance himself from administration policy – for instance, on issues such as climate change. This was not easy to do, the more so as Obama was able to point out that Senate records showed that McCain had voted with Bush on almost all legislation in the Bush years.

Other factors told against Clinton:

- **Internal tensions within her campaign team**, in particular the lack of a clear command structure, poor choices of personnel and the failure to pay sufficient attention to polling.

- **The contribution to her campaign by her husband**, who acquired adverse publicity for his fierce attacks on Obama. In particular, his coded attempts to label Obama as a candidate for black Americans and his put-down of Obama's opposition to the Iraq War as 'the biggest fairy tale I've ever seen' aroused indignation.

- **The timing of key primaries** worked to her disadvantage, for, having been roughly level-pegging with Obama as a result of the votes on Super Tuesday, she needed to follow this up with victories in states in which she was likely to fare well, but the primaries in Ohio, Texas and West Virginia came too late to help her develop momentum. Moreover, two states in which she was the popular choice, Florida and Michigan, did not fully count in the totalling of delegate votes because of a controversy over the scheduling of their primaries.

- **Her inability to attract comparable funding to Obama's.** In the so-called invisible primary season and early weeks of the campaign, Clinton gained generous one-off donations from traditional party backers. However, Obama was highly successful in using twenty-first century techniques, garnering masses of small donations via the Internet. Having proved himself a 'winner' in early contests, his campaign benefitted from a heavy influx of funding after Super Tuesday, far beyond the amount that Clinton could raise. She had counted on winning the nomination by Super Tuesday and was unprepared for a more prolonged campaign.

The public ranking of key issues

Exit polls suggested that the economy was by far the dominant concern in the election. Those who claimed to be 'very worried' by economic conditions were also the strongest backers of Obama, voting by 59% to 38% in his favour.

As to the most important issues facing the country:

- 62% cited the economy;
- 10% cited Iraq;
- 9% cited terrorism;
- 9% cited healthcare;
- 7% cited energy.

Source: The National Election Exit Poll, a sample of 17,856 voters surveyed on election day after they left the polling booth, conducted on behalf of AP and the major US TV networks.

The issue of Iraq was contentious. Obama's early and strong opposition to the war helped him to stand out against the other Democratic candidates during the primaries. It served him well as he stood before a war-weary electorate in the general campaign. He was able to exploit McCain's support for an unpopular war and tried to use the issue as part of his strategy to tie him to President Bush. McCain's backing for the Bush **troop surge** may have won him some support, as the security

> **troop surge**
> The surge refers to President Bush's announcement in 2007 of an increase in the number of American troops in Iraq. Twenty thousand additional soldiers were deployed in order to provide greater security to Baghdad and Al Anbar province.

situation in Iraq was improving at that time. However, Obama could counter that there would have been no need for a 'surge' had there been no war at all.

Party platforms: some key policy priorities

Policy area	Democratic Party: Obama	Republican Party: McCain
Defence	Rebuild the military, strengthen reserves, act with allies	Strengthen military via modernisation of services; effective missile defence
Economy	Reduce tax burden for working families, small and new businesses	Workplace flexibility; lower barriers to trade and streamline taxation
Education	Investment in early years; make college more widely affordable	Support for current 'No child left behind' strategy; more choice for parents
Energy and environment	Support clean energy – for example hybrid cars; save oil; reduce greenhouse gases	Expand oil exploration and production; make country more self-sufficient
Foreign policy	Stop production of nuclear weapons; rebuild alliances; talks with Iran	Pressure on Iran/Syria; pre-emptive attacks against perceived threats; unilateral approach, if necessary
Healthcare	Accessible and affordable healthcare; improvements to public health	Improvements to Medicare; reform healthcare to make it more employer based
Iraq	Phased withdrawal; urge Iraqis to spend oil money on reconstruction; seek improved stability in region	Support counter-insurgency strategy; urge reconciliation; pull out troops as soon as realistically possible
Security	Continue war against al Qaeda; protect against nuclear terrorism; strengthen bio-security	Share intelligence; improve border security, via better screening; improve federal–state cooperation
Taxes	Reduce most taxes; simplify tax system; remove tax on capital gains of small businesses	Lower taxation; streamline tax system; amend to improve agricultural support

The developing financial crisis and fears regarding its implications for the wider economy were further blows to the Republican campaign. In the late summer and autumn of 2008, there was turmoil in the financial markets, which worsened when the bankruptcy of **Lehman Brothers** was announced in mid-September. McCain's response to the developing crisis seemed out of touch with popular feeling. At a time when there was growing public alarm at failures in the banking system and widespread concern about the state of the economy as a whole, he declared that 'the fundamentals of our economy are strong'. His comments about the economy and his seemingly erratic approach to events cast doubt upon his judgement on a key issue. Polls taken in the last few months of the presidential campaign and exit polls conducted on election day showed that anxieties about the economy were the top priority for voters (see box on p. 277). The economy featured strongly in the presidential debates, not to the Republican candidate's benefit.

> **Lehman Brothers**
>
> Lehman Brothers Holdings Inc. was a global financial services firm involved in equity sales, investment management and commercial banking. Its bankruptcy – the largest in US history – led to widespread public fear that the country might plunge into another Great Depression, given the already troubled state of the financial markets.

The outcome

When the votes were counted, it became apparent that Obama had scored a decisive victory, in terms of both the popular vote and seats in the Electoral College. He won in every region of the country by a double-digit margin, other than the South, which McCain won by 9%. The full result, as certified by the Federal Election Commission was as shown in the table below. The turnout was strong at approximately 63%, the highest since 1968. More votes were cast than in any previous presidential election.

2008 presidential election result

Candidate	Party	Home state	Popular vote		Votes in Electoral College
Barack Obama	Democratic	Illinois	69,456,897	52.92%	365
John McCain	Republican	Arizona	59,934,814	45.66%	173
Ralph Nader	Independent	Connecticut	738,475	0.56%	0
Bob Barr	Libertarian	Georgia	523,686	0.40%	0
Chuck Baldwin	Constitution	Florida	199,314	0.15%	0
Cynthia McKinney	Green	Georgia	161,603	0.12%	0
Other			242,539	0.18%	–
Total			131,257,328	100%	538

NB For the outcome of the congressional elections, see p. 225.

Why did Obama win?

From the beginning of the campaign, the odds were heavily stacked against a McCain victory. Past precedent indicated that in the twentieth century only one presidential candidate of the same party as the outgoing two-term president had ever been elected to lead the country for the succeeding four years. When George H. Bush achieved this in 1988, he benefited from the popularity of Ronald Reagan.

So it was true that in 2008 there was a mood for change after eight years of Republican rule. The outgoing president was widely unpopular and, however much McCain tried to distance himself from Bush, Obama was there to remind him that any problems happened during the Republican administration. In the debates, the Democrat was keen to remind voters that the two men were from the same party. He was keen to mention the president at every opportunity; McCain did so only very infrequently.

Whereas, in the eyes of many Americans, McCain represented experience, and continuity with existing policies and practice – however much he might try to show himself to be distinctive – Obama was able to pose convincingly as the candidate of change and renewal. Adopting a phrase once used by Martin Luther King, he spoke of the 'fierce urgency of now' as the country braced itself to tackle the challenges in both domestic and foreign policy. He seemed to be in touch with the national mood. Ultimately, Americans found his inexperience less of a concern than the worry that McCain's association with Bush meant that there would be more of the same.

Obama created a broad grassroots movement across America and a new approach to campaigning by courting and mobilising activists, donations and voters through the Internet. With his formidable organisation and massive funding (see p. 231), he was able to run a skilful, organised and tight campaign. In addition, there were personal issues, with Obama seeming to be the more attractive personality. Whereas McCain could sometimes seem irascible, Obama was cool, reasonable and gifted with a sound temperament. He was able to lift the people's horizons in Kennedyesque oratory. Overall, there was a notable 'enthusiasm gap' between McCain and Obama supporters. One third of the Obama voters were 'excited' by the prospect of his victory, as opposed to just 14% of McCain voters. That enthusiasm translated into more personal contacts, with twice as many Obama supporters having been contacted in person as McCain supporters.

Apart from Obama's ability better to reflect the national mood, he had other advantages over McCain. In particular:

- He made a safe choice in Joe Biden as his running-mate for the vice-presidency, whereas McCain's selection of the indiscretion-prone Sarah Palin proved damaging, not least by reflecting on his judgement. Media interviews suggested that she was seriously ill informed about key issues, which cast doubt among many voters about her qualifications to be vice-president or president. Also, by choosing someone of her inexperience in national politics, McCain undermined his claim that Obama lacked the experience necessary for service in the highest office – a factor that could have proved significant should McCain (aged 72 at the time of the election) have become ill or died in office.
- He reached out to a wider segment of the potential Democratic electorate than John Kerry had done four years previously. His candidature had a stronger resonance with young (18–29 age group) and non-aligned voters. His appeal reached far beyond the more than 90% of African Americans who voted for him; millions of whites, Asian Americans and Hispanics also gave him their support.
- Above all, however, it was the economy that sealed McCain's fate, exit polls showing that it was the leading issue for just over 60% of the voters. In excess of 90% felt that the national economy was in a 'not so good' or 'poor' state. As we have seen, many were particularly troubled about their own personal ability to cope with the economic downturn, fearing that it would adversely affect their own families.

How people voted (percentages)

Sector of the electorate	Obama support	McCain support
Men	49	48
Women	56	43
White	43	55
Black	95	4
18–29	66	32
65+	45	53
Under $15,000	73	25
$30,000–50,000	55	43
$100,000–150,000	48	51
$200,000+	52	46
First-time voters	68	31
Protestant	45	54
Catholic	54	45
Jewish	78	21
Evangelical Christian	24	74
Gun owners	37	62
Urban	63	35
Suburban	50	48
Rural	45	53

Source: NEP.

Some unique features of the election

There were several uniquely interesting aspects of the 2008 election:

- The 2008 election was the first since 1952 in which neither an incumbent president or vice-president participated. Bush was constitutionally unable to run and Cheney chose not to do so.

- It was the first election in which the nominated candidates of both major parties were born outside of the contiguous United States, Obama having been born in Hawaii and McCain in the Panama Canal Zone.

- It was the first election in which both major candidates were sitting United States senators.

Obama was:

- the first African American to be nominated for the presidency by a major political party – and went on to become the first African American to become president. He was also the first of mixed racial background, his mother being white and his father having been a member of the Luo ethnic-linguistic group of Kenya;

- the first president to be born outside the United States;

- the first Democratic president since JFK who was not from the South;

- the recipient of the most votes for any president in US history;

- (with Joe Biden) on the first winning ticket on which neither candidate was a White Anglo Saxon Protestant (Biden is a Catholic, the first to be elected to the vice-presidency);

- (with Joe Biden) on the first winning ticket in which both men were serving senators.

McCain was:

- the oldest first-time presidential nominee in history when the Republicans nominated him in September 2008; he was nearly twenty-five years older than Obama;

- the first Republican nominee to choose a woman – Sarah Palin – as his running-mate.

CONCLUSION

There are various ways in which Americans can participate in political life. Many choose not to do so, having only a limited interest in politics. The vast majority never engage in any political activity between elections and pay little attention to what is going on.

Elections and election campaigns are the processes by which voters in any democracy choose the direction they wish to take in the future. They are the opportunity for voters to have their say. Americans are called upon to participate with great frequency, for there is a theoretical enthusiasm for the ballot box in public life. Yet many of them choose not to take advantage of this.

Those who do vote do so in the light of various influences, of which their long-term party identification has traditionally been the most important. However, in a television age, in which campaigning is conducted in a more visible way than ever before and in which the amount of information available has dramatically increased, the merits of the candidate and issues of the time have become particularly relevant.

REFERENCES

1 A. Grant, *Contemporary American Politics*, Dartmouth, 1995
2 V. Key, *Politics, Parties and Pressure Groups*, Crowell, 1964
3 T. Hames and N. Rae, *Governing America*, Manchester University Press, 1996
4 B. Ginsberg and M. Shefter, *Politics by Other Means*, W.W. Norton, 1999
5 S. Kennedy, 'Americans Have Lost Confidence in Our Social and Legal Institutions', www.huffingtonpost.com, 6 October 2008
6 A. de Tocqueville, *Democracy in America*, vol 2, reissued by Vintage, 1954
7 R. Putnam, *Bowling Alone: The Collapse and Revival of American Community*, Simon & Schuster, 2000
8 F. Bryan (University of Vermont), as quoted in a Vermont Public Television video entitled 'Town Meeting: A Day in the Life', 2000
9 J. Rankin, *Morning Sentinel* (Maine), 26 March 2000
10 J. Zimmerman, *The New England Town Meeting: Democracy in Action*, McGraw-Hill, 1999
11 J. Rankin, as in 9 above
12 F. Bryan, as in 8 above
13 K. Goldstein, 'Presidential Election Negative Ads, 2008: The Least Successful Ever', press release, University of Wisconsin-Madison, 16 August 2008
14 B. Schneider, as quoted in L. Rees, *Selling Politics*, BBC Books, 1992
15 M. Rosenbaum, *From Soapbox to Soundbite: Party Political Campaigning in Britain since 1945*, Macmillan, 1997
16 D. Kavanagh, *Election Campaigning: The New Marketing of Politics*, Blackwell, 1995
17 G. Monbiot, *Captive State: The Corporate Takeover of Britain*, Pan, 2001
18 M. Vile, *Politics in the USA*, Hutchinson, 1978
19 M. Vile, as in 18 above
20 J. Hamilton, J. Madison and J. Jay, *The Federalist Papers*, New American Library, 1961
21 S. Wayne, *The Road to the White House 1996*, St. Martin's Press, 1996
22 M. Wattenberg, *The Rise of Candidate-Centred Politics*, Harvard University Press, 1991
23 A. Campbell, P. Converse, W. Miller and D. Stokes, *The American Voter*, John Wiley, 1960; D. Butler and D. Stokes, *Political Change in Britain*, Macmillan, 1966

24 P. Pulzer, *Political Representation and Elections in Britain*, Allen and Unwin, 1968

25 P. Madgwick, *A New Introduction to British Politics*, Thorne, 1994

26 B. Sarlvik and I. Crewe, *Decade of Dealignment*, Cambridge University Press, 1983

27 P. Kellner, *New Society*, 2 June 1983

28 D. Magleby, 'Direct Legislation in the American States', in D. Butler and A. Ranney (eds), *Referendums around the World: The Growing Use of Direct Democracy*, AEI Press, 1994

29 C. Rabner, majority opinion in New Jersey State Supreme Court, *The Committee to Recall Robert Menendez* v. *Nina Wells*, 18 November 2010

30 D. Magleby, as in 28 above

USEFUL WEB SITES

On elections

www.fec.gov The Federal Election Commission. Provides data on the financing of election campaigns.

www.pollingreport.com The Polling Report. Gives data on elections and campaigning events.

www.ifes.org International Foundation for Electoral Systems. Useful information on election outcomes, systems, turnout and voting.

www.electionstudies.org American National Election Studies site, offering information based on polling research on issues ranging from split-ticket voting to turnout.

www.commoncause.org, **www.democracy21.org** and **www.opensecrets.org** all provide coverage on the role of finance in politics, issues of accountability and democracy.

On the media

www.appcpenn.org The Annenburg Policy Center. Provides analyses of television coverage of politics.

www.newseum.org The Freedom Forum; museum of journalism. Provides insight into changes in the reporting of news over the years.

In addition, most newspapers and television channels have web sites, for example:

www.washingtonpost.com The Washington Post.

www.cnn.com CNN cable network.

www.bbc.co.uk BBC site, extensive topical coverage on presidential election campaigns.

SAMPLE QUESTIONS

1 'Vast amounts of money are spent on elections and electioneering in the US, more than in any other democracy.' Are the elections better for all this expenditure?
2 Why does America have so many elections and why are many Americans so unwilling to vote in them?
3 'Nowadays, American election campaigns are geared to the requirements of television.' Discuss.
4 Evaluate the strengths and weaknesses of the way in which presidential candidates are chosen.
5 To what extent does the method of selection determine the kind of person who will become president of the United States?
6 What is the best preparation for a would-be president of the United States?
7 Should the Electoral College now be abolished?
8 Account for the growth in popularity of methods of direct legislation in recent decades. Are initiatives and referendums a reliable guide to what Americans think?
9 Account for the changes in American voting behaviour since the 1980s.
10 Compare the conduct of elections and the methods of electioneering in Britain and the United States.

Political parties

In any free country, political parties play an important role. They are basic to democracy, in that they organise elections and provide voters with a choice of ideas and personalities. American parties play a significant role, though not a comparable one to those in Britain. US constitutional arrangements impede the development of strong parties and were designed to do so. Many academics and commentators see their role as less important now than it was in the past. This has led to talk of 'the decline of American parties'. Other commentators detect signs of resurgence.

Here, we are concerned with the development of parties; how the party system operates today; what the main parties stand for; whether there are substantial differences between them; and the ways in which they are organised. We can then decide whether or not their role has diminished in recent years.

POINTS TO CONSIDER

- Why were the Founding Fathers suspicious of political parties?
- What role do parties play in American politics?
- Can America be said to have a two-party system?
- What problems beset third parties in America?
- Why have socialist ideas not taken firmer root in the USA?
- What are the main ideas and beliefs associated with the two main parties and whom do they represent?
- What do we mean by describing American parties as decentralised?
- Are American parties in decline or undergoing a resurgence?
- In what respects are British and American parties similar and different?

The role and value of parties

American history reveals a long-standing distrust of **political parties**, which have been portrayed as factions by some writers ever since the days of the Founding Fathers. James Madison (the fourth president) defined a faction in unflattering terms: 'By a faction, I mean a number of citizens, whether amounting to a majority or a minority of the whole, who are united and actuated by some common impulse or passion, or of interest, adverse to the rights of other citizens or to the permanent aggregate interest of the community.'

> **political parties**
> Groups of people of broadly similar views who organise themselves and recruit candidates for election, with a view to achieving office so that they can carry out their ideas and programme. They are not people with identical attitudes and interests, for parties are inevitably coalitions of individuals whose approach on some issues can be widely divergent.

In his Farewell Address (1796), George Washington also made clear his anxieties about 'the baneful effects of the spirit of party generally [with] its alternate domination of one faction over another, sharpened by the spirit of revenge natural to party dissension'. For him, parties 'kindle[d] the animosities of one part against another'. But his warnings were delivered too late to influence the course of events. Since his time, they have been accepted as a 'necessary evil', in that they help to organise the democratic process and present Americans with a choice of candidates and policies.

The main functions of parties are concerned with fighting and winning elections:
1 **They arrange for the choice of candidates.** This was once done in 'smoke-filled rooms' by party bosses who selected their preferred choice, but in the US today it is in most states the voters who choose their preferred candidate in primary elections. By the time of the party nominating conventions the choice is normally clear-cut.
2 **They support the candidates.** Once chosen, by whatever method, candidates need to have a supporting organisation to handle their campaign. Traditionally, the parties have arranged door-to-door canvassing to put their candidate's message across; they also establish phone-banks, arrange lifts to the polling station, assist in fund raising and advertising, and commission the carrying out of private polls. Again, this role has been downgraded in recent years, for with the decline in influence of the 'party machines' candidates have increasingly organised the running of their own campaigns. Moreover, the growth of political action committees has meant that parties have a lower profile in fund raising and advertising than was formerly the case. The 'supportive' function has its uses, however, and at the national conventions the parties are keen to ensure that the presidential campaign attracts the maximum of favourable publicity. They attempt to 'sell' their chosen candidates for the presidency and vice-presidency, and may arrange for 'endorsements' of the ticket by well-respected party dignitaries.

3 **They organise the contest.** Throughout the nation, parties at every level conduct the useful tasks of helping to register voters and arouse their enthusiasm for the contest. Parties help arrange candidate training, research into policy issues, and the publicity that is so helpful in getting the name and message across.

4 **They harmonise the divergent interests within broad sections of society, making them all 'coalitions' of sorts.** In Duverger's[1] words, 'a party is not a community but a collection of communities, a union of small groups dispersed throughout the country and linked by co-ordinating institutions'.

5 **They clarify the issues.** Parties help to simplify the choice that is offered to the voters, for they provide them with information and help to organise the discussion of issues into a 'for' and 'against' format. The arguments on either side are reduced to an appropriate level of public comprehension.

6 **They involve the electorate in the democratic process.** Parties give the individual American a chance to participate in the democratic process. A relative few work as party activists; others who are party members have a chance to vote in primary elections and attend any local meetings. This enables the voter to rally around the party that best fits his or her vision of how American life should be organised. In other words, parties are an outlet for people's interests and enthusiasms, a focal point for their allegiances and loyalties. In providing this outlet, parties are a useful intermediary between the governed and the government – for through parties, the individuals can make their views known and conveyed to those who seek to win and retain their support.

The two-party system

America is a country of great diversity, with marked ethnic, social and regional differences, which one might expect to see represented by parties concerned with their specific interests. Yet it has a two-party system, in which only two main parties seriously compete for political influence and, in particular, every four years seek to capture the presidency. This has always been the case except for rare moments in the country's history. As V.O. Key[2] put it in his classic study of parties: 'While minor parties have arisen from time to time and exerted influence on governmental policy, the two major parties have been the only serious contenders for the presidency. On occasion, a major party has disintegrated, but in due course the bi-party system has reasserted itself.'

A two-party system does not preclude the existence of other parties. In the United States, as in most other western democracies, several other third and minor parties continue to operate. What a two-party system does mean is that only the main parties, the Republicans and Democrats, have a meaningful chance of achieving the highest office or gaining a majority in Congress.

In a two-party system, the two parties may change or adapt; the American Republican Party replaced an established one, as did the British Labour Party. But although there may be transitional phases in which one party is giving way to another, usually within a generation there is a return to normality. In the United States, small parties find it difficult to achieve a breakthrough nationally, although in various states some are well established (see pp. 294–303).

The phrase 'two-party system' is misleading in some respects, for the American pattern of party activity could also be viewed as an 'agglomeration of many parties centred around the governments of the 50 states and their subdivisions',[3] whilst from another point of view it is a four-party system based upon Congress and the presidency. Writers such as Vile[4] have stressed that although the system nominally operates via two parties, this obscures the fact that for most purposes 'America operates under a multi-party system which coalesces into two great **coalitions** for strictly limited purposes'. As he puts it:

> **[electoral] coalitions**
> Alliances of groups of voters representing various interests and ideas that come together for the purpose of fighting elections, especially with a view to capturing the presidency.

> The nature of the Constitution, spreading power as it does to different levels of government, tends to have a disintegrating effect on party structure so that national parties tend to be coalitions of state and local parties forming and reforming every four years, so that what we have is not a single party system. We have 50 state party systems. Politics operate in a framework of 50 systems, for much decentralisation has occurred.

There are a variety of forms of party competition throughout the country. Politics in Minnesota are different to politics in New York, for inevitably, given the size of the country and the constitutional arrangements, political life varies from state to state. In most, two parties compete for power, although the intensity and effectiveness of competition depends on the custom in the individual case. There may well be a genuine alternation of power, with both Republicans and Democrats having a chance to capture the governorship and control of the legislative chamber. In other states, only one party normally ever wins, there never being the realistic prospect of a change of control. A number of major cities – such as Chicago and Detroit – are regular strongholds of the Democrats, just as the states of Kansas, Utah and Wyoming are traditionally loyal to the Republicans. There are also still several non-competitive congressional districts in which one of the two major parties always wins. In 2010, twenty-nine candidates for the House (7%) were elected without opposition, and several others faced only a token battle; the average margin of victory in contested races was 27%, with 49% of congressmen winning by more than 30%. The same is true of several state legislatures, a number of which have regularly been controlled by the Democrats. In state elections held in 2009–10, 1,986 races (33%) were uncontested.[5] Where one party dominates, the battle is between different factions and individuals within the organisation.

In contrast to the one-party dominance we have been discussing, the New York scene is very different. It is not unusual for several parties to take part in any contest. When there is a multi-party situation, there are often candidates from the two regular parties and also from the American Labour Party and the Liberal Party, among others.

If federalism is one reason why use of the term 'two-party system' can be misleading, so too is the separation of powers another. The strict division of constitutional responsibility means that the two parties each have a congressional and a presidential wing. This led James MacGregor Burns[6] to describe the American scene as a 'four-party system' with 'separate though overlapping parties', each with its own distinctive style:

> Presidential Democrats are seen as different from congressional ones, in that they have a different electoral base and appeal to different sections of the people. The presidential party seeks its major support in the urban areas of large industrialised states, whilst the majority of Democratic Senators and Congressmen are responsive to rural and suburban influences.

Congressmen are inevitably concerned with the narrow interests of the locality they represent, whereas presidential candidates must appeal in a much wider constituency. The presidential party is either in office (having captured the presidency), or else it is in a state of oblivion for much of the intervening period between elections, whereas the congressional party, Republican or Democrat, is permanently active. The presidential wings of both parties tend to be closer to each other doctrinally than they are to the respective congressional wings of their own parties.

All of these considerations make it difficult to label the American system straightforwardly as a two-party one. Moreover, recent Pew research indicates that there has been a developing trend for Americans to classify themselves as independents, rather than as supporters of either of the two main parties. In the latest Pew surveys, more Americans considered themselves as independents than support the Democrats or Republicans.

	2010
Number of professed Democrats	33
Number of professed Republicans	25
Number of professed independents	37

Source: *Fewer Voters Identify as Republicans*, Pew Research Publications, 20.3.2010
NB Pew figures for independents include independently-minded Democrats and Republicans; see also p. 265.

Yet, in spite of such observations, it remains meaningful to talk of a two-party system. When people think of politics in America, they think of the battle between the Democrats and the Republicans, and (especially on this side of the Atlantic) they think primarily of the contest for the presidency.

Why does America have a two-party system?

Several factors may be advanced to explain the American system, some institutional, some cultural or historical. Key[7] has suggested that once the basis of the two-party divide had come about at the time of the formation of the Republic, then it was always likely that it would be retained, for 'there is a tendency in human institutions for a persistence of [the] initial form'. Discussion of the form of the Constitution resolved itself into a battle between two opposing viewpoints, and issues thereafter in American history – such as slavery and the Civil War – perpetuated this pattern. Once the two-party system was established, the parties did all that they could to keep it that way and prevent a fractious section of the party from breaking away. In other words, a two-party system tends to be self-perpetuating.

Some would stress the natural tendency for opinion on issues to divide into 'for' and 'against' positions, which often follows the basic distinction between people who generally favour retaining the status quo (the conservatives) and those who wish to see innovation and a quicker pace of change (the progressives). Duverger[8] long ago argued that a two-party system conformed to the basic division in society between those who wish to keep society broadly unchanged, and those who wish to see change and improvement. However, the liberal–conservative, progressive–stay-put distinction has not always been appropriate to American politics, and in either party there have always been those who are more forward looking and those who oppose social advance. Neither has the approach based on social class fitted the picture accurately – the idea that one party represents the working class and the other the middle and upper class (as in the traditional view of the Labour and Conservative clash in Britain) has never had much relevance as an explanation in a country where class plays a less significant part in the political process. In several countries, there is a clear conflict between a socialist and an anti-socialist party, but in the United States there is no large party committed to transforming the social and economic order.

There are more fundamental explanations of the continued dominance of two parties at national and state level:

1 **A single executive:** there is only one vacancy at the highest level, the presidency. The nature of the position means that it is not possible for coalitions of more than one party to share it, as can happen with a cabinet system. To win the presidency is the focus of a party's aspirations, for the office is the focal point of all national political life. The campaigning involved is costly and needs to be planned over a long haul, as today candidates seek to make progress and win support via the primary system. It requires substantial organisational and financial backing. In these circumstances, the best means of winning is to create a coalition behind one man, for any splintering of

support makes success unlikely. The method of election makes a two-party system more desirable, for to win a majority of votes in the Electoral College it is necessary to avoid divisions. As Vile[9] has argued: 'The ability of a party to master the technique of coalition-building is the measure of its ability to command the presidency.'

2 **The broad appeal of the existing parties:** as there is only one supreme prize, it is necessary for any party to appeal as widely as possible. Once the presidential candidate is chosen, the leading parties seek to show that they are attractive to many interests in the country, and this makes it difficult for any smaller party to carve out a distinctive identity that is not already catered for. Both the Republican and Democratic parties are essentially coalitions: large organisations under whose umbrella a variety of groupings can more or less comfortably co-exist. Between them, they cater for all sections of society, being sufficiently flexible to assimilate new ideas that come along and assume importance.

The reasons advanced above (1 and 2) explain why there are only two main parties at the presidential level. They do not entirely explain why it is that in the battle for Congress the various states tend to have two-party competitions.

3 **The mechanics of the electoral system:** the electoral system discourages the formation of third or minor parties. For presidential, congressional and other elections, the British simple plurality or 'first past the post' ('winner takes all') method is employed (see pp. 222–223). Candidates need more votes than their rivals, not an overall majority of the votes cast in any state. A candidate carries any state on election night in which he or she has the highest number of votes. Small parties may total a considerable number of votes nationally or within the region, but it is winning in individual constituencies that counts. Under a proportional electoral system, small parties would have more chance of gaining some representation in the legislature.

4 **Barriers to third or minor party advancement:** in many states, there are real barriers to the formation, progress and survival of third parties. The US is the only nation in which the rules for ballot access in national elections – for Congress as well as the presidency – are written not by the national government but by the states. In several states, legal hurdles have been constructed by the major parties that place third groupings at a serious disadvantage. Many either prohibit 'subversive' ones altogether or make life difficult for them.

Restrictive state statutes have often been challenged in the courts as a denial of 'equal protection' under the law and as a violation of the general right of a party to exist. However, it has been consistently upheld that restrictions are constitutional, and that there is no requirement to extend to small or new parties the same privileges that are granted to others.

Other than issues of ballot access, a further disadvantage of third parties derives from their lack of resources, in particular finance. It is hard for them

Ballot access across the states

Ballot access rules determine the conditions under which a candidate or political party is entitled either to stand for election or to appear on voters' ballot papers. According to Article I, Section 4, of the US Constitution, the authority to regulate the time, place and manner of federal elections is up to each state, unless Congress legislates otherwise. As a consequence, ballot access laws in the United States vary widely from state to state, some being highly restrictive.

On occasion, some states have attempted to ban third parties, such as the Communist Party. More usually, states disadvantage them by requiring them to be of a certain size in order to get their name on the ballot paper. In a few states, the hurdle is so small that it becomes a formality, so that in Arkansas a grouping of at least fifty only needs to hold a convention to qualify. In others, the barrier is much larger, sometimes so much so that it poses a totally unrealistic obstacle. To qualify for the 2010 election ballot, unaffiliated state-wide candidates in North Carolina needed to obtain at least 85,379 signatures.

In certain states, there is no procedure whatever for enthusiasts to qualify to get on a ballot under their own party labels. They must run either as independents or not at all. Georgia and Texas made it very difficult for the veteran consumer rights and environmental campaigner Ralph Nader to get on the ballot paper in 2000. In 2008, he was on the ballot in forty-five states, with write-in status in four of the five remaining states. For ballot access in most states, the Nader campaign had to circulate nominating petitions, with varying numbers of signatures required and deadlines to be met, to be successful. In some states (such as New Mexico), the requirements for ballot access are lower for new parties than for independents, so Nader qualified as a candidate for the Independent Party (composed purely of his personal supporters). In some states, he gained ballot access by associating himself with the Independent-Ecology Party, the Natural Law Party and the Peace and Freedom Party.

to qualify for 'matching funds', the requirement being that they must have received at least 5% of the popular vote in the previous election. Most find this a formidable hurdle; some of them do not even survive long enough to compete in successive elections. The lack of media coverage and well-known personalities make life even more difficult for third parties. Even if they get off the ground, it is difficult for third parties to sustain any momentum over a period, for to stay in business a party needs to be able to maintain an organisation and reward its supporters with the prospect of office or influence.

5 **Fear of a wasted vote:** as voters know that small parties will have difficulty in gaining power, they tend to regard a vote for them as a 'wasted vote'. If these parties cannot eventually win a majority of the votes, they are devoid of real influence; they will not get that majority if people think that they have little chance of achieving it and accordingly fail to vote for them.

Third parties

The late Clinton Rossiter[10] referred to the 'persistent, obdurate two party system'. He went on to observe that:

> There exists in this country today the materials – substantial materials in the form of potential leaders, followers, funds, interests and ideological commitments – for at least three important third parties, any one of which could, under the rules of some other system, cut heavily and permanently into the historic Democrat–Republican monopoly. There is no reasonable expectancy, under the rules of our system, that any such party could make a respectable showing in two successive elections. Indeed, if a new party were to make such a showing in just one election, the majority party closest to it would move awkwardly but effectively to absorb it.

Types of third party

Although the American political system is basically a two-party one, at various times third parties have had a significant impact. Many have existed throughout American history. In recent years, some third-party candidates have won election to public office, and in 1990 Alaska and Connecticut both elected independents in the battle for the state governorships. Vermont re-elected a socialist to the House in the same year. In 1996, Jesse Ventura, a former professional wrestler known as 'the body', was elected as governor for Minnesota, on behalf of the Reform Party (see pp. 295–296). As of October 2011, there are two US senators (Joe Lieberman and Bernie Sanders) who are neither Democrat nor Republican. No governor or member of the House of Representatives hails from outside the major parties.

By a third party, we usually mean one that is capable of gathering a sizeable percentage of popular support and regularly gains seats in the legislature. On occasion, it may win – or threaten to win – enough support to influence the outcome of an election and the control of government, and in particular regions or constituencies it may consistently break through the usual two-party system. We do not usually refer to one that polls only a tiny percentage of the vote and almost never gains representation as a third party. Such organisations are really minor parties.

Most small parties in America are minor ones that may or may not be permanent; they rarely gain more than a minute percentage of the popular vote. From time to time, however, there are those that do erupt onto the national scene and make headline news as they bid for the presidency. These are truly third parties. The terms are often used interchangeably in textbooks, and whether we describe them as third parties, minor parties or small parties we are here concerned with all of those bodies which are parties, but which operate outside the mainstream of the two-party battle.

These small parties differ considerably in type and permanence. They range from those formed to propagate a particular doctrine over a long duration, to those that are more or less transient. The Prohibition and Socialist parties have over long periods been kept alive by bands of dedicated enthusiasts, and regularly contest elections of all types and in several states. But American party history is noted for the turbulence generated by the rapid rise and equally rapid decline of minor parties; they may play a significant role at a particular time, and then become extinct.

In the 2008 batch of elections, fifty-two minor parties had candidates standing in one or more states. In addition, there were some candidates who described themselves as Independent. The list of parties contesting the election included:

Alaskan Independence	Mountain Party
Boston Tea Party	New Party
Ecology Party of Florida	Natural Law Party
Green Independent	Peace Party
HeartQuake '08	US Taxpayers' Party

Along with the Democratic and Republican parties, three other parties nominated candidates with ballot access in enough states to win the minimum 270 Electoral College votes needed for victory in the presidential contest: the Constitution Party, the Green Party and the Libertarian Party. In addition, independent candidate Ralph Nader ran his own campaign, getting on the ballot paper in forty-five states.

Third parties in presidential campaigns

Some third parties arise during presidential elections and continue to have an impact. Often they are based largely around a single person, as with Theodore Roosevelt (Bull Moose) and Perot (United We Stand, America in 1992; the Reform Party in 1996). In 1992, Perot created a high-profile campaign and won the support of activists normally associated with the two main parties. Given his substantial wealth, he could afford to buy extensive advertising on television. For all of the resources at his disposal, he did not win a single state, although he gained an impressive 19% of the popular vote and a couple of good seconds, in Maine and Utah.

Perot's was at first more a personal movement than a formal political grouping, but by 1996 it had been transformed into the Reform Party. The party made little impact in 2000, despite running an expensive campaign. There was a serious clash between hard-line conservative nationalists such as Pat Buchanan (the official candidate) and more socially liberal figures such as Jesse Ventura. Elements among the Reformists seceded and cast their vote elsewhere and the internal schism has continued, with further splintering of the membership. Such events suggest that the party is now in deep trouble.

Some third parties break away from one of the main parties because of disagreement over aspects of the platform that the party currently adopts. John Anderson stood aside from the Republicans in 1980 because he disagreed with the conservative line taken on social issues by the Reaganites, even though he liked the economic approach of the Republican candidate.

Other third parties are more long standing, such as the Libertarians and the Greens. In 1996, and again four years later, the highly visible consumerist Ralph Nader was the official Green candidate. In 2000, he managed to win 3% of the vote and was subsequently blamed by the Democrats for Al Gore's defeat by George W. Bush. In spite of being under pressure to withdraw from the contest in 2004, he stood as an independent, but this time mustered less support. As we have seen above, he made a fourth bid in 2008.

In recent years, a growing number of citizens have defected from the major parties to third-party or independent presidential candidates, who have attracted more support than at any time since the 1920s. Today, many Americans do not see themselves as Democrats or Republicans. They are liable to be tempted by independent candidates and third parties, even if the attraction is short-lived. According to *USA Today*/Gallup findings (27–30 August 2010), the desire of many for a major third political party is as high as it has been at any time in the last decade. Fifty-eight per cent of Americans believe a third major political party is needed because the Republican and Democratic parties do a poor job of representing the American people. Many express wide dissatisfaction with the way things are going and are critical of both Congress and the presidency. Though this rise in support for a third party could be related to the Tea Party movement, Tea Party supporters are just about average in terms of wanting to see a third party created. Sixty-two per cent of those who describe themselves as Tea Party supporters would like a third major party formed, but so do 59% of those who are neutral toward the movement. Tea Party opponents are somewhat less likely to see the need for a third party.

The role and importance of third parties

A source of new ideas

Third parties can think more of principles than power, for they are unlikely ever to have to implement their proposals. They can 'think the unthinkable', before it later becomes the fashion of the day. Through them, ideas and interests that are not catered for within the main parties may find expression politically. They can handle contentious issues on which neither party can take or is willing to take a clear and decisive line. They provide new ideas and issues for the voters to consider. They are not faced with the difficulty of reconciling several views under one umbrella; they can be clear cut in the solutions they offer. They suffer no particularly serious consequences if their solutions are, on analysis, found to be wanting, for they are not putting them into effect. If the ideas do capture the public imagination, then one or other of the main parties may well adopt them. The policy is then translated into established public practice.

At various times the Socialists, Prohibitionists and Progressives have taken up controversial matters, and thereby acted as vehicles for the expression of political discontent. Some of the best ideas have been originally advanced by those outside the political mainstream. The point was well made by the historian Richard Hofstadter.[11] Writing of third parties, he observed that their function 'has not been to win or govern, but to agitate, educate [and] generate new ideas. When a third party's demands become popular enough, they are appropriated by one or both of the major parties and the third party disappears . . . [They] are like bees; once they have stung, they die.'

A healthy democratic outlet

Even if they do not see their ideas adopted and rarely or never win a congressional seat (let alone the ultimate prize of the presidency), small parties have at the very least drawn attention to the way people feel. They form an outlet for those who dislike the character and attitudes of both the main parties, and for those who reject the party battle they provide a haven. They articulate the thoughts of a section of society, and represent a segment of public sentiment. However incoherent or impractical their view may at times be, they have something to say which needs to be considered if only to be rejected. In a democracy, they have a right to exist and put forward their ideas, however weird they may seem to the majority of people.

Holding the balance

At rare times, a third party can be in an influential position, holding the balance of power and/or affecting the outcome of an election. This is unusual, but in 1992 the Perot intervention probably cost George H. Bush the presidency, just as Nader's votes in states such as Florida kept Al Gore out of the White House in 2000.

A CASE STUDY OF FOUR THIRD PARTIES, THEIR OUTLOOK AND IMPACT

The Constitution Party

A conservative party originally founded as the **US Taxpayers' Party**. Members changed its official name to the present one seven years later, although some state affiliate parties continue to use the earlier label. The party's mission, as stated on its website, is 'to restore our government to its Constitutional limits and our law to its Biblical foundations'. Its seven key principles are Life, Liberty, Family, Property, Constitution, States' Rights and American Sovereignty.

The party puts a large focus on immigration and calls for strict penalties on illegal immigrants and a moratorium on legal immigration until all federal subsidies to immigrants are discontinued.

The Green Party

The Green Party of the United States is an informal US affiliate of the left-wing environmentalist European Greens movement. In 1996, it persuaded the prominent consumer advocate, Ralph Nader, to run as its first presidential nominee. In 2000, he raised millions of dollars, mobilising leftist activists and grabbing national headlines with an anti-corporate message. He finished third, with an impressive 2,878,000 votes, a performance that upset many Democrats who felt that his intervention ruined Al Gore's chances of victory. He was under pressure not to stand in 2004, but persisted. His impact was less significant and his vote well down on four years earlier. Nader stresses that he is seeking to build a permanent third party and therefore needs to contest every election, as he did again in 2008.

The Greens have in the past been a largely autonomous collection of local and state-based entities, with only a weak and sometimes splintered national leadership structure. In 2001, they voted to convert from an umbrella coordinating body into a formal and unified national party organisation. Strong local Green parties – with ballot status – exist in a number of states.

The Libertarian Party

Americans are deeply attached to the ideas of personal liberty and limited government. Some are attracted to the Libertarian Party, formed in 1972. Claiming to be neither left nor right, Libertarians feel that neither the Republicans nor the Democrats can be trusted to defend the rights of individuals. They:

- espouse a classical laissez-faire (leave alone) philosophy which, they argue, means 'more freedom, less government and lower taxes';
- wish to see most services run on a private basis, so that there is unrestricted freedom in commerce;
- disapprove of federal and state welfare programmes, and policies which offer subsidies to any group – farmers, businessmen and others;
- dislike any regulatory bodies of a federal nature such as the FBI or CIA, and laws that curb individual freedom, such as those on the wearing of seat belts and motor-cycle helmets.

Whereas most conservatives take a socially restrictive view and wish to limit the sale of marijuana and other soft drugs, gambling, prostitution and pornography, Libertarians would leave such things unrestricted. They would abolish all legislation designed to promote a particular view of morality. On abortion, there is some division, though the founders of the party were more committed to allowing free choice. As might be anticipated, they oppose gun control and are pro home schooling.

Libertarians traditionally billed themselves as 'America's largest third party', and they still usually field more state and local candidates than any other third force. However, in 2000 and again in 2004, the Greens and the Reform Party out-polled them.

The New York Liberal Party

The Liberal Party of New York state claims to be the longest-existing third party in the history of the United States. It was founded in 1944 as an alternative to a state Democratic Party dominated by local party machines that were rife with corruption and a Republican Party controlled by special interests. It has a history of nominating – or more often supporting – candidates on the basis of independence, merit and a progressive viewpoint, regardless of party affiliations; it is interested primarily in whether they are likely to provide good, effective and forward-looking government. Past nominees have included Governor Mario Cuomo, Senator Robert Kennedy and New York City mayors Fiorello LaGuardia, John Wagner and Rudolph Giuliani.

Adopting a broadly centre-left stance, the Liberal Party has been for many years an influential force in New York politics, campaigning on such things as: reproductive freedom (a woman's right to choose abortion); healthcare (the need for a system that is well run and affordable); democracy involvement (encouraging popular participation in civic life); environmental progress (a serious attempt to place environmental considerations at the forefront of policy making); and civil rights (comprehensive legislation to ensure that discrimination on grounds of race, ethnicity, religion, gender, sexual orientation, disability and economic class do not restrict people's lives).

The Liberal Party has declined in influence in recent years. Following a poor showing in the 2002 gubernatorial election, it lost its state recognition, so that it no longer qualifies for automatic ballot paper status. The party ceased operations at its state offices. It is currently struggling to keep going, although dedicated enthusiasts are still proud to label themselves as Liberals. Internal dissension, secession and allegations of corruption against key members have damaged their prospects of making a return to recognised party status. The Working Families Party (formed in 1998) has drawn away much of its support, particularly among the trade unions.

In 2005, it was reported in the *New York Daily News* that incumbent mayor Michael Bloomberg, a Republican liberal on social issues, was seeking to revive the Liberal Party and run on a Republican/Liberal ticket. However, after Bloomberg's re-election under the Republican banner, nothing further came of the rumours. In 2006, there was no Liberal candidate for governor, for the first time since the early 1940s.

Socialism in America: its failure to take root

America has not proved to be fertile ground for socialist thinkers and their ideas. The main writers and philosophers of socialism (see p. 24) have been Europeans, and their ideas and their approach have been developed from European experience. Perhaps because of the influence of German and Jewish believers, Socialism has often been regarded as an alien import unsuited to the conditions of American life.

Socialism in its various forms is traditionally associated with the wish to replace private ownership of the means of production, distribution and exchange with a system of greater public ownership. In the ultimate socialist utopia, property is owned by the state on behalf of the people, and in Marx's words, each receives what is necessary for his needs: 'From each according to his ability, to each according to his needs.' In America, there is more discussion of the rights of private property than interest in public ownership.

American socialists of whatever disposition broadly favour an increased role for government, and wish to place a greater burden on the rich by higher taxation. They would use the revenue thereby obtained to introduce more redistributive policies, including public works schemes to offer work for the unemployed, and more aid to the least well-off.

Socialist doctrine has gained a small but influential following among a section of middle-class intellectuals, but the working classes have never taken up the cause with much enthusiasm or in any significant numbers. Groups have developed to represent the various shades of socialism, most notably the Socialist Party, but, as in Europe, these left-wing organisations have been prone to internal schism, factional strife and secession. There have been socialists on the ballot paper in recent years, standing either as individuals or representing the Socialist Party or groups such as the Socialist Workers or Workers' World.

Small in numbers socialism's adherents may have always been, but much of American socialism has always been of a radical character. It has tended to be Marxist in rhetoric and some of its most well-known characters have used far more revolutionary language than that used by socialists in other countries. European socialists of the late nineteenth century often pointed out that those on the left of the American socialist party more closely resembled the revolutionary **anarcho-syndicalists** of Europe than they did many continental Marxists. Eugene Debs, the party's most prominent

> **anarcho-syndicalism**
> Anarcho-syndicalism is a branch of anarchism that focuses on the labour movement. Supporters portray it as a viable force for revolutionary social change, its goal being to replace capitalism and the state with a new society and an alternative economic system which would be democratically self-managed by workers.

spokesman and five times presidential candidate in the early twentieth century, was noted for his use of revolutionary Marxist terminology, a point noted by Lenin, who singled him out for praise.

Why has socialism failed to make headway in America?

1 **The American Dream.** Most Americans see capitalism as basic to the American way of life, for it promotes enterprise and initiative. It is part of the American Dream that a person, given the right encouragement and incentives, can strike out on his or her own and make a fortune. Working hard, earning their reward, being able to keep most of what they earn, passing on their fortune – whatever its size – to their offspring: these are features of life in which there is much faith. The belief is that people should be able to keep what they earn, use it to buy property of their choice, be it a dream home or a more humble shack, a factory or a farm.

Fundamental to all of this is an almost universal belief in free enterprise. Most voters see doctrines such as communism and socialism as un-American. They don't want to see a redistribution of other people's wealth, they are more interested in having the freedom to go ahead and make their own. Neither do they like the state to take their money via excessive taxation and spend it on costly welfare programmes that discourage other people from being as self-reliant as they are themselves.

2 **The relative absence of class antagonism.** There was never any feudal system in the United States, no society with a hierarchy of lords and ladies at the top, peasants at the bottom. Americans were, in the words of de Tocqueville, 'born equal'. There was never an American class struggle as one group sought to displace the influence of another. There are objective class divisions, but there has rarely been any sense of class consciousness or worker solidarity as seen in Western Europe. The principle of equality is little disputed, even though there are differences of opinion over exactly what it means in policy implementation.

3 **Overriding social factors more significant than class.** Class solidarity is less important than other social distinctions; racial and religious attachments are strong, with distinctive groups such as the Jews in New York, the Irish, the Europeans and so many others. America has a very heterogeneous population, and the massive wave of early twentieth-century immigration has created an ethnic mosaic that is matched by the religious diversity of these peoples. These groups have continued to exist in their social enclaves, though many have moved from inner cities to the outer suburbs. Americans have traditionally been conscious of their roots, even if they also wish to develop an American identity, learn the language and be naturalised as citizens. There is no sense of social solidarity, such as exists in parts of Europe. In particular, race and ethnicity cut across divisions based on other economic and social considerations.

4 **The absence of a tradition of strong, left-wing trade unionism.** Trade
   unionism has never been particularly attractive to many Americans, and unions
   have consequently never gained great influence. Those that did develop rarely
   based their ideas on socialism as a means of overthrowing the established
   economic order, and inclined to individualist rather than collectivist ideas.
   Any attempts to foment industrial strife by militant, left-wing trade union-
   ists have met a hostile response. Such groups have sometimes been banned
   or in other ways actively discouraged.

The Socialist Party USA and its fate

The Socialist Party USA is the official heir to the Socialist Party of America, which had
actually adopted the name Socialist Party USA in 1962. It advocates progress via the
ballot box, rather than militant revolutionary change. Throughout its history, many members have claimed that by participating in the electoral process at all levels of government, they have the opportunity to present socialist alternatives; can educate the public
about socialism; can agitate for progressive reforms and socialist solutions; can help
organise movements of working people; and can win victories of both immediate and
long-term value.

Staunchly anti-communist, the Party was established in 1900 by Eugene V. Debs. In the
first twenty years or so of its existence, it was the third-largest national party. It elected
two members to Congress, was represented in several state legislatures and localities
and at its peak had more than 100,000 members. But even at its peak, it never really
challenged the supremacy of the major parties.

In the decades since World War II, the Socialist Party has suffered from serious internal
schism, control passing from left to right and back again. Since 1973, it has focused
its attention more on grassroots and local politics, and has dealt with the issue as to
whether to stand in presidential elections on a case-by-case basis, although it actively
campaigns against restrictive state laws that deny the party ballot access. In 2004, Walt
Brown and Mary Alice Herbert were the presidential candidates, standing in fifteen states.
Their efforts were rewarded with a meagre national total of around 11,000 votes. In
2008, they fared even worse, shedding more than 4,000 votes. The candidate, Brian
Moore, was at pains to deny Republican scare-mongering that Barack Obama was any
kind of socialist and expressed the view that the Obama campaign was superficial, in
essence little more than a slick public relations exercise.

According to its own mission statement, the party stands for

> the abolition of every form of domination and exploitation, whether based on social
> class, gender, race/ethnicity, sexual orientation or other characteristics . . . and is
> committed to the transformation of capitalism through the creation of a demo-
> cratic socialist society . . . It strives to establish a radical democracy that places
> people's lives under their own control – a non-racist, classless, feminist, socialist
> society in which people cooperate at work, at home and in the community.

5 **The hegemony of the capitalist system in the USA and its control over the media.** Marxist thinkers have often pointed to the dominance of capitalism in the USA and the prevalence of bourgeois culture in what was a new country. Two other theoreticians of the left, Weber and Gramsci, also pointed to America's unique origins and consequent value system as a source of its economic and political development. Gramsci,[12] an Italian neo-Marxist, noted that '"Americanism", uninhibited by the existence of social classes and values derived from a feudal past, is not simply a way of life, it is an ideology.' It was widely and deeply rooted among Americans, who accepted the dominance of their political leaders in part because of the powerful mass media, which were controlled and manipulated by pro-capitalist proprietors. They could carry capitalist values across the nation and into every home, potently proclaiming their own message and denying access to those who peddled ideas that challenged their hegemony or dominance. The bulk of the population was kept in a state of bemused satisfaction, fed as it was by a menu largely consisting of entertainment. As a result, the beliefs and tenets of the controlling elite were so widely held that radical, socialist ideas were not seriously discussed at all.

See also p. 24 for Marx and Engels' explanations for the failure of American socialism.

The two main parties: Democrats and the Republicans

Policy attitudes: similarities and differences between Democrats and Republicans

To non-Americans, the policy differences between the two main parties may seem modest, at times almost non-existent. Lord Bryce[13] once suggested that they were 'two bottles, each having a label denoting the kind of liquor it contains, but each being empty'. The parties have certainly often seemed to have much in common in their policy attitudes.

In fact, the rhetoric of politicians in both parties suggests greater dissimilarity than actually exists. They wish to emphasise the differences and thereby clarify the choice for the voters, but if one looks beyond the speeches and the party literature and examines the record of the parties when they have won the presidency in recent years, then often there has been a broad acceptance of much that has been accomplished by their opponents.

Both parties agree about far more things than they disagree about. Both attach great importance to the Constitution and are committed to maintaining America's present form of government. Both accept the pioneering American values of free enterprise and individualism, on which there is little discord in society. Neither favours root-and-branch change in the economic system. There is certainly no deep ideological divide, and in particular no contest between socialism in its various Western European forms and those who oppose it.

Each party's candidates always closely resemble the others and few contests between them ever present the electorate with a clear-cut choice. Many years ago, one commentator, Denis Brogan,[14] observed that: 'The fact that all Republicans claim to be democrats and all Democrats to be republicans makes the confusion of party names nearly complete.' Both parties recognise the need to appeal to a wide spectrum of groups and interests, and this generally keeps them near to the political centre; they have tended to offer a broad range of rather similar programmes. It is rarely the case for one party ever to be wholly united against the other. This is particularly true when the two parties are in a broadly consensual mould, less so when, as in the early Reagan years, one party veers off on a more distinctive ideological route.

The voters and the parties: their perceptions of what distinguishes them

Ever since the New Deal, those with low incomes – particularly the urban working class, including the blacks and other racial minorities – have leaned strongly to the Democrats. More affluent suburban voters have traditionally been keen supporters of the Republicans, other than a liberal element in the middle class. (See also 'Party support in the 2008 election', pp. 280–281.)

The voters seem to know how to tell the parties apart, and most Americans are quite capable of identifying particular attitudes and approaches within the two parties, each of which is seen as standing for something distinctive. Most of the business and professional people, and large farmers, judge that the Republican party best serves their interests, while workers tend to look to the Democrats as being more helpful to them, 'the party of the little man'. This characterisation owes much to the New Deal, and the subsequent programmes of leading Democrats such as Truman, Kennedy and Johnson. Such an easy division into working and middle class is less clear cut than it once was, and the union-oriented bias of the Democrats has become less apparent than in former years. But polls suggest that the instincts of many voters about the two main parties have not significantly changed.

The Republicans are widely seen as the party that opposes expansion of the role of government, especially in Washington. They are viewed as being more lukewarm about innovations, whereas Democrats tend to see positive action as necessary to promote social welfare and control the worst operations of big business. Their opponents call this traditional 'tax and spend' Democrat thinking.

The roll of interest groups that are broadly supportive of the main parties also tells us something about their respective leanings. Republicans have long been more associated with the American Farm Bureau Federation, the National Association of Manufacturers and the American Medical Association. The Democrats are preferred by many members of the National Farmers Union, the American Federation of Labor and Congress of Industrial Organisations, and the American Political Science Association.

Even when clear differences between the two parties are discernible, it is important to realise that the differences within parties can be more significant than those between them. Massachusetts Democrat Senator John Kerry is a very different political animal from his fellow Democrat, Senator Blanche Lincoln of Arkansas. In the same way, an east-coast Republican often differs sharply in outlook from a Republican elected in the Midwest. However, there are differences of emphasis and style, degree and method, and distinct bases of support. It is to the differences that we now turn.

Since the beginnings of the Reagan era, the political divisions between the Republicans and Democrats have become more apparent. Polling evidence suggests that a higher percentage of today's voters detect differences between them than was the case back in the 1970s. **Ideology** has become more significant; there has been more ideological ferment between and within parties in recent years.

Party differences

(See also pp. 312 and 317 for a listing of party policies at state level in the 2008 election.)

Each party has its own character and image. A 'typical Democrat' might be a member of an ethnic minority, belong to a trade union and the working class, be non-Protestant and an urban dweller. He or she would support measures of social welfare to assist the poor and needy, favour regulation of big business and a fairer distribution of wealth, and support the global role of America as leader of the free world. A 'typical Republican' might be white, male, middle class, college educated and Protestant. He would support law and order, believe in limited government and individualism, support big business and free enterprise, be wary of American involvement overseas and see himself as a **conservative**.

ideology
A set of doctrines or beliefs that form the basis of a political, economic or other system. An ideology needs to provide some explanation of how things have come to be as they are, some indication of where they are heading as a guide to action and some overriding belief to which adherents may make a final appeal when challenged.

conservative
A conservative wishes to preserve traditional customs, ideas and values, and favours social stability and established institutions. He or she tends to oppose – or in some cases is highly resistant to – radical innovation and new thinking, preferring instead gradual development. Most conservatives believe that less government is likely to be better government.

Yet this is too simplistic, as generalisations invariably are. The Democrats have supporters who are white and black, working class and middle class, urban and rural dwellers, combining as they do workers in the northern industrial cities and more wealthy farmers in the West. The Republicans have within their ranks business, professional and working people, many who are small-town religious fundamentalists and some who are city agnostics, many who support curbs on abortion, others who believe in free choice.

If we look at specific issues, there tend to be divergent positions between representatives of the two parties on such contentious matters as:
- abortion, the death penalty and other right-to-life issues;
- civil rights for blacks and other disadvantaged groups;
- affirmative action;
- prayer in state schools;
- the role of the federal government in matters such as education;
- anti-poverty policies and welfare reform;
- the provision of medical care;
- the problems of urban renewal;
- defence spending and the role of America in the post-Cold War era.

One way of distinguishing the parties has in the past been to categorise them as 'liberal' or 'conservative' in tone and outlook, depending on how they view such controversies. Since 1932 the Democrats have generally taken a liberal position, whereas the Republicans have adopted a more conservative stance. The distinction is not always an effective one, for as we can see from the discussion on pp. 308–310 the 'l' word is one that has gone out of fashion in American politics. In recent years, the centre of gravity has moved well to the right. Nevertheless, for a long while after 1932 the division had some validity, and there are some party supporters who remain proud to be a liberal or a conservative. In a Gallup poll in June 2010, 20% of those interviewed identified themselves as liberals, 35% as moderates and 42% as conservatives, findings not dissimilar to other surveys conducted over the last two or three years.

Examples of the likely beliefs of liberals and conservatives

Key policy areas	Liberals	Conservatives
Role of government	Important as regulator in public interest	Distrust, preference for free-market solutions
Spending	Spend more on disadvantaged	Keep spending down
Taxes	Tax the rich more	Keep taxes down
Abortion	Emphasise freedom of choice	Support right to life
Affirmative action	In favour	Wary, wish to make inroads
Crime	Look for causes of crime, respect rights of accused	Be tough on criminals, stress rights of victims
School prayer	Opposed	In favour

NB For information on the conservative Tea Party movement, see pp. 321–323, 341 and 365–366.

American liberalism

Classical liberalism emphasised liberty and individual rights, and a minimal role for state intervention. But by the twentieth century, liberalism became associated with protecting the individual by regulatory action. Today's liberals see government as having a positive role to promote greater justice in society and more equality of opportunity. They talk of individual rights, including the right to own private property, but they also see a need for measures to control the defects of a market economy. Most accept that inequalities of wealth are inevitable and even desirable, but they wish to ensure that everyone has a certain minimum level of wealth, so that they can enjoy life and have a fair deal.

Franklin Roosevelt was the model for American liberals, with his attempt to steer America out of the depression via the **New Deal**. President Kennedy is similarly regarded as a liberal hero, several of his speeches echoing liberal values. In accepting the endorsement of his presidential candidacy by New York's Liberal Party, he sought to clear up some confusion about the term:[15]

> **New Deal**
> The ambitious programme introduced by Franklin Roosevelt in the early–mid 1930s, designed to combat the depressed condition of the United States. It involved measures to bring about the 3Rs, relief, recovery and (long-term) reform. It included a massive increase in public spending to 'prime the pump' and create an upward spiral of economic activity.

> What do our opponents mean when they apply to us the label 'Liberal?' If by 'Liberal' they mean, as they want people to believe, someone who is soft in his policies abroad, who is against local government, and who is unconcerned with the taxpayer's dollar, then the record of this party and its members demonstrate that we are not that kind of 'Liberal'. But if by a 'Liberal' they mean someone who looks ahead and not behind, someone who welcomes new ideas without rigid reactions, someone who cares about the welfare of the people – their health, their housing, their schools, their jobs, their civil rights, and their civil liberties – someone who believes we can break through the stalemate and suspicions that grip us in our policies abroad, if that is what they mean by a 'Liberal', then I'm proud to say I'm a 'Liberal'.

On another occasion, Kennedy gave an insight into liberal beliefs and expressed his commitment to the liberal cause: 'I believe in human dignity as the source of national purpose, in human liberty as the source of national action, in the human heart as the source of national compassion, and in the human mind as the source of our invention and our ideas. It is, I believe, the faith in our fellow citizens as individuals and as people that lies at the heart of the liberal faith.'

The problems of the twenty-first century are different, for the country operates in a more prosperous climate than the days of FDR and the New Deal, but there are still those who are left behind. Modern liberals want to provide better education and housing, are alarmed by inadequate and costly healthcare, and support progressive taxation graduated according to the individual's ability to pay. They are committed to civil rights and affirmative action to overcome the effects of past discrimination against minorities and women; many activists involved in areas ranging from women's liberation and the pro-abortion campaign to the gay and the disabled movements come within the liberal fold. These are all examples of the positive use of government to improve society and remove its defects.

Neo-liberalism and the passing of Rooseveltian liberalism

In the last few years there has been talk of neo-liberals, who are willing to argue the case for traditional liberal beliefs of justice and liberty, and the need for government intervention, but who do not endorse the whole liberal agenda. Neo-liberals are more suspicious of union power, welfare provision and big government with its large, Washington-based bureaucracies. Some also doubt the increasing concern for minority causes. In the words of Irving Kristol,[16] a leading proponent of the idea, they are 'liberals mugged by reality'.

The growth of neo-liberalism reflects the fact that liberalism has rather gone out of fashion. Even those who believe in it are aware of its allegedly adverse effects. Critics, mainly Republicans and southern Democrats, have portrayed liberalism as being too concerned with federal action by the government, with costly programmes which require huge bureaucracies to run them, and with penal taxation which hits the voter in his pocket and tends to destroy his incentive for individual effort. Welfare is seen as damaging to the qualities that made America what it is; it undermines the work ethic and the entrepreneurial spirit. Neo-liberalism has more in common with classical liberalism – laissez-faire, the minimal state and a strong commitment to economic freedom that is interpreted in a different way from what FDR meant by the term.

In 1992 Clinton was concerned to show himself as a new type of Democrat. In the more conservative climate of that decade, he and others were anxious to show that they too believed in the virtues of free enterprise, the perils of communism, the need for tough action against criminals, strong defence and a new emphasis upon traditional patriotism. 'Liberalism' has increasingly become a term of abuse used by those on the political right. Republicans have turned liberalism, the philosophy that dominated politics from the 1930s until the 1980s, into a term of abuse. Accordingly, Democratic politicians are still reluctant to describe themselves as liberal, for fear of losing popular support. The 'l' word was used by George W. Bush against John Kerry, whom it was easy – if in some ways, misleading – to portray as a Massachusetts liberal. So too, the Republicans in 2008 and 2010 were keen to pin the label on Barack Obama.

Liberalism still has its advocates, and, at a time when politicians are reluctant to use the word, there have been academics and journalists who see merit in what it stands for. Thus Arthur Schlesinger could write an article entitled 'Hurray for the L-Word', in which he claimed:[18]

> The presidents we admire and celebrate most – Jefferson, Jackson, Lincoln, Theodore Roosevelt, Wilson, FDR, Harry Truman and JFK – were all, in the context of their times, vigorous and unashamed liberals. They were all pioneers of new frontiers, seeking out the ways of the future, meeting new problems with new remedies, carrying the message of constructive change in a world that never stops changing. From the start of the Republic, liberalism has always blazed the

Barack Obama and liberalism

Aware of the pitfalls surrounding the term, in the election campaign (2008) Barack Obama tended to shun the word 'liberal' and opt for alternatives. He tended to shun the word 'liberal' and portrayed the whole Left–Right conflict as out of date. He talked of it being time for Americans to 'discard ideology', to 'move forward' and to reach a new 'common ground' built around 'broad-based values'. His platform often included references to the politics of 'understanding'. In his inaugural address he declared: 'The question we ask today is not whether our government is too big or too small, but whether it works . . .' This emphasis on what 'works' is his nod to pragmatism, which he implies is almost the opposite of ideological liberalism.

In spite of his avoidance of the 'l' word, many commentators saw Obama as strongly liberal. They noted the range of his plans, as explained in the election campaign. For them, the proposals to end the Bush tax cuts for the wealthy, enact a national health plan, offer a $4,000-a-year tuition reimbursement in exchange for national service and have the government intervene to prevent home foreclosures, had a decidedly liberal tinge.

Opponents placed Obama firmly in the liberal camp, as did a number of writers and journalists. The *National Journal*[17] Washington's leading online and print publisher, has produced a ranking of members of Congress on a liberal–conservative scale. It sifts through the hundreds of roll-call votes taken in any year and selects ones considered to be useful in identifying ideological differences between elected representatives. In 2007, using 99 votes out of the 442 votes cast in the Senate, it voted Obama the most liberal senator. To qualify for a vote rating, a member of Congress needs to participate in half of the selected votes. Obama cast votes in 66 of the 99 roll calls that formed the basis for the Senate ratings. On those 66 votes, he took what were labelled as 'the liberal' position 65 times.

The rating system employed is not without its critics, however. They claim that the terms 'liberal' and 'conservative' are used very subjectively. Moreover, some find the rankings of senators unconvincing, not least because a senator may miss some key votes, and in any case not all representatives are included. For instance, Obama missed thirty-three of the designated votes. Whether he would have taken the conservative position on some of the votes he missed is a matter of conjecture. Again, some senators took the liberal position more often than Obama. But Obama's 65/66 liberal votes earned him the title, as opposed to a senator who might have voted the liberal position eighty times out of ninety.

There was surprise in some other ratings. Joe Biden – usually regarded as a centrist – was rated the third most liberal member of the Senate. Hillary Clinton came sixteenth. Yet despite the disparity in the Obama–Clinton rankings, the voting records of the two presidential contenders were not very different for 2007. As the article that accompanies the listing admits, 'in their yearlong race for the Democratic presidential nomination, Obama and Clinton have had strikingly similar voting records. Of the 267 measures on which both senators cast votes in 2007, the two differed on only 10.' Moreover, John McCain was not even assessed. He did not vote frequently enough to merit inclusion, having missed more than half of the votes in both the economic and foreign policy categories.

trail into the future – and conservatism has always deployed all the weapons of caricature and calumny and irrelevance to conceal the historic conservative objective of unchecked rule by those who already have far more than their fair share of the nation's treasure.

The Democrats

Rossiter[19] was right in suggesting that a usual characteristic of Democratic rule has been a willingness to embrace change. The party accepts innovation, and has since the days of Woodrow Wilson been more willing to extend governmental intervention and welfare programmes. The very names given by presidential contenders to their party platform suggest an acceptance of the need to embrace innovation and move forward with the task of reform. Woodrow Wilson offered the 'New Freedom', Franklin Roosevelt the 'New Deal', Harry Truman the 'Fair Deal', John Kennedy the 'New Frontiers', Lyndon Johnson the 'Great Society', and Bill Clinton the 'New Covenant'.

Since the New Deal, the Democrats have been the party associated with more positive government action to promote social welfare and regulate business activity. They were seen as standing for some redistribution of income, the extension of welfare measures and increased governmental expenditure. Yet in the last decade or so, Democrats have gone some way to shed this image. Bill Clinton's programme in 1992 sounded a far cry from the more liberal ones of some of his party predecessors. It was notably more cautious than the platform adopted by Kennedy and Johnson.

Clinton attempted to blend features of the liberal tradition of positive government with elements of the traditional Republican programme such as controlling the budget deficit. He knew that Americans were growing weary of the problems posed by the urban centres, with such things as the breakdown of law and order, the preoccupation with civil rights and the use of affirmative action. Their anxieties about particular programmes combined with a feeling that government was growing 'too big'. They disliked the spiralling cost of welfare and other public spending, and warmed to promises to 'get Washington off their backs' and of lower taxes. In his New Covenant programme, Clinton was responding to profound changes in American attitudes.

At any one time, there have inevitably been divergent elements within the Democratic Party. Among the present groupings, it is possible to distinguish:

1 **Progressive Democrats**, some of whom are descendants of the New Left tradition. A broadly centrist grouping on economic issues, it is progressive on social ones. Hostile to the economic and social conservatism of the G.W. Bush era, it
   - is sympathetic to government action to rid America of corporate excesses;
   - supports the Obama move for healthcare reform (though it disliked some of the compromises the president made to gain sufficient support);

- advocates interventionist policies to help the disadvantaged, such as blacks, Latinos, gays and the disabled;
- is generally pacific in its approach to foreign policy, having been generally united in its opposition to the war in Iraq.

This element is represented on Capitol Hill by the Congressional Progressive Caucus (CPC).

2 **Liberal Democrats** are to the left of the Progressive Democrats. Once in the ascendancy in party thinking, they lost influence in the Clinton years. Today, they are not easily distinguished from the progressive wing described above, but tend to be more radical on economic and social policy, more committed to civil liberty and particularly opposed to militarism. Edward Kennedy was perhaps their most distinguished standard bearer and Nancy Pelosi, the former House speaker, was also identified as a key supporter.

3 **The unions**, once a powerful part of the New Deal Coalition, are still a force within the party in spite of their declining membership. Among other things, they argue for tighter labour laws and an industrial policy that protects jobs in manufacturing industry. Increasingly, however, on a range of issues they are hard to distinguish from centrist Progressive Democrats and are seen as part of the mainstream party tradition, with its emphasis on governmental intervention in economic and welfare matters. They tend to be more 'hawkish' on foreign policy.

4 Southerners such as Bill Clinton and Al Gore – and others within the **New Democrat** fold – tended to take a more conservative stance on a range of issues. They were less enthusiastic about government intervention, pro-free market in economics and in favour of a robust stance in foreign policy. Traditional liberal nostrums have little appeal for New Democrats, but on civil rights they are markedly more sympathetic than Southern Democrats of the past – relying heavily on black votes for their re-election, in many cases. They appeal otherwise to the white working class and rural voters.

After the 1984 defeat, the **Democratic Leadership Council** (DLC) was formed to organise and co-ordinate the more centrist elements within the Democratic coalition. It continues to serve as a forum for debate on policy and was a dominant force within the party during the Clinton and early G.W. Bush years. A Washington 'think tank' that describes itself as 'the place for pragmatic progressives' – the Progressive Policy Unit (PPU) – is broadly sympathetic and a magazine, the *New Democrat*, continues to propagate its views.

The Republicans

Republicans have traditionally been more cautious than the Democrats in their approach. Sometimes they have been deeply conservative, their pro-business, pro-free enterprise tendencies gaining the upper hand. At other

---

The policy statements of two state Democratic parties in 2010

California

- Promote peace, security, the rule of law, and human rights at home and abroad

- Promote guaranteed support for first responders, military service members, and veterans

- Fight to restore the constitutional balance among the branches of the federal government

- Create a 21st century economy built on a diverse workforce educated by quality public schools and with the right to organize

- Support civil rights, and educational and economic opportunities

- Ensure universal, comprehensive, and affordable healthcare

- Protect a woman's right to choose how to use her mind, her body and her time

- Secure a dignified retirement for our seniors, including social security and Medicare for future generations

- Make California the most energy-independent state, build new industries in the effort to fight global warming and pollution, and protect natural resources

- Build smart, sustainable, safe, environmentally sound, and caring communities

- Support the arts, especially in our public schools

- Insist upon fiscal common sense, responsibility, and accountability in California and Washington.

Texas

The party has faith in democracy. It wishes to build on the sacred values of family, freedom and fairness, to afford every Texan, without exception, the opportunity to achieve their God-given potential. It believes that:

- government exists to achieve as a community, state, and nation what we cannot achieve as individuals, and must not serve only a powerful few

---

times, in the years of the New Deal and after, party spokesman often sounded less hostile to government intervention, recognising the popularity of many Democratic initiatives. But there was always a general unease about the direction in which their opponents had taken the country. Many Republicans were lukewarm about the expanding role of the federal government in economic and social matters. These anxieties have developed since the 1980s, and the modern party wishes to curb the size and scale of governmental activity. It is more interested in economy in government, and the pursuit of the low taxation that reduced expenditure allows.

- citizens have inalienable rights

- there should be freedom from government interference in our private lives and personal decisions

- in equal opportunities for all Texans to receive quality public education; have access to affordable, comprehensive healthcare; find a good job with dignity; buy or rent a good home in a safe community; and breathe clean air and drink clean water

- a growing economy should benefit all Texans

- the people who work in a business are as important as those who invest in it, and should be paid a living wage; good business should offer a fair deal for customers; regulation of unfair practices and rates is necessary; the burden of taxes should be fairly distributed

- our lives, homes, communities and country should be made secure via good emergency services; retirement and pension security; encouraging job security where it is possible; preservation of our precious natural resources and quality of life; and a safety net for those most vulnerable and in need

- America is made stronger by the men and women who put their lives on the line when it is necessary to engage our military to secure our nation, and more secure by competent diplomatic leadership that uses the moral, ethical, economic assets of a powerful, free nation to avoid unnecessary military conflict

- the benefits derived from the individual strengths of our diverse population, including honouring 'family values' through policies that value all our families

- honest, ethical state government that serves the public interest, and not the special interests, will help all Texans realize economic and personal security.

See also the platform of the Democratic Party in the 2008 presidential election (p. 278)

New (Radical) Right

The movement within the Republican Party that advocated laissez-faire economic policies, anti-welfarism and belief in the rights of the individual over those of the community. Its views were more staunchly opposed to abortion and defence cuts than were those of traditional conservatives. The neo-liberal economic policies of this school of thought influenced many other Western governments and have subsequently been adopted by the Christian Right (see pp. 318–321) and other neo-conservatives.

In the 1980s, traditional conservatism – as described – increasingly gave way to a new variety of ultra-conservatism, its adherents often known collectively as the **New (Radical) Right**. Ronald Reagan said that 'government is the problem'. True to this spirit, the Reagan years saw an emphasis upon the market economy, a relaxation of anti-business controls, hostility to organised trade unionism, and low taxation. In as much as

Some common Republican attitudes

- **The economy** – emphasis on the role of laissez-faire economics, free markets, fiscal conservatism, low taxation and the promotion of personal responsibility over welfare programmes.

- **Organised labour** – general dislike of union activity and resistance to the idea of industrial action.

- **The family** – support for conventional and God-fearing families.

- **Minorities** – as descendants of earlier settlers and pioneers (White, Anglo-Saxon Protestants: WASPs), many of its members are suspicious of newer arrivals and of the countries from which they arrived.

- **Foreign policy** – members are often among the sharpest critics of active involvement overseas. Some are deeply isolationist, and even the east-coast establishment tends to be concerned about the scale of commitment made to Western Europe and the use of American troops abroad. There is a strong emphasis upon 'Americanism' and patriotic goals, involving protecting America's status in the world.

government was accepted as necessary, there was a move towards local or state governmental action over that of the federal government. Reagan's approach appealed to many conservatives in America.

Members of the New Right shared much of the ground occupied by other conservatives, but they became associated with particular causes which they wished to see become accepted as public policy. They sought to achieve their programme via greater representation in Congress, and in November 1994 the **Contract with America** was based upon the New Right's philosophical approach.

Contract with America
The policy platform agreed by House Republican candidates for the November 1994 elections. It comprised ten bills that were to be introduced within the first 100 days in office. Conservative in character, it dealt with issues such as shrinking the size of government, promoting lower taxes and greater entrepreneurial activity, and welfare reform.

The New Right wrapped itself in the symbols of nationalism and patriotism, and supporters took a strong stand in favour of business, the death penalty and school prayer, issues which struck a chord with many voters. Today, it has a more distinctive social agenda than its conservative forebears, and its restrictive policies include strict control over abortion, drugs and pornography. It dislikes affirmative action and forced bussing, and is lukewarm in its support for any legislation to advance civil rights.

Moderate Republicans

Some Republicans continue to adhere to the party's more liberal beliefs and traditions, although in recent decades the influence of New Right thinking and of the conservative evangelicals in the Religious Right has left them beyond the mainstream. Republican congressmen who support more moderate ideas and policies may be found in two groupings:

- **The Ripon Society** was founded in 1962, taking its name from the Republican Party's birthplace in Ripon, Wisconsin. It believes that certain Republican values are permanent, whatever the shifts in party opinion at any given time. It claims to represent all Americans through moderate, progressive policy formation that upholds the traditional, common-sense Republican principles of limited but effective government, a free enterprise based economy, a strong, well-maintained, national defence and social tolerance.

  The Ripon Society acts as a haven for Republican moderates and via its journal *The Ripon Forum* circulates its policy ideas. It stresses the need for the party to reach out to all Americans and acts as a haven for Republican moderates. Members are wary of the influence of the Christian Coalition and campaign against the over-representation of small Midwestern states and Western states in the party, seeing these as antagonistic to moderate Republicanism.

- **The Republican Main Street Partnership (RMSP)** is a network supporting moderate Republicans for office. The Partnership, formed following the 1994 House elections, has allied with other moderate Republican groups, including former Governor Christine Todd Whitman's It's My Party Too, Ann Stone's Republicans for Choice, the Log Cabin Republicans, the Republican Majority For Choice, The Wish List, Republicans for Environmental Protection and the Republican Leadership Council.

  In November 2006, many members of the RMSP were defeated in elections that had generally poor outcomes for the Republican Party. This was widely attributed to the fact that moderate Republicans typically hailed from constituencies with a large number of Democratic voters. Seven members from the House of Representatives were defeated by the Democrats, as were one senator and one governor.

  Moderate Republicans do not agree or act in unison on every issue, there being differences over issues such as abortion rights and gun control. But all are committed to a moderate approach to policy issues and are willing to act alongside moderate and conservative Democrats in the party's Blue Dog Coalition, in a spirit of bipartisanship.

In recent years, mainstream Republican thinking has incorporated these New Right attitudes and the more moderate or liberal element of the party has been sidelined. (See box above for information on 'Moderate Republicans'). However, whereas Reaganite conservatives saw government as 'the problem' and wished to curb its influence, supporters of George W. Bush wanted government to act as an enabling force that encouraged citizens to assist themselves. The platforms of George Bush in 2000 and 2004 were based on what he termed 'compassionate conservatism'. Whilst emphasising the party's traditional concerns, it made reference to the need for a caring and inclusive approach that catered for those disadvantaged by the operation of the free market. 'Comcons' envisage a triangular relationship between government, charities and faith-based organisations (churches).

The Bush platforms also reflected the growing influence of neo-conservatives (neo-cons), a grouping within the party whose ideology was in line with New Right thinking on the economy and welfare but took a distinctive – and more interventionist – line in matters of foreign policy. They stressed the use of American military force as the means of defending national interests and spreading democratic ideas throughout the world. This neo-con emphasis on pre-emptive action against dangerous regimes was reflected in the president's State of the Union Address in 2002, when he labelled three states (Iraq, Iran and North Korea) as an 'axis of evil' that posed 'a grave and growing danger'.

The Bush platform also owed much to the outlook of the so-called 'Moral Majority', for the influence of Christian fundamentalists (often known as the Religious Right) is powerful in the United States. Its supporters have been successful at the local level in building a powerful base, and within the Republican Party their position is a strong one. They hold that religious values are the cement that holds the fabric of society together. They are therefore especially concerned with what is taught in schools, for this will influence the attitudes and behaviour of coming generations.

Today, the Republican Party is a conservative coalition, an amalgam of fiscal-, social- and neo-conservatives, moderates and members of the **Libertarian Right**.

compassionate conservatism

Compassionate conservatism is a political philosophy that shows concern for the welfare of society, and particularly for those in need, but emphasises the need to employ traditionally conservative solutions – such as support for low taxes, limited government regulation and the free-enterprise system – in order to achieve it. 'Com-cons' prefer to see social issues tackled via cooperation with charitable bodies, churches and private companies rather than by government, and favour the promotion of personal responsibility and self-reliance.

neo-conservatives (neo-cons)

A label that embraces a set of right-wing policy attitudes espoused by the New Right and Religious Right (for example the free market, limited welfare and traditional cultural values), but adds to them a distinctive approach on international matters. It argues that America should be proactive rather than a reactive, willing to deter other countries and defend the US against any perceived threat.

Libertarian Right

The Libertarian Right promotes a free market economy and criticises the growth in the role of government in economic and other aspects of life. Members see government as a threat to liberty and exalt the freedom of the individual.

NB For further information on the Democratic Party and Republican Party in the 2008 presidential election, see pp. 274–282

The policy statements of two state Republican parties in 2010

Arkansas

The Republican Party will support Republican candidates who are passionate advocates for tax reform, fiscal sanity, less government, smart stewardship of the environment, life, the family, the Second Amendment and individual liberty.

Our basic principles are:

- Faith in God
- The sanctity of life
- Individual responsibility and initiative
- Individual freedom and liberty, secured by a limited government
- Lower taxes to produce economic growth
- Strong national defense
- The personal right to own and bear arms
- The equal and just enforcement of the law.

North Carolina

- *The Family*: the family is the engine of economic progress, a haven of security and understanding; marriage should be limited to the union of one man and one woman.
- *The Economy*: the free enterprise system is the most effective and just economic system. Government should encourage individual initiative and enterprise, unencumbered by excessive regulation and taxation.
- *Individual Liberty*: the State must not interfere with freedom of religion. Recognition of Almighty God is paramount in schools, courts, currency and the Pledge of Allegiance. The Second Amendment is fundamental to liberty.
- *Sanctity of Life*: unborn children have Constitutional rights to life and liberty . . . euthanasia is wrong.
- *State Government*: legislators should be efficient, effective, ethical and responsive. Transparency should exist at all levels of government . . . government should encourage honest, productive work and oppose gambling (including the state lottery).
- *Education*: parents, not the state, should control their children's education . . . schools should encourage patriotism and Western values. Mandatory sex education in public schools should be opposed.
- *Justice*: maintenance of law and order is the first duty of government . . . prisons should pay less attention to inmate comfort, more to security, education and labor. 'We are repulsed by the rise of gratuitous violence and pornography in literature and music.'
- *The Environment*: our God-given natural heritage must be protected. If regulation is needed, the benefits should warrant the cost.
- *Social Security and Health*: Welfare must be placed on a sound financial footing . . . we reject socialized medicine and a government takeover of the health system.
- *National Policy*: The war against terrorism must be waged and rogue nations stopped from obtaining weapons of mass destruction. Participation in international bodies should not jeopardize the sovereignty of the country, which does not require the approval of the United Nations before defending itself . . . borders must be made secure and the Federal Government should enforce immigration laws.

The Religious Right and the Republican Party

Originally known as the Moral Majority, the Religious or Christian Right is the term used to cover a broad movement of conservatives who advance moral and social values. Active in the Republican Party for many years, it seeks to take the American nation back to its true heritage and to restore the godly principles that made the nation great. It represents many of the hopes, fears and prejudices of 'ordinary' white families from small-town or suburban America. It is broadly conservative in its outlook and does not always see eye-to-eye with economic conservatives.

Most members of the Religious Right emphasise that they have been 'born again', in other words their religious life has been dramatically altered by a conversion experience that has made them see issues very differently. They tend to be fundamentalist (accepting the literal truth of the Bible) and are unquestioning in accepting Christian doctrines. Some 15% of the electorate in the United States tell pollsters they are allied with the Religious Right. Many of its supporters can be found in the Christian Coalition (see adjacent box), whose values are consistent with those of the Religious Right.

Supporters of the Religious Right are distinguished by their moral fervour. The telegenic Pat Robertson is a leading spokesman. He founded the Christian

---

THE CHRISTIAN COALITION

The Coalition's website states: 'Christian Coalition of America is a political organisation, made up of pro-family Americans who care deeply about becoming active citizens for the purpose of guaranteeing that government acts in ways that strengthen, rather than threaten, families. As such, we work together with Christians of all denominations, as well as with other Americans who agree with our mission and with our ideals.'

Among current Christian Coalition policies are:

- the abolition of federal endorsement for the arts;
- the elimination of the federal and state departments of education;
- a cap on spending on AIDS research and treatment;
- compulsory reporting of AIDS carriers;
- the mandatory teaching of creationism;
- the abolition of abortion;
- support for capital punishment;
- the restriction of pre-school education;
- the rejection of gun control.

Coalition in 1988 and presided over it until February 2001. In a compilation of answers given on his daily talk show, the *700 Club*[20] – a mixture of faith-healing, hymns and Christian-oriented news – he informs his listeners that, in the outlook of 'liberals', it is wrong to ridicule Hispanics, blacks, the disabled, women, the gays and lesbians, but it is 'open season' to ridicule and humiliate, denigrate and insult the Christians 'as it was with the Jews in Nazi Germany'. He portrays the women's movement as a 'socialist, anti-family, political movement that encourages women to leave their husbands, kill their children, practise witchcraft and become lesbians'. He thunders that: 'God does not want us to turn America over to radical feminists, militant homosexuals, profligate spenders, humanists or world communists'.

Following a loss of influence in the late 1980s, the Religious Right rethought its strategy. Its approach became more sophisticated. It was increasingly based on building up grassroots support, by involving people at the local level on the city council and the school board – as well as aiming for the more obvious congressional targets. In 2000 and 2004, enthusiasts for the cause mailed or handed out millions of 'scorecards', showing the voting records of congressmen on 'issues critical to the family'.

Once in local office, Christian representatives on school boards seek to eliminate 'irreligious' material, particularly books which mention alternative

History and tactics

Under the leadership of Pat Robertson and Ralph Reed, the Christian Coalition quickly became the most prominent voice in the conservative Christian movement. Reed took control of day-to-day operations of the Coalition in 1989. Under his leadership, its approach became more organised and sophisticated. It was based on building up grassroots support, by involving people at the local level on the city council and the school board – as well as aiming for the more obvious congressional targets. Evangelical Christians were encouraged directly to involve themselves in the political process. During sermons, they were exhorted to vote, with the advice usually pointing to the Republicans as the appropriate party for godly Christians to support. This was made easy, for members of the congregation were often given sample ballot papers showing how and where to mark support for the required candidates.

Declining fortunes

The peak of the Coalition's influence culminated in an effort to support the election of a conservative Christian to the presidency in 1996. Since then, the Christian Coalition has made only limited progress. Following Bill Clinton's re-election and Reed's departure in 1997, the organisation declined in influence, financial stability (it had serious problems with the Internal Revenue Service), resources and staffing, although it continues to function on a reduced scale.

lifestyles and such things as abortion or witchcraft: for example, Roald Dahl's *The Witches* has been banned from school library shelves by some boards. Teachers have been told that they should teach 'creation science' (the story of the world's creation as told in Genesis) as well as – or in some cases instead of – Darwinian theories of evolution. The Bible is seen as literally true and to be regarded as the prime resource of learning. Other books which do not meet the necessary criteria include works by Martin Luther King, C.S. Lewis, Rudyard Kipling and A.A. Milne. There are now some 2,250 school boards in the United States, and the Religious Right reckons to control 15% of them.

Within the Republican Party, there is a schism. More traditional party regulars have long feared a takeover of the party. The Christian Coalition is similarly contemptuous of what it portrays as 'country-club' Republicans of the old type, who somewhere along the way lost their conservative agenda and became 'me-tooists', too close to the Democrats. Its policies have much appeal in middle America, which has over the last generation had to come to grips with the sexual revolution and the rise of left-wing radical activism, and doesn't like what it sees. Members stress pro-life policies, and take a firm line on issues such as abortion, birth control, embryonic stem cell research, evolution, gay rights and any other developments that they see as damaging to the nation's moral standards. Some even talk enthusiastically of a wish to export convicts to Mexico, which is prepared to take them for a price and incarcerate them more cheaply.

The Religious Right was temporarily in retreat after the failure of the Clinton impeachment trial, which its supporters strongly backed. But it remains a highly potent electoral force on the American political scene, active at the local level between presidential elections and influential within the Republican Party when those elections take place. White evangelical Christians were targeted by Republican campaign organiser Karl Rove in 2004, for he realised that many of them had not voted four years earlier. Their mobilisation played a key part in getting President Bush re-elected. Exit polls suggested that 'moral values' had been the most important issue in determining the outcome of the vote. Eight out of ten of those for whom such values were the paramount concern voted for George Bush.

The white evangelical Christian vote in 2008

The Religious Right was less active in 2008 than it had been four years earlier. The major reason for its lack of enthusiasm was the absence of a candidate who inspired it. John McCain did not emphasise the issues dear to religious conservatives, although he had long claimed his personal backing for the pro-life position on issues such as abortion.

In spite of Barack Obama's concerted effort to reach out to people of faith, Pew Research suggests that there was still a sizeable gap between the support he received from white evangelical Protestants and his support among the religiously unaffiliated. Sixty-four per cent of the white evangelical Christian vote went to McCain, 35% to Obama.

One of the leading figures of the Religious Right today is the Reverend Rod Parsley, a champion of theocracy ('rule by God' or 'God in power') or what he sometimes calls a 'christocracy'. At his World Harvest Church in Ohio, he and his followers talk of establishing dominion over society in the name of God and of 'reclaiming America for Christ'. Parsley is a critic of liberal attitudes to social issues, particularly the desire to define marriage to include same-sex couples. He has, however, tended to side with more liberal organisations on matters of social justice, such as poverty, justice and women's rights. He personally endorsed the presidential campaign of Republican nominee John McCain in 2007, but the candidate later rejected the endorsement because of Parsley's statement on Islam, which in his view is a false religion that must be destroyed.

The Tea Party movement and the Republican Party

The populist Tea Party movement emerged after the election of Barack Obama to the presidency. Its members are conservatives who dislike many of his policy initiatives, but are also disenchanted with the performance of many Republican politicians in recent years. It describes itself on its website in this way: 'The Tea Party is a grassroots movement that calls awareness to any issue that challenges the security, sovereignty or domestic tranquility of our beloved nation . . . From our founding, the Tea Party is the voice of the true owners of the United States, we the people.'

Tea Party protesters are proud to take their name from the most celebrated anti-government insurrection in American history, the Boston Tea Party of December 1773, carried out by 'the brave men and women . . . who dared defy the greatest military might on earth'. The exact antecedents of the movement are disputed, for there are various claims to its authorship. Most commonly, it is dated back to an observation made in Chicago by Rick Santelli of the CNBC business news cable network. Enraged by the Obama administration's plan to bail out mortgage owners who had taken out loans they could not afford, he asked whether it was time for a 'Chicago Tea Party', at which traders could gather and dump their derivatives in the Chicago River.

The name caught on and Tea Party groups began to take root across the United States. In April 2009, Tea Partiers staged anti-tax protests across the country. Shortly afterwards, rallies were planned to denounce the proposals for healthcare reform that they so much disliked. In September, they staged what was perhaps the largest conservative protest demonstration in US history. The movement has continued to grow. The precise scale of its support is difficult to assess because it is a movement rather than a structured party. One poll for NBC/the *Wall Street Journal* found that 40% of voters had a positive view of it, compared with 35% for the Republicans and 35% for the

Democrats. On this count, it had become the most popular political 'organisation' in the land.

As with any movement, it has some internal divisions. Some individuals and groups compete for influence with others. In particular, the personality of Sarah Palin (see pp. 280–281) is controversial, many Tea Partyers admiring her enthusiasm, forthrightness and pronounced anti-Washington feelings, but being wary of the possibility that she may be seeking to use their movement for her own political ends, and especially to help her win the Republican nomination in the future. They do not want to form a new political structure, nor do they want her as their leader. They wish to change politics from within the existing structure.

The political stance of the Tea Party

Supporters of the Tea Party protest are conservatives of a very fundamentalist and angry variety. It is easier to say what they oppose than what they positively favour, their regular targets being runaway government spending, large deficits, high taxation, Obama's healthcare reform and immigration. The economic stimulus package aroused particular fury, many ordinary Americans being disgusted by some of the events that they associated with it in their minds, such as bailouts of the undeserving – whether greedy Wall Street bankers, incompetent car companies or those who bought homes the price of which was beyond their means. A powerful libertarian, anti-establishment strand pervades all their concerns and feelings. This is why the movement appeals to independents who refuse to align themselves with either established party.

It is, however, the Republican Party that is most affected by the rise of the Tea Partyers, whose goal is to take over the carcass of the Republican Party and reform it according to its original principles. In the short term, the Tea-Partyers' campaigning benefits the Grand Old Party. They are anti-Washington, and Washington was under Democrat control in the early years of the Obama administration. Republicans were keen to galvanise the mood of popular resentment, in order to make substantial gains in the mid-term elections. They were encouraged by the way in which the *Tea Party Express*, the Tea Party movement's paper, lambasted Democratic leaders in the White House and on Capitol Hill. The shock Republican win in Massachusetts (February 2010) in the election to fill Senator Edward Kennedy's former seat illustrated just why the Democrats had reason for concern.

Yet some moderate Republicans detect a potential problem for the future. In 2010, there was a convergence of thought and interest between Republicans intent on regaining political control and activists keen to send more conservatives to Congress. The danger is that the Tea Party will push Republicans so far to the right that the party could become unelectable because of a loss of broad appeal. Moreover, moderate Republicans may increasingly face challenges from conservatives in primary elections, and this could pose problems for party unity and risk a split in the potential Republican vote.

The Tea Party movement and the 2010 mid-term elections

In 2010, Tea Party-endorsed candidates upset established Republicans in several primaries, including Alaska, Colorado, Delaware, Florida, Nevada, New York, South Carolina and Utah, thereby giving a new momentum to the conservative cause in the 2010 elections. The *New York Times* (14 October 2010) identified 138 candidates for Congress who had significant Tea Party support, all of them Republicans (129 were running for the House of Representatives, 9 for the Senate). A *Wall Street Journal*–NBC News poll in mid-October showed that 35% of likely voters were Tea Party supporters, and that they favoured the Republicans by 84% to 10%.

Tea Party-backed candidates generally did well in the 2010 mid-term elections, particularly in elections to the House. While some of the more idiosyncratic candidates lost their races, overall the movement significantly helped the Republicans to gain control of the House. On the other hand, it may have cost the Republican Party victory in the Senate. Rand Paul helped the Republicans convincingly to hold their Senate seat in Kentucky. Marco Rubio triumphed in a three-way fight to become senator for Florida. But in Nevada, the Democrat leader in the Senate, Harry Reid, successfully fought off Tea Party challenger Sharron Angle. There were also defeats for high-profile Tea Partyers such as Christine O'Donnell in the Delaware Senate race and Carl Paladino in the New York gubernatorial battle.

The overall result for the Tea Party was, therefore, mixed. With some races still undecided, MSNBC calculated on 9 November 2010 that only 32% of Tea Party candidates had won. At least eighty-two Tea Party candidates lost their races, though many of those losses had been expected. Identifying Tea Party candidates was an inexact process. MSNBC included anyone who either had been backed by a Tea Party group or had identified themselves as a member of the movement. Toward the end of the election campaign, however, many Republicans were trying to associate themselves with the movement.

Party organisation

Mass party organisation developed soon after the Constitution was designed, and was under way in the 1790s. Since then, the grassroots has always been a significant source of power. Whereas in Britain the party headquarters has substantial control over the local party, in America it is the other way round. Indeed, at a national level, parties only come together four-yearly to bring about the election of their presidential candidates.

American parties are, then, for most of the four-year cycle, loose alliances of state and local parties, and this **decentralisation** reflects the federal nature of the system of government. Indeed, parties are more decentralised than the system of government, which is why Malcolm Shaw[21] described the party system as 'confederal'. There are so many offices for election in the United States at state

decentralisation
Dispersal of decision-making power, in this case to local branches of the party organisation, so that the party is regulated at the state/local level rather than the national level.

and county level, and even lower, that the local party workers have many aspects on which to concentrate their attention. Their concern with Washington seems a far cry from this local preoccupation.

In the more centralised British system of party organisation, agents have a role at the constituency, regional and national level, all of them being trained in and supervised from London. In the US there is no comparable system. Local parties in America are not watched over in the same way. They have a free hand to choose their candidates without referring to headquarters. There is no list of 'approved' candidates provided from the centre, and it is highly unusual for there to be any attempt by the centre at influence or interference. The decision rests with the local party, though the system of primaries and the limitations on funding mean that each individual candidate plays a substantial role in securing his or her own election.

The national role of parties is relatively small. Every four years, Democratic and Republican headquarters come to life; in between, they contract. They do not have the powers to control local or state bodies, issue binding policy positions or censure members or elected representatives who stray from official party policy.

The national and local structure of the two main parties

Generalisation about the organisation of the two main parties is difficult, for the situation undergoes periodic change. For instance, the balance of power between minority activists and traditional party power brokers is liable to fluctuate. Similarly, because the party system is decentralised and the state parties can go their own ways, the structural pattern is not identical throughout the nation. Nevertheless, it is broadly similar, even if it can vary in details from state to state.

The key functions of parties are concerned with choosing candidates for office, perhaps via the organisation of primaries, and especially with mobilising support behind the person who is chosen. Each tier of the party structure is therefore primarily concerned with elections in its own geographical area and is largely autonomous.

The Republican and Democratic National Committees (RNC and DNC) are the main national organisation in each party. The headquarters in Washington DC operates under the direction of the party's national chair, and is run day to day by a small paid office staff plus volunteers. Their job is to prevent the national party organisation fading away completely between presidential elections. Members meet a few times a year, survey the political scene and make pronouncements. The committees do some research work, produce occasional publications for party activists and are involved in raising money. But their main work is to clear up the finances of the party after the presidential election and plan for the next convention four years thence, choosing the location and making organisational arrangements.

The National Convention (see also p. 253–254) of each party is held four yearly. Conventions are the arenas in which key players in the party seek to shape the future direction of party policy, and – if they are successful in capturing the presidency – of the nation as well. Their main task is to choose the presidential candidate. Effectively, candidates have usually already been chosen, having built up sufficient convention votes via the primaries and the party caucuses (held in states where there are no primaries). However, if there were to be any uncertainty, this is where the choice would be resolved. A vice-presidential candidate is also chosen, and a platform on policy is agreed. The Convention then serves as the launch-pad for the bid to win the ultimate prize, the presidency itself.

Traditionally, the essential business at a Republican gathering was done behind closed doors, whereas the Democrats have been more open about their dealings and more willing to have rows in public. Things have changed in recent decades. In 1976 the Reagan supporters staged a challenge to the incumbent Gerald Ford on the Convention floor, and twelve years later the proceedings were again lively and acrimonious as six challengers pleaded for the nomination.

At the state and local levels, organisation is carried out on the same lines. Each state has a state committee, headed by a state chair. Below state level, there are county committees, with varying functions and powers. At all levels, it is the choice and election of candidates for local office that is the key task. For winnable vacancies, there may be a primary contest. Where success is unlikely, it may be more a question of finding a candidate who will allow his or her name to go forward.

Recent trends

Traditionally, American parties have been decentralised coalitions of state and local parties, with a very limited role for the national organisations. However, since the 1960s, there have been a number of contradictory trends in the development of parties. In general, there has been a weakening of their role in selecting candidates, making policy, raising funds, informing the voter and channelling the demands of groups in society. Yet at the same time, via party reforms, there has been a strengthening of national party organisations, especially regarding the selection of delegates to the party Conventions.

The reforms in party organisations originally stemmed from a desire, especially among elements in the Democratic Party, to reduce the power of party regulars from the states and increase participation by the voters in the process of choosing a presidential candidate. The Democrats introduced changes along these lines in the early 1970s and the Republicans also tried to encourage participation by minority groups and ease access to selection meetings. These reforms strengthened the role of the national organisations, but two other developments weakened the power of national parties:

1 The increase in the number of presidential primaries, which led to the growth of more candidate-oriented campaigns.
2 A change in the type of people who participated in the nomination of presidential candidates. Party leaders at state and local levels have less weight and the role of minority groups has increased.

The theses of party decline and of party renewal

The thesis of **party decline**, as developed by several commentators, suggested that the two main parties had been overwhelmed by the range of challenges that confronted them and were unable to adapt to the changing political environment. Writing in 1972, Broder[22] contended that national parties were in retreat in areas they had traditionally dominated, particularly in their most basic function, selecting and running candidates for public office. There was widespread agreement that parties, always weak, were in a seemingly irreversible cycle of decline, unable to respond effectively to changing circumstances.

Since 1980, this sombre view has been questioned and there has been discussion of whether and to what extent the country is undergoing **party renewal**. J. Bibby wrote on *Party Renewal in the Republican Party*[23] and A.J. Reichley on *The Rise of National Parties*.[24] They claimed that the evidence presented in the 1960s had been largely misinterpreted and that (certainly by the 1980s) parties had begun to adapt successfully. They saw evidence of party vitality, indeed of 'renewal'.

party decline
The thesis advanced by many political commentators of the 1970s and early 1980s, which detected that American parties were 'in decline' or even 'in crisis'. They were losing members and were in danger of becoming sidelined.

party renewal
The thesis advanced by political commentators around the turn of the twenty-first century who detected evidence of the renewed vitality of American parties, which were assuming greater importance in electioneering, fund raising and the more partisan atmosphere of Congress.

From this side of the Atlantic, Christopher Bailey[25] saw the 'most clear evidence of the continued vitality of the political parties . . . in the Republican Party', but felt that by the mid-1980s the Democrats were also 'showing signs of continued vitality'. He quoted various commentators who believed that political action committees (PACs), often seen as having 'rendered the parties obsolete', actually supplemented rather than challenged the work of parties; indeed, they 'often follow the party's lead when deciding which candidates to support. Moreover, many PACs have aligned themselves with either the Democratic Party or the Republican Party because of shared beliefs and values.'

There has been a modest resurgence of parties in recent years. They have shown that they can perform a useful, if limited, role. Partly, this has come about because the new issues of the 1960s and 1970s have lost some of their importance, but it is mainly connected with the new emphasis on strengthening party organisation at the federal level and reviving the party role in fund raising. Both parties strengthened their national organisations in the 1980s, making them more professional and effective.

In the Republican Party, a set of structural changes and intellectual and policy initiatives of the late 1970s, known collectively as the 'Brock reforms', strengthened the role of the national party. **William Brock** set out to unify the party's organisation at national, congressional, state and local levels, placing much emphasis on aiding party candidates for elective office. Another important development has been the attempts by the national bodies to regain some of the control over the selection of presidential candidates that they had lost with the increasingly widespread use of primary elections. The choices of George W. Bush over John McCain in 2000 and of John Kerry over Howard Dean four years later both reflected the preferences of members of the party hierarchy.

This increased influence over nomination was made more possible within the Democratic Party by the introduction of **superdelegates**, who were given ex officio seats at the National Convention. As uncommitted delegates who account for some 20% of the delegate votes, there was speculation in 2008 that in the close race between Barack Obama and Hillary Clinton they might play a decisive role in selecting the nominee, a prospect that caused unease among some Democratic Party leaders. In the event, however, Obama won a majority of the pledged

William Brock

Brock was a former member of both chambers of Congress who became chairman of the RNC for four years, from January 1977. His administrative reforms were designed to revive Republican fortunes following the defeat of Gerald Ford' s bid for re-election in 1976. His work provided the foundation for the Republican gains of 1980.

superdelegates

Elected officials, such as party officials and members of Congress, whose uncommitted status at the Democratic Party National Convention can make them influential. (Most convention delegates are selected on the basis of the primaries and caucuses held in each state.)

delegates and of the superdelegates, and won the Democratic presidential nomination. (The Republicans also seat some party officials as delegates without regard to primary or caucus results, but the term 'superdelegate' is usually applied only in the Democratic Party.)

Both parties have developed new techniques of fund raising that make them useful and enable them to play once more a significant role in election campaigning. Candidates challenging for office have been keen to seek help from the increasingly more professional party associations, which can provide them with personal training, information networks, news clippings and research on their opponents, expertise in targeting particular precincts, as well as some financial help. Aldrich[26] concludes that 'they [the parties] have become more truly national parties, better financed, more professionalised and more institutionalised, with greater power to shape the actions of their state and local organisations'.

In 2008, the two main parties retained their predominance in presidential elections, the challenge posed by third-party candidates having effectively been 'seen off'. Other evidence in favour of 'resurgence' includes:

- the high degree of partisanship in the era of George Bush, which provoked many Democrats into uniting against the man who 'stole' the White House in 2000;
- the lack of minority party representation in Congress; even those who have claimed to be independent have normally aligned themselves with one of the main parties;
- greater party unity in Congress;
- the continued importance of the parties in fund raising and campaigning. As Hernnson[27] explains: 'Rather than parties running candidates for office, candidates run for office and seek to attract the resources of parties and other bodies for their own use. [However], it is still easier for most candidates to obtain [resources] from the parties than from alternative sources';
- some evidence of more party activity at the grassroots level, in developing organisations and in campaigning.

If anything, there are today two parties competing for office that are more sharply polarised than for many years. The disappearance of the bulk of the white, conservative element among the southern Democrats and the decline of the liberal element among the Republicans (especially in the northeastern states), has made the two parties more cohesive and provided them with a clearer ideological identity than was the case a few decades ago.

Bailey[28] provides some balance to the debate about resurgence. As he has indicated, 'it is clear that attempts to characterise the developments of the last two decades are extremely problematic'. Because of the fact that different writers draw upon different evidence – or interpret the same evidence in a different manner – some portray a picture of party decline, others one of renewal.

Party weakness and decline: a summary

American political parties are essentially weak and always have been, especially by comparison with parties in many other democracies.

Reasons for the historic weakness of parties include:

- The federal system places emphasis on the role of state rather than national parties.
- The concept of the separation of powers encourages members of a party in Congress to question even a president of their own party.
- The notion of broad consensus in American politics covers a range of fundamental issues.
- The ethos of individualism in American society is a feature of the widely shared American Dream.

Parties became weaker in the twentieth century because:

- The growth of the system of primary elections made candidates less beholden to the parties.
- The development of the mass media led to more candidate-oriented electioneering.
- The 'new issues' that arrived on the political agenda often crossed party lines – for example feminism and environmentalism.
- The increasing importance of pressure groups and PACs provided a new basis of support for candidates.

Parties enjoyed some resurgence in the late twentieth century because:

- Some of the new issues went off the agenda.
- PACs and groups began to work with parties, rather than as a replacement for them.
- Internal party reforms were carried out in the 1970s and thereafter.
- Parties have adapted to the role of working with and supporting candidates and been in the forefront of adopting new electioneering techniques.
- The parties have become more cohesive, having each shed an important element in their former make-up.

Today, most people still think of politics in terms of the Democrat–Republican divide and congressmen are almost entirely elected according to their party label. Parties do matter, both for politicians and for the electorate.

PARTIES IN BRITAIN AND THE UNITED STATES: A COMPARISON

Similarities

- In both democracies, parties fulfil some similar functions, notably clarifying the issues, stimulating public interest, supporting (in Britain choosing) candidates, organising the voters and providing an institutional framework for legislators.

- Both are often described as two-party systems, there traditionally having been only two main parties. Several small parties exist on either side of the Atlantic, but the electoral system ensures that in most situations they are unlikely to have a significant impact on the outcome of elections; there are formidable hurdles for them to overcome.

- Both countries have 'left' and 'right', progressive and conservative, parties. Labour and the Democrats have traditionally been more willing to accept governmental intervention and expand social welfare; the Conservatives and the Republicans have been more attracted by less government and lower taxes. Both Labour and the Democrats have had to accept that the centre of gravity in the political system moved to the right in the Thatcher–Reagan-dominated 1980s, and subsequently responded to this. However, all of the four main parties are aware of the need to adopt policies that make them electable; they see the importance of maintaining a broad appeal.

- Of the two main British parties, one has traditionally been viewed as a socialist party, whereas in America socialism has failed to take root. But in this respect, the two countries have moved closer. The New Labour of the Blair years was not usually described as 'socialist' in any meaningful sense, other than by its opponents. It moved some way to detach itself from the unions, making it more akin in style to the American Democrats. Significantly, both Bill Clinton (New Democrat) and Tony Blair (New Labour) advocated similar 'third way' politics, shunning the old 'big government' and 'tax and spend' attitudes of bygone years and instead being willing to use the power of government, yet also to encourage personal responsibility.

From a British perspective, it is easy to overstate the importance of parties at national level, and stress too much their decline or renewal. Commentators and academics on this side of the Atlantic sometimes place the emphasis on the national parties, especially their role in the nomination of presidential candidates, the most interesting and glamorous aspect of the process. But this is not the main arena for party activists and, as Alan Ware[29] has noted, 'in the federal structure it has always been at the local and state levels of politics that the parties have . . . had their main bases of power; contests for the presidency are merely the smallest but most highly visible apex of party politics'.

Differences

- Britain has party government. Under usual circumstances, a party wins an election and afterwards is in control of both the executive and the legislature. Having had its programme accepted by the electorate, it is expected to govern. To do so, it requires cohesive and disciplined parties if it is to act effectively. America does not have party government in the same sense. Party allegiance is one factor, borne in mind when decisions are made about public policy, but there is no expectation that the 'party line' will be followed. Often, key figures in American government are admired precisely because they do not adopt the party stance on issues of the day. Parties are less disciplined, although in Congress it is true that almost without exception members are identified as belonging to one of the two main parties.

- British parties are more centralised than American ones. Although they often try to assert their independence (particularly in the Conservative Party), the trend has been for British constituency parties to be dominated by the party leadership and the controlling influence of central party headquarters. Americans developed mass party organisations before Britain, partly because universal male franchise was introduced sooner than in this country. Grassroots organisation has long been well established and significant in the US and this – and the lack of strong leadership from Washington – makes for decentralisation. American state and local parties come together every four years to elect their president. At that time, the national headquarters plays an important role in electioneering, but in between presidential contests its role is more modest.

The differences between the role and approach of parties within the two systems have much to do with the American Constitution, which was designed to disperse power in two ways. Firstly, the Founding Fathers established a federal system across the country, and secondly, they were keen to create competitive institutions (the separation of powers). Both have the effect of making party government difficult and do much to undermine tight discipline.

CONCLUSION

Political parties provide an important link between the voters and their elected representatives. In the US, a two-party system has evolved, dominated by the Democrats and the Republicans. Other parties have been unable to make much headway, even if some have been on the political scene a long while. Many voters no longer feel the same loyalty towards the two parties that their parents and grandparents did and neither party can count on a permanent body of supporters. But most Americans still think in terms of the Democrat–Republican divide and are able to detect some difference between them. Parties remain important to candidates and office holders, as well as to the voters.

Parties are essential in any democracy. They fulfil important functions such as organising the competition for public offices, simplifying the policy choices available and helping to translate those choices – once made – into effective action. They may often be written off as being in decline, if not dead. But in many ways, they exhibit signs of renewed vitality.

REFERENCES

1 M. Duverger, *Political Parties: Their Organization and Activity in the Modern State*, Methuen, 1954
2 V. Key, *Politics, Parties and Pressure Groups*, Crowel, 1964
3 G. Wasserman, *The Basics of American Politics*, Longman, 1997
4 M. Vile, *Politics in the USA*, Hutchinson, 1978
5 'Competitiveness of Legislative Elections in the United States', at www.nyc.gov/html/om/pdf/2010/pr507-10_report.pdf.
6 J. Burns, J. Peltason, T. Cronin and D. Magleby, *Government by the People*, Prentice-Hall, 1994
7 V. Key, as in 2 above
8 M. Duverger, as in 1 above
9 M. Vile, as in 4 above
10 C. Rossiter, *Parties and Politics in America*, Signet, 1960
11 R. Hofstadter, *The Age of Reform: from Bryan to FDR*, Knopf, 1955
12 A. Gramsci, *Selections from the Prison Notebooks* (trans.), International Publishers, 1971
13 Lord Bryce, *Modern Democracies*, Macmillan, 1921
14 D. Brogan, *An Introduction to American Politics*, Hamish Hamilton, 1954
15 J.F. Kennedy, acceptance speech to the New York Liberal Party, 14 September 1960
16 I. Kristol, *Reflections of a Neoconservative*, Basic Books, 1983
17 *National Journal: 2007 Ratings*, National Journal Group, 2008
18 A. Schlesinger, *Cycles of American History*, Houghton Mifflin, 1986
19 C. Rossiter, as in 10 above
20 P. Robertson, *Bring it On*, W Publishing Group, 2002
21 M. Shaw, *Anglo-American Democracy*, Routledge and Kegan, 1968
22 D. Broder, *The Party's Over*, Harper and Row, 1972
23 J. Bibby, *Politics, Parties and Elections in America*, Wadsworth, 2000
24 A. Reichley, *The Life of the Parties: a History of American Political Parties*, Free Press, 1992
25 C. Bailey, 'Political Parties', *Contemporary Record* 3:3, February 1990
26 J. Aldrich, *Why Parties? The Origins and Transformation of Parties in America*, University of Chicago Press, 1995
27 P. Hernnson, *Party Campaigning in the 1980s*, Harvard University Press, 1988
28 C. Bailey, as in 25 above
29 A. Ware, 'Party Decline and Party Reform', in L. Robins (ed.), *The American Way*, Longman, 1985

USEFUL WEB SITES

www.democrats.org Democratic National Committee. Details of many aspects of recent election campaign and party platform; issues of interest to the party.

www.rnc.org Republican National Committee. Details of many aspects of recent election campaign and party platform; issues of interest to the party.

Several third parties have interesting sites, explaining their histories and different policy positions:

www.constitutionparty.com Constitution Party.

www.greens.org Green Parties of North America.

www.liberalparty.org New York Liberal Party.

www.lp.org Libertarian Party.

www.perot.org Official Ross Perot site.

www.reformparty.org Reform Party.

www.sp-usa.org Socialist Party.

www.ustaxpayers.org United States Taxpayers Party.

SAMPLE QUESTIONS

1 What are the distinctive features of American political parties?
2 In what sense does America have a two-party system?
3 Why are third parties unable to flourish in the US?
4 Why has socialism failed in the United States?
5 How might the emergence of a successful national third party change the nature and role of the two main political parties? Is such a development likely?
6 'Both American parties have a similar outlook on fundamental issues in American politics.' What are the main areas of agreement and disagreement in their ideologies and policies?
7 Discuss the paradox that although there are few differences between the main parties, they continue to dominate the American political system.
8 Assess the current state and prospects of either the Democratic or the Republican Party.
9 Assess the importance of the Religious Right or the Tea Party movement in American politics.
10 'Party decline' or 'party renewal'? Do parties still play an important part in American politics?
11 Do American parties matter any more?
12 Compare the main British and US parties in respect of their ideas, sources of support and organisations.

Pressure groups: the lobby at work

10

In this chapter, we explore how individuals who share certain opinions come together to press their common outlook upon society and government. We have seen that this may be done via political parties. Here, we are concerned with the ways by which pressure groups lobby to propagate their views.

The leading groups are economic or occupational, but there is a huge variety of other civic, ethnic, ideological, racial and other bodies that have memberships that cut across the large economic groupings. In recent decades, many of them have moved on from lobbying alone and have become far more involved and significant in the electoral process. Concern has been expressed about some of their activities, leading to calls for greater regulation and vigilance.

POINTS TO CONSIDER

- What are the main functions performed by pressure groups in the USA?
- To distinguish the different types of pressure groups that exist in the USA.
- Which interests in American society are best represented by pressure groups?
- How do groups seek to achieve their aims?
- To what extent has the iron gone out of 'iron triangles'?
- To describe the main access points for US pressure groups.
- Why some groups are more effective than others.
- Does it matter that some sections of society are poorly represented?
- Should pressure groups be subjected to greater control?
- In what respects has the nature of group lobbying changed over recent decades?
- Is the influence of pressure groups generally benign or damaging to the workings of American democracy?
- Why are American pressure groups in general so powerful?
- Why is Congress more vulnerable to pressure group activity than the British Parliament?

There is a vast range of **pressure groups** in modern society. Some of these groups are long lasting, others are transient; some are national, others local; some are giants firmly rooted in the public mind, others are little known. They range from the well-known ones recognised by their initials (the American Medical Association and the American Civil Liberties Union, the AMA and ACLU, respectively), to much less high-profile ones, from Prostitutes of New York (a support and advocacy group for all people in the sex industry) to the American Restroom Association (which urges the availability of clean, safe, well-designed public toilets). They cover the whole spectrum of policy issues and are formed for an infinite variety of purposes. Many exist primarily to benefit the interests of members or to advance some specific cause. When such groups are concerned in some way to influence public policy, they are known as pressure groups. Those who do the influencing are known as **lobbyists**.

pressure groups
Pressure groups are organised bodies that seek to influence government and the development of public policy, by defending their common interest or promoting a cause.

lobbyists
Employees of organised groups who exert pressure on members of the legislature and executive, with a view to modifying public policy.

Why Americans join groups

Today, most Americans belong to at least one voluntary association, be it a church, a social or sports club or an organisation concerned to promote civil liberties or rights. Minorities and women have been active in organising to demand access to the social and political benefits long denied to them. Women have sought to ensure that their rights are recognised in law, as well as to speak out on the central issues of procreation and reproduction. Forming groups is a natural thing for people to do, for man is essentially a social creature. But there is also another sound motivation for joining together with other people. Individuals are rarely sufficiently influential on their own that they can hope to influence policy and decisions that affect their lives. Therefore, they act together in order to secure the introduction, prevention, continuation or abolition of whatever measures they feel are important to them. After visiting the United States in the 1830s, Alexis de Tocqueville[1] was impressed by the way in which 'Americans of all ages, all conditions, and all dispositions constantly form associations' which had, in his view, become a 'powerful instrument of action'. In his view their existence was to be celebrated as an indication – indeed a bastion – of a healthy democracy.

This associative tendency constitutes a country's **civil society**. It includes those public groups that are above the personal realm of the family but

civil society
Civil society comprises mainly voluntary organisations and civil associations that allow individuals to work together in groups, freely and independently.

beneath the state. It covers a variety of bodies such as registered charities, development nongovernmental organisations, community groups, women's organisations, faith-based organisations, professional associations, trade unions, self-help groups, social movements, business associations and advocacy groups. These are areas of social life – the domestic world, the economic sphere, cultural activities and political interaction – which are organised by voluntary arrangements between individuals and groups, outside and beyond the direct control of the state.

The scale of lobbying

For many years, lobbyists have played a significant role in the legislative process, a role that has increased with the enlargement of governmental activity in the era since the New Deal. The term 'lobby' includes a vast array of groups, operating at several levels and covering commercial and industrial interests, labour unions, consumer associations, ethnic and racial groups. In the mid-1950s, the *Encyclopaedia of Associations* listed less than 5,000 national organisations. In the early twenty-first century, it lists some 25,000. Representation of companies in Washington has greatly increased, but more dramatic has been the explosion in the number of public-interest organisations and grassroots groups. These barely existed at all before the 1960s; today, they number in the tens of thousands and collect more than $4 billion per year from 40 million individuals.[2] More than nine out of every ten Americans belong to at least one voluntary grouping, be it a church, civil rights organisation, social club of some kind or other public body. On average, each American will belong to four groups.

Under the Legislative Reorganisation Act (1946), lobbyists were required to register with the relevant offices of the Senate and the House, and provide details of their work and funding. At that time, there were fewer than 2,000 registered lobbyists with Congress, but now the number registered approaches 9,000. But this figure omits the vast array of individual corporations, state and local governments, universities, think-tanks and other organisations in the private sector that engage in lobbying at some level, as well as the myriad of Washington representatives, ranging from lawyers to public relations agencies, which do similar work.

Organisations such as the Ford Motor Company not only belong to the appropriate interest group; they also maintain their own lobbying staff in Washington. Most other business corporations retain a sizeable lobby in the city, partly for reasons of prestige but also as a means of using any opportunity to influence laws and regulations. Similarly, labour unions and groups representing sections of society, such as the elderly, and causes, such as the environment, maintain well-manned permanent offices. All wish to exert pressure at some level of government, many of them in Washington (either at

The top fifteen lobbying organisations in 2009, based on total spending

Organisation	Total spend on lobbying ($)
Chamber of Commerce	144,496,000
Exxon Mobile	27,430,000
Pfizer Inc.	26,619,268
Pharmaceutical Research and Manufacturers of America	26,150,520
General Electric	25,520,000
Blue Cross/Blue Shield	23,310,439
AARP (formerly the American Association of Retired Persons)	21,0010,000
American Medical Association	20,830,000
Chevron Corporation	20,815,000
National Association of Realtors	19,477,000
American Beverage Association	18,850,000
American Hospital Association	18,347,176
ConocoPhillips	18,069,858
Verizon Communications	17,680,000
Boeing Co	16,850,000

Source: The Center for Responsive Politics at www.OpenSecrets.org.

the White House or on Capitol Hill). However, in recent years there has been a marked extension of lobbying activity within the states as well. The American political culture is tolerant of pressure group activity, and this encourages the creation of an array of organised interests. There are many **access points** for group representatives to explore. Because of their success, the average citizen looks as much to his or her voluntary groups for political satisfaction as to his or her elected representative.

> **access points**
> Those formal parts of the governmental structure that are accessible to pressure group influence. There are many such outlets via which groups can present their case, the more so given America's constitutional structure.

The key developments in pressure group formation

Period	Type of group	Example
1830–60	Creation of first national organisations	YMCA and anti-slavery groups
1880–1900	Creation of many business and labour bodies, in era of industrialisation	National Association of Manufacturers, American Federation of Labour
1900–20	Peak period for group formation	American Medical Association, Chamber of Commerce
1960–80	Creation of many environmental and public interest bodies	Common Cause, National Organisation for Women

Adapted from table in R. Hrebenar and R. Scott, Interest Group Politics in America, Prentice Hall, 1997.

NB An updated version might indicate the rise of groups associated with the Religious Right (such as the Christian Coalition) and the range of socio-moral causes on which they campaign. For instance, many groups exist to advance stem cell research (Texans for Advancement of Medical Research and The Michael J. Fox Foundation for Parkinson's Research) and civil marriages (Freedom to Marry).

Some relevant definitions

By the **lobby** we mean all those groups that seek to influence public policy, whether they are primarily promotional or propaganda bodies or those that seek to defend the interests of their group or organisation. The word 'lobby' originally derives from the location where the process occurred, the anteroom or lobby outside the chambers of Congress where representatives could be intercepted and urged to support a particular cause when they voted. Hotel lobbies have sometimes provided a similar venue, and lobbyists are those who wait there hoping for a chance meeting. To lobby is to seek to bring influence on legislators and officials. Lobbyists are therefore employees of associations who try to influence policy decisions, especially in the executive and legislative branches of government.

By **pressure groups** we refer to associations of people who come together on the basis of shared attitudes to try to influence public policy. This may involve lobbying governmental institutions or their representatives or seeking to influence voters at election time. Such groups are different from political parties, which are also bodies that include within their membership people who share a broadly agreed approach to the conduct of affairs.

Pressure groups and political parties

Pressure groups are voluntary associations formed to advance or defend a common cause or interest. They are unlike political parties in that:

- They do not wish to assume responsibility for governing the country, rather they seek to influence those who do so.

- They have a narrower range of concerns than parties, which seek to draw together a variety of interests in order to broaden their appeal; pressure groups have a limited focus, many of their aspirations being non-political.

Because their concerns are liable to be affected by government decisions, pressure groups need to be organised in order to influence policy makers and respond to what they propose.

Some writers dislike speaking of 'pressure groups', for the term may seem to imply the use of force rather than persuasion. American academics tend to use the term 'interest groups' instead. As we shall see, this label does not cover the whole range of associations with which we are concerned. Whichever term is used – and we will use the broader term 'pressure groups' – there is a further distinction which can be made between **interest or protective groups** (for example the American Medical Association), which are primarily self-interested and seek to protect or defend the position of their members, and **promotional groups** (for example the American Civil Liberties Union), which are primarily concerned with propaganda.

Insider and outsider groups: applying the Grantian distinction to the US

The British academic Wyn Grant[3] developed a different categorisation of groups to the long-standing protective/promotional one. He made a distinction between **insider and outsider groups**.

Insider groups are those that have most influence with government because of the expertise they can provide and the help they can offer in making and implementing policy (for example in Britain, the British Medical Association and the National Farmers Union). In the United States, the American Medical Association and the American Farm Bureau Federation are examples of bodies that have a close relationship with the relevant government department. Outsider groups are less influential, being able to give little assistance or trade-off in return for policy influence. Some groups are outsiders because they cannot achieve insider status. Other – often ideological – groups do not want such status.

There are difficulties with this distinction, as Grant himself later conceded. It is not clear cut because: some groups pursue insider and outsider strategies at the same time; more groups have insider status than Grant originally suggested (governments consult very widely with a range of groups, even if in some cases their influence is marginal); and the distinction is in any case less valid

> **insider and outsider groups**
>
> Insider groups are groups with access to senior government officials, are often recognised as the main representatives for particular interests and sometimes are formally incorporated into the official consultative process. They tend to represent business, professional and food-producing interests, examples being bankers and industrialists, doctors and lawyers, farmers and wine growers.
>
> Outsider groups are groups with no access to senior government officials. They lack the privileged position of insider groups, either because they lack bargaining power, are too critical of government or prefer to be on the outside and remain detached from government.

today because new forms of politics have arisen since it was first made in the 1980s. Pressure group politics have changed in several ways. In particular, there has been a growing emphasis on mass protest and direct action. Popular protest – often lacking formal leadership and relying on loose networks of activists – has benefited from communications technology and careful use of the media, both of which make it easier for popular movements to erupt suddenly and achieve their goal. Such activity does not fall easily into the classic typologies and methods of pressure group activity. It relies more on the implied threat that the government will lose votes in the next round of elections. In the United States, the Tea Party movement (see also p. 341) does not have, and may never have, an organisation. It is a loose collection of many groups. There does not appear to be strong impetus to form a third political party. It has no formal figurehead.

The insider/outsider categorisation works less well in the United States than in Britain because of the different structure of government in the two countries. As Grant later wrote:[4] 'Pressure groups remain a litmus test of where power is concentrated in a polity and, uniquely among the OECD countries, ultimate power in the US resides in the legislature on many issues. Hence, there is an understandable emphasis in US work on the Congress.' This is a key point, for the separation of powers in the US gives the legislature a greater role than it has in Britain. An American administration lacks the capacity of a British government to push its programme through the legislative chambers, so that there is much more concentration by large pressure groups on Congress, which has a key role in shaping legislation. In Britain, the most powerful groups concentrate their lobbying primarily on Whitehall rather than Westminster, for that is where decisions are made.

The former category includes the most influential American associations, which wield substantial economic power. Those in the latter category are usually less influential, promoting as they do some cause, idea or issue not of direct benefit to themselves or to those who belong, but of general benefit to society. Promotional groups tend to be smaller than protective ones, and comprise dedicated people who commit themselves to what are sometimes minority concerns.

The distinction above is not adopted by all writers, some preferring to speak of the lobby, others just using the terms 'interest groups' or 'pressure groups' to cover every type of association involved in the process. Woll and Zimmerman[5] employ the term 'interest groups' and define interests as 'concerns, needs, benefits, or rights that groups or individuals have or would like to have'. The areas in which people have interests include, among other things, business, the workplace, education, the environment, health and religion. These interests are shared by a number of people, who organise into groups to mobilise their common feelings. Hence, according to the two writers, interest groups are 'associations of persons who share common concerns, needs, benefits or rights and have as their purpose the satisfaction of claims to these. Usually, the claims are made on the government, and are met as a result of pressure.'

Inevitably, there are some organisations that do not fit neatly into the division referred to. A number of them protect the interests of their members and also do a fair amount of promotional work that increases their acceptability to the community at large. One of the most prominent of these **hybrid** bodies is the National Rifle Association (see box below). There are different motives for people to join together in this organisation. Some belong for reasons of commercial protection (they make or sell guns), others for ideological or

---

The National Rifle Association (NRA)

The NRA is perhaps the best-known American pressure group and the most successful in lobbying on Capitol Hill. It has over three million members, who are enthusiasts for shooting as both recreation and protection. It has successfully resisted most national attempts since the late 1960s to limit the ownership of guns, even though on occasion pressure for gun control has gained ground. In the last few years, it has paid more attention to state governments, for it is to that level that supporters of restriction have increasingly turned their attention.

The NRA's Institute for Legislative Action exercises a watching brief over any attempt by the federal or state governments to introduce limitations on the manufacture and sale of guns or on gun ownership. If there are any such initiatives, members are immediately alerted so that they can mount strong resistance, by phoning or e-mailing relevant officials, writing to newspapers, appearing on television or by any other appropriate method.

The NRA is currently seeking to widen its appeal, so that some of its recent propaganda has been targeted at minority groups and women.

self-interested reasons (owners of guns who see it as their constitutional right to bear them or who simply feel that they are necessary).

Distinguishable from such groups, by whatever label we adopt, are **movements**. A movement is a wider and more all-embracing organisation, and it includes all those people and groups who are interested or involved in a particular cause. Movements often develop from local activity and become part of a larger national campaign – in the way that individual small groups of women in the United States took up particular concerns that then became national causes to which many more women were committed. Within the Women's Movement today, there are several groups which pursue their own distinctive agendas, whether peace, child welfare or low pay. They share some ideas and approaches, but may differ on controversial issues such as abortion, as well as over the tactics to adopt in seeking the fulfilment of their aims. The Civil Rights Movement for equal treatment for black Americans has similarly spanned several organisations, as do those on animal rights and the environment.

The Tea Partyers: pressure group, movement or party?

The Tea Partyers, a grassroots network of discontented right-wingers, emerged in the first two years of the Obama administration, in protest against a number of its policies. Supporters are in some respects a rather disparate group, but they are united in their opposition to the president's healthcare programme, public spending and the growth of government, among other key causes. Tea Party enthusiasts can be found in several organisations and have contested elections, an illustration of the overlap that can exist between pressure groups, movements and political parties.

The Tea Party is a movement in that it spans a number of organisations that would individually qualify as pressure groups, including the Nationwide Tea Party Coalition, Americans for Prosperity, Tea Party Express, Tea Party Nation, Tea Party Patriots and the National Tea Party Federation. As is often the case with movements, there are disagreements within and between such bodies over the direction they follow, the goals they pursue and the methods they employ, with some competing with others for supremacy within the movement. There is also tension between the national and statewide groups, some Tea Partyers being wary of the large organisations that are trying to take them over; others dispute the exact path that should be taken in the future. In particular, there is a fear that Republican Party leaders might try to influence them in order to mould their agenda in a way more comfortable to many traditional Republicans.

Unlike a political party, the Tea Party movement has no official national spokesperson and no organised structure. Some supporters would like to turn the movement into a structured party, and indeed it does contest some primary and other elections; some of its supporters were elected in November 2010. Yet to become a party might weaken its appeal, for the creation of a leader, an internal bureaucracy and a detailed policy programme might give the impression that it is just another party, factional and unwilling to act in the national interest. (See pp. 321–323 and 365–366, for further explanation of the Tea Party phenomenon.)

Categories of American pressure groups

It is convenient to classify the lobby into broad groups. This can be done either by opting for the protective/promotional typology, or by categorising organisations according to the sector they claim to represent. The second approach is the one we will adopt here.

Business groups

Business is the most effective area of group activity, because it has the advantages of expertise, organisation and resources. It includes organisations that speak up for small firms (for example the National Federation of Independent Business), and much larger bodies such as the National Association of Manufacturers, which represents large corporations. The Chamber of Commerce claims a membership of some 300,000 businesses. In addition, there are 3,000 state and local chambers, some of which choose to affiliate with the US organisation.

Such **umbrella or peak organisations** have not tended to stress a Washington role, for their individual members often have representatives based in the capital. General Electric, Ford, General Motors and other industrial giants such as Union Carbide are also well represented in Washington. These corporations are so large and so vital in the American economy that politicians of all persuasions will listen to their concerns.

> **umbrella or peak organisations**
> These are broad-based organisations representing the interests of capital or labour to those in government. They speak for a range of similar interests, their members being other organisations rather than individuals. The National Association of Manufacturers represents many businesses across the country.

The business lobby is a powerful one, though it would be wrong to assume that the large range of groups (about 20% of all pressure groups) operate together as a powerful bargaining sector. 'Corporate America' is not a single entity with but one agreed objective. The interests of America's 15 million businesses diverge. In the 1980s, some leading manufacturers favoured high protective tariffs to fend off foreign competition. Others who operated more in the export market feared that such an approach would invite retaliation and damage their overseas prospects. Also, as we have seen, not all of these organisations focus on the same areas of decision making. Some operate in Washington, others elsewhere; some favour one target, others another. Because of such considerations, umbrella business organisations have much less influence in the United States than does the Confederation of British Industry in Britain.

Labour groups

Unions have always been less prominent in American politics than in Britain and other European countries, for the US workforce is less unionised than in many democracies. Unions lack the clout of many large corporations, and moreover they are numerically in decline, and suffer diminishing membership. They have more influence in the industrial areas such as the Northeast than in the South, which has traditionally been dominated by agrarian interests.

The largest umbrella body representing organised labour is the loose alliance known as the American Federation of Labour and the Congress of Industrial Organisations (AFL-CIO), to which ninety-six unions belong; it represents about 12% of the workforce. In common with other union organisations, it lobbies government on workers' conditions and rights (for example the minimum wage and job security) and business/trade matters of concern to the workforce. Long-standing individual unions include the United Automobile Workers (UAW), the International Brotherhood of Teamsters (lorry drivers), the International Ladies Garment Workers Union (ILGWU) and the United Steelworkers of America.

In industrial matters, unions can be militant in defence of workers' interests, but politically they play less of a role than in Britain. They carry more weight with the Democratic Party and may give it funds, although there have never been the formal, institutional links that exist between British unions and the Labour Party.

Professional groups

Professional bodies cater for the needs of accountants, doctors, educators, lawyers, scientists and others, and those groups within this category often have no interests in common other than their status. They may, as with the doctors and the lawyers, sometimes come into conflict – as, for instance, in a case concerning medical malpractice. Among the foremost professional associations in Washington, the American Bar Association and the National Education Association have been notably influential, the former having a substantial voice in the selection of judges, the latter having forced education to the forefront of national debate – to such an extent that in 1988 George Bush senior promised to run as the 'education president'.

In the area of health provision, the American Medical Association is the largest association of medical doctors and medical students in the United States. Its stated mission is to promote the art and science of medicine for the betterment of the public health, to advance the interests of physicians and their patients, to promote public health, to lobby for legislation favourable to physicians and patients, and to raise money for medical education (see box).

The American Medical Association

The American Medical Association is a federation of fifty state associations representing about 250,000 members, two-thirds of the nation's doctors. Throughout its history, it has been actively involved in a variety of medical policy issues, ranging from **Medicare** to public health, from reform of US health provision to climate change. In the early 1990s, it was much involved with other relevant interests in the struggle over the attempted reform of medical care. This led to a massive attempt to influence the thinking of congressmen and the general public, in an attempt to tone down the nature of the Clinton proposals.

> **Medicare**
>
> Medicare is a national social security programme introduced by President Johnson. It provides health insurance for Americans of 65 years and over.

Aware of the Clinton experience and of the influence the AMA carries, Barack Obama was careful to address the annual conference of the Association in June 2009, with a view to keeping the organisation on board. It subsequently issued a series of statements indicating support for Obama's goal of making health insurance accessible to all, but came out against a crucial component of his proposal, the creation of a publicly run insurance plan to compete with private plans.

While not the political behemoth it once was, the association probably has more influence than any other group in the healthcare industry. Lawmakers seek its opinion and support whenever possible. In recent years, it has repeatedly persuaded Congress to cancel or postpone cuts in Medicare payments to doctors.

Agricultural groups

Historically, farm organisations were particularly influential, for the agrarian community has been generously represented in the Senate and the House. This influence resulted in the passage of a number of emergency bills in the late 1970s. Much of the campaigning for these laws was conducted by the American Agriculture Movement, which often took a more militant line than the more conservative American Farm Bureau Federation, whilst both often found themselves in disagreement with the National Farmers Union.

As the number of family farms declined (the owners having often gone into debt), so agribusinesses, vast farms owned by large corporations, developed in their place. The arrival of business people – familiar with different and more sophisticated techniques of lobbying – has helped to change the image of agriculture. Professional lobbyists are now commonly employed in this field.

Public interest groups

Public interest groups include those that are concerned with the quality of government, consumerism and the environment. Common Cause, 'a national citizens' lobby', has both Democrat and Republican members. It seeks to 'open up' the processes of government, by such means as electoral reform and strict control over the financing of election campaigns. The League of Women Voters is also keen to promote better government, through greater public involvement. There is less disagreement between the various organisations operative in this area than in some other sectors. All are seeking to achieve goals designed to benefit the entire population.

Ideological and single-issue groups

Within the ideological sector there is a wide divergence of viewpoints between far left and far right. However, members of the groups are likely to share a broad philosophy and outlook, whatever the diversity of their backgrounds. The sizeable and well-known American Civil Liberties Union (ACLU) has been known to defend the rights of the American Nazi Party, a body which it abhors and which would, given power, almost certainly destroy the ACLU. It sometimes cooperates closely with very different organisations, such as the National Abortion Rights Action League, which is determined to retain the right to abortion and stresses a women's right to choose.

There is a vast array of associations that can be described as single-issue ones, and the abortion ones are currently among the most prominent (see pp. 392–393). Such issue groups have mushroomed since the 1960s, and gain public attention by a variety of techniques – ranging from writing to congressmen to taking action in the courts, from attending demonstrations to participating in other forms of direct action. Generally, they lack the funds available to large interest groups, and their influence often derives from their ability to show that they have the support of many voters.

How groups operate

Groups pursue their goals at various access points in the American system of government, partly depending on the objective to be achieved and the location where relevant decisions are made. Any organisation wishes to concentrate its attention at the level where it can have the greatest influence. Groups have traditionally operated at four main levels, the executive, the legislature, the judiciary and the public at large.

The executive

Lobbying is a proven way of applying pressure on government, and most groups employ full-time persons to perform the task; others may hire a professional lobbyist as necessary to represent their interests. Lobbyists are 'persuaders' who inhabit the world of Washington or the states, and they understand the functioning of the political system and often have useful personal contacts. As the seat of the federal government, Washington is the focus of much of their activity. More than 4,000 corporations are represented in the capital, and some 3,000 associations have an office there. According to one recent estimate,[6] in 2007 there were more than 17,000 federal lobbyists based in the capital.

Many corporations spend vast sums on lobbying in Washington, their lobbyists working in the so-called **K Street corridor**. They seek to influence legislation, some 2,000 having made submissions on the **Economic Stimulus Bill**, more than 1,200 on the **Health Care Reform Bill** and just over 1,000 on the American Clean Energy and Security Act of 2009.[7] On occasion, lobbyists devise bills that can then be introduced by members of Congress.

Some lobbyists have been lawyers, others have moved from working for the administration into lobbying. Lobbyists are highly skilled, and are selected because they are likely to be able to gain access where others cannot. Any lobbyist wishes to know the key personnel in the various agencies and bureaux of government, for more and more legislation derives from initiatives from within the executive branch. Interest groups have much to offer by way of specialist information, and the group lobbyist and members of the bureaucracy will often seek to develop a sound working relationship. Some writers refer to so-called 'iron triangles' (see p. 348) to describe the networks of mutually self-supporting lobbyists, bureaucrats and members of congressional committees, where key decisions of government are made.

Americans speak of the 'revolving door' to describe the easy movement of personnel between the executive and the interest groups. The suspicion lingers that, in making decisions whilst they are in office, politicians may bear in mind their possible need for a business position in the future with the very companies whose fate they are determining. Sometimes, the door – when opened – reveals a murky

K Street corridor

A Washington street in which many of the offices of powerful lobbying groups – covering activities in the realms of business, social sciences, international affairs, education, law and government – are headquartered. Examples include the Alliance for Aging Research, Leather Industries of America and the National Association of Water Companies.

Economic Stimulus Bill

The $787 billion economic stimulus package introduced by President Obama and subsequently approved by Congress in February 2009. The package was intended to jump start economic growth and save between 900,000 and 2.3 million jobs. See also The American Recovery and Reinvestment Act (February 2009) on p. 92 for further information.

Health Care Reform Bill

The bill passed in March 2010 to extend healthcare insurance to 32 million more people, predominantly the poorest, giving the country 95% coverage. It requires most Americans to purchase health insurance and provides higher subsidies to those who cannot afford it. (See also The Patient Protection and Affordable Care Act (March 2010) on p. 92, for further information).

world of behind-the-scenes influence. In the Reagan–Bush years there were many examples of dubious behaviour. Woll and Zimmerman quote[8] as an example the way in which many of Reagan's appointees earned themselves a fortune as lobbyists in the HUD episode. For calling up old friends at the Department of Housing and Urban Development and obtaining lucrative contracts for clients, they received millions of dollars.

Sometimes it works the other way round. A person with a business background goes into politics. Dick Cheney was a former chairman and chief executive of Halliburton, an oil and gas services company. He directed the National Energy Policy Development Group, commonly known as the Energy Task Force. Comprised of people in the energy, this group included several **Enron** executives. Because of the subsequent Enron scandal, critics accused the G.W. Bush administration of improper political and business ties.

Enron

Enron Corporation was a US energy company based in Texas which filed for bankruptcy after its perilous financial position was revealed. It became apparent that its reported financial condition over previous years had been sustained by some creative accounting procedures. Enron has since become a popular symbol of wilful corporate fraud and corruption.

The legislature

Congress is a key target for lobbyists, for the bulk of the work done there can be traced to its various subject committees. Committees determine the nature of legislation, or indeed prevent it from being passed. They discuss legislation with individual congressmen and provide evidence, written and oral, for committee hearings.

Members and staffers develop specialised expertise in the policy areas of agriculture, education, science, the federal budget and a host of other topics. This expertise, in addition to the committee connections they bring with them, makes congressmen prime picking for lobbying firms, whose clients are seeking to shape policies that affect their industry. The most powerful committees, such as Energy and Commerce, Appropriations, and Ways and Means are of special interest to lobbying firms.

Lobbyists are keen to develop close ties with committee figures, inviting elected representatives to dinners and various entertainments. Abramson[11] has high-lighted the bonds that bind together the two sides. Nearly a quarter of ex-representatives move over into lobbying, and members of their families are often similarly involved, an indication that the so-called revolving door includes congressional officials and ex-congressmen, as well ex-members of the executive, all of whom are liable to spin in and out of the private and public sectors.

Iron triangles and issue networks

For many years, there were particularly close links in America between interest groups, committee chairmen and government departments, an arrangement often referred to as 'iron triangles'. The three elements were often in close contact with each other and enjoyed cosy relationships based on interdependent self-interest. Sometimes, there was movement of personnel from one position within the triangle to another. Such iron triangles often dominated areas of domestic policy making, possessing a virtual monopoly of information in their sector. One example was the smoking/tobacco triangle (the Department of Agriculture, the House and Senate agricultural committees and the tobacco lobby of farmers and manufacturers), in which there was a focus on crop subsidies to tobacco farmers. Others covered areas such as defence, agriculture and, more specifically, the sugar industry. In all cases, there were tight bonds within the triangular relationship.

The defence triangle comprised the Pentagon, the relevant committee chairmen of the two chambers of Congress and members with a constituency interest in arms manufacturing and/or the armed forces, and representatives of the arms industry who were keen to see their business benefit from federal purchases of the weapons they produced. In his farewell speech on leaving the White House (1961), President Eisenhower issued a warning about the power of the bonds within the armaments industry. He felt that what was good for those with a vested interest in developing costly armaments and weapons systems was not necessarily beneficial to the country as a whole: 'We must guard against the acquisition of unwarranted influence by the military-industrial complex . . . in order to balance and to integrate these and other forces, new and old, within the principles of our democratic system.'

Among the titans of influence in Washington, is former Senator Trent Lott, the senate majority leader from 1996 to 2001. In 2007, he left Congress shortly after it passed a comprehensive ethics reform bill, the Honest Leadership and Open Government Act (see p. 358). By leaving when he did, Lott bypassed the newly approved restrictions that would have otherwise prevented him from lobbying his former colleagues immediately. With former Senator John Breaux at his side, he co-founded the Breaux Lott Leadership Group. Lott's firm has since become one of the leading lobbying groups.

The courts

Some groups carry little weight with the executive or the legislature. When these avenues are closed, they may rely on the courts instead, and hope that they can use their knowledge of the law to gain a favourable interpretation in court rulings. Anti-abortion, consumer and environmental groups have sometimes used litigation, as have other groups that lack a strong congressional base.

In the last two decades, the autonomy of such triangles or sub-governments in America has been challenged by alternative centres of power, often known as 'issue networks'. Issue networks are wider and looser, and – in addition to the three elements above – describe other players involved in discussion of a policy area, including the research institutes and the media. Media scrutiny and the attentions of consumer protest groups have led to a more critical analysis of policy-making processes, so that secret deals and mutual back scratching are now less frequent or effective. As Hague and Harrop[9] have explained, 'the iron has gone out of the triangle; now influence over decisions depends on what you know, as well as who you know'. In America, the policies supported by the tobacco triangle came under challenge from health authorities that had been excluded from the area of tobacco policy making. In defence policy, at times when the danger to America seemed to be less evident, expenditure on weaponry was curbed – suggesting that influences other than the elements of the triangle were a factor in determining the level of military capability.

In the issue networks of today, relationships are not continuous or particularly close and there is less interdependence than was the case in the days of iron triangles. They have lost much of their stranglehold over policy making and new participants, be they environmental or human rights activists, research bodies or consumer groups, have come into the equation. Grant and Ashbee[10] have illustrated the vast array of groups now involved in the development of health policy, ranging from healthcare providers (the AMA and the American Dental Association) to the health insurance companies (Health Insurance Association of America), pharmaceutical and medical equipment manufacturers (Health Industry Manufacturers' Association), employers (National Federation of Independent Business) and representatives of big business (Chamber of Commerce).

One group that gained successes via this route was the National Association for the Advancement of Coloured People (NAACP). By using the courts, it was able to bring about pressure for a change in the status of African Americans. In 1954, it won a particularly significant victory in a case that resulted in the judgment that segregation was inherently unequal, and therefore illegal (see pp. 205 and 378–379).

In those countries in which there is a strong tradition of judicial review, activists tend to use the courts more readily. Accordingly, in the USA, the method is well established, not least because Americans are traditionally a litigious (ready to go to law) people. American judges have wide constitutional powers to overrule decisions of the executive and considerable latitude in interpreting the meaning of legislation, so that bringing test cases may prove invaluable in winning a friendly judgment. Of course, much depends who is on the bench. US groups often seek to influence the selection of judges, pressing the claims of those whose political and social leanings they find acceptable.

It is not just campaigning promotional groups that have used this route. 'Going to law' requires substantial resources, so that it is often the large and powerful business corporations that have been successful in adopting this approach. They regularly challenge government statutes and regulations, and have their own lawyers to advise them and handle the passage of cases through the courts. In other cases where they might not be a party to the litigation, groups may submit an **amicus curiae** ('friend of the court') brief, in order to have their views represented and taken into account.

amicus curiae
A brief filed by an individual or group with the permission of the court. Such briefs provide information and argument additional to that presented by those immediately involved in a case. In effect, a group is acting in the privileged position of being an adviser to the court, a role popular with campaigners in the debates on abortion, consumerism, law and order, and the environment.

Main targets for group activity: a summary

Tier of government	Executive	Legislature	Judiciary
Federal	President, cabinet, civil servants	House of Representatives, Senate, congressional committees	Supreme Court, federal courts, other
State	Governor, departmental heads, officials	Two houses of legislature committees	State Supreme Court, courts of appeal
Local	Mayors, elected and non-elected officials	Councils, school boards, other local boards	Other state courts

Adapted from 'Access Points', in Alan Grant, *The American Political Process*, Dartmouth, 1994.

The public

American groups have always placed great emphasis on the use of campaigns directed at the 'man in the street'. By mailing, by advertising, and especially through television, an attempt is made to influence opinion. Propaganda is often targeted towards certain groups, such as the voters in a congressman's home state, in the hope that the electorate will, in turn, pressure their representative to vote as the group wishes when he or she is in Washington. Congressmen are only too aware that their re-election could depend on keeping the electors happy.

Business organisations spend heavily on advertising, often using professional companies to organise a campaign. Many groups once employed indiscriminate mailing, based on names from the phone book. However, with the development of computers, mailing has become a more sophisticated technique, for letters can be personalised and directed at those likely to be sympathetic, such as members of environmentalist groups.

Direct action

In pursuing their aims, some groups resort to direct action. The anti-abortion associations that are prepared to injure or – at worst – kill those who carry out abortions are but one example. Others are prepared to use less dramatic forms of protest, ranging from demonstrations and strikes to law breaking in the form of withholding tax or rioting.

Direct action, an attempt to coerce those in authority into a change of viewpoint, can be very effective. It may be militant, but peaceful; sometimes, it may involve ignoring or breaking the criminal law and can easily spill over into violence. What has made its use more commonplace is that extreme behaviour can get publicity and command prime television exposure in news and current affairs programmes.

History confirms that direct action can be effective, and many great social changes have come about because of the willingness of some people to resist what they see as unjust laws. The NAACP engaged in a policy of passive resistance, and Martin Luther King and his followers were ready to break laws they felt to be immoral. This could involve deliberately seeking service at a restaurant which operated a colour bar, or riding on a 'whites only' bus. American blacks took more violent direct action in 1992, when riots broke out in Los Angeles; allegations of police racism provoked the black community into desperate action.

Lobbying over health reform pre the 2010 mid-term elections

Under a report entitled 'Health Sector a Big Spender in Fall Election', the *Washington Post* quoted research into health spending conducted by the Center for Responsive Politics in the run-up to the 2010 election. It found that the healthcare industry spent $267 million on lobbying efforts through the second quarter of 2010 – more than any other industry – in hope of guarding its interests amid challenges to the health reform law.

Data on lobbyist spending for the first half of 2010 show that the industry directed 54% of its contributions to Democrats and 46% to Republicans. The sector also spent $91 million toward candidates' mid-term election campaigns. Analysts noted that at that stage it remained unclear whether physicians, drug companies and hospitals wanted to preserve or revamp the reform law.

According to CRP, the leading lobbyists in 2010 were:

- the National Community Pharmacists Association;

- the American Dental Association;

- the American Hospital Association;

- Pfizer, the drug manufacturer.

D. Eldridge, *Washington Post*, 26 September 2010.

POLITICAL ACTION COMMITTEES

Political Action Committees (PACs) have mushroomed in the last two decades. They represent the political wing of pressure groups and are legally permitted to raise funds to distribute to candidates and parties. Business, labour and trade associations, among others, have PACs to further their political goals. They seek to persuade congressmen to vote as the group wishes and they offer advice and information to candidates, as well as the financial assistance that is their most important role. Elections are expensive, and candidates need substantial funds from their backers for such things as their advertising campaigns.

Groups have always wanted to influence election results and PACs existed as long ago as the 1930s. However, it was in the 1970s that they assumed a much greater significance, largely as a result of reforms introduced after Watergate. Now, there are some 4,500 PACs registered with the Federal Election Commission and the scale of their participation in the political process has dramatically increased.

Nearly two-thirds of PACs represent corporations, trade associations and other business and professional groups. Alliances of bankers, lawyers, doctors, farmers, manufacturers and merchants all sponsor PACs. They range from the American Bankers Association PAC to the National Beer Wholesalers' Association PAC. Labour unions also sponsor hundreds of PACs, as do ideological, public-interest and non-profit groups seeking to advance a particular cause. For instance, the National Rifle Association and the Sierra Club each operates a PAC, as does EMILY's List, the organisation that has raised and donated millions of dollars to women candidates for political office.

The five leading PACs in 2009–10, judged by the scale of
their contributions to candidates

PAC	Contributions ($)
Honeywell International	2,968,600
AT & T Inc.	2,779,875
International Brotherhood of Electrical Workers	2,608,873
National Beer Wholesalers Association	2,495,000
American Association for Justice	2,375,000

Based on information provided by Open Secrets: www.opensecrets.org/pacs/.

The cases for and against PACs

In favour

1 They are the modern way to make money available for costly election campaigns. The methods employed are open and are preferable to the situation before they became widespread, when the sources of finance were often disguised and unknown to the public. Indeed, it is the very availability of information that has led to criticism of them, criticism that is better directed to the whole system of campaign funding.

2 Such is the cost of campaigning that politicians cannot afford to be unduly beholden to particular PACs. They need a diversity of sources of funding, and this prevents

any undue influence – the more so as the $5,000 a PAC can donate is the level fixed two decades ago.

3 PACs represent a legitimate interest in a pluralist system, and the fact that there are nearly 5,000 of them serves to prevent any one of them from gaining excessive influence. Their actions are open to scrutiny, and the media are constantly on the lookout for examples of undue favours being granted.

4 As with groups in general, they offer an outlet through which people can be involved and express their ideas and opinions. On the one hand, they educate the voters, but they also act as a means of communicating their views.

Against

1 The central allegation against PACs revolves around the idea that money can buy influence and power. A congressman who has the backing of a PAC is likely to give favours in return, and so they are associated with undue influence. In the words of one writer,[12] PACs are 'a huge coalition of special interest groups dedicated to perverting the political process for private gain'. The fact that some PACs have actually been willing to back rival candidates is seen as evidence of their determination to gain such influence.

2 Most PACs give money primarily to incumbent congressmen, and this makes it more difficult for a challenger to mount a successful campaign against a person already in office. In as much as this is true, it is seen as undermining the democratic process, for it makes a contest less meaningful and fair.

3 The costs of campaigning in congressional elections have spiralled out of control, a reflection of the easy availability of money collected by PACs. It is not due to the escalating costs of advertising, but more to the fact that congressmen have used this 'easy money' to equip themselves with needlessly large offices and staffing levels.

4 The usual criticism of pressure groups, the lack of internal democracy, is often mentioned as well. Alan Grant quotes[13] the example of the decision of the AFL-CIO to back Walter Mondale as the Democratic presidential nominee in 1984, even though less than a quarter of union members were asked their preference.

A note on 527s

'527s' are tax-exempt organisations named after a relevant section of the US tax code. They are groups created primarily to influence the nomination, election, appointment or defeat of candidates for public office. Although PACs are also created under Section 527, the term '527' is generally used in reference to political organisations not regulated by the Federal Election Commission and not therefore subject to the same contribution limits as PACs. They are able to raise and spend freely to influence elections, as long as they do not coordinate their activities with a candidate or a party and directly advocate the election or defeat of any candidate for federal elective office. Many 527s are run by interest groups and used to raise money to spend on issue advocacy and voter mobilization, as a means of evading the restrictions placed on PACs.

Groups and the electoral system

Pressure groups seek to influence the conduct of government, not to assume responsibility for administering policy. They do not contest elections, but wish to influence their outcome. In particular, they may wish to see certain candidates elected and certain ideas advanced. This may involve publishing the voting records of sitting congressmen in an attempt to show how suitably they fulfil the group's requirements.

The regulation of party funding in the 1971 Federal Election Campaign Act and the Campaign Act of 1974 spawned the growth of the **Political Action Committees** (PACs), the political arms of pressure groups. These can assist candidates in several ways – by providing research material and publicity, by raising election funds and by providing organisational backup to a candidate who lacks a strong personal political organisation or party machine. For a candidate lacking such party or organisational support and who lacks private funds, PACs can provide invaluable assistance (see box 352–353).

> **Political Action Committees (PACs)**
>
> PACs are the means by which organisations such as corporations, labour unions and other pressure groups collect money from their members and then give it to candidates and political parties who support their interests. PACs have grown in number since campaign finance reform legislation was introduced in the 1970s.

Of course, not all pressure groups so involve themselves in determining the outcome of election contests. They may wish to reach out to people associated with either party and therefore take a non-partisan approach. The American Telephone and Telegraph Company, and Western Electric, are examples of groups who prefer to concentrate on educating the voters and parties in their viewpoint.

The strength of group activity

Why pressure groups are strong in America

The American system of government offers much scope to the lobbyist. It provides many layers of government to target, and the relatively weak party system provides an opportunity for groups to step in and fill the gap. As parties do not have rigid doctrinal platforms, congressmen are less likely to follow the party line. They have to decide what is best in the national interest and for their geographical area, in the light of the information they receive from all quarters. Much of this comes from the interests who seek to persuade them.

There are other factors that serve to strengthen the influence of pressure groups. Via the Bill of Rights, the Constitution offers protection for groups who are quick to proclaim their rights of free speech under the First Amendment; any ban on unions or restrictions of freedom of assembly and expression would be likely to be deemed 'unconstitutional'. Moreover, the freedom of information legislation provides access for group activists to relevant documentation, and a generally open system of government creates an atmosphere in which groups can flourish. Finally, in America there are many influential bodies representing a variety of highly diverse and often ethnic and racial backgrounds (the Irish and Jewish lobbies, the Italian community etc.).

Factors making for group success

It is not easy to generalise about the factors which make group action successful, for there are exceptions to most sweeping generalisations. The party in control may be relevant, for business interests are traditionally catered for by the Republicans who – as in the Reagan era – tend to show greater hostility to organised labour. Yet the Democrats won praise from some manufacturers who were pleased by President Clinton's backing for the North Atlantic Free Trade Area, an issue on which the more conservative party failed to offer him much support. For many years, the Democrats have been viewed as sympathetic to the unions rather than big business, though the bargaining power of organised labour has been reduced under any administration now that membership has so declined.

Size is relevant to influence, for an association able to claim the backing of 2 million voters is one that cannot be easily ignored. One with 20,000 supporters has less electoral clout. Much, of course, depends on the commitment and organisational skills of those involved, and sometimes an active and persistent small group can be effective.

If a body has nationwide support – such as the AMA, with its local organisation in almost every congressional district – it is likely to be more influential than a group whose support is localised, unless the concern being voiced is a purely local one. Also, as with British groups, resources (especially money and professional expertise) are important. Those groups that can present an impressive case based on soundly researched data are more likely to be listened to. This can be costly.

Sometimes, timing is the key factor. Groups arise because of a growing interest in particular concerns. The environmentalists have been important in recent years, and many associations have sprung up and flourished. In the present mood of widespread social and political conservatism (and particularly with the growing influence of the Religious Right), anti-abortion groups are likely to be listened to with greater respect than those who advance the cause of a woman's right to choose.

Indeed, any group with a liberal agenda is likely to find present circumstances less congenial than two decades ago. This applies especially in the area of civil

The ability to make strategic alliances

Some groups supplement their own resources by forming coalitions with other bodies sharing similarity of outlook on key issues. For under-resourced promotional groups, this is a useful tactic, enabling them to maximise their impact. So too, is it for powerful groups that are keen to demonstrate to government the broad backing for or against a particular measure. Interest groups are likely to be more effective if they can work with other groups.

An Energy Bill Coalition of renewable energy, energy efficiency and bio-fuels organisations was galvanised in 2010, in response President Obama's call for clean energy legislation, following the BP oil disaster. Its members include: the Alliance to Save Energy, the American Wind Energy Association, the Biomass Power Association, the Business Council for Sustainable Energy, the Energy Recovery Council, the Geothermal Energy Association, Growth Energy, the National Hydropower Association and the Solar Energy Industries Association. Members of the coalition urged the Senate in mid-summer 2010 to pass comprehensive energy legislation that would create millions of American jobs and decrease US reliance on fossil fuels.

One of the companies involved in previous energy alliances is the US Chamber of Commerce, which itself is a member of more than 300 coalitions. In its fight for free enterprise before Congress, the White House, regulatory agencies, the courts, the court of public opinion and governments around the world, it regularly works with other organisations. It also has a number of affiliated bodies, including the Business Civic Leadership Center and the Center for International Private Enterprise.

In the same way, the Christian Right works with right-to-life groups, groups professing taxpayers' rights and conservative think-tanks such as the Heritage Foundation. On the pro-choice side of the abortion argument, the American Humanist Association campaigns alongside more well-known advocates such as NARAL Pro-Choice America, Planned Parenthood Federation of America and the YWCA.

Groups that belong to coalitions recognise that by joining together in common cause they are likely to have: more impact on congressmen (to whom grassroots members of all affiliated associations can write or e-mail their views); a wider network of contacts; and improved access to the resources that are so useful for the employment of researchers and the propagation of their views via TV ads.

---

liberties, where women and racial minorities find less support for affirmative action than was previously the case. The president and congressmen are mindful of election considerations. No cause is likely to be endorsed if it is potentially damaging to their popularity and therefore a threat to their chances of re-election.

The mass media can be very relevant, for favourable attention from broadcasters and journalists can help a group to project its image and address a wider audience. Moreover, if the organisation can convey via the media the impression that its outlook is in the general interest and shared by many people, then those in power or seeking to obtain office will be especially attentive.

The regulation of group activity

The First Amendment to the American Constitution guarantees the right of free speech and to petition for the remedy of grievances. Interest groups have used this protection over many years as a defence of their activities against the threat of excessive regulation. Some controls were introduced at state level as far back as the early nineteenth century, and within a few decades there was pressure for more to be done. Public anxiety increased because of the widespread influence of big business, in particular the influence wielded by rich corporations who were able to influence congressmen to gain valuable concessions – especially rights to land where it was hoped to build railroads.

Not until after World War II was anything done by national government to tackle the problems posed by the growth in lobbying. Then, it was felt that there was a need to regularise group activity, whilst recognising its legitimate role in the political process. This was achieved by encouraging groups to disclose details of their aims, membership and funding.

The **1946 Federal Regulation of Lobbying Act** required the registration of lobbyists and details of the concern that employs them. It was largely unenforced, and frequently the details were either not given or were incomplete. Some groups evaded registration by arguing that lobbying was not their primary role. An attempt to stiffen the law in 1976 (the Lobby Disclosure Bill) failed because of powerful opposition from lobbyists who felt that it would needlessly complicate their task and waste their time on pointless form filling.

However, because of the alarm about some of their activities in the late 1960s and 1970s (notably about the cost of campaigning and the funding of candidates for elective office), further legislation was devised, in the form of the **Federal Election Campaign Act** (FECA). The Act, passed in 1971, replaced all earlier statutes. In its present form, thrice amended, it requires candidates and parties to disclose details of their income and expenditure. Individuals and PACs have to declare the costs they incur in providing them with any financial backing. The effect of tightening the control has, ironically, been to increase the number of PACs and the scale of their contributions.

Following an unsuccessful attempt in the 103rd Congress to amend the definition of lobbying so that more individuals would be required to register, a further attempt at reform was made by the 104th Congress. In 1995, it passed the Lobbying Disclosure Act (1995), which defined lobbyists and required those who are compensated for their actions to register with the clerk of the house and the secretary of the Senate, respectively, and to report on their activities.

Further legislation in 1998 made further refinements to the earlier Act, so that between them the two bills required the production of a report accounting for the lobbyists' major expenditures.

In July 2005, Public Citizen published an influential report that pointed to the need for further legislation, 'The Journey from Congress to K Street'. The report analysed hundreds of registration documents filed under the terms of the 1995 and 1998 legislation. It drew attention to the fact that following its passage, 43% of the 198 members of Congress who had subsequently left government had registered to lobby. It highlighted several examples of illustrate the scale of their activities, noting particularly the case of former speaker-elect Bob Livingston, who had resigned his seat in Congress in 1999 and within six years had developed his lobbying firm so successfully that by the end of 2004 it had earned $40 million and via his two PACs contributed extensively to the campaigns of several candidates.

An attempt to bring greater transparency was made by the two congressional chambers in 2007, with the passage of the **Honest Leadership and Open Government Act**, which President George W. Bush signed into law. The Act was a comprehensive ethics and lobbying reform bill that amended parts of the Lobbying Disclosure measure. It strengthened public disclosure requirements concerning lobbying activity and funding, placed more restrictions on gifts for members of Congress and their staff, and provided for mandatory disclosure of **earmarks** in expenditure bills.

On the day after he entered the White House, President Obama signed two executive orders and three presidential memoranda in a bid to ensure that his administration would be more open, transparent and accountable than its predecessors. They represented an attempt to rein in the influence of lobbyists, bring increased accountability to federal spending and limit the influence of special interests. They also include a lobbyist gift ban and a **'revolving door' ban**. In May 2009, the **Recovery Act Lobbying Rules** established new and tougher limits on special-interest influence.

The world of pressure groups is now more open than was formerly the case. Deals between representatives of interest groups and congressmen are

earmarks
Earmarks are defined by the Congressional Research Service as 'provisions associated with legislation . . . that specify certain congressional spending priorities or in revenue bills that apply to a very limited number of individuals or entities'. In other words, they direct approved funds to be spent on specific projects or direct specific exemptions from taxes or mandated fees. Earmarks are controversial, viewed by critics as being synonymous with pork-barrel legislation.

'revolving door' ban
President Obama required a pledge from all appointees entering his administration: 'I will not for a period of two years from the date of my appointment participate in any particular matter involving specific parties that is directly and substantially related to my former employer or former clients, including regulations and contracts.'

today more likely to be exposed. Congressmen are less likely to be in the pay of any one major lobby. Should there be a suspicion of too close an arrangement, then there is always another competing group willing to 'blow the whistle'. In the light of these considerations, many congressmen and groups such as the American Civil Liberties Union do not recognise a need for more stringent regulation, a reflection of the prevailing American view that the influence of interest groups is generally beneficial to the process of government and in the public interest as well.

The merits and demerits of pressure groups

Most academics and politicians accept that groups have a legitimate role in American government, and recognise that it is inevitable that they will seek opportunities to advance their own interests. Many members of the general public might concede that they offer some advantages, but none the less remain perturbed by their ever-growing influence.

The case against

The names employed to describe the activity of interest groups are themselves a cause for concern to some people. The term 'pressure group' smacks of sinister and harmful behaviour, and when a small number of groups resort to violence or the threat of intimidation to achieve their ends there is understandable alarm. The use of death threats by the anti-abortion lobby can damage the cause, by offending many Americans who themselves are perturbed by the practice of termination. In some respects, the term 'interest group' is no better. It has obvious overtones of self-interest and serves to fuel the fear that such groups are concerned to promote their own advantage rather than the general interest of the community.

Moreover, among these 'interests', some are more powerful than others. They have greater financial resources and can therefore develop highly professional organisations and great expertise. Rivals in the field cannot hope to match the funds and resources of a big corporation. Business and labour are well organised, whereas the voice of consumers was for many years less effectively conveyed. Consumers are now protected by many active individuals and associations, but other interests – the racial minorities, the disabled, the elderly and the unemployed lack the income and bargaining power within the economy to enable them to achieve their goals – unless they can create enough public support as an election approaches. Abramson quotes[14] an analyst who regards Washington as a 'capital so privileged and incestuous in its dealings, that ordinary citizens believe it is no longer accessible to the general public'.

Concern has also been voiced about the unrepresentative character of some group leadership. Some leaders are elected by a small percentage of the membership, others are appointed. Once in their position, they can purvey their own ideas and attitudes, irrespective of whether these reflect the views of those whom they are supposed to represent. One writer has noted[15] that 'the system is skewed, loaded and unbalanced in favour of a fraction of a minority' – those in the highest socio-economic and educational categories.

Above all, much of the public anxiety is related to fear of behind-the-scenes influence. It is widely suspected that there is something distasteful about lobbying. It may not be illegal, the influence may be legitimate, but there is a suspicion of deals from which the bulk of the public are excluded. There have been enough cases involving corruption and malpractice to make people question the secrecy of lobbying activity, and assume that either side is out to maximise its own advantage.

The case in favour

Pluralism provides an important perspective on the role of pressure groups in a liberal democracy. Many Americans view competition between freely organised groups as an expression of democracy, rather than a threat to it. All kinds of interest can have their say, and no one group dominates a particular sector; other groups can exercise a countervailing pressure. There may not always be equally balanced groups on either side of some particular issue, but whatever the preponderance of views, the arguments for and against a question are usually reasonably well aired. For instance, the influence of the energy companies is matched by that of the anti-nuclear groups that wish to halt the development of nuclear energy plants. The desire of management and unions in the Northwest woodlands to cut down trees is countered by the complaints of the environmentalists, who are active in demanding that the practice is controlled. Again, in the impassioned abortion and gun control debates, the influence of pro-lifers in the former is balanced by those who are pro-choice, just as the influence of the National Rifle Association is matched by that of Handgun Control.

> **pluralism**
> Pluralism (literally, rule by the many) describes a political system in which there are numerous groups competing to exert influence over the government. New groups can easily be created, so that further competition can emerge in the marketplace. The state is more umpire than player, responding to interests expressed to it.

Groups can provide positive benefits to the community and to those in authority. They allow a large number of citizens to participate in the political process as members of associations. Some are passive supporters who pay their dues and do little else. Others, usually a small minority, are more deeply committed enthusiasts who try to galvanise the less active members into giving more positive support.

The presence of many groups ensures that the attitudes and outlook of all groups in society are articulated. It is surely healthier for all people to have an outlet for their views, however extreme, rather than for them to resort to underground methods. They also convey ideas to and from the elected and appointed officials who make decisions. As intermediaries between the government and the governed, they help to make government accountable. In these respects, rather than being a threat to the democratic process, they actually underpin democracy.

They also provide government with specialist information and expertise, and may help in carrying out policies that law makers have laid down. They meet congressmen and officials of the administration at regular intervals, and assist by providing evidence, submitting proposals and attending hearings. This flow of information to the agencies and institutions of government is again an important part of the democratic process. By becoming involved in this way, groups help to modify government decisions and public policy. Some may not like it, but that is what has come to pass.

Apart from the specific arguments quoted above, supporters of group activity often point out to the inevitability of group activity in a **pluralist society**. This view was developed by David Truman[16] in 1951 and has been widely accepted over the last fifty years. For those who belong to this school of thought, the formation of groups is an obvious method by which people with shared ideas and circumstances cooperate to achieve their goals. They are a natural, desirable and healthy democratic outlet. Any problems in their operation can be controlled by appropriate regulatory machinery.

pluralist societies

In pluralist societies (for example Australia, Canada, the UK and the USA), the power of the state is limited and there is a political marketplace in which group activity can flourish. Governments are responsive to group interest. In the words of Hague and Harrop,[17] 'politics is a competitive market with few barriers to entry'.

Recent trends: the changing pressure group landscape

For a long while, the lobbying scene in Washington was dominated by three major interests: agriculture, business and labour. These no longer carry the weight that they once did. We have seen that the American Farm Bureau Federation and National Farmers Union, the large peak organisations, have now lost some of their influence to the product or regional associations. As with agriculture, so with business. The National Association of Manufacturers and the U.S. Chamber of Commerce are still important players, but other organisations have developed, and corporations increasingly organise more of their own lobbying. Similarly, the status and impact of unions has been in long-term decline. Their membership peaked at above 30% of the workforce in 1945; today it is just over 12%. They remain important in the American economy, but many groups of workers – especially in newer, smaller, high-tech industries – are non-unionised. There are some localised signs of a recovery. In 2007, the

Department of Labor reported the first increase in union memberships in twenty-five years and the largest increase since 1979. Most of the recent gains in union membership have been in the service sector, while the number of unionised employees in the manufacturing sector has continued to decline. Many of the gains in the service sector have come in west-coast states such as California, where union membership is now more than 4% above the national average, at 16.7%.

The days when congressmen from the industrial states were desperate to avoid offending the unions, or those from the South and Midwest had to show immense sympathy for agrarian interests, have changed. These interests are still important, but the industrial and farming vote are both less crucial than was once the case. Democrats fear being portrayed as too close to labour, and Reagan and Bush were prepared to cut agricultural subsidies in spite of the preferences of the small farmers of Iowa, Kansas and other farm states. Given the large number of groups, it is now less easy for congressional committees to be too close to one particular interest; similarly, an individual congressman cannot afford to be beholden to one group only. They are open to many influences, and would be unwise to fail to meet delegations from any association, irrespective of their private view.

Recently formed bodies and those that have acquired increased significance

The nature and pattern of group activity has significantly altered in recent years. Today, there are far more groups than ever before. We have already noted the proliferation of cause or issue groups that seek to advance particular areas of concern – from abortion to the environment, from gender to the right to bear arms. One reason for this development is the growth of federal welfare and regulatory activities in the 1960s and 1970s. Several groups were formed in response to these initiatives, by groups of people who found their lives affected by the changes. Other factors might be the weakening of political parties and the increased opportunities for lobbying in Congress.

Lobbying is done also by various **think-tanks** that seek to convert policy makers to their approach on a whole series of issues. The Heritage Foundation and the American Enterprise Institute are broadly conservative research bodies that have become an important part of the Washington lobbying network. So too are the state and local governments that now

think-tanks
Think-tanks are policy institutes that carry out detailed research and provide analysis of and information on a range of policy options. They are often ideologically based, their ideas sometimes being influential with the parties that share a broad affinity of perspective. Think-tanks such as the Progressive Policy Institute have taken on much of the work of developing new policy options. The role of parties in this area has diminished.

often employ the services of professional lobbyists to influence the federal government – again, via an office in Washington.

If the range of groups has proliferated over the last generation, so has their relative importance changed (see the current rankings, listed in the box below). There are many variables that combine to determine the impact of groups at any given time, ranging from their size and the geographical distribution of their membership to their resources and the skills of their leadership. In the last few years, the American Association of Retired People (AARP) has consistently come out at or near the top. This is hardly surprising in an age when more people are living longer than ever before. The AARP ranks as America's largest pressure group, with offices in all fifty states, the District of Columbia, Puerto Rico and the U.S. Virgin Islands. Its support from the 'over-fifties' is readily mobilised when issues affecting their lifestyles and prospects are up for national debate.

THE MOST INFLUENTIAL GROUPS IN AMERICA TODAY

The ten most powerful groups in Washington

1 National Rifle Association of America

2 American Association of Retired Persons

3 National Federation of Independent Business

4 American Israel Public Affairs Committee

5 American Association of Trial Lawyers

6 American Federation of Labor and Congress of Industrial Organisations (AFL-CIO)

7 Chamber of Commerce of the United States of America

8 National Beer Wholesalers' Association

9 National Association of Realtors

10 National Association of Manufacturers

The top five most influential groups in the states

1 Schoolteachers' organisations (National Education Association)

2 General (umbrella) business organisations (Chambers of Commerce)

3 Utility companies and associations (those covering electricity, gas etc.)

4 Lawyers (state bar associations and trial lawyers)

5 Traditional labour groups (AFL-CIO)

Information for the Washington scene adapted from an article in *Fortune* (a business magazine), 'The Power Twenty-five' survey, 28 May 2001. The survey was based on a questionnaire in which congressmen, professional lobbyists, White House aides and many others ranked on a scale of 0 to 100 the influence of 87 different associations. Information on the states adapted from R. Hrebenar, *Interest Group Politics*, Prentice Hall, 1997.

There are many more recent groups that compete with the traditional ones in the economic area and in the professions. In medicine, the AMA has long been a leader and it remains very important. However, in addition there are numerous other influential organisations operating in the medical field. Some are concerned with specialist work such as that of paramedics (the National Association of Emergency Medical Technicians) and nurses (Filipino Nurses Association), some represent hospitals and clinics, whilst others speak for the increasingly active insurance companies in this sector.

At the federal level, the amount of interest group activity around educational issues has exploded. According to lobbying disclosure reports filed with the secretary of the Senate's Office of Public Records, the number of registered groups lobbying on educational issues rose by 55% between 1998 and 2005. Additionally, the amount of money spent on these activities during the same period increased by $50 million. As a result of this rise in the numbers of groups involved and the amounts they spend, research carried out by the Center for Responsive Politics shows education to have been the tenth most active lobbying issue in Washington in 2005.

The rise of the professional lobbyist

Lobbying is carried out by a variety of actors, ranging from large interest groups to the government relations divisions of large corporations. In addition to these 'in-house lobbyists', there are those lobbyists who operate as professional intermediaries, such as political consulting firms or lawyers specialising in offering political advice, sometimes referred to as professional or contract lobbyists. In this more recent form of lobbying, as well as mingling with members of Congress and the executive branch and monitoring new policy developments, professional lobbying firms package issues, mobilise voters and raise campaign funds on behalf of their clients.

By using professionals in this way, groups know that they are obtaining the services of former government personnel, ex-congressmen and other people with experience of life in Washington, who know how government works and who also may have a recognisable name and presence. Groups such as the government relations law firm Dickstein Shapiro, which 'represents and develops partnerships with Fortune 500 and Global 1000 companies in various industries across diverse geographies' (www.dicksteinshapiro.com/experience/) employ high-profile figures, including former speaker Hastert and ex-congressman Albert Wynn, for the expertise and insights they can offer. One of its rivals, Ogilvy Government Relations, states clearly on its website (www.ogilvygr.com) the advantages that a public relations firm can provide:

OGR's partners have each served in senior-level positions throughout the legislative and executive branches of the federal government. Additionally, many have played key roles in both presidential and congressional campaigns. This professional experience – coupled with a long-standing belief that intelligence, strategy, and dedication can solve virtually any problem in Washington – has enabled OGR to successfully represent its clients on a wide variety of issues.

The increased importance of non-federal access points

For the lobbyists too, things have changed. Not only are there more of them, there are also more targets to influence at national and state level. Nationally, there are more agencies and congressional subcommittees to contact, and as we have seen (pp. 346–347), many who do the lobbying are professional lobbyists who find themselves seeking to influence the very people for whom they once worked. (see box on 'The rise of the professional lobbyist'). In addition, state governments have become a new focus of attention. Business organisations are particularly active in some states, often employing former state legislators, governors and officials to do their work. Since the days of Reagan's New Federalism, more policies are operated and financed at the state rather than the federal level, particularly in the welfare field.

Finally, a very recent development in the world of political campaigning has been the emergence of the Tea Party movement (see also pp. 321–323 and 341). Within a short time, this network of conservatives – with affiliated organisations across the states – has provided an outlet for the views of many

Another group that offers strategic advice, and consulting and lobbying services, to a wide range of firms and organsations, such as state and local governments, is the Breaux Lott Leadership Group (see also p. 348). Acquired in 2010 by Patton Boggs, one of the nation's highest-revenue producing public policy law firms, it too can open the doors of the federal government to the interest groups for whom it works. As Hague and Harrop[18] put it, this and the other consultancy firms are 'technicians of influence: hired guns in the business of interest group communication . . . they keep a close eye on proposed regulations under consideration by legislative committees'. The two writers explain why such firms are increasing in number:

1 Government regulation has expanded, often impacting on areas directly relevant to companies and other interests groups such as trade unions.

2 The world of public relations campaigning is becoming increasingly sophisticated and refined, providing scope for other advisers to come into their own, planning and delivering campaigns of a type that are too integrated and complex for any group to manage on its own.

3 As so many American groups now lobby in Washington directly, rather than working through a trade association of some kind, they find it really useful to use a company that has access to a government agency or sympathetic legislator. Hence McKay's[19] observation that in recent years 'there is overwhelming evidence that individual firms have taken a more active part in public policy-making. Most major corporations now have Washington offices and employ professional lobbyists to advance and protect their interests.'

Americans who are dissatisfied with the Obama administration and the direction of the policies with which it is associated.

Pressure groups in Britain and the United States: a comparison

	Britain	United States
Size and character of country	Small, compact and fairly homogeneous, though growing percentage of ethnic minorities and non-Christians.	Vast country with marked regional variations and diverse ethnic and religious backgrounds. Very pluralist society with influential groups such as Italian community and Jewish lobby etc.
Nature of constitution	Uncodified, rights of groups not guaranteed – for example removal of rights of protestors to freedom of assembly by Criminal Justice Act, 1994.	Written constitution, with group rights more secure. Legislation to take away rights of protestors would have fallen foul of First Amendment.
Level of centralisation in a unitary and federal country	Leading groups target Whitehall/Westminster, where key decisions are made, though devolution has created additional targets in other parts of the UK; local action groups lobby councils.	Much activity in the states – for example many key decisions on welfare are made in state capitals; also, much local lobbying.
Targets or 'access points'	Interest groups (insiders) tend to concentrate on executive, but Parliament and public are other targets. More recently, EU and other pressure groups.	Separation of powers encourages groups to lobby three areas of government; also, public at and between elections, states and other groups.
Party system	a. Two-party system, but three- or four-party politics, offers opportunities for some groups to work with and through parties – for example Welsh-language groups and Plaid Cymru b. Strict party discipline discourages main groups from seeking influence at Westminster as a priority, though unions have Labour links.	a. Fairly strict two-party system encourages activists to form groups rather than find parties to express their viewpoint. b. Looser party discipline, so more point in groups seeking to persuade congressmen and committees.
Funding of election campaigns	Conducted mainly through parties, Conservatives having links with some sections of industry (though not what they were) and Labour having union financial backing.	PACs, the financial and political arm of pressure groups, have a central role in funding more candidate-centred electioneering.
Open/closed system of government	Much interest group activity behind closed doors (for example NFU, as powerful insider group) and less open to public scrutiny. A traditionally secretive system of government which keeps activities of executive as closed as possible.	More open government. Media have protection of First Amendment, and effective freedom of information legislation provides access to documentation. Pressure group activity more open to public examination.

CONCLUSION

The United States has a vast array of pressure groups that operate at several access points and have highly significant influence. In recent decades, the extent of lobbying in Washington and the fifty states has increased and the role of PACs has become a key element in the financing of election campaigns. Group activity provokes much controversy and there have been regular calls for more regulation and control. Debate about groups has centred upon the contribution of groups to the democratic process.

In particular, Washington has become a hub of pressure group activity. On any given day, group activists will be involved in many arenas. Some will be testifying for or against proposed legislation in congressional hearings. Others will be arguing in the Supreme Court, perhaps for stricter enforcement of regulations or for the protection of the rights of a section of the American people. Yet others will be meeting with bureaucrats in government departments, perhaps discussing ideas about legislation.

There is an interesting paradox about the participation of Americans in their political system. Many are reluctant to turn out and vote in elections, yet they are willing to involve themselves in pressure-group activity. As Schlozman and Tierney[20] have written: 'Recent decades have witnessed an expansion of astonishing proportions in the involvement of private organisations in Washington politics.' They might have referred to the other outlets as well, for many groups are now very active in working the many sub-governments in the American system.

REFERENCES

1 A. de Tocqeville, *Democracy in America*, vol. 2, reissued by Vintage, 1954
2 J. Rauch, *Demosclerosis: The Silent Killer of American Government*, Times Books, 1995
3 W. Grant, *Pressure Groups, Politics and Democracy in Britain*, Harvester Wheatsheaf, 1995; and – for an update on Grantian thinking – *Pressure Groups in British Politics*, Palgrave Macmillan, 2000
4 W. Grant, 'Is the Study of Pressure Groups a Fading Paradigm?', paper delivered to the Political Studies Association, Edinburgh, 2010
5 P. Woll and S. Zimmerman, *American Government: The Core*, McGraw-Hill, 1992
6 *Washington Representatives* (32nd edn), Columbia Books, 2007
7 Open Secrets at www.OpenSecrets.org, October 2010
8 P. Woll and S. Zimmerman, as in 5 above
9 R. Hague and M. Harrop, *Comparative Government and Politics: An Introduction*, Palgrave, 2007

10 A. Grant and E. Ashbee, *The Politics Today Companion to American Government*, Manchester University Press, 2002

11 J. Abramson, 'The Business of Persuasion Thrives in Nation's Capitol', *New York Times*, 29 September 1998

12 C. Griffin, *Cleaning out Congress*, Griffin Associates (New York), 1992

13 A. Grant, *Contemporary American Politics*, Dartmouth, 1995

14 J. Abramson, as in 11 above

15 G. Wasserman, *The Basics of American Politics*, Longman, 1996

16 D. Truman, *The Governmental Process: Political Interests and Public Opinion*, 1958

17 R. Hague and M. Harrop, as in 9 above

18 R. Hague and M. Harrop, as in 9 above

19 D. McKay, *American Politics and Society*, Blackwell, 2005

20 K. Schlozman and J. Tierney, *Organised Interests and American Democracy*, Harper and Row, 1986

USEFUL WEB SITES

www.influence.biz *Influence*, a trade publication for the lobbying industry, chronicles the relationship between lobbyists and their clients.

www.policy.com Lists various think-tanks and issue groups.

Two sites with a broadly ideological perspective are:

www.conservativenet.com Conservative Net.

www.turnleft.com Turn Left.

Individual pressure groups have their own sites dealing with the specific issues of interest to them. Examples are:

www.commoncause.org Common Cause, a non-partisan, non-profit advocacy organisation, which acts as a vehicle for citizens to make their voices heard in the political process.

www.naacp.org National Association for the Advancement of Colored People.

www.now.org National Organisation for Women

SAMPLE QUESTIONS

1 What is the role of interest groups within US politics?

2 Which 'access points' are most likely to provide opportunities for US pressure groups to achieve their objectives? Does influence vary according to the type of group involved?

3 Discuss the role and value of pressure groups in the American legislative process.

4 'It is possible to overestimate the effects of pressure group activity. Ultimately, groups cancel each other out.' Discuss.

5 Does lobbying play too large a part in the American political process?

6 Should there be more restrictions on the activity of Political Action Committees?
7 Are pressure groups beneficial to American democracy or do they undermine it?
8 Are American pressure groups too powerful?
9 Are pressure groups more useful than parties in American politics?
10 'In Britain and America, the producer lobby is far more powerful than that representing consumers.' Is this true and if so, does it matter?

Civil liberties and civil rights have already been briefly discussed in Chapter 2. Civil liberties are areas of social life in which governmental power should rarely intrude upon the free choice of individuals. Civil rights are areas of social life where government must act to ensure that all citizens are treated fairly and enjoy equality of opportunity. This involves the protection of the rights of minorities from the unfair actions of state and local governments, individuals and groups.

In this chapter, we explore the protection offered by the Bill of Rights to all Americans. We assess how well First Amendment freedoms are protected, before proceeding to examine the rights of America's ethnic minority populations, women and (briefly) other groups, the policy of affirmative action and the conflict that it engenders.

POINTS TO CONSIDER

- How do civil liberties and civil rights differ?
- To what extent have First Amendment freedoms been upheld in the USA?
- What have been the significant landmarks in the campaign by black Americans to achieve their civil rights? How effectively are they protected today?
- Why did the Equal Rights Amendment fail?
- What has been the impact of the issue of abortion on the women's movement?
- What are the different forms of affirmative action and why has it gone out of fashion?
- What problems have been experienced by gays in their bid for equal recognition?
- How effective is the Bill of Rights in securing the freedoms of all Americans?

Throughout American history those in government have had to draw a line between areas of social life in which individual choice should be largely unrestricted and areas in which certain sorts of choices will be constrained or prohibited. The issue has been when and for what purpose the power of government should be brought to bear on individual citizens, to affect their patterns of choice and activity. The term '**civil liberties**' refers to those areas in which governmental power should rarely intrude on the free choice of individuals, such as free speech and freedom of worship. In these cases, citizens are protected against arbitrary or excessive governmental interference. The term '**civil rights**' covers those areas where government must act, intruding upon what individuals might otherwise choose to do, in order to see that everyone is treated fairly and that opportunities are available to all who are able and prepared to seize them. Here, government is acting positively to protect individuals against discrimination or unreasonable treatment by other individuals or groups.

civil liberties
Areas of social life such as freedom of speech, religion and the press, in which the Constitution restricts or prohibits governmental intrusion on the free choice of individuals.

civil rights
Areas of social life in which the Constitution requires government to ensure equal treatment of individuals – for example by granting all of them the right to vote. Whereas civil liberties (sometimes known as negative rights) are legal protections against governmental restriction of First Amendment freedoms, civil rights are legal protections against discrimination because of such things as ethnicity, gender or religion. In these cases, the government positively confers rights on disadvantaged groups, by passing anti-discriminatory legislation.

Most Americans are theoretically comfortable with the two concepts of liberties and rights, which combine to ensure that they can do as they please unless they discriminate against others. Yet in a society whose Constitution proclaims protection of the laws for all, some sections of the community have seen their rights denied. In particular, members of ethnic minorities and women have long experienced disadvantage, even if much has been done to redress the balance in recent decades. It remains the case that on average they earn much

First Amendment freedoms
The basic freedoms of religion, speech, press and assembly, as set out in the First Amendment to the Constitution.

less than white males. They also find that when they seek to advance up the occupational hierarchy, all too often they hit a 'glass ceiling' that limits their progress. As part of the attempt to reverse historical disadvantages, the Great Society programme of the 1960s contained measures of affirmative action. Today, critics of the idea see this as 'reverse discrimination'.

Civil liberties: First Amendment freedoms

The key freedoms to protect citizens from an abuse of governmental power are to be found in the First Amendment, which is why they are commonly referred to as '**First Amendment**' freedoms. The Amendment states:

Congress shall make no law respecting an establishment of religion, or prohibiting the free exercise thereof; or abridging the freedom of speech, or of the press, or the right of the people peaceably to assemble, and to petition the Government for a redress of grievances.

These are the essential civil liberties that allow democracy to work, for they concern the right of people to communicate freely with each other and with the government. They allow the public, the press, lobbyists and congressmen to 'go public' and organise an attempt to change government policy. It was Justice Oliver Wendell Holmes who argued that in a democratic society there is as much need for competition among ideas as there is in an economic marketplace for competition among producers. It is through free discussion that ideas can be tested, allowing all options to be explained and erroneous ones to be challenged. In Holmes's view, good ideas would ultimately drive out bad ideas and the public could be relied upon to reject what was wrong and opt for what was true.

Inevitably, there must be restraints upon freedom of speech, but these are kept to a minimum, the emphasis being on maximum tolerance unless there is a clear threat to society or a serious violation of the rights of others. Justice Holmes is renowned for his remark that no one has a right to shout 'fire' in a crowded theatre when there is no fire. But in the overwhelming majority of circumstances, the free and uncensored expression of opinion is protected. This is because freedom of speech and expression are vital elements of any democracy. Political participation, open debate of alternatives and majority rule all depend upon it.

As we have seen in Chapter 2, the requirement set out in the American Constitution has been broadened to cover state as well as central governments. So too has it been extended to cover not only oral speech, but also gesturing, mimicking, wearing buttons and armbands, raising signs and leafleting passers-by.

The First Amendment also protects the rights of Americans to refuse to utter things they do not believe. When some children of Jehovah's Witnesses objected to repeating the Pledge of Allegiance in schools – because in the view of the parents this was worship of 'graven images' (the flag) – the nine justices of the Supreme Court overturned their suspension from school, in the case of *West Virginia State Board of Education* v. *Barnette* (1943). The ruling declared that: 'No official, high or petty, can prescribe what shall be orthodox in politics, nationalism or religion, or other matters of opinion, or force citizens to confess by word or act their faith therein.'

In *Watchtower Bible and Tract Society of New York Inc* v. *Village of Stratton, Ohio* (2002) there was further protection for the same religious group. The Court protected the rights of people who go from door to door – whether for political, religious or other reasons. The Jehovah's Witnesses had challenged a

Stratton law that required their officers to get a permit before they did so, but the ruling declared that 'it is offensive . . . to the very notion of a free society, that in the context of everyday public discourse a citizen must first inform the government of [his] or [her] desire to speak to [his] or [her] neighbours and then obtain a permit to do so'.

The Court has in the past also upheld state laws that ban seditious behaviour (any conspiracy to overthrow the government by force), but it has not allowed convictions of communists solely on account of their membership of the Communist Party, for to do so would infringe the right of freedom of association. In other words, merely to believe in the violent overthrow of those who rule is not in itself a crime, nor is membership of any body that advocates such a policy. It is actually attempting to overthrow the government that is prohibited. This position was made clear in the case of *Whitney* v. *California* (1927). Whitney was convicted under state law of engaging in Communist Party organisational activities. The Supreme Court upheld the Californian statute, although a dissenting justice (Louis Brandeis) argued that 'only serious danger to the state . . . an emergency can justify repression'. Forty-two years later, in *Brandenburg* v. *Ohio*, the line taken by Brandeis was supported in the Court, which adopted the 'clear, present, and imminent danger' test in such cases.

Protection under the Constitution is also granted in cases of 'speech plus', those that exceed the normal understanding of what speech involves. These may concern such things as wearing buttons and burning flags, '**symbolic speech**' or speech-related activities. The anti-war students who entered a courthouse with the words 'F . . . the draft' on the back of his jacket was held in contempt of court by the judge, but the Supreme Court did

> **symbolic speech**
> Speech-related acts such as flag burning, gestures and even the wearing of certain types of clothing that are protected under the First Amendment, because they relate to the communication of ideas or opinions.

not concur. The justices ruled that: 'While the particular four-letter word being litigated here is perhaps more distasteful than most others of its genre [kind], it nevertheless is often true that one man's vulgarity is another's lyric.' Flag burning too was protected towards the close of the twentieth century. In *Texas* v. *Johnson* (1989), the Court took the view that: 'If there is a bedrock principle underlying the First Amendment, it is that Government may not prohibit the expression of an idea simply because society finds the idea itself offensive or disagreeable.'

Legal rights: the rights of the accused

The Fifth and Fourteenth Amendments prevent national and state governments from depriving citizens of their lives, liberty or property without due process of law. Due process, a phrase used in the Fourteenth Amendment, provides the guarantee of fairness in rulings and actions of government officials, especially those in the courtroom. In criminal trials, the right of due process includes:

- the right to free counsel if you cannot afford a lawyer, and to have a legal representative present at any police questioning;
- the right to reasonable bail after being charged;
- the right to a speedy trial;
- the right to confront and cross examine any who accuses or testifies against you, and to remain silent;
- the right to an impartial judge and a jury selected without racial bias;
- the right of appeal to a higher court if legal errors are committed by a judge;
- protection from double jeopardy ('nor shall any person be subject for the same offence to be twice put in jeopardy of life and limb').

In the landmark case of *Miranda* v. *Arizona* (1966), the Supreme Court outlined a set of procedures to be followed by the police before any individual

---

LEGAL RIGHTS DENIED: ANTI-TERRORIST LEGISLATION

After the 9/11 attacks on New York and Washington, there was widespread debate in the United States and elsewhere about the threats to freedom and security. By their actions, the terrorists involved had destroyed the most basic right of all – the right to life – of nearly 4,000 Americans, and had threatened the 'life, liberty and pursuit of happiness' of many more.

Almost every American could agree on the need to ensure greater security of the person by rooting out terrorists and preventing the danger of further attacks. But critics of the Bush administration claim that its package of anti-terrorist measures ('Uniting and Strengthening America By Providing Appropriate Tools Required To Intercept and Obstruct Terrorism' – more usually known as 'the USA Patriot Act') – went far beyond what was necessary to achieve these objectives. They detected signs of a serious erosion of accepted freedoms, in particular: the way in which new powers tilted the balance of power towards the executive branch and removed from the judicial system some of its power to review the actions of the administration; the dedication to secrecy, which made it difficult to find out information relating to the six hundred or so detainees held in federal prisons; and the undermining of the traditional distinction between foreign intelligence gathering and criminal investigation at home.

Critics claimed that the situation created by 9/11 was being used to launch an unnecessarily broad attack on civil liberties in America. The *New York Times*[1] felt inspired to launch a ferocious attack on the limitations being imposed on personal freedom. In an editorial, it was claimed that: 'Civil liberties are eroding, and there is no evidence that the reason is anything more profound than fear and frustration . . . Two months into the war against terrorism, the nation is sliding toward the trap that we entered this conflict vowing to avoid.'

can be questioned. Once an investigation is under way with the focus on one individual, he or she must receive the following warning:

You have the right to remain silent.
Anything you say may be used against you in a court of law.
You have the right to be represented by an attorney of your choice.
If you cannot afford an attorney, a public defender will be provided for you if you wish.

These **Miranda rules** apply when a person has been taken into custody or otherwise significantly deprived of freedom of movement by the police. Although some exceptions have been created, in essence they still govern all police interrogations. Courts have often thrown out confessions obtained where the rules have not been followed.

Miranda rules
The list of guidelines concerning the treatment of people during 'custodial interrogation', as established by the *Miranda* v. *Arizona* ruling.

Detention at Guantanamo Bay

The growing anxiety about the threat to freedom came to a head in early 2002 over the issue of the treatment of terrorist suspects at Guantanamo Bay in Southeast Cuba, an area leased by the USA as a naval base in 1903. They were held in one of three detention areas: Camp Delta, Camp Iguana and Camp X-Ray. The plan was to try them before special military courts, against whose decision there would be no right of appeal. The defense secretary labelled them as 'unlawful combatants' rather than as 'prisoners of war', thus denying them the full protection of the Geneva Convention. But under international law they were not to be subjected to torture, nor to inhumane treatment. Civil libertarians around the world were disturbed by reports concerning the conditions in which they were being held.

Many critics could accept that it was understandable that America wished to glean as much information as possible from the Taliban and Al Qaeda detainees. They felt little sympathy for their alleged actions and recognised that they might have been part of a dangerous terrorist conspiracy against Western targets. Yet they recognised that detainees still had rights. If they were not covered by the Geneva 'laws of war', then they were ordinary criminals. As such, if tried in the United States they would have been protected by the Sixth Amendment, which insists that in 'all criminal prosecutions' in the United States inalienable rights apply, including the right to a jury trial. But they were being held in a place beyond the remit of normal US jurisdiction.

Legal challenges to the Bush policy

The arrest and detention of Guatanamo detainees aroused strong criticism among many individuals and groups in the USA. In November 2003, the Supreme Court announced that it would listen to cases brought on appeal by Afghan war detainees who challenged their continued detention at the camp as being unlawful. It subsequently made a number of rulings that undermined the detention policy, most notably:

- In **Rasul v. Bush** (2004), the Court ruled that detainees at Guantanamo were entitled to constitutional protections.

- In **Hamdi v. Rumsfeld** (2004), it recognised the power of the government to detain unlawful combatants, but ruled that detainees who were US citizens must have the ability to challenge their detention before an impartial judge.

- In **Hamdan v. Rumsfeld** (2006), it decided that the military commissions established by executive order to try detainees were unlawful and violated the American Uniform Code of Military Justice, the 1949 Geneva Conventions and various human rights standards relating to fair trials. The justices also disagreed with the administration's view that the laws and customs of war did not apply to the armed conflict with Al Qaeda and Taliban fighters in Afghanistan.

- After the Republican majority in Congress had passed the Military Commissions Act in response to the Hamdan verdict, in **Boumediene v. Bush** (2008) the Court found the

Civil rights: the search for equality

In the Declaration of Independence, Thomas Jefferson decreed that 'all men are created equal'. By this, he was not saying that everybody was alike and that there were no differences between human beings. Indeed, throughout his life, he clearly believed that there were differences, for he took the view that black Americans were genetically inferior to whites. But a further clue to his meaning is to be found in the same declaration, when it speaks of the 'inalienable rights' to which all are entitled. He wanted everyone to have the same chance, in other words, equality of opportunity. What individuals made of that chance was, in his view, a matter dependent on their abilities and efforts. He did not favour equality of outcome, with its emphasis on equal rewards, but he did think that in a moral sense all had the right to equal consideration.

The struggle for equality has been the rallying point for all groups demanding an end to discrimination against them and the attainment of their full civil rights, among them African Americans, women, and others such as gays and lesbians and the disabled. The list could be extended to cover the victims of discrimination on grounds of age (the old and the young), people with AIDS and the homeless. Here we concentrate on the campaign for civil rights associated with ethnic minorities and women, and more briefly take on board the issue of gays and the disabled. All of these groups have presented challenges to mainstream America.

Military Commissions Act was an unconstitutional suspension of habeas corpus, for it failed to provide adequate provisions to guarantee a fair trial.

Guantanamo today

In the election campaign of 2008, Barack Obama described the events at the Guantanamo camp as 'a sad chapter in American history' and pledged himself to close it down as soon as possible. In January 2009, the White House announced that the detention facility would be shut down within the year. Obama subsequently ordered a review of all the detainees' cases, to determine whether and how prosecution might proceed. However, the plan encountered a setback when officials within his administration discovered that in many cases there were no comprehensive files concerning the detainees, so that merely assembling the available evidence about them could take months. In December of that year, the president ordered the preparation of the Thomson Correctional Center in Illinois, in order that Guantanamo prisoners could be eventually moved there. However, at the time of writing (May 2011), 171 prisoners remain at Guantanamo. Moreover, the passage of the Defense Authorization Bill in early January 2011 contains provisions preventing the transfer of Guantanomo prisoners to the mainland or to other foreign countries. This effectively stops the Obama policy of closing the detention facility.

If minorities and women have achieved partial success and seen a considerable expansion of their civil rights, other groups too have found it difficult to progress as far as they would, in today's conservative social climate. In particular, gays and lesbians still feel that their campaign for the same rights as those enjoyed by heterosexual Americans has a long way to run. So too do the disabled and the growing band of American's elderly feel that their rights need greater recognition.

Civil rights for black Americans

The treatment of black Americans up until the 1950s

Until the late nineteenth century, black Americans were primarily subjugated by custom and economic conditions rather than as a result of legislation. But around the turn of the century, several laws were enacted which allowed persecution and separation to exist. It became illegal for black and white people to travel together, or to share other public facilities such as hospitals and swimming baths. The statutes were often known as the **Jim Crow laws**, a name derived from a runaway slave who composed a song and dance in which the name was

Jim Crow laws
The generic name for all laws and practices that enforced segregation of the races in the American South, from the late nineteenth to the mid-twentieth centuries.

used. It was taken up by white comics and came into general use as a label for all black Americans. As a result, blacks were excluded from the electorate and from most worthwhile job opportunities.

According to the Constitution, the 'equal protection' clause of the Fourteenth Amendment decreed that no state could 'deny to any person within its jurisdiction the equal protection of the laws'. Yet this requirement was easily evaded, because the *Plessy* v. *Ferguson* ruling (1896) of the Supreme Court determined that racial segregation was not discrimination if 'equal accommodations' were provided for members of both races. In fact, there never was such equality, and for many years black Americans experienced inferior conditions, and – denied the vote – had no effective means of protest. There were a few challenges in the Supreme Court, but these never produced significant changes.

The lot of the majority of African Americans was to suffer three indignities: **segregation**, discrimination and intimidation. The latter came in the form of terror from the **Ku Klux Klan** and other secret societies, and beatings and lynchings by their members were commonplace.

segregation
The practice of creating separate facilities within the same society for the use of a minority group.

Ku Klux Klan (KKK)
The KKK is the collective name used in reference to several past and present secret terrorist bodies that are part of a white supremacist, anti-Semitic movement whose supporters share a commitment to extreme measures to achieve the goal of racial segregation.

At the turn of the twentieth century, 90% blacks lived in the South and the vast majority of them were employed in agriculture. But between the wars there was a drift to the North as they and their offspring looked for work in the developing towns and cities, where they hoped to make a better life for themselves and their families. Their social status remained low; life was hard and many were poverty-stricken.

It was American involvement in World War II that created jobs for people of all colour and race. Once the fighting was over, returning black soldiers wanted a better deal for their families than they had known before. In the North, the number of blacks was growing, so that in Washington there was a black majority by 1961. They were becoming frustrated with their rate of advance. There were among them some articulate and able leaders who began to make an impact in their chosen field – business, education, the church, the law and the arts. The majority of their race had no such good fortune, and resentment was becoming more overt.

Postwar progress on civil rights to the 1960s

A major step forward had already come about by then, for in 1954 the Supreme Court reversed the 1896 'separate but equal' judgment, and declared that separate facilities were 'inherently unequal'. The case was *Brown* v. *Topeka Board of Education*, which concerned the issue of desegregation. At that stage, there were still seventeen states that segregated schools in accordance with their own laws. The Court said that segregated schools were illegal, for 'segregation is itself discrimination'. It had to be ended with 'all deliberate speed'. This judgment of the Warren Court shocked conservative America, members of which disliked such judicial liberalism. Although several states implemented it speedily, there were others where the dominant whites were determined to retain their privileged position. Governors in the Deep South sought to use the law to evade the ruling, but over the coming years the Supreme Court struck down many attempts to frustrate its will.

In 1957, President Eisenhower had to send in federal troops to Little Rock, Arkansas, to ensure that black children were allowed to enter the white school. The president saw the attitude of the governor as a challenge to federal authority, and it was probably his determination to insist on central power as much as his determination to enforce civil rights which influenced his action. Over the following years, segregation gradually disappeared. In 1969, the Supreme Court decreed that 'all deliberate speed' must be interpreted as immediately. Dual schools were brought to an end.

Much of the progress in the 1960s came about as a result of the campaigning of the Civil Rights Movement. In particular, the National Association for the Advancement of Colored People (NAACP) had achieved a significant victory in 1955, when a **bus boycott** by blacks in Montgomery ended in the

> **bus boycott**
> The bus boycott was a technique of popular protest first used in the 1940s by black activists to challenge segregation in South Africa. The method was borrowed by black American activists in the US, against a background of heightened civil rights activity and a rising tide of massive resistance.

Dr Martin Luther King

Martin Luther King (1929–68) was born into a well-educated and relatively prosperous family whose members understood the ways in which the church and the NAACP strengthened the black community.

Initially, he wanted to become a minister, but he became active in the black boycott of Montgomery's segregated buses (1955), helped to establish the Southern Christian Leadership Conference, which campaigned for greater equality for American blacks (1957) and thereafter was involved in anti-segregation sit-ins and freedom rides. He stressed the importance of non-violent, passive resistance, although his activities often led to his arrest. In 1963, he made his inspirational 'I Have a Dream' speech (see pp. 387–388) in the March on Washington, his actions encouraging President Johnson to obtain civil rights legislation.

Towards the end of his life, he was increasingly criticised by some black as well as white Americans. In 1968, he was assassinated by a social misfit, James Earl Ray, who had long derided him as 'Martin Luther Coon'.

company relenting and ceasing to reserve seats for white people. This episode led to the emergence of Dr Martin Luther King as a leader in the crusade for racial justice.

There were many protests and demonstrations in the early 1960s, during which Dr King won over much white liberal opinion with his 'dream' of racial equality. President Kennedy was sympathetic on the issue of civil rights, but after his assassination it was Lyndon Johnson who introduced the Great Society legislation which included many measures to end racial injustice – among them, the Voting Rights Act of 1965 and the Civil Rights Acts of 1964 and 1968 that tackled discrimination in jobs and housing. (For a listing of civil rights legislation, see p. 391.) The integrationist phase of the Civil Rights Movement reached its peak in the 1960s.

An important and controversial feature of the progress in that decade was the introduction of special programmes – sometimes backed by federal money – to help promote racial or gender balance. The policy was known as **affirmative action**, and involved a set of procedures designed to correct the effects of past discrimination against minority groups (and women). Specific targets were laid down and quotas sometimes applied in recruitment for jobs and university places, with the intention of boosting the representation of minorities. Since the late 1960s, affirmative programmes have been adopted by national, state and local governments, by public institutions such as state colleges and universities, and by some private employers and organisations.

Affirmative action
Better known in England as positive discrimination, affirmative action programmes are designed to increase the chances of women and minorities being selected for positions in public life, such as on university courses or in management positions. The topic has become one of fierce debate in the last two decades.

NB See pp. 401–405 for further details of affirmative action programmes and the intense debates they have subsequently inspired. Much of the information there is highly relevant to this section on the advancement of civil rights for black Americans.

The rise of Black Power

In the 1960s, much was being done to improve the rights of blacks and to remove some of the worst forms of discrimination, but many of them still found that their conditions in areas such as education, employment and housing were markedly worse than those of white Americans. Many felt powerless, and unrest in the underclass of black Americans was beginning to gather pace.

Dr King preached passive resistance and non-violent direct action, arguing that violence stood little chance of success against the might of the American government. He disliked the 'hate whitey' language adopted by some of his younger, more militant critics who wanted to see a different approach. They questioned the desirability of integration, the strategy on non-violence and the presence of white liberals in the leadership of the cause. King was particularly condemnatory of the tone adopted in the early 1960s by Malcolm X, a leader of the radical black Nation of Islam that had been established back in 1930 and had spread through some of the northern cities in the 1950s and afterwards. Many of its supporters were anti-Semitic (anti-Jewish) and sexist, Malcolm X describing the best position of women as 'horizontal'. He rejected political activity through the orthodox channels and urged racial separation.

Malcolm X (1926–65)

Born into a ghetto background, Malcolm Little spent his early life in petty crime, drug abuse and pimping, before being converted in prison to the Nation of Islam. He replaced his 'slave name' Little with X.

Malcolm X's prominence increased in the 1950s, his preaching of black pride appealing to ghetto blacks. He went on several speaking tours and helped establish several new mosques. He was eventually assigned to be minister of the mosque in New York's Harlem area. Founder and editor of *Muhammad Speaks*, he rejected integration and racial equality and instead advocated black power. He denounced the 'Farce on Washington' in 1963, but left the Nation of Islam a year later to engage more fully in the civil rights struggle.

In his last years – after a pilgrimage to Mecca – he rejected his former separatist beliefs and advocated world brotherhood. He blamed racism on Western culture and urged African Americans to join with sympathetic whites to bring discrimination to an end. He was prepared to cooperate with whites against racism and apologised for his attacks on King. He was murdered in 1965, three black Muslims being later convicted of the murder.

The assassination of King (April 1968) confirmed many blacks in their belief that society was so rotten that peaceful change would not work. Some leaders were more confrontational, among them Stokely Carmichael, who felt that the whites would never surrender their supremacy. Whereas King talked the language of integration, Carmichael was committed to separatism. He and other 'Black Power' activists called on blacks to reject white society; they urged the use of the term 'blacks' rather than 'negroes', a term with overtones of past humiliations. They wanted to see black children taught pride in their black culture, so that a generation would grow up willing to challenge those who suppressed them. A more militant group was the Black Panther organisation, which believed in armed revolution, an open war with white society.

Within the black leadership, there were many divisions. Many of the older generation still believed in the methods of Martin Luther King, others believed that the pace of advance was too slow if they relied on seeking to secure white goodwill. Some of the spokesmen were unimpressive, and there was discord over personality and tactics. None the less, the emphasis upon 'Black Power for Black

---

Black Power

The Black Power movement developed out of the Civil Rights Movement, which had steadily gained momentum through the 1950s and 1960s. Although not a formal movement, the movement for black power marked a turning point in black–white relations and also in how blacks saw themselves.

Power was the demand of the militant Stokely Carmichael, who rejected the King approach to black campaigning for civil rights. He urged the burning of 'every court house in Mississippi' and proclaimed 'black power', a term taken up by his supporters.

Enthusiasts rejected the integrationist ideas of King, who was concerned not to alienate white liberals. They felt that integration was no longer possible or even desirable, and instead argued for black and white separation. Supporters believed that the only route to attaining equality in positions of power was to oppose the evils of white authority by every possible means, including violence. The Black Power movement was concerned to develop a sense of black consciousness, which is why it rejected the earlier ethnic term 'negro', which was associated by many white Americans with the idea of 'subservient niggers'.

Some hailed the movement as a positive and proactive force aimed at helping blacks achieve full equality with whites. Others reviled it as a militant, sometimes violent faction whose primary goal was to drive a wedge between whites and blacks.

People' helped to make many black Americans more proud of their race and their individuality. They were gaining a personal dignity that many had never had before.

Economic and social progress since the 1960s

As we have seen, the affirmative action programmes launched in the 1960s provided special benefits to those in the community who had been traditionally disadvantaged. In providing enhanced opportunities, it was anticipated that there might also be other benefits, such as enriching the nation's economic, social and cultural life and creating greater harmony and stability. This might result from reduced tension on the part of disaffected blacks, and also from the creation of a larger black middle class which would feel it had a stake in society and would demonstrate to others that advancement is possible.

Affirmative action programmes did assist many black Americans in improving their status and opportunities. But such was the weight of past injustice and disadvantage that in education, entrance to medical school and gaining skilled employment, access was likely to be denied to many of them for years to come. Moreover, in recent years, a succession of Supreme Court judgments has restricted the use of racial preference in areas such as admissions to educational institutions and awarding grants and contracts.

After the burst of activity in the 1960s, the rate of progress has been patchy. There have been legislative and other advances, but in many areas of life much remains to be done:

- In **housing**, it has proved difficult to end discrimination, for white residents and estate agents in some districts combine to ensure that 'undesirable' elements are kept out.
- In **employment**, blacks still suffer twice as much unemployment as whites, and access to jobs can be limited by factors such as poor educational attainment and covert or indirect discrimination. Some blacks have 'made it' and done well, and act as a role model for others, but the majority who work do so in low-paid positions.
- Black **poverty** actually increased in the later 1970s and 1980s, and remains a serious problem. Whilst there are some examples of successful black Americans, one in three live in poverty (one half of black children), and many are very deprived. Recession, the impact of Reaganite policies and the increasing number of one-parent families were all contributory factors. The gap between black and white earnings actually increased towards the end of the century.
- The black **infant mortality rate** of 19% was higher than in some countries in the developing world.
- Poor, ghetto **living conditions** and **lack of employment** opportunities were associated in the minds of many white Americans with black crime, contributing to a white backlash against measures designed to help promote black progress. The violence that erupted in Los Angeles in 1992 showed that race relations between black and white Americans were poor. Four white policemen used unnecessary force to arrest Rodney King in March 1991. Following their acquittal by a white jury, four days of rioting resulted, culminating in forty-seven deaths, more than 2,000 injuries and 9,000 arrests.

Black gains in the 1960s via legislation (see below) and affirmative action programmes created much white resentment. Many whites could accept black legal and political rights and appreciate the contribution made by black sporting celebrities, but widespread class prejudice and racism remained. If any proposed solution to black poverty involved higher taxation, many whites were not keen to hear the message.

Progress in political life

In the last few decades, the focus of black politics in the United States has changed from being primarily concerned with southern blacks' acquisition of the right to vote, to an emphasis on acquiring significant representation in the major institutions of American political life at national, state and local levels. This transformation in the approach to political participation is perhaps best characterised as a move away from the politics of protest, operating on the outside of the political system, to a commitment to working within the political system as the best means of securing real gains.

THE BLACK VOTE

Traditionally, it has been the Democrats who have been more active in the field of civil rights, and they have been rewarded with overwhelming support from black voters. Lyndon Johnson won 94% of the black vote, the highest figure recorded for one party, but Clinton won over 80% in 1992. Clinton won massive backing from many black leaders during the impeachment process. They claimed that one of the reasons he was under attack was because of his policies towards black Americans. He was their friend, in the words of one civil rights activist:[1] 'Someone called Bill Clinton our first black president, and I do think he is a man who understands race. He identifies with black people and has black friends outside politics.' Al Gore was unable to enthuse blacks so much, but he also scored well among them in the 2000 election. In 2004, by which time African Americans constituted 11% of the electorate, exit surveys indicated that Kerry won 89% of the black vote. Unsurprisingly, Barack Obama did even better. By then, they made up 12.1% of the electorate, 95% of them voting Democrat.

Black voter turnout in the 2004 and 2008 elections

Much of the surge in black voter participation in 2008 was driven by the greater participation among black women and younger voters, their turnout rates respectively increasing by 5.1% and 8.7% over the presidential election of four years earlier. Overall, the greatest increases in turnout between the two elections were in the southern states, with large black populations eligible. In Mississippi, turnout was up 8.5%, in Georgia 7.5%, in North Carolina 6.1% and in Louisiana 6.0%. (In Washington DC it was up 6.9%.)

This increased size of the potential and actual black vote was highly significant in some southern states. In North Carolina, 74% of the state's registered African American voters turned out, as opposed to 69% of North Carolinians in general. According to exit polling,[2] Obama won the support of almost 100% of black American females and of black Americans aged 18 to 29. This was the case in Virginia as well, where much higher turnout among African Americans propelled Obama to victory in the former Republican stronghold.

The growing size of the ethnic minority vote in presidential elections (percentages)

Presidential election	White voters	Black voters	Hispanic voters	Asian voters
1988	84.9	9.8	3.6	
1992	84.6	9.9	3.8	1.2
1996	82.5	10.6	4.7	1.6
2000	80.7	11.5	5.4	1.8
2004	79.2	11.0	6.0	2.3
2008	76.3	12.1	7.4	2.5

Figures in this table are adapted from M. Lopez and P. Taylor, Dissecting the 2008 Electorate: Most Diverse in US History, Pew Research Center Publications, 2009.

NB The figures for whites, blacks and Asians do not include Hispanics in these groups. The Asian share is not available pre-1990.

Prior to the passage of the 1965 Voting Rights Act (VRA), few black Americans held political office as members of Congress or state legislatures, mayorships or other important public offices. Following its implementation,

The black conservative vote

In spite of the traditional association between black voters and the Democratic Party, the voting behaviour of blacks is no longer as predictable as it once was. The black conservative is less of a rarity than in the past, Clarence Thomas and others being testimony to this phenomenon. Alan Keyes made history as the first African American to seek the Republican nomination for the White House for 1996. If his attempt was short lived, it none the less suggested that there is a growing willingness among more prosperous blacks to abandon past allegiances. Such voters share with middle-class whites an antipathy to the usual pro-black policies such as the welfare state and affirmative action, believing that these liberal shibboleths sap African American pride and foster a black dependency culture. There was some evidence of these trends in the 2004 election.

The Joint Center for Political and Economic Studies, a Washington DC-based black political research institute noted that between 2000 and 2004 there was an 11% fall in the percentage of the registered Democrat vote, with one in three of the under-35s describing themselves as independent. In the same period the percentage of blacks registered as Republican tripled, albeit from a low base. This feature was evident in the 2000 election in Florida, where a record black vote in Democratic precincts almost tipped the disputed election to Democrat Al Gore. Four years later, a much-reduced black turnout, combined with the 13% of the black votes Bush received (double his figure in 2000) helped the president to win the state outright. Republican gains among the black voters of Ohio were more dramatic, for Bush picked up nearly 20% of the vote.

Under their strategist Karl Rove, the Republicans in 2004 were keen to redefine the fight for black rights, in a bid to appeal to young, upwardly mobile blacks. For them, rights were not about more entitlement and more government welfare, but rather pro-business and homeownership, pro-social security privatisation and/or decentralisation to the states, and pro-family values. Rove also recognised the emergence of black evangelicals as a potent political force. They warmed to the anti-abortion and anti-gay rhetoric of many Republicans. Conservative values have begun to spread lower down the social scale. In the anti-abortion movement and the Christian Coalition, attitudes can be shared by Americans of different colours and classes.

In seeking to broaden their appeal to black and other ethnic minority voters, the Republicans are recognising that their concerns are going to become increasingly important in determining the outcome of federal and state elections in the years to come. In 2008, they failed to capitalise on their performance in 2004, but as the mid-term results indicated in 2010, the Democrats cannot take the votes of the three largest minority groups – blacks, Hispanics and Asians – for granted.

southern blacks were able to exercise their newly acquired political clout to elect members of their own race, and northern blacks increased their influence to the extent that they were able to gain representation in districts where they did not constitute a majority.

According to the National Council of State Legislatures, in 1970, 179 blacks served in national and state legislatures; by 2000, there were 570; and by 2009, there were 628 such legislators. When Barack Obama won the senatorial race in Illinois (November 2004), his victory was won against a black opponent. (He became the only black member of the Senate, and only the third ever to be elected.) In early 2009, there were more than 640 black mayors in American towns and cities, nearly fifty of them in places of more than 50,000 population and many more for localities in which there was a minority black population. In the 112th Congress, there are forty-four blacks in the House and none in the Senate.

In 1969, the overall total of black elected officials was around 1,200; by 2000, it exceeded 7,500; and by 2007, it had risen to more than 9,400. The figures indicate substantial progress, even if most of those elected still serve at the municipal level. Their election in part reflects increased black voting in inner-city ghetto areas, but the willingness to elect a black representative in several other areas there exists a white majority has been noticeable.

Of the presidents of the last half century, Lyndon Johnson appointed the first black to a cabinet post, Nixon appointed four African American ambassadors, Bush senior nominated Clarence Thomas to the Supreme Court and Bill Clinton proved himself to be more willing to put forward black appointees to the judiciary than any of his predecessors. George W. Bush selected Colin Powell as his first Secretary of State and Condoleezza Rice as his National Security Adviser and then – from early 2005 – as Powell's successor. President Obama included three black appointees in his cabinet (Eric Holder, Ron Kirk and Susan Rice).

Although the scale of black political advancement can be exaggerated, its magnitude is illustrated by the prominence over many years of Jesse Jackson within the Democratic Party, and most dramatically by the election of a black president. The son of an illiterate South Carolina sharecropper, Jackson rose to prominence in the Southern Christian Leadership Conference and hoped to take over the leadership from Martin Luther King. He was so keen to advertise their closeness that on the day of King's assassination he appeared on television with what he claimed was his hero's blood on his shirt. By 1984, and again in 1988, his appeal was such that he campaigned (unsuccessfully) for the Democratic nomination for the presidency, although the mainstream of the party did not consider him the man to take on Ronald Reagan. On the second occasion he won markedly more support from white party members, his 'rainbow [all colours] coalition' faring especially well in New York, among blacks, whites and Hispanics. Jackson remains a leading figure who commands respect and whose backing is much sought after by potential presidential candidates.

Of course, the most dramatic and visible indication of black advancement has been the election of Barack Obama – born in Hawaii to a black Kenyan father and a white American mother – to the presidency. If his background is distinctive from that of many African American politicians and civil rights activists of recent decades, he none the less possesses the oratorical skills characteristic of many of them; his use of language having been compared to that of Dr King.

Postwar progess reviewed

The Democrats have been more committed than the Republicans to the active pursuit of racial justice in the United States. Truman (1945–53) was the first president to take active measures to help black Americans. He established a liberal civil rights committee to investigate violence against them and used its report, 'To Secure These Rights', as ammunition in his attack on the problems they faced. In his State of the Union address (1948), he had proclaimed that: 'Our first goal must be to secure fully the essential human rights of our citizens.' He drew attention to the disparity between the words of America's Founding Fathers ('All men are created equal') and the actions of their descendants. He acted to end discrimination in the armed forces and to guarantee fair employment in the civil service.

Thereafter, progress followed in the Kennedy, Johnson, Carter and Clinton presidencies, whether in the appointment of black judges, the greater willingness to adopt black candidates for public office, the pursuit of policies based on affirmative action or legislation against discrimination. Black voters recognised that the Democrats were more likely to pursue policies advantageous to them (see p. 384), and the party's presidential candidates have benefited from their generally solid support over many years.

But what has been achieved? How different is the America of today from the country to which Martin Luther King addressed his message in Washington more than forty years ago? On that occasion, he reminded his audience of the past situation, before proceeding to outline his future vision:

> Five score years ago, a great American, in whose symbolic shadow we stand today, signed the Emancipation Proclamation. This momentous decree came as a great beacon light of hope to millions of Negro slaves who had been seared in the flames of withering injustice . . . One hundred years later, the life of the negro is still sadly crippled by the manacles of segregation and the chains of discrimination . . . we have come here today to dramatise a shameful condition . . .

So I say to you, my friends, that even though we face the difficulties of today and tomorrow, I still have a dream. It is a dream deeply rooted in the American dream, that one day this nation will rise up and live out the true meaning of its creed – we hold these truths to be self-evident, that all men are created equal . . .

With this faith we will be able to tear out of the mountain of despair a stone of hope. With this faith, we will be able to transform the jangling discords of our nation into a beautiful symphony of brotherhood . . .

The passage of civil rights legislation two years after that speech drew a line under the civil rights era for many Americans. Since there were no legal barriers to black participation, some chose to ignore the economic, social and political barriers that remained. Not only would they come to resist demands to address the legacy of segregation and slavery through affirmative action. They would do so with King's own words, insisting that candidates for university and

A NOTE ON RED POWER AND THE PROGRESS MADE BY NATIVE AMERICANS

At the turn of the 1960s, the disadvantages endured by Native Americans were worse than those experienced by many African Americans. Many of the problems were the same – inadequate housing, poverty and unemployment, and a lack of educational opportunities. More than half of them lived on reservations, where, at 44 years, life expectancy was twenty years less than the national average, tuberculosis was a regular killer and suicide rates were alarmingly high – not a problem that affected the black population. Native Americans, even more than other minority groups, suffered from low self-esteem, for they felt despised not only on account of their ethnicity but also on account of their distinctive culture.

The National Congress of American Indians (NCAI) had been established in 1944 and it had made some gains, preventing reservation rights from being terminated under the Eisenhower administration and winning support from President Kennedy for a jobs strategy to boost employment opportunities. Like the NAACP, it used the courts to achieve social and political progress, but unlike the more famous pressure group it did not advocate racial integration. Its goal was to ensure the survival of the unique cultural identity of Native Americans.

Red Power

The Red Power movement sought equal rights and justice for Native Americans. As a group, they were inspired by the campaign for equality so ably pursued by American blacks. Like them, many adopted an increasingly militant approach in the 1960s. Young activists tired of the NCAI approach, which in their view involved too close cooperation with the Bureau of Indian Affairs (BIA). Many turned to the American Indian Movement (AIM), the most overtly confrontational organisation. It developed in the ghettos of

employment should be 'judged not on the colour of their skin but the content of their character'.

For King, the March and speech were a beginning. He told reporters shortly before his death that 'it is now absolutely necessary now to deal massively and militantly with the economic problem. The grave problem facing us is the problem of economic deprivation, with the syndrome of bad housing and poor education and improper health facilities all surrounding this basic problem.'

Integration has won for many African Americans the right to eat in any restaurant, but only more equal facilities and opportunities can ensure that more of them have the funds to finance the meal. Further progress continues to be hampered by divisions within the black leadership, racial tension, the white backlash and the sheer difficulty for many African Americans of steering themselves out of the ghetto poverty trap.

Minneapolis-St Paul and demanded reform of ghetto conditions and an end to harassment of Native Americans by the police.

In common with the approach of their militant black equivalents, the AIM leaders wanted to present a more positive image of Native Americans. They spoke of Red Power, indulged in acts of civil disobedience, occupied BIA offices and committed sporadic violence. Such tactics inspired a backlash among some white Americans, as did those of Black Power supporters. However, white Americans were generally more sympathetic to Native Americans, seeing them as less of a threat to the white position.

Progress in recent years

In the late twentieth century, Native Americans made some progress within American society, a process begun during the Great Society years as a result of the War on Poverty programme. They were assisted by other federal policies. Money was made available for several forms of tribal development. By 1980, Congress had authorised substantial payments to compensate for previous unjust land losses; many Indian studies programmes had been created within the higher educational system; and tribal museums had opened. Useful though such programmes were, it was also true that some of the improvement in Native American economic status owed more to a growing tourist influence in Native American culture than it did to government action.

Overall, there has been some modest increase in the living standards of many Native Americans, but they remain more than twice as likely to fall below the poverty level than African Americans and have a significantly lower level of educational attainment. Under 2 million in number, they are a declining proportion of the population. AIM continues to fight over rights to lands; protest over athletic team Indian mascots; and seek repatriation of sacred objects once removed from Native American land.

The struggle for women's rights

For many years, American women experienced the same treatment as their counterparts in Europe. It was widely assumed that their responsibilities involved the domestic role of caring for their children and husbands, for whom they were expected to be attractive and dignified adornments. They were seen as goods and chattels, dependants of their fathers and husbands. They had few legal rights and were unable to vote. Neither was there much opportunity to further their interests through educational advancement. This sense of powerlessness and dependency inspired some pioneering women to involve themselves in the women's movement. Under a hundred of them gathered in New York State in 1848, where they proclaimed the Seneca Falls Declaration of Rights and Sentiments and demanded 'the rights and privileges which belong to them as citizens of the United States'.

As elsewhere, the position of the minority of women who were striving for greater recognition was a difficult one. They were excluded from a political system dominated by men, and their chances of securing their rights and improving the lot of women in society were therefore dependent upon elected male representatives. Most men were unwilling to share the exercise of power, for they took the view that the world of politics and decision making was one for which they were peculiarly well suited. Those women who tried to involve themselves in political action to persuade men to allow them to open up the citadels of power found themselves ridiculed, slandered or even arrested.

As in Britain, the vote was an initial target for many campaigners for female rights. Suffragists engaged in a variety of persuasive tactics to gain attention, some peaceful and educational, others militant and more intimidatory. Moderates were more willing to argue their case patiently, in countless leaflets and public meetings. Militants were more likely to cause a stir by chaining themselves to the railings of the White House. When they did such things, they were liable to be jailed and force-fed, among other indignities.

However, in the late nineteenth century, some states began to grant women the vote, and gradually it was extended across the country. In 1920, the Nineteenth Amendment made it legally binding for all states to provide for the female franchise. The right to vote was an important equality gain in itself. More than that, it empowered women, for once they had a voice in political life, they were able to use it to campaign for other rights – on matters such as child welfare, anti-lynching and prohibition.

In World War II, the labour shortage created a demand for extra workers. Although many women workers were considered expendable once hostilities were over, there were still 6 million in work, many of them wives rather than single women and a number of them black. Since then, several factors have helped women to advance their position in American society, similar ones to those which apply in Britain:

- the spread of education, especially higher education;
- the need for labour in the economy;
- the increased availability of labour-saving devices in the home;
- the increased ability of women to control their own fertility, via birth control;
- legislative action (see box below).

KEY CIVIL RIGHTS LEGISLATION AFFECTING MEMBERS OF ETHNIC MINORITIES AND WOMEN

Civil Rights Act (1957)

This made it a federal offence to seek to prevent persons from voting in federal elections and authorised the Attorney-General to take legal action when a person was deprived of his or her voting rights. This was targeted at ethnic minorities.

Civil Rights Act (1964)

This has been the most sweeping anti-discriminatory statute. It prohibited discrimination on grounds of race, sex, religion or national origin, and in public accommodation and federally funded programmes. It created the Equal Employment Opportunity Commission. The impact of the measure has been significant for ethnic minorities and women. The impact of the measure, part of the Great Society programme, has been significant for ethnic minorities and women. (At the same time, the Democratic president, Lyndon Johnson, was also committed to a policy of affirmative action, which was popular with many people in both sections of the community.)

Civil Rights Act (1991)

This placed the onus on employers to justify any practices that negatively impacted upon ethnic minorities and women. They were required to defend such practices as being necessary for the job in question, there being no alternative approach available. Compensatory damages could be awarded for intentional discrimination, and punitive damages in the case of employers found guilty of acting with malice or reckless indifference to rights based on sex, religion or disability (they could already be awarded in cases of racial discrimination, under earlier legislation).

The 1991 legislation also established a commission to enquire into the issue of 'glass ceilings', those invisible barriers that served to prevent minorities and women from becoming executives or assuming other important positions in management.

The women's movement

The women's movement today is a broad umbrella, and within it there are several groups pursuing their own agendas. Even where there is agreement on the goals to be pursued, there may be differences of opinion about the means by which they should be attained. All agree, however, on the need to advance rights for women.

ABORTION: A FEMINIST AND A MORAL ISSUE

Abortion, the deliberate termination of a pregnancy, is a highly controversial issue in the United States. It has sometimes been referred to as a 'new Vietnam' because of the way in which it has so sharply polarised popular opinion. What makes it different from most other questions is that it involves a clash of absolutes. To its supporters, it is a matter of a woman's fundamental right to do what she wishes with her own body. To its opponents, it is about the fundamental right to life of the as yet unborn child. Opponents, be they Catholics or supporters of the Christian Right, regard abortion not just as another symptom of a general decline in moral standards, but as a sin. For them, it is a contravention of the divine law of the scriptures, and for the more militant, one they cannot accept.

Abortion is sometimes portrayed as a defining issue between liberals and conservatives, and this is broadly true. But the degree of religious involvement in the debate makes the categorisation less clear cut. Many Catholics who might be liberal on a range of social questions concerning such things as employment rights would find themselves in the conservative camp in discussion of the rights to life of the unborn.

Abortion before and after the 1973 *Roe* v. *Wade* judgment

In the nineteenth century, many states introduced laws against abortion, but by the early 1970s nineteen states permitted it. The American Law Institute and the American Medical Association came out in favour of terminations in certain situations such as foetal abnormality. Their members were also worried about the danger to desperate women who resorted to dubious back-street treatments. They were joined by elements in the growing women's movement, who also campaigned for the removal of restrictive state laws. On the other side of the argument, there were important developments too. Foremost among them was the increasing involvement of the Catholic church in the debate. Its role was crucial to the anti-abortion movement, which resisted any liberalisation of the law. It established the National Right to Life Committee (NRLC) in 1971. Abortion, originally a state concern, had come to assume national importance.

Then, the Supreme Court delivered the much-quoted *Roe* v. *Wade* judgment (1973). It found that state laws against abortion were unconstitutional, for they violated the right of a woman to terminate her pregnancy and thereby have control over her own person. This denied a woman her right to privacy, as laid down in the Fourteenth Amendment. In other words, there was a constitutional right to have an abortion. Abortion thereafter became legal across the United States.

Opponents and supporters of abortion were galvanised into action by this Court judgment. Supporters formed the National Association for the Repeal of Abortion Laws, now known as the National Abortion and Reproductive Rights Action League (NARAL). They felt it necessary to mount a defence of the newly proclaimed right, in order to fend off

Among those who come within the women's movement are some who see women's inferior treatment as part of a more general problem of social disadvantage for minority groups, others who stress the right to work or the

the attacks of those who would seek to undermine it. Many opponents were to be found in the Catholic church, but there were soon stirrings among religious evangelicals. Opposition to abortion became a key issue in the emergence of what was to become the Christian Right (see pp. 318–321).

Limitations upon abortion by the judiciary and legislature

Since 1973, there have been numerous attempts to reverse the legal position, mostly through the courts. In 1989 the Rehnquist Court made a significant inroad into the 'right to choose', in the *Webster* v. *Reproductive Services* case. Instead of overruling the 1973 decision, the justices reduced its impact by acknowledging the constitutional right to an abortion, but also granting more power to individual states to impose restrictions (though not to ban the operation completely). In 1992, in *Casey* v. *Planned Parenthood*, states were given the power to regulate abortion even in the first three months of pregnancy (the period in which the *Roe* v. *Wade* judgment had denied any right of interference) and to ban it once the foetus was deemed to be 'viable'. Yet the basic right was upheld, and state regulations were not to infringe that right unduly.

Clinton's two appointments to the Supreme Court tilted its balance in a more moderate direction, making further Court restrictions less likely. In the 1990s the pressure to limit abortion further came from the legislative branch, following the change of party control in 1994. In late 1995, the House voted to ban a rare, late-term abortion procedure used in cases where there is a severe foetal abnormality or the health of the mother is under threat (partial birth abortion) and to jail doctors who carried it out. The Senate similarly gave the bill a speedy passage. Twice, Bill Clinton used his veto to prevent the measure from reaching the statute book, and in 2000 the Supreme Court ruled against a state law that sought to ban such abortions. The issue remained contentious, for the anti-abortion movement saw it as one on which it could make progress with its campaign to make further inroads into the constitutional right to have an abortion. In 2003, George W. Bush (who opposed abortion except in the most extreme cases) signed a ban on partial birth abortions into law. Because of its limited use, pro-choice groups were outraged at what NARAL called 'the most devastating and appalling attack on a woman's freedom to choose in the history of the House'. Anti-abortionists portrayed the operation as being tantamount to infanticide.

Party reactions

Polls show that Americans are more or less evenly divided on the rights and wrongs of abortion. Even women who favour women's rights in other areas may take a pro-life stance. Both parties are worried by internal fission over the issue. Democrats tend to favour the right to legal abortions and most feminists who campaign for it are committed to the party.

need for greater educational opportunity, and yet more whose interest relates to a single controversial issue such as abortion or lesbianism. Even on abortion, there is a division of opinion (see box on pp. 392–393 for a fuller discussion of the issue), for whereas the majority would stress the mother's right to choose, a minority of activists emphasise the rights of the unborn child. There are also differences over tactics, a variety of approaches having been advocated by campaigners. Some want to change the constitution. Others are content to work for concrete legislative gains, large or small. Some want to work with sympathetic men. More strident voices sometimes portray men as the enemy and see little hope of winning concessions from them – and may indeed find it demeaning to seek them.

Tensions over goals and tactics are liable to surface in many campaigning organisations, but in the 1970s and 1980s there was a general recognition of the need to work for the passage of the **Equal Rights Amendment (ERA),** which was designed to guarantee 'equality or rights' under the law for both sexes. This was an ambitious project that inevitably provoked an anti-feminist backlash, not just from men, but from socially conservative groups as a whole, including religious evangelicals and powerful business interests. Passed by Congress, it was never ratified by enough states to become part of the Constitution and ultimately lapsed in 1982. Many Americans were too anxious about the extent of social change that the amendment might unleash, to allow their support.

Working for constitutional change was successful in 1920 (votes for women), failed sixty-two years later (the ERA) and was again proposed in the 1990s. NOW (see the box below) had been in the forefront of the battle for the ERA and enhanced its reputation and membership in the process. In 1995, it began its campaign for a Constitutional Equality Amendment, bolder, lengthier and more explicit than the original proposal. In article one, it demands that 'women and men shall have equal rights throughout the US and every place and entity subject to its jurisdiction: through this article, the subordination of women to men is abolished'. Elsewhere, it strikes out discrimination on account of 'sex, race, sexual orientation, marital status, ethnicity, national origin, color or indigence' and prohibits 'pregnancy discrimination and guarantees the absolute right of a woman to make her own reproductive decisions including the termination of pregnancy'. Overall, it seeks 'to bring the authority of the Constitution to work on entrenched beliefs about gender difference, as well as equality'.[3]

Despite the pressure of the women's movement for equal rights, women hold only 7% of public offices in the early twenty-first century and women's wages remain on average considerably lower than those of men. Women are more likely to work in white-collar employment, more than a quarter of them performing clerical or office-related work. Their jobs tend to be in sectors that

Some prominent organisations within the women's movement

Created in 1966, the **National Organization for Women (NOW)** is a multi-issue, multi-strategy organisation that takes a holistic approach to women's rights. It campaigns on a broad front, its interests spanning issues such as abortion access, childcare, employment discrimination, the law on marital property and international women's rights. t has over a half a million members across the US, with branches in all fifty states. They employ a variety of campaigning methods, ranging from the traditional electoral and lobbying work to bringing lawsuits, from mass marches to non-violent civil disobedience.

Several women's organisations are concerned with more specific issues, such as the relatively small number of women in key positions in public life. Among these:

EMILY's List (EMILY = Early Money Is Like Yeast) was formed with the intention of getting more pro-choice women elected as representatives of the Democratic Party. It has been very successful at fund raising, and is currently one of the largest donors among American political action committees. Other features of its work include the recruitment and training of candidates and campaign managers. It also acts as a consultancy, offering advice to those interested in its area of concern. EMILY's List targets its money on winnable seats. The Republicans set up a similar (pro-choice) body, the **Wish List**.

The **Fund for a Feminist Majority** targets all seats, whatever the chance of success. It likes to field female candidates at every opportunity.

On the other side of the fence, two right-wing organisations, **Concerned Women for America** and **Eagle Forum**, believe that feminists pose a threat to American society, the more so because of their espousal of the pro-abortion cause. Concerned Women actively opposes NOW and its proposed constitutional amendments. Relying mainly on education and use of the media, it focuses its case on Biblical principles. Among its special causes are education, religious liberty and the sanctity of life (for), and abortions, gay adoptions and pornography (against). Eagle Forum's mission is to enable Christian, conservative pro-family men and women to participate in the political process: work to expose radical feminists; oppose their goals of 'federally financed and regulated child care and feminisation of the military', tax-funded abortions and same-sex marriages; and honour the institution of marriage and the role of the full-time home maker.

pay less well (such as teaching); management/industrial positions are still dominated by men. The fight to upgrade the level of female incomes is an important plank of the women's movement, whose members point out that twice as many women as men have incomes around the minimum-wage level.

The political involvement of women

Women in political office

Some women served in public office even before the introduction of the female franchise. Back in colonial days, the Pennsylvanian assembly appointed a woman as a tax inspector in 1715. Such examples were rare, but it was not unknown for women to gain such responsibilities.

The first woman to stand for Congress received twenty-four votes when she campaigned in 1866. It was to be another fifty years before Jeannette Rankin became the first woman to become a representative. In 1872, Victoria Claflin stood for the presidency on behalf of the Equal Rights Party. Whilst two of her gender have stood as vice-presidential candidates (Geraldine Ferraro for the Democrats in 1984, Sarah Palin for the Republicans in 2008), no woman has served as vice-president. Hillary Clinton's unsuccessful run for the Democratic nomination against Barack Obama did result in her getting a very senior appointment in his administration (secretary of state). She is the most high-profile woman in public office at the time of writing, although until 2011 Speaker Pelosi was third in line of presidential succession.

The number of women in elected office has traditionally been markedly lower than the proportion of women in the American electorate. Several factors may be involved. They are more reluctant to come forward as candidates, they have difficulty in getting nominated and the electoral system makes it harder for them to succeed if they are chosen.

The progress of women in elective public office, 1979–2011

Year	US Congress (%)	State-wide executive offices (%)	State legislatures (%)
1979	3	11	10
1989	5	14	17
1999	12	28	23
2009	14	26	23
2011 (112th Congress)	17	22	23

Figures adapted from those provided by the Center for American Women and Politics (CAWP).

NB Fifty of the 315 available positions are as state governor. To date, forty-nine states have elected a woman to this position. Only Maine – in which the only executive office is that of governor – has not yet had a female state-wide executive.

In the federal legislatures, women are usually better represented in the Democratic Party, which has been more willing than the Republicans to adopt them as candidates. In the 112th Congress more than two-thirds of the women in the two chambers are Democrats (sixty out of eighty-nine); there are seventeen women in the Senate, and seventy-two in the House. In addition, three delegates to the House (from Guam, the Virgin Islands and Washington DC) are women. Of the women in the two federal legislatures, 27% are described as 'women of color'. Delaware, Iowa, Mississippi and Vermont are the only states never to have had a woman represent them in either house of Congress.

Within the fifty states, women fare better, so that some states that have had little female representation in either chamber of Congress have had many women serving in one of their state bodies. In January 2011, 1,718 out of 7,382 state legislatiors were female, 1,266 of them Democrats and 519 Republicans. Since 1971, there has been a fivefold increase in the number of women in state legislatures, although there is a considerable variation in performance. Washington, Colorado, Maryland, California and Connecticut currently head the list, with more than 30%, whilst South Carolina has below 10%.

Women who hold political office in federal or state legislatures tend to view themselves not just as representatives of their local area. Rather, they see themselves as representing 'all women' – not just in other parts of their state but across the country. According to one survey,[4] they tend to be actively involved in promoting legislation to improve women's position in society. They tend to prioritise women's concerns such as childcare, domestic violence, health provision, reproductive rights and the welfare of family and children (even if this was not their original intention), have a strong interest in the policy agenda on equality and work for more open and participatory government. Overall, on social issues their broad stance tends to be more liberal than that of men.

Jane Mansbridge[5] refers to 'surrogate representation' to describe the tendency of women representatives to see themselves as spokespersons for women beyond their own electoral district. She notes how women in public office feel a special responsibility to represent the interests of women: 'In practice, it seems that legislators' feelings of responsibility for constituents outside their districts are considerably stronger when the legislature features few, or disproportionately few, representatives of the group in question.' This sense of surrogate responsibility has been articulated by the Democrat Senator Barbara Boxer, who points out that: 'Women from all over the country really do follow what you do and rely on you to speak out for them on the issues [which matter]'.[6]

Bill Clinton was more receptive to the claims for female representation in appointed offices in public life than were his predecessors. He included three women in his first Cabinet, appointed a second to the Supreme Court and made useful progress towards achieving a more balanced judiciary. His Democratic successor, Barack Obama, has continued the trend, there being six women in his Cabinet, four secretaries and two others (United Nations Ambassador Susan Rice and Environmental Protection Agency Administrator Lisa Jackson). He has appointed two more women to the Supreme Court (to replace men) and has also shown a commitment to broadening the range of judicial appointments.

At state level, women hold 68 out of 315 (22%) of the elective executive offices across the country. To date, they have been elected to executive offices in forty-nine states, only Maine failing to have followed the general trend.

THE SLOW PROGRESS IN INCREASING FEMALE REPRESENTATION IN POLITICS

Women have a long history of activism in local and community work, but their role in the partisan political arenas has not matched this degree of social participation. Some of the barriers have begun to diminish and women are entering politics in greater numbers at state and national levels. Yet in spite of this improvement, Congress remains overwhelmingly male at the beginning of the twenty-first century. There has been some progress, most obviously in 1992, which was dubbed the 'Year of the Woman', when women won a record forty-seven seats in the House. This advance has been most apparent within the Democratic Party and it often occurs on occasions when there is an open race in which candidates for election stand in seats held by retiring male incumbents.

Women currently make up 59% of the workforce and 51% of the population, but only about 20% of state and local government officials and only 10% of national government officials. Progress in female representation remains slow within the United States, the US being relatively backward in world terms. Basing its figures on representation in the House (considerably higher than for the Senate), the Inter-Parliamentary Union's listing of countries ranked it 73rd out of 186 assessed. (Women in National Parliaments, November 2010 – see www.ipu.org/). Optimists cling to the belief that, as more women acquire graduate qualifications and/or professional experience and become more willing to work outside the home, and the public shows its willingness to support women politicians, there is a likelihood that the slow increase in female representation will continue into the future.

What have been the barriers to female representation?

As a group, women still possess obvious disadvantages over men. In the past, they suffered from more limited educational opportunity and from a lack of role models to emulate, for politics has traditionally been a man's world. More importantly today, opportunities for active participation continue to be limited by child-bearing and home-making responsibilities. Within the Republican Party in particular, there are many women who would see these as their primary concerns. This limits the number willing to come forward as candidates. Those who do come forward tend to do so at a stage in their lives when family responsibilities have diminished.

Women and voting

The traditional picture of women in politics suggests that they are less likely to vote and participate at all levels of activity, that they are more partisan and more likely to support right-wing parties. For many years, it was true that they turned out less enthusiastically, but this situation was reversed in the 1980 election. In every subsequent presidential election, the *proportion* of eligible female adults who voted has exceeded the proportion of eligible males who did so. The *number* of female voters has exceeded the number of male voters

Male predominance tends to be self-perpetuating. Much political discussion is conducted in a macho manner, sometimes by sexist males. It requires great determination and self-confidence for any woman to resist the slings and arrows likely to be endured, and to advance her claims. This can act as a deterrent for women who might be more willing to seek other professional positions. Some of the groups mentioned in the box on p. 395, such as EMILY's List, have been active in encouraging women to come forward and in helping them to overcome likely obstacles – for example by fund raising and offering training programmes.

Beyond these considerations, there are institutional factors that explain the under-representation of women. One is the electoral system. Women tend to fare better in countries that employ some variant of proportional representation. They are more likely to receive party encouragement to stand in multi-member constituencies. When voters are able to choose 3 or 4 names from a wide range of candidates in a multi-member constituency, women are more likely to get elected in higher numbers.

The low turnover of legislators in Congress is another factor. Once elected, men tend to retain their office for several terms, the feeling being that 'one good term deserves another'. When many seats are being contested by male incumbents, the chances of a woman challenger are diminished. With very high rates of incumbent re-election, a bottleneck is created.

Melissa Harris-Lacewell,[7] a specialist on (black) women in politics, suggests that cultural norms and structural barriers act as deterrents for women considering a career in politics. Noting that 'women tend to help men get elected, but don't run themselves', she observes that:

> Women can be deterred from seeking office for themselves by the amount of money they need to raise to run a political campaign, the time it will take away from their families and the sometimes unpleasant, 'un-ladylike' battles they may have to wage against their opponents . . . [in addition], women candidates have to guard against negative campaigning, which alienates voters and ultimately hurts the female in the race.

in every presidential election since 1964, a reflection of the fact that for many years there have been more females in the country than males.

Similarly, there is little evidence today that women are more conservative in their voting allegiance. In recent presidential elections it is the Democratic Party that has benefited from their support. Whereas in 1980, 47% voted for Ronald Reagan and 45% for Jimmy Carter, twelve years later they supported Bill Clinton over George Bush senior by 46% to 37% (17% for Ross Perot). Al Gore and John Kerry maintained the Democrat lead among women voters, but whereas the former won 54% of the female vote, the latter achieved only 51%. President George W. Bush's ability to increase his share of the women's vote to 48% in 2004 (up from 43% in 2000) was a major reason why he substantially increased his share of the popular vote. In 2008, Barack Obama proved a very popular candidate amongst women, 56% of whom voted for him – as opposed to 43% for Senator McCain.

Defined as the difference between the proportion of women and the proportion of men voting for the winning candidate, the gender gap in presidential elections varied from 4% to 11% and averaged 7.7% between 1980 and 2000, peaking in 2000 at 10%. In 2004 and 2008, it was 7%.[8] In state-wide elections too, the same gender gap prevails, with women disproportionately voting for Democratic candidates, though being willing to vote Republican if the candidate appeals to them on the issues. Early research into the 2010 mid-term elections suggests that gender gaps in voting were evident in almost all Senate and gubernatorial races. In spite of the media attention to high-profile Republican women candidates, polling showed that the presence of a Republican woman candidate in a race did not eliminate the gender gap or reverse its direction. Women were more likely than men to prefer the Democratic candidate, regardless of the gender of the candidates.

It may be that women have leaned to the left in the last few years because they associated Reagan, George Bush senior, Gingrich and George W. Bush with serious cuts in welfare expenditure, and – in the case of Reagan and George W. Bush – with a hawkish attitude on issues of foreign policy. In contrast to the Bushes and McCain, Clinton and Obama appeared more interested in the domestic agenda, as well as being widely seen as more attractive candidates.

Opinion polls quoted in CAWP research have consistently shown clear differences in gender positions on the issues. Women are less militaristic, less inclined to support the death penalty and less critical of a positive role for government in business and social affairs. They are more likely to favour regulation and control of social 'vices' such as drugs, gambling, pornography and prostitution; wish to limit the number of guns in circulation; favour protection of the environment; and support legislation to promote the interests of the disadvantaged. Such positions are ones often espoused by Democratic candidates.

Women in other areas of political life

Other than voting, there are other outlets for those who wish to play a part in politics in some capacity. Traditionally, women have been rather unwelcome in trade unions, which tend to be male-dominated institutions. However, there are other technically non-political bodies such as pressure groups in which women seek to influence public policy on social, moral and local issues. Women are often active in the anti-poverty lobby and areas where involvement can be reconciled with family ties.

The debate over affirmative action programmes

As we have seen, affirmative action programmes are those that are intended to correct the effects of individual and societal discrimination in the past. They provide special benefits to those in the community such as blacks, women and other disadvantaged groups that have traditionally been the victims of discrimination. Usually, these programmes involve a special effort to recruit and promote members of these groups. Affirmative action programmes may be of the hard or soft kind. Hard forms involve setting particular quotas as to how many people of a certain type should be recruited to an organisation, irrespective of whether they have the appropriate qualifications (for example 20% of a police force must be black). Soft forms may involve measures to encourage minority applications. They are intended to boost minority representation by ensuring that when people of equal qualifications present themselves, then – in order to boost diversity – the member of the disadvantaged group is chosen.

The introduction of and debate surrounding affirmative action programmes

Although segregation and discrimination had already been made illegal by the mid-1960s, many supporters of equal rights saw this as insufficient. Neutral treatment would do little or nothing to equip women and racial minorities (primarily African Americans, Hispanics and Native Americans) with genuine opportunities, and they would still be denied the chance to participate fully in American life. In particular, because African Americans had suffered from the continuing burden of disadvantage for so long, they would never have equal opportunities in areas such as access to education or medical school, skilled employment or winning government contracts. This, then, was a well-intentioned – and not unsuccessful – attempt to give modest preferences to those long denied their full citizenship and a fair chance in life. In the process, it might have other benefits, such as improving the nation's economic and social life (enriching it by bringing in a diversity of talents and experience) and removing a cause of disaffection and thereby promoting social order and stability. It might also help create a black middle class, which could provide a useful role model for any aspirational African Americans.

The affirmative action policy became highly contentious in the 1990s and remains controversial today. Its opponents believe that it is a form of reverse discrimination that replaces one form of discrimination by another. They feel that appointment, progress and promotion should be organised on the basis of merit rather than any other consideration. In particular, they dislike the quotas that are often written into programmes; these establish a target number of women or members of a minority group who must be employed. When there is work for everyone, the quota might seem more acceptable. When it is in short supply, or when a few particular jobs are much in demand, there tends to be a backlash against the concept. Similar controversy is stirred over educational provision. To achieve the target of a certain number of minority representatives in universities involves allowing some students to be enrolled who are less academically qualified than others, who are being rejected.

Northern whites began to be upset by the policies designed to promote opportunities for black people, such as bussing and affirmative action. Many of the programmes derived from the Civil Rights Act (1964) and the way it was to be interpreted. It was the Supreme Court that had to decide whether the Act was constitutional. Could equality of treatment be obtained by providing opportunities for some groups that were themselves inherently unequal?

The legality of affirmative action

Within the Supreme Court there has been uncertainty over affirmative action, just as there has been throughout the nation. The Fourteenth Amendment to the Constitution laid down the notion of 'equal protection' before the law. The Court has, on occasion, argued that quota programmes in government or instigated by it are a violation of that idea. The Burger Court (1969–86) generally approved the principle of affirmative action (for example *The University of California Regents v. Baake, 1978*), but was unhappy with the details of particular programmes. The details can vary and these variations may be very important in their constitutional implications. In *Firefighters v. Stotts*, 1984, the Court would not accept the principle as the only or even most important consideration.

> **The Baake Case, 1978**
> A landmark judgment on affirmative action which stated that race could be taken into account in admissions decisions, as long as the institution did not set aside a specific number of seats for which only minorities were eligible. The Court ruled by 5–4 that Baake (a white American with high grades who was unable to get into medical school) had been the victim of discrimination, but by the same margin judged that positive discrimination was not inherently unlawful. This was an ambiguous judgment that came to be regarded as favourable to the existence of affirmative action programmes, even if quotas were unacceptable.

In subsequent cases, there has been a division of opinion in the attempt to apply the 'equal protection' clause of the Constitution. Sandra Day O'Connor, herself the first woman to make it onto the bench, expressed grave doubts as to whether race-sensitive remedial measures could ever be justified, whereas others have taken the view that they can be necessary if the commitment to equality is to be honoured and past injustice righted.

Many votes have been very close, 5–4 or 6–3. In 1990, by 5–4, the Court upheld the right of Congress to adopt 'benign race-conscious measures' designed to increase the number of minority-held radio and television licences issued by the Federal Communications Commission. Similarly, the Supreme Court has often been willing to accept policies designed to help women overcome past disadvantages. In 1987, it upheld the California county agency's scheme allowing consideration of gender in making appointments to positions where women had fared badly in earlier years. It recognised that there had in the past been unfairness in representation and that it was therefore reasonable to use the issue of gender to correct the imbalance.

Bill Clinton was aware of the unpopularity of affirmative action, but generally resisted the temptation to trim his support and tried to encourage a 'mend it, don't end it' approach. His appointments to the judiciary helped to ensure that the policy continued, in spite of the doubts and hesitancy revealed by members of the Rehnquist Court. Rehnquist[9] had doubts about the policy, once arguing in a dissenting submission that 'the Fourteenth Amendment was adopted to ensure that every person must be treated equally by each state regardless the color of his skin . . . Today, the Court derails this achievement and places its imprimatur on the creation once again by government of privilege based on birth.'

In the 1990s, there was increasing scrutiny of affirmative action at all levels in the political system. Some states meanwhile took their own line on affirmative action. Via a 1996 proposition (no. 209), Californians voted to end it in education and the public services. There was a year-long delay in the state courts before the policy was enacted (1997). In 1998, Washington became the second state to outlaw affirmative action, passing the Initiative 200 law. In 2000, Governor Jeb Bush's 'One Florida' initiative succeeded in banning race as a factor in college admissions policies. Such moves reflected a growing hostility to the whole idea. Conservatives in many states were resistant to the idea, and this opposition was not confined to white Americans. Some successful African Americans shared the sense of resentment about programmes that tended to devalue success achieved on the basis of merit. Shelby Steele,[10] a black commentator, wrote *The Content of Our Character*, in which he argued that not only was the value of qualifications being undermined, but, more seriously, affirmative action tended to reinforce feelings of black inferiority to white Americans.

From time to time, a particular issue arises that brings the issue into national prominence once again. The case of *Taxman* v. *Township Board of Education* (1997) concerned events in Piscataway, New Jersey. The school board, faced with the need to make economies, fired a white teacher, Sharon Taxman, rather than her black colleague, and made the racial basis for the decision explicit. The Supreme Court decided that diversity was not a sufficient rationale for considering race, except 'to remedy past discrimination or as the result of a manifest imbalance in the employment of minorities'. The governmental review accepted that 'a simple desire to promote diversity for its own sake . . . is not a permissible basis for taking race into account'.

The University of Michigan and its admission policies

In 2002–3, the Supreme Court had to decide its attitude in a case concerning affirmative action at the University of Michigan. Two white students claimed that the University acted unconstitutionally in denying them places in 1995 because of their race-scoring policy, and a third argued that the law school (which took race into account but did not explicitly score applicants) did the same to her in 1997. The University claimed that its policies were essential to its goal of assembling a diverse student body 'which is critical to the quality of the educational experience students receive'. In most departments, it point-scored applicants, who needed to acquire 100 out of 150 to qualify for entry. Whilst full marks in a high school SAT reasoning test (formerly Scholastic Assessment Test) provided 12 points, membership of an ethnic minority qualified candidates for 20. Other supporters (including the NAACP) argued that affirmative action policies were needed for a different reason: 'race conscious admissions policies are justified to remedy both past and present discrimination at the University'.

As we have seen, fixed quotas have been outlawed since the Baake case, which none the less was in many ways a victory for affirmative action because it ruled that the broad goal of classroom diversity was 'a compelling state interest'. But in preparation for the Michigan ruling, the Bush administration filed papers with the Supreme Court, urging it to decide that the University policy was 'unconstitutional'. It wanted a once-and-for-all

Bill Clinton had called for a modification of affirmative action programmes in the light of court judgments. But in the private sector, such programmes continued to be popular with many large companies that see them as a means of winning or maintaining a market share for their products among minority communities. Their approach was a relevant factor in the policy of the University of Michigan over admissions (see box above for further details). By its rulings in 2003, the Supreme Court maintained its commitment to diversity as a laudable goal and accepted that race could be a factor, among others, in making decisions over recruitment. In *Gratz* v. *Bollinger* and *Grutter* v. *Bollinger*, the justices reaffirmed the spirit of the Baake judgment. They found against the admissions policy of the university (based as it was on additional points for being a member of an ethnic minority), but allowed the approach adopted by the Law School (considering issues of race and diversity on a practical basis) to continue.

In *Parents Involved in Community Schools* v. *Seattle School District No. 1* (2007), in a 5–4 ruling the Supreme Court prohibited assigning students to public schools solely for the purpose of achieving racial integration and declined to recognise racial balancing as a compelling state interest. Five justices, led by John Roberts, held that the school board did not present any 'compelling state interest' to justify the assignment of school places on the basis of race. However, Anthony Kennedy, in supporting the majority verdict,

decision that racial preference had no place in admissions policy. It accepted that the goal of diversity was a worthy one, but argued it must not supersede equal rights and individual opportunity, for this was reverse discrimination. Moreover, because of the backlash created, any attempt to grant preference on minority grounds could end up harming the people it was intended to support.

The case proved to be hugely controversial. General Motors, which employs many graduates from the University, urged that diversity-admissions policies be allowed to continue. The company is a global enterprise and it argued that 'diversity equips American students to deal with people from different backgrounds, cultures and races – to be better business people'. Other supporters also pointed out that another crucial factor in Michigan admissions policies favours white students – namely, the allocation of extra points to those whose parents attended the institution.

The Bush administration, keen to emphasise its commitment to diversity at a time when ethnic minorities in the United States were rapidly growing in numbers, talked about a third stance – it supported 'affirmative process', policies which led to diversity without specifically targeting race. This stance did not satisfy all members of the administration, some of whom backed the then secretary of state, Colin Powell, who wanted to see a continuation of affirmative action policies geared to ending racial imbalance.

delivered a more nuanced concurring opinion. He argued that schools may use 'race conscious' means to achieve diversity, but that the school involved in this particular case did not use a sufficiently narrow tailoring of its plans to sustain such a goal.

Affirmative action remains contentious. Its opponents are aware of ambiguities in recent Court judgments and are likely to feel encouraged to continue their campaign to put the policy finally to rest.

Gay rights and same-sex marriages

In recent years, the Supreme Court has supported the principle of marital privacy, but it has refused to extend recognition to gays and lesbians. In 1986, it decided that a Georgian law that criminalised consensual sodomy as practised by homosexuals was acceptable within the Constitution. As such behaviour usually occurs in privacy, many people would argue that the state has no right to intrude into the home except in extreme circumstances. But this was not the view of a majority of the justices.

The issue of the degree of tolerance to be accorded to gays and lesbians is highly contentious in the United States and in many other democracies. Gay campaigners first began to organise to air their views in the 1970s, presenting their case in positive terms by emphasising the discrimination from which they suffered and their entitlement to the full range of civil rights. Their greater bold-ness in espousing the cause created a backlash from religious conservatives, who were assisted in proclaiming their arguments by the spread of AIDs in the following decade. This was portrayed by right-wing Christians as God's retribution for immoral behaviour.

Gay activists succeeded in obtaining federal funding for AIDs research and treat-ment, although most relevant legislation included clauses designed to prevent such money being used to advance homosexuality. Gays secured other gains in the 1990s, although they could not overturn the ban on gays serving openly in the military.

In his election campaign in 1992, Bill Clinton gave assurances to the gay com-munity which aroused high expectations. Some advances were made by gay activists during his presidency. He established the first official liaison office for the gay community and in 1998 signed an executive order prohibiting civilian federal departments and agencies from discriminating on the basis of sexual orientation. Other gains in the 1990s were the repeal of many state laws ban-ning homosexual sex, and the creation of court orders and legislation in a small number of states to provide partner benefits for public employees in some areas such as health insurance.

But there were also disappointments. On the issue of the rights of gays to serve in the military, Clinton had to compromise under pressure from the Pentagon and top military brass. He came up with a fudge, the 'Don't Ask, Don't Tell' formula; officers could not ask about a soldier's sexual proclivities, but neither could a lesbian or a gay man in uniform 'come out' or engage in sexual activities whilst on duty or special assignments. (See p. 93 for details of the progress on reversal of this policy by the Obama administration.) Gays also disliked the Defense of Marriage Act (1996), which banned people in same-sex marriages from eligibility for those federal benefits available to married couples, and allowed states not to recognise unions conducted in another state.

The issue of such same-sex liaisons was to become a controversial one in the new millennium. Religious conservatives were determined to achieve a ban on gay marriages. They campaigned to do so at national, state and even local level.

Civil unions and same-sex marriages

New England has been at the centre of the push towards legalisation of same-sex marriage. In 2000, Vermont became the first state to adopt a civil unions law, providing legal recognition of same-sex partnerships and most of the legal entitlements and obligations of marriage. In 2004, Massachusetts went a size-able step beyond Vermont, by becoming the first state to recognise gay mar-riages, the first taking place in May of that year. The governor himself was against the initiative and invoked an old law to stop same-sex couples from outside the state from coming in to get married, although many city clerks said that they intended to ignore his move. It soon became apparent that there was a real doubt as to whether these same-sex marriages would be recognised in more conservative areas of the country, particularly in the thirty-eight states that have banned them by specifically stating that marriage can only involve a man and a woman.

The events of early 2004 unleashed powerful forces on either side of the debate. Gay marriage became a touchstone social issue, with both candidates opposed and President Bush saying that he would support an amendment to change the constitution to define marriage as a heterosexual institution. John Kerry argued that decisions on such matters should be taken at state level. Both men supported civil unions, conferring some marriage benefits.

Cynics said that in 2004 presidential advisers were pushing Bush to take up the case for an amendment as a political manoeuvre. He knew that the chances of securing an amendment were very small. But by so doing, he would be creating a 'wedge issue' that would serve to unite the Republicans and divide the Democrats and enable him to portray his opponent as a stereo-typical liberal. Some commentators pointed out that a president who believed so strongly in states' rights in other contexts should be prepared to let the states do their jobs and work out their own marriage laws, before resorting to a constitutional amendment.

In 2008, Barack Obama and John McCain shared the view that marriage is a union between a man and a woman. Neither backed a constitutional amendment on the matter, arguing instead for the states' right to determine their own positions.

Four of the six New England states now allow same-sex couples the legal right to marry, but in the rest of the United States the issue remains highly divisive.

States tolerant of same-sex marriages (October 2010)

State	Current status of same-sex marriage
Connecticut, Iowa, Massachusetts, New Hampshire and Vermont; and Washington DC and Coquille tribe (Oregon)	Recognised as legal; ceremonies performed.
California	Briefly performed in 2008, before a constitutional ban was introduced, following passage of an initiative; ban challenged in federal court, where judge deemed it illegal. Issue currently before federal appeals court.
Maryland, New York State and Rhode Island	Recognition of legality of marriages performed in other states; no licences granted to allow them to be performed within state.

The rights of the disabled

Many Americans with disabilities have in the past suffered from discrimination, often being denied education, jobs and rehabilitation services. Throughout much of the country's history, the blind, deaf and mobility-impaired found buses, stairs, telephones and other necessities of life designed in such a way as to make it impossible for them to use them to full advantage, if at all. As one campaigning slogan put it: 'Once, blacks had to ride at the back of the bus. We can't even get on the bus.'

In the 1970s, the disabled began to be viewed as a minority group within society that wanted equality and recognition, in the same way as did other groups whose civil rights were in need of protection. This rights-based model provided a new framework for looking at disabilities, based around the ideas of inclusion, empowerment and economic independence. Advocates of this 'rights model' saw the need for new laws to address the rights and concerns of this minority. The legislation that they urged was concerned with the accessibility of facilities such as buildings and air travel, opportunities in education and housing, and voting rights.

The first 'equality' measure introduced was the Rehabilitation Act, 1973 (twice vetoed by President Nixon), which added people with disabilities to the list of those protected against discrimination. Progress continued with the passage of the Americans with Disabilities Act (ADA), passed by Congress during the presidency of another Republican, George Bush senior. This was the real breakthrough, for as Bush recognised when he signed the law, it represented a 'dramatic renewal not only for those with disabilities but for all of us, because along with the precious privilege of being an American comes a sacred duty to ensure that every other American's rights are also guaranteed'.

The ADA defined a disabled person as anyone possessing a mental or physical impediment 'that substantially limits one or more activities of life'. It prohibited discrimination based on disability in employment, places of public accommodations and public services (for example buses, trains and subways); required that facilities be designed to make them accessible and usable by those with disabilities; and required them, to the extent feasible, be redesigned to do so. Its passage both reflected changes in attitude and helped to promote them, as it provided the legal language and framework for discussing issues and cases. With the advent of the ADA, people began to look not only at making life easier for those with disabilities, but also for ways to help them integrate with others and participate fully in all aspects of life.

The introduction of the ADA has resulted in dramatic improvements in wheelchair access to facilities ranging from churches to hotels, from restaurants to universities. Phone companies have provided special facilities for those with speech and hearing impairments. But the attainment of civil rights for the disabled has not been achieved without substantial opposition. Whilst few people would wish to be seen as overtly hostile to a group already enduring emotional and/or physical handicaps, goodwill has not always been apparent in their attitudes and actions. Even when passed into law (sometimes in the face of considerable opposition), enforcement has sometimes been sporadic and sluggish. The problem is the same one that influenced President Nixon in 1973: cost.

Civil liberties and civil rights: an assessment

The existence of civil liberties on paper is no guarantee that they will exist in practice. In times of peace and prosperity, they are more likely to be acted upon, although this was not true of the 1920s, when – in a 'golden decade' – those suspected of adhering to any progressive creed were liable to be branded as 'reds' and treated illiberally. Such intolerance was again apparent in the early post-1945 era, when the **McCarthyite** witchhunt against alleged 'subversives' was at its peak. In the 1960s, some of the methods used by the FBI, including the phone-tapping of Dr Martin Luther King and the surveillance of other protesting individuals and groups, suggest that the civil liberties of those who dissent from the American way of life are liable to be ignored. Few people will spring to their defence, especially when the cause is unpopular with majority opinion. In the atmosphere created by the attack on the Twin Towers on September 11, many Americans have been able to reconcile themselves to some alarming limitations of personal freedom, and the rights of many detainees have not been respected or defended.

McCarthyism
The practice of making unsubstantiated accusations of disloyalty or communist leanings, associated with the Republican Senator Joseph McCarthy. McCarthy led the notorious investigations into 'un-American activities' by members of the US government and other people prominent in public life such as artists and intellectuals, between 1949 and 1954. Many Americans of socialist or even liberal persuasion were hounded from public life as a result of the hysteria of his anti-communist crusade.

Such cases might seem to be a violation of the Bill of Rights, yet throughout American history they have occurred. The 1960s was a decade in which interpretation of individual rights often revealed surprising latitude, but this has been less true since the 1980s. The nation has been more conservative, as witnessed by the growing influence of the Christian Coalition and of the Religious Right, and by the advances made by the more cautious and conformist Republican Party in capturing the presidency for twelve years up to 1992 (and again in 2000 and 2004) and gaining control in Congress in 1994 and 2010. The Supreme Court has recognised this change of mood. On issues of individual freedom, it has generally been less liberal, although the more conservative tide has not been widely reflected in rulings concerning freedom of speech.

Many Americans, alarmed by a wave of terrorism and of violent crime, are broadly willing to accept restrictions on their lifestyle, such as greater electronic surveillance, helicopter searches, roadblocks and urine tests. A case can be made for many of these developments, but when viewed together they do suggest that respect for individual liberties and rights is less than it was a generation ago. Also, on matters involving criminal procedure, judicial opinion has moved. The liberal decisions of the Warren and Burger courts (see pp. 204–208) have not subsequently been overruled, but their application has been reduced in scope.

The liberties and rights of people in Britain and the United States: a comparison

Issue	Britain	United States
Existence of Bill of Rights	No, but Human Rights Act (HRA); protection of the law, but no entrenchment. Faced with the perceived terrorist threat, some ministers could in 2006 contemplate amending the HRA, in order to ensure that their legislation was not imperilled in the courts.	Yes, many rights guaranteed by Constitution. Rights are entrenched and therefore unlikely to be amended. Where change has occurred (for example Thirteenth Amendment banning slavery), it was to provide stronger protection of rights.
Language and interpretation	Articles of HRA require interpretation: several qualifications in articles of European Convention. Much depends on judicial interpretation.	Broad phraseology of Constitution, but terms not qualified. Much depends on judicial interpretation.
Freedom of expression	Now protected by HRA, Article 10, but traditionally more restricted than in US, as in the case of libel.	Guaranteed by First Amendment: much toleration over symbolic speech, but not always towards minority rights – for example communists.
Punishment: rights of suspects, defendants and detainees	Power of police strengthened in recent years, concern over criminals 'going free'. But also concern for right of accused and over causes of crime. No death penalty.	Err on side of police powers. Rights of accused often questioned, tougher regime for many detainees, especially terrorists at Guantanamo Bay. Many states employ the death penalty.
Rights of women	Gained vote in 1918 and 1928. Anti-discrimination measures passed from 1970 onwards.	Vote via Nineteenth Amendment, 1920. Anti-discrimination legislation (1964), before Britain. Women's liberation movement developed here.
Rights of ethnic minorities	Anti-discriminatory laws on race relations passed from 1960s. Much still to do.	Anti-discriminatory legislation (1964) earlier than in Britain. Much still to do.

New rules have placed more emphasis on society's need for public order than on the rights of the accused.

Since the 1960s, there has been a vast expansion in the civil rights of Americans. The process began with redress of the very obvious grievances of black Americans; it spread to tackle the rights of other ethnic minorities and of women; more recently, it has been extended to gays and lesbians, the disabled and the elderly. The interests of women and minorities converged on the issue of affirmative action, the collective term for policies requiring a special effort to be made to help advantaged groups. But as we have seen, this has run into substantial opposition today.

CONCLUSION

It would be wrong to see the United States as anything other than broadly liberal in matters of personal freedom. Few other countries have such an enviable record, whatever the occasional lapses. A human rights rating of 90% was awarded in the latest edition (1993) of the *Humana Guide*. The *Guide* made the point that achieving a good record in a large, culturally heterogeneous country is inherently more difficult than doing so in a small country. It denied points only on the issue of capital punishment and the existence of widespread inequalities. It accepted that in the United States there is a widespread respect for freedom, even if the position on matters such as homosexuality and abortion varies between the fifty states.

The civil rights umbrella is a large one. Increasing numbers of groups seek protection for their rights, be they older and younger Americans, those with disabilities, homosexuals, or victims of AIDS and other chronic and debilitating conditions. It is difficult to predict what controversies the new century will yield, but those categorised as belonging to disadvantaged minorities – blacks, Hispanics, gays, the disabled, and the elderly among them – now constitute a very significant element in the population and are likely to be active in demanding greater recognition of their rights.

REFERENCES

1 The observation was originally made by black novelist Toni Morrison in a *New Yorker* essay, 1998. Its validity is discussed in D. Wickham, *Bill Clinton and Black America*, Ballantine, 2002

2 'How Black Democrats won North Carolina and the Election: Massive Turnout, Week of November 13–19, 2008', *The Wilmington Journal*, 24 November 2008

3 NOW website: mission statement

4 J. Flammang, *Women's Political Voice: How Women Are Transforming the Practice and Study of Politics*, Temple University Press, 1997

5 J. Mansbridge, 'The Many Faces of Representation', working paper delivered to JFK School of Government, Harvard University, 1997

6 Quoted in S. Carroll, *Representing Women: Congresswomen's Perceptions of their Representative Role*, Rutgers University Press, 2000

7 M. Harris-Lacewell, keynote address at Ready to Run: Campaign Training for Women programme, Eagleton Institute of Politics, Rutgers University, 2008

8 Center for American Women and Politics (CAWP), press release, 1 January 2005

9 W. Rehnquist, dissenting opinion in *Fullilove v. Klutznick*, 1980

10 S. Steele, *The Content our Characters*, Harper Collins, 1990

USEFUL WEB SITES

There are a variety of sites providing information and/or argument about the range of social policies covered, some governmental, others belonging to pressure groups. These are some relevant ones among them:

Civil liberties

www.aclu.org/ The site of the American Civil Liberties Union contains information on issues ranging from torture to voting rights, as well as maintaining a watch on decisions of the Supreme Court and the voting records of members of Congress.

Affirmative action

www.bamn.com/ A forum for campaigning groups in favour of affirmative action (particularly in California).

www.acri.org The anti-affirmative action site of the American Civil Rights Institute, covering gender and racial issues.

Civil rights

www.census.gov Information gathered from the official census on the ethnic and racial characteristics of Americans in every region and state.

www.naacp.org The official site of the National Association for the Advancement of Colored People.

www.now.com/ The official site of the National Organization for Women (NOW).

www.cawp.rutgers.edu/ The Center for American Women and Politics.

SAMPLE QUESTIONS

1 Discuss the significance of ethnicity in American politics.
2 'The days of radical protest are largely over, because so many black Americans are now finding opportunities for advancement in American society.' Discuss.
3 'Black Americans have significantly improved their position in recent decades, but other groups still face formidable barriers.' Discuss.
4 Assess the impact of women and the women's movement on American politics.
5 Why is abortion such a controversial issue in the United States?
6 What is meant by affirmative action and why has it proved controversial in American politics?
7 Why has the idea and practice of affirmative action gone out of fashion in recent years?
8 What does the treatment of gays and lesbians tell us about the state of civil rights in the United States?
9 Why do issues of civil rights continue to arouse so much controversy in the United States?
10 Has the existence of a Bill of Rights been effective in securing the civil liberties and rights of the American people?
11 Are civil liberties and rights better protected in the UK or the USA?
12 Examine the means and assess the effectiveness of protecting rights in the UK and USA.

Conclusion: the state of American democracy 12

The meaning of democracy

The ancient Greeks were the first to give a democratic answer to the question of how to organise a political system. Athenian democracy was practised in a small city-state, where the citizens made some political decisions directly, and controlled others. This was **direct democracy** in action, with people coming together to make decisions whenever necessary. Debates in the assembly were free, open and wide ranging, each citizen having a single vote.

> **direct democracy**
> Government in which citizens come together in one place to make laws; refers to populist measures such as the initiative, recall and referendum.

After the Greeks, the notion of democracy went out of fashion, being associated in the eyes of many rulers with factional conflict and violence. Until the early nineteenth century, far from government being rule by the many, it was actually in effect rule by the very few, who were not subject to popular control. The majority of people were seen as unfit to rule, and members of the nobility who possessed governing skills did not feel that they should be subject to the whims of the illiterate and ill-informed majority. In *The Federalist*, James Madison[1] echoed the outlook of many of his co-framers of the American Constitution when he wrote: 'Such democracies [as the Greek and Roman] have ever been found incompatible with personal security or the rights of property; and have in general been as short in their lives, as they have been violent in their deaths.'

The word 'democracy' is not used in the US Constitution. The framers preferred the term 'republic' to describe the form of government that they wished to create. It lacked the connection with direct democracy, with its possible associations with demagogues, mass rule and the mob. The vision of the Founding Fathers was of a **representative system**, a republic in Plato's sense, by which all those in power obtain and retain their position as a result of winning elections in which all free adults are allowed to take part.

> **representative system**
> A form of government in which the people rule indirectly through elected representatives.

The nineteenth century saw the spread of representative democracy, a system under which a person stands for and speaks on behalf of another. Today, it is widely accepted that this is the only viable form of democracy in a vast country. The mass of people cannot rule, in the sense of making binding decisions. Instead, representatives of the people, freely elected, decide. What is crucial is that there should be effective popular control over the rulers or decision makers. A system is democratic to the extent that those who have power are subject to the wishes of the electorate. Abraham Lincoln put it more succinctly: 'government of the people, by the people and for the people'.

The past workings of American democracy: blemishes and virtues

Democracy is seen as a pre-eminently American value. Yet the United States has not always acknowledged the democratic rights of all its citizens, and some of the developments in the twentieth century have cast doubt upon the genuine attachment to democratic values. For instance, the existence of the right to vote is seen as a major criterion of any democracy. If broad categories of the public are denied the opportunity to express their preference between candidates, then this must be a blot on the landscape. Women obtained the vote in 1920, and in theory all men had the vote from the time the Constitution was created, subject originally to a property qualification. Yet slaves were not allowed to participate in elections, and when slavery ended, ruses were adopted in various southern states to prevent blacks from exercising their democratic rights.

In the absence of an effective universal franchise, there must be doubts about the American commitment to democracy. True, the property qualifications were pitched at a relatively modest level, and by the early nineteenth century some 80% of American men owned sufficient property to qualify. True also that the US was relatively speedy in extending the popular suffrage to include all women. But they were white men and white women, and it was not until the 1960s that the majority of black Americans were able to use their entitlement, if they so wished.

On the score of recognising and respecting minority rights, the Americans again did well in theory. Crucial liberties were granted in the Constitution, most obviously in the first ten amendments that make up the Bill of Rights. These are inviolable, unless there is a further constitutional amendment to change them. Yet, again, there have been blemishes upon the record. Two sets of factors ruin the record of the Americans in protecting and respecting such rights:

1 **The anti-communist hysteria that has at times characterised American society**. The 1920s was a markedly intolerant decade, in which the liberties of many individuals were infringed, and anyone whose views were mildly progressive was liable to be branded as a 'red'. Similarly, the McCarthy witch-hunt against those portrayed as communists was at a fever pitch in the early

1950s. His techniques of investigation, with their emphasis upon smear and innuendo, displayed little respect for constitutional niceties. 'Un-American activity' was interpreted very widely, and there was much harassment of individuals and groups. There was in both eras a desperate desire for conformity, and those who did not conform to the American ideal of being White Anglo-Saxon Protestants (WASPs) were hounded.

2 **The slow progress towards achieving equal opportunities and rights.** The ideal of equality, as proclaimed in Jefferson's resounding cry 'We hold these truths to be self-evident, that all men are created equal', is seen as an American contribution to humankind. Certainly, privilege and rank count for less in America than in Western Europe, and an egalitarian fervour is in a way a part of the American Dream – that each person can go out and make a fortune, by using his or her gifts and exhibiting a pioneering spirit. But the position of black Americans and other minorities until comparatively recently suggested that in practice not everyone benefited from the Jeffersonian dream.

States adopted many differing rules to prevent political and legal equality of white and black from becoming a reality. Segregation and racial discrimination may be particularly associated with the Deep South, but in many northern cities there was much *de facto* segregation well into the 1960s. Even today the opportunities available to many black Americans are more theoretical than real.

If, in several respects, reality has fallen short of the democratic ideal, yet the commitment to democracy of many Americans has always been apparent, and to their credit many have always felt uneasy about lapses from that ideal. It would also be fair to point to other areas of political life in which the theory and practice of democracy has been evident:

1 In the Progressive era (1900–14), the introduction of direct election of senators and the spread of primary elections to defeat the power of the party-machine bosses were moves that reflected a true concern for democracy.

2 The US has practised direct democracy as well as the representative form. Devices such as the referendum, the initiative and the recall are practical demonstrations of direct democracy in action, whatever their weaknesses. More unusual is the use of the town meeting in small rural areas of New England. Originally, such meetings were vehicles through which the mainly Puritan religious leaders informed and led other members of the community – a means of seeking a consensus via a guided discussion. They were not opportunities for the expression of majority will on issues of the day and those who declined to agree to the general will were likely to be driven out of the area. However, such meetings have developed into a more acceptable democratic form, and in them citizens gather together to make decisions for their community.

American democracy today

America has long been regarded as a model democracy, but some commentators believe that today the system is not working well. Indeed, Kenneth Dolbeare has written[2] of 'the decay of American democracy' and asks whether the condition is a terminal one. He sees the problem as one compounded by the sheer scale and power of the government in Washington, for this has meant that it is 'increasingly connected only to a steadily shrinking proportion of its affluent citizens'.

Dolbeare discerns several factors that have contributed to the 'decay':
- the decline of political parties;
- the rise of television;
- the dominance of money as a means of access to television and electioneering in general;
- the rise of political action committees;
- near-permanent incumbency in Congress;
- a general abandonment of leadership to the latest opinion poll.

More seriously than any of the above factors, however, he sees the 'thirty-year trend toward abandoning political participation' as the most alarming indication of decay. In particular, this means a more or less continuous decline in voter participation, particularly a problem for those in the bottom one third of the social pyramid. He notes the paradox that has emerged: 'The growing underclass has rising needs for education, jobs, training, health care etc., but these very services are being held to a minimum or even cut – and yet the voting participation of this same underclass is declining faster than that of any other population group.'

Other writers have also noted that at the very time that the Soviet control of Eastern Europe has broken down and given rise to the creation of 'new democracies', the American version of that same system has shown severe signs of fatigue. Paul Taylor[3] is an exponent of this viewpoint: 'As democracy flourishes around the globe, it is losing ground in the United States.'

The debate on the state of American democracy was given renewed impetus as a result of the limitations on civil liberties introduced in the light of 9/11 and the War on Terror (see p. 107). Those within America who have criticised aspects of administration policy, and challenge US foreign and defence policy objectives, have often been attacked as unpatriotic or anti-American. One writer[4] has written of the 'new McCarthyism' and pointed out that it sits uneasily in a country supposedly noted for its 'freedom of thought and speech, for diversity and dissent'. The case he and other civil libertarians expressed was well articulated in a news release of the American Civil Liberties Union (ACLU):[5]

> Whilst we at ACLU feel as strongly as anyone that the perpetrators of these monstrous crimes [i.e. the 11 September attacks] must be brought to justice, we also feel that America's freedom – the very essence of our national character – must be protected as we respond to the threat of terrorism within our border. Americans can be safe and free. Unfortunately, the government has implemented measures that go light years beyond anything necessary to combat terrorism.

Democracy is sustained by public scepticism, and it is essential that people are allowed to challenge, and to express dissent. At the same time, a democracy under attack must have the means for its own defence. Getting the balance right between security and liberty is one of the most difficult tasks for any government at a time of national danger.

Future possibilities

We have examined some of the problems associated with the operation of democracy in the late twentieth and early twenty-first centuries. Some fears may be

---

Democracy in Britain and the United States: a comparison

In Britain, some of the same anxieties about the health of democracy exist. There is a disaffected underclass that is largely ignorant of and uninterested in political life. Many of its members do not turn out to vote. Indeed, turnouts generally have been in long-term decline (a trend particularly evident in the 2001 general election), although there was some improvement in that for the 2004 local and European elections. There is the same scepticism of politicians, but for many people it is more than a sensible wariness about those who exercise authority. Rather, it is a deep and cynical distrust of those who rule.

In Britain, there is concern about the existence of numerous quangos, power having been handed over to a new lay elite whose members increasingly run a wide range of services. American experience is different, for wherever there is a public office to fill across the Atlantic, the tendency is to hold an election. In Britain, the passion for election does not extend to those who serve on various boards and trusts; neither does it (yet) extend to the second chamber.

In both countries, the media at best provide reflective analysis and commentary on national events, and expose alleged or real corruption, the abuse of power and other forms of public scandal. In so doing, they contribute to the workings of democracy. In other respects, they present a threat to its values. Concentration of ownership in too few hands, the lack of diversity of opinion and intrusive and sometimes shamelessly biased reporting are dangers in the press.

Television can be said to aid democracy by informing voters, via news bulletins, current affairs programmes, and other scheduling which often conveys information in an entertaining form. But the tendency to trivialise, to concentrate upon personalities and personal 'weaknesses' and to express serious issues in a shorthand, sound-bite form has reduced the educative role which, at its best, the medium can offer.

overstated, and different writers and politicians have their own particular misgivings and complaints. There is general agreement among many that all is not currently well with the body politic, and that American democracy is today under strain.

As to the future, new forms of democratic involvement have become a possibility with the development of media technology. E-mail has become well established as a means of transmitting opinions and exerting pressure on those in office. More recently, blogs and tweets have given a voice to anyone with a computer and a web connection. Americans increasingly look to the Internet for news and information. Pew Research[6] indicates that in 2008 it surpassed newspapers as the source of national and international news, nearly doubling from the year before. It now ranks third behind national and local television as the major source for news. Barack Obama channelled the power of the Internet to reach millions during his presidential campaign, and his administration has launched innovative methods to use the Internet to govern.

The basic liberties associated with democratic rule are written into the American Constitution, whereas Britain has traditionally had a negative approach to freedoms. Few of them were guaranteed by law, so that we could do or say something provided that there was no specific law against it. Unlike the situation in other Western democracies, there was no bill or rights or document setting out basic entitlements. With the passage of the Human Rights Act in 1998, the European Convention on Human Rights has been incorporated into British law, so that for the first time there is a written record of the liberties and rights of the subject.

Since the 1960s, there has been an expansion of individual rights in Britain and the United States. Positive freedoms have been proclaimed, with legislation and – in the US case – court judgments ensuring that the rights of women and minority groups have been enforced. However, in both countries, the events of 11 September 2001 have led to anti-terrorist legislation that some libertarians see as too all-embracing, and out of proportion to the threat that exists.

Finally, on one freedom, that of the right of access to information, the US performance still leaves Britain trailing. America has had a Freedom of Information Act since 1966. Whatever the doubts about the costs of its implementation or its effects on carrying out confidential investigations, most Americans and consumer groups welcome the fact that the legislation is strong and effective, giving Americans a 'right to know'. The more recent British legislation, which took effect in 2005, has been widely criticised for its timidity, even though significant concessions were extracted from ministers during its passage in 1999–2000. The range of exemptions it includes is wider than in the comparable legislation passed by other democratic states.

Such technology empowers voters, and provides new means for them to be more actively involved in political dialogue. It opens up the possibility that they will be able to pass information to one another, so that the overall level of knowledge of the American citizenry will be increased. Voters may wish to use these developments to their advantage, and those elected to public office will need to be more conscious of those whose vote placed them there. This does not mean that they have to be subservient to public pressure, but certainly their performances will be more effectively monitored.

In the longer term, another possible development is that the computer-literate might conduct some form of referendum on the net, giving many people a greater opportunity to participate in the political process than ever before. There may be dangers in 'electronic populism' and 'mobocracy', but for others, such as Kevin Kelly,[7] 'the Internet revives Thomas Jefferson's 200-year-old dream of thinking individuals self-actualising a democracy'.

REFERENCES

1 J. Madison in J. Madison, A. Hamilton and J. Jay, *The Federalist Papers* (no. 10), 1787–88, re-issued by Penguin, 1987

2 K. Dolbeare, *Political Issues in America Today: 1990s Revisited*, Manchester University Press, 1999

3 P. Taylor, 'Democracy and Why Bother Americans', *International Herald Tribune*, 7 July 1990

4 G. Monbiot, *Guardian*, 16 October 2001

5 ACLU press release, 14 December 2001

6 *Internet Overtakes Newspapers as News Outlet*, Pew Research Paper, 23 December 2008

7 K. Kelly, *Wired* magazine, quoted in the *Guardian*, 22 February 1995

SAMPLE QUESTIONS

1 Examine the condition of American democracy today.

2 'A flawed democracy.' Discuss this verdict on the American political system.

3 'Democratic in theory, but less impressive in practice.' Discuss the fairness of this assessment of the operation of the political system on either side of the Atlantic.

Index

Bold indicates a definition

abortion 13, 92, 207, 209, 210, 212, 213, 306, 308, 320, 345, 355, 356, 385, 392–393, 394
Adams, J. 118, 119, 122, 193
advertising (on television) 232, 238, 248–251
affirmative action 7, 101, 207, 209, 356, **380**, 383, 391, 401–405
Afghanistan/War on Terror 80, 107, 276, 417
African-Americans (American blacks) 6, 7, 20, 351, 377–389, 416
  economic and social progress 7, 14–16, 17–18, 382–383, 387–389, 401–405, 416
  progress in political life 3, 68, 176, 178, 180, 191, 192, 214, 237, 282, 383, 389
Alito, S. 198, 199, 214
American Civil Liberties Union 198, 208, 338, 345, 359, 363, 417–418
American Dream **10**, 16, 20, 23, 103–104, 301, 329, 416
American Farm Bureau Federation 304, 339, 344, 361
American Federation of Labor and Congress of Industrial Organisations 304, 343, 353
American Medical Association 97, 304, 338, 339, 343, 344, 355, 364, 392
American Recovery and Reinvestment Act (2009) 92, 149, **346**
American Socialist Party 223, 302
Americans with Disabilities Act (1990) 408

anarcho-syndicalism **300**, 301
apportionment 5, 146–147
Articles of Confederation 28, 50–51
Asian-Americans 9, 16, 176, 180, 191, 385
attack on Twin Towers/World Trade Centre (9/11) 11, 17, 60, 81, 93, 100, 107, 139, 374, 409, 417

Baake Case (1978) 207, **402**
baby boomers **4**
Bible Belt **3**
Biden, J. 118, 121, 280, 282, 309
Bill of Rights 29, 31, 39, 42, 43–45, 46, 354, 409, 415
  see also First Amendment freedoms and ch11
bills 148, 149, 150, 346
  see also Congress: legislative process
Black Power 380–382
block grant **56**
Brock, W. **327**
Brown v Topeka Board of Education (1954) 205, 378–379
Budget and Impoundment Control Act (1974) 159, 170–171
bureaucracy see federal bureaucracy
Burger W. (Chief Justice) 206, 207–208, 402, 410
bus boycott **379**
Bush, G. H. 233, 244, 263, 264, 297, 400
  conflict with Iraq/Gulf War 80, 97
  judicial appointments 191, 196, 199
  presidential style and performance 57, 80, 86, 87, 91, 97, 156, 237, 246, 248, 399, 408
  Vice President 112, 121

Bush, G. W. ('Dubya') 112, 118, 328
  2000 election 11, 198, 210–211, 223,
    248, 296, 315, 328, 400
  2004 election 101, 198, 308, 313, 400
  Afghanistan/War on Terror 80, 107,
    276, 417
  appointments to the Supreme Court
    195, 196, 198
  approach to federalism **59**–60, 64
  'axis of evil' speech (2002) 316
  compassionate conservatism **316**
  'decline' of administration 101, 106,
    108–109, 276
  election campaigner 224, 233, 256
  handling of banking crisis/recession
    60, 277, 278, 279, 281
  Iraq War 107–108, 276, 277, 278
  judicial appointments 191, 198
  Libertarian Right **316**
  neo-cons **316**
  presidential performance and style 87,
    88–89, 91, 99, 100, 101, 106,
    108–109, 125, 141, 156, 161,
    232, 310, 315, 358, 385, 386,
    393, 400, 407
  reaction to terrorist threat 87,
    374–377 *see also* War on Terror
  relationship with Cheney R. 122–123
  troop surge **278**
  see also unitary executive theory
Bush v Gore case (2000) 107, 198,
  210–211

Cabinet 123–128
  choice of membership 125–126
  conduct and use of 123–125
  role and practice 127–128
candidate-centred electioneering **228**
career politicians **65**
Carter, J. 58, 62, 79, 85, 86, 87, 104,
  112, 118, 121, 124, 130, 173,
  196, 246, 257, 258, 387
categorical grants **55**
caucus **219**, 251, 258–259, 275–276
Cheney, R. 99, 103, 118, 122–123, 125,
  240, 282

Christian Coalition 12, 318–320, 337,
  385, 409
  see also Religious Right
civil liberties (ch11) 206, 209, 214,
  371–376, 409–411
  comparison with Britain 410
  legal rights 373–376
  see also Patriot Act 2001
civil rights (ch11) 205, 209, 311, **371**,
  409–411
  comparison with Britain 410
Civil Rights legislation (1957, 1964,
  1968, 1991) 380, 391, 402
Civil Rights Movement 12, 341, 379–388
Civil War (1861–1865) **2**, 7, 53
Clinton, B. 4, 16, 18, 20, 79, 80, 107,
  112, 121, 125
  affirmative action 403, 404
  appointments to Supreme Court
    195–196, 393
  approach to federalism 57–59, 62
  assessment 104, 105, 106
  character and appeal 96, 97, 102, 104,
    105, 106, 256, 384, 387, 397,
    399, 400
  choice/use of, and relationship with,
    Gore, A. as Vice President 118,
    121
  electioneering 105, 106, 246, 248,
    254, 257, 264, 399–400
  gay rights 406
  healthcare reform 87, 97, 344
  impeachment proceedings 94–96,
    166, 196, 240, 320
  judicial appointments 77, 191,
    195–196
  New Covenant 310
  party attitudes 308, 310, 311
  presidential style and performance 78,
    79, 80, 86, 89, 91, 101, 104, 105,
    106, 125, 126, 135, 140–141,
    159, 160, 166, 225, 355, 386,
    387, 393
  scandals (infidelity, Lewinsky,
    Whitewatergate etc) 86, 94–96,
    104, 106, 120, 162, 175, 257

Clinton, H. 126, 161, 245, 274–282,
    309, 327, 396
Cold War **2**, 90, 100, 227, 246
Confederation **28**, 50–51
Congress (ch5)
    107th 178, 179
    109th 178
    111th 37, 92–94, 149
    112th 149, 150, 178–179
    as a microcosm of nation 176, 177,
        178–180
    assertiveness 86, 91, 170, 175
    comparison of pay and facilities of
        elected representatives with
        Britain 184
    criticism of 170, 175–177
    facilities and pay of members 182–184
    finance 162–163
    functions 152–164
    impeachment 94–96
    investigative function 162
    legislative process 153–161
    members' backgrounds 176, 177,
        178–180
    members' roles and responsibilities
        164–170, 290
    organisation of 146–152
    party loyalty 160–161, 166–167
    powers 150–151
    public image 22, 176, 181–182, 184
    reform 156, 170–177
    relations with presidents 90–96
    representation **152**–153
    term limits 181–182
    use of filibuster 157
    war-making powers *see* War Powers Act
    see also House of Representatives and
        Senate
Congressional Budget Office 171
Congressional committees 38, 148, 149,
        153–157, 163–164, 171–174
    chairmanships 148, 172, 173, 348
    comparison with Britain 164–165
    seniority in 156, **171**–172, 173
    types 154–155
    see also Congress: legislative work

Congressional districts *see*
    apportionment
Congressional elections 150
    mid term 224–225
    Nov 1994 37, 58, 86, 91, 97, 105,
        140, 148, 160
    Nov 2006 101, 109
    Nov 2010 92–93
Conservatism 305–306, 310, 311–313
    compassionate **316**
    neo-cons **316**
    Libertarian Right **316**
    see also Republican Party
conservative **305**
Constitution (ch2) 20, **28**, 77
    amendments 34–39, 52, 61, 96–97,
        184, 197 *see also* Bill of Rights
    assessment 39–42
    characteristics and underlying
        principles 29
    checks and balances **33**–34, 35
    comparison with Britain 42, 45
    compromises 29–34
    Philadelphia Convention (1787) 28,
        29, 34, 49, 50, 72
    ratification 28, 29, 31
    separation of powers **33**, 46, 84, 160,
        162, 188, 290
    take-care clause **288**
    see also federalism, Founding Fathers
        and Fourteenth Amendment
Constitution Party 298
Contract with America 37, 148, 166,
        181, **314**
courts (ch7) 348–349
    federal 190–216
    types 188–189
Cuban Missile Crisis (1962) 81

Declaration of Independence (1776) 20,
        23, 28, 30, 376
democracy (ch12) 20, 21, 45, 234
    comparison with Britain 418–419
    definition and criteria 20, **32**, 414–415
    practice in America 20, 411, 415–420
    see also direct democracy

Democratic Party (ch9) 2, 12, 171
  2004 election 3
  2008 election 274–282
  activist, 'progressive' attitudes 58,
    310–311
  areas of key support 2, 68, 256
  characteristic attitudes and policies
    290, 308–309, 310–311,
    312–313, 355, 387–389, 391
  number and profile of supporters 13,
    261–262, 265, 290, 302, 305,
    384–385
  see also direct democracy
de Tocqueville, A. 18, 24–25, 241, 335
devolution 50
direct action 351
direct democracy/direct legislation 32,
    45, 241, 266–274, 414, 416
  2010 proposals 269–270
  comparison with Britain and Europe
    271–273
  forms of 266–268
  issues, frequency and growing use
    224, 266–271
  merits and demerits 272–274
  participation and turnout 271–272
disability rights 408–409
'due process' clause 32, 373–375

earmarks 358
Economic Stimulus Bill (2009) 346
Eisenhower, D. 256, 258
  appointment of, attitude to Earl
    Warren 194, 196, 204
  presidential style and performance
    105, 106, 120, 125, 126, 127,
    348, 379
elections, electioneering and voting
    (ch8)
  campaigns 228–230, 238, 275–279
  candidate-centred electioneering
    228
  comparison of turnout in main
    democracies 235
  comparison with Britain 230
  congressional (mid-term) 224–225

Nov 1994 37, 58, 86, 91, 97, 105,
    140, 166, 182, 224
  Nov 2002 224
  Nov 2006 101, 109
  Nov 2010 92–93, 224–225,
    322–323, 341, 385
electoral system 222–227
how people get elected 219–222,
    250–261
importance, frequency and timing
    219, 222
mass media 242–245
  see also television
method of choosing presidents
    250–261
money and state funding 230–234,
    277, 280, 328
  see also FECA legislation and
    Political Action Committees
political advertising 232, 238,
    248–251
presidential
  1952 248, 256, 263
  1960 234, 246, 254
  1968 263
  1976 246
  1980 263, 399
  1984 253
  1992 22, 246, 254, 264, 297, 399
  1996 22, 236, 237, 263
  2000 11, 106, 107, 121, 210–211,
    223, 236, 237, 248, 255, 275,
    296, 297, 298, 385, 400
  2004 3, 13, 101, 107, 198, 234,
    302, 385, 400
  2008 3, 112, 199, 218, 231, 235,
    244, 245, 247, 263, 274–282,
    302, 327, 385, 400
presidential debates 245–247, 279
primary elections 220–221, 251, 252,
    258–259, 275–277
turnout 234–238, 239
use of political consultants 228,
    229
voting behaviour 261–266
electoral coalitions 289

Electoral College **4**, 37, 107, 118, 210,
    223, 226, 255–261, 274–282, 292
  assessment 257, 259–261
electoral system (FPTP) 179, 180,
    222–227, 292
  comparison with Britain 227
  experimentation with use of
    proportional representation
    226–227
Enron **347**
equality 20, 376–377, 416
Equal Rights Amendment 39, 394
exceptionalism 18–19, 23
executive agencies **137**
executive agreements **102**
Executive Office of the President 82,
    102, 128–134
  assessment of 132–134
  elements of 130–131
  establishment and operation of
    129–132
executive orders **88**, 101, 377
executive privilege **78**, 207

Fannie Mae and Freddie Mac **60**
federal bureaucracy 54, 98, **134**–143
  appointment of 135–136
  Bush Management Agenda 141–143
  definition and extent 134–139
  presidential initiatives to improve the
    functioning of 139–143
  Reinventing Government 140–141
Federal Election Campaign Acts (FECA)
    (1971, 1974 and 1979) 231–232,
    354, 357
Federalism (ch3) 324, 290
  benefits 49, 70–72
  coercive federalism **55**
  comparison with Britain 71
  competitive federalism **64**
  cooperative federalism **54**
  creative federalism **54**
  decentralisation and the growth of
    state power since 1980s 54–66,
    72
  devolutionary federalism **58**

dual federalism **49**, 51–52, 53, 72
federal-state government relations
    reviewed 50–51, 61–64
  long-term trend towards central
    control 51–54, 72
  meaning and workings 33, 49, 51, 72,
    97, 330
  New Federalism **55**–57, 58, 140,
    365
  Supreme Court decisions 52, 56, 57,
    62, 63, 65
Federalist Papers **31**, 34, 200, 414
Federalist Society for Law and Public
    Policy **198**
Fifth Amendment 32, 43
filibuster 157
First Amendment freedoms 43, 44, 207,
    208, 209, 213, 354, **371**–376
  symbolic speech 373
flag and flag desecration 37, 39, 40, 208,
    372
focus groups **228**
Ford G. 38, 106, 110, 111, 196
  presidential style and performance 78,
    85, 156, 246, 325
foreign policy
  'axis of evil' 316
  crisis management 81
  machinery of 81–82
  National Security Advisor 82
  National Security Council 82
  presidential role 79–80, 81–82, 102
    see also individual presidents
  Secretary of State/State Department
    81–82
  see also war against Iraq, War on
    Terror and War Powers Act
Founding Fathers (framers of
    Constitution) **17**, 21, 30, 33, 34,
    40, 41, 42, 49, 76, 84, 96, 219,
    259, 269, 287, 414
Fourteenth Amendment (due process,
    equal protection of the law) 32,
    43, 44, 205, 373–375, 402, 403
Frost-belt x, 4
Fundamentalism **3**

Gays/gay rights 208, 307, 320, 377,
        405–407
    in the military 93, 97, 406
    same sex marriages/unions 68, 208,
        406–407
Gingrich, N. 148–149, 400
Gore, Al 11, 107, 118, 120, 121,
        140–141, 198, 210–211, 223,
        296, 297, 384, 385, 399–400
government corporations 138–139
government (executive) departments
        137
    see also state department
grants-in-aid 53, 56
Great Depression 52, 53, 82, 102, 128,
        200, 201, 261
Great Society programme 54, 55, 61–62,
        172, 386, 391
Green Party 296, 298
Guantanamo Bay detention 375–377

healthcare and health reform 22, 37,
        307, 344
    Clinton attempt at reform 87, 97, 344
    Medicare 344
    Obama and reform 22, 60–61, 92, 97,
        310, 344, 346, 351
    Patient Protection and Affordable Care
        Act (2010) 92
Hispanics (Latinos) 7–9
    economic and political position 8–9,
        14–16, 176, 178, 180, 191, 194,
        198, 237, 387
    voting significance 9, 93, 385
House of Representatives (ch5) 161
    elections to 150, 224
    majority and minority leaders 148,
        149
    membership 146–147
    role and powers 150–152
    Speaker 148–149, 159
Howell, W. 99, 100–101
Hurricane Katrina 276

impeachment procedure 94–96
incumbency in Congress 182, 224, 399
independent agencies 137–138

individualism 14, 19–20, 23, 329
initiatives 32, 266, 268–270, 271,
        272–274
Internet 242, 280, 419
Iran Contra Affair (Irangate) 85, 81, 82,
        162, 240
iron triangles and issue networks 172,
        348–349
issue advertisements 232

Jackson, J. 12, 23, 386–387
Jefferson, T. 28, 376, 416
Jim Crow Laws 377–378
Johnson, L. 54, 112, 118, 120, 122–123,
        196
    presidential style and performance 55,
        61–62, 84, 87, 89, 91, 99, 101,
        105, 106, 119–120, 160, 172,
        190, 194, 380, 384, 386, 387, 391
judges
    appointment 190–192
    comparison with Britain 203–204
    federal 190–192
judicial activism 194, 204, 210, 215,
        216
judicial independence 188
judicial restraint 194, 210, 215
judicial review 35, 46, 197–200, 203
Judiciary (ch7)
    civil and criminal law 188
    comparison with Britain 203–205, 215
    definition 187–188
    range of US courts 188–192
    see also Supreme Court

Kennedy, J.F. 13, 54, 68, 88, 89, 91, 97,
        101, 102, 103, 105, 112, 118,
        120, 122, 123, 125, 127, 139,
        196, 254, 257, 260, 304, 307,
        380, 387, 388
    TV debates with Richard Nixon 246
Kerry, J. 3, 11, 13, 151, 152, 257, 281,
        305, 308, 399–400, 407
King, Dr M.L. 12, 275, 351, 379,
        380–382, 386, 387–388, 409
K. Street Corridor 346
Ku Klux Klan 209, 378

Latinos *see* Hispanics
Legislation
  legislative process: how bills become
    laws 153–161
  pork-barrel **168**
  role of presidents 158–161
Lehman Brothers **279**
Lewinsky, M. 94, 104
Liberalism 19–20, 21, 68, 306–310
  see also Democratic Party
Liberals 19, 68, 195, 199, 270, 299,
    306–310, 311, 382
Libertarian Party 298–299
limited government 23, **31**
Lincoln, A. 2, 32, 53, 88, 89, 105,
    123–124, 415
line item veto **66**, 159
local government 48–49, 59, 69–70
Locke, J. 19, 20, 21
Lott, T. 348, 365

McCain, J. 151, 231, 232, 233, 244, 247,
    248, 274–282, 309, 320, 321,
    400, 407
McCain-Feingold Finance Reform Act
    (2002) 232, 233
McCarthy, J. and McCarthyism **409**,
    415–416, 417
Madison, J. 30, 31, 34, 41, 287, 414
Malcolm X. 381
Marbury v Madison (1803) 35
Marx, K. 24, 300–303
Marshall, J. (Chief Justice) 192–193, 211
Massachusetts
  politics 146, 152, 270, 305
  same sex marriage 59, 67, 68,
    406–407
  state government in action; case study
    67–68
mass media 17, 97, 100, 102, 228–230,
    238, **242**–251, 356–357, 417,
    418–419
  comparison with Britain 249–251
  new media 419–420
Medicaid 57, 60
Medicare **344**
melting pot **10**

messianism **19**
mid-term elections *see* congressional
    elections
Miranda rules 375–376
Mondale, W. 118, 121, 353
  Motor Voter Act (1993) 236–237

Nader, R. 295, 296, 297, 298
National Association for the
    Advancement of Coloured People
    (NAACP) 349, 351, 379–380
National Association of Manufacturers
    304, 341, 361, 363
National Farmers Union 304, 344, 361
national nominating conventions 219,
    253–254, 325
  superdelegates **327**
National Rifle Association 42, 340, 352
National Security Council 125, 131
national security directives **89**
Native Americans 9–10, 388–389
  Red Power 388–389
Neustadt, R. 87–90, 99–100
  'power to persuade' 90, 98, 99
New Deal programme **41**, 53, 54, 57,
    58, 61, 200, 201, 302, 307
New (Radical) Right **313**
news management **244**
New York Liberal Party 299, 307
Nixon, R. 4, 87, 91, 99, 104, 105, 118,
    120, 122, 124, 126, 130, 131,
    156, 170, 246, 248, 386, 408,
    409
  appointment of judges 190, 192,
    194–195, 196, 206, 207
  approach to federalism 55–56, 58
  Vice President 112
  Watergate **38**, 78, 94, 96, 104,
    207–208

Obama, B. 4, 11, 102, 106, 121, 131,
    133, 141–143, 149, 386, 387, 407
  2008 112, 199, 218, 231, 233,
    244–245, 247, 248, 274–282,
    302, 308, 309, 320, 321,
    327–328, 384, 397, 400, 407,
    419

Obama, B. (*Continued*)
  2010 mid-term elections 3, 92–93,
      224–225, 308, 322–323, 341, 385
  appointment of federal judges 191,
      198–199, 397
  appointment of Supreme Court
      justices 194, 196, 198–199, 397
  approach to federalism 60–61
  choice of Biden, J. as Vice President
      118–119
  Guantanamo detention camp 377
  health reform ('Obamacare') 22,
      60–61, 92, 97, 310, 322, 344,
      346, 351
  legislative record 60–61, 78, 92–94,
      161, 322, 346, 358
  liberalism? 308, 309
opinion polls and pollsters 229, 251,
      276, 279, 400
Oregon's suicide law 59

Palin, S. 244, 281, 282, 396
participation 19, 32, 234–242
party organisation 232, 323–326
  Brock reforms 327
  decentralisation **324**, 325–326
  recent trends 325–326
  role of national headquarters
      324–325, 327
  superdelegates **327**
  see also national nominating
      conventions
Patient Protection and Affordable Care
      Act (2010) 92
  see also health care
Patriot Act (2001) 374
Pelosi, N. 149, 396
Perot, R. **22**, 253–254, 295, 297
Philadelphia Convention (1787) 28, 29,
      34, 49, 50, 72
photo-opportunities 244
platform **221**
Pledge of Allegiance **23**, 372
plurality systems **222**
Political Action Committees 229, 230,
      231, 287, 327, 352–353, **354**

  see also Elections and voting: role of
      money
political advertising 232, 238, 248–251
political consultants **228**, 229
political culture **17**–24
political parties (ch9)
  comparison with Britain 330–331
  decentralisation **324**, 325–326
  decline/renewal? 229, **326**–330
  definition **287**
  Founding Fathers' fears regarding 287
  organisation 232, 323–326
  role and value 287–288, 331–332
  role of ideology **305**
  similarities/difference of two main
      parties 303–306
  third parties 294–303
  two party system 288–293, 331
  voter perceptions of two main parties
      261–262, 265, 280–281, 290,
      304, 305, 384–385, 398–400
  see also Constitution, Democratic,
      Green, Liberal (New York),
      Libertarian, Reform, Republican,
      Socialist Party and third parties
popular sovereignty (sovereignty of the
      people) 21, **32**, 45
pork-barrel politics **168**
poverty 16
presidential debates 245–247
presidential system **34**
presidential veto 89, 158
presidents and the presidency (ch4, ch5)
  academic debate 84–85, 99–101,
      109–110
  backgrounds of presidents 111–112,
      122–123, 151, 282, 387
  Cabinet 123–128
  choice of Vice Presidents 118–119
  comparisons or president with British
      prime minister 112–113
  crisis management 81
  different presidential attitudes
      towards office 104–105
  Executive Office of the Presidency
      128–134

federal bureaucracy 134–143
handling of foreign policy 81–82
Imperial 84–**85**, 87, 99, 114
leadership 98, 102–103, 106, 107,
    108, 109, 112
limits of presidential power (ch3)
    especially 87–98, 99–100
modern presidency **83**, 98, 100
National Security Advisor/Council
    131
popular expectations, ratings and
    reactions 75, 100, 103–104, 107,
    109, 114
power (ch4)
presidential 'success' 106–109, 112
rankings of presidents 107, 109–110
relations with Congress (ch4, ch6) *see*
    presidential power and limits to it
    and Congress and
    legislation/reform
role 76–80, 88–89, 114
support for (ch5) *see also* Bureaucracy,
    Cabinet, Executive Office and
    Vice Presidency
veto power 158–159
Vice-Presidency 118–123
White House Office 130
Wildavsky and the 'two presidencies'
    101
see also individual presidents
pressure groups and lobbying (ch10) 97,
    166, 240
527s 353
access points **337**, 350
and political parties 338
assessment 359–361
business organisations 336, 337, 340,
    342, 347, 350, 355, 365
civil society **335–336**
classifications and examples 334,
    337–345
comparison with Britain 366
definition and scale **335–336**, 337,
    338–341, 367
direct action 351
insider and outsider groups **339**

iron triangles and issue networks 172,
    348–349
labour groups 343
    see also trade unions
lobbyists **355**
membership and why members join
    335
methods adopted 345
movements 341
pluralism and pluralist societies
    360–361
professional lobbying 348, 364–365
regulation 336, 357–359
strength and reasons for success 97,
    240, 337, 354–357, 363
trends 361–366
umbrella or peak organisations **342**
see also Political Action Committees
primary elections **220–221**, 251, 252,
    275–277
criticism of 258–259
proclamations **89**
Progressive Era/Movement of early C20
    226, 416
pseudo-events **249–250**

race and racial discrimination *see*
    affirmative action, Afro-
    Americans, Asian Americans,
    Hispanics, Native Americans
Reagan, R. 4, 80, 121, 233, 305, 347
    approach to federalism 56–57, 62, 69
    Irangate **85**, 81, 82, 162, 240
    judicial appointments 190–191, 194,
        195, 196
    popularity 68, 103–104, 112, 256,
        263, 325
    presidential style and performance
        85–86, 89, 100, 101, 126, 130,
        136, 156, 190, 225, 313, 315,
        400
    skill as communicator via media 91,
        102, 104, 112, 244
recall 32, 268–269
Reconstruction **2**
Red Power 388–389

referendum 32, 241, **266**, 270–274
Reform Party 22, 295–296
regulatory commissions **137**–138
Rehnquist W. (Chief Justice) 198, 201,
   208–211, 393, 403
Religion
   importance of 3, 12–13, 23
   religious diversity 10–12
   see also 'born again' Christians,
      Christian Coalition and Religious
      Right
Religious Right **12**–13, 59, 166, 191,
   355, 356, 393, 409
   see also Christian Coalition
representative system **414**
Republican Party (ch9) 225
   2004 election 3, 409
   2008 election 274–282
   2010 midterm elections 409
   areas of key support 2, 3, 171
   characteristic attitudes and policies
      63, 311–317, 387, 392–94
   compassionate conservatism **316**
   Contract for America 37, 148, 166,
      181, **314**
   Libertarian Right **316**
   Moderates 312, 315, 320
   neo-cons **316**
   New (Radical) Right **313**
   number and profile of supporters 13,
      262, 265, 290, 302, 305, 385
   role of Religious Right 13, 316,
      318–321
   role of Tea Party 225, 321–323
revolving door and ban 346–347, **358**
Roberts, J. (Chief Justice) 198, 201,
   211–214, 404–405
Roe v Wade (1973) 206, 207, 212,
   213, 392–393
Roosevelt, F. 41, 57, 82, 129, 225
   court-packing scheme 194, 201–202
   New Deal **41**, 53, 96, 200, 307
   popularity 103
   presidential style and performance 82,
      86, 91, 96, 98, 101, 102, 105,
      120, 143, 190

Roosevelt, T. 91, 104–105, 295
rugged individualism **3**
rule of law **32**, 45
Rules Committee 148, 154, 156, 172

same sex marriage 59, 67, 68, 149, 208,
   406–407
Schlesinger, A. 84–85, 99
Segregation (ch11) 205, 207, **378**, 401,
   416
Senate (ch5) 31
   Advice and Consent role **77**, 79
   elections to 150, 224
   Majority Leader 160, 348
   Prestige 151–152
   Role and Powers 150–152
seniority system
separation of powers 46, 84, 160, 162,
   188, 290
signing statements **89**
social class 13–14
social inequality 13–16
socialism in USA **23**, 300–303
Socialist Party USA (formerly Socialist
   Party of America) 302
'soft money' **232**
Sotomayor, S. 194, 198, 214
sound-bites 244
South 2–3, 5, 6, 166, 237, 416
Speaker of House of Representatives
   148–149, 150
   Boehner, J. 149
   Gingrich, N. 148–149, 400
   Hastert, D. 149, 364
   Pelosi, N. 149, 396
spin 245
spin-doctors 245
split-ticket voting 263–264
State Department 81–82, 139
states and state government (ch3)
   decentralisation of power/revival of
      states 54–66, 72
   federal-state government relations
      reviewed 61–64
   innovation 58, 59, 60, 62,
      63–64

long-term trend to central control
51–54
pressure group activity 365
state government in Massachusetts
67–68
state and local government in action:
relations between the two tiers
64–72
see also devolutionary federalism
Sun-belt x
superdelegates **327**
Super Tuesday **236**, 277
Supreme Court (ch7) 49–50, 78, 96, 102,
181, especially 192, 216, 393
affirmative action 402–405
amicus curiae **350**
appointments 193–196
attitude to Constitution 192, 199, 200,
206
briefs 196
Bush v. Gore 107, 198, 210–211
concurring opinions 197
conference work 197
constitutional change 192–193
dissenting opinions 197
Guantanamo rulings 375–376
judicial review **197**
loose constructionism **206**
New Deal programme 200, 201–202
political controversy 201–203,
204–205, 215–216
procedure 196–197
role 197–201
size and membership 190, 193–196
strict constructionism **206**
see also Burger W., Rehnquist W.,
Roberts J., Warren E. and
individual cases

take-care clause **88**
Tea Party movement 225, 269, 296,
321–323, 339, 341, 365–366
television and politics 97, 102, 103, 228,
242, 244–251, 417, 418
and election campaigns 228–230, 236,
244–251, 257

political advertising 232, 238,
248–251
presidential debates 245–247, 279
term limits 37, **65**
terrorist attack September 11th 2001 11,
17, 60, 81, 93, 100, 107, 139,
374, 409, 417
anti-terrorist legislation 374–376,
410, 419
see also War on Terror
think-tanks 166, **362**
third parties
barriers to their development 292–293
types and range 294–296
role and importance 296
town meetings 32, 68, 241, 242–243,
416
trade unions 302, 311, 314, 353, 355,
361–362
Truman, H. 105, 124, 128, 196, 387
Truman Doctrine (1947) 84
trust in government/politicians 19, 23,
176, 181–182, 184, 238–240
turnout *see* elections: turnout
two party system 288–293
reasons for 291–293

unfunded mandates **58**
unitary executive theory (UET) **88–89**,
100–101
unitary state 49, 50
United States
background information (ch1)
class 13–14
economy 14–16
education 14
income 15–16
inequality 14–16, 20
patriotic feeling 23
population 4–10, 24
religion

Vice Presidency 118–123
Cheney in office 103
choice of Vice President 118–119
responsibilities and role 119, 150

Vice Presidency (*Continued*)
  frustrations of office 119–120
  increasing influence 120–123
Vietnam War **84**, 80, 104, 106, 119,
     127, 240
voter registration 235, 236
voting behaviour 261–267
  2008 274–282, especially 280–281
  Afro-American vote 384–385
  changes over recent decades 262–264,
    267
  comparison with Britain 265–267
  female vote 398–400
  Hispanic vote 8–9, 281
  importance of state of economy 264,
    277, 278, 279, 281
  increased importance of candidate
    262, 267
  increased importance of issues 262,
    264, 267
  party identification and its declining
    significance 262–265, 267, 290,
    296
  retrospective and prospective voting
    264
  social class 262, 267
  split-ticket voting 263–264
  white evangelical vote 320
  see also candidate-centred
    electioneering
Voting Rights Act (1965) 236, 380, 385

war against Iraq 107–108, 276, 277,
    278
  troop surge **278**
War of Independence 20
War on Poverty 54, 56
War on Terror 80, 107, 276, 417
War Powers Act 1973 **80**, 91, 170
Warren, E. (Chief Justice) 193, 194,
    196, 199, 202, 204–206, 207,
    210, 216, 410
Washington, G. 21, 30, 77, 123, 287
Watergate 84, 85, 104, 162, 240
  welfare reform/Welfare Reform Act
    (1996) 57, 62
West 3–4, 5, 6
White Anglo-Saxon Protestants (WASPS)
    13
White House Office 102, 127, 130,
    132
Wildavsky, A. 101
Wilson, W. 40, 64, 79, 91
Women
  in Congress 176, 178–180,
    396–399
  in judiciary 191, 198, 214, 397, 402
  in public life 17–18, 390–400
  in state government 396–399
  legislation affecting 391
  voting 398–400
Women's Movement 391–395
Write-in vote **222**